I0897041

# Handbook of Research on Emerging Business Models and Managerial Strategies in the Nonprofit Sector

Lindy Lou West
*Griffith University, Australia*

Andrew Worthington
*Griffith University, Australia*

A volume in the Advances in Public Policy and Administration (APPA) Book Series

IGI GLOBAL
DISSEMINATOR OF KNOWLEDGE

www.igi-global.com

Published in the United States of America by
IGI Global
Business Science Reference (an imprint of IGI Global)
701 E. Chocolate Avenue
Hershey PA, USA 17033
Tel: 717-533-8845
Fax: 717-533-8661
E-mail: cust@igi-global.com
Web site: http://www.igi-global.com

Copyright © 2017 by IGI Global. All rights reserved. No part of this publication may be reproduced, stored or distributed in any form or by any means, electronic or mechanical, including photocopying, without written permission from the publisher. Product or company names used in this set are for identification purposes only. Inclusion of the names of the products or companies does not indicate a claim of ownership by IGI Global of the trademark or registered trademark.

Library of Congress Cataloging-in-Publication Data

Names: West, Lindy Lou, editor. | Worthington, Andrew C., editor.
Title: Handbook of research on emerging business models and managerial strategies in the nonprofit sector / Lindy Lou West and Andrew Worthington, editors.
Description: Hershey : Business Science Reference, [2017]
Identifiers: LCCN 2017005027| ISBN 9781522525370 (hardcover) | ISBN 9781522525387 (ebook)
Subjects: LCSH: Nonprofit organizations--Management. | Nonprofit organizations--Marketing. | Personnel management.
Classification: LCC HD62.6 .H3456 2017 | DDC 658.4/012--dc23 LC record available at https://lccn.loc.gov/2017005027

This book is published in the IGI Global book series Advances in Public Policy and Administration (APPA) (ISSN: 2475-6644; eISSN: 2475-6652)

British Cataloguing in Publication Data
A Cataloguing in Publication record for this book is available from the British Library.

All work contributed to this book is new, previously-unpublished material. The views expressed in this book are those of the authors, but not necessarily of the publisher.

For electronic access to this publication, please contact: eresources@igi-global.com.

# Advances in Public Policy and Administration (APPA) Book Series

ISSN:2475-6644
EISSN:2475-6652

MISSION

Proper management of the public sphere is necessary in order to maintain order in modern society. Research developments in the field of public policy and administration can assist in uncovering the latest tools, practices, and methodologies for governing societies around the world.

The **Advances in Public Policy and Administration (APPA) Book Series** aims to publish scholarly publications focused on topics pertaining to the governance of the public domain. APPA's focus on timely topics relating to government, public funding, politics, public safety, policy, and law enforcement is particularly relevant to academicians, government officials, and upper-level students seeking the most up-to-date research in their field.

COVERAGE

- Government
- Law enforcement
- Political Economy
- Politics
- Public Administration
- Public Funding
- Public Policy
- Resource Allocation
- Urban Planning

IGI Global is currently accepting manuscripts for publication within this series. To submit a proposal for a volume in this series, please contact our Acquisition Editors at Acquisitions@igi-global.com or visit: http://www.igi-global.com/publish/.

The Advances in Public Policy and Administration (APPA) Book Series (ISSN 2475-6644) is published by IGI Global, 701 E. Chocolate Avenue, Hershey, PA 17033-1240, USA, www.igi-global.com. This series is composed of titles available for purchase individually; each title is edited to be contextually exclusive from any other title within the series. For pricing and ordering information please visit http://www.igi-global.com/book-series/advances-public-policy-administration/97862. Postmaster: Send all address changes to above address. Copyright © 2017 IGI Global. All rights, including translation in other languages reserved by the publisher. No part of this series may be reproduced or used in any form or by any means – graphics, electronic, or mechanical, including photocopying, recording, taping, or information and retrieval systems – without written permission from the publisher, except for non commercial, educational use, including classroom teaching purposes. The views expressed in this series are those of the authors, but not necessarily of IGI Global.

## Titles in this Series

*For a list of additional titles in this series, please visit: www.igi-global.com/book-series*

*Ideological Messaging and the Role of Political Literature*
Önder Çakırtaş (Bingol University, Turkey)
Information Science Reference • copyright 2017 • 317pp • H/C (ISBN: 9781522523918) • US $175.00 (our price)

*Therapeutic Jurisprudence and Overcoming Violence Against Women*
Debarati Halder (Centre for Cyber Victim Counselling (CCVC), India & Unitedworld School of Law, India) and K. Jaishankar (Raksha Shakti University, India)
Information Science Reference • copyright 2017 • 344pp • H/C (ISBN: 9781522524724) • US $230.00 (our price)

*Public Sector Entrepreneurship and the Integration of Innovative Business Models*
Mateusz Lewandowski (Jagiellonian University in Kraków, Poland) and Barbara Kożuch (Jagiellonian University in Kraków, Poland)
Business Science Reference • copyright 2017 • 309pp • H/C (ISBN: 9781522522157) • US $190.00 (our price)

*Handbook of Research on Citizen Engagement and Public Participation in the Era of New Media*
Marco Adria (University of Alberta, Canada) and Yuping Mao (California State University Long Beach, USA)
Information Science Reference • copyright 2017 • 503pp • H/C (ISBN: 9781522510819) • US $265.00 (our price)

*Global Perspectives on Development Administration and Cultural Change*
Gbenga Emmanuel Afolayan (Murdoch University, Australia) and Akeem Ayofe Akinwale (University of Lagos, Nigeria)
Information Science Reference • copyright 2017 • 277pp • H/C (ISBN: 9781522506294) • US $170.00 (our price)

*Handbook of Research on Managerial Solutions in Non-Profit Organizations*
Vojko Potocan (University of Maribor, Slovenia) Mustafa C. Üngan (Sakarya University, Turkey) and Zlatko Nedelko (University of Maribor, Slovenia)
Information Science Reference • copyright 2017 • 609pp • H/C (ISBN: 9781522507314) • US $300.00 (our price)

*Achieving Open Justice through Citizen Participation and Transparency*
Carlos E. Jiménez-Gómez (Department of Justice of the Autonomous Government of Catalonia, Spain) and Mila Gascó-Hernández (Institute of Public Governance and Management, ESADE Business and Law School, Spain)
Information Science Reference • copyright 2017 • 296pp • H/C (ISBN: 9781522507178) • US $190.00 (our price)

IGI GLOBAL
DISSEMINATOR OF KNOWLEDGE

www.igi-global.com

701 East Chocolate Avenue, Hershey, PA 17033, USA
Tel: 717-533-8845 x100 • Fax: 717-533-8661
E-Mail: cust@igi-global.com • www.igi-global.com

# List of Contributors

# Table of Contents

# Detailed Table of Contents



Big Data refers to large volumes of information – on diseases, ticket sales, and so on – that standard database tools such as MySQL and Oracle, cannot easily process. Thus, data analytics tools, such as InfoGram and Google Fusion Tables, are required to manage the information. The processed data is useful in several ways. For instance, public health officials may use the results of the analysis to explain the spread of viruses including the H1N1 virus. Airplane companies may use the results to predict changes in ticket prices. Apart from the medical and aviation industries, institutions of higher learning also collect significantly large quantities of data. Hence, the analysis of Big Data also takes place in higher education. The beneficiaries of the analysis include students and administrators.



The objective of this chapter is to delineate the sustainability problems encountered by not-for-profit organisations and to explore how these challenges can be can be managed through shared value creation by the stakeholders. Case study-abductive research methodology was adopted to explore stakeholder shared values and sustainability. This method of study is especially useful for trying to test theoretical models by using them in real world situations. Findings revealed that the sustainability strategy in not for profit organizations must be a holistic approach. Such an approach needs to build upon value-creation that is integrated to develop social entrepreneurship and create social capital along the three dimensions which includes innovative, proactive, and risk management behavior. This chapter contributes to the shared value with stakeholders to provide a social enterprise pathway for a not for profit organization to achieve long-term financial sustainability while maintaining the core social mission and objectives.

Project Portfolio Management is a relatively new practice for the majority of non-government organisations. Project portfolio management is important in the areas of management and education of third sector practitioners. However, project portfolio management, corporate management tools are usually used in the business sector with very little research undertaken in the non-government sectors. This chapter fills that research gap by identifying and analysis of project portfolio management practices in non-governmental organizations. Findings suggest that non-government organisations manage multiple projects simultaneously but that project portfolio management could support them to build their portfolio in accordance with a strategic plan that can fulfil their strategic objectives efficiently and effectively.



Twenty-first century organizations face a challenge and an unprecedented opportunity: to build a new model of relationship with current and potential clients which is more efficient and innovative. And this necessarily implies to acquire a completely new corporate culture in which the collection, management and interpretation of information will inspire the entire business. Under this new business scenario, the data is not understood as part of a process but instead to be part of the core business as a decision tool. Only if companies can manage this flood of information will be able to understand what we do and where they are going; identify the tastes and preferences of consumers and, more importantly, anticipate their decisions to adapt the services in real time and in a personalized way. The Big Data points companies beyond the facts: transforms the actions into predictions.



This chapter considers the lack of knowledge by both non-profit and for-profit organizations in building business models and developing global managerial strategies; as well as, considers the need for organizations to understand open transformation of organizational structure with an autonomous mindset of each stakeholder and unification of the organizational system. The focus of perspectives points to what is needed to understand behavior stemming from the culture of the organization and what it takes to structure or restructure its culture to fit with the 21st century's demands and growing global perspectives. Explanations are given as to how some theories and disciplines need to band together to bring out deeper meanings of phenomena to address managerial and leadership strategies. There are six figures and one table highlighting developmental processes of successful organizational systems. These will be used as roadmaps in developing on-going constructs to navigate assessments, training, and transformation processes of an organization.

Crowdfunding has been applied to equity investments as well as in a preproduction consumer purchase model. Crowdfunding is projected to become a $US90-96 billion industry by 2025, and is being touted as a valuable tool for fundraising for charitable non-profits. For leading non-profits around the globe a critical question is whether charitable crowdfunding is a threat or an opportunity for them. This chapter demonstrates that charitable crowdfunding represents a powerful new fundraising tool for leading, start-ups and not for profit organisations. This discussion contributes to the financial knowledge, specifically in the online crowdfunding and non-profit organisations and concludes that non-profit organisations through crowdfunding has the potential to expand the donor base.



The suitability of current Information System (IS) adoption models is anachronistic when uniformly applied across regions in developing economies, including Latin American (LAT) countries where the context varies from the accepted norm. From the premise that the major ingredients of adoption studies are drivers whose relationships are encapsulated into theoretical models, this chapter present a comprehensive Systematic Literature Review (SLR) process convergent towards the critical selection of reliable scholarly sources in order to identify empirically supported drivers of IS adoption successes and assesses their applicability in public organizations situated in LAT, as not for profit environments. Participants from Public Ecuadorian Organizations were sought out as a focus case to gather opinions and scrutinize identified drivers to demonstrate the depth of this problem. The study offers an overall comprehensive rationalization of proposed drivers, and the identified need for an adapted IS adoption theory for LAT contexts.



This chapter proposes conceptual framework that explores factors that influence managerial career orientations (self-perceived talents and abilities, basic values and the evolved sense of motives and needs that influences a person's career-related decisions. The argument put forward is that demographic (age, gender, social class, marital status, ethnicity, professional and educational qualifications); societal and organisational factors (government policies, labour market conditions, diversification of income streams, organisation size, structure and culture) will influence small third sector manager's career orientations. Identifying and understanding the career orientations of managers provide organisations with greater awareness of employee career needs and the ability to target career management effectively. The results indicate positive outcomes in organisational commitment, improved productivity and staff retention. This chapter concludes with a summary of finding, implications and future research directions.

Nonprofit organisations should be at the forefront in implementing corporate social responsibility in their actions and in disclosing these practices, not only to improve their image but also to enable access to corporate social responsibility information to be used as an effective instrument for continuous improvement. This chapter analyses perceptions of online transparency and web-usage as a means of online corporate social responsibility disclosure practices. Data is obtained from nonprofit case study analysis of Spanish Verdiblanca. The results reveal a contradiction between the corporate social responsibility information that is considered most important and actual practices of information disclosure. In particular, the information disclosure that is most highly valued concerns the social impact made by the organisation, compared to information on economics which is the most visible on the organisational webpage.



This chapter empirically investigates the Turkish chambers of commerce and industry's social media usage. Specifically, the research explores the prevalence, types, frequency, reasons, and the most importantly effectiveness of social media usage among the Turkish Chambers of Commerce and Industry (TCCI). A web based survey conducted to gather data from the TCCI. The chapter consists of five main parts: Introduction, social media as a modern business imperative, survey about social media usage in Turkish chambers of commerce and industry, and conclusion.



As social and environmental struggles intensify, the raising economic and social role of not for profits will continue to expand globally. Not for profit organizations have the potential to mobilize digitally-enabled communities and to work on various global challenges, overcoming the limitations of governmental institutions, local and short-term perspectives of public administration and private interests of business organizations. The present research aims to reassess the business models and value creation behind NFP operational models, their role for social innovation, the impact of the new technologies and the characteristics of the emerging digital communities. Further, there will be discussed the new perspectives for NFP development as innovative instruments, protecting social interests between government and private organizations, and contributing to solve increasing social problems.

The recent global economic crises and the decline of the traditional welfare state are challenging the development of third sector organisations involved in the provision of public services. With the support of the Italian case and the experiences of different Italian third sector organisations, this contribution highlights how organisational survival and growth require reinvention of the business model, commencing with the concept of social, economic and environmental sustainability. The scope of third sector organisations depends on the type of government, the stage of economic development, the model of civil society, the existence of philanthropic traditions and the law and regulation. All these variables affect the business model of third sector organisations. This chapter contributes to the third sector knowledge in Italy and concludes with a discussion on solutions that are able to incentivize the use of entrepreneurial principles, stimulate networking, cooperation and growth while maintaining the relationship with the territories.



Little scholarly research has systematically examined impact investing in the nonprofit realm. In the overview, the paper presents a case study of a U.S.-based private foundation that has transformed itself from a grant-maker to an impact investor, and the associated challenges of institutional entrepreneurial motivations, successful strategy for institutional adaptation, and the ensuing lessons for the field of impacting investing. The paper has two main objectives: to identify the motivation and enabling environment for such strategic change, and to analyze the issues and changes of the managerial model when evolving from traditional grant-making to impact investing. We argue that organizations that are mission-driven, entrepreneurial in spirit and structure, with embedded business/philanthropy principles acting as a source of change in the institutional field. However, it faces technical and legitimacy problems resulting from the new practice's lack of institutional saturation in the field.



The concept of strategy in non-profit higher education is a contested issue. It is argued that strategy, in the business sense, does not apply to a substantially public and more institutionalized sector such as higher education and is not achievable in complex, loosely coupled organizations such as universities. Additionally, strategy does not sit easily with organizations operating in regulated contexts limiting competitive market pressures. This chapter discusses the regulatory environment of non-profit higher education by focusing on one of the most highly regulated disciplines: medical education and research.

The chapter will begin by developing a context for discussion by firstly mapping the landscape of Australian medical education and research. Subsequently, the chapter argues that medical schools and research institutes need to exercise as much discretion as they can in the area under their control, develop sound strategies to deal with their changed circumstances, and develop a coherent and defensible basis for decision making through assessing their environment.



The last few years have witnessed the emergence of hybrid business models, in particular, social enterprises, which combine social and economic concerns in the same extent. Social enterprises are ambidextrous organizations that conduct activities to meet the social needs of their target beneficiaries simultaneously with income generating activities. This hybrid operational nature raises new questions about the definition and identification of an effective operations management strategy. The present chapter aims to identify the main operational challenges faced by hybrid organization in order to open avenues for future research. Drawing on current literature, the main concepts, the definition of an operations strategy and the social enterprises as hybrid organizations, are discussed. Findings suggest that the main operational challenges arise from hybridity. This chapter contributes to the theory and practices of social enterprises and concludes by identifying some opportunities for future research.



This chapter aims to contribute to the debate about performance measurement and management in the social business sector through the analysis of the critical issues that arise in the implementation of impact assessment models in social business organizations. To this aim, the social impact measurement approaches, which are suggested in the literature, are analyzed and the strengths and weaknesses of different frameworks are highlighted. Then, the critical issues that could emerge in the implementation of social impact assessment practices are identified and discussed base on the case of an Italian social enterprise working in the education field, Cometa. Finally, the paper provides some guidelines and recommendations aimed to mitigate these critical issues.



Innovative business model development, understood as a static phenomenon neglects the dynamic influences on both for-profit and not for profit sectors. Business model development is a complex process which has been well researched in corporations, but predominantly remained under-researched in not for-profit organisations. An exploratory study during 2011-2015 is undertaken to examine business development process in the areas of stability, sustainability and resistance in a local not for profit public enterprise.

# Preface

Globally, nonprofit (also not-for-profit) organizations, entrepreneurial startups and hybrid nonprofit entrepreneurial organizations, operate in a dynamic world of increasing competition, commercialism, technologically inter-connected and ever-changing environments with finite government funding, challenging regulatory requirements, emergent policies, business analytics and big data models where the dominant constants are perpetually in transition, transformation or termination. With funding changes, new capitalization models, big data infrastructure, mergers and acquisition, strategic performance management and business analytics are becoming increasingly important to the sector.

To gain new insights, increase funding sustainability, adhere with contractual obligations, deliver quality goods and services outcomes, improve customer satisfaction in line with laws, regulation, standards and compacts, nonprofit organizations, entrepreneurial startups and hybrid nonprofit entrepreneurial startups globally, are constantly searching for new ideas, models, concepts and systems. The contributing chapters in this book examine, synthesize, and evaluate diverse theories, concepts, frameworks, typologies, knowledge information, and data across and within interdisciplinary subjects as they relate to the nonprofit sector and individual organizations. Authors identify gaps and recommend potential solutions, provide a bridge between traditional and contemporary business models, systems and visions, information and business analytics and qualitative and quantitative research. The chapters in this book also propose a contemporary research agenda for the ever deconstructing and reconstructing nonprofit sector, the internal and external nonprofit marketplace, existing challenges, emerging issues, future research, and practical directions.

In Chapter 1, Marta Vidal, Javier Vidal-García, and Rafael Barros examine the use of the large volumes of information known as big data that standard database tools such as MySQL and Oracle cannot easily process and that important in the context of nonprofit entities. Thus, data analytics tools, such as InfoGram and Google Fusion Tables, are required to manage the information. The processed data is useful in several ways. Public health officials may use the results of the analysis to explain the spread of viruses, while higher education institutions also collect significantly large quantities of data, the better analysis of which can assist a wide range of nonprofit stakeholders.

Tony Kandaiya and Meena Chavan seeks to understand the survival strategies for nonprofit organizations and to identify the approaches used to meet the challenges of long-term sustainability in Chapter 2. Two main challenges are examined: 1) the overreliance of trustworthiness theory on the nondistribution constraint, and 2) the failure to explain why this constraint does not destroy the motivation of undertaking social entrepreneurial activities. To better understand these issues, Meena's chapter provides real-life case study observations, a theoretical framework of social enterprise entrepreneurship business and nonprofit sustainability and a better understanding of the way financial sustainability influences the development of a business strategy and business models, combined with the shared values with stakeholders and the role of the social enterprise pathway for nonprofit organizations.

In Chapter 3, Kenneth Strang examines the concept of the effectiveness of business models and managerial strategies in nonprofit organizations. Kenneth argues that effectiveness is a perspective conditioned by social culture and that naturally nonprofits in emerging countries have different priorities and perspectives to those in the developed world. Obviously, nonprofit goals usually differ from those of for-profit enterprises, but problematically most best-practice strategic management studies are only concerned with the latter. Effectiveness also differs based on organization size and mission, and Kenneth generalizes his findings toward a number of alternative contexts and institutional sizes.

In Chapter 4, Sarah Caflisch observes that many social service nonprofits must abide by codes of ethics when serving vulnerable populations, as well as when holding fundraisers, and they usually follow all of these codes because they know that an organization gains social and financial capital only by publicly embodying its values. Lately, scrutiny and concern over the ethical "private face", internal management, and overall day-to-day business dealings of nonprofits, has been increasing. In her chapter, Sarah examines more than 20 nonprofits operating in the Minneapolis/Saint Paul region of Minnesota in the US and considers the number of nonprofits currently with effective policies and procedures in this regard, and the potential costs, in both financial and social capital, of not following ethical practice.

Amir Manzoor examines the potential role of crowdfunding for the nonprofit sector, and whether these organizations can couple crowdfunding with social media to produce radical changes in the way they obtain funds in Chapter 5. The chapter examines applications and the impact of crowdfunding as an additional source of revenue for nonprofits. There is particular attention on the regulatory changes needed for keeping up with technological developments in the nonprofit sector and the way crowdfunding can facilitate an increase in funding.

In Chapter 6, Beata Jałocha and Ewa Bogacz-Wojtanowska consider the relatively new role of project portfolio management in management and education in third-sector practitioners. Unfortunately, most project portfolio management to date emphasizes corporate management tools typically used in the business sector with very little research undertaken in nongovernment sectors. The chapter addresses this research gap by identifying and analyzing project portfolio management practices in nongovernmental organizations. The findings suggest that while nongovernment organizations manage multiple projects simultaneously, project portfolio management could support them to better build their portfolio in accordance with a strategic plan that could fulfil their strategic objectives more efficiently and effectively

In Chapter 7, Javier Vidal-García, Marta Vidal Rafael, and Hernández Barros examine the challenge and unprecedented opportunity for modern organizations to build a new model of relationship with current and potential clients which is more efficient and innovative. This necessarily implies acquiring a completely new corporate culture in which the collection, management and interpretation of big data will inspire the entire business. Under this new business scenario, data is understood not as part of a process, but instead as a core business decision tool. The authors argue that only if companies can manage big data will they be able to understand what they do and where they are going, identify the tastes and preferences of consumers, and, more importantly, anticipate their decisions to adapt services in real time and in a personalized way.

Bessie Rean Bowser considers the lack of knowledge by both non-profit and for-profit organizations in building business models and developing global managerial strategies in Chapter 8. She also considers the need for organizations to understand the open transformation of organizational structure with an autonomous mindset of each stakeholder and the unification of the organizational system. Bessie explains how some theories and disciplines need to band together to bring out deeper meanings of phenomena to address managerial and leadership strategies and highlights the developmental processes of successful organizational systems that potentially can be used as roadmaps in developing on-going constructs to navigate assessments, training, and the transformation processes of an organization

In Chapter 9, Amir Manzoor makes the case for the nonprofit sector to couple crowdfunding with social media to produce effective and efficient changes in the way they seek, obtain and sustain funds. However, while crowdfunding is potentially an effective and cost efficient mechanism for nonprofit organizations to raise revenue, some conventional nonprofits and charities consider it as a threat. Amir explores how nonprofits can launch a successful crowdfunding campaign by providing insights into crowdfunding and the changing economic landscape of fundraising in the nonprofit space. The chapter also includes the characteristics of a successful nonprofit organization and discussion of the business models and strategies required for successful crowdfunding.

In Chapter 10, Nayeth Alcivar, Louis Sanzogni and Luke Houghton discuss how information systems (IS) in government organizations of developing economies are often overlooked by those conducting studies on technology acceptance and adoption. The authors argue that local governments, as nonprofit organizations, often struggle with such technology because it is undeveloped, under resourced and often does not live up to the expectations of those who have developed it. To address this problem, the authors identify the drivers of IS adoption, and the factors contributing to information system success, and software usage associated with the successful adoption of IS in organizations.

Chi Maher proposes a conceptual framework that explores factors that influence managerial career orientations (self-perceived talents and abilities, basic values and the evolved sense of motives and needs that influences a person's career-related decisions) in Chapter 11. The argument is that demographic (age, gender, social class, marital status, ethnicity, professional and educational qualifications); societal and organizational factors (government policies, labor market conditions, diversification of income streams, organization size, structure and culture) will influence small third-sector manager career orientations. Identifying and understanding these career orientations of managers then provides organizations with greater awareness of employee career needs and the ability to target career management effectively.

In Chapter 12, Juana Alonso-Cañadas, Maria Del Mar Galvez-Rodriguez, Maria Del Carmen Caba-Pérez and Laura Saraite consider the role of corporate social responsibility (CSR) in nonprofit organizations. CSR is the procedures and actions that organizations adopt in order to apply best practices in the management of the economic, social and environmental impact of their actions. However, while CSR and online transparency arouse considerable interest among nonprofits, little is known about best practices in this regard. To address this, the authors consider the case of the Spanish nonprofit organization Verdiblanca. Data are obtained by questionnaire and the organization's webpage examined, with a particular focus on the extent of the accountability mechanisms used, especially the Global Reporting Initiative (GRI) reporting model.

In Chapter 13, Ali Acilar and Muzaffer Aydemir conducts the findings of an online survey of 133 members of the Union of Chambers and Commodity Exchanges of Turkey in regard to usage by these nonprofits of social media. The authors find that most of the participant chambers operate a website (98.4%) and use social media officially (95.1%), with Facebook and Twitter being the most popular platforms. In addition, 55.2% report that they have a clear official social media use policy/plan, and 65.5% have a designated department responsible for social media. Overall, 62.1% of chambers had a positive experience with social media usage experience, 34.5% as average, and only one negative. Most participants (79.3%) agreed that social media was useful for the nonprofit chambers.

In Chapter 14, Albena Antonova argues that as social and environmental struggles intensify, the economic and social role of nonprofits will continue to expand globally. This is because they have the potential to mobilize digitally-enabled communities and to work on various global challenges, overcoming the limitations of governmental institutions, the local and short-term perspectives of public administration, and the private interests of for profit businesses. Albena examines the business models and value creation underpinning nonprofit operational models, their role for social innovation, and the impact of the new technologies and emerging digital communities. She also discusses the new perspectives for nonprofit development as innovative instruments, protecting social interests between government and private organizations, and contributing to solving social problems

Dario Cavenago and Laura Mariani consider the impact on Italian third sector organizations of the type of government, the stages of economic development, and the model of civil society, the existence of philanthropic traditions and law and regulation using a case study and content analysis in Chapter 15. They find that third sector organizations that are incentivized, use entrepreneurial business models, social networking, and cooperation to ensure their survival and growth. In doing so, Dario and Laura reduce that knowledge gap and enhance our understanding of the role and behavior of third sector organizations in the Italian context.

In Chapter 16, Lijun He, Jessika Graterol-Alfronzo and Kilian Tep examine how impact investment has emerged as a financial tool that allows nonprofit foundations to achieve their mission through the use of endowments, and to generate social impact. Such activity also allows foundations to tackle social issues and generate social changes in a more sustainable way than is possible through grant allocation. Using an in-depth qualitative case study of a pioneering grant-making foundation in the US that has shifted its strategic focus to impact investing, the chapter identifies the motivation and enabling environment of this strategic change and analyzes the issues and changes confronting the managerial model when evolving from traditional grant-making to impact investing.

In Chapter 17, Marian Mahat and Alan Pettigrew argue that every nonprofit organization needs a strategy—a set of unified actions undertaken to advance its organizational mission by leveraging its competitive advantage. In higher education and research, key issues shaping the competitive landscape compel nonprofit institutions to make strategic choices in order to make use of their resources effectively and efficiently. However, the concept of strategy in nonprofit higher education in particular is a contested issue. This chapter discusses the regulatory environment of nonprofit higher education in Australia by focusing on one of the most highly regulated disciplines in the field: medical education and research. The chapter develops a context for discussion by firstly mapping the landscape of Australian medical education, training and research, including its regulatory contexts. Subsequently, it discusses strategy formulation in nonprofit medical schools and research institutions.

Liliana Ávila and Marlene Amorim discuss the proliferation of hybrid organizations and diversification of the organizational and competitive landscape, where social enterprises as hybrid organizations are attracting growing interest among academics and practitioners in Chapter 18. The authors present the main concepts behind the definition of an operations strategy and the main reasons why social enterprises are labelled as hybrid organizations, as well as the tensions emerging from their hybridity. The chapter also identifies key operational challenges faced by social enterprises motivated by the ambidexterity of their activities and proposes some future research derived from the specificities of operations management in social enterprises.

In Chapter 19, Tomaso Amati, Marika Arena, Irene Bengo and Debora Caloni contribute to the debate on performance measurement and management in the social business sector through an analysis of the critical issues that arise in the implementation of impact assessment models in social business organizations. They first analyze the approaches suggested to measure performance with specific reference to social impact in social business organizations, highlighting the strengths and weaknesses of different approaches related to their implementation. They then present the case of an Italian social business organization, Cometa, that operates in the field of education and outline its paths in connection to social impact measurement. Based on the case evidence, the authors highlight the key problems that have emerged in the implementation of social impact assessment practices and how these problems could be addressed.

In Chapter 20, Beata Maria Staszewska argues that business model development is a complex process which while well researched in companies, is little considered in the context of nonprofit organizations. To address this, Beata reports the findings of an exploratory study conducted during 2011–15 to examine business development process in the areas of stability, sustainability and resistance in a local nonprofit public enterprise. The findings suggest that a balanced approach to economic, ecological and social characteristics, organizational coping capabilities during volatile phases of business model development, and organizational capability to manage during times of instability contributes to the type of business model development process.

Lastly, in Chapter 21, Xunyu Xiang, Cheryl Chui, Lucy Porter Jordan and Min-Hsiu Chiang investigate the opportunities for the implementation of business-like strategic models in the Chinese nonprofit sector. The chapter focuses on a single case in China's context—the nonprofit incubator—to assess how a business-like strategic model can be applied successfully in an authoritarian regime. Drawing from the theoretical frameworks of policy windows and balanced scorecard, first introduces current trends regarding the convergence of business-like strategies and the nonprofit sector, followed by an overview of nonprofit support organizations (NSOs). The authors then explore the development of NSOs in contemporary China through statistical data and conduct an analysis of managerial systems and strategic planning and how a nonprofit incubator can execute business-like strategies.

The themes explored in the chapters include nonprofit sector organizations, strategic performance management models, innovative business analytics, social ventures, big society and small government concepts, funding, information technology and methodological advances, consumerism, commercialism, borders and boundaries of the status of NFP organizations, competitive behavior and social ventures. While diverse in topic, purpose and approach, these chapters share a common focus on strategy, strategic business models and strategic performance management in the critically important nonprofit sector. These topics and themes will therefore be of immense interest and value to academics, practitioners, entrepreneurs, philanthropists, funders, business analysts and consultants, legal advisors, and researchers working in the field.

*Lindy Lou West*
*Griffith University, Australia*

*Andrew C. Worthington*
*Griffith University, Australia*

# Chapter 1
# Big Data in Higher Education

**Marta Vidal**
*Complutense University of Madrid, Spain*

**Javier Vidal-García**
*University of Valladolid, Spain*

**Rafael Hernández Barros**
*Complutense University of Madrid, Spain*

## ABSTRACT

*Big Data refers to large volumes of information – on diseases, ticket sales, and so on – that standard database tools such as MySQL and Oracle, cannot easily process. Thus, data analytics tools, such as InfoGram and Google Fusion Tables, are required to manage the information. The processed data is useful in several ways. For instance, public health officials may use the results of the analysis to explain the spread of viruses including the H1N1 virus (Mayer-Schönberger & Cukier, 2014, p. 2). Airplane companies may use the results to predict changes in ticket prices. Apart from the medical and aviation industries, institutions of higher learning also collect significantly large quantities of data. Hence, the analysis of Big Data also takes place in higher education. The beneficiaries of the analysis include students and administrators.*

## INTRODUCTION

The educational environment in the institutions of higher learning has considerably improved. Technological advancements are mainly responsible for the positive changes. Specifically, the introduction of data analytics in higher education – universities and colleges –made it easier for the management to make progress in key areas such as finance, student evaluation, and resource allocation (Bichsel, 2012). In other words, Big Data analytics aids college and university administrators to make predictions with respects to campus operations.

Before delving further into the uses of Big Data analytics in higher education, it is necessary to explain a few concepts about Big Data. Prior to the introduction of Big Data analytics, regular computers collected, contained, processed, and managed raw information. However, soon the data became so

DOI: 10.4018/978-1-5225-2537-0.ch001

Copyright © 2017, IGI Global. Copying or distributing in print or electronic forms without written permission of IGI Global is prohibited.

voluminous that the traditional computers could not process it efficiently. This prompted engineers to overhaul the existing data analytics tools (Mayer-Schönberger & Cukier, 2014, p. 6). As a result, processing technologies such as MapReduce and Google's Hadoop were developed. These technologies manage terabytes of data by arranging the information in structured database tables. Thus, the database tables provide the raw materials for data analytics.

## BACKGROUND

### How to Use Big Data Analytics in Higher Education

The data analysis is a five-stage process. Firstly, the researcher needs to state the research question or objective that will drive the study. Thereafter, data that is relevant to the research question is collected. Thirdly, the analysis takes place. Normally, the objective of the data analysis is to establish forecasting parameters. Fourthly, the data analytics tool presents the results of the analysis in a manner that is simple to understand and interpret. In addition, the findings or recommendations should be actionable or practical (Bichsel, 2012). Lastly, the application generates reports that provide the feedback needed to evaluate the entire process. If the report shows that the analysis did not achieve the objective, then new research questions may need to be identified or different sets of data collected or both. So, do the institutions of higher learning follow the five-stage process?

According to Bichsel (2012), while a majority of colleges and universities are collecting large volumes of data, few use the information strategically. In other words, the use of Big Data analytics is not as extensive as it should be. Even when the tools are available, a considerable number of the users employ the applications in rudimentary tasks such as creating reports and filling credentials. However, some administrators are attempting to use Big Data analytics correctly. In this case, they employ the tools in enrollment management and budgeting. Sadly, the school managers have not yet tested Big Data analytics in resource optimization and administration, which are key aspects of higher education management.

Big Data analytics is effective if there is commitment, partnership, and investment. To begin with, the readiness of an institution to engage in the venture determines its commitment (Bichsel, 2012). Secondly, if research institutions, executives, and functional leaders work together, the users of the tools will reap optimal gains. Finally, the implementation of Big Data analytics succeeds if the managers of the institutions of higher learning perceive the technology as an investment rather than an expense. That said, implementing Big Data analytics is costly. This is because the institutions have to invest in expensive means of data collection (Bichsel, 2012). Additionally, often, the schools have to hire professionals to identify the key requirements for generating data models and provide suitable recommendations.

Besides the mentioned applications, Big Data analytics can significantly influence higher education in another way. Online tutorials are quickly replacing traditional lectures. In this case, instead of travelling to attend a class, a considerable number of students opt to take part in lectures through the internet. This is because the online tutorials enable students to save not only transport and accommodation fees, but also the time wasted in moving around campus from class to class (Guthrie, 2013). As a result, the institutions of higher learning have introduced massive open online courses (MOOCs). The MOOCs are a product of Big Data analytics.

In addition, Big Data analytics will enable educators to prepare effective assignments easily. Normally, the lecturers give students assignments and continuous assessment tests to gauge their understanding of taught concepts. After, collecting the responses, the data should be stored. This information will aid the instructors in designing customized assignments that will assist the learners to work on the identified weaknesses (Guthrie, 2013). Thus, Big Data can aid in the creation of a model that accelerates the learning process.

Furthermore, the use of Big Data analytics can aid students to develop skills and abilities. For instance, after identifying the strengths of the learners through customized assignments, the educators can create exercises that will aid the students build up on their abilities and hence qualify for certain vocations (Guthrie, 2013). In other words, the instructors can use the analytical information to direct the students to focus on their talents. Big Data analytics is, therefore, a tool that contributes toward student achievement.

Again, through the online tutorials, Big Data analytics enables the students to interact effectively with their instructors (Guthrie, 2013). Normally, universities assign a lecturer to a considerable number of students. As a result, only the learners who can initiate discussions with the tutors during class hours establish relationships with them. Unfortunately, a significant number of the learners fail to initiate interactions with their teachers and hence miss the benefits of having interpersonal relationships with the lecturers such as receiving extra tutorials. The online tutorials created through Big Data analytics give the shy students an opportunity to communicate with the lecturers.

Lastly, the use of Big Data analytics will aid in transforming the universities from institutions that transmit information into institutions that enhance learning. In this case, while MOOCs cannot completely replace conventional classes, they give a significant number of students an opportunity to enjoy the benefits of customized learning (Guthrie, 2013). In contrast, conventional classes have become avenues for spoon feeding students.

## MAIN FOCUS OF THE CHAPTER

### What Universities Can Learn from Big Data

Before the introduction of Big Data analytics into higher education, other industries experimented with the technology, for instance, health, banking, and retail sectors (Groves et al., 2013). In this regard, the leaders of the institutions of higher learning can learn valuable lessons in relation to how the other professionals use the systems. Specifically, the health sector provides useful information in that respect.

The health care industry benefitted tremendously from utilizing Big Data analytics. For instance, the institutions managed to identify the appropriate precautionary measures that aid in the fight against preventable diseases by using Big Data analytics tools. That is, through the applications, health professionals have been able to collect and analyze data on right living, right provider, and so on (Groves et al., 2013). In this case, right living means adopting lifestyle choices that promote good health. Right provider refers to seeking treatment from certified health professionals. Thus, the Big Data applications enhance the quality of care provided to patients.

Besides causing an improvement in service delivery, the use of Big Data analytics in health care has resulted in the introduction of innovative treatments. For instance, Asthmapolis, a healthcare company, installs GPS transmitters in its inhalers to track the usage of the devices (Groves et al., 2013). The transmitters send the usage data to a central database. Thereafter, the analytical tools analyze the information to identify areas that have elements that can trigger asthma attacks. This means that Big Data analytics facilitates asthma prevention and management.

Similarly, the universities should seek to use Big Data analytics to optimize the quality of education. In this case, it is worth noting that some of the institutions have already taken the initiative to adopt the use of Big Data analytics. These include colleges in Texas and so on. The details on how the higher education organizations employ or should employ Big Data analytic are provided under student enrollment, student course major selection, and student retention.

## Student Enrollment

Big Data analytics is also relevant in student enrollment. Initially, the learners were wholly responsible for making career choices and selecting the institutions that would provide the relevant training. Nowadays, the institutions of higher learning use the Big Data analytics tools to collect and analyze information on various disciplines and thereafter provide feedback that assists incoming students in selecting the right subject combinations that will aid them to qualify for their chosen professions. This means that data can be the driving force behind engagement in universities across the United States (Smith, 2014).

Additionally, there are analytical tools that provide web interfaces that guide the learners in selecting the right institutions for training. For instance, Texas students have access to MyFutureTX, which is the ideal college shopping platform. Through the web interface of the application, the prospective students input data such as SAT scores, location, and household income (Smith, 2014). Thereafter, the application evaluates the data and identifies a suitable institution and course on behalf of the learner. Additionally, the prospective students obtain information on expected earnings after graduation.

The College Board is another institution that hosts a data-driven website known as Bigfuture. In this case, Bigfuture generates a sequence of queries aimed at determining what the potential students would like to achieve from their college experience. Thus, the learners can shortlist several career choice options. Thereafter, the system generates requirements for enrollment into several colleges that provide the courses that will enable the potential students achieve their career ambitions (Smith, 2014.).

Another Big Data analytics platform that aids the student in enrollment is StatFuse. This website allows the learners to create and develop individual profiles. The personal profiles include data such as preferred extracurricular activities, GPA, and ethnicity. The application then checks the data against the enrollment requirements of a considerable number of universities. Subsequently, StatFuse uses a 'Chanculator' to determine the probability of a college admitting the student (Smith, 2014). Thus, the platform effectively helps the students in selecting colleges that will most likely accept their applications.

In addition, Big Data analytics can assist in marketing colleges. For instance, in Ithaca College, the enrollment team devised data experimentation methods for marketing. One of the means includes a private social network known as myIthaca, which they launched in 2011. The myIthaca site allows the students to share their photos and profiles among themselves (Smith, 2014). This means that no information is accessible to extended families. As a result, the system enhanced student engagement and hence improved student enrollment.

Lastly, Big Data analytics can aid in student recruitment in another way. In this case, colleges can collect and analyze information on course preferences (Kellen, Recktenwald & Burr, 2013, p. 11). Analytical tools can then analyze the data to generate smart course recommendations. That is, when the prospective student generates a list of course options, the individual is able to view the recommendations of learners who completed the selected programs. Thus, this reference model may provide information that will assist in student enrollment. Such a model is similar to the recommendation engine that Amazon operates; the engine enables new consumers to assess existing products based on the findings of other customers who purchased the goods.

One must accept that Big Data analytics greatly enhances student enrollment. In this case, a considerable number of institutions – such as MyFutureTx, Bigfuture, StatFuse, and myIthaca – are increasingly relying on Big Data analytical tools to lure more students into their campuses. In other words, such sites make the identification of relevant courses simpler than before.

## Student Course Major Selection

Big Data analytics is also applicable in student course major selection. Normally, after joining campus, college students have to select a course to major in. In some instances, the learners can major in more than one discipline (Kanar, 2014, p. 7). A course major prepares an individual for a career. Hence, the learners require advice in selecting their majors. Big Data analytical tools can provide the needed information in case a student does not have access to an academic advisor.

Before explaining how the Big Data analytical tools can aid in student course major selection, it is important to explain the conventional process of course major selection. According to Kanar (2014, p. 7), course major selection is a five-step process. Firstly, the learners prepare academic plans. The plans consist of a list of courses that the students qualify to pursue. Secondly, the students assess their values and interests. In other words, the learners establish the extent to which they are motivated to perform specific duties or jobs. Normally, a three-column table aids in the assessment (Kanar, 2014, p. 8). The students can name the first column 'personal values', the second 'major(s)', and the third 'career(s)'. If, to take an example, a learner's value is 'creating wealth', then the major may be 'business,' and the career 'financial advisor'.

Thirdly, the student should thereafter consult other parties. In this case, the learner needs to discuss the course content with other students who major in the selected program (Kanar, 2014, p. 7). This will enable the leaner to know how much effort to put in the studies and so on.

Fourthly, careers are life-long commitments that reflect what an individual wants to achieve in life (Kanar, 2014, p. 7). Thus, after obtaining advice, the learner should make an independent choice in relation to the selected major. That is, proceed with the course, select another one, and so on.

Lastly, the student may not be ready to select a major at that moment. In this case, the learner will have to pursue an associate of arts (AA) degree (Kanar, 2014, p. 7). The AA allows the student to study general courses related to some majors. After studying for some time, the learner may develop a keen interest in some topics and hence use that as the basis for selecting a major.

However, some students may not be aware of the five-step process, especially if they do not have academic advisors. In this case, the Big Data analytical tool can play the role of the advisors. The applications access the learners' records, including results of aptitude tests and high school performance (Kellen, Recktenwald & Burr, 2013, p. 24). The scores are checked against the profiles of other students who have enrolled into different programs. Thereafter, the systems advice the students to major in the courses pursued by the students whose profiles match theirs.

Besides that, the Big Data analytical tools may provide information on workplace demands or required skills for the chosen professions. In this respect, the tools serve the same purpose in course major selection and student enrollment.

Time is also a factor to consider in student course major selection. A significant number of tertiary institutions give the learners a time limit to declare their majors. For instance, a considerable number of universities that offer four-year courses demand that the students make the decision by the end of the second year study. A few colleges require students to make up their minds upon entry into campus. Pushing the learners to declare their course majors upon entry into college is inappropriate. This is because the students will not have had enough experience to make the right choice. In other words, they need to accumulate credit hours before they are in a position to make decisive career choices (Tobolowsky et al., 2009, p. 54). The institutions of higher learning should provide the Big Data analytical tools to students upon entry or during sophomore year so that they can key-in enough data that will enable the systems to give proper recommendations in relation to course major selection at the end of the second year of study.

One must agree that Big Data analytics plays a significant role in student course major selection. The analytical tools simplify the decision-making process, particularly in instances where the students do not have educational advisors. Additionally, one has no option but to accept that the colleges should provide the tools as soon as students join campus. In this case, doing so will enable the systems to collect enough profile data for analysis and thereafter offer recommendations in relation to course major selection.

## Student Performance

Normally, the lecturers rely on hardcopy assignments and exams to gauge the level of understanding of their learners. After marking the assessments, a significant number of the teachers plan revision sessions. In this case, the objective is often to just point out the correct answers. Thus, the teachers seldom give feedback on the specific subjects or topics that the learners should study again. Worse still, they provide no recommendations on how the students can improve their study habits to enhance their performance. The Big Data analytical tools deal with such shortcomings of conventional assessments (West, 2012).

For instance, consider Samantha, a student who takes a course to nurture her reading skills. Her tutor expects that she will read a considerable number of short stories. To gauge her progress, every week, the lecturer may give her comprehension and vocabulary tests. Once she does the assessments, the teacher may take several days to mark the paper, issue grades, and returns the results to Samantha (West, 2012). Before returning the results, the tutor may insert comments into the paper if Samantha performed poorly; for instance, the lecturer may recommend that she should work harder. In this case, one can see that Samantha has to wait for some time before she receives feedback that does not provide specific instructions on how to improve her comprehension ability and vocabulary.

Now, consider a student – Richard – who uses a software program to improve his reading skills. The application records the period he takes to complete going through the stories. At the end of each study session, the computer displays a quiz that tests his comprehension ability and vocabulary skills. In this case, Richard receives feedback after submitting every answer. In addition, the software provides links to sites that explain the difficult concepts (West, 2012). Besides that, the application sends updates on Richard's reading progress – including information on the amount of time he spends reading, the supplemental materials he reviews, and more – to the instructor every time he signs out. Thus, the teacher can intervene if the reports show that the learner is not making progress.

The second example shows how Big Data analytics can improve student performance. The analytical tools enable the students to refer to the sources that provide information that will aid them in eliminating their academic weaknesses (West, 2012). Additionally, the systems send detailed reports to the lecturers who can then use the feedback to design customized intervention plans for the learners.

The Big Data analytics tools can also improve student performance in other ways. To begin with, the applications aided in the design of a high school learning model known as Connected Chemistry. Connected Chemistry covers the molecular theory. This means that the program enables the students to gain a better understanding of how submicroscopic elements and macroscopic particles are related (West, 2012). Additionally, the use of the software allows the instructors to mine learning methodologies. That is, the teachers are able to find out how their students understand experimental designs, chemistry, and so on. For instance, the systems may show that a considerable number of students do not understand the relationship between volume and gas pressure. This means that the teachers may improve their students' performance by elaborating further on the misunderstood concepts.

Another application that relies on Big Data analytics to improve student performance is WebQuest. In this case, the teachers encourage their students to use WebQuest to conduct online research. The reason for that is that the application trains the learners on how to filter internet-based content (West, 2012).

A study was carried out to investigate the impact of the use of WebQuest. The results showed that the instructors agreed that the application significantly improved the ability of the students to do their assignments correctly (West, 2012). Additionally, WebQuest enabled the learners to interact and collaborative while doing their homework. Thus, the analytical tool fosters teamwork.

One must agree that Big Data analytics can improve student performance. It enables both the learners and tutors to take note of the time taken to go through a topic, provides immediate feedback on the students' progress, and recommends the specific steps that the learners can take to improve their performance. In addition, the Big Data analytical tools enhance teamwork among students.

## Student Retention

Big Data analytics also plays a role in student retention. In this case, student retention means stopping the learners from dropping out of school. One of the main reasons for quiting school is poor performance. Normally, some students opt to terminate their studies if they do not receive adequate help while facing academic difficultuies (Willis, 2013). Often, this happens if the instructors are unable to timely predict the performance of the learners. The Big Data analytics tools provide a feedback mechanism that alerts the students and lecturers if the leaners are in danger of performing poorly, hence prompting both parties to take measures that will prevent the students from dropping out.

For instance, Purdue University employs a data analytics program known as Signals. The application is able to predict student performance based on data such as the individual's academic history, demographics, current performance, and so on (Willis, 2013). After analyzing the data, Signals provides three types of feedback. If the screen shows a red light that means the student's study methods will not lead to success. Hence, the learner should immediately seek help from the lecturers. A yellow light indicates that the student should take precautionary measures to avoid failure. Finally, a green light means the leaner's performance thus far is satisfactory.

Because of introducing Signals, the student retention rates improved within the four years, from 2004-2007. Within that period, the educators noted that for students who did not use Signals, the retention rate was 69.40%. For students who used Signals in at least one course, the retention rate was 87.42%. Finally, for students that employed the application in two courses, the retention rate was 93.24% (Willis, 2013). The encouraging retention rates were attributable to the fact that Signals prompted the students to improve their standardized test (SAT) scores.

## Student Profiles

It is not necessary to utilize sophisticated analytical tools to process the data concerning a small number of students. This is because the educators can easily track each individual learner. However, for a large population of students, it becomes difficult for the management to track the progress of every one of them (Lane, 2014, p. 132). Fortunately, the Big Data analytical tools aid in solving this problem in several ways.

To begin with, the Big Data analytics tools help in the creation of student profiles. A student profile is a collection of information that shows educational progress, individual identity, and so on of a learner. Thus, the profiles are a representation of the student population. In reference to that, the student profiles do not portray a group ideology. Instead, they provide information on unique attributes concerning individuals (Lane, 2014, p. 132). Therefore, the Big Data analytics tools can help in revealing the specific traits of each learner that contribute to better interaction among the learners. This is important in bringing out each student's identity in a diverse setting.

Additionally, (Jeffreys, 2012, p.56) states that student profiles play a role in student retention. This is because student profile attributes directly influence cultural values, beliefs, motivation, and academic performance. If to take an example, consider the nursing course. Before joining the program, the students must submit their profile data, which includes information on age, educational background, ethnicity, language, gender, and so on. Having the information enables the educators to know the individuals' weaknesses in areas such as language beforehand and hence create modules that will aid the learners to build on their shortcomings. That is, the instructors are able to plan for the development of other skills that are important to nursing. Catering to individual needs increases the likelihood of the students staying in school.

Creation of student profiles assists in the customization of education in another way. In this case, the data obtained enables the identification of the learners who possess similar study styles or challenges. Thereafter, the students are grouped together to share resources. In this way, the instructors can come up with personalized teaching courses for the unique classes (Akerkar, 2014, p. 60). To add to that, Big Data analytics can aid in the analysis of the learners' responses to different instruction methods and hence optimize teaching.

One must agree that Big Data analytics enables the development of student profiles. The profiles portray individual identities through attributes such as gender and ethnicity. The analysis of the student profiles is useful in the creation of personalized teaching courses, which improve student retention. The building of student profiles also enables the institutions of higher learning to adopt the best teaching strategies and models, all of which can aid in assessing teacher effectiveness.

## Teacher Effectiveness

The Big Data analytics tools significantly improve the means of evaluating instructor effectiveness. In this case, the powerful applications facilitate the provision of prompt feedback, which in turn enhances teacher preparation. That is, the tutors are able to improve their lectures in time and hence influence the performance of the students facing difficulties after receiving the results of the analysis of their results in a quick and comprehensive manner (Walsh, 2014). To elaborate further, the Big Data analytics tools enable the instructors find out the subjects that students have not mastered prior to issuing quizzes and exams. Hence, the lecturers can come up with intervention measures promptly and thus improve learning. These concepts will be clearer once one reviews the tools that aid in the evaluation of teacher effectiveness.

One of the devices that have revolutionized teaching is the iPad. The hand held device consists of a touch screen, a powerful processor, and different types of applications. The utilization of the powerful processor and applications ensures that the users of the device obtain accurate and instantaneous feedback. This is what has prompted the educators to adopt the use of the electronic device in teaching and evaluation. The lecturers can install the Big Data analytics applications in iPads and then use the devices to evaluate student performance even while lectures are ongoing. For instance, one of the performance measures may be the learners' thinking process. That is, the teachers are able to determine why students answer questions in a particular manner during a lesson (Walsh, 2014). Such insight enables the tutors to alter the structure of their lessons to cater to students' academic deficiencies.

Already, elementary schools have shown how the installation of the Big Data applications into such devices can make a difference in learning. For instance, in Roosevelt Elementary School, which is close to San Francisco, the teachers utilize an application known as DIBELS (Walsh, 2014). DIBELS contains reading assignments. After doing their assignments through the application's interface, the instructors assess the pupils' responses through the program to determine the topics than need further elaboration. For that matter, the teachers can immediately follow up on the identified problems in subsequent lessons since the applications provide the results of the analysis instantaneously. Additionally, given that the software sends feedback to the school officials, they are in a position to evaluate the lecturers to determine whether there are changes to make in teaching arrangements. Institutions of higher learning can acquire similar applications.

Besides that, Big Data technology improves teacher effectiveness by optimizing data privacy. In this case, the students with excellent grades often look down upon their counterparts who face academic difficulties. As a result, it becomes difficult for the learners with poor records to participate in class. One of the ways of protecting the students from psychological abuse is by keeping their academic reports confidential. The Big Data analytics tools enable the teachers to provide feedback to individual students (Walsh, 2014). The optimization of privacy in such a manner makes teaching more effective.

Additionally, the Big Data analytics tools facilitate continuous teacher evaluation. In this case, the management of the learning organizations can use the applications to collect data on teaching appraisal elements such as leadership ability, problem-solving skills, and so on. Normally, such evaluations aid in the monitoring of the progress of lecturers and hence the institutions as well (Campbell et al., 2003, p. 132). The Big Data analytics tools facilitate access to information that is useful in the evaluation of teacher progress and provide the results of the analysis in real time.

Finally, the Big Data applications can help in identifying changes that can improve teacher effectiveness. For instance, after analysis, the systems may show a downward slope in teacher performance over several years. This will necessitate a change in the teaching strategy including introduction of job rotation, swopping of classes, and more (Campbell et al., 2003, p. 132). Such necessary adjustments improve teacher effectiveness.

## Bookstore Effectiveness

Big Data analytics is not only applicable in higher education, but also in businesses related to learning. Specifically, retail enterprises such as bookstores may find the utilization of the applications beneficial. There are several ways to show that (Schmarzo, 2012).

Before delving into how bookstores can utilize Big Data analytics, it is worth mentioning how the retail industry ended up using the technology. For a long time, the retail enterprises employed several data-reading devices and techniques – including point-of-sale (POS) scanners, radio-frequency identification (RFID), universal product code (UPC) – and analyzed the supply chain to obtain customer loyalty data. In this case, customer loyalty data refers to information on the consumers' habits. Some of the major retail players that utilized the techniques include Wal-Mart and Amazon. After using the technologies for several years, retail giants, such as Wal-Mart, were able to develop innovations for their supply links. The developments resulted from the use of Big Data applications.

Through the Big Data analytical tools, the retailers capture voluminous data on customer loyalty. Initially, the information is collected via online or hardcopy questionnaires. The surveys capture data on the strengths and failures of product placement, advertising, and so on. Thereafter, the Big Data applications analyze the data and hence enable the users to come up with appropriate recommendations for improving the overall customer experience. The collection of customer loyalty data led to the creation of loyalty cards. Shoppers use the cards to collect points that shop owners award them because of frequently buying merchandise from their outlets. Hence, this is an indirect benefit of using Big Data analytics in the retail industry (Atzori, Iera & Morabito, 2010).

The institutions of higher learning may adopt similar approaches to attract clients to their bookstores. That is, the store operators should use the Big Data applications to collect and analyze data on the shopping trends of students and hence have the relevant information that will aid them in marketing the books. Additionally, they can issue loyalty cards to attract more buyers to their stores.

Specifically, the use of the Big Data applications in analyzing consumer trends may reveal information on product demand. Normally, seasons influence consumption. For instance, the sales of boots and socks increase during winter. In this respect, the analysis of bookstore-sales may also reveal some relationships. If to take an example, at the beginning of the year, storeowners may sell more books, stationeries, and so on than at any other time. Hence, the Big Data analytics tools aid in determining when bookstores should engage in aggressive promotion exercises to maximize revenues.

Product assortment also changes during particular seasons depending on demand. In this case, the retailers stock more quantities of the goods that have incremental demand than other products. Researchers obtained this information after using Big Data analytics to study consumer purchase-patterns during local events or in different seasons. The information is relevant to inventory stores including bookshops. That is, the business owners use the data to project demand and hence ensure they have sufficient supplies of the needed commodities. Another benefit of Big Data analysis in retail stores, including bookshops, is reduction in costs. In this case, the ability to predict shopping patterns is crucial for creating savings. That is, the forecasts are vital in making decisions pertaining to storage, transportation, and replenishment. For instance, the costs associated with the processes decrease if one is able to avoid surpluses during low seasons and vice versa. The Big Data analytical tools aid in creating such forecasts.

Lastly, the Big Data analytics tools enable the bookstore owners to analyze social media sites to obtain information on new products, market insights, and customers preferences. For instance, the applications mine data from Twitter, Pinterest, and Facebook to determine customer sentiments and interests and hence identify emerging opportunities (Vidal, Vidal-García & Hernandez Barros, 2016, p. 140). That is, determine which types of books are on demand.

One must agree that Big Data analysis results in bookstore effectiveness. This is because the applications enable the collection of customer loyalty data, which is useful in several ways. For instance, the data facilitates demand forecasting, cost reduction, and so on. In addition, the tools can derive useful information from social media platforms for use in identifying consumer trends in relation to reading materials.

## Big Data to Promote Decision-Making

Decision-making is an element of financial management. In any organization, the administrators make choices that dictate the direction taken. Therefore, the managers require useful information to aid them in decision-making. In this regard, the Big Data analytical tools provide a data-driven means of facilitating efficient decision-making in business development, inventory management, product pricing, and so on.

To begin with, business development relies on the data-driven approach. This means that components such as digitization, data/technology, emerging trade models, and accelerating competition facilitate growth (IRIS Group7). In this case, digitization requires the use of the Big Data analytics tools to create the necessary data-driven development models. That is, it directly influences data storage, movement, and so on. The higher the digitization level, the easier it is to collect, store, and process data.

Data/ technology provide information for use by managers. The data undergoes analysis to provide the relevant information. Hence, the management relies more on data than experience in making choices (IRIS Group 8). The Big Data analytics tools significantly enhance the collection and analysis of facts to create information.

In relation to decision-making, Big Data analytics has other applications. The technologies aid emerging businesses or enterprises in transition in dealing with external competition. This is because it is relatively easy to develop new concepts for existing products through the applications (IRIS Group 8). Data is vital for developing a new service or product. Hence, the continuous data collection approach that Big Data analytical tools facilitate allows industrial firms to move toward new trade models.

In addition, the competitive environment determines the trends in Big Data analytics. This is particularly the case with companies that provide similar services (IRIS Group 8). That is, while the international enterprises focus on price, the local businesses may rely on the Big Data analytical tools to gain the competitive edge.

One must agree that the four components are useful. The elements help managers in making strategic decisions. In addition, the components provide a platform for the continuous development of any company. An example will elaborate the benefits further.

In December 2013, the IRIS Group, in collaboration with the Danish Business Authority, published a report explaining how the Big Data analytics tools can radically enhance the development of Danish small and medium enterprises (SMEs). The researchers identified several barriers to effective use of Big Data analytics as a resource in decision-making (Vidal-García & Vidal, 2016, p. 220). Firstly, executives are unaware that the technology can significantly aid in the management of their organizations. Hence, very few firms use the applications (IRIS Group 15). This means that the leaders make calculated decisions concerning sales opportunities, productivity gains, and so on without the use of Big Data analytics and thus the process is inefficient.

Secondly, there is lack of inspiration to use Big Data analytics in decision-making. In this case, the private sector does not have the skills required to employ the systems. In addition, there are limited sources that provide information on Big Data analytics applications in management (IRIS Group 15).

Thirdly, the cost of implementing the Big Data analytics tools is prohibitive. That is, the users must acquire software, hardware, professional expertise, and other resources (IRIS Group 15). The SMEs find it hard to raise capital for all the requirements.

However, such challenges may be catalysts for the adoption of Big Data analytics in decision-making in the higher education institutions. That is, the managers of the colleges can easily solve the problems. To begin with, Big Data resource centers are an investment rather than a cost (Guthrie, 2013). The construction of such research and development (R&D) centers is a long-term plan in higher education. Secondly, data mining of data-driven decision models provides valuable information to universities as well as SMEs. Hence, despite the cost, the institutions are motivated to embrace the technology. Thirdly, the creation of university networks enables the organizations to share information on the applications of Big Data analytics.

One must agree that data-driven models are useful in decision-making. This is particularly evident in business development where data/technology is a driving force. In addition, the management requires data to make informed decisions on new products, sales opportunities, product mix, and so on. One has no option but to accept that the SMEs provide useful case studies on the use of Big Data analytics that can aid the college managers in implementing the technology.

## Using Big Data to Predict Student Success

Student success is vital for the survival of educational institutions. Hence, the managers of schools, colleges, and universities require information on probable student performance for planning purposes. Normally, learning analytics aids in providing such predictive data. In this case, learning analytics entails the collection, measurement, and analysis of student data to optimize education. Thus, the learning analytics enables the faculty to make decisions concerning student success. The learning analytics is an aspect of Big Data analytics. Further elaboration will make the importance of the tool clearer.

Several institutions adopted the learning analytics for a variety of reasons. These include improving student performance, retention, and courses. The University of Maryland Baltimore County (UMBC) is a one such institution. In this case, the organization utilizes Blackboard Learning Course Management System (LCMS), a learning analytics tool, to foresee student success and track performance (Dietz-Uhler & Hurn, 2013). Hence, the educators obtain information on possible student success prior to quizzes and/or exams.

The LCMS collects limited data on student academics. This is because the learning analytics systems are restricted to using few parameters including the frequency of student logins, assignment grades, and comments in online chats (Junco & Clem, 2010). Fortunately, such information still provides a relatively strong basis for prediction. That said, the learning analytics systems might become more accurate by incorporating additional data. These data includes student involvement, self-stated confidence level, and academic records.

Some learning analytics systems use other means to predict student success – analysis of reading strategies. Reading strategies include taking notes, re-reading, highlighting, outlining, and listing. Research has revealed several facts concerning the reading strategies. For instance, the lowly skilled learners are more likely to highlight texts than their highly skilled counterparts are. In addition, the extent to which one covers a textbook determines the individual's test scores. Finally, the students who read digital texts have high rates of academic success. The LCMSs provide digital copies of resources. Big Data analytics plays a part in predicting student success. The applications use several techniques to do that including analyzing reading strategies. The systems can be more useful if the designers enable the applications to use more student data parameters in the prediction of success (Vidal-García, Vidal & Hernandez Barros, 2017).

## Big Data Analytics and Cloud Computing

Big Data analytics relies on advanced technologies. That is, the users must have access to software and hardware that are costly. Consequently, a significant number of businesses have been unable to adopt the technology in their operations. Fortunately, cloud computing can change the situation. It provides a cost-effective means of Big Data analytics management.

Cloud computing is a means of accessing computing resources through an online network and hence the technology is implemented in three ways. These are software as a service (SaaS), platform as a service (PaaS), and infrastructure as a service (IaaS). In PaaS, the users can use the service providers' platform to create customized applications (Purcell, 2013). The sharing of the platform presents little risks and minimizes the development costs. In SaaS, the users can access and operate virtual servers. In this case, the organizations pay for time and bandwidth allocation. Finally, in IaaS, the clients hire the service providers' equipment such as servers, networking devices, and so on. Thus, through IaaS, the organizations can access services including data storage, disaster recovery, and computing. In all the cases, the sharing of resources minimizes cost.

There are three different types of clouds. To begin with, a private cloud is an in-house data hub that is inaccessible to the public. This means that it is secure and self-managed. The users access services through an intranet. Additionally, the client company owns the cloud resources. Hence, implementing a private cloud is costly.

Secondly, there is a public cloud. It is accessible to the public. In addition, it operates on a pay-as-you-go basis. Hence, the ownership of the resources remains with the service provider. As a result, using the public cloud is relatively cheap.

Thirdly, a hybrid cloud combines the services of the private and public clouds. That is, the organization can use the private cloud for storage of sensitive and confidential data, while the public cloud handles non-private data. In addition, the public cloud can expedite tasks that the internal data hub cannot easily manage.

Cloud computing provides viable options for dealing with the costs associated with Big Data analytics. The managers of institutions of higher learning may adopt cloud computing deployment solutions, such as IaaS, SaaS, and PaaS, depending on their needs and capabilities (Purcell, 2013). In addition, the administrators may select any of the three types of clouds – private, public, and hybrid – depending on security and management requirements.

## CONCLUSION

One must agree that Big Data analytics is relevant in higher education. The analytical tools aid in creation of customized curriculums, course selection, success prediction, and monitoring student performance, which is vital for student retention. In reference to that, the administrators that view the applications as an investment rather than an expense tend to benefit the most from the use of the systems. In addition, the Big Data analytics tools aid in building student profiles, evaluating teacher effectiveness by providing prompt feedback, and enhancing bookstore effectiveness. Besides that, the managers of the educational institutions can employ data-driven models in decision-making. Thus, the beneficiaries of Big Data analytics in higher education include students and administrators. The technology is expensive, but the introduction of concepts such as cloud computing can significantly bring down the associated costs and hence encourage more organizations to utilize the applications.

## REFERENCES

Akerkar, R. (2014). *Big Data Computing*. Boca Raton, FL: CRC Press.

Atzori, L., Iera, A., & Morabito, G. (2010). The Internet of Things: A survey. *Computer Networks*, *54*(15), 2787–2805. doi:10.1016/j.comnet.2010.05.010

Campbell, J., Muijs, D., Robinson, W., & Kyriakides, L. (2003). Measuring teachers' performance: A case for differentiation. *Education, 3*(31), 4-8.

Dietz-Uhler, B., & Hurn, J. E. (2013). Using learning analytics to predict (and improve) student success: A faculty perspective. *Journal of Interactive Online Learning*, *12*, 16–19.

Jeffreys, M. R. (2012). *Nursing student retention: Understanding the process and making a difference*. New York, NY: Springer Publishing.

Junco, R., & Candrainna, C. (2010). *Evaluating sow the courseSmart engagement index predicts student course outcomes*. Purdue University Working Paper.

Kanar, C. C. (2014). *The confident Student*. Boston, MA: Wadsworth, Cengage Learning.

Kellen, V., Recktenwald, A., & Burr, S. (2013). *Applying Big Data in higher education: A case study*. Arlington, MA: Cutter Consortium.

Lane, J. E. (2014). *Building a smarter university: Big Data, innovation, and analytics*. Albany, NY: State University of New York Press.

Mayer-Schonberger, V., & Cukier, K. (2014). *Big Data: A revolution that will transform how we live, work, and think*. Boston, MA: Houghton Mifflin Harcourt.

Purcell, B. M. (2013). *Big Data using cloud computing*. Holy Family University working paper.

Tobolowsky, B. F., Mary, S., Hunter, L. A., Schreiner, J., Gardner, N., & Pattengale, J. A. (2009). *Helping sophomores succeed: Understanding and improving the second year experience*. San Francisco, CA: Jossey-Bass Publishing.

Vidal, M., Vidal-García, J., & Hernandez Barros, R. (2016). Big Data and business decision making. In M. K. Singh & K. G. Dileep (Eds.), *Effective Big Data Management and Opportunities for Implementation* (pp. 140–157). Hershey, PA: IGI Global. doi:10.4018/978-1-5225-0182-4.ch010

Vidal-García, J., & Vidal, M. (2016). Big Data in financial services. In Effective Big Data Management and Opportunities for Implementation (pp. 217-230). Hershey, PA: IGI Global.

Vidal-García, J., Vidal, M., & Hernandez Barros, R. (2017). Computational business intelligence, Big Data and their role in business decisions in the age of the Internet of Things. In I. Lee (Ed.), *The Internet of Things in the Modern Business Environment*. Hershey, PA: IGI Global.

West, D.M. (2012). *Big Data for education: Data mining, data analytics, and web dashboards.* Brookings Institution working papers.

Willis, J. E. III. (2013). *Ethics, Big Data, and analytics: A model for application.* Instructional Development Center Publications, Purdue University.

## ADDITIONAL READING

Bichsel, J. (2012). *Analytics in higher education: Benefits, barriers, progress, and recommendations.* Louisville, KY: EDUCAUSE Center for Applied Research.

Groves, P., Kayyali, B., Knott, D., & Van Kuiken, S. (2013) *The 'Big Data' revolution in healthcare.* McKinsey Report.

Guthrie, D. (2013). The coming Big Data education revolution. *USNews.*

IRIS Group (2013). *Big Data as a growth factor in Danish business – potentials, barriers and business policy implications.* Danish business authority report.

Schmarzo, B. (2012). *Big Data in traditional retail-part 1.* InFocus Blog.

Smith, D. F. (2014). *4 ways Big Data is giving students an edge in the college hunt.* EdtechMagazine.

Walsh, K. (2014). *Understanding how Big Data can help improve teaching, with 2 examples.* Edu1world.org

## KEY TERMS AND DEFINITIONS

**Big Data:** Term employed to describe large data sets, it is commonly used to describe analytical methods to obtain value from data. The proper use of Big Data may improve the decision making process.

**Data Analytics:** Examining data with the objective of using this information for decision-making purposes.

**Educational Environment:** The physical locations and cultures, in which students learn. School policies and its governance are also considered as characteristics of the educational environment.

**Faculty:** A department in a college or university that includes one or several subject areas.

**Higher Education:** It includes the final stage of education after attending secondary education institutions. Students obtain academic degrees or professional certifications. Third level education for non-degree seekers is known as further education.

**Universities and Colleges:** An institution of higher education which provides and confers academic degrees at the undergraduate and graduate level.

**University Administrator:** It is the Section responsible for the organization of the institution and separate from the academic departments.

# Chapter 2
# Shared Value Creation for Sustainability in Not-for-Profit Organisations

**Tony Kandaiya**
*Partners in Micro-Development (PIMD), Australia*

**Meena Chavan**
*Macquarie University, Australia*

## ABSTRACT

*The objective of this chapter is to delineate the sustainability problems encountered by not-for-profit organisations and to explore how these challenges can be can be managed through shared value creation by the stakeholders. Case study-abductive research methodology was adopted to explore stakeholder shared values and sustainability. This method of study is especially useful for trying to test theoretical models by using them in real world situations. Findings revealed that the sustainability strategy in not for profit organizations must be a holistic approach. Such an approach needs to build upon value-creation that is integrated to develop social entrepreneurship and create social capital along the three dimensions which includes innovative, proactive, and risk management behavior. This chapter contributes to the shared value with stakeholders to provide a social enterprise pathway for a not for profit organization to achieve long-term financial sustainability while maintaining the core social mission and objectives.*

## INTRODUCTION

Partners in Micro-Development (PIMD) adopted a social enterprise model and introduced a commercial training arm which would provide training at subsidized rates to staff from donor corporations and the sales proceeds. This division would support the diminishing donations which will enable PIMD to continue with the social mission and provide sustainability. The contention in this discussion is that nonprofit organizations would benefit from the development of an entrepreneurial sustainability strategy to survive. The findings suggest that an innovative business model for the creation of shared value with

DOI: 10.4018/978-1-5225-2537-0.ch002

Copyright © 2017, IGI Global. Copying or distributing in print or electronic forms without written permission of IGI Global is prohibited.

the stakeholders provide a pathway to achieve long-term financial sustainability while maintaining the core mission objectives.

The objective of this chapter is to understand the survival strategies for not for profit organizations and to identify approaches to meet the challenges faced by them for long-term sustainability. The intention here is to advance the theory of corporate social responsibility in the context of social enterprise sustainability. To this end, financial sustainability challenges faced by a not for profit organisation (NPO), PIMD is explore and two main challenges are examined:

1. Over reliance of the trustworthiness theory on the non-distribution constraint.
2. Failure to explain why this constraint does not destroy the motivation of undertaking social entrepreneurial activities.

In this discussion, the challenges of financial sustainability faced by not for profit organisations but particularly the case of PIMD highlights those challenges. Drawing from the academic literature and the intellectual and human capital experiences of PIMD, an explorative case study investigates the challenges of financial sustainability faced by NPOs Data was collected through a structured interview. This chapter advances the theory of corporate social responsibility in the context of social enterprise entrepreneurship to expand the understanding of survival of not for profit organizations. To achieve this outcome, corporate social responsibility and social enterprise entrepreneurship theories are explored to illustrate the complexities of a not for profit organization as it transitions and shifts to a new business model where the production of multiple goods with social value attracts funding for sustainability.

A conceptual framework influences the theoretical framework of sustainability which contributes to the development of a new business model for PIMD. Such an approach capitalized upon value-creation that is integrated to develop social entrepreneurship and which creates social capital along the three dimensions of:

1. Innovative.
2. Proactive.
3. Risk Management.

This chapter contributes to the understanding of long-term financial sustainability, entrepreneurial social enterprise business model development. Commencing with an introduction and literature overview, this chapter then provides real-life case study observations which in turn guides the research methods. Second, the theoretical framework of social enterprise entrepreneurship business and not for profit sustainability are analysed. Third, understanding financial sustainability influences the on the development of a business strategy and the application of the development of a business model. Fourth, shared values with stakeholders and a social enterprise pathway for not for profit organisations to achieve long-term sustainability while maintaining the core social mission and organisational objectives are highlighted. Fifth, multiple challenges are identified, solutions are suggested and future research directions concludes this chapter.

## LITERATURE REVIEW

Salamon & Sokolowski's (2003:13-27) study on NPOs in India illustrates the wide variations in definitions of NPOs along the dimensions of economics, services, financing, legal structure as well as regional patterns. These views are supported by Salamon and Anheier (1997:11-51), Boris and Steuerle (2003: 66-110) and PRIA (2002). The NPO industry has also grown exponentially in the developing countries of Asia, Africa and Latin-America due in part to the increasing reliance of governments and international agencies on the third sector to deliver services, innovations in information and communication technology and the media (Te'eni & Young 2003), and growing demand for change in socio-economic conditions, politics, human rights, environment, rise of advocacy, volunteerism, and community groups.

Partnerships and channeling of funds between NPOs in the developed world and those in the developing world have also been a contributing factor (Salamon & Anheier 1997: 321-467; Salamon & Sokolwski, 2003: 1-13; UN NGO/Civil Society Forum 2004). More governments are turning to the not for profit sector to deliver goods and services to communities that are underserved. As a consequence, there is extensive research on not for profit organizations Dees and Economy (2001).More recently this research has branched out in the areas of social enterprises and social entrepreneurship (Kourula and Laasonen, 2010). Literature on these topics is a progression from not for profit research in the 1970-1980.

However, diminishing trend of the traditional donor-based funding model precipitated by the global financial crisis is threatening the survival of many not for profit organizations. To overcome this challenge, not for profit organizations need to explore new financial sustainability strategies that will provide financial independence to continue the core mission of service delivery to the community as well as building social capital. Dees and Economy (2001) have argued the case for NPO leaders to be particularly enterprising to meet the challenges and demands for greater accountability from donors, as well as new forms of competition from the business sector. The commercialisation of not for profit organisations has also gained wider acceptance due to the global economic downturn Weisbrod (1998).

## PARTNERS IN MICRO DEVELOPMENT

Partners in Micro Development (PIMD) an Australian-based volunteer supported not for profit organisation delivers primary education in underserved communities in the northern and eastern provinces of Sri Lanka. For the past eight years, PIMD's programs have focused on English as a second language (ESL) and computer literacy (CL) for primary grades in remote rural village schools. The organisation has developed curriculum and lesson plans, designed and delivered teacher training programs and provided computers, educational software, printers and other accessories for the sixty participating schools. This work constitutes the early stages of the teacher training e-learning and m-learning strategies as illustrated in Figure 1.

The aftermath of the conflict in Sri Lanka and the 2004 tsunami have devastated the economic, social, physical and human capital of the North and East provinces. Sri Lanka is now confronted with challenges on many fronts (social, political, economic, psycho-social, residual ethnic tension and divisions, gender and other issues) in its post-conflict recovery, reconstruction, and reconciliation programs. PIMD investments in social, human, intellectual capital, and infrastructure and other resources have also been lost. This has left the organisation with no choice but to make a fresh start on its education programs in a very challenging post-conflict environment.

*Figure 1. PIMD e-Learning and m-learning strategy: Five Pillars*
*Source Adapted from Ministry of Defense (2000)*

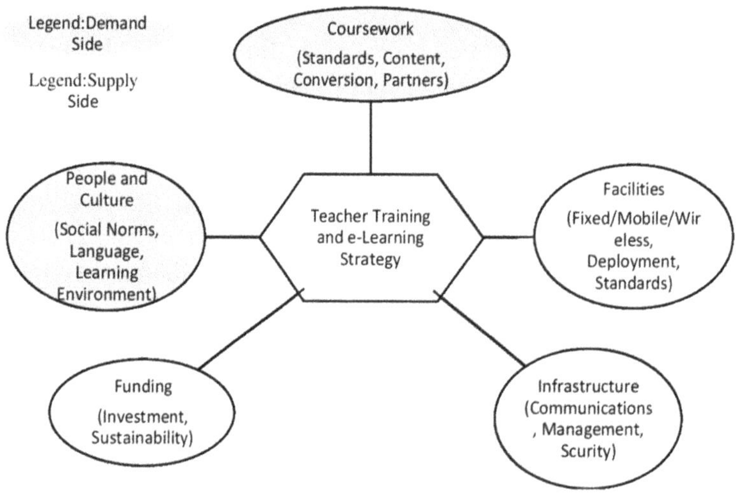


Post-war reconstruction in the north and east of the country commenced in the latter half of 2009 with the help of international donors to rebuild the basic infrastructure in the war ravaged areas to sustain and rehabilitate the communities returning from the IDP camps UN (2010). In the final years of the war, the relationship between the government of Sri Lanka and western donor aid agencies was strained (Samath, 2010) and has since continued to be an impediment to the reconstruction effort in the early stages (Goodhand et al. 2002; Ofstad 2000; Senanayake 2009).

As a part of the reconstruction effort in the northern and eastern provinces and as recognition of the success of PIMD programs in the past the Ministry of Education, Sri Lanka has approved the restart of the ESL and CL programs in the northern and eastern provinces. The current donative (Hansmann, 1987) PIMD business model which is dependent exclusively on revenue from donations is unsustainable. New entrepreneurial strategies and business models for sustainability are explored if PIMD is to survive and grow upon the trust and confidence that the communities and government have in the organisation to deliver outcomes.

## THEORETICAL FRAMEWORK

Numerous case studies on social enterprises and social entrepreneurship (Kernot & Mcneill 2011) are a testament to the phenomenon of social and economic business model development. However some scholars have argued that the demand-side and supply-side theories are incomplete as they do not consider the interactions between supply and demand. They advocate the need for an integrated approach and holistic understanding of NPOs where various elements are inter-related to each other and the roles of each sector (Ortman 1996; Steinberg 2006: 129-134; Valentinov 2008b).

A number of interesting academic contributions on the complete or integrative theories on not for profit organizations (Ortman, 1999, Steinberg, 2006, Valentionov, 2008b) but for different reasons are not relevant in this discussion. For example, Ortman (1996) have proposed theories based on the division of labour and game theory. Steinberg (2006: 29-134) proposed a framework to clarify thinking on developing complete and integrated theories. Valentionov (2008b), like Ortman (1999) have proposed theories based on the division of labor and game theory.

To further enhance the understanding of the adoption and implementation of a social enterprise business model for PIMD, two ground-breaking contributions Weisbrod (1975) and Hansmann (1980) are of particular relevance in this case study analysis. Weisbrod (1975) in public goods theory and Hansmann (1980) in trustworthiness and non-distribution constraint theory provide insights into the challenges and successes of not for profit organizations. Furthermore, theories categorized as demand-side economic theories takes into account the role and need of NPOs and supply-side theories considers the objectives and motivation of entrepreneurs. The contributions of Weisbrod's (1975) public goods theory and Hansmann (1980) trustworthiness and non-distribution constraint theory have both argued that NPOs exist due to market and state failure to satisfy the demand of the citizens.

## Public Goods Theory

Weisbrod (1975), argued that not for profit organisations fulfilled the demand for public goods which remain unsatisfied by government agencies. For example, while satisfying the demand for the median voters, the government overlooks the needs of some citizens which are then provided by not for profit organizations that receive donations from citizens. Although some not for profit organization would like to increase their financial sustainability and subsequently the availability of public goods based on the definition of the NPF, policies are restricted in terms of profit distribution, financial management and accountability. Furthermore, managers of not for profit organizations continue to lack the incentive of profit maximization that could possibly misrepresent the provision and delivery of goods and services (Weisbrod 1998: vii).

According to Weisbrod (1975), the public goods theory also be offered as semi-public or private goods. For instance, playing music in the open area is a public good but if the same music is played in a concert and fees applied, it will be considered as a private good (Heitzmann, 2000). These theories and subsequent theoretical and empirical studies are categorized as demand-side economic theories which conceptualize the role and need for NPOs, and supply-side theories which conceptualize the objectives and motivation of entrepreneurs (Krashinsky 1997; Valentinov 2006). What is noteworthy is the subsequent extension of these two theories to explain the complexities of the not for profit sector as it developed new business models and moved to the production of multiple goods with social value in order to attract funds.

## Non-Distribution Constrain Theory

According to the non-distribution constrain theory of Hansmann (1980) NPOs are legally prohibited to distribute their net earnings to their controlling members such as directors, managers, trustees and so on. In spite of the limitation imposed upon them, nonprofits may succeed in distributing some of their net earnings through inflated salaries, various perquisites granted to employees and other forms of excess payments (Hansmann 1980: 844)

This non-distribution constraint therefore renders not for profit organizations attractive to donors in terms of trustworthiness on efficient utilization of their funds. Hanmann's (1980) trustworthiness theory (or contract failure approach) explains that NPOs exist due to asymmetric information in the marketplace.

In most cases, the producer or supplier of goods and services have much more information than those who demand it. Commercial organizations have their own incentives in exploiting this information to increase their profit margin. However, since NPOs are not profit-oriented and legally obliged to refrain from using net earnings for personal use, they are assumed to be more trustworthy by the donors.

Both Hansmann and Weisbrod theories are based on the assumption that NPOs and other profit-making enterprises are competitors. For instance, that not for profit organizations satisfy the service delivery demands which government fail to meet. However, Salamon (1997) argues that in many countries, NPOs and the state operate jointly rather than separately. Empirical study performed in Austria revealed that NPOs which operate jointly with the state-owned organizations received funding from the public institutions although amounts varied significantly (Heitzmann, 2000).

Kingma (1997) and Valetinov (2008a) have criticized the over reliance of the trustworthiness theory on the non-distribution constraint and the failure to explain why this constraint does not destroy the motivation to undertake social entrepreneurial activities. Valentinov (2008a) and DiMaggio & Anheir (1990) contend there are other motivational factors such as sympathy, altruism, reciprocity and prestige that enhance the utility function of stakeholders in being engaging, participating and enjoying the process, akin to the diverse motivations of the members of PIMD for participating in social capital building programs.

The crucial issue confronting not for profit organisations is how to achieve financial sustainability to manage and sustain projects for extended periods in a complex, competitive and unpredictable environment (Hugget 2009; Landsberg 2004). Furthermore, commercialisation in the NPO sector is not a new phenomenon (Hansmann 1990) but one that has gained wider acceptance due to the global economic downturn and competition for diminishing funding pools (Bradley 2004: xiii-xvi; Tuckman 1998; Weisbrod 1998: 1-22).

The paradox of a not for profit mission and the for-profit commercialisation, mission creep and motivational dilemmas facing volunteers and stake holders can erode the trust and social capital built by the not for profit mission. Tuckman and Chang (2006) have enunciated the necessary conditions for successful commercialisation of the NPOs including establishing the need for financial resources to sustain social programs such as through the sale of goods and services, the existence of opportunities for commercial activity, and to ensure that there is no or minimal mission conflict between the not for profit and for-profit objectives.

Not for profit commercialisation requires the adoption and implementation of for-profit business models, governance regimes and market orientation without compromising the core not for profit mission. This contradiction has spurred the entrepreneurial social activists to create a new form of hybrid organisation, the social enterprise. The social enterprise draws from business, charity and social models (Alter 2007: 13-22; Mair & Noboa 2006:121-135; Nicholls 2006: 1-23). The drivers behind the growth of the social enterprise business model in the NPO sector can be attributed to the adoption of hybrid business models for sustainability by the corporate sector through corporate social responsibility programs. Figure 2 illustrates a sustainability strategy to achieve sustainability equilibrium through dual value creation strategies.

Current studies have focused on the not for profit and public policy domains are social entrepreneurship phenomenon-driven and lack a cross-disciplinary theoretical framework (Dees 2001; Mair & Marti 2006; Short et al. 2009). However, existing studies focused on the social enterprise and social entrepreneurship fields are nascent areas of scholarly research (Dees, 2001, Mair and Marti, 2006, Short et al, 2009).

*Figure 2. Sustainability equilibrium*
*Source Adapted from Alter (2007:15) 2*

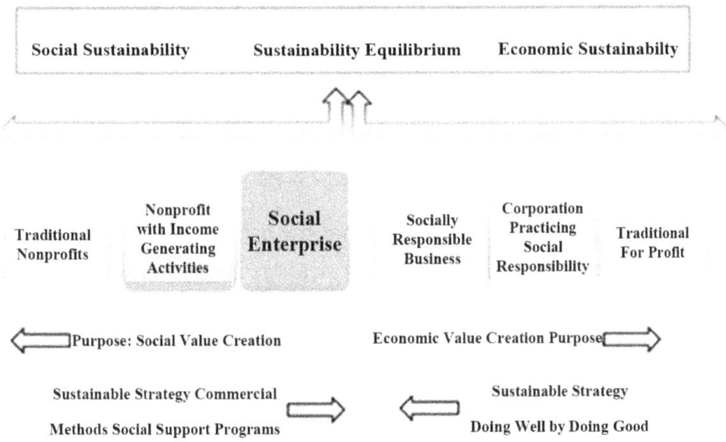


The conceptual framework in Figure 3 encapsulates key elements of a sustainable business model. It draws from, and integrates key dimensions of financial sustainability and frames the questions raised by an NPO such as PIMD by addressing the key sustainability challenges.

The ultimate goal is to achieve a balance between a sustainability economic equilibrium and social value creation as referred to by Alter (2005). Given that some NPO sectors have embraced and implemented social enterprise business models, hence the adoption of this model has been considered a practical proposition for PIMD to achieve financial sustainability. Based on the above-mentioned observations, adapting a social enterprise business model as a sustainability strategy for NPOs is an economically viable response to the challenge of financial sustainability.

*Figure 3. Conceptual sustainability framework*

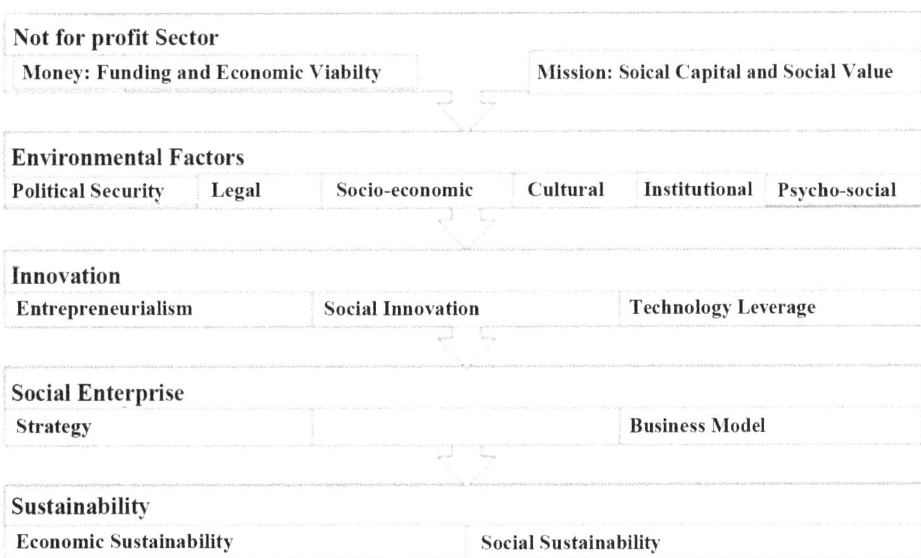

## CASE STUDY

According to the grounded theory of sustainability (Seel, 2006) NPOs can no longer follow the traditional pattern of small incremental changes, but instead require multiple and organizational-wide transformation and adaptation of organizational culture. A specific approach for PIMD is therefore to develop a transformative business strategy and model for the long-term financial sustainability for the organisation. This can be achieved by asking two questions:

1. Drawing on theory and literature relating to the not for profit and particularly social enterprise and financial sustainability, what is the sustainability strategy that can ensure long-term economic and financial sustainability for an organisation such as PIMD?
2. What is the conceptual business model that will ensure the feasibility of the identified sustainability strategy?

A case study methodology was thought to be appropriate for this research project. This method of study is especially useful for trying to test theoretical models by using them in real world situations. A case study provides more realistic responses than a purely statistical survey. Furthermore, qualitative case study methodology provides tools for researchers to study complex phenomena within their contexts.

As outlined by Blumberg, Cooper and Schindler (2008), the case study method is appropriate for explanatory, descriptive and exploratory research and most appropriate to accomplish the research objectives. This view was supported by Yin (1989:23) who defined case study research as an empirical inquiry that investigates a contemporary phenomenon within its real-life context when the boundaries between phenomenon and context were not clearly evident and in which multiple sources of evidence are used. In the real world case study examined in this chapter, an abductive research methodology is best suited to gain insights into the complexities experienced by not for profit organizations.

Kovacs and Spens (2005) argue that the inductive and deductive research approaches look for relations between existing constructs and are not conducive to the creative process which leads to an intuitive leap to creating knowledge. The abductive research process is viewed as systematic creativity or intuition to discover/develop new knowledge (Saraniemi 2009: 23). Chamberlain (2006) observes that the literature on formulation of business strategies leans more towards the traditional normative and descriptive outputs (Haugstad 1999; Ortner 2007).

These approaches however do not consider research methodology as a critical research task and can lead to methodological problems. Chamberlain (2006) for example contends that business strategy formulation is a subjective social construct as is the case of PIMD. Chamberlain (2006) advocates instead the adoption of an interpretive approach as suggested by Blaikie (2004). The interpretive version of abductive research focuses on the subjective social constructs such as business strategy formulation. In particular where the researcher is engaged or immersed in the interpretivist reality of the situation to perceive remarkable or noteworthy and then insightfully speculate on likely associations or causations thereof (Chamberlain, 2006: 295). It is also argued that the abductive research approach is commonly used in both action research and case studies (Saraniemi 2009: 22-24) due to the parallelism of data collection, theory development and theory building element common to both methods (Dubois & Gadde 2002; Kovacs & Spens 2005)

In the case of PIMD, the prior theoretical knowledge (step 0) discussed in this chapter, the real-life observations (step 1) drawn from its work to date are used to match relevant theories (step 2). The development or extension of an integrated theory of financial sustainability (step 3 in Figure 4) form the basis for the development of a business strategy and the application of conclusions (step 4 in Figure 4) leads to the development of a business model for PIMD.

## TRANSFORMING PIMD INTO A SOCIAL ENTERPRISE

While the discussion so far suggests that adapting a social enterprise business model as a sustainability strategy for NPOs is an appropriate and economically viable response to the challenge of financial sustainability, the decision to embark on a new business strategy and model demands disciplined and meticulous analysis of the business opportunity underscored by entrepreneurial creativity and innovation, pro-activeness and risk management. It also involves a learning process in which theoretical and empirical studies are used to add clarity to defining objectives, managing stakeholder expectations and setting realistic performance targets (Dees 2004: 3-18; Caesar & Baker 2004:207-223). The cost of failure is much more devastating to NPOs compared to the government or corporate sectors who are better positioned to withstand the loss and move on.

The findings of Weerawardene et al (2010) empirical research on sustainability of not for profit organisations emphasize that NPO sustainability should be a strategic issue and not an operational one. Adoption of multiple strategies that consider competition, opportunity recognition, governance, operational efficiency, revenue enhancement and cost reduction should be part of the overall business strategy which underpins the social enterprise business strategy and model.

Chesbrough and Rosenbloom identify the functions of a business model as follows: articulate value proposition, identify market segment, define the structure of the value chain, estimate cost structure and profit potential, describe the position of the firm within the value network and formulate competitive strategy (Chesbrough & Rosenbloom 2002: 536).

*Figure 4. The Abductive Research Process*
*Source 3 Adapted from Kovacs and Spens (2005)*

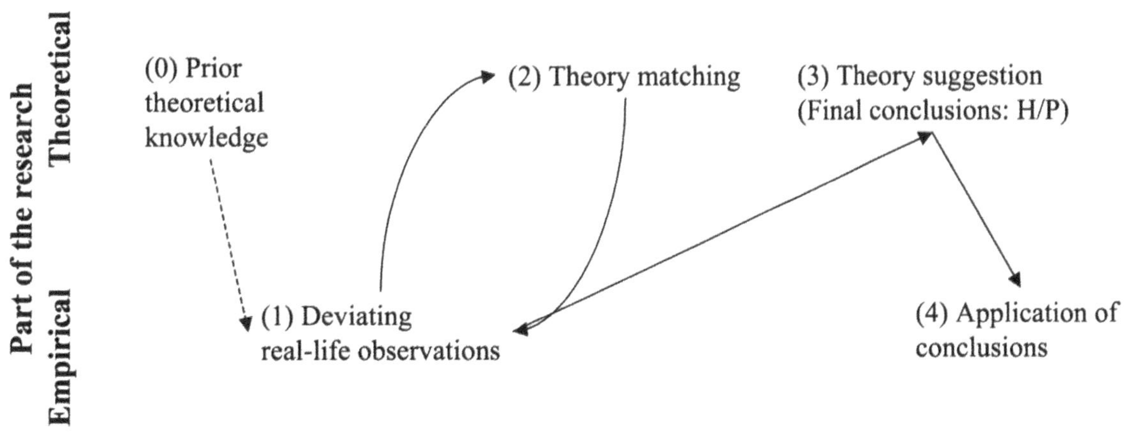

It was decided that PIMD's social enterprise can therefore be designed using the above functional framework as a basis. It is an entrepreneurial response (Steinberg, 2003) to ensure the long-term sustainability of PIMD's social projects in Sri Lanka. The question relating to strategy should draw on Weerawardene and Mort's, 'Bounded multidimensional model of social entrepreneurship' as the foundation of PIMD's sustainability strategy. The strategy in turn will be based on a holistic perspective of a social enterprise and built around themes which are integrated to develop an approach in which social entrepreneurship creates social capital along three dimensions: innovative, proactive, and risk management behavior. These behaviors are constrained by the need to fulfill the social mission and ensure sustainability of the organization within the environmental dynamics in which it operates. Thus, the sustainability dimension of the social enterprise strategy will underscore PIMD's conceptual business model for financial sustainability.

A similar but pragmatic approach as above can be adapted for the second question relating to the social enterprise business model itself, due to the real life application to PIMD. Literature on financial sustainability issues in social enterprises, entrepreneur business models, adoption of commercial practices in NPOs, functions of business models and business models will serve as a guide in developing PIMD's e-business model based on Chesbrough and Rosenbloom business model framework. It was determined that PIMD would adopt a social enterprise model and introduce a commercial training arm which would provide training at subsidized rates to staff from donor corporations and the sales proceeds from this division would support the diminishing donations which will enable PIMD to continue with the social mission and provide sustainability. Besides, a PIMD fund would be created which would be supported by the Government, donations from donor corporations and small voluntary donations from benefit recipient families and candidates. This would enable the creation of shared value by all the stake holders and sustain PIMD.

## CONCLUSION

The demand side and the supply side of nonprofit organization should be viewed as complementary to each other, rather than mutually exclusive. In this paper we focused on the demand approaches to nonprofits through the public good approach based on Weisbrod's path-breaking paper from 1975 and the trust approach, which stems from Hansmann's influential paper from 1980.

Weisbrod's theory delineates that public good provision dilemmas are solved by collective action of the affected individual. He stresses more donative financing necessarily leads to more provision of public good. Extensions of Weisbrod's approach identifies altruistic behavior, possible integration with Hansmann's trust approach which rationales for nonprofit entrepreneurship and a variety of stakeholders with partly conflicting interests. Many of these models maintain donations as a key feature (Kingma 2003)

PIMD's education projects for underserved rural communities in Sri Lanka are unsustainable in the long-term due to financial constraints. Donations are essential for its survival. As a volunteer-based not for profit organization, PIMD's reliance on a donative financial model to support its programs is untenable. The development of a new approach to achieve long-term financial sustainability and independence without compromising the core social mission and jeopardizing the social capital building projects is a matter of urgency and survival. Contributions to the third sector literature from academics and practitioners emphasize the imperative for the sector to adopt entrepreneurial and innovative business strategies and models and to leverage technology (Dart 2004b; Dees & Economy 2001: 1-18) which is supported by Hansmann's trust approach which rationales for nonprofit entrepreneurship

Organizations such as PIMD should adopt the social entrepreneurship (SE) model which will enable the creation of shared value. It was suggested that PIMD should therefore adopt an abductive research methodology in order to formulate an entrepreneurial sustainability strategy and innovative business model for the creation of shared value with the stake holders to provide a pathway for PIMD to achieve long-term financial sustainability while maintaining the core mission objectives. The literature review served as a starting point to help formulate the key questions for the PIMD case study.

It needs to be acknowledged that the PIMD case is focused exclusively on a single aspect of –financial sustainability which is part of a much wider sustainability strategy. While the social enterprise business model is the beginning of the journey to commercialization of PIMD, other elements of the transformational process such as organizational, stakeholder and volunteer strategies will require the organization to also address social, cultural, economic and socio-psycho issues.

Future research will explore and scrutinize varied social entrepreneurial models which are in existence and operating successfully to deliver continuous growth to a region and benchmark these to develop a best practice and customized cross cultural model suited to wide-ranging environments. SE models from different regions of the world need to be compared in terms of their firm specific factors, external environment, orientation of the owner manager and their current regional growth and sustainability contribution. The aim is to get an understanding of the different existent models of social entrepreneurship and investigate the success factors of these models and recommend a customized regional best practice model suitable to adapt with in a not for profit organization.

## REFERENCES

Alter, K. (2007). *Social Enterprise Typology*. Retrieved from http://rinovatios.edublogs.org/files/2008/07/setypology.pdf

Anheir, H. (n.d.). *Reflections on the Global Economic Downturn, Philanthropy and Nonprofits*. Retrieved from http://www.csi.uni-hd.de/downloads/Anheier%20-%20CSI%20zur%20Krise_EN.pdf

Blaikie, N. (2004). Abduction. In M. S. Lewis-Beck, A. Bryman, & T. F. Liao (Eds.), *The Sage Encyclopedia of Social Science Research Methods* (Vol. 1, p. 1). London: Sage.

Bradley, B. (2004). Foreword. In S. Oster, C. Massarsky, & S. Beinhacker (Eds.), *Generating and Sustaining Nonprofit Earned Income* (pp. xiii–xvi). San Francisco: Jossey-Bass US.

Caesar, P., & Baker, T. (2004). Fundamentals of Implementation. In S. Oster, C. Massarsky, & S. Beinhacker (Eds.), *Generating and Sustaining Nonprofit Earned Income* (pp. 207–223). San Francisco: Jossey-Bass.

Chamberlain, G. (2006). Researching Strategy Formation Process: An Abductive Methodology. *Quality & Quantity*, *40*(2), 289–301. doi:10.1007/s11135-005-8094-3

Chesbrough, H., & Rosenbloom, R. (2002). The Role of the business model in capturing value from innovation: Evidence from Xerox Corporations technology spin-off companies. *Industrial and Corporate Change*, *11*(3), 529–555. doi:10.1093/icc/11.3.529

Dart, R. (2004). b. Being 'Business-Like" in a Nonprofit Organization: A grounded and Inductive Typology. *Nonprofit and Voluntary Sector Quarterly*, *33*(2), 290–310. doi:10.1177/0899764004263522

Dees, G. (2001). *The Meaning of Social Entrepreneurship.* Retrieved from http://www.caseatduke.org/documents/dees_sedef.pdf

Dees, G., & Economy, P. (2001). Social Entrepreneurship. In G. Dees, J. Emerson, & P. Economy (Eds.), *Enterprising Nonprofits: A toolkit for Social Entrepreneurs* (pp. 1–18). New York: John Wiley and Sons Inc.

Dees, J. (2004). Putting Nonprofit Business Ventures in Perspective. In S. Oster, C. Massarsky, & S. Beinhacker (Eds.), *Generating and Sustaining Nonprofit Earned Income* (pp. 3–18). San Francisco: Jossey-Bass.

DiMaggio, P., & Anheir, H. (1990). The Sociology of Nonprofit Organizations and Sectors. *Annual Review of Sociology*, *16*(1), 137–159. doi:10.1146/annurev.so.16.080190.001033

Dubois, A., & Gadde, L. (2002). 'systematic combining: An abductive approach to case research. *Journal of Business Research*, *55*(7), 553–560. doi:10.1016/S0148-2963(00)00195-8

Goodhand, J., Hulme, D., & Lewer, N. (2002). Social Capital and the Political Economy of Violence: A case study of Sri Lanka. *Disasters*, *24*(4), 390–406. doi:10.1111/1467-7717.00155 PMID:11138373

Hangman, H. (1990). The Economic Role of Commercial Nonprofits: The Evolution of the US Savings Bank. In H. Anheier & W. Seibel (Eds.), *The Third Sector: Comparative Studies of Nonprofit Organizations* (pp. 65–75). Berlin: Walter de Gruyter & Co.

Hansmann, H. (1980). Role of Nonprofit Enterprise. *The Yale Law Journal*, *89*(5), 835–901. doi:10.2307/796089

Hansmann, H. (1987). Economic Theories of Nonprofit Organization. *VOLUNTAS: International Journal of Voluntary and Not For Profit Organization*, *89*(2), 93-96.

Haugstad, B. (1999). *Strategy Theory- A short review of the literature.* Retrieved from http://www.kunne.no/upload/Gamle%20publikasjoner/Nedtegnelser/Strategy%20Theory_N0299_Haugstad.pdf

Heitzmann, K. (2000). *The role of third sector organizations in specific policy fields: Contrasting non-profit theory and empirical findings—The case of Austria.* Paper prepared for the Fourth International Conference of the ISTR, Dublin, Ireland.

Hugget, J. (2009). *The challenges nonprofits face in the current uncertain economic environment.* Retrieved from http://www.csi.edu.au/assets/assetdoc/985b7df93006c9d4/Lecture%20Series%20No.%206%20-%20Inaugural%20John%20B%20Reid%20Lecture.pdf

Kernot, C., & Mcneill, J. (2011). *Australian Stories of Social Enterprise.* Retrieved from http://www.csi.edu.au/assets/assetdoc/81476e838a4e4d61/Australian%20Stories%20of%20Social%20Enterprise.pdf

Kingma, B. (1997). Public Good Theories of the not for profit sector: Weisbrod Revisited. *Voluntas*, *8*(2), 135–14. doi:10.1007/BF02354191

Kingma, B. R. (2003). Public Good Theories of Nonprofit Sector: Weisbrod Revisited. In H. Anheier & A. Ben Ner (Eds.), *The Study of the Nonprofit Enterprise: Theories and Approaches*. Kluwer Academic / Plenum Publishers. doi:10.1007/978-1-4615-0131-2_3

Kourula, A., & Laasonen, S. (2010). Nongovernmental Organizations in Business and Society, Management and International Business Research: Review and Implications from 19982007. *Business & Society*, *49*(1), 35–67. doi:10.1177/0007650309345282

Kovacs, G., & Spens, K. (2005). Abductive Reasoning in Logistics Research. *International Journal of Physical Distribution & Logistics Management*, *35*(2), 133–141. doi:10.1108/09600030510590318

Krashinsky, M. (1997). Stakeholder theories of the not for profit sector: One cut at the economic literature. *Voluntas*, *8*(2), 149–161. doi:10.1007/BF02354192

Landsberg, B. (2004). The Nonprofit Paradox: For-Profit Business Models in the Third Sector. *International Journal of Not-for-Profit Law*, *6*(2).

Mair, J., & Marti, I. (2006). Social entrepreneurship research: A source of explanation, prediction, and delight. *Journal of World Business*, *41*(2), 36–44. doi:10.1016/j.jwb.2005.09.002

Mair, J., & Noboa, E. (2006). How Intentions to Create a Social Venture are formed. In J. Mair, J. Robinson, & K. Hockerts (Eds.), *Social Entrepreneurship* (pp. 121–135). Palgrave McMillan. doi:10.1057/9780230625655_8

Nicholls, A. (2006). *Social Entrepreneurship: New Models of Sustainable Social Change*. New York: Oxford University Press.

Ofstad, A. (2000). *Countries in conflict and aid strategies: The case of Sri Lanka*. Retrieved from http://bora.cmi.no/space/bitstream/10202/248/1/WP2000.18%20Arve-07202007_12.pdf

Ortner, J. (2007). *A Literature Review of Strategy and Complexity Theory*. Retrieved from http://api.ning.com/files/qx6YCvp40dLkRffS1iZUOHb9OVYxoyud8bYyAEBHHLAlob839ZsHYOjDLN-NA7zg7Us8QqotWRx4d3AWSv0uC3TqDNQksP7Nv/aliteraturereviewofstrategyandcomplexitytheory.pdf

Salamon, L., & Anheier, H. (1997). The Challenge of Definition: Thirteen realities in Search of a Concept. In L. Salamon & H. Anheier (Eds.), *Defining the nonprofit sector: A cross-national analysis* (pp. 11–99). Manchester, UK: Manchester University Press US.

Salamon, L., & Anheier, H. (1997). *The Third World's Third Sector in Comparative Perspective*. Retrieved from http://adm-cf.com/jhu/pdfs/CNP_Working_Papers/CNP_WP24.pdf

Salamon, L., & Sokolwski, W. (2003). *Global Civil Society: An Overview*. Retrieved from http://adm-cf.com/jhu/pdfs/Books/BOOK_GCS_2003.pdf

Samath, F. (2010). *NGO's Brace for Tighter Government Control*. Retrieved from http://ipsnews.net/news.asp?idnews=50507

Saraniemi, S. (2009). *Destination Branding in a Country Context-A case study of Finland in the British market*. Retrieved from http://www.scribd.com/doc/54035096/3/The-scientific-approach-%E2%80%93-abductive-logic

Seel, K. (2006). *Boundary Spanning: A Grounded Theory of Sustainability in Canada's Nonprofit Sector*. Retrieved from http://www.mtroyal.ca/wcm/groups/public/documents/pdf/npr06_bound_thesis.pdf

Senanayake, D. (2009). *Sri Lanka's Post-Conflict Transition: Reconstruction, Reconciliation and Aid Effectiveness*. Retrieved from http://www.isas.nus.edu.sg/Attachments/PublisherAttachment/ISAS_Insights_86_29102009120637.pdf

Short, J., Moss, T., & Lumpkin, G. (2009). Research in Social entrepreneurship: Past contributions and future opportunities. *Strategic Entrepreneurship Journal*, *3*(2), 161–194. doi:10.1002/sej.69

Steinberg, R. (2006). Economic Theories of Nonprofit Organizations. In W. Powell & R. Steinberg (Eds.), *The Nonprofit Sector: A Research Handbook* (p. 117). London: Yale University Press.

Teeni, D., & Young, D. (2003). The Changing Role of Nonprofits in the Network Economy. *Nonprofit and Voluntary Sector Quarterly*, *32*(3), 397–414. doi:10.1177/0899764003254900

Tuckman, H. (1998). Competition, Commercialization, and the Evolution of Nonprofit Organizational Structures. *Journal of Policy Analysis and Management*, *17*(2), 175–194. doi:10.1002/(SICI)1520-6688(199821)17:2<175::AID-PAM4>3.0.CO;2-E

Tuckman, H., & Chang, C. (2006). Commercial Activity, Technological Change and Nonprofit Mission. In W. Powell & R. Steinberg (Eds.), *The Nonprofit Sector; A research Handbook* (pp. 629–642). London: Yale University Press.

UN. (2010). *Mid-Year Review-Common Humanitarian Action Plan (CHAP)*. Retrieved from http://reliefweb.int/node/361967

Valentinov, V. (2006). Toward an Economic Interpretation of the non-distribution constraint. *International Journal of Not-for-Profit Law*, *9*(1).

Valentinov, V. (2008a). The Economics of the Non-Distribution Constraint: A Critical Reappraisal. *Annals of Public and Cooperative*, *79*(1), 35–52. doi:10.1111/j.1467-8292.2007.00351.x

Weerawardena, J., McDonald, R. E., & Sullivan Mort, G. (2010). Sustainability of nonprofit organizations: An empirical investigation. *Journal of World Business*, *45*(4), 346–356. doi:10.1016/j.jwb.2009.08.004

Weerawardene, J., McDonald, R., & Mort, G. (2010). Sustainability of nonprofit organizations: An Empirical Investigation. *Journal of World Business*, *45*(4), 346–356. doi:10.1016/j.jwb.2009.08.004

Weisbrod, B. (1975). Toward a Theory of the Voluntary Not for profit Sector in a Three-Sector Economy. In E. Phelps (Ed.), *Altruism* (pp. 171–195). New York: Morality and Economic Theory.

Weisbrod, B. (1998). The nonprofit mission and its financing: Growing links between nonprofits and the rest of the economy. In B. Weisbrod (Ed.), *To Profit or Not to Profit: The Commercial Transformation of the Nonprofit Sector* (pp. 1–22). Cambridge, UK: Cambridge University Press. doi:10.1017/CBO9780511625947.003

# Chapter 3
# Integrating Theory and Practice to Identify Contemporary Best Practice Factors in USA Not-for-Profits

**Kenneth David Strang**
*State University of New York, USA*

## ABSTRACT

*This chapter used a critical analysis of the current NFP literature followed by a practitioner activity analysis using a purposive nonprobability sample of 880 NFP institutions. The current literature was integrated with the practitioner activity data to identify contemporary best practices. Eight categories emerged from the text analytics. Several insightful recommendations were provided to guide future NFP research as well as to overcome the limitations of this study. The results of this research should generalize to the key stakeholders of NFP organizations, namely to the managers and the board of director members, as well as to their volunteers and to other researchers focused on studying these entities. In particular, this research will be of interest to government social assistance agencies to inform policy development as well as to higher educational institutions for curriculum content.*

## INTRODUCTION

This chapter emphasizes effective business models and managerial strategies utilized by a not-for-profit (NFP) organization. The key word effective is based on the perspective of a standard or measurement scale.

Paradoxically, effectiveness is a perspective which is conditioned by social culture. Naturally a NFP in an emerging country has different priorities and perspectives as compared to a similar organization in a developed nation. As discussed in earlier chapters, NFP goals are usually different than those of a for-profit enterprise so another assertion is that NFP business models and managerial strategies differ. A constraint embedded within the literature is that most strategic management best practice studies were based on for-profit businesses. Likewise, NFP effectiveness differs based on organization size and mis-

DOI: 10.4018/978-1-5225-2537-0.ch003

Copyright © 2017, IGI Global. Copying or distributing in print or electronic forms without written permission of IGI Global is prohibited.

sion. This chapter examines medium to large multinational NFP organizations. Thus, the findings should generalize across social-cultures, towards larger NFP entities rather than small associations.

On the other hand, the scholarly literature can define NFP effectiveness factors and identify the requisite techniques to measure that. This is the approach here. This chapter develops a NFP effectiveness model driven by factors grounded in the literature and it is subsequently modified by using data collected through theoretically-sampled case studies. Then unique interdisciplinary methods are explained to measure the effectiveness of not NFP. The models and strategic management methods proposed in this chapter should be of interest to established NFP organization members as well as to their stakeholders, including funding sources and consultants.

There are very few scholarly best practice studies focused purely on contemporary NFP organizations. Much of the NFP best practices were popularized in the post-industrial era of the late 1990's or prior to 2012. More importantly a critical downfall of the existing NFP scholarly literature concerns its credibility. Some of the NFP best practice claims in the literature do not show a source or validation of effectiveness factors. This is an essential issue for NFP decision makers. NFP leaders and board of director members must be able to reduce risks by following best practices. This chapter articulates what those NFP best practices are.

This chapter articulates NFP best practices by citing the literature and by surveying effective NFP organizations in a USA sample frame. Generally accepted research design methods are applied to ensure the results are statistically reliable and will generalize to NFP stakeholders. Despite this optimistic value proposition, a practical limitation that readers need to be aware of right up front is that the authors are from USA so their western social-culture and case study organization data ultimately impact the ability of the findings to generalize outside of this context. The reason that we used a purposive nonprobability sampling technique of the USA population was that we used state accreditation as both a selection criterion and to designate the NFP as effective. State-registered NFPs contribute slightly under $1 trillion USD annually to the American economy (5.4% of the US GDP) according to their tax documents and they employ over 11 million people (more than 10% of the American workforce). We do not mean that the results of this study would not generalize to emerging nations but rather it is just that we can only statistically conclude that our hypotheses are supported for the given population. The ideas published in this chapter may be useful for a NFP stakeholder in any country or social-culture to consider.

## METHODOLOGICAL APPROACH

The authors held a positivistic ideology so this chapter utilized techniques to review the empirical literature, collect evidence of the proposed important factors, and then develop an inductive framework to guide future research into NFP best practices. The population of interest for this chapter was accredited state-registered NFPs operating in any industry and located in continental USA. This population was selected because the chapter goal was to gain a better understanding of the critical success factors of NSPs in developed and emerging nations. USA is not a perfect proxy for the goal but it an excellent source of best practices since it is a successful developed nation with many NFPs. We used a sampling frame of NFPs listed with a state government because it would be difficult to locate every single NFP in USA and survey them. We could not apply any of the probably sampling techniques such as random, systematic, stratified, proportion or cluster (Lucas, 2014) because our research goal was to examine effective successful NFPs judged effective by the state government and by an independent accrediting agency. Thus, we used purposive nonprobability sampling, which is a technique to select a case or participant according to a best-fit match with a theory or research goal.

Critical analysis within the literature review constituted the major research technique for this chapter. This is an appropriate technique when attempting to review the state-of-the-art literature to integrate or validate theory with actual practice (Strang, 2015c). Theoretically-sampled case study participants, descriptive statistics and text analytics were employed to collect actual data and to summarize the empirical evidence. Tables and other visual summary techniques were utilized to organize the findings.

A critical analysis and integration of the theoretical literature with practitioner activities is considered appropriate to explain the grassroots functions of case study participants (Duraj, Felt, & Singhal, 2014). This approach was chosen because Duraj, Felt and Singhal (2014) determined that most researcher-interpreted evaluations of data insufficiently capture participant knowledge, and therefore miss documenting the meaning of local grassroots ways of knowing. According to Strang (2015b), the critical analysis starts with a literature review and is supplemented by data collection from practitioners in order to validate or extend theoretical models with empirical evidence. An exploratory study such as this chapter would conclude with a list of the key factors and then propose recommendations for future research.

### Case Study Participants

We contacted 46 state-level NFP accreditation associations in USA but we were able to evaluate only 44. Each NFP association contained on average 20 member charities thus making the entire sample frame 920 institutions. The sample characteristics are described in the next section.

It made sense to purposively-sample accredited state-registered NFP associations in USA because this indicates they are operating, they are able to pay their accreditation fees, and observing these organizations would meet the research goal. While this may limit how the findings could generalize to other countries, it seems reasonable to assume that the best practices of accredited NFPs based in USA would at least be of interest to book chapter readers. It establishes significance of the sample when considering that according to National Council of Nonprofits (NCN, 2016) NFPs in USA account for $887 billion USA (5.4%) of the USA economy each year, they employ 11.4 million people (constituting 10.3% of the entire American workforce). These economic demographics are higher than the gross domestic production of many other countries.

The data was collected through the Internet, emails, phone calls, and newspaper articles. The data was saved into word processing documents and then records were grouped together (not changed or interpreted) as a way to summarize it.

## SCHOLARLY NFP LITERATURE REVIEW

### What is NFP Effectiveness?

NFP effectiveness is an ambiguous term (NCN, 2016). Effectiveness, especially in the NFP sector, depends on the perspective of those doing the measuring (Schalock et al., 2014). The National Council of Nonprofits (NCN) is considered an authority on the subject in USA – 46 of 52 states have a centralized NFP association that provides accreditation and best practices. The NCN have a detailed list of criteria used to accredit a NFP including solvency, community good standing, possessing a professional code of ethics, and other elements. We adopt the NCN designation of accredited as indicating a NFP is effective. The centralized NFP associations and the national council best practices are cited by the Internal Revenue Service as guidelines for registered charities under the 501[c][3] corporation tax legislation (IRS, 2016). The NCN asserts that NFP effectiveness are best practices of accountability, transparency, prudent fiduciary oversight, legal, ethical, and responsible fundraising (NCN, 2016, para. 4). In that statement NCN refer to the how – the way things are done - as the measure of NFP effectiveness rather than the monetary outcomes which would be the emphasis of a for-profit business. NCN indicate that accredited NFPs do not fail otherwise they would lose their accreditation. Effectiveness for a NFP according to NCN and IRS generally means being ethical, accountable and transparent. Evidence-based effectiveness is a contemporary term attributed to NFP organizations (Hurlburt et al., 2014) – this refers to having factual results of program outcomes from the customers served which are often in the form of customer-testimonial forms, service receipts or authentically written case-worker reports.

NFP effectiveness is a well-known issue documented in the literature, or rather finding evidence of NFP effectiveness is most likely the actual root cause of the problem. Knife, Haughton and Dixon (2014) conducted a meta-analysis which revealed that there has been a proliferation of endowments, foundations, non-government-organizations (NGOs) and other organizations operating within many developing countries over the past 20 years as social entrepreneurs/enterprises under NFP or charity status. They explained that while many NFP organizations have been supporting and working in developing countries, attempting to transform the quality of lives of their beneficiaries and in doing so, creating social value. They claimed that there was some evidence on measuring NFP effectiveness based on outcomes from programs but they found there was little evidence of meaningful, sustained impact and hence effectiveness, despite millions of dollars being spent. Thus, the lack of this evidence for NFP effectiveness poses the question of the justification for continued funding, state benefits and tax exemptions (Knife et al., 2014). Additionally, the question of uncertain NFP effectiveness raises the issue of sustainability of the intervention process provided by a NFP in society, given that the primary source of funding for many of these organizations comes in the form of government grants and/or philanthropic donations.

A different version of NFP effectiveness emerges when looking at the strategic management literature. The NFP business model differs from the commercial environment so this also carries forward into the effectiveness measure. According to Foster, Kim, and Christiansen (2009) a NFP is more complicated to operate than a business because in most instances a NFP must first obtain the revenue to fund the service or product offered and separately find a client whereas a business creates a product/service to be sold to an identified target segment customer (Strang, 2016). Therefore NFP effectiveness means to be accredited, to both obtain funding and then deliver the product/service whereas only the last criteria would necessarily be measured in a business as it would generate the profit. In other words, a NFP would not be considered effective if they obtained funding but did not deliver the intended service but a business would be considered successful if they generated revenue. This disconnectedness and reverse sequence of revenue-to-client adds a second level of risk to NFP strategic planning because they must continually generate income and also solicit customers.

In a more scientific perspective, NFP effectiveness means achieving the factors required for a relevant accreditation association (and the taxation department of a government), plus remaining solvent by obtaining funding, and achieving their goals by spending the funding to help target segment client(s) along with collecting evidence to show that the outcome was accomplished as intended. We accept the definition of NCN effectiveness in this study which is indicated by accreditation and by state government registration.

## Contemporary NFP Effectiveness Factors

The NFP effectiveness factors are those components which allow the institution to achieve meet the criteria of association accreditation and government, as explained in the previous topic. The effectiveness factors also refer to key success factors or competencies that we assume an effective NFP would possess to continue to be in business. These factors would include intuitive elements such as good leadership but a scientific research approach requires that the scholarly literature be reviewed to first establish the state-of-the-art for NFP effectiveness factors. Contemporary means up to date: No older than six years. A current relevant literature review is important to establish research credibility because the world-wide business macro-environment is changing rapidly due to key megatrends such as the continuing economic instability after the 2008 global fiscal collapse (Mataira, Morelli, Matsuoka, & Uehara-McDonald, 2014; Read, 2012; Strang, 2012c), longitudinal global terrorism-data security threats, (Strang, 2014c; Strang & Alamieyeseigha, 2015) and increased cross-cultural sharing of knowledge through the Internet (Goodwin & Strang, 2012; Strang & Vajjhala, 2015).

Leadership tops the list of competencies that a NFP needs in order to be effective, at least according to the literature (Alsudairi & Tatapudi, 2014; Beynaghi et al., 2016; Germak, 2014; Koski & Lee, 2014; Lan, Zhu, Ness, Xing, & Schneider, 2014; Mataira et al., 2014). Additionally, as reviewed in this section, a NFP needs to have other requisite skills to be effective, namely: A clear operational governance for members, information technology assets and skills, capable human resources, ethical accountability and financial management, marketing communications for benefit promotion, and strategic planning skills for fund raising and longevity.

Operational governance and human resource training are related. Having operational governance is two-part: First documentation needs to be created and thereafter human resources, staff and volunteers, need to be continuously trained. Cantrell-Bruce and Blankenberger (2015) suggested that NFPs should outsource generic skills training, including leadership, marketing communications, and fund raising because these are services that universities may deliver more economically and also maintain the content of such programs. They advised that NFPs should partner with universities that offer NFP management skill sets necessary for working across the increasingly blurred boundaries of service delivery. They referenced two types of degrees of primary interest to NFP staff management and leaders: Master of Public Administration (MPA) and Master of Public Policy (MPP) programs that embrace the key role of relevant skills that NFPs need. An insightful point they made was to place students into NFP internships during their program so that they may benefit from authentic experiential learning. This idea could also benefit the NFP for human resource recruiting because they could informally evaluate a prospective candidate for 3-6 months before making a hiring decision.

While there is no doubt that transformational leadership is an important factor for NFP effectiveness (Lan et al., 2014; Strang, 2012b), strategic planning must be done to ensure there is a strategy in case the leader needs to be replaced due to attrition or unexpected risks occurring (Hamilton & Brown, 2016). Successor planning is an important component of strategic planning since less human resources and finances may be available to undertake a full recruiting program, especially to fill a key position requiring knowledge of the products or services (Hoefer & Sliva, 2014). Contingency planning is related to successor planning. Contingency planning is as important for NFPs as it is for commercial businesses (Lock, Fansler, & Webb, 2016), and perhaps more so given the scarcity of assets owned by most NFPs (Hamilton & Brown, 2016).

A number of researchers identified technology as an important factor for NFP effectiveness (Zlotnikova & van der Weide, 2015). Technology generally refers to business software but it could also include individual devices such as laptops and cell phones (CÃ³rdoba, Jansen, & GonzÃ¡lez, 2014; Trencher, Yarime, McCormick, Doll, & Kraines, 2014). Bos and Brown (2014) claimed that socio-technical systems such as enterprise resource systems help large institutions manage their complex processes and technology is essential in a modern business world. Two key points they conferred were that technology systems must be customized to support the programs and that training must be provided to transition new employees and volunteers joining the institution.

Being ethical and socially responsible seems like a de facto process for a NFP but articulating a recognizable social benefit is mandatory for a contemporary NFP (Dedeurwaerdere et al., 2016; Gebauer & Saul, 2014; Khieng, 2014). This is known in the strategic management literature as the balanced scorecard triple bottom line: Outcomes that produce profit that are environmental ecological friendly and socially responsible (Rasoolimanesh, Jaafar, Badarulzaman, & Ramayah, 2015; Strang, 2010b). Jayashankar, Ashta and Rasmussen (2015) asserted that in our current climate of fiduciary capitalism, NFP funders have begun fulfilling non-financial goals in order to address the concerns of a broader range of their stakeholders: Socially responsible investors with a strong emphasis on making capital circulate locally, especially within agricultural and healthcare industries. Therefore a contemporary NFP may have to re-examine older product/service goals to ensure they are still meeting the needs of current donors and funders. Jayashankar, Ashta and Rasmussen (2015) developed a seven-item taxonomy for the healthcare industry to show how NFP decision makers could strategically address the financial, social and environmental returns demanded by their patients and investors in agriculture and other local enterprises. The critical element in their taxonomy was the requirement for communication of the long term triple bottom line impact associated with the use of donations or funds and in turn publicize if any are dispensed for agricultural or healthcare research. There is additional support in the literature for this idea of a NFP focusing on agriculture, organics and other good-citizen aspirations (Clark & Martinez, 2016; Wohlgemuth, 2014).

Theoretical divergence is a valuable triangulation technique and there is literature in stark contrast to the above, suggesting that a NFP ought to take a narrow strategic goal focus. Senses-Ozyurt (2015) clearly found the triple bottom line strategy was not a best practice, at least for a female Muslim NFP association. Her study evaluated the effects of a political institutional environment and management culture on the performance of a nongovernmental/nonprofit organization, specifically an international Muslim association covering members located in the Netherlands and USA. She interviewed six female informants – who were founders of the organization - and then performed narrative analysis of in-depth interview transcripts. She found that when performance was evaluated as goal attainment, the NFP performed satisfactorily. However, when performance was assessed using financial sustainability and social image factors the results were mixed and not satisfactory. Overall, the findings confirmed that political institutional environment had a significant impact on NFP performance, and that ethnic culture played a role in how the NFP practices were developed. These results are not clear in terms of NFP effectiveness except to infer that having singular goals focused on the mission may be better than adding financial as well as a corporate responsibility mandate – only for the sake of satisfying donors or funders. In other words, a NFP should not add financial or social responsible goals unless those are part of their core mission.

In contrast to the recommendations of Senses-Ozyurt (2015) there are strong arguments in the literature that NFPs should be more financially responsible and self-sustainable instead of focusing on social goals (Martin, 2015; Stecker, 2014). Stecker (2014) asserted that although NFPs serve the community in significant ways, their heavy reliance on philanthropic and government funding was not sustainable, especially in the wake of the economic instability noted earlier. Interestingly though Stecker argued that a NFP could leverage social entrepreneurial principles - including social enterprise activities – to improve the sustainability of the NFP business model while bolstering management capacity and enhancing the mission. This could be achieved by strategically disrupting the de facto gift-giving dependency of contemporary NFPs in exchange for a financially sustainable mission focused on identifying target customers and collaborating with donors to develop products/services to deliver to that segment as would a commercial business. Sanzo (2015) also stressed that a business-oriented marketing approach would work well in a NFP.

Marketing communication and benefit dissemination are important NFP functions (Brink-Danan, 2015; Vallejo & Wehn, 2016). Brink-Danan (2015) reviewed the activities of a religious NFP and found that while external communications to stakeholders were essential to be effective, the content needed to be authentic. More so, given the increased attention given to diversity in the workplace, a NFP should also strive to adhere to diversity principles but not at the expense of survival and not merely ascribe to false pretenses of supporting diversity (Vallejo & When, 2016).

Business intelligence gathering may become everyday strategic planning functions for a NFP. Javalgi, Hall and Cavusgil (2014) studied international business-to-business institutions including NFPs. They emphasized the import role that salespeople play because they often have more direct, prolonged, and intimate contact with customers. In a NFP there may not be a distinction between salespeople and staff. Nonetheless, Javalgi, Hall and Cavusgil (2014) argues that the client-facing staff (sales people) should collect business intelligence data about their customers and use single-informant surveys as a way to collect data on specific needs. The concept of surveying NFP customers is certainly not new – Beecham (2014) published a study showing how this could be done to collect qualitative special services outcome data in Australia. It is interesting to see business intelligence and big data analytics techniques proposed as a NFP effectiveness factor. Perhaps this is a direction of the future. A further concept proposed by Diver and Higgins (2014) was to create and publish research as a service or product, or as a complement to other outcomes.

A further dimension to business intelligence is research. NFPs may benefit from conducting and publishing research (Haegeman, Spiesberger, Veselitskaya, Sokolov, & Weiss, 2015). In fact, this is what many drug and health related institutions practice (McGoey, 2014). Publishing research establishes credibility and it achieves dissemination of the benefits to customers. Haegeman, Spiesberger, Veselitskaya, Sokolov and Weiss (2015) advocated employed expert workshops, a Delphi survey, mind mapping and prioritization techniques to select relevant topics for a joint research call intended to raise funds for a NFP. They claimed that proposing future research would attract support and funding from important donors including the Russian federal government and the European Commission. Their idea is distinct from applying to a grant RFP – instead their idea would be to create the RFP or simply bypass it by convincing the funders to financially support their motive if it were research-oriented. This seems a good idea albeit it would apply to a limited range of NFP product/services. Puljak and Vari (2014) examined the use of research networking to enhance research productivity in a NFP. They found that nurturing non-governmental research networks, spreading awareness in scientific community of practices and establishing research consortium partnerships helped NFPs identify funding opportunities and to obtain more funding that otherwise would be possible on an individual basis. Their study took place in a Regional Cooperation for Health, Science and Technology which was a consortium led by the Cedars-Sinai Medical Center, a NFP hospital with a mission to promote medical education, through scientific communication. Not surprisingly, there seems to be a larger volume of literature advocating a NFP should become more involved in research to be effective.

Collaborating on research as a NFP participant has interesting potential. Lewis, Yerby, Tucker, Foster, Hamilton, Fifolt, Hites, Shreves, Page, Bissell, Lucky and Higginbotham (2015) published an action research project with a NFP. The purpose of their study was to determine if cultural competency, trust, and research literacy can improve the strategic planning and effectiveness of a NFP. They found that NFP research partnerships led to sustainable grant funding based on community-based participatory research. They recommended the development of a pilot grant request for application before embarking on a full scale partnership. A sampled NFP in their study went on to win a grant to investigate obesity, which in turn led to promoting scholarly NFP collaborations between academic researchers and the healthcare community. Additional sampled NFPs were successful, in fact 75% of the collaborative NFO teams successfully submitted grant application to fund intervention projects to address rural and minority obesity disparities. They concluded that collaborative NFP research activities were successful in developing productive scholarly relationships between researchers and community leaders, which resulted in grant funding. This activity makes sense for a NFP that is focused on products/services that may be investigated through research. Another strategic approach may that comes to mind based on their ideas would be to research the product/service casual factors through grant funding even if the NFP is involved in only the delivery of interventions or remedies for the causes. For example, here in New York State there has been a significant rise in heroin addiction so a NFP offering drug rehabilitation treatment could partner with a university or other research-oriented NFP to win a grant in order to explore preventative measures to complement their post-addiction services.

As noted earlier, global terrorism and other unexpected risks have impacted the NFP sector. Hamilton and Brown (2016) reviewed the literature to determine how NFP institutions such as libraries and universities were conducting strategic planning in this new era of economic instability and global crises. In particular they found there was an emphasis on contingency planning due to increased risks (natural disasters, especially floods). They also cited a potential risk of losing valuable assets, which is not often considered for a NFP but certainly it is a concern for museums, universities, schools, historic societies and libraries. Floods have always been a common risk for libraries and other asset-based NFPs (Chaudron, 2016; Guzzo, Ferri, Grifoni, & Firus, 2012; Mabe, 2016) but global terrorism seems to be the newest uncertainty for schools and universities (Strang, 2015a; Trencher et al., 2014). Interestingly, Hamilton and Brown (2016) believed the strategic planning focus should be on continuing business operations rather than asset recovery – which may seem surprising given they were based in hurricane-prone Louisiana. They also alluded to the important social role that NFP organizations such as libraries, schools and universities play in society, serving as centers of communication during important events and crises. The specific best practice was to have a document continuity plan authored by those responsible for maintaining or updating it, and also for carrying it out, should it be needed.

Lock, Fansler and Webb (2016) expanded on the above study (Hamilton & Brown, 2016) by looking specifically at risk management at NFP institutions based in North Carolina. Their suggestion was to focus on information dissemination within strategic planning which is a component of the communicating and reporting factor already identified as a NFP best practice. They also mentioned the importance of training protocols. Finally they pointed out that a best practice for any NFP would be to conduct ongoing strategic risk planning reviews using a small dedicated core committee to avoid getting bogged down in details or administrative procedures. The core committee could be the executive strategic planning group or in some cases the board of directors at the NFP.

Few scholars have investigated the NFP effectiveness factors within an emerging nation scenario outside of the USA (Karikari, Quansah, & Mohamed, 2015; Omoruyi & Omiunu, 2014; Watkins, Papaioannou, Mugwagwa, & Kale, 2015). Stewart (2015) is one of the few to do so. She worked with a group of international capacity building practitioners to identify key success factors for South African NFP organizations. Her ideology was pragmatic and she employed a variation of reflection-in-action as she collaborated with her team. The project was based at the University of Johannesburg and the goal was to identify best practices for leveraging evidence in NFP decision making. Stewart's (2015) findings revolved around five best practices. First a NFP needed to establish relationships with a local community of practice to provide an ongoing sustainable source of experts (policy makers, researchers and research facilities). We assume these experts could be staff, volunteers or consultants. Second was to use training or mentoring to develop capacity for conducting research related to the NFP mission. This was a strategic proposition and it is recommended by other researchers (vanderHeiden, Pohl, Bin Mansor, & van Genderen, 2015). Third was to attract the correct human resources, those having baseline skills in monitoring and evaluation and with the motivation to work. This seemed redundant with the first two steps. Next was to build relationships with national governments especially with departments having cross-jurisdictional program monitoring and review responsibility. This seemed an insightful concept because it would allow the NFP to understand how to improve their government grant winning and perhaps increase their reputation with the funding decision makers. Finally she recommended NFPs must ensure partners are committed by asking the right questions to potential funders (Stewart, 2015). While Stewart's work mentioned developing an important contemporary NFP competency – research skills – her study did not include enough details or mention the other commonly proposed effectiveness factors.

In summary, the critical analysis of the scholarly literature did not reveal much elaboration into the core factors of NFP effectiveness such as leadership, ethical accountability, operational governance, human resourcing and training, information technology, fund raising and marketing communications. The core NFP functions have been well-researched in the management literature. Instead, the scholarly literature review of NFP effectiveness identified insightful variations of the resourcing and marketing factors. In particular, partnering and collaborating with other NFPs or with the funding source organizations was a unique effectiveness factor revealed. This may extend to trading off collaboration in lieu of hiring staff as resources, or to use shared technology of a NFP university instead of acquiring it. Additionally, conducting research with other NFPs most likely a university was viewed as a critical success factor in order to identify needs for goals and to uncover new grant opportunities. These two ideas could work synergistically if a NFP collaborated with a university to leverage their intellectual research capacity, their information technology, and credibility with government funders to leverage grant proposals.

## NFP PRACTIONER ANALYSIS

The western world, USA and English-speaking European Union member countries in particular, have traditionally led the world in the production of scholarly managerial best practices literature. This is clear from a scan through the well-known citation index producers (Cabell's, Proquest, EBSCO, Scopus, etc.) and search engines (Google Scholar, Research Gate, etc.). The dearth of relevant findings in the scholarly literature about NFP effectiveness best practices may be due to more emphasis being placed on the outcomes of NFP product/service research as opposed to analyzing internal productivity. NFP effectiveness should also include elements of quality judged against best practices in the field (Walker, 2014). Therefore, research into NFP practitioner activities can expand upon the scholarly literature and in some instances support or refute earlier empirical findings.

In this section, we review NFP accreditation best practices rather than conduct action research into the NFP member institutions. This may be considered a theoretical sampling approach whereby we focus on examining participants with positive outcomes to better understand what leads to an effective NFP, at least in the context and perspective of USA. In USA, NFP effectiveness parallels higher education whereby a key benchmark starts with accreditation from a recognized state, national or international association, which itself is overseen by government or another transparent public entity. NCN and their state affiliates provide accreditation of NFP and through that process a framework for measuring effectiveness is established. As with higher education, it is not mandatory to be accredited to operate, but accreditation carries a powerful marketing appeal to donors and fund grantors. Therefore, selecting accredited NFPs represents a theoretical-sample of positive NFP best practices that we may assume to point towards effectiveness. Certainly a better scientific methodology would be to measure NFP effectiveness but this would require enormous effort and funding beyond the budget of this study (that would be a recommendation for future research).

We reviewed NFPs registered with the state-level government and who were also accredited by the NCN association, as summarized in table 1. This was the sample frame no the population since we had no way of identifying NFPs accredited by other organizations not listed with NCN (some do exist). We originally contacted two additional NFP associations but they requested to be excluded from our sample. The entries are sorted in descending order of the largest first. This table includes the formal name of the NFP association, the state where they were formally registered, and contact information such that other researchers may reproduce the data or follow up to extend this study. Each entry also includes a best practices web site (with exception that New York State [NYS] did not have one as of the time of writing). Most NFP state associations were registered charities but some were government (NYS) or consultant-driven (Alaska and Illinois). The states lacking a central NCN accreditation authority were Virginia, Ohio, Rhode Island, South Dakota, New Mexico, Georgia, and the territories (Puerto Rico, Guam, US Samoa, Mariana and Virgin Islands).

After collecting the best practices from each of the 44 NFP associations, the data was iteratively categorized to obtain a logical reduction to present (not interpret) the findings. The NFP practitioner best practices are summarized below

Leadership was not necessarily described as an individual activity in the practitioner best practices, but instead it was explained as governance, board of directors, and roles. We often assume there must be a single passionate leader for a NFP to be effective but the best practice was to use a group of people, the board of directors. Leadership or governance in a NFP constitutes expertise in the products/services advocated along with ethical character. An ethical NFP organization is governed by an independent and voluntary board of directors or board of trustees (board) that bring various invaluable skills and expertise to the operation of the NFP. The composition of the board should be representative of the community it serves, reflecting the diversity and interests of the entire community, and acting as a passionate advocate for the organization's mission. At least a portion of the board must include stakeholders familiar with the major funding sources or revenue generating models.

*Table 1. Sampling frame of not-for-profit accreditation associations in USA (N=44)*

| **Pennsylvania**<br>Penn State Association of Nonprofit Organizations<br>717 236-8584<br>http://pano.org | North Carolina<br>NC Center for Nonprofits<br>919-790-1555<br>http://ncnonprofits.org | South Carolina<br>SC Association of Nonprofit Organizations<br>803-929-0399<br>http://scanpo.org | Maryland<br>Maryland Nonprofits<br>410 727-6367<br>http://marylandnonprofits.org |
|---|---|---|---|
| Massachusetts<br>Providers' Council<br>617-428-3637<br>http://providers.org | Michigan<br>Michigan Nonprofit Association<br>517-492-2400<br>http://mnaonline.org | Minnesota<br>Minnesota Council of Nonprofits<br>651 642-1904<br>http://minnesotanonprofits.org | Tennessee<br>Alliance for Nonprofit Excellence<br>901 684-6605<br>http://npexcellence.org |
| Florida<br>Florida Nonprofit Alliance<br>407 694-5213<br>http://flnonprofits.org | Louisiana<br>Louisiana Association of Nonprofit Organizations<br>225 929-LANO<br>http://lano.org | Washington<br>Washington Nonprofits<br>253 330-8850<br>http://washingtonnonprofits.org | Texas<br>Texas Association of Nonprofit Organizations<br>512 287-2043<br>http://tano.org |
| West Virginia<br>WV Nonprofit Association<br>304-667-2248<br>http://wvnpa.org | Mississippi<br>Mississippi Center for Nonprofits<br>601 968-0061<br>http://msnonprofits.org | Missouri<br>Nonprofit Missouri<br>573 340-1634<br>http://nonprofitmissouri.org | California<br>California Association of Nonprofits<br>800 776-4226<br>http://calnonprofits.org |
| Colorado<br>Colorado Nonprofit Association<br>303 832-5710<br>http://coloradononprofits.org | Connecticut<br>Connecticut Association of Nonprofits<br>860 525-5080<br>http://ctnonprofits.org | Delaware<br>Delaware Alliance for Nonprofit Advancement<br>302-777-5500<br>http://DelawareNonprofit.org | Vermont<br>Common Good Vermont<br>802 862-1645<br>http://commongoodvt.org |
| Arkansas<br>Arkansas Nonprofit Alliance<br>501 375-1223<br>http://arkansasnonprofits.org | Arizona<br>Alliance of Arizona Nonprofits<br>602 279-2966<br>http://arizonanonprofits.org | Maine<br>Maine Association of Nonprofits<br>207 871-1885<br>http://NonprofitMaine.org | DC<br>Center for Nonprofit Advancement<br>202 457-0540<br>http://nonprofitadvancement.org |
| Montana<br>Montana Nonprofit Association<br>406 449-3717<br>http://mtnonprofit.org | Nebraska<br>Nonprofit Association of the Midlands<br>402 557-5800<br>http://nonprofitam.org | Nevada<br>Alliance for Nevada Nonprofits<br>702 483-1266<br>http://alliancefornevadanonprofits.com | Alabama<br>Alabama Association of Nonprofits<br>205 879-4712<br>http://alabamanonprofits.org/ |
| New Jersey<br>Center for Non-Profits<br>732 227-0800<br>http://njnonprofits.org/ | Alaska<br>The Foraker Group<br>907 743-1200<br>http://forakergroup.org/ | New Hampshire<br>NH Center for Nonprofits<br>603 225-1947<br>http://nhnonprofits.org/ | Iowa<br>Iowa Nonprofit Resource Center<br>319 335-9765<br>http://inrc.law.uiowa.edu/ |
| Wisconsin<br>Wisconsin Nonprofits Association<br>414 412-0408<br>http://wisconsinnonprofits.org/ | Kentucky<br>Kentucky Nonprofit Network<br>859 963-3203<br>http://kynonprofits.org/ | Hawaii<br>Hawai'i Alliance of Nonprofit Organizations<br>808 529-0466<br>http://hano-hawaii.org | Idaho<br>Idaho Nonprofit Center<br>208 424-2229<br>http://idahononprofits.org/ |
| Illinois<br>Forefront<br>312 578-0090<br>http://myforefront.org/ | Indiana<br>Indiana Nonprofit Resource Network<br>800 457-1450<br>http://inrn.org | Oregon<br>Nonprofit Association of Oregon<br>503-239-4001<br>http://nonprofitoregon.org | Oklahoma<br>Oklahoma Center for Nonprofits<br>800-338-1798<br>http://OklahomaCenterforNonprofits.org |
| North Dakota<br>ND Association of Nonprofit Organizations<br>701 258-9101<br>http://ndano.org/ | Utah<br>Utah Nonprofits Association<br>801 596-1800<br>http://utahnonprofits.org/ | Wyoming<br>Wyoming Nonprofit Network<br>307 772-9148<br>http://wynonprofit.org/ | New York<br>NYS Associations (through Secretary of Government)<br>Best-practice web site not available |

NFP leadership or the leader per se, should be a role that is democratically elected, and thereby changes to ensure fresh ideas emerge and to promote the continuity of the NFP. The board determines the mission of the organization, establishes governing policies and strategic plans, gives and solicits resources adequate to those plans, and monitors the organization's financial, executive, and programmatic performance. The entire board must be accountable for the NFPs annual budget, insurance coverage, executive compensation, and choice of auditor, as well as the findings of the organization's audit, and strategic planning outcomes. The actual structure and titles of the NFP are not important here but generally a Chief Executive Officer/President and other appropriate positions would be included in the governing body and report to the board. The board is responsible for defining the organization's mission and for providing overall leadership and strategic direction to the organization. NFP boards must actively set policy and ensure that the organization has adequate resources to carry out its mission. The board employs and provides oversight and direction for the executive director without usurping authority to manage financial and human resources. As will be discussed below, NFP boards have must evaluate their own effectiveness as governing bodies in upholding the mission and ensure the public interest is served by the organization.

Strategic planning is a critical process that defines a nonprofit's overall direction and activities to be employed to fulfill its mission. NFP boards have a duty to engage in sound planning to define a clear vision for the future and to set specific strategies for reaching established goals. NFP strategic planning should include input from constituents and should be intentional and ongoing to position organizations to achieve their goals. NFPs are obligated to understand their role as entities that engage and inspire individuals and communities for public benefits, and to conduct their activities with transparency integrity, and accountability. The outcomes of strategic planning should involve portfolios of related products/services, along with approved projects when new products/services need to be developed or changed whereas ongoing products/services would be a program within a portfolio (Strang, 2010a, 2011b). Projects are a best practice for NFPs to undertake new work because a project manager is delegated the responsibility to manage it but a sponsor or committee is identified to control it through gating mechanisms using milestones that ensure progress is on schedule, under budget, within scope, and of acceptable quality otherwise a struggling project may be cancelled before it fails entirely (Strang, 2010a).

Research is a strategic planning function that NFPs must do. Many NFPs scan grant opportunities from government but they often miss request-for-proposals from private companies or other NFP agencies. This is a factor that scholarly literature extended what practitioners reported doing. NFP staff or their partners must become more active in research focused on their mission and goals. This may not always be possible for a small NFP – approximately 90% of NFPs in USA have a budget less than $1 million USD (NCN, 2016). This factor is also discussed under the fund raising factor. A decision making methodology or several techniques should be available and applied to allow the NFP to make objective choices rather than allow subjective emotional perceptions influence the institution. Objective strategic planning decision making techniques may include Analytical Hierarchy Process, Factor Analysis, Weighted Scoring Models, Economic Payoff Tables and so on (Strang, 2012a, 2012c, 2014a, 2014b).

The operations of the NFP are closely tied to the products/services offered. Often these processes are not publicized. The important point to make about NFP operations or work processes is that they need to be documented to facilitate recruiting and training. Documentation of NFP processes is called 'Standard Operating Procedures' according to the operations research body of knowledge (Strang, 2011a). Interestingly, a NFP could become ISO 9001 certified by having their processes well documented and this would provide additional credibility to their funding sources and donors. Furthermore, training must be developed or outsourced to allow new staff or volunteers to come on board as needed. This is also a factor where the scholarly literature extended practitioner activities. Universities are best-suited to develop, maintain and deliver education of all types, particularly for general skills such as research, communications, professional ethics, accounting, marketing, writing, public speaking, data analytics and so on. Thus, a NFP should arrange a cost-effective partnership to outsource basic skill training. A strategic action would be to hire staff who already possess the basic competency needed. The NFP will need to provide customized training for their unique products/services, as noted above, but the development and maintenance of this could also be outsource to a university if it is cost-effective.

The strategic management of human resources is essential for a NFP to be effective. The board is responsible for oversight of the leader and that role is responsible for oversight of paid or volunteer staff. NFP organizations should exercise fair and equitable human resources and volunteer (including board members) management practices that attract and retain qualified individuals. NFPs have an obligation to adhere to all legal employment practices and to provide a safe work environment. NFP organizations should establish specific policies and practices that promote mutual cooperation to advance the organization's mission. An ethical NFP organization has a 'Human Resources Manual' in place that outlines policies that address paid employees. These policies establish that the organization is responsible to hire and manage employees in a fair and effective manner and ensure compliance with local, state and federal employment laws. In particular the EEOC have general guidelines that NFPs may follow. For example, it would be essential for a NFP to have fair nondiscriminatory policies that condone a 'No Harassment/No Discrimination' philosophy in the workplace. As with operations training, a NFP could outsource some of the human resource management function but it is best to retain the selection of the board and leaders.

The scholarly literature extended the human resource factor by showing how strategic alliances and partnerships could benefit a NFP. The effectiveness of a NFP depends on successful relationships with other community institutions. Regardless of form – partnership, collaboration, cooperation or coordination – these relationships or strategic alliances, can serve a variety of purposes, including resource sharing, policy interpretation, and improved operational efficiency through common function sharing (e.g., intake services, office administration, security, etc.). Function sharing strengthens both the capacity of individual organizations and the sector as a whole because they allow the NFP staff and board to focus more on mission-critical activities rather than the administrative functions. A NFP should be open to strategic alliances to strengthen their capacity to achieve documented goals that are mutually beneficial. A NFP should initiate and promote the cooperation and coordination of resource activities between a variety of entities to avoid unnecessary duplication of services to maximize the resources available to the communities they serve. A good example of this is FEMA and Red Cross frequently share resources and delegate emergency management services to the NFP in the best position to respond to a crisis event.

Technology management is often cited in NFP practitioner activities as though this means to have laptops, tablets and cell phones. Technology management is more than that. Certainly the basic policies of proper technology usage would apply, but a NFP strategic plan for technology should include researching enterprise resource planning software in order to collect and manage the information it collects. A NFP is no different from a commercial business in as far as it may collect useful behavioral data from its clients and stakeholders that could be analyzed to reveal important product/service provisioning opportunities. Three important technology software requirements arose from the NFP practitioner research. First, NFPs need basic accounting transaction software to record all financial activities. This actually saves money later because it facilitates the preparation of tax returns and annual reports, which are often done with the help of volunteers (at least in the smaller NFPs). A best practice identified from NFP practitioners was to use Excel or Google Calc spreadsheet software to analyze the key financial ratios reported in the IRS 990 form. The key ratio is that fundraising should be three times the expenses, or in other words, for every $1 invested in fundraising expenses, the NFP should raise at least $3. The other two key software models for a NFP would be a Client Relationship Management/Sales Prospecting tool and a basic research analysis software. The basic research analysis software could be a spreadsheet or more strategically the NFP could look to their partners such as a university to use more powerful data analytics or statistical software.

The scholarly literature has also extended the NFP practitioner best practice activities by pointing out the importance of risk management, particularly in observance of global or domestic terrorism. Both human and technology (including data) must be protected through policy and active control. Staff and volunteers should be checked through the police records and national terrorism blacklists (operated by the USA Department of Homeland Security). Technology should be protected from unauthorized access and unexpected viruses, the latter of which could quickly make a NFP unproductive. Data backup and protection is also needed. Although having an enterprise resource planning system and other software give the NFP staff more analytical capability, it also opens the door to additional risks such as data loss, corruption or theft. A NFP should have technology policies that address federal legislation such as Confidentiality of Information. An ethical NFP will have policies in place in the Standard Operating Procedures manual that identify who has access to certain information and the security procedures in place to prevent unauthorized access. Given the rise in domestic terrorism, besides new staff or volunteer criminal records check screening, clients, employees and anyone entering the NFP offices should be documented and cleared where needed. NFP practitioners particularly identified data backup as a needed step. The scholarly literature also identified data backup and recovery as a major risk and needed step in contingency management.

The NFP practitioner best practice statement for technology management was: A successful NFP manages information with regard to confidentiality, safety, accuracy, integrity, reliability, cost effectiveness, and legal compliance. It incorporates appropriate technology into its work to improve its efficiency, efficacy and accuracy in the achievement of its mission, and has information systems in place that provide timely, accurate and relevant information.

Financial management refers to acting as responsible stewards in managing NFP financial assets. A NFP must comply with all legal financial requirements. They should adhere to sound accounting principles that ensure fiscal responsibility and build public trust. A NFP should use their financial assets, human and technology resources to accomplish their mission in an effective, efficient manner and should establish clear policies and practices to regularly monitor how funds are used. Enterprise resource planning or accounting software can automate the data collection, analysis and reporting but the responsibility rests with the board and leader(s). An ethical NFP organization conducts periodic financial reviews to address regulatory and liability concerns, plus it creates and maintains financial reports on a timely basis that accurately portray its financial status and activities. More importantly, an NFP should make its annual reports available to the board, staff and the public.

Additional NFP practitioner financial management activities include providing staff and volunteers with a confidential means to report suspected financial impropriety or misuse of its resource assets – and when a report is file a fair independent investigation must be undertaken. The key financial policies required by NFP practitioners were those to cover the following:

1. Investment of its assets;
2. Internal control procedures;
3. Purchasing practices;
4. Reserve funds; and
5. Others as required.

Some NFP organizations offer an advocacy role or a voice to citizens. A NFP may play a central role in the democratic process of a society by providing a means for individuals to deliberate public policies and decisions that affect them. To the extent possible, NFP organizations should engage constituents in public policy and advocacy activities as a means to fulfilling their missions and promoting community interests. Open communication and consultation between policy makers and constituents of nonprofit organizations contribute to well-informed policies and the effective implementation of them.

An ethical NFP organization must be aware of and comply with all applicable federal, state, and local laws. This may include, but is not limited to: complying with laws and regulations related to fundraising; licensing; financial accountability; human resources; lobbying and political advocacy; and taxation. In particular, taxation compliance with the IRS is the most important best practice for a NFP practitioner. An ethical NFP organization that solicits donations from the public is 1) properly organized as a tax-exempt charity and registered with the IRS under 501[c][3] legislation, 2) registered in all states in which it actively solicits donations, and 3) is in compliance with both the spirit and the letter of all local, state and federal laws governing charitable solicitations (IRS, 2016). An ethical NFP organization offers proof of its tax-exempt status by providing its IRS Determination Letter on request (IRS, 2016). An organization that is not eligible to receive tax-deductible contributions discloses this fact at the time of solicitation (IRS, 2016).

NFPs must also be professional, which means to be ethical and moral. As entities that serve the public, NFPs have an ethical obligation to conduct their activities with accountability and transparency. NFPs should engage in ongoing efforts or openly convey information to the public about their missions, activities and decision-making processes. This information should be easily accessible to the public and should create external visibility, public understanding and trust in the organization. Keywords that NFP practitioners mention included: Integrity, public trust, and ethical. NFPs are expected to offer products/services based their mission. NFPs are also expected to follow best practices such as those discussed in this chapter. A NFP should be accountable which means that outcomes must be measurable to provide evidence of the delivery of effective programs and services. According to NFP practitioners, the true measure of NFP success is whether individual lives—and our communities—change for the better as a result of products/services. This is perhaps a differentiating feature of a NFP – that the products/services must benefit human lives, instead of merely making an outcome or a report. A NFP should respect the diverse needs of individuals and communities served. NFPs should respect the dignity and autonomy of each person and the integrity, privacy, pride, beliefs, and cultures of our varied constituencies—the people we serve, our employees, donors, volunteers, and others. The human resource and standard operating policies cited above should reflect that. For example, a technology management policy should address the data accuracy and integrity requirement that ensures information is accurate and is used only as intended in a database.

Fundraising is the revenue generating engine of a NFP. As explained earlier, this requires identifying revenue for carrying out a product/service program and finding relevant clients to deliver it to (in most cases). This is why communications goes hand-in-hand with fundraising for a NFP. It must practice truthful communications during fund solicitation and in promotional materials that 1) contain accurate and truthful product/service benefit statements, 2) identify the organization, 3) reflect its IRS status, 4) reflect its mission, and 5) state its intended use of funds received. Marketing staff must use non-coercive tactics that are not intimidating or deceptive, especially to disadvantaged members of society. More importantly, a NFP must not sensationalize publicity for its own purposes, meaning to respect the integrity and privacy of its clients or patrons. Specifically, it must not use clients, their pictures or their case histories in any publicity or fundraising activities without prior written consent.

Donor gifts or grant funds must respect the restrictions or constraints placed upon their intended use. An ethical NFP must accurately record and receipt gifts or grants. As discussed above, it reports to donors and the public in a timely way on the use and management of contributed funds. It promptly acknowledges all donations, including in-kind gifts, and states, if applicable, the value of goods and services provided in return for those donations. Specifically, a NFP should provide the last two years IRS 990 filings, in their entirety, and two last years of its annual reports, on its website as well as in any printed prospectus.

Performance effectiveness evaluation is perhaps the most understated NFP practitioner activity. The practitioner activities refer to accurate reporting and filing IRS 990 forms. However, this does not satisfy the effectiveness criteria explained in the previous two sections of this chapter. The de facto performance activity involves reporting funds received and their use. Effectiveness must be measured by correlating quantitative as well as qualitative outcomes with the mission and goals. An enterprise resource planning system will facilitate this by using activity based coding for all transactions, by linking pre-established goal codes with every dollar of revenue and expense recorded. This is known as direct cost accounting or activity based costing. However, it is more difficult to relate outcomes to the goals. A separate system of accounting is needed to measure program outcomes, quantitative and qualitative, with respect to goals. Here the scholarly literature provides some useful advice where the NFP practitioner activities fail to offer a solution. The best place and time to record an NFP outcome is when the product/service is delivered. This is often finalized by a salesperson or front line worker. Software should be used to facilitate this, and it need not be a fancy system, merely a basic transactional application, including one that would function on a smart phone. The front line person should record what was delivered, select the best-fitting goal from a pre-determined list (perhaps more than one could be permitted), and record client satisfaction either as a yes/no binomial or better to use an ordinal scale of 1 to 5 (where 5 is highest or most satisfied). If this were consistently applied across the NFP for all products/services delivered, the resulting data could be easily analyzed using basic statistics software to measure the effectiveness. Descriptive statistics such as the median, mean, standard deviation and coefficient of variance would suffice. Additional analysis such as correlation and cause-effect regression could provide insight into the NFPs product/service delivery. Although the scholarly literature studies tended to rely on surveys given to samples, this approach refers to a population data collection close to the source delivery point and time – this will be the most accurate measure of effectiveness.

Measuring qualitative or quantitative outcomes could be accommodated through the above methodology. Additional reflection could be undertaken on the above measurements, by having experienced NFP staff look at the results in the overall context of the macro environment and client population.

Some trends may be attributed to factors beyond control of the NFP while others may highlight program improvement areas – all of which should be added to the annual reports. Objectivity could be achieved by ensuring the reflection of previous effectiveness is done by someone outside of the specific product/service delivery responsibility. This may be another opportunity where the NFP could collaborate with a university partner to have both the quantitative/qualitative results analyzed as well as to have a reflective improvement trend analysis conducted on the effectiveness results. Furthermore, reflective analysis could lead to new product/service development opportunities for the NFP, which could be missed if the NFP were to do their own in-house statistical analysis. A university may also have access to other NFP performance data and could thereby perform meta-analysis by industry, geographic or other category, perhaps performing big data analytics when the volume and complexity of the information increases.

### Text Analytics of NFP Practitioner Best Practices

We conducted a text analytics of the NFP practitioner best practices from the 44 state level accreditation associations. The text analytics settings were adjusted to eliminate common grammar and to retain the 100 more frequent words captured in the practitioner best practices after we integrated the extensions identified from the scholarly literature review (e.g., technology management, partner collaboration on research and performance effectiveness measurement).

In summary there were eight core NFP effectiveness best practice factors emerging from the above results, as enumerated below:

1. Leadership and structure.
2. Strategic planning.
3. Documented procedures and training.
4. Human and technology resource management.
5. Financial management and accountability practices.
6. Ethics and professional communications policies.
7. Collaborative fundraising and marketing initiatives.
8. Performance effectiveness evaluation.

## CONCLUSION AND RECOMMENDATIONS

This chapter has reviewed the current literature to identify contemporary NFP best practices needed to be effective in a modern environment facing increased economic instability, global terrorism, and ubiquitous sharing of information through the Internet. A current literature review was undertaken to identify contemporary NFP best practices that could make an institution more effective. This was followed by a practitioner analysis of 44 state level NFP accreditation associations based in USA that averages 20 member NFP institutions. Thus the sampling frame contained over 880 NFPs. A critical analysis was performed on the literature and then the most relevant findings were integrated with the results of the practitioner data collected from the NFP institutions.

The first interesting finding was that the current scholarly literature researchers tended to avoid de facto competency skills needed in any business such as leadership and decision making, owing to their extensive coverage in older managerial best practice studies. The scholarly literature did identify several valuable extensions to contemporary NFP best practices, namely to form strategic alliances for resource sharing and to conduct research as part of the grant funding processes. The scholarly literature offered ideas for technology management, especially the use of enterprise resource software, and statistical analysis/data analytics through collaborations with another NFP (primarily a university).

Finally, the practitioner data clearly displayed a focus on leadership and structure, accountability, ethical conduct and financial management. However, the practitioner activities were weak in strategic planning, decision making, technology management and performance effectiveness measurement. Once the scholarly literature was integrated with the practitioner data, eight overall contemporary NFP best practice factors emerged: Leadership and structure, strategic planning, documented procedures and training, human and technology resource management, financial management and accountability practices, ethics and professional communications policies, fundraising and marketing initiatives, and performance effectiveness evaluation.

## RECOMMENDATIONS FOR FUTURE STUDIES

Future research should examine NFP best practices from individual member institutions and drawn from additional populations outside the USA. This study used a theoretical-sample of 44 state-level NFP accreditation institutions each of which contained an average of 20 member companies. The member companies were not included in the data or analysis due to budget constraints (no external funding was received for this study).

Additional research should be undertaken to illustrate how to measure NFP performance using both quantitative as well as qualitative product/service outcome data. For example, this study discussed using descriptive statistics and trend analysis (including correlation and regression). Advanced data analytics were also mentioned. However, no actual examples were given as to how to apply those techniques on NFP product/service program outcome data.

Future studies should expand on strategic management and decision making techniques. Several objective decision making techniques were cited, including AHP, payoff tables, and weighted scoring models. However, no examples were given about how to apply those techniques within strategic planning. Furthermore, there was no mention or examples of common strategic planning techniques such as SWOT/TOWS, House of Quality or other advanced product/service decision making model – many exist. There was no mention of fuzzy logic strategic planning approaches (except for AHP), but these are examined in detail within the operations research literature so they could be discussed within the NFP context as a potential collaborative study with a university. For example, there was a recent study published using AHP with NFP data (Zhao, Zu, Li, & Li, 2014) and another using DEA for NFP capacity building analysis (Medina-Borja & Triantis, 2014). More research of this nature is required to further advance the NFP best practice practitioner body of knowledge.

## REFERENCES

Alsudairi, M. A. T., & Tatapudi, G. (2014). Social innovation: Can it be a strategy for influencing GCC public welfare? *Innovation: Management. Policy & Practice*, *16*(2), 273–282. doi:10.1080/14479338.2014.11081988

Beecham, R. (2014). Measuring SpICE (Specialist Integrated Community Engagement). *Australasian Journal of University-Community Engagement*, *9*(1), 56–76.

Beynaghi, A., Trencher, G., Moztarzadeh, F., Mozafari, M., Maknoon, R., & Leal Filho, W. (2016). Future sustainability scenarios for universities: Moving beyond the United Nations Decade of Education for Sustainable Development. *Journal of Cleaner Production*, *112*(4), 3464–3478. doi:10.1016/j.jclepro.2015.10.117

Bos, J. J., & Brown, R. R. (2014). Assessing organisational capacity for transition policy programs. *Technological Forecasting and Social Change*, *86*(1), 188–206. doi:10.1016/j.techfore.2013.09.012

Brink-Danan, M. (2015). Value and meaning: Paradoxes of religious diversity talk as a globalized expertise. *Language and Communication, 44*, 44-58.

Cantrell-Bruce, T., & Blankenberger, B. (2015). Seeing Clearly: Measuring Skill Sets That Address the "Blurred Boundaries" of Nonproit Management Education. *Journal of Public Affairs Education*, *21*(3), 367–380.

Cãrdoba, D., Jansen, K., & Gonzãlez, C. (2014). The Malleability of Participation: The Politics of Agricultural Research under Neoliberalism in Bolivia. *Development & Change, 45*(6), 1284-1309.

Chaudron, G. (2016). Managing the commonplace: Small water emergencies in libraries. *International Journal of Risk and Contingency Management*, *5*(1), 42–61. doi:10.4018/IJRCM.2016010104

Clark, P., & Martinez, L. (2016). Local Alternatives to Private Agricultural Certification in Ecuador: Broadening Access to â€˜New Marketsâ€™? *Journal of Rural Studies*, 1.

Dedeurwaerdere, T., Admiraal, J., Beringer, A., Bonaiuto, F., Cicero, L., Fernandez-Wulff, P., & …, Luis Vivero, J. (2016). Combining internal and external motivations in multi-actor governance arrangements for biodiversity and ecosystem services. *Environmental Science & Policy*, *58*(1), 1–10. PMID:28149197

Diver, S. W., & Higgins, M. N. (2014). Giving Back Through Collaborative Research: Towards a Practice of Dynamic Reciprocity. *Journal of Research Practice*, *10*(2), 1–13.

Duraj, L., Felt, L. J., & Singhal, A. (2014). What counts? For whom? Cultural beacons and unexpected areas of programmatic impact. *Evaluation and Program Planning*, *44*(1), 98–109. PMID:24662404

Foster, W. L., Kim, P., & Christiansen, B. (2009). Ten nonprofit funding models. *Stanford Social Innovation Review*, *13*(1), 32–39.

Gebauer, H., & Saul, C. J. (2014). Business model innovation in the water sector in developing countries. *The Science of the Total Environment*, *488-489*(1), 512–520. doi:10.1016/j.scitotenv.2014.02.046 PMID:24612490

Germak, A. J. (2014). Building Nonprofit Capacity: A Guide to Managing Change Through Organizational. *Human Service Organizations: Management. Leadership & Governance*, *38*(1), 116–117.

Goodwin, Y., & Strang, K. D. (2012). Socio-cultural and multi-disciplinary perceptions of risk. *International Journal of Risk and Contingency Management*, *1*(1), 1–11. doi:10.4018/ijrcm.2012010101

Guzzo, T., Ferri, F., Grifoni, P., & Firus, K. (2012). Flood risk awareness: An experiment using school students to inform families and friends. *International Journal of Risk and Contingency Management*, *1*(1), 49–63. doi:10.4018/ijrcm.2012010104

Haegeman, K., Spiesberger, M., Veselitskaya, N., Sokolov, A., & Weiss, G. (2015). FTA supporting effective priority setting in multi-lateral research programme cooperation: The case of EUâ€"Russia S&T cooperation. *Technological Forecasting and Social Change*, *101*(1), 200–215. doi:10.1016/j.techfore.2015.04.009

Hamilton, R., & Brown, D. (2016). Disaster management and continuity planning in libraries: Literature review. *International Journal of Risk and Contingency Management*, *5*(1), 26–41. doi:10.4018/IJRCM.2016010103

Hoefer, R., & Sliva, S. M. (2014). Assessing and Augmenting Administration Skills in Nonprofits: An Exploratory Mixed Methods Study. *Human Service Organizations: Management. Leadership & Governance*, *38*(3), 246–257.

Hurlburt, M., Aarons, G. A., Fettes, D., Willging, C., Gunderson, L., & Chaffin, M. J. (2014). Interagency Collaborative Team model for capacity building to scale-up evidence-based practice. *Children and Youth Services Review*, *39*(1), 160–168. doi:10.1016/j.childyouth.2013.10.005 PMID:27512239

IRS. (2016). *Instructions for Form 990. Return of Organization. Exempt From Income Tax. Under section 501(c), 527, or 4947(a)(1) of the Internal Revenue.* Internal Revenue Service (IRS). Retrieved June 20, 2016, from the World Wide Web: https://www.irs.gov/pub/irs-pdf/i990.pdf

Javalgi, R. G., Hall, K. D., & Cavusgil, S. T. (2014). Corporate entrepreneurship, customer-oriented selling, absorptive capacity, and international sales performance in the international B2B setting: Conceptual framework and research propositions. *International Business Review*, *23*(1), 1193–1202. doi:10.1016/j.ibusrev.2014.04.003

Jayashankar, P., Ashta, A., & Rasmussen, M. (2015). Analysis: Slow money in an age of fiduciary capitalism. *Ecological Economics*, *116*(1), 322–329. doi:10.1016/j.ecolecon.2015.05.007

Karikari, T. K., Quansah, E., & Mohamed, W. M. Y. (2015). Developing expertise in bioinformatics for biomedical research in Africa. *Applied & Translational Genomics*, *6*, 31-34.

Khieng, S. (2014). Funding Mobilization Strategies of Nongovernmental Organizations in Cambodia. *Voluntas: International Journal of Voluntary & Nonprofit Organizations*, *25*(6), 1441–1464. doi:10.1007/s11266-013-9400-7

Knife, K. A. H. N., Haughton, A., & Dixon, E. (2014). Measuring sustainability and effectiveness of social value creation by social sector actors social enterprises within developing countries. *Academy of Entrepreneurship Journal*, *20*(1), 1–22.

Koski, C., & Lee, T. (2014). Policy by Doing: Formulation and Adoption of Policy through Government Leadership. *Policy Studies Journal: the Journal of the Policy Studies Organization*, *42*(1), 30–54. doi:10.1111/psj.12041

Lan, H., Zhu, Y., Ness, D., Xing, K., & Schneider, K. (2014). The role and characteristics of social entrepreneurs in contemporary rural cooperative development in China: Case studies of rural social entrepreneurship. *Asia Pacific Business Review*, *20*(3), 379–400. doi:10.1080/13602381.2014.929300

Lewis, D., Yerby, L., Tucker, M., Foster, P. P., Hamilton, K. C., Fifolt, M. M., & Higginbotham, J. C. A. et al. (2015). Bringing Community and Academic Scholars Together to Facilitate and Conduct Authentic Community Based Participatory Research: Project UNITED. *International Journal of Environmental Research and Public Health*, *13*(1), 35. doi:10.3390/ijerph13010035 PMID:26703675

Lock, M. B., Fansler, C., & Webb, M. (2016). Revolutionary emergency planning: Adding resilience through continuous review. *International Journal of Risk and Contingency Management*, *5*(2), 47–65. doi:10.4018/IJRCM.2016040103

Lucas, S. R. (2014). Beyond the existence proof: Ontological conditions, epistemological implications, and in-depth interview research. *Quality & Quantity Journal*, *48*(1), 387–408. doi:10.1007/s11135-012-9775-3

Mabe, M. R. (2016). Libraries to the rescue. *International Journal of Risk and Contingency Management*, *5*(1), 62–81. doi:10.4018/IJRCM.2016010105

Martin, M. (2015). Building Impact Businesses through Hybrid Financing. *Entrepreneurship Research Journal*, *5*(2), 109–126. doi:10.1515/erj-2015-0005

Mataira, P. J., Morelli, P. T., Matsuoka, J. K., & Uehara-McDonald, S. (2014). Shifting the paradigm: New directions for non profits and funders in an era of diminishing resources. *Social Business*, *4*(3), 231–244. doi:10.1362/204440814X14103454934212

McGoey, L. (2014). The philanthropic state: Marketâ€"state hybrids in the philanthrocapitalist turn. *Third World Quarterly*, *35*(1), 109–125. doi:10.1080/01436597.2014.868989

Medina-Borja, A., & Triantis, K. (2014). Modeling social services performance: A four-stage DEA approach to evaluate fundraising efficiency, capacity building, service quality, and effectiveness in the nonprofit sector. *Annals of Operations Research*, *221*(1), 285–307. doi:10.1007/s10479-011-0917-0

NCN. (2016). *Principles and Practices*. National Council of Nonprofits (NCN). Retrieved June 1, 2016, from the World Wide Web: https://www.councilofnonprofits.org/tools-resources/principles-and-practices

Omoruyi, F. E. O., & Omiunu, S. E. (2014). Strategies for strengthening vocational skills development programme for women in Benin metropolis. *Journal of Educational Review*, *7*(1), 127–131.

Puljak, L., & Vari, S. G. (2014). Significance of research networking for enhancing collaboration and research productivity. *Croatian Medical Journal*, *55*(3), 181–183. doi:10.3325/cmj.2014.55.181 PMID:24891275

Rasoolimanesh, S. M., Jaafar, M., Badarulzaman, N., & Ramayah, T. (2015). Investigating a framework to facilitate the implementation of city development strategy using balanced scorecard. *Habitat International*, *46*(1), 156–165. doi:10.1016/j.habitatint.2014.12.003

Read, C. (2012). Review of key risk and uncertainty theories influencing contemporary financial economics. *International Journal of Risk and Contingency Management*, *1*(4), 18–27. doi:10.4018/ijrcm.2012100102

Sanzo, M. J., Álvarez, L. I., Rey, M., & García, N. (2015). Business as Nonprofit Partnerships: Do Their Effects Extend Beyond the Charitable Donor-Recipient Model? *Nonprofit and Voluntary Sector Quarterly*, *44*(2), 379–400. doi:10.1177/0899764013517770

Schalock, R. L., Lee, T., Verdugo, M., Swart, K., Claes, C., van Loon, J., & Lee, C.-S. (2014). An evidence-based approach to organization evaluation and change in human service organizations evaluation and program planning. *Evaluation and Program Planning*, *45*(1), 110–118. doi:10.1016/j.evalprogplan.2014.03.012 PMID:24762778

Senses-Ozyurt, S. (2015). Political institutional environment and management culture as determinants of nongovernmental / nonprofit organizations' performance. *International Journal of Organization Theory and Behavior*, *18*(3), 269–303.

Stecker, M. J. (2014). Revolutionizing the Nonprofit Sector Through Social Entrepreneurship. *Journal of Economic Issues*, *48*(2), 349–358. doi:10.2753/JEI0021-3624480208

Stewart, R. (2015). A theory of change for capacity building for the use of research evidence by decision makers in southern Africa. *Evidence & Policy Journal*, *11*(4), 547–557. doi:10.1332/174426414X1417545274793

Strang, K. D. (2010a). *Complexity and project portfolio selection.* Paper presented at the Lille Project Seminars, Helisinki, Finland.

Strang, K. D. (2010b). Education balanced scorecard for online courses: Australia and USA best practices. *Journal of Cases on Information Technology*, *12*(3), 46–51. doi:10.4018/jcit.2010070103

Strang, K. D. (2011a). Applying multidisciplinary logistic techniques to improve operations productivity at a mine. *Logistics Research Journal*, *3*(4), 207–219. doi:10.1007/s12159-011-0058-5

Strang, K. D. (2011b). Portfolio selection methodology for a nuclear project. *Project Management Journal*, *42*(2), 81–93.

Strang, K. D. (2012a). Applied financial nonlinear programming models for decision making. *International Journal of Applied Decision Sciences*, *5*(4), 370–395. doi:10.1504/IJADS.2012.050023

Strang, K. D. (2012b). Group cohesion, personality and leadership effect on networked marketing staff performance. *International Journal of Networking and Virtual Organisations*, *10*(2), 187–209. doi:10.1504/IJNVO.2012.045734

Strang, K. D. (2012c). Man versus math: Behaviorist exploration of post-crisis non-banking asset management. *Journal of Asset Management*, *13*(5), 348–467. doi:10.1057/jam.2012.14

Strang, K. D. (2014a). Dimensional analysis of real estate portfolio selection methods. *Global Business and Economics Review*, *16*(3), 269–265. doi:10.1504/GBER.2014.063069

Strang, K. D. (2014b). Investment selection in complex multinational projects. *International Journal of Information Technology Project Management*, *5*(2), 62–80. doi:10.4018/ijitpm.2014040105

Strang, K. D. (2014c). Nonparametric analysis of global risk management techniques. In Information Resources Management Association (Ed.), Crisis management: Concepts, methodologies, tools and applications (Vol. 1, pp. 687-711). Hershey, PA: Information Science Reference. doi:10.4018/978-1-4666-4707-7.ch033

Strang, K. D. (2015a). Exploring the relationship between global terrorist ideology and attack methodology. *Risk Management Journal*, *17*(2), 65–90. doi:10.1057/rm.2015.8

Strang, K. D. (Ed.). (2015b). *Matching Research Method with Ideology and Strategy* (Vol. 1). New York: Palgrave Macmillan. doi:10.1057/9781137484956_4

Strang, K. D. (Ed.). (2015c). *Selecting Research Techniques for a Method and Strategy* (Vol. 1). New York: Palgrave Macmillan. doi:10.1057/9781137484956_5

Strang, K. D. (2016). Exploring Marketing Theories in Business Web Service Procurement Behavior. In IRMA (Ed.), Web-Based Services: Concepts, Methodologies, Tools, and Applications (Vol. 2, pp. 221-250). Hershey, PA: Information Resource Management Association (IRMA). doi:10.4018/978-1-4666-9466-8.ch011

Strang, K. D., & Alamieyeseigha, S. (2015). What and where are the risks of international terrorist attacks: A descriptive study of the evidence. *International Journal of Risk and Contingency Management*, *4*(1), 1–18.

Strang, K. D., & Vajjhala, N. R. (2015). Impact of Socialized Uncertainty on Group Decisions: An Experiment with Emerging Executives. *International Journal of Risk and Contingency Management*, *4*(2), 45–58. doi:10.4018/IJRCM.2015040104

Trencher, G., Yarime, M., McCormick, K. B., Doll, C. N. H., & Kraines, S. B. (2014). Beyond the third mission: Exploring the emerging university function of co-creation for sustainability. *Science & Public Policy*, *41*(2), 151–179. doi:10.1093/scipol/sct044

Vallejo, B., & Wehn, U. (2016). Capacity Development Evaluation: The Challenge of the Results Agenda and Measuring Return on Investment in the Global South. *World Development*, *79*(1), 1–13. doi:10.1016/j.worlddev.2015.10.044

vanderHeiden, P., Pohl, C., Bin Mansor, S., & van Genderen, J. (2015). The role of education and training in absorptive capacity of international technology transfer in the aerospace sector. *Progress in Aerospace Sciences, 76*(1), 42-54.

Walker, R. M. (2014). Internal and External Antecedents of Process Innovation: A review and extension. *Public Management Review*, *16*(1), 21–44. doi:10.1080/14719037.2013.771698

Watkins, A., Papaioannou, T., Mugwagwa, J., & Kale, D. (2015). National innovation systems and the intermediary role of industry associations in building institutional capacities for innovation in developing countries: A critical review of the literature. *Research Policy*, *44*(1), 1407–1418. doi:10.1016/j.respol.2015.05.004

Wohlgemuth, N. H.-M. (2014). Alternatives to Rural Development: Organic Agriculture and Indigenous Communities in Chiapas, Mexico. *Journal of Latin American Geography*, *13*(1), 67–88. doi:10.1353/lag.2014.0003

Zhao, Y., Zu, B., Li, Z., & Li, C. (2014). Corporate social responsibility assessment: A multi-dimensional and dynamic perspective. *Mining Technology*, *123*(4), 230–239. doi:10.1179/1743286314Y.0000000071

Zlotnikova, I., & van der Weide, T. (2015). Community outreach projects as a sustainable way of introducing information technology in developing countries. *International Journal of Education & Development using Information & Communication Technology, 11*(1), 55-79.

## KEY TERMS AND DEFINITIONS

**Business Analytics:** Business intelligence involves collecting data from competitors while business analytics may be the analysis performed on this data or on the data collected through the normal process of business (such as the transaction processing system records).

**Client Relationship Management (CRM):** A CRM is an application used to contain customer profiles and sales forecasting data. CRM's are intended to allow the organization to assist customers by using past transactional behavior, along with client-modified profile purchase preferences, to predict future needs and behavior. The CRM may be linked to other organizational software such as the ERP.

**Enterprise Resource Planning (ERP):** An ERP contains the chart of accounts for the organization and it links the separate operations models across all departments or functions of an organization. It facilitates strategic planning and business analytics by providing the data with links to the goals through activity based costing and using codes for all transactions.

**Models:** Models are analog or digital. Analog models are conceptual diagrams or figures intended to show how a system behaves. Digital models are operational versions of conceptual models, generally programmed in a language or in a spreadsheet, able to accept variables to provide an expected value in order to predict an outcome for planning purposes.

**NCN:** The National Council of Nonprofits (NCN) is considered an authority on the subject in USA – 46 of 52 states have a centralized NFP association that provides accreditation and best practices. The NCN have a detailed list of criteria used to accredit a NFP including solvency, community good standing, possessing a professional code of ethics, and other elements. We adopt the NCN designation of accredited as indicating a NFP is effective. The centralized NFP associations and the national council best practices are cited by the Internal Revenue Service as guidelines for registered charities under the 501[c][3] corporation tax legislation (IRS, 2016).

**NFP Effectiveness:** In the research scope, if refers to a USA-based NFP being solvent, registered with state government, and accredited by the NCN. The NCN asserts that NFP effectiveness are best practices of accountability, transparency, prudent fiduciary oversight, legal, ethical, and responsible fundraising (NCN, 2016, para. 4). In that statement NCN refer to the how – the way things are done - as the measure of NFP effectiveness rather than the monetary outcomes which would be the emphasis of a for-profit business. NCN indicate that accredited NFPs do not fail otherwise they would lose their accreditation. Effectiveness for a NFP according to NCN and IRS generally means being ethical, accountable and transparent.

**Not for Profit (NFP):** A NFP may be a registered charity with a government department (most countries have this governance) or a NFP may simply an organization that does not have an owner or stock owners to share the profits – therefore in this latter situation a NFP shares the difference between revenue – expenses as a reinvestment into the organization or a distribution to the public.

**Strategic Planning:** Planning for a business or entity that extends beyond one year, generally for three to five years. This type of planning will involve senior management and it will be focused on achieving the mission of the organization.

# Chapter 4
# The "Private Face" of Nonprofits:
## Legal and Ethical Human Resource Practices

**Sarah Caflisch**
*Hamline University, USA*

## ABSTRACT

*Financial and social costs for nonprofits that do not follow legal and ethical human resources policies, procedures and practices, are substantial for social welfare nonprofit organisations. Especially, a knowledge deficiency in the area of employee discipline and discharge suggest that nonprofits struggle when these challenges occur. Often, such deficiencies have led to costly litigation, loss of funding and diminished public good will. Data is obtained from nonprofit social welfare service providers using surveys and interviews. This chapter contributes to the generation of knowledge in the areas of legal and ethical human management particularly as these relate to employee performance management and discipline, discharge and termination issues and concludes with alternative solutions, approaches and future research directions.*

## INTRODUCTION

*If you build both the moral and the ethical foundation, as well as the business and the experience foundation, then the building won't crumble. Henry Kravis, financier and investor*

The introduction of human resource policies, procedures and practices contributes to a safe, productive and ethical workplace environment (Malloy & Agarwal, 2001). As Gross-Schaefer & Zaller (1998) pointed out, social service non-profit organisations must abide by codes of ethics and ethical behaviour when serving vulnerable populations, fundraising, securing social and financial capital and maintain organisational reputation and public credibility. However, as the Panel on the Nonprofit Sector (2007) revealed although many nonprofit organisations are expected to adhere with numerous codes of ethics, ethical behaviour and ethical human resource management, internal organisational management poli-

DOI: 10.4018/978-1-5225-2537-0.ch004

Copyright © 2017, IGI Global. Copying or distributing in print or electronic forms without written permission of IGI Global is prohibited.

cies, processess and practices, organisational day-to-day operations, board of directors, management capabilities of nonprofit social welfare service providers, are increasingly scrutinised.

Still, very little research has been undertaken to examine the number of nonprofit social welfare providers with current and up-to-date effective and ethical human resource policies, procedures and practices, the social and financial capital resources and costs associated with not following ethical human resource practices and the barriers prohibiting small and mid-size nonprofit social welfare organisations from adhering to legal and ethical human resource management policies, procedures and practices. Of particular interest in this discussion is the -prevalence of organisational failure to enforce ethical human resource management practices.

The introduction lays the foundation for the remaining chapter followed by a background on US-based non-profit social welfare service providers. A qualitative approach is adopted to explore small and mid-size nonprofit social welfare organisations in the Saint Paul regional area of Minneapolis, Minnesota, United States (US). The discussion is limited to four legal and ethical human resource management challenges, each are further elaborated following the background section. These four legal and ethical human resource management challenges are:

1. General Legal and Human Resource Management.
2. Resource (social and financial) Management.
3. Organizational Culture.
4. Mediation and Early Intervention.

## BACKGROUND

Internal Revenue Services (IRS) Form 990, introduced in 2010, is the accountability and transparency methods for American non-profit social welfare services providers. The IRS Form 990 are also provides an avenue for donor research giving opportunities and includes questions about employee and industrial relations such as whistle-blower policies and other personnel guidelines, policies and procedures and provides a human resource management framework (O'Connell, Hurd, & Spurlock, 2007). Many labor experts correctly predicted that an increase in labor-friendly laws and practices in the US would be mandated by President Obama's administration, such as protection for non-union employees under union rules and a demand for third-party witnesses for any disciplinary or termination procedure (Lian, 2008). Major philanthropists and lawmakers are growing more and more vigilant about holding nonprofits accountable for ethical work enviroments and practices (Panel on the Nonprofit Sector, 2007). Indeed, for the past decade, funders and governmental agencies that fund nonprofits are using performance management, effective supervision, and infrastructure more and more as methods of evaluation and accountability (Martin & Kettner, 1997).

According to Van Bogaert & Gross-Schaefer (2005) one of the most costly human resource management practices is discipline, discharge or termination. Although the non-profit sector is driven by values, one unethical non-profit workplace environment incident can result in devastating financial and social costs, capital loss and also negatively impact organisational capacity and productivity (Davenport, 1999). Consequently, the financial and social risks and costs associated with unethical, ineffective and inefficient human resource management. are high. A viable alternative would be a best practice and early interventionist approach to execute workplace discipline, discharge or termination. This view is supported by findings based on the data collected from surveys and interviews (Caflisch, 2016). Caflisch (2016) highlighted that understanding labor, industrial law and mediation contributes positively to the resolution of legal and ethical discipline, discharge or termination policies and procedures.

## General Legal and Human Resource Management

It may seem obvious, but it is hard to discipline for breaking workplace policy and rules if you don't actually have any—or if you have them but have kept them a secret (Sroypetch & Kleiner, 2006). It is paramount that an organization have disciplinary rules and that they are communicated to the staff. A way to ensure that staff have seen these rules is to have employees sign and date a document outlining them (Sryopetch & Kleiner, 2006). To avoid legal trouble, and in the spirit of ethical management, these disciplinary rules and procedures should be followed consistently (Depree & Jude, 2007). For example, if Mary comes in 10 minutes late every day, but has never been spoken to or disciplined for this behavior, Gary will feel very picked on if he gets a reprimand the first time he comes in to work tardy.

Many guidelines exist to ensure legal compliance while conducting a discipline interview. Among them are a fair and timely investigation into the alleged wrongdoing and a fully documented interview (Sryopetch & Kleiner, 2006). But other guidelines are helpful as well to ensure compliance and changed behavior, such as setting ground rules for the exchange, focusing on the behavior or incident and not the person, and a follow-up meeting. Another is using the interview as an opportunity for the manager to listen to the employee and to get to the root of the deviant behavior (Sryopetch & Kleiner, 2006).

Some might think that such practices are a lot of bother for something that, if done wrong, could cause an employee to get disgruntled and sue the organization. Why even bother with discipline policies at all? According to the Nonprofits Cut Legal Risk (2996), the possibility of being sued increases when discipline interviews and performance management are not taking place. One impotant reason for this is that workplaces are obligated by law to provide a safe space for all, and if harassment (racial, religious, sexual, or otherwise) goes unchecked and undisciplined, an organization is leaving itself open for a major legal hassle, not to mention victimized employees (Sorenson & Robinson, 2009). This is also why it is important to have clearly communicated discipline policies consistently executed for all employees; if an organization does not do this, an accusation of discrimination sticks a lot easier (Teratanavat & Kleiner, 2005). When leaders of organizations do not take timely and consistent measures to discipline deviant or underperforming employees, productivity and morale of all employees worsens and the organization is seriously weakened (Light, 2004). If one cares not about employee morale but only about cold hard cash, know that much of that cash is lost by not addressing underperforming, absent, or deviant employees (Gislason & Wilson, 2009).

What if management at an organization has meted out discipline to an underperforming employee in a timely, fair, and consistent manner but the employee still can't deliver performance outcomes and is constantly a liability on the nonprofit? Then, it may be time to terminate the employee, and if that organization thinks executing legal discipline is difficult, they haven't seen anything yet. But, can terminate at any time, for any reason! many nonprofit human resource managers might fuss. Why do we have to worry about legal problems when we fire someone? Here's why: Since a 1980 California Supreme Court case, *Tameny v. Atlantic Richfield 3*, had a ruling that allowed employees to sue former employers for emotional distress caused by firing, employees have been a lot more willing to travel down the road of litigation after being fired (Van Bogaert & Gross-Schaefer, 2005). Other ways and reasons for terminating that could lead to litigation include (but are not limited to) alleged discrimination due to race, age, or gender; and violations of the American Disability Act or the Family and Medical Leave Act. Additionally, reasons such as the employee perception that there was a written or verbal contract and continued violation of the constructive discipline policies or procedures outlined in the employee handbook have been used in termination disputes. (Van Bogaert & Gross-Schaefer, 2005).

But wait! someone might say. Could just having discipline policies—communicated to an employee, in writing, in a personnel policy manual—actually lead to litigation when terminating an employee? Indeed, it can. Minnesota's Small Business Assistance Office (SBAO) recommends that specific discipline policies not be included in a personnel policy manual, for the very reason that such statements could be a perceived as a sort of contract, which, if not carefully followed, could be grounds for violation of procedures when attempting to terminate an employee (Minnesota Department of Employment and Economic Development, 2006). Another resource made specifically for nonprofits, the personnel policy templates of the National Council of Nonprofit Associations, includes a very complete subsequent discipline policy, including written and verbal warnings, suspensions, and grievance hearings (National Council of Nonprofit Associations, 2004).

There are steps to take to ensure that terminating an employee will not end in litigation. A crucial step is to review the personnel file of the employee to be terminated. If it contains warnings and other documentation about communication regarding behavior or performance that needs to be modified, and proof of lack of improvement, this is a good start. If a long-time employee has a personnel file filled with performance reviews that show good or even just average performance, the employer will have a harder time putting forth the argument that the termination was for some non-performance-related reason (Teratanavat & Kleiner, 2005). In this same vein, if a manager is tempted to immediately terminate an employee who seems to be suffering from chemical dependency or even using on the job, care must be taken, for two reasons: (a) Alcoholism and other drug usage sometimes puts the employee in a protected class, because it is viewed as a disease, and (b) if the employee's personnel file has nothing but good performance reviews, suspension may be the most prudent and fair step to take (Van Bogaert & Gross-Schaefer, 2005).

Other important steps include the following, the step-by-step discipline and discharge policies and procedures outlined in the employee handbook, and also documenting, in writing, the reason for discharge (Depree & Jude, 2007). If an organization really wants to be thorough and manage all risk of litigation, documentation should happen all throughout the journey of the employee. Keeping the job posting, offer letter, and all training documentation will help build an employer's case that all efforts to be fair and communicate expectations were made (Sidebotham, 2005).

Termination is not just about judicious filing and documenting and protecting an organization from all legal rebuttals; there are the issues of ethics, fairness, and how the termination is perceived by the remaining staff, the board, and external stakeholders (Van Bogaert & Gross-Schaefer, 2005). Not communicating effectively about the termination and the workplace norms and performance expectations violated can lead the staff to perceive that politics are at play, which can drastically lower morale as well as productivity (Rosen, Harris, & Kacmar, 2009). And communication about the termination can serve as reinforcement of the formal expectations of the whole staff (Cox & Kramer, 1995). Finally, employers should not terminate in anger: Take time and thought (not only about how the termination is done, but when). For example, do not terminate directly before the Christmas break (Van Bogaert & Gross-Schaefer, 2005).

## Social and Financial Resource Management

If a nonprofit was operating on manual typewriters, one could almost forgive it for not having well-thought-out discipline and discharge procedures—almost, as they would also have to be using carrier pigeons for all external communication. An embarrassment of free and highly accessible riches exists online or is accessible with a quick telephone call for any small or midsized nonprofit looking for instructions on how to author personnel policies and what they are legally required to do in regard to discipline and discharge—in their state and municipality and at a federal level.

In the United States of America, the Department of Labor (www.dol.gov) has a website with all federal labor laws, and the U.S. Equal Employment Opportunity Commission (www.eeoc.gov) covers everything from sexual harassment laws to mediation services. The EEOC also has full descriptions of all laws that prohibit discrimination in hiring and on the job, such as the Age Discrimination Act of 1967, which protects workers 40 and older, and the Civil Rights Act of 1991, which allows for financial retribution in the event of job discrimination.

The Alliance for Nonprofit Management (http://www.allianceonline.org), an organization devoted to capacity building, has a wonderful area on discipline and discharge for nonprofit organizations. The aforementioned Panel on the Nonprofit Sector (www.thenonprofitpanel.org) is also an invaluable resource, an ethical compass when making decisions in a nonprofit. If an organization has no time to do its own research on the vast array of free templates, literature, and research available for nonprofits, worry not, as the Hauser Center at Harvard University (http://www.hks.harvard.edu/hauser) has done the search for you with 10-plus pages of results. Finally, the Society for Human Resource Management (www.shrm.org) is a wonderful tool for keeping up to date on any new development in the areas of discipline and discharge, or, for that matter, any human resource issue.

Nonprofit and nongovernmental organizations (NGOs) operating outside of the United States have ample online resources as well, such as the European Commission's web page entitled Employment, Social Affairs and Inclusion (www.ec.europa.eu/social). Helpful, non-geographically-specific human resource policies and manual templates can be found at Network Learning (www.networklearning.org), a site devoted to offering free manuals, templates, and scholarly articles for NGOs, and also at NGO Connect (www.ngoconnect.net). NGOs that operate outside of the United States, but are funded by U.S. dollars or organizations, can find information on what is expected for their human resource management at USAID, the United States Agency for International Development (www.usaid.gov).

## Organisational Culture

Sometimes a nonprofit has grown so fast that the policies and procedures have not caught up to the realities of the organization (Hall, 2006). Usually, the programs or services provided have been given the most attention, training, and money, and the nonprofit is operating at a level far above its infrastructure (Stevens, 2001). This is not all the nonprofit's fault, however, as most funders think only of giving money toward an exciting new program, with little thought to the administrative needs. Having strong human resource policies grow right along with the programs has been shown to increase employee morale and productivity and help ease transistions from one lifecycle to the other (McIntyre, 2004).

Although aligning human resource management with strategic growth is a best practice for keeping legal and ethical infrastructure up to speed with program and services development, a study of Canadian nonprofits revealed that almost no nonprofits do this (Akingbola, 2006). Some might assume that people work at nonprofits for reasons other than great management, and that the passion for the mission will keep the talent on board, even if the infrastructure is weak. This assumption, though widespread, is false. Good management, especially in the area of human resources, is critical to prevent turnover, regardless of the employee's attachment to the mission (Kim & Lee, 2007).

What if a nonprofit is handed all of the tools to create and execute legal and ethical discipline and discharge policies, but doesn't have a culture that supports their use? There is currently no consensus among scholars as to how to most accurately define "culture," but a common working definition is that culture encompasses the tools and knowledge necessary within an organization to get things done (Jaskyte & Dressler, 2004). This can be knowledge given formally through channels such as employee training and manuals, and informally through stories, gossip, and modeling. Employees are, of course, individuals, and within organizations employees can vary greatly in their understanding and following of the dominant organizational culture (Jaskyte & Dressler, 2004).

Recent findings suggest that Human Resource Practices that are ability and opportunity focused (recruitment and training focused) as opposed to motivationally focused (bonuses and commissions), tend to breed a more ethical, as opposed to egotistical climate (Radaelli & Siletti, 2015). In addition, research suggests that organizations that have clear (and often union-sanctioned) discipline and termination policies actually offer supervisors an easier time of disciplining employees, as the steps are agreed upon by consensus, have methods for transparency, and are formally communicated (Franklin & Pagan, 2006). In organizations where employees are not unionized and do not have formal procedures, supervisors must rely on more informal cultural cues when attempting to discipline or fire an employee, such as approval and support from their peers, the rest of the staff, and the people above them (Franklin & Pagan, 2006). Ancedotes and stories of what has happened to past supervisors when they have attempted to discipline employees will also play a big role in organizations that have mainly informal cues for how to supervise (Franklin & Pagan, 2006).

When supervisors pick up on these informal cues about discipline and discharge, yet find little support in the culture or from upper management in dealing with underperforming or deviant employees, they rely on their own personal feelings when making decisions about termination and discipline. A dislike of confrontation and the dismissal process is an overriding personal reason for not firing an employee (Cox & Kramer, 1995). Other common personal, informal reasons for not dismissing or disciplining an employee can include the pleasing personal attributes of the employee being disciplined, social friendship between supervisor and employee, and the supervisor having hired and invested time in the employee (Cox & Kramer, 1995).

Sometimes the lack of formal cues and documentation in an organization can lead to a lack of confidence in supervisors who must carry out discipline procedures, especially when they have not been trained as managers, which is the case in many small to midsized nonprofits (Hader, 2006). Indeed, although it has been documented that the financial cost of deviant and inappropriate behavior in the workplace is great and debilitating to the organization, it is more often ineffective supervision, lack of disciplinary action, and the organizational culture as a whole that will predict inappropriate behavior, more so than the individual characteristics of employees (Litzky, Eddleston, & Kidder, 2006).

## Mediation and Early Intervention

David Allyn (2011) has suggested that nonprofit organizations and collaborations can experience "mission mirroring," where the same challenges and conflicts that the organization has formed to solve happen internally. For example, a social justice nonprofit will most likely attract employees with great knowledge about, and keen sensitivity to, the problems of inequality in the workforce, both on a micro and macro level. This can lead to nonprofit organizations overaccommodating "internal terroists," or employees who engage in nonviolent and surreptitious bullying or deviant behavior when they perceive injustice.

Gender of supervisor and employee, not formal policies, can play a major role in accomodation (van Fleet & van Fleet, 2006). Top nonprofit managers and leaders of both genders will feel like they earn their paycheck when they hear that they, more than the organization mission or workplace peers or work groups, and even individual factors like gender, dictate an ethical climate and culture (Malloy & Agarwal, 2001).

Mediation in labor settings typically means that a neutral third party tries to negotiate a dispute between an employee and a supervisor so it can be worked out before going into arbitration or litigation (Equal Employment Opportunity Commission, 2009). Mediation is the recommended way for dealing with discipline or discharge issues that employees are grieving because it is inexpensive, serves to find a good and fair solution for both parties, and often gets to the root of systematic concerns (in addition to those of individual employees) in the organization. Mediation is most common in public agencies or in organizations with unionized employees (Equal Employment Opportunity Commission, 2009).

It may be worthwhile for nonprofits of every size to integrate mediation and grievance procedures into their human resource repertoire. Providing a forum for employee complaints and disagreements and using mediation to address discipline concerns early on enhances all employees' perception of organization justice, ethics, and commitment, and therefore increases loyalty and productivity (Chang, 2005). In fact, just having grievance and mediation procedures, and not necessarily the outcome from these procedures, has been correlated with employees' perception of organization fairness, and this is true regardless of the size of the organization (Daley, 2007).

Having mediation and grievance policies, along with accessible channels for problem solving and voicing dissent, actually helps engender a culture of problem solving and helps align the way conflicts are handled internally with a nonprofit's mission, vision, and values (Society of Professionals in Dispute Resolution, 2001). For years, mediation, grievance hearings, and alternative dispute resolution techniques were seen as the purview of large corporations and only the largest of nonprofits in the private sector, but that trend is changing. Midsize and small organizations are seeing the value in addressing labor issues in a thoughtful and productive way, primarily because increased productivity and good employee morale are ultimately good for business (Lipsky, Seeber, & Fincher, 2003)

## INTERVIEWS AND SURVEYS

The objective of the research was to examine the application of discipline and discharge policies, procedures and perceived barriers in small to mid-sized nonprofits with fifty or fewer full time employees. Questions for consideration included:

1. Do policies exist, and if so, has there been cause to use them?
2. Do organizations have mediation or other early-intervention methods?
3. Do small to midsize nonprofits perceive barriers to executing legal and ethical policies? If so, what are they?

Toward this end, a survey was created and sent to human resource managers and professionals currently working at nonprofits located in the United States of America, specifically in Minnesota.

In addition to exploring the current state of discharge and discipline procedures in small to midsized nonprofits, in-depth interviews with two nonprofit professionals and two lawyers specializing in labor law and mediation in nonprofits were conducted to find out their recommendations for policies and procedures in small to midsized nonprofits, and their perceptions of special barriers to creating and executing those recommendations faced by the organizations.

A 10-question online survey on discipline and discharge practices was created through the online survey creation tool Survey Monkey (www.surveymonkey.com). This instrument was developed with the hope of determining how many small to midsized nonprofits actually have policies and procedures regarding discipline, whether they include the progressive steps recommended by the law and current research (e.g. written warnings, suspensions, grievance hearings), and whether they have had cause to use these policies in the last 5 years (not including layoffs due to economic reasons).

This survey was distributed via e-mail to more than sixty (n=60) nonprofit human resources or upper-management professionals. The e-mail addresses were procured through the following: Minnesota Council for Nonprofits human resources group, an arts and culture human resources support group, and the social media site Facebook (www.facebook.com). All participants gave permission to be included in the survey. Participants received an e-mail explaining that the results would be anonymous and used for a graduate student's research paper, and that all who answered the survey would be entered in a drawing to win a gift certificate to a local restaurant.

The survey was developed in late February 2009 and distributed throughout the months of March and April 2009. In total, 25 professionals completed the survey. The survey was divided into three sections: demographic information, policy information, and discipline and discharge execution. How many full-time employees, age of organization, and purpose of the organization comprised the demographic information. Size was included, because this study concentrated on 50 or fewer employees. Age and purpose were included to investigate if either of those factors plays a part in how and what discipline and discharge are executed. Next, do policies exist? And if so, how are these communicated to employees (are they internal procedures? Or are they communicated to all employees through the personnel manual?)

Since all nonprofits answering the question were from Minnesota, the choices for this question were developed using Minnesota's SBAO resources and recommendations (Minnesota Department of Employment and Economic Development, 2006) for legally compliant personnel policies, and the human resource templates found on the website of the Minnesota Council for Nonprofits. Also explored were these questions: Do small nonprofits have uses for these procedures? Have people actually been disciplined and discharged recently? If not, should I really be making all of this fuss? Finally, do they perceive barriers to executing legal and ethical policies in their organization, and if so, what are the barriers? The choices given for this question were developed from the literature exploring how organizational culture affects supervisor decisions on when and how to terminate (Franklin & Pagan, 2006).

Having twenty-five (n=25) professionals as a sample size is a woefully small number, and even the most lax scientist would be loath to generalize to the whole population of incorporated 501(c)(3) organizations in the United States, because, as of last count in 2006, over one million organizations were incorporated as such (National Center for Charitable Statistics, 2007).

As the literature and previous research suggested, although authoring policies and procedures is an important step toward having fair and legal disciplinary and discharge execution, it is actually the training, sensitivity, and wisdom of the supervisors, supported by a healthy organizational culture, that actually and ultimately encourages it. Therefore, in-depth interviews within the field of nonprofit management, law, and mediation were important. However, there was little success to find participants willing to discuss barriers in their organization to executing discipline and discharge procedures.

A little more success was obtained contacting nonprofit professionals who were known for having best practices in the areas of employee performance management. Additionally, interviews with two lawyers involved with labor and employment law and arbitration issues provided excellent insights. Face to face interviews with David Larson, professor of law at Hamline University School of Law, and Aimee Gourlay, director of training and services for the Mediation Center in affiliation with the Dispute Resolution Institute at Hamline University in March and April of 2009.

## DISCUSSION AND POSSIBLE SOLUTIONS

Because many of the participants were recruited from the Minnesota Council of Nonprofits human resources group and from the arts and culture human resources group, 44 percent of the organizations represented in the survey have full-time employees of 50 or more, and a vast majority (84%) have been incorporated as a 501(c)(3) for 20 years or more. This may have skewed the results of the survey; it may show greater knowledge and better systems in human resources in nonprofits than one taken from a truly general nonprofit organization population, especially since many of the participating nonprofits are focused enough on human resource management to spend time and effort to form a group committed to the subject!

Keeping in mind that the results from this survey may be only a look at the nonprofits that are most committed to human resource management, the result that 20 percent of those surveyed had no discipline or discharge policies or procedures, either in a personnel policy manual or internally. When cross-tabulating this question with organizational size, the results highlighted that of the 20 percent of organisations with no policies and procedures were nonprofits with 50 or fewer full-time employees. Although the results were not unexpected, what was surprising was that nearly 100 percent of the organisations have been in operation for six or more years and more than fifty percent were in business for 20 years or more.

Fifty-two percent have discipline policies explained in the personnel manual, and 36 percent have discharge policies (in addition to "at will") outlined there as well. Eighty-four percent of those who have policies or procedures use written and verbal warnings, and 52.6 percent used suspension, two of the progressive discipline steps suggested by the research on the subject (Depree & Jude, 2007; Sroypetch & Kleiner, 2006). It is impressive that the percentage of nonprofits that include mediation or other early-intervention meetings with a neutral third party (42.1%) and that have grievance hearings for employees disagreeing with a discipline or discharge action (42.1%). Almost half of organizations that include these steps have 1–25 employees, which is also suprising, one would expect these results to have come from bigger organizations, who are more likely to have union as well as nonunion employees.-

Is there an actual need for smaller nonprofits to have policies and procedures? According the survey, seventy-six percent of the organizations had formally discplined at least one employee in the last 5 years, and that same percentage had to terminate at least one employee (not including layoffs for economic reasons) in the past 5 years. Almost half of these disciplines and discharges came from organizations with fewer than 50 employees. What small nonprofits should pay attention to, especially those who think they are too small to need policies, is that almost a third of the organizations surveyed who answered that they had to formally discipline and discharge someone in the last 5 years came from organizations who have fewer than 15 employees.

Forty-four percent of the nonprofits surveyed felt that there are barriers to executing timely discipline and discharge, and this percentage included an equal representation of large and small nonprofits. The barrier that got the most votes was staff relationships and friendships (72.7%), with discipline and discharge being at odds with organizational culture (63.6%). This is not surprising, as friendships between supervisor and employee can hamper timely discipline (Cox & Kramer, 1995), as well as friendships and relationships between employees and other upper-management leaders. This is not necessarily the direct supervisor, as lack of support for discipline and discharge from a supervisor's peers or colleagues can also stop execution (Rosen et al., 2009). Untrained supervisors (54.5%) did not follow policies and procedures and supervisors and senior staff (45.5%) did not follow policies and procedures.. As mentioned earlier, professionals who may be highly trained in one area, such as social work, nursing or art, may not be trained in supervising or managing other professionals, and can impact disciplinary action (Hader, 2006). All the policies and procedures in the world, no matter how legally and ethically sound, means nothing if they are not used or not used well. Summaries from interviewees who use policies and procedures well, and, in some cases, had completely overhauled, formally or informally, systems that weren't working or did not fit the culture of the organization. Although they all had distinct things to say, some overriding common themes emerged. Effective human resource practices impact the whole organization (Chang, 2005), especially affecting employee morale and productivity (Daley, 2007); and a strong and ethical leadership makes a big difference (Malloy & Agarwal, 2001). Findings revealed that:

1. Organisational culture was not conducive to honest or accurate appraisals and that employees did not take performance management seriously.
2. Terminate underperforming employee resulted in litigation procedures.
3. Court cases were expensive.
4. Discipline and dischange policy manuals were difficult to execute the action.
5. The conversation about performance commences begins with the performance management evaluation.
6. A timeline of coaching is useful to use after an evaluation has been undertaken and evidencing the process and procedures are imperative.
7. An employee improvement plan is followed by an evaluation of the progress and an employment improvement plan with a specific feedback schedule. Though his process is not driven by documentation, Sisson did stress that documenting every step of the process is imperative.
8. Standards should be set for the whole staff and followed by the whole staff.
9. Weekly formal documented performance reviews is helpful, as well as constant feedback, to help coach employees into more productive habits.
10. Communicating clear consequences is also helpful. If an employee still fails to meet expectations, it is a clearer and less litigious decision to move to terminate.
11. Legal restraints, were biggest barrier to giving fair and honest reviews.

12. Leaders not having the courage to do what's right and fair in regard to performance management and disciplinary procedures.
13. Personal ethics as a leader will create the organizational culture that supports fair, honest, and helpful employee management. (personal communication, April 10, 2009).

Larson (2009) stressed the importance of following not just the federal laws and mandates for employers, but the state and municipal laws as well, as these can all vary. For example, take the Family and Medical Leave Act; any employer with 50 or more employees must follow the dictates of this federal act (including letting an employee have time off for having a child or adoption). Under Minnesota labor laws, any employer with 21 or more employees must follow this rule, under the State Parental Leave Act (Minnesota Department of Labor & Industry, 2009).

Although Larson agrees that documentation can help reduce litigation and confusion when attempting to discipline or discharge an employee, the act of documenting alone does not protect an employer from being sued; one should be aware of what one is documenting. For example, if a supervisor puts in writing in an employee's personnel file that the supervisor is not promoting the employee because the supervisor thinks he or she is overweight and that's a sign of laziness, such an act will hurt an organization's chances of staying out of legal trouble in regard to employment law. This may seem like a ridiculous example, but Larson relayed that when employers get to the point of documenting disciplinary action, great emotion is usually involved, and this can cloud common sense.

Mitigating poor performance or employee deviance early, has the potential to prevent the problems from escalating and can engender constructive and productive conversations. Larson (2009) suggested that organizations of every size have early-intervention methods based on alternative dispute resolution practices. Also important is giving employees methods to voice issues and providing avenues of complaint other than the person they directly report to in cases where the supervisor is actually the problem employee.

Communication issues can be at the heart of cross-cultural exchange in the workplace, and especially during disciplinary interviews or grievance hearings. Larson (2009) contended that employees would attend hearings as if they were just telling long, personal stories about their childhoods, their families, their lives.

For Gourlay (2009), mediation as a default for all workplace problems instead of addressing an individual's behavioral problem directly is an alternative communication tool. Mediators start their work by investigating the issue or conflict they are to help resolve before the conversations and negotiations even begin. Sometimes the conflict is a relationship issue between two employees, and sometimes it is a systematic problem, with the conflict being merely a symptom of an overriding organizational sickness. For example, if there is a prelitigation mediation between a supervisor and an employee who is being disciplined or discharged, the problem might not be just between those two individuals, but a conflict born out of inadequate personnel policies or insufficient training. Or it could be an outgrowth of a culture that doesn't respect employees or encourage open communication. Sometimes the conflict being mediated ends up not having to do with the employee involved at all, but rather mis-communication from upper management. Mediation has a valuable place in opening avenues for employees who have legitimate gripes about discriminatory personnel practices, and is a safeguard against abuses of these kinds. Along with being a safeguard for employees, it is also one for organizations who are unaware of their supervisor's misguided or unsanctioned behavior, and they can address the problem before it gets to litigation.

Nonprofits provide some special opportunities for in-depth conversation and negotiations during the mediation process. A typical conversation to have during a mediation or workplace conflict resolution session is about values: what values drive people to work where they work, and how people make meaning in work (Gourlay, 2009). This is a powerful question to pose to a nonprofit staff, as passionate personal values are usually the impetus for choosing to work where they work, and to work in the sector generally.What can cause deep conflict in nonprofits is people operating from the belief that everyone they work with feels exactly the same way they do and brings the exact same values to the work place. Day to day, this assumption can actually stifle conversation, as opposed to stimulating it, and cause great rifts when people think they are dismissing or not honoring shared values. Deliberate communication about values can help get to the root of organizational conflict, or better yet, give powerful tools to deal with conflicts as they arise.

According to Gourlay (2009), some common factors that lead to mediation in nonprofits are weak boards and founders staying on as executive directors. Having a weak or ineffectual governing body can lead to poor oversight, especially with an executive director who has a strong or, perhaps, immovable position. If this visions starts becoming at odds with the best strategies for strategic or financial health of the organization, an outside party may be needed to facilitate a conversation. Although people who work at nonprofits are highly skilled professionals, they may not be skilled managers or come to their jobs equipped with knowledge on how to best handle staff. But the root cause of conflict and discord in nonprofits has seen the most is finances (Gourlay, 2009). Due to lack of finances, organisations are struggling to survive in a changing environment.

## CONCLUSION

Four main points in this discussion focused on general legal and human resource management, social and financial resource management, organisational culture and mediation and early intervention. Human resources practice is an area in need of great improvement for many small to midsized nonprofit organizations. It is cost exercise not to think about implementing appropriate policies and procedures. Implement discipline and discharge policies and procedures is there critical to not for profit organisations. As Kime and Lee (2007) stated, the legal costs, the costs of losing productivity, morale, and talent are risks for nonprofits not committed to fair, timely, and ethical human resource practices, are prohibitive. Light (2004) argu7ed that to keep great talent working in a nonprofit organization because of the lack of resources, and that can leave an organization with a lot of dead weight. Commitment to the mission and a quality work environment are two ways to keep great talent around and, ultimately to build capacity (Light, 2004). Liz Flinn's narrative is a great example of how a leader's commitment. For Flinn (2009), quality and ethical work environment makes for productive and happy current and former employees.

The need to improve discipline and discharge practices in small to midsized nonprofits.Organisational mission statements, vision and values, followed by discussions with employees and the board about how human resources practices and management of employees fit in with the overall values of the organization (Franklin & Pagan, 2006; Panel on the Nonprofit Sector, 2007). Communication about values, are a great start to engendering a culture that supports fair and honest communication about performance. A crucial next step is examining what policies and procedures, if any, exist and where they exist. I would recommend that progressive discipline steps be outlined in the personnel policy manual, for several reasons: Having transparent and communicated policies affects employee satisfaction positively (Chang,

2005); it also encourages supervisors to actually follow the procedures and helps to communicate a culture of fairness (Daley, 2007); and having them communicated actually staves off litigation as opposed to leaving the organization open to it, because they encourage rational, fair, and consistent disciplinary practices (Sroypetch & Kleiner, 2006).

These procedures should include verbal and written warnings and suspensions, and every communication should be only about the observed deviant or underperforming behavior (for example, do not include personal or nonwork criticisms or opinions in your documentation) (Sidebotham, 2005). Even if you are only giving a verbal warning, make sure to document it on your personal calendar (Sroypetch & Kleiner, 2006). Suspensions, not termination, should be the next progressive step after discipline interviews and verbal and written warnings, and should only be given if the behavior or underperformance has been directly observed by you, or completely, fairly, and thouroughly investigated (Depree & Jude, 2007).

But having those steps and documentations in place means nothing if they are executed poorly or executed not at all. As my research suggests, most nonprofit organizations of every size have discipline policies and procedures imagined and written down somewhere, yet almost 50% reported that untrained supervisors are a barrier to these policies being followed. There must be a commitment to training all supervisors in the art of people management (Daley, 2007). Disciplinary interviews should be seen as a great opportunity for coaching and partnering with an employee to perform his or her best work. Liz Flinn talked a lot in her interview about taking the time to listen and to really be committed to finding out what the employee needs to succeed. Jim Sisson gave great advice about making concrete goals and creating timelines and opportunities for check-ins and feedback. The disciplinary process doesn't end with the interview and documentation; it just begins there. It must be communicated to supervisors that part of their job is to help their employees succeed, and a big part of that success is communicating when employees are not meeting expectations and then finding out what they need to meet them (Gislason & Wilson, 2009).

One of the best ways to communicate is by example, by the leader's unwavering commitment to honest and timely performance assessment, as this will lead the culture at the organization (Cox & Kramer, 1995). An atmosphere of support—for hard conversations and for supervisors holding all of their employees to the same standards of performance—is an important culture-building step as well (Franklin & Pagan, 2006). As David Larson and Aimee Gourlay suggested (as well as the literature), opening multiple avenues for communication before times of conflict and crisis is a good way to stop trouble before it even starts. Letting employees have ways of communicating dissent or problems (not necessarily to their supervisor if their supervisor is the cause of the problems) is an effective way of stopping harassing or other illegal behavior before it starts. An organizational culture that does not support these kinds of conversations was seen as a barrier by large number of organizations surveyed; this means the organization has a culture that breeds poor performance and therefore, poor results (Litzky et al., 2006). This correlation—nay, causation—should be impetus enough for nonprofit leaders to work on encouraging a culture of honest and direct communication about values and performance.

Almost 75% of the organizations surveyed who felt there were barriers to executing discipline and discharge in a fair and timely manner cited "staff friendships and relationships" as the barrier.

Terminate an employee, if all steps have been followed and all efforts made to assist the employee, it should be no surprise to the employee or the employee (Van Bogaert & Gross-Schaefer, 2005). Having the option of grievance hearings listed in the policy manual is a great way to communicate that a commitment to due diligence when firing someone exists in the organization (Society of Professionals in Dispute Resolution, 2001).

As scrutiny increased, the decreased opportunities to find funding, and the growing need for the valuable services that nonprofits provide make this an unfortunate time to not have systems in place for effective performance management. Since nonprofits are rich in human capital, such organizations can get the most out of this investment that will perform the best, serve the most, and ultimately survive in this economy (Davenport, 1999). But it has been affirmed by the research and interviews in this paper that values (not necessarily success) drive nonprofit organizations. If this is the case, those values should be translated to the ethical and fair management of the staff. There is no excuse not to. Future research directions could include exploring

1. Underperforming expectations and what the employee has to do to meet organisational performance outcomes.
2. Research could further explore coaching in small to mid-size welfare social service non-profit organisations. Specifically coaching employees achieve higher productivity and develop productive habits would be an interesting contribution to the overall organisational communication strategy. Additionally, evaluation of the progress and an employment improvement plan with a specific feedback schedule and documentation processes.
3. Further research can be also be undertaken in the areas of discipline, discharge and termination in non-profit social welfare organisations and exploring whole of organisational standards would benefit non-profit organisational understanding of legal and ethical human resource management policies, procedures and practices.
4. Finally, an organisational communication plan can include a disciplinary, dis and termination philosophy which includes regular weekly formal performance reviews, feedback and achieving outcomes, that way side-stepping costly litigious decision associated with discipline, discharge and termination.

## REFERENCES

Akingbola, K. (2006). Strategy and HRM in nonprofit organizations: Evidence from Canada. *International Journal of Human Resource Management*, *17*(10), 1707–1725. doi:10.1080/09585190600964350

Allyn, D. (2010). Mission mirroring: Understanding conflict in nonprofit organizations. *Nonprofit and Voluntary Sector Quarterly*, *40*(4), 762–769. doi:10.1177/0899764010370869

Chang, E. (2005). Employees overall perception of HRM effectiveness. *Human Relations*, *58*(4), 523–544. doi:10.1177/0018726705055037

Cox, S. A., & Kramer, M. W. (1995). Communication during employee dismissals: Social exchange principles and group influences on employee exit. *Management Communication Quarterly*, *9*(2), 156–190. doi:10.1177/0893318995009002002

Daley, D. M. (2007). If a tree falls in the forest: The effect of grievances on employee perceptions of performance appraisal, efficacy, and job satisfaction. *Review of Public Personnel Administration*, *27*(3), 281–296. doi:10.1177/0734371X06297621

Davenport, T. O. (1999). *Human capital: What it is and why people invest in it*. San Francisco: Jossey-Bass.

Depree, J. C., & Jude, R. (2007). Ten practical suggestions for terminating an employee. *The CPA Journal*, *77*(8), 62–63.

Equal Employment Opportunity Commission. (2009). *Facts about mediation*. Retrieved from http://www.eeoc.gov/mediate/facts.html

Franklin, A. L., & Pagan, J. F. (2006). Organization culture as an explanation for employee discipline practices. *Review of Public Personnel Administration*, *26*(1), 52–73. doi:10.1177/0734371X05277335

Gislason, M., & Wilson, J. (2009). *Coaching skills for nonprofit managers: Creating a culture of contribution, self-motivation, accountability, and high performance*. San Francisco: Jossey-Bass.

Gross-Schaefer, A., & Zaller, Z. (1998). The ethics audit for nonprofit organizations. *PM Network*, *12*(4), 43.

Guerci, M., Radaelli, G., Siletti, E., Cirella, S., & Rami Shani, A. B. (2015). The impact of human resource management practices and corporate sustainability on organizational ethical climates: An employee perspective. *Journal of Business Ethics*, *126*(2), 325–342. doi:10.1007/s10551-013-1946-1

Hader, R. (2006). Put employee termination ettiquette to practice. *Nursing Management*, *27*(12), 6. PMID:17159553

Hall, H. (2006). Getting over growing pains: Life-cycle analyses help charities deal with the challenges of aging. *The Chronicle of Philanthropy*, *12*(3), 15.

Hamline School of Law. (2009). *Faculty, staff, and administration*. Retrieved from http://mitchellhamline.edu/biographies/person/david-larson

Jaskyte, K., & Dresssler, W. W. (2004). Nonprofit organizations studying culture as an integral aggregate variable: Organizational culture and innovation in a group of nonprofit organizations. *Field Methods*, *16*(3), 265–284. doi:10.1177/1525822X03262281

Kim, S. E., & Lee, J. W.Seok Eun Kim; Jung Wook Lee. (2007). Is mission attachment an effective management tool for employee retention? An empirical analysis of a nonprofit human services agency. *Review of Public Personnel Administration*, *27*(3), 227–248. doi:10.1177/0734371X06295791

Lian, R. G., Jr. (2008). *The potential impact of the Obama administration on the labor and employment legal landscape*. Retrieved from http://washlaborwire.com/2008/11/13/the-potential-impact-of-the-obama-administration-on-the-labor-and-employment-legal-landscape-4

Light, P. C. (2004). *Sustaining nonprofit performance: The case for capacity building and the evidence to support it*. Washington, DC: Brookings Institution Press.

Lipsky, D. B., Seeber, R. L., & Fincher, R. (2003). *Emerging systems for managing workplace conflict: Lessons from American corporations for managers and dispute resolution professionals*. San Francisco: Jossey-Bass.

Litzky, B. E., Eddleston, K. A., & Kidder, D. L. (2006). The good, the bad, and the misguided: How managers inadvertently encourage deviant behaviors. *The Academy of Management Perspectives*, *20*(1), 91–103. doi:10.5465/AMP.2006.19873411

Malloy, D., & Agarwal, J. (2001). Ethical climate in nonprofit organizations. *Nonprofit Management & Leadership, 12*(1), 39–54. doi:10.1002/nml.12104

Martin, L., & Kettner, P. (1997). Performance measurement: The new accountability. *Administration in Social Work, 21*(1), 17–29. doi:10.1300/J147v21n01_02 PMID:10166757

McIntyre, T. L. (2004). A model of levels of involvement and strategic roles of human resource development: Professionals as facilitators of due diligence and the integration process. *Human Resource Development Review, 3*(2), 173–182. doi:10.1177/1534484304265444

Mediation Center. (2009). *Mediation center staff.* Retrieved from http://law.hamline.edu/mediation-center/mediation-center-staff.html

Minnesota Council of Nonprofits. (n.d.). *Templates and samples.* Retrieved from http://www.minnesotanonprofits.org/nonprofit-resources/templates-samples

Minnesota Department of Employment and Economic Development. (2006). *An employer's guide to employment law issues in Minnesota.* Retrieved from http://www.mnsbao.com/PDFs/empllaw.pdf

Minnesota Department of Labor & Industry. (2009). *Federal family and medical leave act; state parental leave act.* Retrieved from http://www.doli.state.mn.us/fmla.html

National Center for Charitable Statistics. (2007). *Number of nonprofit organizations in the United States, 1996–2006.* Retrieved from http://nccsdataweb.urban.org/PubApps/profile1.php?state=US

National Council of Nonprofit Associations. (2004). *Managing nonprofit employees.* Retrieved from https://www.councilofnonprofits.org/tools-resources/managing-nonprofit-employees

Nonprofits cut legal risks with better personnel policies. (1996). *Risk Management, 43*(5), 3–5.

Northwest Area Foundation. (n.d.). *About us.* Retrieved from http://www.nwaf.org/

O'Connell, F. J., Jr., Hurd, G., & Spurlock, R. (2007). New Form 990 aims for transparency, accountability, and oversight. *Tax Adviser, 38*(9), 501–502. Retrieved from www.nonprofitlawblog.com/form-990-policies-is-it-better-to-check-yes-or-no

Panel on the Nonprofit Sector. (2007). *Principles for good governance and ethical practice: A guide for charities and foundations.* Retrieved from https://www.independentsector.org/uploads/PrincipleResources/The_33_Principles.pdf

Rosen, C. C., Harris, K. J., & Kacmar, K. M. (2009). The emotional implications of organizational politics: A process model. *Human Relations, 62*(1), 27–57. doi:10.1177/0018726708099836

Sidebotham, E. J. (2005). How to use documentation to decrease the likelihood of litigation. *The Psychologist Manager Journal, 8*(2), 131–140. doi:10.1207/s15503461tpmj0802_4

Society of Professionals in Dispute Resolution. (2001). *Designing integrated conflict management systems: Guidelines for practitioners and decision makers in organizations (Cornell Studies in Conflict and Dispute Resolution, No. 4). Ithaca, NY: Cornell/PERC Institute on Conflict Resolution and Washington*, DC: Association for Conflict Resolution.

Sorenson, R. B., & Robinson, S. K. (2009). What employers can do to stay out of legal trouble when forced to implement layoffs. *Compensation and Benefits Review*, *41*(1), 25–32. doi:10.1177/0886368708329213

Sroypetch, N., & Kleiner, B. H. (2006). How to conduct discipline interviews. *Nonprofit World*, *24*(6), 25–27.

Stevens, S. K. (2001). *Nonprofit lifecycles: Stage based wisdom for nonprofit capacity*. Long Lake, MN: Stagewise Enterprises.

Teratanavat, R., & Kleiner, B. (2005). When it's time to say good-by. *Nonprofit World*, *23*(2), 12–14.

Van Bogaert, D., & Gross-Schaefer, A. (2005). Terminating the employee-employer relationship: Ethical and legal challenges. *Employee Relations Law Journal*, *31*(1), 50–69.

van Fleet, D., & van Fleet, E. W. (2006). Internal terrorists: The terrorists inside organizations. *Journal of Managerial Psychology*, *21*(8), 763–774. doi:10.1108/02683940610713280

## KEY TERMS AND DEFINITIONS

**Alternative Dispute Resolution:** The use of methods such as mediation and arbitration to resolve a dispute instead of litigation.

**Grievance Policy:** Step by step process an employee must follow to get his or her complaint addressed satisfactorily.

**Human Resource Management:** The process of hiring and developing employees so that they become more valuable to the organization.

**IRS Form 990:** Form 990 is the United State's Internal Revenue Service (IRS) form entitled *Return of Organization Exempt from Income Tax*. This federal form must be filed annually by American tax-exempt organizations.

**Social Capital:** The networks of relationships among people who live and work in a particular society, enabling that society to function effectively.

**Mediation:** Intervention in a dispute in order to resolve it; arbitration.

**Organizational Culture:** The values and behaviors that contribute to the unique social and psychological environment of an organization.

# Chapter 5
# Running Successful Crowdfunding Campaigns for Non-Profits

**Amir Manzoor**
*Bahria University, Pakistan*

## ABSTRACT

*Crowdfunding is a method to raise revenue and funding from a large number of people. First used by entrepreneurs as a way to attract small-sized investments to for-profit ventures, the crowdfunding platform has grown substantially over the last five years. Today, a valuable mechanism for fundraising for not for profit organisations, the crowdfunding platform is projected to realise nearly a US$100 billion by 2025. Non-profit leaders, employees and volunteers can benefit by successful crowdfunding campaigns as a means to raise revenue.*

## INTRODUCTION

Crowdfunding is an innovative mechanism to raise funds from a large number of people (a crowd). The funds obtained from the individual is usually small-to-medium (Ordanini, 2009). According to Mulvey, (2013), the non-profit sector can couple crowdfunding with social media to produce effective and efficient changes in the way non-profits organisations seek, obtain and sustain funds. Crowdfunding has changed the dynamics of funding and has become an instrumental pathway for not for profit fundraising for non-profits to do so social good (Hobey, 2014). One of the reasons for this growth could be because crowdfunding platforms directly connect donors with requestors.

Crowdfunding is a very effective and cost efficient mechanism for not for profit organisations to raise revenue and funding. However, some conventional nonprofits and charities consider it as a threat (Maldonado, 2012). Despite a small group considering online crowdfunding as a threat, existing stakeholders in non-profit sector would benefit from seriously considering crowdfunding for its revenue raising potential and evaluate then make informed decision about their organizational long and short term objectives and business models. It should be acknowledged though that the dynamic growth in the online crowdfunding

DOI: 10.4018/978-1-5225-2537-0.ch005

Copyright © 2017, IGI Global. Copying or distributing in print or electronic forms without written permission of IGI Global is prohibited.

platform has been compared as analogous to what digital file sharing once was for the major players in the music industry (Southin, 2013). Southin (2013) suggests that the fundraising environment is changing and that the growth of online funding is just at the beginning stages of development.

This chapter explores how a non-profit can launch a successful crowdfunding campaign. Following the introduction, a brief overview of the crowdfunding landscape provides insights into crowdfunding and the changing economic landscape of fundraising in the non-profit space. The characteristics of a successful not for profit organization crowdfunding campaign are then discussed followed by specific recommendations for not for profit organizations to embark on a crowdfunding business model and crowdfunding strategies are provided for successful crowdfunding campaigning is outlined. This chapter contributes to the financial knowledge in the not for profit space and concludes with three additional future research project recommendations.

## CROWDFUNDING LANDSCAPE

Businesses and nonprofits have raised funds by using small number of donors are able to donate large amounts of money. However the landscape of fundraising is changing. Crowdfunding is one method of fundraising that relies upon getting small amounts of money from a large number of donors. Crowdfunding is normally done online (Bray, 2015).

The recession of 2008 has produced significant negative impact on the trend of philanthropic giving. In this scenario, crowdfunding represents a unique opportunity to obtain funds from individuals who may provide a smaller amount of donation and feel that they can make the difference in the success of the mission of nonprofits (Becher, Entsch, Frey, 2011). Crowdfunding as an innovative approach of fundraising has quickly grabbed the attention of nonprofit sector. Around the globe thousands of individuals and nonprofits are using crowdfunding to impact the lives of needy people. Crowdfunding has provided opportunities of philanthropic giving out of a small group of wealthy donors (Andrew, 2013; Belleflamme, Lambert, & Schwienbacher, 2010).

Crowdfunding is not a new concept. This concept has been around for hundreds of years. This concept of collective fundraising was used as early as in 17th century to fund publications (Carvajal & García, 2012). Today, the modern notion of crowdfunding is deeply rooted in the very old business model that nonprofits have used in which the funds were generated by collecting micro-donations from individuals to achieve the cause of nonprofits (Belleflamme, Lambert, & Schwienbacher, 2010). The term crowdfunding was first coined by Michael Sullivan. He launched a fundraising campaign to create an incubator for projects involving creation of video blogs. The basic principles behind crowdfunding approach were reciprocity, transparency shared interest and getting funding from the crowd. However the concept of crowdfunding was fully operationalized when Kickstarter.com, one of the largest crowdfunding platforms, adopted it (Prive, 2012).

By 2011, many more crowdfunding platforms emerged. These platforms were able to raise US dollar 5 billion in 2013. 30% of this amount was devoted for social causes (Morgan & DiGiammarino, 2014). While the figures speaks themselves the novelty and success of today's crowdfunding is due to the modern Internet technologies and the new philanthropic mindset of the people that have provided crowdfunding practices of big push. Crowdfunding projects can be used by both nonprofits and commercial firms.

The crowdfunding projects initiated by nonprofits are community-based and offer no financial gain for donors (Estellés-Arolas & González-Ladrón-de-Guevara, 2012). While crowdfunding can provide many alternatives nonprofits are mostly interested in the donation crowdfunding. The basic philosophy behind this option is that people are invited to invest in the project initiated by nonprofits because these people have a passion for the mission of nonprofit. The investors expect intangible return of the investment that can be personal satisfaction coming from doing good for the community.

While crowdfunding is helpful for nonprofits it should be noted that nonprofits cannot use it as an approach to generate funds on an ongoing basis. Crowdfunding should be used to supplement the other techniques of fundraising such as personal solicitations, fundraising lunch, and direct mail campaigns. Crowdfunding should be used as a short-term technique to raise funds that should be integrated into a balanced mixed of fundraising techniques. As such crowdfunding should not be considered a replacement of other traditional fundraising techniques. For example crowdfunding can be a great way to raise funds for a specific cause such as launch of a new service.

Before launching a crowdfunding campaign nonprofits need to ensure that they set the campaign timeline and funding goal. They should then make efforts to generate genuine excitement around the cause for which the campaign is being run. Doing so the nonprofits can easily engage the support of existing and new followers. They can also encourage their followers to engage their friends and family in the cause. If nonprofits properly leveraged the power of social media and personal interaction there crowdfunding campaign can grow exponentially (Hemer, 2011).

Many times donors are motivated when they have a connection to the cause and are inspired not only by the work of the nonprofit but also by the mission of nonprofit and the people being helped. Crowdfunding is a great technique for nonprofits to supplement existing fundraising techniques. However successful crowdfunding campaign required developing a strategy plan. The nonprofits should start crowdfunding campaigns by first creating a description of the crowdfunding project. This description should outline how this project will benefit both the nonprofit and the community it serves. This project description should be considered as the pitch that nonprofit will be using to support and promote the crowdfunding campaign. The next step is the identification of the people that are likely to support the crowdfunding campaign. The nonprofit should pay attention to determine the needs expectations and values of the people being targeted for fundraising (Lambert & Schwienbacher, 2010).

The identification of incentives for the donors is the next step. The incentives are very important for crowdfunding campaigns launched by nonprofits. This is because there is no financial benefit or return associated with the investment that donors make into the crowdfunding campaign. Cost of the reward is not important and many studies show that donors of crowdfunding campaigns sponsored by nonprofits are not interested in any gift or return for their donation. The important thing for them is the personal satisfaction they derive by helping the people in the community they feel connected to (Pitschner & Pitschner-Finn, 2014). However, public recognition is one significant motivation behind donation. Nonprofits should ask their donors if they would like to be acknowledged for their donation. This acknowledgement can be made, for example, by prominently listing the name of the donors on the nonprofit's website. Besides providing a letter of thanks to the donors, the nonprofit can also provide donors the letter of appreciation from people or organizations that were helped by their money (Garecht, 2016). These letters can provide great emotional impact.

Nonprofits can also hand over small items, such as stationery or bags with nonprofit's name and logo printed on them, to the donors. They can also provide some distinctive experience for donors by arranging meetings of leaders of nonprofits with the donors or arrange the donors' visit to the facilities of nonprofits. Creativity is a key to success for every crowdfunding campaign. Nonprofits should think out-of-the-box and consider every option that can help build the support of the crowd they are targeting for fund raising. Nonprofits can leverage the power of visual elements in their campaigns. Short but powerful videos can be created to highlight the cause and strengthen the connection between the nonprofit and its supporters. The marketing plan should include an outreach plan that clearly outline how the crowd would be approaches e.g. through personal meetings or email (StartSomeGood, 2016).

## CHARACTERISTICS OF A SUCCESSFUL CROWDFUNDING CAMPAIGN

Success of crowdfunding lies in generating interest with group of targeted people who are eager and willing to give for a cause. By increasing the number of people touched by the message of the crowdfunding campaign, nonprofits can increase the chances of success of the campaign by getting higher levels of funds. Nonprofits should develop a consistent, well-developed pitch for their crowdfunding campaign that can ignite support among the crowd and encourage them to use their individual influence and bring their friends and family to support the cause (Lamson, 2013).

Marketing efforts should continue throughout the campaign. These efforts should continue to make sure that campaign is sustaining and new energy is generating. It is a fact that donors are more comfortable supporting successful campaigns. Therefore, setting examples of early success is very important. Nonprofits should encourage their supporters to make early donations. Irrespective of the amount of individual donation, promoting the fact that a large number of donors are donating can encourage others to donate as well. This can help build the required momentum for the campaign. On most platforms, project creators can post updates about the project. Xu et al., (2014) found that success rate of crowdfunding projects that provided regular updates was fifty-nine percent of as compared with a success rate of thirty-nine percent among crowdfunding projects that provided no updates..

There are no limits in a crowdfunding campaigns and nonprofits can use both traditional and non-traditional methods to raise funds. However, nonprofits must have a funding goal. Non-profits should also make every possible effort to explain in a concise and clear manner to the donors how the donated money will be used. The promotional materials should provide a clear and easy-to-follow call to action that could drive the donation by the donors. Registering with tax authorities and using an established payment mechanism can help build reputation and trust among donors. A fast and trusted online payment mechanism can also make the process of giving fast, safe and with less complications (Read, 2013).

Crowdfunding can help nonprofits in their development plans by providing the needed cash and by generating awareness of the mission of the nonprofit. This awareness can then be used by the nonprofit to gain new supporters and potential donors. Crowdfunding campaigns are short in duration, but these campaigns provide a high level engaging and personal relationship building with the people. These relationships can help nonprofit strengthen its brand and reputation, expand its presence, and attract new fans. With increasing use of crowdfunding by the nonprofits and for-profits, there is also a need to develop standards and expectations. Without standards it will be difficult to use crowdfunding to reproduce the success (Carvajal, Garcia-Aviles, & Gonzalez, 2012).

Crowdfunding global platforms are varied and diverse. A brief overview highlights a few crowdfunding projects in the global community crowdfunding space. To start, Kickstart, one of the largest and most successful crowdfunding projects, deserves some mention followed by a brief overview of other global crowdfunding platforms and projects

Kickstarter is a very large global community developed to support creative projects. Around the globe, more than 10 million donors have supported Kickstarter project. In July 2016, Kickstarter was running 108,651 successful projects. The successful project is the one that achieved its funding goal. Cummulatively Kickstarter raised approximately $US2.53 billion worth of donations between 2012 and 2016 (Kickstarter, 2016). The basic model of Kickstarter is based on a reward for donation. Kickstarter solely operates in US. Fundly is another large online crowdfunding platform that operates exclusively for nonprofits and charities.

Fundly only services U.S-based crowdsourcing campaigners and donors. Despite this limitation, by 2013, Fundly was running more than 3000 campaigns. These campaign raised more than US$ 300 million in donations (Fundly, 2013). Fundly charges a platform fee (4.9%) and credit card processing fee (2.9% + $.30) transaction to set up a fundraising page (Fundly, 2016).

Indiegogo is one of the world's largest crowdfunding platforms. With social media integration, direct email, and announcement features users can easily spread the word, raise awareness, and increase funding. For 501 (c) (3) nonprofits and charities in the US IndieGoGo offers a 25% fee reduction (indiegogo.com, 2016). In general, this exemption is applied to not-for-profit organizations (scientific, charitable, educational, religious, etc.) that must be registered and verified by the US Government through the IRS. 501(c) (3) tax exemptions and deductions are only available in the United States.

Besides these very large crowdfunding platforms, many other small-to-medium sized crowdfunding platforms for nonprofits. For example, *Causes* is a crowdfunding platform for GuideStar-verified 501(c) (3) nonprofits. Users can create a cause to support a nonprofit and integrate the campaign page with social media to mobilize their network to make donation. *CauseVox* is an online crowdfunding platform that nonprofits can use to create customized fundraising websites for campaigns. *Crowdrise* is an online crowdfunding platform that followers of nonprofits can use to create personal fundraising pages where their friends and family can donate. *Giveffect* is exclusively for charitable crowdfunding where donations go directly to partner nonprofits (Chung, 2013) (Chung, 2013). *Donate Now/Network for Good* provides free and economical fundraising tools that nonprofits can use to obtain donations on their own websites and on social networks. *DonorsChoose* is a platform that individuals can use to obtain donations for needy students.

*FirstGiving* can be used by individuals to obtain online donations. *Fundraise.com* can be used by both individuals and organizations to manage their online fundraising activities. *FundRazr* is a social fundraising tool for both individuals and nonprofits. *Givezooks!* Can be used by nonprofits to create custom online crowdfunding campaigns and integrate their campaign sites with social media to increase donor base. *GoFundMe* is a do-it-yourself online fundraising service for nonprofits. *Help Attack!* Uses social media to collect donations. JustGive (www.justgive.org) is crowdfunding platform where donors can give to nonprofit organizations through e.g. fundraising registries. *Pay It Square* is a crowdfunding platform to create customized fundraising pages and collect donations online. *Razoo* is a platform that individuals and organizations can use to create fundraising pages and accept donations. *StayClassy* is used by small- and medium-size nonprofits for online crowdfunding.

Each crowdfunding platform has features and expectations. Each nonprofit must carefully consider these features and expectations. All the platforms invite any nonprofit to set up an online fundraising campaign. Each fundraising page includes narrative, videos and pictures. These fundraising pages can link to social media sites or to the nonprofits' website. Nonprofits can either use their own payment mechanism to accept donations on these fundraising pages or use the payment mechanism provided by the platform. In former case, the burden of record keeping/processing and pushing the traffic to the fundraising page lies with the nonprofit.

## Success Stories

Globally, crowdfunding success stories are emerging of which only a few will be briefly mentioned here. Kids Company is a UK-based well-established charity that supports vulnerable children with food, clothing etc. Kids Company used crowdfunding to raise more than £100,000 online and became the leading UK innovator in fundraising by crowdfunding (Ratty, 2015).

AH20 is another UK-based newly founded charity dedicated to provide clean water for children and families in Nicaragua. Other such programs have also been set up. But AH20, has built an extensive reputation for its crowdfunding success.

The Canadian Hero Fund was started to provide scholarships to children of fallen Canadian soldiers. Since its inception in 2010, the Canadian Hero Fund has raised over $175,000 in scholarships revenue. Fifteen children of fallen Canadian soldiers (CanadaHelpsa, 2014) have benefitted from the scholarships.

The Canada-based The LEMON LOVE RIDE initiated the crowdfunding campaign to raise funds, enhance the profile of and acknowledge the role of hospice care in Canada. The LEMON LOVE RIDE aimed to help hospitals to fund operations and expansion plans. Since its inception, The LEMON LOVE RIDE set an initial funding goal of $10, 000 (Canadian) but within three weeks had reached its objective and the continued support of donors (CanadaHelpsb, 2014).

## CROWDFUNDING BUSINESS MODEL

Ratty (2015), suggests that there are 4 Ps of giving. From Ratty's point of view, people give because they wish to participate, support, contribute and feel rewarded as an included member of society who have contributed to valuable cause. Figure 1 summarizes why people contribute finances to social and community projects.

*Figure 1. 4 Ps of giving*
*Source Ratty (2015) 1*

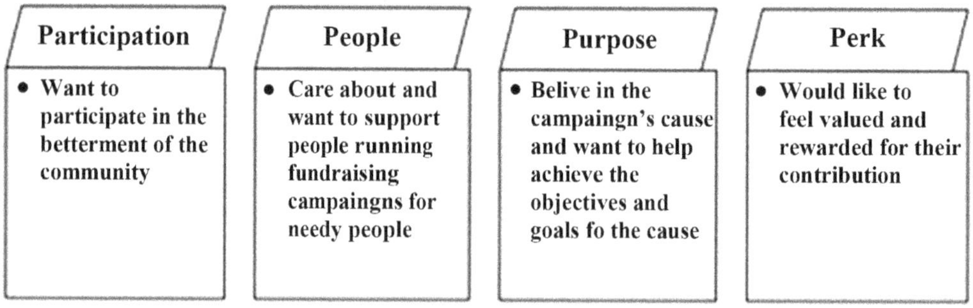

Including the 4 Ps into their organizational business model and designing a crowdfunding strategic plan could provide not for profit organizations with the following benefits which include:

1. Building meaningful relationships with communities
2. Connect and reconnect with new and existing supporters
3. Communicate the impact of their mission
4. Building a recognizable brand
5. Access to and open up new networks
6. Generate funds
7. Generate organizational awareness
8. Generate organizational and program profiles

Crowdfunding presents a cost-effective way to gain support of community and to raise funds. There are few recommendations that nonprofits can use to build and sustain successful crowdfunding campaigns. Not for profit organizations should strategically consider Ratty's 4 Ps in the design of their crowdfunding campaigns. For example, to obtain funding, nonprofits must identify and offer incentives to the prospective donors. Realistic expectations, regarding the scope and reach of the organization, can help nonprofit avoid undesirable results. Nonprofits should set an achievable funding goal keeping in view the amount of expected support they can get (Wu, 2014). Figure 2 shows some important characteristics of crowdfunding campaign that are described below.

*Figure 2. Crowdfunding campaigns characteristics*
*Source Wu (2012), Zorn (2015) Emma (2016) 1*

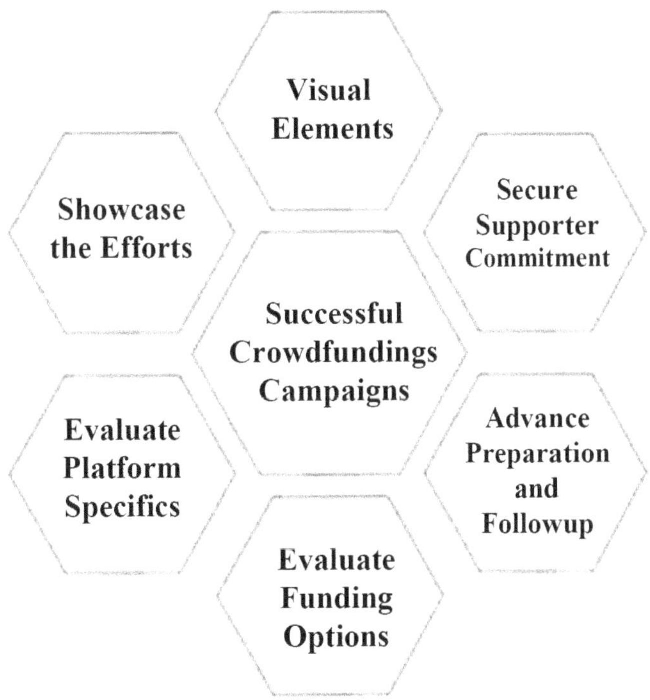

## Visual Elements

Visual elements are a vital element of any crowdfunding campaign. It can not only help introduce the cause but also make it easier for supporters of nonprofit to share it with their friends and family. With cost-effective video editing tools, these videos can be economically produced and provide great return. MPW Media conducted a study that found medium was crucial when it comes from taking campaigns from idea to reality. The study analyzed 7,196 projects on Kickstarter and discovered that crowdfunding campaign pages with video were 85% more likely to achieve their funding goals (Emma, 2016).

## Early Commitment by Supporters

Establishing early success stories is vital for crowdfunding campaigns. These success stories give donors confidence in the campaign and increase probability of their giving. Nonprofits should make every possible effort to ensure all the stakeholders, including supporters, are aware of their crowdfunding campaign before the campaign is launched (Wu, 2014). According to Zorn (2015), all successful crowdfunding campaigns are initially funded between 20-35% through the project creators pre-campaign awareness efforts within the first two weeks of launch.

## Showcase the Effort

Showcasing efforts made in crowdfunding campaign can help nonprofit increase campaign success rate. For example, nonprofits can create an infographic providing highlights of the use of donated funds. Such highlights may include number of kids sent to school, number of people fed etc. This sharing of accomplishment can not only provide emotional impact but also help build momentum in the campaign.

## Advance Preparation

Due to their limited duration, crowdfunding campaigns are highly dependent on how they are planned. An outreach plan should be developed and the supporters should be contacted well in advance of the launch of the campaign. It is important that committed donors be given advance notice of crowdfunding campaigns so that they have ample time to alert their social network about it (Bechter, Jentzsch, & Frey, 2011).

## Follow Up

It is important to let supporters and donors know how the campaign is doing. This is because the crowd supporting a campaign feels the ownership and responsibility of the campaign. Updates and news of campaign on regular basis can keep this crowd informed and actively engaged in the campaign throughout. This follow up can also include appreciating the early supporters and offering them incentives to continue their philanthropic giving in future (Wu, 2014).

### Evaluate Funding Options

Crowdfunding platforms can offer a fixed-funded model or flexible funding model. Under fixed-funding model crowdfunding campaign is given a pre-established timeline and financial goal (Cumming, Leboeuf, & Schwienbacher, 2015). If that goal is not achieved within the designated time frame, the organizers do not collect any funds. It is an "all or nothing" situation. Under the flexible funding model, organization can set the length of the campaign (e.g. 45-60 days) and the financial goal. If the organization fail to achieve the goal, they would still receive the funds but a large proportion would go to the platform provider. Kickstarter.com offers a fixed-funding model while Indiegogo.com offers an option of choosing between fixed or flexible funding model. If an organization feels that, they are short of time and unsure of the possible support they could get, flexible funding model is a better choice.

### Evaluate Platform-Specific Features

While choosing a crowdfunding platform, the nonprofit should carefully evaluate the following options. According to Hogue (2015), if a crowdfunding campaign is able to raise at least twenty percent of its goal, it is very probable that the campaign will be able to reach its target. Around seventy-nine percent of the campaigns on Kickstarter that raised more than twenty percent of their target ended up being successfully funded. However, crowdfunding campaign is not easy to setup, manage and sustain. The look and feel of the campaign is important for successful outcomes. Marketing and social media is increasingly playing an important role, selecting the appropriate fee paying and payment processing portal and the ease of using the online crowdfunding platform are all elements that contribute to the success or failure of a crowdfunding campaign. The up-front effort and full buy-in options from the organizational leaders are prerequisite for measureable success.

## CROWDFUNDING CAMPAIGN STRATEGY

### Look and Feel

The platform should include visual elements that appeal to your audience and donors.

### Ease of Use

Evaluate your abilities to design and run a crowdfunding page. It is preferable that the nonprofit should be able to design and manage the fundraising page with minimum requirements of specific skills (like HTML) to operate the site.

## Payment Processing

The chosen platform should offer the preferred choices of payment mechanisms that nonprofit can use to accept donations online. It is preferable that platform should provide a variety of payment options. It is especially important if the nonprofit would like to handle the payment processing using its preferred payment processor.

## Fees

Nonprofit should carefully evaluate the available platforms any set-up, maintenance, or credit card processing fees. They should perform a comparison of costs with the amount of money they are willing to invest in building and managing the fundraising page.

## Marketing and Social Networking Capabilities

Marketing on social media is essential to build rapport, gain new supporter, and reconnect with existing loyal followers. The chosen platform should provide integration of fundraising site with various social media platforms.

## Traction

The chosen platform should provide nonprofits ability to monitor the donors' visits on the fundraising site. Nonprofits should monitor the visits and the amount of donations collected to see if they are meeting their funding goal.

The organizational business plan and the organizational crowdfunding strategy are both important to achieving crowdfunding objectives (Hogue, 2015). The investment is such a strategy is not easy. Various organizational elements require careful consideration. However it is anticipated that the initial initiative could produce exceptional outcomes. Careful consideration is required and the crowdfunding business plan and crowdfunding business strategy as depicted here are merely sketches. Figure 3 depicts how crowdfunding strategy relates to the crowdfunding outcomes.

*Figure 3. Crowdfunding strategy*
*Source: Wu (2012), Zorn (2015) Emma (2016 2*

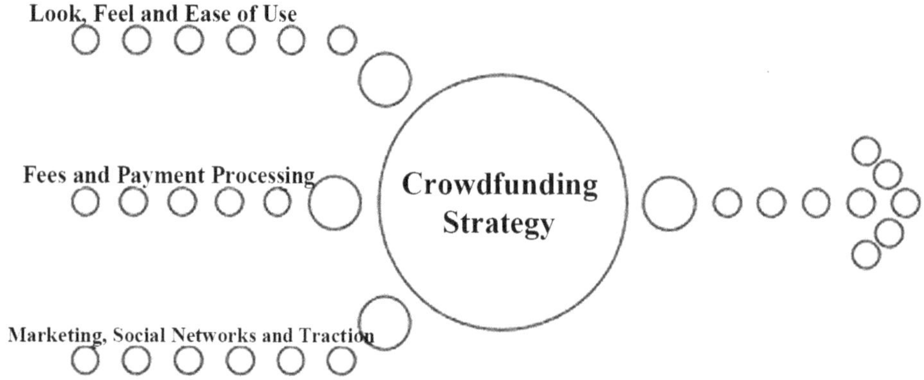

## CONCLUSION

Crowdfunding is rapidly and dynamically gaining popularity. Due to the cost efficiency, scope of and reach of diverse online communities, the opportunities provided for not for profit organizations who seek to raise revenue, are extensive. However, crowdfunding campaign is not easy to setup, run, and sustain. A good amount of up-front effort and full buy-in from the organization's leaders are prerequisite for measureable success.

Taking the four Ps of crowdfunding into careful strategic consideration, can help nonprofits build meaningful relationships with community, connect with new supporters and reconnect with existing supporters, communicate the impact of their mission, build a recognizable brand, open up new networks and generate funds, as well as awareness.

The crowdfunding campaign environment is a new phenomenon in the not for profit environment. Further research would generate knowledge on future directions in this space. Future research in the not for profit and crowdfunding space could include:

1. Comparative analysis of crowdfunding platforms that are used around the globe. This would enhance the understanding of crowdfunding being undertaken and the types of platforms that other not for profit organizations are operationalizing elsewhere.
2. Knowledge on similar crowdfunding platforms is lacking but understanding the differences between crowdfunding platforms would generate new knowledge and provide new insights on the mechanisms of different types of not for profit organizations, the use of similar crowdfunding platforms and the donor response rate. Such knowledge would greatly extend the knowledge and understanding of the success rate of crowdfunding and not for profit organizations
3. The impact of organizational brand, how it influences donor decision to contribute to the campaign, would provide insights to the success and failure of crowdfunding campaigns.

## REFERENCES

Andrew, B. A. (2013, June 18). *How start-ups can tap cash from ordinary people and give the prospect of huge profits in return... What is crowdfunding and how does it work?* Retrieved July 9, 2016, from http://www.thisismoney.co.uk/money/smallbusiness/article-2333399/Crowdfunding-does-work.html

Becher, C., Entsch, S., & Frey, M. (2011). (Forthcoming). From wisdom to wisdom of the crowd and crowdfunding. *Journal of Communication and Computer*.

Belleflamme, P., Lambert, T., & Schwienbacher, A. (2010). Crowdfunding: An industrial organization perspective. In *Workshop Digital Business Models: Understanding Strategies* (pp. 25–26).

Bray, I. (2015). *Using Crowdfunding to Raise Money for Your Nonprofit*. Retrieved July 9, 2016, from http://www.nolo.com/legal-encyclopedia/using-crowdfunding-raise-money-your-nonprofit.html

CanadaHelps. (2014a, August 20). *Lemon Love Ride – A Fundraising Success | CanadaHelps - Donate to any charity in Canada*. Retrieved July 9, 2016, from https://www.canadahelps.org/en/giving-life/fundraising/lemon-love-ride-a-fundraising-success/

CanadaHelps. (2014b, November 5). *Canadian Hero Fund Launches 11 for 11 Campaign | Canada-Helps - Donate to any charity in Canada*. Retrieved July 9, 2016, from https://www.canadahelps.org/en/giving-life/community-happenings/canadian-hero-fund-launches-11-for-11-campaign/

Carvajal, M., & García, J. (2012). Crowdfunding and non–profit media: The emergence of new models for public interest. *Journalism Practice*, *6*(5-6), 638–647. doi:10.1080/17512786.2012.667267

Cumming, D. J., Leboeuf, G., & Schwienbacher, A. (2015). Crowdfunding models: Keep-it-all vs. all-or-nothing. *All-Or-Nothing*.

Emma. (2016). *The Videos of the 10 Most Funded Crowdfunding Campaigns Ever*. Retrieved September 11, 2016, from https://ignitiondeck.com/id/the-videos-of-the-10-most-funded-crowdfunding-campaigns-ever/

Estellés-Arolas, E., & González-Ladrón-de-Guevara, F. (2012). Towards an integrated crowdsourcing definition. *Journal of Information Science*, *38*(2), 189–200. doi:10.1177/0165551512437638

Fundly. (2013, February 26). *World's Largest Crowdfunding-for-Good Platform, Fundly, Announces Campaign of the Year Winners*. Retrieved July 8, 2016, from http://www.prnewswire.com/news-releases/worlds-largest-crowdfunding-for-good-platform-fundly-announces-campaign-of-the-year-winners-193240701.html

Fundly. (2016, July 7). *Pricing*. Retrieved July 8, 2016, from http://fundly.com/pricing/

Garecht, J. (2016). *How to Use Crowd-Funding Sites to Raise Money for Your Non-Profit*. Retrieved July 9, 2016, from http://www.thefundraisingauthority.com/internet-fundraising/crowd-funding-your-non-profit/

Hemer, J. (2011). *A snapshot on crowdfunding*. Working papers firms and region.

Hobey, E. (2014, July 4). *Fundly: Crowdfunding for the Greater Social Good Interview with Dennis Hu, CEO of Fundly*. Retrieved July 7, 2016, from http://www.crowdfundinsider.com/2014/07/43251-fundly-crowdfunding-greater-social-good-interview-dennis-hu-ceo-fundly/

Hogue, J. (2015, November 23). *How to Set Realistic Crowdfunding Goals*. Retrieved September 11, 2016, from http://www.crowd101.com/setting-realistic-crowdfunding-goals/

https://www.statista.com/statistics/310218/total-kickstarter-funding/

Indiegogo.com. (2016, July 7). *How to Raise Tax-Deductible Funds*. Retrieved July 8, 2016, from http://support.indiegogo.com/hc/en-us/articles/202444736-How-To-Raise-Tax-Deductible-Funds

Lambert, T., & Schwienbacher, A. (2010). An empirical analysis of crowdfunding. *Social Science Research Network, 1578175*.

Lamson, B. (2013, November 14). *How to Successfully Crowdfund for Your Nonprofit*. Retrieved July 9, 2016, from http://www.huffingtonpost.com/ben-lamson/how-to-successfully-crowd_b_4274202.html

Maldonado, M. (2012, August 5). *Crowd-funding campaigns gaining popularity with Canadians*. Retrieved July 7, 2016, from http://www.nationalpost.com/m/wp/news/blog.html?b=news.nationalpost.com/2012/08/05/crowd-funding-campaigns-gaining-popularity-with-canadians

Morgan, E., & DiGiammarino, B. (2014, May 22). *Crowdfunding for Nonprofits | Stanford Social Innovation Review*. Retrieved July 9, 2016, from http://ssir.org/articles/entry/crowdfunding_for_nonprofits

Mulvey, J. (2013, March 13). *Crowdfunding executive living the dream through his job | MNN - Mother Nature Network*. Retrieved July 7, 2016, from http://www.mnn.com/money/green-workplace/stories/crowdfunding-executive-living-the-dream-through-his-job

Ordanini, A. (2009, March 23). *Crowd Funding: Customers as Investors - WSJ*. Retrieved July 7, 2016, from http://www.wsj.com/articles/SB123740509983775099

Pitschner, S., & Pitschner-Finn, S. (2014). Non-profit differentials in crowd-based financing: Evidence from 50,000 campaigns. *Economics Letters*, *123*(3), 391–394. doi:10.1016/j.econlet.2014.03.022

Prive, T. (2012, November 27). *What Is Crowdfunding And How Does It Benefit The Economy - Forbes*. Retrieved July 9, 2016, from http://www.forbes.com/sites/tanyaprive/2012/11/27/what-is-crowdfunding-and-how-does-it-benefit-the-economy/#1146a2be4ed4

Ratty, J. (2015, May 14). *Crowdfunding Charities: 9 of the best UK charity crowdfunds*. Retrieved from http://www.crowdfunder.co.uk/blog/crowdfunding-charities-9-of-the-best-uk-charity-crowdfunds/

Read, A. (2013). *Crowdfunding: an empirical and theoretical model of non-profit support*. Academic Press.

Southin, T. (2013). *Harnessing the Fundraising Potential of Charitable Crowdfunding in Canada*. Retrieved from http://travissouthin.com/images/pdf/CharitableCrowdfunding-TravisSouthin.pdf

StartSomeGood. (2016). *How it works – crowdfunding for non-profits, social entrepreneurs and changemakers*. Retrieved July 9, 2016, from http://ssg.startsomegood.com/HowItWorks

Wu, R. (2014, November 24). *5 Best Practices in Nonprofit Crowdfunding*. Retrieved July 9, 2016, from https://www.causevox.com/blog/5-best-practices-nonprofit-crowdfunding/

Xu, A., Yang, X., Rao, H., Fu, W. T., Huang, S. W., & Bailey, B. P. (2014). Show me the money! *Proceedings of the 32nd annual ACM Conference on Human Factors in Computing Systems*. doi:10.1145/2556288.2557045

Zorn, M. (2015, November 27). *10 steps to Crowdfunding Success | Vision Launch*. Retrieved September 11, 2016, from http://www.visionlaunch.com/10-steps-to-crowdfunding-success-2/

## KEY TERMS AND DEFINITIONS

**Branding:** Refers to aligning what an individual or firm want people to think about itself with what people actually do think about the individual or firm.

**Business Plan:** A business plan defines business goals, explain why they are attainable, and plans for reaching them.

**Community:** Refers to a group of people who share some common interest.

**Crowdfunding Platform:** Refers to a website used to develop and run a fundraising campaign.

**Crowdfunding:** Refers to raise funds for a venture using a large group of people.

**Donor:** Refers to a person who donates something, especially money to charity.

**Non-Profit:** Refers to an organization that uses its surplus revenues to further achieve its purpose or mission.

**Recognition:** Refers to public acknowledgement of person's status or merits.

**Social Networking:** Refers to the use of dedicated websites and applications for people interaction.

**Sponsor:** Refers to a person who pays for a specific item to be released.

# Chapter 6
# Project Portfolio Management:
## Tool for Strategy Implementation in Non-Governmental Organizations

**Beata Jałocha**
*Jagiellonian University, Poland*

**Ewa Bogacz-Wojtanowska**
*Jagiellonian University, Poland*

## ABSTRACT

*Project Portfolio Management is a relatively new practice for the majority of non-government organisations. Project portfolio management is important in the areas of management and education of third sector practitioners. However, project portfolio management, corporate management tools are usually used in the business sector with very little research undertaken in the non-government sectors. This chapter fills that research gap by identifying and analysis of project portfolio management practices in non-governmental organizations. Findings suggest that non-government organisations manage multiple projects simultaneously but that project portfolio management could support them to build their portfolio in accordance with a strategic plan that can fulfil their strategic objectives efficiently and effectively.*

## INTRODUCTION

The NGO sector in Poland is growing. There are nearly one hundred thousand foundations and associations (100,000), two hundred thousand other organizational forms, including semi-formal, large groups and Catholic organizations (200,000). Despite the increase in number of NGOs in the last 26 years of transformation of the country, Polish NGOs still face many difficulties. In particular the lack of permanent funding for activities, a strong focus on project work, lack of funds for hiring full-time employees, as well as a common distrust of society, resulting from disclosure of unethical and illegal practices of some NGOs. The most important feature of Polish NGOs is their not for profit character, hence the interchangeable use of two terms: non-governmental and non-profit. However, taking into considerations diverse conditions of formation and nomenclature of third sector organizations, the term NGO used in

DOI: 10.4018/978-1-5225-2537-0.ch006

Copyright © 2017, IGI Global. Copying or distributing in print or electronic forms without written permission of IGI Global is prohibited.

this chapter is similar in its meaning to the concept of non-profit organization described by Salamon and Anheier (1999). Many NGOs implement large projects and contributes to building and developing a strong and credible third sector in Poland.

Project management is a widely used business management concept used in NGOs globally and regardless of the type of activities that are managed (Khang & Moe, 2008; Golini, Kalchschmidt, Landoni, 2015). It is not a new approach to the implementation of tasks in organizations in general – dating back to the construction of the Egyptian pyramids and Roman aqueducts. Traditional project management was focused on the management of a single project in a single location. However, the 1990's technological change, the globalization process and the different needs of customers projected project management into new forms (Kloppenborg & Opfer 2002). In the field of project management, three main areas have been identified (tactical, operational, strategic) and particularly, project management, program management and project portfolio management have increasingly attracted attention. One important differentiating point as pointed out by Jugdey (2003) is that program management and project portfolios concern the management of groups of individual projects and differ from managing a single project (Jugdev, 2003). This is an important distinction in understanding project portfolio management in non-government organizations, which is the main objective of this discussion.

Although project management has been traditionally used in NGO's globally, Project Portfolio Management (PPM) is a relatively new practice for the majority of non-government organisations, and particularly so in Poland. PPM is important in the areas of management and education of third sector practitioners. However, project portfolio management, corporate management tools are usually used in the business sector with very little research undertaken in the non-government sectors. This chapter fills that research gap by identifying and analysis of project portfolio management practices in non-governmental organizations.

Following the introduction, the concept of projectification provides an overview of the conceptualisation of project portfolio management and its application in non-government organizations. This is followed by a discussion on project portfolio management, stages of project portfolio management and project portfolio management in non-government organizations. The chapter concludes with the importance of project portfolio management in non-government organizations and provides future research recommendations.

## BACKGROUND

Similarly to the business and the public sector, the sector of non-governmental organizations is strongly influenced by projectification processes. Projectification is a phenomenon that can be observed in all areas of economics, and which results in an increasing, sometimes even predominant, part of organizational tasks being executed in the project-based form. Moving away from operating on the basis of repeatable processes, organizations execute short, one-off projects. In the case of NGOs projects are a natural form for their activities, since funds obtained outside the organization have a limited time frame and a specific purpose. Moreover, contracts concluded on performance of public tasks have a form of projects, as do tenders announced by grant-giving foundations (Bogacz-Wojtanowska & Jałocha, 2016). Projectification processes in NGOs also support models and principles of cooperation with other organizations, particularly public ones. Projectification of projects occurs in contracts for the performance of public services which exist in the Anglo-saxon model of NGO operations as well as in many Eastern European countries.

Project management, usually as a task performance method, is identified with a flexible, innovative and effective approach to management. However, with increasing frequency these shifts are being criticized, also in the NGO sector, and the criticism does not concern solely governmentalization processes. Project-oriented approaches are short-term focused and influences the stability and sustainable development of non-government organization (Bogacz-Wojtanowska & Jałocha, 2016). Subsequently, the long-term strategic planning and achieving long-term strategic objectives of non-government organisations are impacted by the short-termism of project-oriented approaches. For example, instead of thinking about their long-term development and achieving strategic objectives, NGOs may have to focus on seeking new projects to sustain the funding.

Sustaining income in turn funds the continuity of employment of staff who deliver the services and subsequently achieve the project objectives, organisational objectives and organisational mission. Failure to strategically plan perilously impacts the stability, sustainability and growth of the organization. The continuation of non-government projects is important for another reason, sustaining public trust. Sustaining public trust in services obtained from non-government services, strengthens community confidence and thereby contributes to a balanced approach to delivering services to the public.

Project Portfolio Management (PPM) attempts to shift the focus from the constant pursuit of new funding, and allows management to adopt a strategic approach where each project is observed as part of a jigsaw puzzle which when combined reflects the organisational strategy linked together in as a holistic and balanced phenomenon. Adopting PPM as a method which focuses on an inter-linking of projects to achieve the organisational objectives, prevents a pathological destabilising and distrust of non-government organisations.-

Golini, Kalchschmidt and Landoni (2015) indicate that NGOs apply varied methods related to project work. Golini et al (2015) argued that the level organizational maturity in terms of project management depended on the organisational ability to execute project management processes as well as document, measure, control and continuously development. Furthermore, Golini et al (2015) suggested that better project knowledge management leads to effectiveness of non-government organisations. The contention in this study is that the application of PPM could assist non-government organization in the effective knowledge management, strategic management, strategic planning and strategic implementation of projects and programs. To this end, the next section provides an overview of strategic management followed by a discussion of project portfolio management.

## STRATEGIC MANAGEMENT

Strategic management is a set managerial decision-making tools and organizational activities which are used to create an organizational competitive advantage and facilitate long-term operations (Powell 2001; Bryson, Gibbons, 2001; Anheier 2006). Strategic management can be used by NGOs to develop their long-term organisational vision and programs (Powell 2001; Bryson, Gibbons, 2001; Anheier 2006). Furthermore, with the increasing pressure to measure performance and social impact, adopt a business model and professionalise non-government service delivery, adopting a strategic management approach is becoming an important approach for non-government organizations to achieve results (Reid, Brown, McNerney & Perri D, 2014). However, according to Zharp and Brock (2012) substantial research demonstrated that nonprofits still exhibit a significant level of resistance in response to strategic planning process.

Bryson (1989) identified that third sector organisations needed to adapt to the application of strategic management as an answer to the changing circumstances and conditions for conducting third sector and non-governmental activities. This is a challenge third sector organizations continue to face. Interestingly, Wilson (1993) argued that there were two distinct sets of strategies which non-government organisations could consider. Wilson (1993) referred to the pluralistic strategies and the competition strategies. Pluralistic strategies was oriented towards the cooperation between organizations executing similar goals while competition strategies were pro-market orientation and focused on acquiring the largest market possible or overtaking market niches of interest to the organization.

However, Mulhare (1999) and Eisenberg (1997), questioned the usefulness of strategic planning in NGOs, indicating that it involved adapting inappropriate commercial practices, and strategic planning is an end in itself, eclipsing the essence of NGOs' functioning. Burdney and Murray (1998) argued that it is difficult for non-government organisations to adopt strategic management as both internal and external stakeholders must be taken into account. Despite the debates for or against strategic management, support of strategic performance management in the third sector has grown over the years Golensky and Mulder 2006, Miller 2002, van der Pijl, Sminia 2004). Fredericks (2008) and Domanski (2009) outlined strategic management application, methods and techniques for third sector organizations. Mara (2000) suggested that one of the most essential functions of strategic management in non-government organisations is the efficient allocation of resources which strengthened the organisational financial capacity and determined organisational survival.

Marucello (2001) suggested that since non-government organisations had to constantly seek new funding to continue the organisational objectives and service delivery outcomes, it has become increasingly more important for non-government organisations to focus on increasing resources than on providing services. Hafsi and Thomas (2005) and Ridder and McCandless (2008) argued that non-government organizations should consider the factors influencing the operations of the organisation. Bryson, Ackermann and Eden (2007) focused on the key competencies of strategic management. Renshaw and the need for strategic knowledge management in these organizations Renshaw and Krishnaswamy (2009), contended that strategic knowledge management in non-government is important to achieve organisational outcomes. However, strategic management, while it allows for the effective execution in long term strategy, strategic objectives focuses on strategic process with two separate process of strategic planning and strategic implementation. Project Portfolio Management, with its focus on achieving-strategic objectives through the executed projects, enhances strategic management.

## PROJECT PORTFOLIO MANAGEMENT

Project Portfolio Management (PPM) distinguishes between two phases of the strategic process: strategic planning and strategic implementation (Ansoff, 1987) but relates to both the strategic planning and strategic implementation phases. PPM has its origins in business and particularly from project-oriented enterprise where projects play a key role in the process of executing activities to achieve the desired and planned outcomes. The fundamental objective of project-oriented enterprises is to synergise and execute projects to maximise as profits gained from project execution. PPM is therefore a strategic approach where the emphasis is on the strategic dimension of strategic planning and strategic implementation.

Meskendahl, (2010) argues that as the main premise of a project portfolio is the maximization of its financial value, combining the portfolio of projects with strategic organisational objectives and balancing the projects within the portfolio, levels the potential profitability, risk and financial gain. To achieve the maximisation of financial gain, PPM treats different projects as a combined and coordinated project which enables the execution of long-term strategic objectives (Meskendahl (2010). Gerais (2007) summarises that PMM is a project portfolio collection of all projects which a project-oriented organization conducts at a given time., and relationships between these projects. Similarly,

Archer and Ghasemzadeh (2007) define a project portfolio as a group of projects financed by a given organization. Meskendahl (2010) adds that a project portfolio is a collection of projects which compete for the same resources of an organization. In this sense, PPM assists organisations to cope with the increasing number of project activities (Meskendahl, 2010, Rad and Levin, 2006). Project portfolios differ significantly depending on the industry (Killen 2008; Archer, Ghasemzadeh, 2007). However, projects and programs are strategic initiatives combined into portfolios to create and maximise value for the organization.

According to Rad and Levin (2006), the portfolios of projects are created for the strategic management of project activity of the organization. PPM scope and objective, as opposed to individual projects, changes with the change of the strategic objectives of the organization. Programs and portfolios are different concepts. Programs are considered as a manifestation of strategic actions of the organization. However, programs restricted to one narrow area or an organisation rather than in a holistic organisational dimension. Project portfolios, on the other hand are considered as holistic organisational dimensions that like a jigsaw puzzle, fit together to make a complete whole. PPM fits the needs of project oriented non-government organisations.

## Portfolio Management Process

According to one of the most popular definitions of the Project Portfolio Management formulated by the Project Management Institute, the process is the coordinated management of portfolio components to achieve specific organizational objectives (PMI, 2008). Project Portfolio Management can be defined as a process of managing organizational projects and programs at different stages of their life cycle, which are analyzed, prioritized, monitored and controlled in the course of a dynamic process (Jałocha, 2014). However, PPM is above all a strategic action and requires the organization's management to make a series of strategic decisions.

The most critical decision is to decide whether a particular project is going to be executed or not. This is the most fundamental decision in the entire process, with key impact on the shape of the portfolio and the process of its management (Jafarizadeh, Khorshid-Doust, 2008: 613). Due to the fact that very often in organizations different – both individual and group – interests clash, (e.g., interests of particular divisions, branches, departments), deciding which projects should be approved for execution and which to reject, is oftentimes very difficult. Sometimes the so-called "pet projects" promoted by important employees of a given organization in senior management positions, are chosen for realization, even though they should not.

In a correct PPM process, the selection of project for execution should be decided on the basis of the most objective criteria available, based on strategic organizational objectives. This is undoubtedly no mean feat, especially in the case of organizations whose main criterion of organizational success is not the financial profit, but e.g. social development, or welfare of the people, like in the case of non-governmental and public organizations. The selection of projects for the portfolio is usually conducted by a commission – an appropriate committee is appointed, equipped with relevant authorizations for making decisions concerning the choice of projects for the portfolio. In order to ensure the transparency of this process and avoid forcing at all cost only projects favoured by particular decision-makers, it is necessary to provide a set of tools supporting this process and ensuring – as much as possible – impartial assessment of particular enterprises (Jałocha, 2014). The process of selecting projects for the portfolio cannot be too complicated – the selection of optimal projects should be based on relatively simple criteria.

Therefore, to ensure that the process of selecting projects for the portfolio proceeds correctly, a well thought-out concept of its construction and management is necessary. The basic question which should be posed is whether a particular project would allow our organization to develop further, and whether it fits into our strategy. Of course, we should also reflect on what we need to perform a particular undertaking and whether we have the potential and capacities for its successful execution.

Project Portfolio Management is a complex process derived from decision making about the future, operating in a dynamic turbulent environment with constantly changing circumstances, different stages of different project life-cycles, competing for available resources which are limited and decision making about the execution of one project decreased resources assigned to another for completion complexity results, among others, from the following factors (Jałocha, 2014). Jonas (2010: 822) argued that tasks connected with portfolio management can be grouped into four basic phases comprising the life cycle of a project portfolio as follows:

## Phase One: Portfolio Structuring

Portfolio structuring involves strategic planning of activities and defining long-term objectives. This phase is also when proposals of projects, which could be placed in the portfolio, are evaluated and selected. It is repeated regularly, according to the cycles of the organization's strategic planning. Due to the importance of this phase and its impact on the final shape of the portfolio, it features strong involvement of senior management (Jałocha, 2014). The selection of projects for the portfolio is a periodic action consisting in making the selection from among new project proposals or organizational programs, as well as ones being currently executed (if it is not the first attempt at portfolio assessment), which comply with organizational objectives and do not exceed available resources and other organizational limitations (Archer, Ghasemzadeh, 1999: 208). Certain elements taken into account in the process of selection are strategic objectives, financial benefits, intangible benefits, availability of resources and the level of portfolio risk.

## Phase Two: Portfolio Resources Management

Portfolio resource management involves planning the division of resources between projects, formally confirming the allocation of resources and managing conflicts concerning resource allocation (if they arise). Moreover, resources are allocated again, if a new, previously unplanned, need for them occurs.

## Phase Three: Portfolio Steering

Portfolio steering comprises such activities as monitoring the portfolio strategic compliance, determining correction methods in the case of deviations from the set portfolio objective, identifying synergies between projects, or coordinating projects in departments.

### Phase Four: Organisational Learning and Portfolio Exploitation

Organizational learning and portfolio exploitation. Portfolio results are subjected to evaluation; and post-project reviews are carried out to enable tracking the benefits gained. Furthermore, knowledge obtained through project execution is gathered and analysed, for the purpose of later application of best practices in future endeavours.

Problems accompanying the selection process result from several factors (Ghasemzadeh, Archer, 2000:73):

1. The organization has many different objectives which sometimes contradict one another, some of them are qualitative, and not quantitative – hence the difficulty in measuring and comparing them;
2. Uncertainty and risk influence projects – the selected portfolio may need balancing in terms of risk and time remaining until the end of particular projects;
3. The number of possible combinations in the portfolio is often very large, which makes the choice more difficult.

An array of portfolio project selection methods exists, yet there is no single leading method perceived as the ultimate or the most universal (Jałocha, 2014). Each portfolio organization should select its own set of indicators, which would best enable to characterize the executed projects and place emphasis on the most important factors, from the organization's point of view, which should determine the project's place in the portfolio. The largest differences between particular criteria will depend on the industry within which a particular organization operates. In the business sector, the main criterion for building the portfolio will usually be the financial profit generated for the organization. In public and non-governmental organizations, whose strategic principles are based on different objectives, the profit is not always the main criterion of the project selection. Of course, the Project Portfolio Management process does not end at a one-time selection of projects which fit organizational strategic objectives. It requires constant portfolio reviews and reprioritization of projects it contains, as well as including new initiatives.

## PROJECT PORTFOLIO IN NON-GOVERNMENT ORGANISATIONS

### Research Methods and Findings

Four non-governmental organisations operating in Poland were selected for participation in the Project Portfolio Management project. These organizations were identified as having a previously existing project portfolio. Due to a lack of detailed preliminary research on PPM in non-governmental organisations, an exploratory multiple case study approach (Streb, 2010) was used to investigate PPM in non-government organisations. Exploratory case study is very often applied as a preliminary step of an overall causal or explanatory research design exploring a relatively new field of scientific investigation (Streb, 2010). Exploratory studies provide an initial understanding of the situation.

However, conclusions based on exploratory case study are limited and requires enhanced quantitative and qualitative research. Non-governmental organizations with identified project portfolios of 4-5 projects executed annually provided a purposive sample of non-government organisations that have been operating for at least 7 years and have continuously executed projects for selected groups of stakeholders.

The participating organisations were socially legitimate non-government organisations with employed paid staff and had reputations as reliable non-government organisations that fulfilled their objectives, worked in a professional manner and adopted an ethical approach and an organisational structure that coped with portfolio management (Suchman, 1995).

Qualitative studies were conducted in 2016 in Poland. On the basis of data analysis four case studies (Yin, 1984) of exploratory character were prepared. The study consisted of:

1. Conducting an in-depth interviews with persons managing the organization (served as our primary source of data in the current analysis);
2. Analyzing organizational documents, in particular strategic and project documents,
3. Analyzing websites and social media profiles.

In-depth interviews were conducted on the basis of a structured interview scheme. Interview questions were based on a preliminary analysis of the literature and related to aspects such as: process of portfolio selection (Archer & Ghasemzadeh, 2007), PMO's role (Desouza & Evaristo, 2006), portfolio management process (Project Management Institute, 2008). At the same time, when a given issue was significant, interviewees were allowed to express free, in-depth reflection on the subject. Each interview lasted at least an hour. Data analysis followed the transcription of the interviews. Due to the small number of interviews, computer software was not used for the analysis. Interviews were repeatedly read in order to identify emerging categories. Among the identified threads, in each of the studied organizations particular attention was brought to such issues as: the process of projects' selection, the role of PMOs, project knowledge management and managing the portfolio risk. These categories are discussed below.

## Projects in Researched Organizations

The studied organizations were quite diverse in terms of their size and the number of executed projects. Table 1 features the characterization of the studied organizations.

A common feature of the studied organizations is that projects are very important for them, but at the same time they are neither the principal nor the only way of financing their activities. Contrary to organizations which base the entirety of their operations on projects, the studied organizations are determined to have, apart from uncertain, contract-based initiatives, also stable source of funding for their activities, based mainly on fixed membership fees or the conducted business activity.

*Table 1. Characteristics of the studied organizations*

| NGO | Area of Activity | Number of Employees | Number of Projects Executed (Annum) | Value of Projects Executed (Annum) | Project Budget Within Total Budget (%) |
|---|---|---|---|---|---|
| 1 | Public assistance | 80 | 40 | 11m | 60 |
| 2 | Local and regional development | 31 | 6 | 1m | 30 |
| 3 | Financial support for NGOs and social enterprises | 3 | Between 50-100 micro | Between 500 and 1m | 10-30 |
| 4 | Local government development, support for the Polish diaspora | 5 | 5 | 900,000 | 40 |

NGOs' leaders are convinced that the key is financial stability obtained by diversification of financial sources. It is quite difficult to achieve, because external sources of funding and projects undergo significant fluctuations, collapses, and by the year are hedged with increasingly complex bureaucratic regulations. According to some leaders, they often do not bring profit to beneficiaries, neither do they bring the organization closer to the fulfilment of its mission.

Diversification of funding sources is very important for the studied organizations and building organizational stability together with projects, but not based on them. In two of the studied organizations, the share of projects in the financing of the activities was usually larger than 50% of the budget. All organizations acknowledge that projects fit the strategic aspects of their activities, although none of the organizations has a formal strategy – they are either documents created by leaders but unpublished, preliminary guidelines for the strategy, or strategic guidelines, functioning in organizations only informally. In two organizations, to a large extent intentionally, innovative objectives are realized through projects – e.g. testing innovative products for stakeholders, which could not have been funded from the primary budget. It can be noted that these are research and development projects, which enable development of innovative services.

It could therefore be concluded that without securing financial stability based on constant revenues, the studied organizations are reluctant to diversify their project activities. In practice, the studied NGOs try to manage the project portfolio in their own way (adjusting structures, implementing regulations concerning planning and project selection), yet very rarely it is a deliberate, planned process of managing all of the organization's projects as a single, cohesive portfolio. PPM in the studied NGOs is partly an intuitive process, deprived of systematic approach.

## Selection of Projects for the Portfolio

Ideas for projects emerge both on the part of leaders or managers of the studied organizations, and junior employees. Interviewees remarked as well that sometimes ideas for projects come directly from their stakeholders and beneficiaries, and sometimes they are the result of certain opportunities created by the institutional context. All project initiatives, in each of the studied organizations, align or coincide with key areas of activity, resulting from statutory objectives, as well as the specificity of organizations' operations. Established areas of activity, usually developed by the organization for years, are executed within the obtained own funds, or in the framework of its business activity. In order to strengthen, expand and make their offer more attractive, organizations seek and select projects for these areas.

## Role of a Project Management Office

In two of the studied organizations, a separate unit was deliberately formed, to fulfil the function assigned to Project Management Offices. These divisions create projects, prepare grant applications, manage projects and prepare settlings of reports from them. They are a kind of a project centre for the organization. But such divisions exist only in two large organizations. In the case of smaller ones, project tasks are not assigned to divisions – individual persons are in charge of them. The need to create a PMO unit within the organizational structure arises with the increase in the number and the level of complexity of project activities, as well as in the situation where project tasks are doubled in various organizational units. It is noteworthy that one of the studied organizations intentionally left all *de facto* project tasks to one person, who in a manner of speaking manages the project portfolio (with the NGO's board mandate), selecting projects in a way which maintains the balance in the area of employment and necessary own contribution.

## Project Knowledge Management

Project knowledge management processes are not usually formalized in the studied organizations. Sharing knowledge happens mostly during face-to-face encounters, or via internal training or semi-formal meetings with stakeholders. One of the organizations deliberately introduced weekly managerial staff meetings, also to exchange knowledge.

There are also cases of gradual codification or organizational knowledge, in the form of preparing summary publications or long-standing project activities' portfolios. What is also deemed important for sharing knowledge is networking within mother or partner organizations. However, most frequently even many years of project experience is weakly codified, and sometimes it is mainly focused on the person of the leader or the main manager of the organization. Such cases, when knowledge is informally concentrated in the hands of one person, are quite dangerous for the organization. Most importantly, managers are aware of this situation, partly believing that this is a safety buffer, protecting them from movements of organizations' management boards. Two organizations experienced the departure of employees trained in the area of project management, either voluntarily, or in the situation when project activities were closed. Developed procedures with regard to project management, or knowledge sharing were lacking. This kind of approach may constitute a menace to the stability of portfolio management in the already mentioned, and very common situation for the third sector, namely staff turnover.

## Project Reviews, Reprioritization Processes

In the studied organizations, mechanisms of portfolio review and its reprioritization occurred. On the basis of project reviews, preventive actions are undertaken, as well as reactions to problems emerging within projects. However, it has not been found that reviews are conducted on the basis of sophisticated business tools. The most advanced tool used for the analysis was MS Excel software, used for entering current data about the status of particular projects. The studied projects do not use advanced IT tools supporting the management process (e.g. MS Portfolio Server).

## Managing Portfolio Risk

The key element of the portfolio management process, which interviewees approach with particular commitment, is portfolio risk management. It is understandable and stems from NGOs' attributes, their functions and ways of securing funds. The risk of losing any financial means can be triply dangerous: the danger concerns not only funds of the organization, but also the abuse of social trust in the NGO, as well as problems with securing other projects from public institutions (institutional limitations). The studied organizations emphasise that the analysis of risk connected to the enterprise is conducted for each project and on this basis, decision whether to initiate the project is taken.

At the same time, similarly to most managerial actions concerning the portfolio, they are not based on advanced procedures. Mainly simple financial analyses are conducted, which enable the organization to establish whether it is financially prepared to take on a particular project, and if so – when. Moreover, the risk is assessed mostly before including a particular project into the portfolio, and substantive risk management process is not conducted at any later stage. In the situation when crisis occurs, remedial actions are taken ad hoc.

## RECOMMENDATIONS

### Adaptation of PPM in NGOs

According to Courtney (2002: 6) in the nonprofit sector "there is perhaps a tendency to create a simple caricature of strategic planning or strategic management in the private sector in order to refute its relevance for the nonprofit sector". To avoid such misunderstanding in terms of Project Portfolio Management, it has to be unambiguously stated that it is impossible to employ business methods of Project Portfolio Management in non-governmental organizations without their prior adaptation and adjustment to the needs of a particular NGO and conditions of the environment in which it operates. At the same time, by building their portfolio in a conscious and previously planned manner, NGOs can fulfil their strategic objectives more efficiently, and effectively work for their stakeholders. Among recommendations which could help in the adaptation of Project Portfolio Management methods, we could list:

### Project Registry and Archive

Regardless of their size and the scope of activities, NGOs can create project registries which include planned, currently executed, and rejected projects. Such a registry would enable to gather information about various project initiatives in a systematic way, and allow for cyclical reviews in order to assess which initiatives should be taken up anew, which should be continued, and which – rejected. In addition, NGOs should consider the creation of a project archive, containing information about concluded projects, achieved results or applied methods and project approaches. The project archive can be also an element of a comprehensive evaluation system for organizational activities and the assessment of the progress with regard to fulfilling their mission, which is crucial for any NGO.

### Strategy

Strategic planning is the key to portfolio management. Without a well-planned and developed strategy it is difficult to select appropriate projects, leading to the development of the organization and stakeholders' satisfaction. NGOs should have a prepared strategy, which serves as a reference point for all undertaken tasks. Both a certain way of strategy formalization and the participation of numerous stakeholders in its creation should be suggested.

### Strategic Analysis of the Projects to be Included in the Portfolio

Such an analysis would be helpful in the process of selecting optimal projects, i.e., those fitting statutory objectives and the resulting strategic objectives of a given organization. Only the execution of projects related to strategic objectives should be recommended. Projects which do not fit the strategy should be rejected, unless they serve to offset the portfolio, e.g., through acquiring funds, which in turn would enable the development of statutory activities. However, the latter solution is ridden with traps connected to the decrease of social trust, the necessity for temporary employment of additional staff, and finally the so-called "grantosis", i.e., project dependency.

## Criteria for the Selection of Projects for the Portfolio

When working on the criteria for the selection of projects for the portfolio, particular attention should be devoted to intangible criteria. Apart from purely economic factors, every NGO should establish criteria connected with its mission-related non-material activities. These are difficult to formulate, as their nature is often not measurable. Yet they are indispensable for the proper balance in the project portfolio.

## Implementation of Project Knowledge Management Principles

Gathering knowledge in projects can proceed in various ways, both more formalized (e.g., in an electronic application, printouts) and less formal (e.g., during employee meetings in organizations aiming at the exchange of project-related experiences). However, the key is project managers' awareness in this respect. The formalization of knowledge gathering can protect the organization from its loss, in the situation of employee turnover, a very common occurrence in the third sector.

## Creation of a Unit Serving as a PPM Office/Center of Project Knowledge

Such a unit could absorb and diffuse knowledge about concluded projects, as well as provide specialist support to project executors. It is particularly important in the case of organizations with significant employee turnover. Since this is when the hidden knowledge acquired by employees in projects is not retained in the organization.

## Methodologies and Principles of Project and Portfolio Management

In the case of large NGOs, executing a significant number of projects, it would be beneficial to develop a set of principles concerning their selection and execution. These principles may take the form of a methodology, based on selected elements of widely recognized approaches to project management (Prince2, PMBoK). In smaller organizations, introducing strict methodologies seems unnecessary. However, it would be advisable to develop guidelines for project and portfolio management, based on the gathered experiences and best practices.

## Project Portfolio Management Risks

Consistent with the findings of the non-government organisations, Jalocha (2014) pointed out that a lack of project knowledge management, incorrect estimation of the projects' budgets, weak communication process and not using previously acquired project experience are cited as some of the main reasons of project management failures in organizations (Jałocha, 2014).

Dai and Wells (2004: 527) organisations must have a willingness to:

1. Achieve a cohesive approach to project management,

2. Achieve a more effective way to use organizational resources, including human resources in a multi-project environment,
3. Link project management to strategic objectives and thus building competitive advantage.

Desouza and Evaristo (2006: 416), argued that knowledge management permeated three organisational levels:

1. Strategic,
2. Tactical,
3. Operational.

Strategic level, projects must comply with strategic objectives and growth. Tactical level, the integration between projects, execution and monitoringand compliance are imperative to ensure success. Operational level, integration of knowledge developing a source of expert knowledge, and regularly reports to the senior management on the status of particular projects in the portfolio (Dexouza and Evaristo, 2006:416, Jałocha, 2014).

In order to apply previous experiences and manage new initiatives, projects and programs more effectively, many organizations create Project Management Offices (PMO). A PMO can fulfil various functions – from supporting project managers, to realizing project training, to strategic support for management boards of organizations. Above all, one of its most crucial functions is the role of a knowledge hub, a center for gathering and managing project knowledge (Project Office Management, Jalocha, 2014).

## CONCLUSION

The maximization of the portfolio financial value which motivates the idea of building and managing the project portfolio in business organizations has little application in the case of the studied non-governmental organizations. These NGOs do not aim at the maximization of the financial profit as a main criterion in selecting projects to be realized. In their activities, they aim to fulfil their statutory objectives and mission, and their projects are tailored to the needs of the organization's beneficiaries and stakeholders.

Among the studied organisations, in large and professional NGOs with an established reputation, Project Portfolio Management is rather intuitive and informal. There is no standardized approach to portfolio management, neither are there formal methods of comparing and monitoring projects as a whole. However, the study revealed that despite the low level of portfolio management professionalization, NGOs cope well with managing multiple projects simultaneously.

The studied organizations feature both single-person PMO units, and teams or offices charged with project management. Absorption and diffusion of project knowledge is significant in each of the studied organizations, but they are not highly formalized, and largely concentrated in the hands of main leaders or managers of the organization.

Undoubtedly, there is a need to expand the knowledge about Project Portfolio Management in non-governmental organizations. However, we should remember that this approach cannot serve chiefly the maximization of the financial value, and can only be a means to enable more effective realization of strategic objectives for the beneficiaries of a particular organization.

## FUTURE RESEARCH DIRECTIONS

1. Despite the increasing marketization of the third sector, project execution still constitutes the basic form of third sector organizations' activities. It is a certain paradigm in NGO management, both in small and large organizations. The latter increasingly often have a project portfolio, yet they do not achieve the business level of portfolio management. A comparative analysis of large and small third sector organisational project execution would provide further insight into the business level of portfolio management in non-government organizations.
2. There is a shortage of good practices in the area of portfolio management in NGOs, which would facilitate particularly the implementation of management methods, as well as project tools which are useful and universal in business practice. Further research in the definition of good practice in the area of portfolio management in non-government organisations would facilitate and generate knowledge on future implementation of management and business models.
3. The present study is easily replicable, and acquiring data from NGOs is easy, perhaps due to a strong uncertainty of managers in this area, as well as their willingness to share doubts and problems. There are clearly limitations to the exploratory case study, although the propositions formulated in this chapter may be subjected to broader quantitative and qualitative analysis. However, it would be beneficial to consider further in-depth qualitative research of Project Portfolio Management practices in other countries, especially against the background of different institutional solutions in the area of financing projects from public funds, addressed to and executed by NGOs.

## REFERENCES

Anheier, H. K. (2006). *Nonprofit organizations. Theory, management, policy*. London: Routledge Taylor&Francis Group.

Archer, N., & Ghasemzadeh, F. (2007). Project portfolio selection and management. In P. Morris & J. Pinto (Eds.), *The Wiley Guide to Project, Program and Portfolio Management* (pp. 94–113). John Wiley and Sons. doi:10.1002/9780470172391.ch11

Bogacz-Wojtanowska, E., & Jałocha, B. (2016). The bright side of social economy sector's projectification: a study of successful social enterprises. *Project Management Research & Practice, 1*(1).

Brudney, J., & Murray, V. (1998). Do International Efforts to Improve Boards Really Work? The Views of Nonprofits. *Nonprofit Management & Leadership*, *8*(4), 333–348. doi:10.1002/nml.8403

Bryson, J. M. (1989). *Strategic Planning for Public and Nonprofit Organizations. A Guide to Strengthening and Sustaining Organizational Achievement*. San Francisco: Jossey- Bass Publishers.

Bryson, J. M., Ackermann, F., & Eden, C. (2007). Putting the Resource-Based View of Strategy and Distinctive Competencies to Work in Public Organizations. *Public Administration Review*, *67*(4), 702–717. doi:10.1111/j.1540-6210.2007.00754.x

Bryson, J. M., Gibbons, M. J., & Shaye, G. (2001). Enterprise Schemes for Nonprofit Survival, Growth, and Effectiveness. *Nonprofit Management & Leadership*, *11*(3), 271–288. doi:10.1002/nml.11303

Dai, C. X., & Wells, W. G. (2004). An exploration of project management office features and their relationship to project performance. *International Journal of Project Management*, *22*(7), 523–532. doi:10.1016/j.ijproman.2004.04.001

Desouza, K. C., & Evaristo, J. R. (2006). Project management offices: A case of knowledge-based archetypes. *International Journal of Information Management*, *26*(5), 414–423. doi:10.1016/j.ijinfomgt.2006.07.002

Eisenberg, P. (2000). The non-profit sector in a changing world. *Nonprofit and Voluntary Sector Quarterly*, *29*(2), 325–330. doi:10.1177/0899764000292007

Gareis, R. (2007). Management of the Project-oriented company. In P. Morris & J. Pinto (Eds.), *The Wiley Guide to Project, Program and Portfolio Management* (pp. 250–270). John Wiley and Sons. doi:10.1002/9780470172391.ch6

Golensky, M., & Mulder, C. A. (2006). Coping in a constrained economy: Survival strategies of nonprofit human service organizations. *Administration in Social Work*, *30*(3), 5–24. doi:10.1300/J147v30n03_02

Golini, R., Kalchschmidt, M., & Landoni, P. (2015). Adoption of project management practices : The impact on international development projects of non-governmental organizations. *International Journal of Project Management*, *33*(3), 650–663. doi:10.1016/j.ijproman.2014.09.006

Hafsi, T., & Thomas, H. (2005). Strategic Management and Change in High Dependency Environments: The Case of a Philanthropic Organization. Voluntas. *Voluntas*, *16*(4), 329–351. doi:10.1007/s11266-005-9146-y

Jafarizadeh, B., & Khorshid-Doust, R. R. (2008). A method of project selection based on capital asset pricing theories in a framework of mean–semideviation behaviour. *International Journal of Project Management*, *26*(6), 612–619. doi:10.1016/j.ijproman.2007.09.004

Jałocha, B. (2014). *Zarządzanie portfelem projektów. Koncepcje biznesowe a praktyka organizacji publicznych*. Kraków: WUJ.

Jonas, D. (2010). Empowering project portfolio managers: How management involvement impacts project portfolio management performance. *International Journal of Project Management*, *28*(8), 818–831. doi:10.1016/j.ijproman.2010.07.002

Jugdev, K. (2003). *Developing and sustaining Project management as a strategic basset: A multiple case study using the resource-based view*. University of Calgary.

Khang, D. B., & Moe, T. L. (2008). Success criteria and factors for international development projects: A life cycle based framework. *Project Management Journal*, *39*(1), 72–84. doi:10.1002/pmj.20034

Killen, C. P. (2008). *Project portfolio management for product innovation in service and manufacturing industries*. Retrieved September 10, 2011 from http://minerva.mq.edu.au:8080/vital/access/manager/Repository/mq:6279

Kloppenborg, T., & Opfer, W. (2002). The current state of project management research: Trends, interpretations and predictions. *Project Management Journal*, *33*(2), 5–18.

Kong, E. (2008). The development of strategic management in the non-profit context: Intellectual capital in social service non-profit organizations. *International Journal of Management Reviews*, *10*(3), 281–299. doi:10.1111/j.1468-2370.2007.00224.x

Lipsky, M., & Smith, S. R. (1989). Nonprofit Organizations, Government, and The Welfare State. *Political Science Quarterly*, *104*(4), 625–648. doi:10.2307/2151102

Mara, C. M. (2000). A Strategic Planning Process for a Small Nonprofit Organization: A Hospice Example. *Nonprofit Management & Leadership*, *11*(2), 211–223. doi:10.1002/nml.11206

Marcuello, C. (2001). *Approaching the Third Sector from a Management Perspective: What Does This Offer? The Third Sector from a European perspective*. University of Trento.

Meskendahl, S. (2010). The influence of business strategy on project portfolio management and its success – A conceptual framework. *International Journal of Project Management*, *28*(8), 807–817. doi:10.1016/j.ijproman.2010.06.007

Miller, K. D. (2002). Competitive strategies of religious organizations. *Strategic Management Journal*, *23*(5), 435–456. doi:10.1002/smj.234

Mulhare, E. M. (1999). Mindful of the Future: Strategic Planning Ideology and The Culture of Nonprofit Management. *Human Organization*, *58*(3), 323–330. doi:10.17730/humo.58.3.975v78735176943v

Powell, T. C. (2001). Competitive advantage: Logical and philosophical considerations. *Strategic Management Journal*, *22*(9), 875–888. doi:10.1002/smj.173

Project Management Institute. (2008). The Standard for Portfolio Management (2nd ed.). PMI.

Rad, P., & Levin, G. (2006). *Project portfolio management. Tools and techniques*. New York: IIL Publishing.

Reid, M. F., Brown, L., McNerney, D., & Perri, D. J. (2014). Time to raise the bar on nonprofit strategic planning and implementation. *Strategy and Leadership*, *42*(Iss: 3), 31–39. doi:10.1108/SL-03-2014-0019

Ridder, H. G., & McCandless, A. (2008). Influences on the Architecture of Human Resource Management in Nonprofit Organizations: An Analytical Framework. *Nonprofit and Voluntary Sector Quarterly*, *39*(1), 124–141. doi:10.1177/0899764008328182

Rymsza A. (2005). Partnerzy służby publicznej? Wyzwania współpracy sektora pozarządowego z administracją publiczną w świetle doświadczeń amerykańskich. *Kwartalnik Trzeci Sektor, 3*, 53-66.

Salamon, L. M. (2003). *The Resilient Sector: The State of Nonprofit America*. Washington, DC: Brookings Institution Press.

Salamon, L. M., & Anheier, H. K. (1999). *The emerging Sector Revisited. A Summary Revised Estimates*. CNP The Johns Hopkins Comparative Nonprofit Sector Project, Phase II.

Speckbacher, G. (2003). The economics of performance management in nonprofit organizations. *Nonprofit Management & Leadership*, *13*(3), 267–281. doi:10.1002/nml.15

Streb, Ch. (2010). Exploratory Case Study. In A. J. Mills, G. Durepos, & E. Wiebe (Eds.), *Encyclopaedia of Case Study Research*. SAGE.

Suchman, M. C. (1995). Managing Legitimacy: Strategic and Institutional Approaches. *Academy of Management Review*, *20*(3), 571–610.

Suchman, M. C. (1995). Managing Legitimacy: Strategic and Institutional Approaches. *Academy of Management Review*, *20*(3), 571–610.

Van der Pijl, K., & Sminia, H. (2004). Strategic management of public interest organizations. Voluntas. *Voluntas*, *15*(2), 137–155. doi:10.1023/B:VOLU.0000033178.54004.e9

Wilson, D. C. (1993). Organizational Structures in the Voluntary Sector: Theoretical Overview. In Issues in Voluntary and Non-profit Management (pp. 149-166). Addison-Wesley Publishing Company.

Yin, R. (1984). *Case study research*. Beverly Hills, CA: Sage Publications.

Zharp, Z., & Brock, D. (2012). Implementation Through Risk Mitigation: Strategic Processes in the Nonprofit Organization. *Administration & Society*, *44*(5), 571–594. doi:10.1177/0095399711418325

## KEY TERMS AND DEFINITIONS

**Diversification of Funding Sources:** The process of financial management in NGOs involving the intentional exploration and use of funds from various financing sources, i.e. private or public that influences and corresponds to the Project Portfolio Management process.

**Economic Analysis of Projects:** A kind of simplified financial analysis used in NGOs' projects. It is based in particular on the analysis of their own resources and simple risk analysis.

**Project Knowledge Management:** The process of capturing, developing, sharing, and using lessons learned and project knowledge in general for continuous improvement of the organization.

**Project Management:** The process of planning, executing, controlling, and closing the work to achieve specific goals in a specific time under predefined success criteria.

**Project Management Office:** A department within an organization that defines standards for project management, maintains them and support employees in project execution.

**Project Portfolio:** A collection of projects and/or programs financed and executed by a given organization.

**Project Portfolio Management:** A process of managing organizational projects and programs at different stages of their life cycle, which are analysed, prioritized, monitored and controlled in the course of a dynamic process.

# Chapter 7
# Business Applications of Big Data:
## Considerations for Not-for-Profits

**Javier Vidal-García**
*University of Valladolid, Spain*

**Marta Vidal**
*Complutense University of Madrid, Spain*

**Rafael Hernández Barros**
*Complutense University of Madrid, Spain*

## ABSTRACT

*Twenty-first century organizations face a challenge and an unprecedented opportunity: to build a new model of relationship with current and potential clients which is more efficient and innovative. And this necessarily implies to acquire a completely new corporate culture in which the collection, management and interpretation of information will inspire the entire business. Under this new business scenario, the data is not understood as part of a process but instead to be part of the core business as a decision tool. Only if companies can manage this flood of information will be able to understand what we do and where they are going; identify the tastes and preferences of consumers and, more importantly, anticipate their decisions to adapt the services in real time and in a personalized way. The Big Data points companies beyond the facts: transforms the actions into predictions.*

## INTRODUCTION

There is a trend in technological development that have created a new era in the understanding and decision-making, which is used to-develop new business and increase profitability using Big Data applications (See Vidal, Vidal-García & Hernandez Barros, 2016, p. 140).

The computational business intelligence and Big Data is applied to all that information that cannot be processed by traditional methods. A database is a collection of interrelated data. When speaking of

DOI: 10.4018/978-1-5225-2537-0.ch007

Copyright © 2017, IGI Global. Copying or distributing in print or electronic forms without written permission of IGI Global is prohibited.

relational database reference is made to the theory of relational data model of IBM researcher Edgar Codd in 1970 and has a strong mathematical basis. The relational model is characterized for providing that all the information should be contained in tables and the relationships between data must be represented an explicit reference in the same way. What is achieved with this model is always work on interrelated tables. Avoiding duplication of records and ensuring the referential integrity is to say if you delete a record, you delete all related records. The great disadvantage is the time required to handle large amounts of data, but this is achieved thanks to Big Data. On the other side, what is achieved when working with databases is to combine different types of data in a formalized manner.

The use of Big Data is used in all economic activities and generating new business opportunities for companies worldwide, this was inconceivable just a decade ago. Exploiting the potential of Big Data is an important challenge for companies as they have to adjust the way they make decisions about their business operations. Companies should leave the intuition when making decisions and learn to examine reliable information, creating structures and new roles that will transform organizations (Hartmann, Zaki & Feldmann, 2014).

The top performing companies are in a good position in the learning curve and technological development with regard to the development of analytical competence, although a lot of companies are still discovering the process and have to overcome different challenges to become technological competitive. The difficulties identified as the most important depend on the source of the information. Some of these studies indicate technical barriers associated with the use of software for managing Big Data

In this chapter we will explain the major challenges associated with the use of Big Data and computational business intelligence in business organizations and examine the case of Capital One, which has managed to implement a successful strategy based on Big Data. We will use this example to show the characteristics of a company that clearly favors the development of its analytical capacity, the ability of the company to use Big Data and computational business intelligence to improve performance. Finally, we will discuss how the development of analytical capacity is not restricted to few companies, but instead traditional companies and relatively small ones can incorporate Big Data analysis into their business operations, with benefits for their performance (Kruschwitz, 2001).

## BACKGROUND

The term Big Data refers to all those datasets whose size exceeds the ability to search, capture, storage, management, analysis, transfer, display or legal protection of conventional tools. Under that name it also includes infrastructure solutions and models needed to extract value from these groups of information in the most economical way, fast and flexible as possible for intelligent decision-making (Lazer, Kennedy, King & Vespignani, 2014).

The data sets included under this concept are characterized also by its variety in both origin and formats; the speed at which they occur; and the veracity or implied to their nature and mode of use.

In essence, the Big Data enables intelligent study and exploitation of millions of bytes of information on all kinds of events and activities-from atmospheric variations to daily patterns of consumption -, produced, disseminated or stored through mobile phones, social networks or, for example, machines connected to the Internet of Things (Mian, Rao, & Sufi, 2013). In 2012, and in around two-year period, it is estimated that humanity had generated by these means about 2.5 zetabytes information, ie, the ninety percent of all produced throughout his history.

This milestone is the result of adding all data from blog comments, emails, online books and articles, online consultations or financial transactions by electronic payment systems, among other sources (Vidal-García & Vidal, 2016, p. 220).

Today it is estimated that Internet is used -the main vehicle of this unprecedented revolution-about 3,000 million people and there are active more than 2,300 million mobile phone accounts. Other 2,000 million people dedicate to Facebook and QZone 20,000 million hours and generate from these services around 70,000 million comments a month. By 2020, in addition, experts predict that there will be some 30,000 million wireless devices, such as those employed by the Spanish firm Inditex to know the cycle of use and rotation of its products, releasing information network independent and steadily (Mayer-Schönberger & Cukier, 2014, p. 23).

Such figures explain why the Big Data in the last five years has gone from defining a concept to become a label used for virtually any intelligent data analysis,

## THE MAIN FOCUS OF THE CHAPTER

### Main Benefits of an Intelligent Data Management

The economic impact of Big Data is difficult to estimate, especially in a global environment, and in permanent technological revolution. Some firms have ventured that the investment that in coming years will go to its implementation and development in companies will exceed one hundred billion Euros and that this trend will be part of the main activities of nine out of ten companies from the selected circle of Fortune magazine.

It is also estimated that three out of five EU businesses already use some system to process the data generated by nearly 370 million users of the Internet Community. The great attraction of massive data is their potential to predict events, forecast behaviors, expectations and future needs of a particular group of consumers, make more effective and less costly the analysis processes and take smarter business decisions (Choi & Varian, 2012).

In general, the following are recognized benefits for Big Data:

#### Detecting Trends and Behavior

The Big Data allows us to find patterns behavior and consumer trends that with traditional methods and techniques are almost impossible to detect. This advantage, which supports the development of market segments and specific study is possible thanks to the collection and integration of data from multiple channels, including physical stores, call centers, mobile devices, trade mail or social media, among others (McGuire, Manyika & Chui, 2012).

The Federal Bureau of Investigation's United States, better known by its acronym, FBI, in 2011 carried out the largest operation of its history against fraud by analysis Big Data. Following his example, it is estimated that the UK Treasury could save taxpayers of the country between 20,000 and 41,000 million Euros (See Hoffmann & Birnbrich, 2012).

## Customer Knowledge and Product Development

It can be used as a tool to discover and measure the influence of customers and non-customers on each channel; how they impact on their networks contacts, friends and followers; analyze links between influencers and their networks and variations of their messages and those of its competitors. Wal-Mart and Coca-Cola, in fact, study the information in real time (for example, through the vending machines) for "experimental" product developments at any scale and know its impact (Barney, 1991).

United Nations, together with the World Food Programme and the Ministry of Planning Development of Indonesia, launched in 2012 and 2013 a pilot project to design a system of indicator to identify the variation in supply and demand in the Asian country and adopt the necessary policies at all times and in each place to ensure adequate food supply to the population. To do this, through the initiative International Global Pulse, collected millions of open conversations in Twitter about the price of meat (beef and chicken), the onion and chili, and developed a model based on the daily correlation between patterns posted on the platform and variation prices of those foods (Cavallo, 2012).

The interesting thing about this tool is that not only allows a better understanding of domestic market but also equip s the country with an alert system against unexpected fluctuations of prices.

## Predictive Analysis

Big Data can help organizations to anticipate market behavior and customers and respond in a proactive way. To this end, the objectives are identified and appropriate methodology is applied to respond to questions such as "what would happen if…" (Edelman, 2015).

The platform about film and television on demand Netflix, invested 100 million dollars in the consecutive production for HBO, the two first seasons of the series House of Cards. The success of his bet was guaranteed: the daily knowledge of the interests and preferences of his thirty million users around the world.

## Agility in Decision-Making

Big Data can activate instantly, from certain responses, actions that otherwise would require complex controls and relatively long time. To do this, it relies on visual models which are easy to understand and close to what is happening: heat maps, scatter diagrams, visualizations 3D, word clouds, etc (See Purcell, 2013; and Vidal-García, Vidal & Hernandez Barros, 2017).

RocketFuel, a company founded by scientists from NASA and experts from Yahoo, DoubleClick or Sales Force has real time platform that learns in real-time from results that obtains from advertising campaigns and modifies automatically, based on the results, the audience that wants to reach. It can evaluate up to 28,000 million impressions per day and predict when and where a person will respond to an advert. As a result, putting together Big Data and artificial intelligence, it has increased the profitability of shares of their customers up to 229%.

## Process Optimization

The emergency customer service of Telefónica uses predictive models for determine the number of calls that will receive receive in very specific dates and thereby improve their troubleshooter levels up

50%. The McKinsey Global Institute estimates that the exploitation of massive data has a potential of generating 240,000 million Euros for the US Health and a value of 200,000 million Euros for European public administration.

## Attraction and Customer Loyalty

Thanks to the capture and management of massive data it is possible to quickly adapt and convert information into knowledge, using techniques of data mining, machine learning, or natural language processing. This, in turn, is a valuable mechanism to meet, attract and retain customers. To do this, Big Data gives marketing departments the opportunity to segment their audiences as their actions and preferences over time; analyze the propensity to buy other products or services; determine the best time to offer cross-selling and up-selling and know more accurately the impact of their campaigns (McAfee, Brynjolfsson, Davenport, Patil & Barton, 2012).

Procter & Gamble, for example, is able to integrate into a single tool –designed from a dozen technologies- how consumers from 80 different countries use about 4,000 million of its products on a daily basis. Financial Times uses the analysis of mass data to optimize rates from its according to the immediate demand from their subscribers.

We can say that the revolution of Big Data, driven both from the public sector as from the private, it is producing transformation and evolution in the economy, the business community and even the society in general. There are numerous and interesting success stories referenced in fields such as education, health, culture, safety, research, tourism or advertising. However, there is also a long way to go in the exploitation of the information.

We describe some examples of the use of Big Data in different sectors:

## Financial

Traditional banking has a vast amounts of customer information on accounts, products and contracted services, credit card transactions, ATM operations office management operations, online banking, means of payment used, etc, whose analysis enables to recommend and customize business deals according to specific needs and client capabilities, improve cross-selling of financial products or know the causes of customer dissatisfaction and identify those who are more likely to reduce prices (Jiménez, Ongena, Peydro & Saurina, 2014). Also new patterns behaviors are identified and detected that enable better risk management and optimization in credit operations or fraud detection and prevention in the means of payment (Barker, D'Amato & Sheridon, 2008).

PayPal, the system allows its users make payments and transfers through Internet without sharing financial information with the recipient, predicts, identifies and prevents fraudulent activities in real time. It establishes patterns of activity from transactions, currency, origin, point of sale, purchased products, IP address, information browser and other technical data. The figures speak for themselves: in 20115 the official data reposts around 157 million active accounts, a presence in 203 countries, 26 currencies, an average of 9.7 million transactions per day and a very low index fraud, only 0.33%.

## Transport

From the data generated from logistics operators, the traffic, the type of merchandise, weather conditions or the destination, it is possible to optimize the distribution routes for goods and services to increase productivity, save costs and anticipate demand in the field of transport.

Reduce traffic congestion and decrease consequently air pollution is also possible. In a city like Los Angeles, since 2012, it has been possible reduce by 10% this congestion by shortening the time that drivers spend looking for a place to park. Sensors have been installed in parking spaces to provide real-time information to drivers on free spaces, it can be consulted on the website of the city in a mobile application and the plan is to incorporate the data to the navigation systems for vehicles that can point automatically drivers to free parking which is closer to their destinations. In this sense, the system management of parking slots, LA Express Park, has the ability to change parking rates decreasing them in those places that help to redirect traffic to less congested areas.

## Health

The health sector suffers constant pressure to reduce costs, ensure patient safety and quality service. There are various studies estimating at hundreds of millions the savings of the public health system thanks to Big Data through the integration of various data sources and analysis for reducing administrative inefficiencies, detection of fraud and abuse, improving care coordination with citizens, optimizing medical processes or the proper material distribution of health and medicine, among others.

In the field of clinical research it is possible to obtain correlations and information to determine which treatments are the most effective under certain conditions or with certain symptoms; identify related patterns with adverse drug effects; determine the causes of some diseases. Initiatives such as the Medroom project, a platform that analyzes, summarizes and presents easily contained medical information in all electronics clinical records, for its use in clinical practice, it has been the winner of the project Call to Innovation 2014 that is granted by the Singularity University.

Similarly, wereables devices and mobile apps, are now a technological revolution in the healthcare area. They allow carrying out the remote patient monitoring and populations affected by disease but provide real-time information about biological data, diet, physical activity or sleeping guidelines. All this information makes available other relevant factors that help patients and doctors detect early disease, to establish custom treatments or perform more effective or monitor and evaluate the progress of these treatments.

## Sport

In Formula 1, the variables measured are countless (elements of the car, engine consumption, tire condition, gearbox activity, pilot biorhythms, circuit conditions, and atmospheric conditions) and are subjected to detailed analysis during and after the race to tune the cars and drivers, determine where they can improve times or avoid the problems that can arise.

The German football team, winner of Brazil World Cup in 2014, used the program SAP Big Data to improve the sport performance of their players during the training period. The players train with sensors whose data are transmitted from an antenna to the analysis system that provides information to coaches and players on performance, ball possession, passing, shots on goal, speeds. Thus, they were able to reduce the average possession of the ball for each player an average of 3.4 seconds to 1.1 increasing the speed of passes. The system also allows analyzing the performance of rival team from the positional records of the players using data obtained from images of the games.

The technology is applicable to the design of the training and competition strategy more convenient to operate at maximum performance, detect possible injury, monitoring of athletes outside sport environment (nutrition, sleep, emotionally), control elements (shoes, balls, golf clubs, t-shirts), and it also serves to clubs or sports federations to manage the services they offer to customers, selling entrance tickets, or providing merchandising or unique experiences to their supporters.

### Energy

The demand for electricity, gas or water in a particular time and the establishment of mechanisms that fit consumption based on this time represents one of the great energy savings and a more sustainable and environmentally friendly growth. This demand is also deeply affected by the weather, so that the analysis of meteorological information, the phases of the tides, satellite images, deforestation maps or historical records of temperature and other data are fundamental for forecasting supply and the performance of renewable energy systems such as wind or solar.

In order to change the behavior of energy consumers, companies like Opower, allow customers to compare their electricity consumption with its neighbors as a measure to encourage reduction of consumption. If thanks to this initiative the creation of a power plant is avoided or the improvement of the network, this will result in savings for the company and its customers.

Another major generator of information in the energy sector are the smart meters. They are meters capable of transmitting data consumption and receive remote information from pricing, connection instructions or disconnection, alarms and indicators of whether there is a waste, change the type of consumption to prepaid mode. Thus, consumers benefit from better information and more accessible and companies eliminate the requirement to reading the meter manually, ensure accuracy in the invoices and generate and distribute energy in a more profitable way (Osterwalder & Pigneur, 2010, p.15).

## Big Data in Health Organizations

Patients, managers, service providers and, of course doctors, surgeons, nurses, etc., could benefit from the advantages and efficiency that imply to gain insights from the data. This is where several experts in the field speak of the future Medicine 5P, the crossing between health and Big Data (Feldman, Martin & Skotnes, 2012):

### Customize

The eternal dream of medicine. To give a unique and specific diagnosis of each patient needs treatment. With Big Data, the huge amount of data, and context that describes each of the patients, this is possible. Only a matter of “code” in data which has not been done in a matter of clinical issues such as mood, emotions, pain expression, etc.

## Predictive

It would be transitioning from a reactive model of health to a much more efficient active and predictive model where the health system and their staff, would warn the patient directly of potentially dangerous situations. The statistics to the service of our health.

## Preventive

It would be to prevent the onset of disease, based on a set of medical procedures and analysis of patterns and historical data. We know that is always better to prevent that to cure later on that in medicine makes more sense than any other area of life.

## Participative

The importance that all the agents we have discussed above are well coordinated. Working with patients not only has an impact on the therapeutic aspects, but also in the management and processes, so that does not escape any details, in European countries where there is n important fragmentation of the health organization into different systems would be a relevant advantage.

## Population

For the entire population. The possibility of making more efficient the system could bring with the same resources, could serve a larger population size. In short, do not leave anyone unattended.

This fit would be simple either. Much of the health knowledge is expressed in unstructured sources. That is, without any structuring data matrices. Technologies to process this knowledge are much more complicated and costly than structured data processing.

On the other hand, a lot of medical treatments work in a given context, but not in others. This makes coding data in this context an important element. And in turn, generates more complexity the generation and data management, such as processing. Moreover, the complexity of the data (from the genomic, through biomarkers, as well as social aspects) is important and the organization is vital to get the value from the data.

As often happens with Big Data, this is not without risk. Collecting performance data of patients with sensors, it generates data. And where they are? And who owns this data? These are issues that, as often happens, the law still does not provide an answer. Social and communication aspects are critical in this point. We must not forget aspects of privacy. And finally, the "profiling" of user and the possibilities of decision making outside ethics that brings decisions. will a customer be attended that according to the data is at high risk? would not be covered with an insurance policy a person with a high probability to die? These may seem obvious issues, but it is not so easy to find a solution.

Many sectors bring opportunities and challenges with Big Data. The health field is not different in this sense. Big Data and health go hand in hand for a better society and well-being of all. Scientific institutions also notice it. It is important to start changing this situation in colleges and universities. First we must get people to want to acquire an engineering culture. We are looking at the forge of a future explosion in public opinion that will redefine the boundaries of what can be done with the personal information of the digital consumer.

In the next decade, the progress of new technologies based on the analytical, safety or the cloud model will have a major impact on the internal processes of healthcare organizations. Like other sectors faced with the challenges of adapting to the new changes brought about by the digital explosion, the health care system will follow the same route.

The main trends that will transform activities in hospitals and other health institutions refer to those responsible for the need to place investments in technology among its priorities to support the process of technological integration. Overall, the research companies find that Big Data plays a crucial role in the internal organization of the health system. The costs do not stop growing, which will directly influence the quality of hospital operations. By the end of 2016, it is estimated that the solution to the operational inefficiency will force health organizations to invest a portion of their budgets on a digital strategy based on the data.

Among the main costs, those related to the management of patients with chronic diseases will create a greater demand for intelligent systems of macro data and analytical capacity to support management initiatives. Consequently, 70% of global health institutions will invest in mobile applications, and remote monitoring systems (Feldman, Martin & Skotnes, 2012).

## Big Data Types

There are basically three types of data in big data:

1. Structured data,
2. Unstructured data,
3. Semi-structured data.

### Structured Data

Structured data is data that have well-defined length and format. This data is usually numbers, strings of characters and are stored in tables. In companies, this data is found in information obtained from CRM and ERP. This data are usually stored in a Data Warehouse and if contain a lot of information and if the company does not generate so much data will have a relational database. Access to this data is made using SQL queries. Most cases for business intelligence and business analytics work with this type of data (Chen, Chiang, & Storey, 2012).

Where we get structured data:

1. Data generated by machines.
   a. **Data From Sensors:** There are many examples like from a GPS, electricity meters, tachometers, medical equipment, etc....
   b. **Web Log Data:** Servers, networks, applications, etc.. generate large amounts of structured data.
   c. **Data From Selling Points:** A good example would be a hypermarket with a cashier passing products by a bar code reader.
   d. **Financial Data:** Many banking and trading operations are automatically generated from structured data.
2. Data generated by people.

   a. Structured data generated by people are also varied and go from the records of an accounting ERP through the fact to fill in a form on a website or even our movements in one of those online games that we are now in Facebook.
   b. Structured data is the cornerstone of relational databases. In relational models, all information is stored in a table scheme and the tables have defined some fields and relations between them.

## Unstructured Data

Unstructured data are the opposite to structured data, they lack a specific format. These are generated by:

1. Data generated by machines and computers.
   a. Satellite images.
   b. **Scientific Data:** seismic graphs, weather, etc...
   c. Photography and video surveillance cameras.
   d. Data collected from sonar and radar (Smartphone positioning...)
2. Data generated by people, data introduced by people on a computer.
   a. Texts included within the internal information systems of organizations: documents, presentations, emails, etc...
   b. **Data From Social Networks:** Twitter, Facebook, LinkedIn, Flickr, Instragram, Tuenti. The number of social networks is growing every day; it is becoming more common to see different social networks that refer to different groups.
   c. **Data From our Mobile Devices:** Think of the messages we send with our mobile phones.
   d. **Content Websites:** From YouTube videos to website content or blogs.

Around 80% of company data is unstructured, and thanks to big data these can now be examined and obtain useful information for organizations. However it should be emphasized that the big data is not only focuses on unstructured data, but it uses all them, both structured and unstructured, as well as semi-structured.

## The Semi-Structured Data

Semi-structured data is a mixture of structured and unstructured, this data follow a kind of implicit structure but not as regular as to be managed and automated as structured information. Examples of these are the websites. This data have the peculiarity that maintaining a small structure it is possible to get useful information. The format is evolving into a generally accepted protocol or formula, with a number of defining characteristics. We could say that these semi-structured data have their own "semi-structured metadata", describing the objects from the text and the relationships that can be inferred. Examples of these data are the notes of death, applications for employment, real estate listings, legal notices or bank account names.

## Big Data Model Implementation

IBM and the Saïd Business School, University of Oxford, created a report on the use of Big Data in the real world, and they have identified four main phases in the process of adoption of Big Data, with the activities which are characteristic of each one of them.

### Educate

The education phase focuses on awareness and knowledge development. Most companies at this stage are studying the potential benefits of technology and Big Data analytics and trying to understand how this can help them address significant business opportunities in their own sectors or markets.

The main activities carried out are:

- Expand knowledge focusing on those use cases where the Big Data provides a competitive advantage to the company, both inside and outside their sector.
- Work with business units to identify opportunities and most critical business challenges that can be addressed with a better and timely access to information.
- Focus on strengthening the environment and infrastructure information management, including the development of a Big Data project.

### Exploration

In this phase, the focus is on developing the roadmap of the company for the development of Big Data for a quantifiable business case. Data, technology and existing skills are taken into account, and then it is set where to start and how to develop a plan in line with the business strategy of the company.

The activities that will to turn plans into action are:

- Ensure that there is active support from a leader within the company as the strategy and Big Data roadmap develops.
- Develop the business case of one or two key business opportunities or challenges that can be addressed through pilot projects or proof of concept.
- Planning the longer-term requirements, verifying that the basis of information management and IT infrastructure are able to support the technologies and capabilities necessary for Big Data POC or pilot project.
- Evaluate current governance processes and providing information to address new aspects of Big Data.
- Analyze the skills of internal resources and put in place mechanisms to develop in those areas where deficiencies are detected, or hire external resources.

## Interact

In the interaction stage companies begin to see the business benefits of Big Data, as well as to carry out an assessment of their technologies and skills. Companies work within a defined and limited field to understand and test the technologies and skills needed to exploit new sources of data..

The activities carried out are:

- Actively promote the success of the pilot projects to maintain momentum within the company.
- Fleshing out the business case with validation and quantification of ROI and the expected
- benefits, including the criteria and parameters of defined success.
- Identify the changes and improvements that could be made in the process of business with better and more timely information (eg, marketing, sales, customer service and social networks).
- Develop a plan to confirm the availability of appropriate and necessary technical skills to achieve goals both short and long term.
- Documenting the detailed project plan to migrate pilot projects to production. This plan should include confirmation of the business valuation, costs, resources and expected project schedules (Varian, 2014).

## Execution

In the implementation phase, the level of operation and implementation of analytic functions and Big Data is greater within the company.

The activities carried out are:

- Documenting the measurable results of the first successes to reinforce future initiatives.
- Implement formal communications about Big Data across the company to continue to increase the support and momentum.
- Focus on expanding the technologies and skills necessary to tackle new Big Data challenges in all business units, functions and geographic locations.
- Stay alert on government information, privacy and security (Heffetz & Ligett, 2014)
- Continue to evaluate the tools and Big Data technologies of rapid development.

## Capital One: Learning From a Successful Case

Not only by their initial success, but because its models has served as format for countless banks and credit institutions; Capital One is a case that allows us to understand, in depth, which changes should be made in an organization to develop their analytical skills.

Originally under the name of Signet, Capital One worked as a traditional regional bank based in Richmond, Virginia. Its credit decisions were based on very careful consideration that allowed the bank to offer one of the lowest rates in the market but at the same time limiting its growth. At the beginning of the decade of the 90s, under the direction of two new directors in the company, bank managers began implementing a new method for making credit decisions. The method was based on analytical models constructed with data that included not only the demographic customer information, as was the industry standard at the time, but also information about their transactions. The fundamental assumption of new managers was that crossing the two types of information it was possible to create models of consumer behavior (risk, preferences, etc.) that would allow make credit decisions with higher levels of confidence, customize credit cards features and cross-sell other services. Although this idea is not extraordinary today, at that time most banks, with the aim of reducing costs, used to recycle computer tapes in which old customer transactions were recorded, completely losing any possibility to gain perspective of customer behavior over time. The results of this innovation were surprising. The credit card division of Signet separated from the matrix becoming Capital One in 1994 and went from being the subsidiary of a small regional bank to the seventh largest credit card company in the country. Since its IPO in 1994 and until 2000, the value of the share capital increased by more than 1000%, while the S&P 500 index did by about 300%. The average annual growth rate of the company, 46%, was the largest in the industry (excluding growth as a result of mergers and acquisitions).

Analytical models served as a base, but it was the design of the Capital One organization which ensured the successful implementation of this business idea. One of the key design features of the organization of Capital One was the integration of new analytical of its call center models and the Internet operations to the sales and customer operations with Big Data, in other words, what we can define as analytical effectiveness. Call center operators were able to provide customers personalized answers based on analytical models generated by customer responses, they knew what to offer to achieve cross-selling or when was the best time to meet customer requirements. Another important feature of the organization of Capital One was the creation of a business development process to routinely analyze demographic data and customer transactions to create new analytical models and identify business opportunities, that is, analytical intelligence.

Business analysts took advantage of the ideas generated from the customer data and created prototypes of new financial services that were tested in pilot studies applied to small samples of customers. The continuous nature of this innovation activity based on data required close collaboration between the area responsible for information technology and call center, especially since every year a lot of tests that included more than 40,000 customers were made.

Analytical intelligence was instrumental to decide when it should stop offering a product so that the portfolio of Capital One maintained their levels of complexity and constant effectiveness over time. The tests that were successful were transferred at a later stage to general analytical models to make them available to all bank customers.

Three factors, analytical infrastructure, analytical culture and the structure of analytics government did enable Capital One to develop and maintain its effectiveness and analytics.

The analytical infrastructure was to have an IT department able to handle the world´s largest database from Oracle, with about 23 terabytes of data, or what is the same, forty information pages, single spaced, for each one of the citizens of the United States each year (Philip, 1997). This database won the award for technological excellence of the Gartner Group, granted to only one company in the USA per year (Gordon & Wilson, 1999).

The analytical infrastructure Capital One was flexible, in the sense that it was able to quickly accommodate new analytical models, as they were available. Likewise, it was scalable, meaning that it had the ability to grow rapidly when new analytical models made possible the launch of successful products. The success of the business model of Capital One would not have been possible without the establishment of an analytical culture.

This analytical culture rejected the decision based on subjective judgments and fostered the perception that credit decisions should be made based on actuarial scientific criteria and experimental evidence. The logic of making decisions based on facts was showed mainly hiring business analysts, potential employees were subject to standardized psychological tests whose results were compared with employees who were successful in the company. In addition, candidates for positions of business analyst must pass the filter of senior executives.

Finally, the design of the organization of Capital One was characterized by analytical government structure overseeing all aspects of Big Data strategy. When Capital One separated from Signet, the creators of the strategy of Big Data took command of the organization: Richard Fairbank became the president of the executive board and CEO, while Nigel Morris was named president and COO of the company. The presence of a "patron" of Big Data at the highest level of the organization ensures that the company devotes its efforts to achieve four key objectives of government, namely (i) ensure good long-term decisions are taken and that investment in analytical tools and models generate business value, (ii) protect and manage data. Also providing the information derived from the data and the products generated based on analytical tools safely, ethically and in accordance with established trends (iii) ensure allocation of responsibilities, transparency and traceability of managers in charge of finance, develop and make use of the resources associated with the analytical organization and (iv) provide an organizational structure that will ensure that resources are available to those in need in their role of development and use of analytical tools; and that data, information derived from the use of analytical and products

*Figure 1. Overview of the Big Data and Computational Intelligence Model for Capital One*

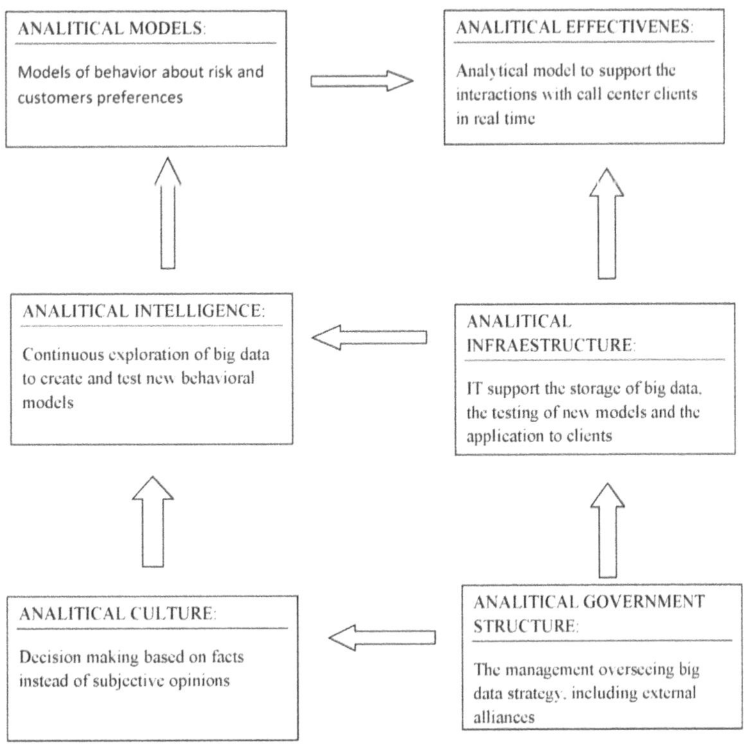

generated based on these tools evolve based on continuous learning and dissemination of best practices in the organization and between it and other entities that would make part of the ecosystem of Big Data (Grossman & Siegel, 2014).

## Companies Using Big Data and Computational Business Intelligence

### Yelp

Yelp is an urban and electronic guide that helps people find the best places to eat, shop, drink, relax and have fun. It is based on the opinions OF a vibrant and active community of local residents. Yelp is a fun and easy way to find, watch and talk about great (and not so interesting) things in the world. It was founded in 2004 but 6 years later it became an international phenomenon. In November 2010, it had over 39 million visitors and over 14 million reviews.

Yelp used Big Data technology and computational business intelligence to revise all reviews or messages left by users. By doing this, it performs automated filter review to identify suspicious content and minimize exposure to the consumer. In addition to using Big Data technology, it stores information about consumers to then be able to offer a personalized catalog of sites of special offers, events, like Amazon with its virtual store. The company manages all created free accounts and uploaded photos. It also add all the information collected by mobile applications like Smartphones and tablets.

The technology used is owned by Amazon:

- **Amazon Elastic MapReduce:** To obtain information of interest for users.
- **Amazon Storage Service (Amazon S3):** To store the photos and records of daily users.

### Shazam

Shazam is an application designed for mobile devices like Smartphone and tablets. Its function is to allow instantly know the song title, author and album of the song being played, and being able in only a few seconds to hear the song with the device. It has a database of over 60 million songs, more than 200 million registered users. It is available in 33 different languages in 200 countries in which it operates.

Shazam uses Big Data technology from Amazon:

- **Amazon Web Services:** Shazam gets a complete set of infrastructure services and applications that allows to run everything from the cloud.
- **Amazon DynamoDB:** With this service Shazam gets a NoSQL fast and fully managed data that allows to store and retrieve easily any amount of data.
- **Amazon Elastic Compute Cloud (Amazon EC2):** Web service that provides resizable compute capacity in the cloud, so that in the great events in which many users use Shazam they can attened properly.

With this technology Shazam has managed to be in the ranking of the 10 most downloaded applications of all portable operating systems (Android, IOS, Windows Phone, Blackberry,...).

## Etsy

It is an online marketplace that specializes in handmade items, antiques and craft materials. In Etsy anyone can upload his own shop and it offer products by category. It was founded in 2005 and in 2012 had with over 800,000 stores, more than 1.4 billion monthly visits and over 18 million products for sale.

Etsy also uses Big Data technology belonging to Amazon:

- **Amazon EC2:** Web service that provides resizable compute capacity in the cloud, for the great peaks of simultaneous users.
- **Amazon Web Services:** Where it hosts Adtuitve, a company that acquired as ad server. With this got to target retail announcements at a rate of 100 million visits per month.
- **Amazon S3:** Information storage.
- **Amazon Elastic MapReduce:** AEM is able to run dozens of algorithms on hundreds of machines to obtain recommendations of interest to users.

## Telefónica

Telefónica is a Spanish multinational company operating telecommunications services (fixed telephony, mobile telephony, ADSL, FTTH, etc.) with headquarters in Madrid.

What Telefónica gets thanks to Big Data and computational business intelligence:

- Mobile consumption by region, through which it is possible to obtain a socioeconomic status of a country. This it could be done through surveys few years ago, and today it is a reality thanks to Big Data.
- End-to-end Big Data solution that includes a phase of identifying internal and external sources, an audit to erroneous processes of data and various model predictions depending on the target customers.
- Risk assessment for predicting defaults.
- Prediction studies about best prices.
- Studies identifying ways to advertise products
- Studies about locations for opening new stores.
- Improved response time and reduced costs.

The technology used Big Data by Telefónica is:

- **Instant Servers:** It is similar to Amazon EC2 as discussed above, but with more limited functionality. However, this technology is also sold by Telefonica like Amazon does with its Amazon EC2. The advantage regarding EC2 servers is its simplicity when managing private networks while EC2 is more complex. Another advantage is cost, Instant Servers are cheaper. However, EC2 has more features.

## Paypal

It is an eBay company which has implemented a quick and secure way to pay online without the need to share financial information from credit accounts with vendors. It operates in 195 countries with 25 different currencies and more than 128 million active accounts.

PayPal like other companies like Amazon or Google thanks to the Big Data technology and computational business intelligence have developed patterns of fraudulent activity. PayPal has a number of filters for Fraud Management. This is achieved by collecting data from fraudulent sites such as financial data, IP addresses, browser information, different types of information with which they can identify and prevent fraudulent transactions. PayPal is the most reliable internet payment and trusted by more users worldwide.

## eBay

It is a web portal for buying and selling on the Internet: a place where buyers and sellers meet to exchange almost anything. EBay in 2012 had more than 100 million active users according to official reports.

EBay obtains the following benefits thanks to Big Data technology and computational business intelligence

- Intelligent searches and ads.
- Smart Catalog.
- Finding patterns of fraudulent sellers.
- Storing user accounts, ads, and photos.
- Find items faster.

EBay engineers report that using Hadoop they are able to access more than 300 million business ads, additionally they get lots of historical information allowing them to understand all customers.

In 2015 Ebay had a turnover of 86 billion euros, this level of transactions would not be possible without the Big Data technology.

## Facebook

Facebook is a social network that grows every day and has more than 100 peta bytes. Much of the income of Facebook is through advertising. Thanks to Big Data computational intelligence Facebook manages all advertising intelligently directing to users that require it. Another clear example of the use of Big Data is the smart labeling that detects the faces of users. But the clearest example is the management of databases of Facebook which stores photos, profiles, conversations, and users in more than 50000 servers.

It also collects information from the mobile devices and browsers, the users can imagine the vast amount of data that Facebook has to handle.

Hadoop is used to store copies of internal register and dimensional data sources and it is used as a source for reporting / analysis and learning.

The company has 2 big groups:

1. A group of 1100 machines with 8,800 cores and 12 PB of storage.
2. A group of 300 machines with 2,400 cores and about 3 PB of storage.

Each node has 8 cores and 12 TB of storage.

## Spotify

Spotify is currently the most known music platform. Spotify offers multiple services but the main one is to offer music in "streming" via internet, for it has a database with more than 10,000 songs. However music is not offering its unique service, like LastFM it provides musical recommendations, it offers interactive radios, the chance to connect with different users to see the music they listen or even to connect to various social networks. And we must not forget that Spotify is not a free service and has to implement secure payment forms like EBay and PayPal.

Data collected by Spotify in Hadoop includes:

- 200 GB of compressed data of users per day.
- 100GB of data services per day.
- 60GB of data generated by Hadoop per day.
- 190 nodes per cluster of 4 PB storage capacity.

## Twitter

Twitter is a microblogging web application that combines the advantages of blogging, social networking and instant messaging so users can stay in touch in real time with people of interest with messages of no more than 140 characters. Currently Twitter has stored about 12 terabytes of Tweets created daily, so as to manage this huge number needs of Big Data technology. For its purposes it uses:

- **Web and Social Media:** It is a type of Big Data content collected on social networks.
- **Cassandra:** It is a non-relational distributed database. It allows handling large volumes of data.
- **Hive:** It is a Data Warehouse infrastructure that facilitates managing large volumes of data.

# CONCLUSION

The importance of Big Data lies in that it impacts both in industry and in the society in general and offers a considerable competitive advantage. The amount of data currently generated is enormous and extremely complex for analysis. Companies increasingly require that the analysis is as close as possible to real time. And Big Data is the key, as involve the variables of speed, variety and volume required by companies in today business competitive market.

Big Data is created from the need to respond to a range of current market needs, requirements that progress have driven and that can only be satisfied by technological means. Nowadays, customers want to be treated in a completely personalized manner. That is why, companies should be able to detect their preferences, it has become a first class necessity to increase the sales volume, directing sales in a much more direct way to achieve the expected success.

*Table 1. Overview of companies using big data and computational business intelligence models*

| COMPANY | BUSINESS | TECHNOLOGY USED |
|---|---|---|
| YELP | Urban and electronic guide | -Amazon Elastic MapReduce.<br>-Amazon Storage Service. |
| SHAZAM | Application to hear songs with Smartphone. | -Amazon Web Services.<br>-AmazonDynamoDB.<br>-Amazon Elastic Compute Cloud (Amazon EC2). |
| ETSY | Online marketplace | -Amazon EC2.<br>-Amazon Web Services<br>-Amazon S3<br>-Amazon Elastic MapReduce. |
| TELEFÓNICA | Telecommunications company | - Instant Servers. |
| PAYPAL | Online payment website | - Hadoop.<br>-Spark. |
| EBAY | Online selling platform | - Hadoop. |
| FACEBOOK | Online social network | - Hadoop. |
| SPOTIFY | Music platform | - Hadoop. |
| TWITTER | Microblogging web application | -Web and Social Media.<br>-Cassandra.<br>-Hive. |

In addition, it worth keeping in mind that each individual relates to others, whose analysis allows both learn more about the client, as well as increase the number of potential customers. These data are transformed into a knowledge base of incalculable value for the business.

The exploitation of data enables a greater understanding of the business, and also provides the ability to rethink the services offered. In fact, Big Data represents an opportunity for the IT department to influence the business in a really significant manner. The CIO must lead the adoption of a set of technologies -such as Big Data, Analytics or language technologies- and best practices to extract value from the data, for which will be necessary to redefine new features and make an organizational redesign. In particular Big Data requires a new role that is the data scientific. The lack of talent is one of the obstacles of the organizations that will have to rely in third-party services.

A large majority of companies think that Big Data will transform business operations as Internet did in the past. Most companies also feel that Big Data will dramatically change the way they are doing business. Companies agree that organizations that do not use big data will lose their competitive position and might even disappear.

The first companies that use Big Data perceive that it implies a competitive advantage and are advancing quickly to revolutionize their own operations related to data, rather than let competitors overtake them. Perceptions about the disruptive power of Big Data are not limited to technology organization; companies perceive that a new competitive weapon can be used by across industries and companies, from sectors such as financial services and insurance, to postal services and governments (See Nickerson & Rogers, 2014).

Companies are moving quickly to take advantage of new technologies that investigate and consume increasingly diverse data from an even greater number of sources and, producing results faster and with greater impact than imagined. Companies are structuring projects and expecting results in weeks or months instead of lose years in the design stage. The result is an exponentially more complex and interesting environment: the data gathering and analysis are always operating; large volumes of data are obtained continuously, which must be consumed and analyzed with great speed; more data means being able to make decisions quicker when companies perceive the right signals.

## REFERENCES

Barker, K. J., DAmato, J., & Sheridon, P. (2008). Credit card fraud: Awareness and prevention. *Journal of Financial Crime*, *15*(4), 398–410. doi:10.1108/13590790810907236

Barney, J. (1991). Firm resources and sustained competitive advantage. *Journal of Management*, *17*(1), 99–120. doi:10.1177/014920639101700108

Cavallo, A. (2012). Online and official price indexes: Measuring Argentinas inflation. *Journal of Monetary Economics*, *60*(2), 152–165. doi:10.1016/j.jmoneco.2012.10.002

Chen, H., Chiang, R. H., & Storey, V. C. (2012). Business intelligence and analytics: From Big Data to big impact. *Management Information Systems Quarterly*, *36*, 1165–1188.

Choi, H., & Varian, H. (2012). Predicting the present with Google Trends. *Economic Inquiry*, *88*, 2–9.

Edelman, B. (2015, April). How to launch your digital platform. *Harvard Business Review*.

Grossman, R. L., & Siegel, K. (2014). Organizational models for Big Data and analytics. *Journal of Organization Design*, *3*(1), 20–25. doi:10.7146/jod.9799

Hartmann, P. M., Zaki, M., & Feldmann, N. (2014). *Big Data for Big Business? A Taxonomy of Data-driven Business Models used by Start-up Firms.* University of Cambridge Working Paper.

Heffetz, O., & Ligett, K. (2014). Privacy and data-based research. *The Journal of Economic Perspectives*, *28*(2), 75–98. doi:10.1257/jep.28.2.75

Hoffmann, A., & Birnbrich, C. (2012). The impact of fraud prevention on bank-customer relationships. *International Journal of Bank Marketing*, *30*(5), 390–407. doi:10.1108/02652321211247435

Jiménez, G. S., Ongena, S., Peydro, J. L., & Saurina, J. (2014). Hazardous times for monetary policy: What do 23 million loans say about the impact of monetary policy on credit risk-taking. *Econometrica*, *82*, 463–505. doi:10.3982/ECTA10104

Kruschwitz, N. (2011). First look: The second annual new intelligent enterprise survey. *MIT Sloan Management Review*, *52*, 87–89.

Lazer, D., Kennedy, R., King, G., & Vespignani, A. (2014). The parable of Google flu: Traps in Big Data analysis. *Science*, *343*(6176), 1203–1205. doi:10.1126/science.1248506 PMID:24626916

Mayer-Schonberger, V., & Cukier, K. (2014). *Big data: A revolution that will transform how we live, work, and think*. Boston, MA: Houghton Mifflin Harcourt Print.

McAfee, A., Brynjolfsson, E., Davenport, T. H., Patil, D., & Barton, D. (2012). Big Data. The management revolution. *Harvard Business Review*, *90*, 61–67. PMID:23074865

McGuire, T., Manyika, J., & Chui, M. (2012). Why Big Data is the new competitive advantage. *Ivey Business Journal*, *76*, 1–4.

Mian, A., Rao, K., & Sufi, A. (2013). Household balance sheets, consumption and economic slump. *The Quarterly Journal of Economics*, *128*(4), 1687–1726. doi:10.1093/qje/qjt020

Nickerson, D., & Rogers, T. (2014). Political campaigns and Big Data. *The Journal of Economic Perspectives*, *28*(2), 51–74. doi:10.1257/jep.28.2.51

Osterwalder, A., & Pigneur, Y. (2010). *Business model generation: A handbook for visionaries, game changers, and challengers*. Wiley.

Purcell, B. M. (2013). *Big data using cloud computing*. Holy Family University working paper.

Varian, H. (2014). Big Data: New tricks for econometrics. *The Journal of Economic Perspectives*, *28*(2), 3–28. doi:10.1257/jep.28.2.3

Vidal, M., Vidal-García, J., & Hernandez Barros, R. (2016). Big Data and business decision making. In M. K. Singh & K. G. Dileep (Eds.), *Effective Big Data Management and Opportunities for Implementation* (pp. 140–157). Hershey, PA: IGI Global. doi:10.4018/978-1-5225-0182-4.ch010

Vidal-García, J., & Vidal, M. (2016). Big Data in financial services. In Effective Big Data Management and Opportunities for Implementation (pp. 217-230). Hershey, PA: IGI Global.

Vidal-García, J., Vidal, M., & Hernandez Barros, R. (2017). Computational business intelligence, Big Data and their role in business decisions in the age of the Internet of Things. In I. Lee (Ed.), *The Internet of Things in the Modern Business Environment*. Hershey, PA: IGI Global.

## ADDITIONAL READING

Feldman, B., Martin Ellen, M., & Skotnes, T. (2012). *Big data in healthcare. Hype and hope*. DrBonnie360.com working paper.

Gill, P. J. (1997). Objects at the Core. *Information Week*, (August): 25, 99–102.

Gordon, G. J., & Wilson, A. E. (1999). Credit card industry picture book. Paine Webber, May, p.13.

Shroeck, M., & Shockley, R. (2012). Analytics: The real-world use of big data. IBM Institute of Business Value in collaboration with Said Business School, University of Oxford.

## KEY TERMS AND DEFINITIONS

**Big Data:** Large volume of data that inundates a business on a day-to-day basis.

**Business Analytics:** Skills, technologies, practices for ongoing exploration and investigation of previous company performance to gain insight and drive business planning.

**Business Decision Making:** Decision making is an essential aspect of business success.

**Business Intelligence:** The methodology for the acquisition and transformation of raw data into useful information for business analysis.

**Computational Intelligence:** The ability of a computer to learn a specific task from data or experimental observation.

**Data Management:** Development and execution of policies and procedures to manage the information of a company in an effective manner.

**Electronic Commerce:** A business model that enables to conduct business over the internet.

**Information Technology:** It is the use of any computers, storage, networking and other processes to create, store and exchange electronic data.

# Chapter 8
# Banding Organization, Management, and Leadership Theories to Identify Managerial Strategies

**Bessie Rean Bowser**
*Khayruh Enterprises, USA*

## ABSTRACT

*This chapter considers the lack of knowledge by both non-profit and for-profit organizations in building business models and developing global managerial strategies; as well as, considers the need for organizations to understand open transformation of organizational structure with an autonomous mindset of each stakeholder and unification of the organizational system. The focus of perspectives points to what is needed to understand behavior stemming from the culture of the organization and what it takes to structure or restructure its culture to fit with the 21st century's demands and growing global perspectives. Explanations are given as to how some theories and disciplines need to band together to bring out deeper meanings of phenomena to address managerial and leadership strategies. There are six figures and one table highlighting developmental processes of successful organizational systems. These will be used as roadmaps in developing on-going constructs to navigate assessments, training, and transformation processes of an organization.*

## INTRODUCTION

This chapter brings awareness to leaders concerning unified concepts of management, leadership, and adaptability of change or new mindsets for developing modeled global-friendly non-profit and for-profit organizations. An organization's behavior relates to organizational cultural norms. Leaders/owners who realize their cultural norms are not working in their favor may look for ways to adapt to change. The 21st century brings concepts of diversification and unity among stakeholders, with a global perspective implying that leaders must exercise visions of open transformation, prosperity, and unity for sake of

DOI: 10.4018/978-1-5225-2537-0.ch008

Copyright © 2017, IGI Global. Copying or distributing in print or electronic forms without written permission of IGI Global is prohibited.

peace and a healthier organizational environment. The discipline of the organization does not matter (i.e., psychology, sociology, medical, political, family system, education, nutrition, etc.).

A "make or break me" phenomenon exists for organizations in the 21st century. This means that technology is forcing our hands in competition and existence. For instance, when one must fill out an employment application, they must do it online. If one's computer skills or economic situations are not up to par, it will have a negative impact in moving from point A to point B. Some organizations may be slow in entering the reality of ongoing transformation of the world that navigates through time and space. Most organizations have outdated management and leadership systems suffering from deteriorating false and old structures. This could stem from an unwillingness, not knowing how, or not understanding what leadership and management competencies are needed to be able to change or bend with the ages of time. Through the investigation and analysis of an organizational unit's behavior, organizational scholars can present managerial strategies that consider the deeper meaning of the causes that stifle growth and change. Business and management strategies are needed in every aspect of for-profit and non-profit business operational procedures of accountability.

Several theories (cultural leadership theory, implicit leadership theory, double ABCX theory, organizational system theory) are discussed in order to explore the concept of how one understands the deeper meanings in the behavior of societal organizations. The author attempts to explain factors that connect thoughts and behaviors in one's individual and group actions. An organization can increase understanding of reasoning to operate in unity and have a global mindset with knowledge of reality of working mechanism that can spearhead ethical organizations. Globalization is not a new concept to spiritual truth and unity. However, misdirection and selfish leadership ethics have made society weak when making organizational changes to benefit stakeholders.

The goal of this chapter is to awaken the power within non-profit organizational leaders to critically think in unity of the functions of social business development, acknowledging spirituality connection in everyone and everything, whether individually or as an organization. Many people have heard of "putting the cart before the horse" as in this case "putting the actions and reactions before the known factors." In order to be innovative, generate new knowledge, or adapt a new mindset, true factors are needed to gain true actions and reactions. To strengthen the chapter's delivery and understanding of its goal, a guide with factors supporting critical thinking and stabilization of a new mindset and change is developed and presented that may help all types of business and social organizations.

## BACKGROUND

Managerial strategies are essential to growth, change, and development of a new mindset for the adaptability of ongoing economic advancement for both non-profit and for-profit organizations. For decades, managerial strategies focused on the analysis of a for-profit organization's strengths, weaknesses, opportunities, and threats (SWOTs). Non-profit organizations are known to mimic these types of strategic concepts, although they are proven to be ineffective (Alexander, 2000; Eisenberg, 1997; Kong, 2008); but, why ineffective? Once SWOTs are discovered, what should be done next? Managerial strategies are on-going and must consider the next step to maintain strength, improve weakness, take advantages of opportunities, and diminish the threats. Organizations not knowing what to do after finding SWOTs appears to have a direct cause of ineffectiveness. According to Eisenberg (1997: 334), much of the non-profit world has adopted some of the worst, not best, practices of corporations.

Sound managerial strategies should come from the under level (the root) to bring up the principles of ethics, human relations, social development, spirituality, and organizational unity serving all stakeholders. To build and strengthen the effectiveness of all facets of managerial strategies, organizations have to review the deeper meaning and reasons behind ineffective management techniques. Factors to be considered in developing any type of organization in management and leadership are ground-root factors that spearhead vision and growth internationally. According to findings in a study by Bowser (2015), using a grounded theory approach for understanding cultural adaptation of families in international assignments sheds light on overall adaptability to change or a new mindset. Organizations that collect data from all stakeholders for strategic managerial development should learn and understand grounded theory as a method to study organizational history, culture, experiences, communications, and behavior.

Grounded theory methods will help you get started, stay involved, and finish your project (Charmaz, 2006: 2), which generate new ideas and build leaders and managers' analytic and decision-making skills and competencies. In better understanding organization's experiences through the grounded theory approach, the author incorporated hermeneutic phenomenology as theory to find and analyze the deeper meanings of actions and reactions of the organization (Bowser, 2015). Managerial strategies or strategic management, according to Kong (2008) is based on intellectual capital (IC) in social service non-profit organizations (SSNPOs) context because non-profit organizations attend to social needs, investing in citizens instead of profits. The concept of IC is the creation of wealth by investing in intellectual property, information, experience, and knowledge (Stewart, 1997). Edvinsson and Malone (1997) added to the concept of IC by including investments in technology, skills, and customer relations. Kong (2008) argues that IC focuses on indicators that are non-financial for strategic vision.

However, IC is derived from management techniques of a for-profit, which has become a conceptual model for non-profits. Therefore, some for-profit organizations are in the same 21st century managerial and leadership confusion as some non-profits. Kong (2008) concluded that non-profit organizations need more knowledge in order to adapt to change in operating and managing businesses. SSNPOs need a strategic management competent model to support organizations to remain autonomous and pursue sociable missions while enhancing organizational effectiveness. Additionally, organizations are not effective when serviced citizens as well as consumers are disconnected. Consumers and serviced citizens are considered stakeholders and view non-profit and for-profit organizations through the same lens.

How do consumers view non-profit and for-profit organizations? This question led Aaker, Vohs, and Mogilner (2010) in their inquiry, finding that people stereotype organizations based on identifying them as for-profit or non-profit. In addition, they found that people look to see whether the organization is competent or warm. Consumers may be willing to buy from for-profit organizations more than non-profits because of the notion of perceived competence. This is true even when there is a lack in warmth and endorsement. However, with non-profit organization endorsement, consumers perceive competence and warmth. Aaker et al. (2010) show that consumers would rather buy from non-profit organizations because of warmth and competence. Therefore, there is a growing number of non-profit organizations that were once run by for-profit organizations.

Are for-profit organizations getting into the realm of non-profit organizations? Aaker et al. (2010) believe this to be true and argue that non-profits, as well as for-profits, may be seen as warm and competent but the consumer's reasoning for preference is applied. Bailly and Chapelle (2012) focus on France and Europe when questioning whether or not there is a risk to the boundaries between non-profit organizations and for-profit organizations becoming blurred due to for-profits awareness of their social responsibilities and non-profit organizations losing their specificity. The types of specificity Bailly and Chapelle (2012) mention are the:

1. Output of non-profit organizations linked to the output of for-profit organizations
2. Managers/leaders/founders of non-profit organizations
3. Types of governance and management, especially in human resources management

Bailly and Chapelle (2012: 651) aim to identify the factors influencing the behavior of the organizations that provide continuing training for jobseekers and in particular the impact of their status, be it for-profit or non-profit. It is clear that a deeper phenomenological analysis is warranted to produce more evidence and shed knowledge on restructuring the foundation of both non-profit and for-profit organizations. Changing mindsets, adapting behaviors, and developing a stronger and professional organizational structure can be less challenging with an efficient managerial strategic business leadership model and a list of factors leadership and management essentials.

Challenges exist in navigating the redevelopment of our society. It is the social responsibility of organizations to uplift mankind through leadership and management. The overall purpose of an organization will be strengthened through knowledge of the external environment (economic, social, educational and political) as it relates to a family system structure, community awareness, and global awareness. To support the development of business models with managerial strategies for organizations to adapt to a new mindset, change, and diversification, open transformation is warranted. The factors to be considered must be connected to doing the right thing, respect, trust, selfish less, and reclaimed spirituality (goodness within or self-actualization) in leadership, management and training.

## FACTORIAL PERSPECTIVE OF GROWTH AND CHANGE

Most organizations face challenges with leadership when making decisions when lacking knowledge (Bowser, 2015). In order to be innovative, knowledge of different concepts is needed to support adjustment, change, and adaptation. By critically thinking through reasoning and acting according to facts, organizations will gain true actions and true reactions. Connecting human nature, human relations, critical thinking, spirituality, the environment, and global unity could be the necessary mode of thinking and acting for successful organizations, especially non-profits. In an organizational transformation process, cultural leadership theory (CLT) (Dorfman, Javidan, Hanges, Dastmalchian, & House, 2012) helps to identify the behavior of leaders and managers. Implicit leadership theory (ILT) is used to analyze leadership in the organizational culture in order to predict the behavior of leaders (Lord & Maher, 1991; Shaw, 1990).

Many research studies have used CLT for predicting cross-cultural adaptation (Bader, Berg, & Holtbrügge, 2013; Bauer & Taylor, 2001; Bowser, 2015; Caligiuri, Hylan, & Joshi, 1998; Dorfman et al., 2012; Gupta & Gupta, 2012; Harrison, Shaffer, & Bhaskar-Shrinivas, 2004). The author considers CLT in discussing challenging issues non-profit and for-profit organizations acknowledge when adjusting and adapting to change. Knowledge, skills, abilities, and leadership characteristics promoted through organizational system theory (OST) and CLT could make adjusting to change and adapting to a new mindset clearer when learning the deeper meaning of behavior associated with reasoning behind the development of organizational cultural intelligence (OCQ).

## ORGANIZATIONAL SYSTEM THEORY

The goal of organizational systems theory (OST) is to modify the present rather than explore and interpret the past. The past is a measuring instrument in providing support for an organization's present and future mindset and change through intervention (Bowser, 2015; Minuchin, 1974). Therefore, transformation in organizational system structure produces possibilities for change. The organization will maintain the change once it is proven to be effective and continues to be validated through the organization's stakeholder experiences. In the organizational system each stakeholder is affected by the behavior of others, whether employee, member, volunteer, owner, supporter, etc. The goal in any organization is to focus on and maintain equilibrium as it goes through developmental milestones (Konopaske, Robie, & Ivancevich, 2005). Internal and external factors can affect the equilibrium of the organizational system. Studies focusing on organizational system unity are limited. Is it because society has become selfish, arrogant, unethical, jealous, uncaring, and mean-spirited? The author found insufficient literature on 21st century OST regarding organizational system unity. However, more seminal literature was found. In 1972, Kast and Rosenzweig argued:

*Biological and social scientists generally have embraced systems concepts. Many organization and management theorists seem anxious to identify with this movement and to contribute to the development of an approach which purports to offer the ultimate— the unification of all science into one grand conceptual model. Who possibly could resist? General systems theory seems to provide a relief from the limitations of more mechanistic approaches and a rationale for rejecting "principles" based on relatively "closed-system" thinking. This theory provides the paradigm for organization and management theorists to "crank into their systems model" all of the diverse knowledge from relevant underlying disciplines. It has become almost mandatory to have the word "system" in the title of recent articles and books.*

Kast and Rosenzweig (1972:448) asked, "But where did it all start?" This question led them to the 19th and early 20th centuries' philosophical arguments concerning mechanistic and organismic models, quoting Deutsch (1968):

*Both mechanistic and organismic models were based substantially on experiences and operations known before 1850. Since then, the experience of almost a century of scientific and technological progress has so far not been utilized for any significant new model for the study of organization and in particular of human thought [12, p. 380].*

The field of management and organizational theory is familiar with the unit systems perspective. A basic system framework was used by Barnard (1938), detailing a cooperative system (Kast & Rosenzweig, 1972: 448):

*A cooperative system is a complex of physical, biological, personal, and social components which are in a specific systematic relationship by reason of the cooperation of two or more persons for at least one definite end. Such a system is evidently a subordinate unit of larger systems from one point of view; and itself embraces subsidiary systems—physical, biological, etc.—from another point of view. One of the systems comprised within a cooperative system, the one which is implicit in the phrase "cooperation of two or more persons," is called an "organization" [3, p. 65].*

The development of the organizational system unit depends on significant contributions of interpersonal skills, global interactions, self-efficacy, discretion, culture diversity, and role ambiguity for successful organizational behavior. OST research shows little attention to the whole organizational unit structure's cohesiveness and the ability to function with a systematic relationship of all stakeholders. The organizational unit is a system that functions openly in development, transformation, and adaptation (Bowser, 2015; Caligiuri, Hylan, & Joshi, 1998; Caligiuri & Tarique, 2009). Positive transformation is based on truth, vision, ethical behavior, a constant evolving mindset, adjustment, and adaptability. To understand organization's adaptation experiences with a new mindset or culture, descriptive science looks and rediscovers first experience through phenomenological reductions to the originality of awareness. The author's advice is to focus on the organization unit as a whole, including all stakeholders, in order to support development, transformation, and adaptation to change. Organization, management, and leadership expert consultants could assist with the analysis of the position of organizations with recommendations of business models and managerial strategies.

## CULTURAL LEADERSHIP THEORY

In the author's earlier study on global diverse adaptability and change, findings showed that an organizational system is self-perpetuating and should be structured to last indefinitely. This should depend on all stakeholders' "mutual nurturance, socialization, support, and regulations to maintain and preserve its effectiveness" (Bowser, 2015: 96). Internal and external factors impact an organization, calling for readjustment, flexibility, vision, change, and solid decisions made on facts, honesty, and ethical conduct with strong adaptability focusing on organizational equilibrium. Figure 1 depicts a prototype taxonomy of an organization based on a "constructivist and phenomenological analysis behind the actions" (Bowser, 2015: 97) according to analysis of adaptation abilities, skills, and characteristics of an effective strong organizational structure.

Gaining knowledge and awareness of CLT provides a better understanding of changing environments, diversification, and global unity. Figure 2 depicts a prototype taxonomy of cultural leadership theory (CLT) as a "constructivist and phenomenological analysis behind actions" (Bowser, 2015: 98) according to analysis of an organization's new mindset adaptation process. Considering the constructs of CLT, the author demonstrated the holistic view of an organizational structure and how the constructs shape ILT (Lord & Maher, 1991; Shaw, 1990) of each organizational stakeholder (employees, members, owners, etc.) regardless of geography.

## IMPLICIT LEADERSHIP THEORY

Implicit leadership theory (ILT) is the organization's cultural level of analysis of the structure and content of the belief systems shared amongst its members (Bowser, 2015; Javidan, Dorfman, de Luque, & House, 2006). CLT gives organizations a global perspective in understanding behavioral factors, psychology, philosophy, social structure, and reasons for accepting and adapting to change. When an organization is faced with challenges from external and internal factors, employees/stakeholders are affected by the actions and decisions of others (Bowser, 2015; Minuchin, 1974). The organizational unit's attitude toward a new mindset, adaptability, and adjustment stems from the culture of the organization.

*Figure 1. Prototype Taxonomy of Effective Organisation Adaptation Concept*

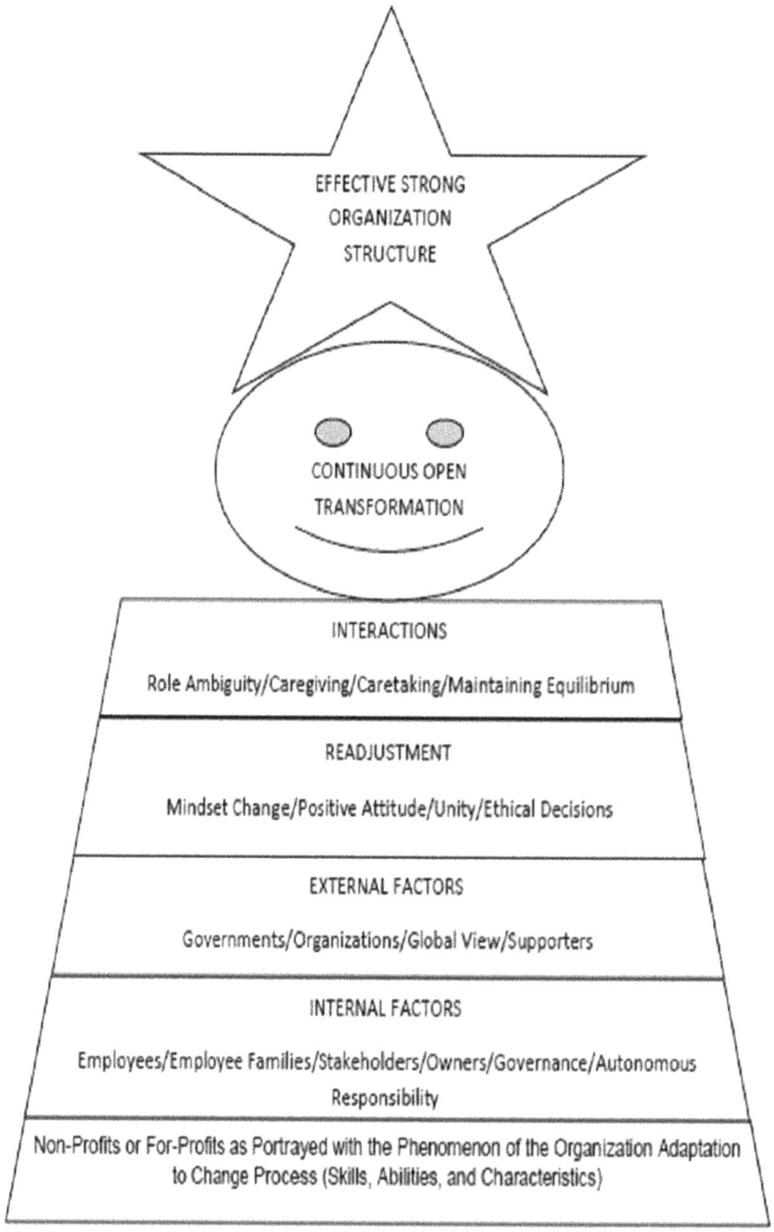


Organizational scholars and researchers have been concerned with the effectiveness of behavior in organizations. For instance, the Global Leadership and Organizational Behavior Effectiveness (GLOBE) project (House & Javidan, 2004) had 200 international researchers from a variety of disciplines connected with their project. The project considered the ILT foundation to develop the organization's CLT, which is based on honesty and respect (Bowser, 2015). The GLOBE project focused on cultural organizational and leadership effectiveness. Shortly after its start, they learned that economic competition and human conditions of societies significantly impacted behavior. These scholars, as well as other organizational,

*Figure 2. CLT Prototype Taxonomy of Organisation New Mindset Adaptation Process*

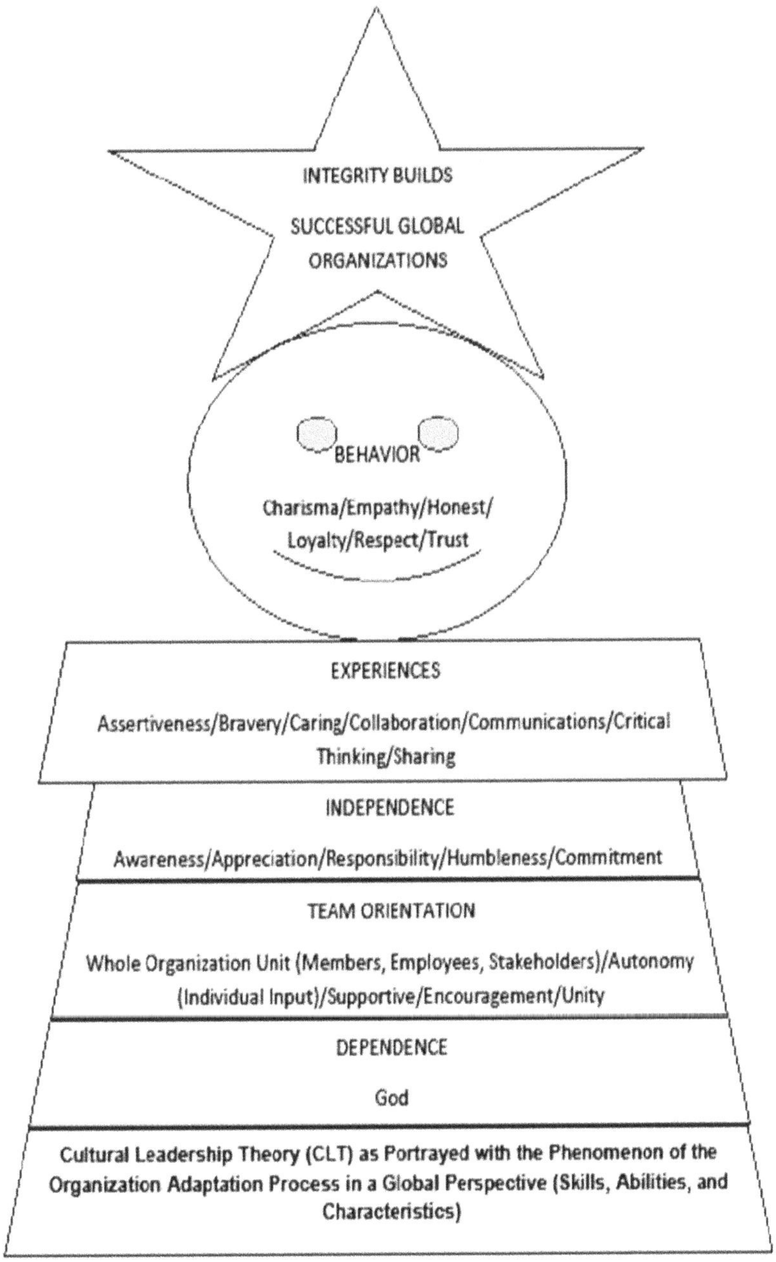


management, and leadership researchers, aimed to provide global cultural awareness, sensitivity, knowledge, and understanding to non-profit and for-profit organizations. Six leadership dimensions surfaced from the GLOBE analysis:

1. Charismatic/value-based
2. Team-oriented

3. Participative
4. Humane-oriented
5. Autonomous
6. Self-protective.

As mentioned, Figure 2 shows the CLT as the author demonstrated by a holistic structure of organizations and how the ILT is shaped (Bowser, 2015; Lord & Maher, 1991; Shaw, 1990).

## CULTURAL INTELLIGENCE

Cultural intelligence (CQ) is being assertive in one's ability to understand other organizational cultural context, engage others, and adapt to change, new mindsets, and the environment (Bowser, 2015). Organizations that successfully adapt are highly motivated to venture out and adopt new skills and behavior. Once organizational stakeholders advance through cognition and motivation, they exhibit adaptability behavior that constitutes CQ (Ang, van Dyne, Koh, Ng, Templer, Tay, & Chandrasekar, 2007; Earley & Ang, 2003). Although CQ skills training increases knowledge and develops sensitivity to diversity, personal behavior, and awareness, "perspective-taking affects the developmental process" (Bowser, 2015: 34). Some management scholars emphasize building networks that may prove to be effective. However, networking may turn out to be ineffective in a host country (Farh, Bartol, Shapiro, & Shin, 2010). Organizational information and support (models and managerial strategies) should focus on assisting stakeholders in building ties and diverse relationships with individuals willing to be of assistance.

Based on a study by Farh et al. (2010), a five-stage process model can help researchers explain how and when individuals are effective when interacting with others/actors (peer members/stakeholders, a host country, or diverse individuals) to develop communication ties (Bowser, 2015). The five stages are that the:

1. Organization unit must have the motivation to seek support from actors
2. Organization must contact potential actors
3. Actors must be willing and able to assist
4. Organization must perceive and acknowledge actors' responses as positive and supportive
5. Experiences must be encouraging and enhancing in order to adapt to change, as well as add the actor to the support network as being available for future request for support.

This five-stage process model addresses frameworks of advice-tie generation (Nebus, 2006), cross-cultural adjustment literature (Earley & Ang, 2003), and social support processes (Iida, Seidman, Shrout, Fujita, & Bolger, 2008).

Cultural intelligence is evident through normal adaptive behavior, which is learned and instilled by society and contributes to the organization's diverse adaptability (Bowser, 2015; Sternberg, 1982) and new mindset. However, further research is suggested (Farh et al., 2010) to determine how individual differences affect the tie-information process, how CQ's components relate to the importance at each stage of the tie-formation process, and how to identify diverse cultural contexts in which the organization and its stakeholders' CQ is rated as necessary in the tie-formation process.

Based on the process model by Farh et al. (2010), tie formation in this perspective begins with a leader's ability to identify the benefits of diverse organizational unity, and have the assertiveness and motivation to seek global managerial models, strategies, and support for open transformation. Leaders will be approachable by all stakeholders, support autonomous behavior, and support diverse language skills, training, and development. The organization is able to absorb and translate the new knowledge promoting and enhancing adjustment. Chin, Gu, and Tubbs (2001) support the argument of needing more development of global leadership CQ competencies to maximize potential for global opportunities and support.

OST seeks to modify the present rather than explore and interpret the past. CLT aims to be self-perpetuating and indefinitely structured. CQ promotes assertiveness in on-going learning, autonomism, socialization, change, and advance through cognition and motivation. The wheel that connects these theories is the perspective-taking process. This process is a cognitive concept of seeing the world from another viewpoint or lens (Bowser, 2015; Park & Abbott, 2011; Wang, 2006), which benefits unity, social behavior, stereotyping, and an organization's effectiveness.

## Perspective-Taking Process

In the process of developing and maintaining an organizational unit's interactions and social contacts with global diverse environments, perspective-taking is necessary to make the process effective. Perspective-taking organizations are highly experienced in communication; their contextual performance and adjustment to change are strong and successful. According to Park and Abbott's (2011) perspective-taking model, influences are based on the types of duties, flexibility of role orientation, and an organization's diversification. Activation of perspective-taking can differ depending on the types of duties (e.g., functional, strategic, technical, or developmental; Park & Abbott, 2011) and responsibilities assigned. Organizational unit members/stakeholders with high flexibility of role orientation are expected to go where there is a need. They are expected to go without hesitation and to behave honorably. This will allow them to gain understanding of the environment and cultural diversities. Organizations that are strongly engaged in active perspective-taking are high in awareness of differences in mindset, simulation in values, morals, spirituality, and unbiased in decision making (Bowser, 2015).

This chapter provides five factors from Park and Abbott (2011) as contributing to the influence and effectiveness over the relationship of active perspective-taking. These factors are the accessibility of perspectives, situational-specific knowledge, prior experience, cultural distances, and psychological capital. Individuals or organizations with high levels of psychological capital, situational-specific knowledge, and experience accurately understand situations, behaviors, and feelings. Low accessibility of another's perspective and high cultural distance may decrease the accuracy of active perspective-taking (Bowser, 2015). Since, psychological capital requires high levels of emotional and cognitive resources to identify stressors, change and adjustment with a new mindset, organizational training, and development support models may be helpful for organizational stability and to "increase the levels of psychological capital" (Bowser, 2015: 37).

Situational-specific knowledge is knowledge about an organizational unit's culture and language. This improves communication and stakeholder effectiveness in the perspective-taking process. An organizational unit with more than one language will assess local and global social expectations more accurately, according to Bell and Harrison (1996) (as cited in Park & Abbott, 2011). Park and Abbott (2011) also cited Firoz and Ramin (2004) as stating that during an unexpected situation, cultural knowledge strengthens the stakeholder's confidence to effectively address the situation. Experienced managers and leaders who have been challenged through trial and error have the foresight and ability to view an organization's behavior more accurately than someone who is inexperienced. Experienced leaders have developed cognitive schemata and comprehension on a much higher level (Bowser, 2015; Park & Abbott, 2011).

Cultural distance can cause barriers in the perspective-taking process because it is positively related to active motivation of perspective-taking. Some researchers argue that organizational stakeholders have more challenges with new mindset adjustment when faced with cultural differences between home and work. Perspective accessibility is an important factor in perspective-taking tasks (Bowser, 2015). Breaking down barriers between external and internal groups is critical in creating well-adjusted stakeholders. Perspective-taking is a strategy to help achieve that challenge. Organizational management and leadership should seek ways to encourage the activities of perspective-taking training and extend it to stakeholder families because family members influence the outcome of the organizational unit's social behavior (Caligiuri et al., 1998).

## Competencies in Leadership

Technical expertise is not a sufficient reason to assign the duties of managers and leaders. Leadership without leadership competencies is detrimental to the success of an organization. To better understand adaptability to a new mindset and change, the author explains leadership competencies by way of Maslow's (1943) hierarchy of needs. Maslow's pyramid has contributed enormously in stability of health, wealth, and family structure, as well as business structure (Bowser, 2015). Since many are familiar with Maslow's (1943) hierarchy of needs pyramid concept whereas each step or level conquered according to a needs adaptability transformation process is mastered. This high level of transformation is sometimes called the mastery stage (Chin, et al., 2001; Sanchez, Spector, & Cooper, 2000) as depicted in Figure 3 using three transformation concept steps. CQ is explained while focusing on leadership competencies in three steps:

*Figure 3. Prototype Taxonomy of Effective Organisation Adaptability*

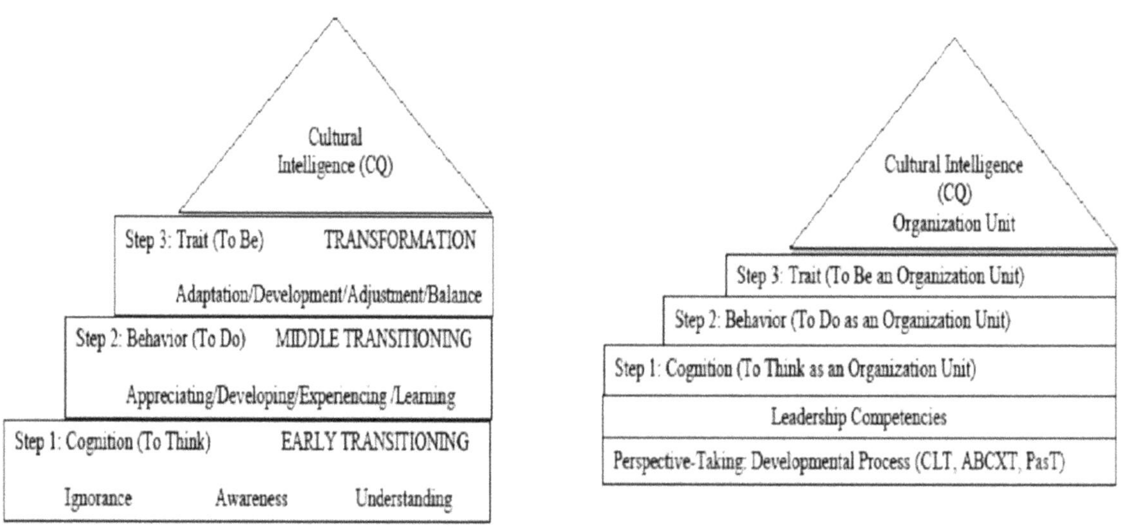

## Step 1: Cognition Step

The cognition step means "to think." It is the levels of ignorance, awareness, and understanding. Ignorance is a mindset without knowledge of successful organizational system structure. There are signs of discord in Step 1. Yet, organizations assume their current organizational culture is perfect. According to Stoltz (1997), this is known as unconscious incompetence (Bowser, 2015). Awareness is obvious once organizational stakeholders interact and notice other cultural habits. At this point, impressions are formed and a bond is established. However, there may be an ethnocentric attitude because of unconscious denial (Bowser, 2015; Chin et al., 2001). At the level of understanding, one becomes conscious of their efforts of wanting to know more and begins to ask why, what, when, and how diverse individuals and organizations do, act, and react as they do. Then, organizational stakeholders show interest in the environment, history, and organizational cultural value systems. They begin to develop tolerance, respect for others, and acceptance of new concepts. Sanchez, Spector, and Cooper (2000) refer to this level as "early transition." Eventually, the organization gains knowledge, becomes aware, and displays understanding and willingness to focus on a new mindset and change for their organizational system.

## Step 2: Behavior Step

The Behaviour step means "to do." This includes levels of appreciation, learn, and adapt. Appreciation develops as stakeholders venture out, seeking experiences with different points of views, appreciating diversification, and preferring new activities and new cultural ways over their own. Learn is developed through training, language courses, history, art, leadership, ethics, etc. Adapt is relevant when one comfortably communicates in an unbiased manner and sees alternative avenues of business practices, displaying appreciation and ways of living in unity. This mindset allows organizations/stakeholders to see through someone else's viewpoint (Chin et al., 2001) or lens, referred to as the "middle transition stage" in organizational developmental process. According to the phenomenological perspectives, all organizational stakeholder mindsets change as they begin to see the big picture from an adaptive point of view.

## Step 3: Trait Step

The trait step means "to be." This is the level where organizational stakeholders are acknowledged and identified as transforming, managing, and successfully leading the organizational unit or structure. The three levels of the Trait Step are transformation, manager, and leader. Transformation is living and leading with a celebration of reality, while having visions of universal values that could apply globally. The manager level is digesting, analyzing, reflecting, and evaluating the experiences and knowledge gained. This level is called internalization (Chin et al., 2001) as it verifies experiences and learning. The organizational leadership perceives change, growth, diversity, and globalism as authentic and realizes globalization as a way of life. The for-profit organization also perceives world competition as authentic. Through the phenomenological view, organizational stakeholder behaviors present themselves as having charisma, competence, integrity, and balance (Bowser, 2015). At the leader level, behavior is effortless and globalization is seen as a normal way of life.

Leader traits are seen as integrity, ethical, competent, charismatic, empathetic, balanced, stakeholder-friendly, family-friendly, organization unit-structured, and autonomist supportive. In some leadership literature, according to Avolio (2007), not all traits and competencies are fixed as to the success of the developmental, adjustment, and adaptive process. Traits are constantly evolving and changing based on interactions and reformation of organizational unit system structure. Traits shape organizational leadership, effectiveness, adjustments, and development in degrees, displaying an organizational unit's strength and growth. The most important perspective in developing and understanding traits is the spirituality that connects everyone and everything in unity. The author explains this through hermeneutic (van Manen, 1990) phenomenology after the next section.

Understanding CQ, CLT and OST can help to identify or predict organizational behavior. However, the author attempts to make a clearer picture of meeting or not meeting demands by considering and explaining the constructs of Double ABCX theory (ABCXT) (Creed, 2006; Hill, 1949; McCubbin & Patterson, 1982, 1983), in how it helps maintain organizational equilibrium after organizations possess the trait qualities.

## DOUBLE ABCX THEORY

Integrity, cooperation, and autonomy will maintain equilibrium of the whole organizational structure. The Double ABCXT's constructs are stressors, resources, perception, crisis, etc. This theory states that organizational members/stakeholders are knowledgeable and efficient enough to identify challenges or organizational stressors by critically thinking and expanding resources by way of social skills learned to understand what need to be done. If or when a crisis occurs and the organization cannot meet demand, that situation could cause maladjustment and organizational stagnation and/or added stress.

Balance and equilibrium are achieved between organizational members/stakeholders and the organizational unit as a whole by strengthening, maintaining, and developing united integrity and united independence. Imbalances and deterioration in organizational unit's behavior, functioning, integrity, and independence cause growing incompetence and blind sight to a new mindset. According to the ABCXT, Figure 4 depicts a flow chart emphasizing the concepts of the components. Component A represents organizational stressor events over time. Component B represents organizational resources within the organizational unit. Component C represents organizational concepts, definitions, or perceptions of events throughout the organizational unit structure. Component X represents the occurrence of an organizational unit crisis due to the inability to meet demands and resulted in maladjustment and maladaptation.

Acculturation is to modify the organizational culture. How is this done? An organizational system unit divides adjustment and adaptability into several levels, such as the individual member/stakeholder, a department group, and the whole organizational unit as a group. Acculturation strategies relate to sociocultural adaptation and psychological adjustment (Bowser, 2015; Searle & Ward, 1990). Psychological acculturation (Berry, 1990) focuses on individual adjustments to a new mindset and new organizational behavior. Psychological adjustment targets internal processes of emotions (i.e., anxiety, tension, fatigue, depression, psychological well-being), which Creed (2006) refers to as cultural maintenance (Bowser, 2015). Social support, life changes, and individual personality influence psychological adjustment (Ward & Rana-Deuba, 1999). Sociocultural adaptation is concern with the ability to communicate, negotiate, and easily accept the new culture or mindset, which is known as contact/participation (Creed, 2006). The author proposed that the organizational unit "adopts certain adjustment and psychological strategies" (Bowser, 2015: 34). From an eco-systemic point of view (Bronfenbrenner, 1979), the individual member/stakeholder ventures out from their comfort zone of the organization and communicates with local and global cross-culture communities. However, the author sees this combination of theories as a

*Figure 4. Organisational Flowchart of Double ABCX Theory Components*

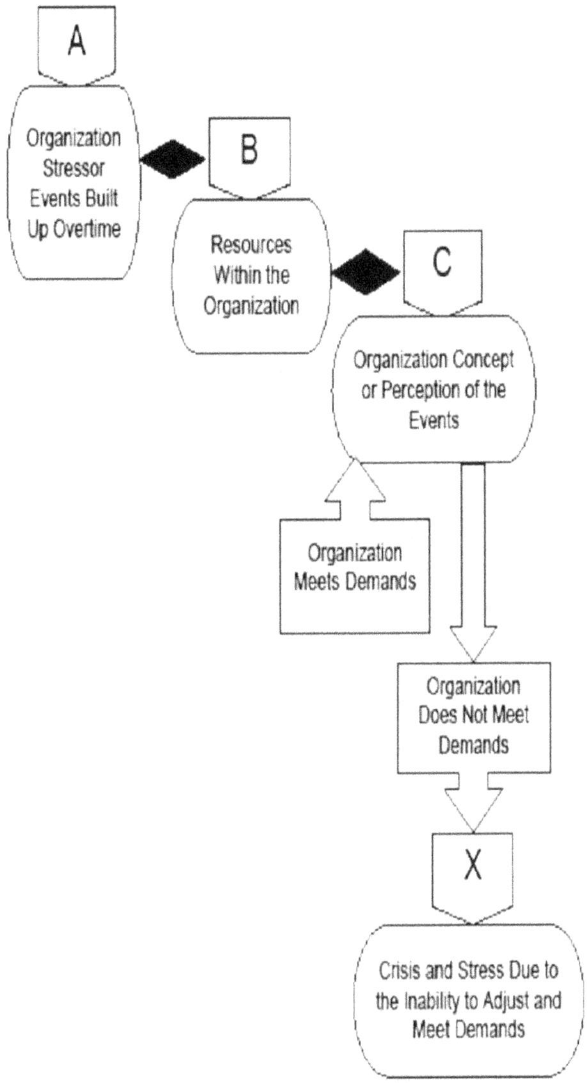


guide or roadmap to get to the root of why some organizations could easily adapt to a new mindset and others could not through examining the deeper meaning through the Phenomenology as Theory (PasT) perspective (Bowser, 2015).

## HERMENEUTIC PHENOMENOLOGY AS THEORY

Hemeneutic phenomenology as theory (PasT) describes the phenomenon as presented through objects, thoughts, and feelings from investigated lived experiences (Bloomberg & Volpe, 2012). It creates patterns and relationships of the meaning. Hermeneutic phenomenology is concerned with lived human experiences (Ehrich, 2005). Ontologically (van Manen, 1990, 1991), the concern is the meaning of being.

Therefore, scholars such as Todres and Wheeler (2001) argued that "phenomenology can become shallow without hermeneutics" (Bowser, 2015: 41). Phenomenology is appropriate for understanding how organizational leaders/members (stakeholders) experience the adaptation of new mindsets and change. This approach is holistic and poetic. It is holistic because phenomenology can reveal deep insights into the experienced condition; it is poetic because it is sensitive and reflective (Ehrich, 2005). Phenomenology, as a descriptive science, rediscovers the foundation or first experience. Through phenomenological reduction, it reaches originality of awareness, viewing experience in a new light to gain true knowledge and new vision into organizational unit structure of adaptability to change and a new mindset. The focus is on all organizational stakeholder perspectives, which brings diversity and competing expectation to the organizational system (Osula & Ng, 2014).

## UNDERSTANDING ORGANIZATIONAL TRANSFORMATION PROCESS

The successful organizational structure is an ongoing open transformation system including every individual/stakeholder. It operates efficiently with autonomous thinking and behavior toward transitions. As members/stakeholders constantly change, grow, and adapt, demands on organizational leaders and managers to support and allow an open system within the organizational structure is developed. Depending on organizational stakeholder support, nurturance, socialization, training, communication, ethical conduct, and vision of unity, transformation will be evident and give rise to change and adaptability. The stakeholders will bring diverse or competing expectations to the organization. The organizational system becomes self-perpetuating (Minuchin, 1974) as seen in Figure 5, the organizational unit structure open transformation system model. Organizational transformation will continue, will be maintained, and will be preserved for its effectiveness. Organizations are strengthened by open transformation promoting autonomous, social, and transitioning behavior of stakeholders. Stakeholders constantly adapt to the environment and change according to autonomous experiences and insight. Therefore, the organizational unit changes and adapts to different challenges and circumstances as the transformation process continues. The author believes that non-profit organizations may best accept and apply this transformation system because it is feasible, ethical, stable, and makes sense of unification. For-profit organizations can be just as accepting to this model. However, some for-profit organizations may have a hard time breaking the cycle of their management and leadership concept.

Some successful non-profit and for-profit organizations may have a similar system already in place. Based on the study (Bowser, 2015), the open transformation system is an on-going process of incoming and outgoing communication addressing new demands, increasing CQ and knowledge on organizational behavior in view of social, psychosocial, philosophical, and psychological development. When organizations consider the 21st century's competition on a global scale, competent and diverse managers/leaders/stakeholders are limited. According to Silvanto and Ryan (2004), the war for talent is progressing for non-profit and for-profit organizations. Therefore, it would be beneficial for organizations to understand, tailor, and craft a talent mobility diverse strategy. Organizations that are not functioning as an open

*Figure 5. Organisation Unit Structure Open Transformation System Model*

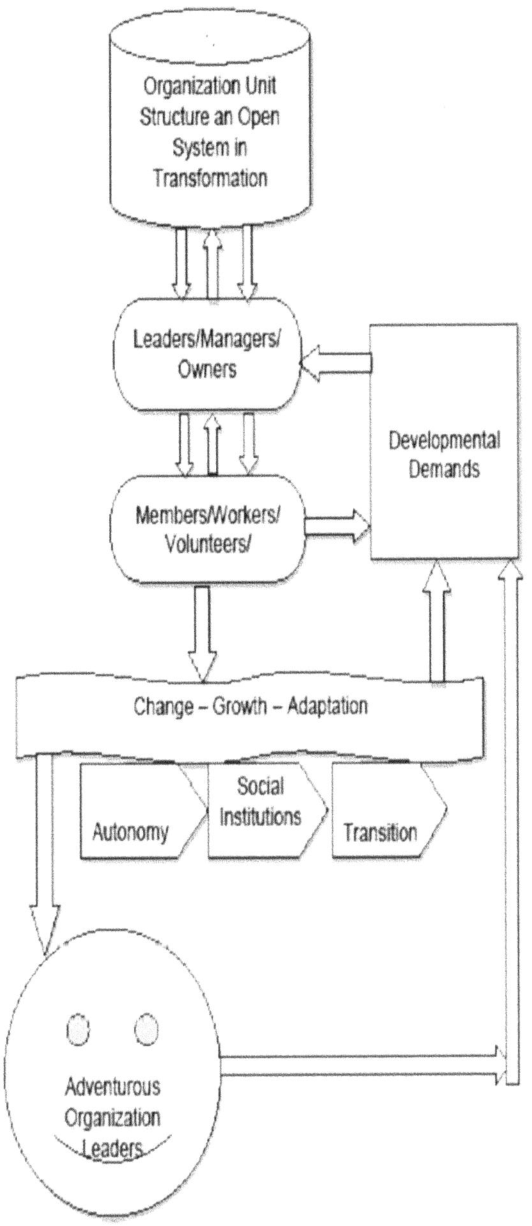


transformation system unit, may find that experienced and competent stakeholders may move on. The organizational structure's transformation process attracts open-minded workers and view each member/stakeholder as a helper and not as the helped (Minuchin, 1974). Diversified transactional patterns will develop. Reinforcement of adaptability and adjustment in a new mindset will create a successful organization. Next, the chapter will consider factors that can help guide the development of a non-profit organization's business model and successful managerial strategies.

## Factors Contributing to Managerial Strategic Success

Bowser (2015) argues, the identified list of factors in Table 1 contributes to organizational unit success and is needed to better understand and support the creation of non-profit business managerial strategic models. These factors will increase understanding of organizational management and leadership's views of global perspective involving training, development, and unity in diversified adaptation. The factors were assigned to four groups based on the phenomena that best serves particular characteristics "based on analysis, underlying logic, and the common sense of the researcher" (Bowser, 2015:119; White, Woodfield, & Ritchie, 2003). These factors identify reasons for the ability or inability to adapt to change and diversity, as well as for understanding cultural differences. In a 21st century global perspective, one must be aware of organizational management and leadership factors that are the foundation of change and growth within an organizational unit structure. The OAP model (Figure 6) demonstrates the flow of the organizational managerial process as strategies to recognize the need for global leadership competences, support, and training for successful adaptation and continuous transformation of the organizational unit. This applies to both non-profit and for-profit, as well as governmental agencies. Whatever the stakeholder's relationship or duty, there should be proper steps to take to ensure training and support are available.

## SOLUTIONS AND RECOMMENDATIONS

It can be overwhelming when a non-profit organization or other type of organization reshapes its cultural behavior. Some organizations may have similar managerial strategies in place but need a revision due to the demands of the 21st century. Selfish and arrogant behavior of leaders and managers have stagnated business opportunities on a global scale. These types of behavior effect the life and growth of an organization, as well as stakeholder families and communities. As organizations take the initiative to build a unified structure with empathic leaders while taking in consideration CQ or the lack of it, demands can be addressed that will transform organizations with equilibrium. The OAP model (Figure 6) can serve as a guide to start the process of assessing the organizational unit structure and stakeholders. Some organizations may need an expert consultant to help with the process of developing assessment programs for all areas of the business and individual stakeholders' behavior. Assessments will help identify problem areas, challenges, or demands facing the organization. Analysis of the assessments will show leaders and managers the necessary action to bring about adaptability and equilibrium. New and upcoming non-profit organizations are in the best place to begin business with ethical and directional managerial strategies focusing on organizational unity and transformation.

The author recommends promoting a diversified mindset dictated by the 21st century. Concentrate and focus on righteousness through spirituality that connects every human being, which is the lifeline to unity and success. Do not mix spirituality with religious ideologies. An organization should be identified by the work it does, rather than by showcasing personal religious preference. The author argues that this may push away positive stakeholders who want to be a part of the organizational unit because it is the spirituality of that person that looks to connect with the same natural spirituality; however, hesitant due to perceived or experienced behavior of disunity, etc. of that particular organizational cultural ideology. Striving for unity and peace should be the goal of all organizations, especially non-profit organizations. "How can I help?" is the question to brand in one's heart and organizational structure.

*Figure 6. Organisational Adaptive Process*

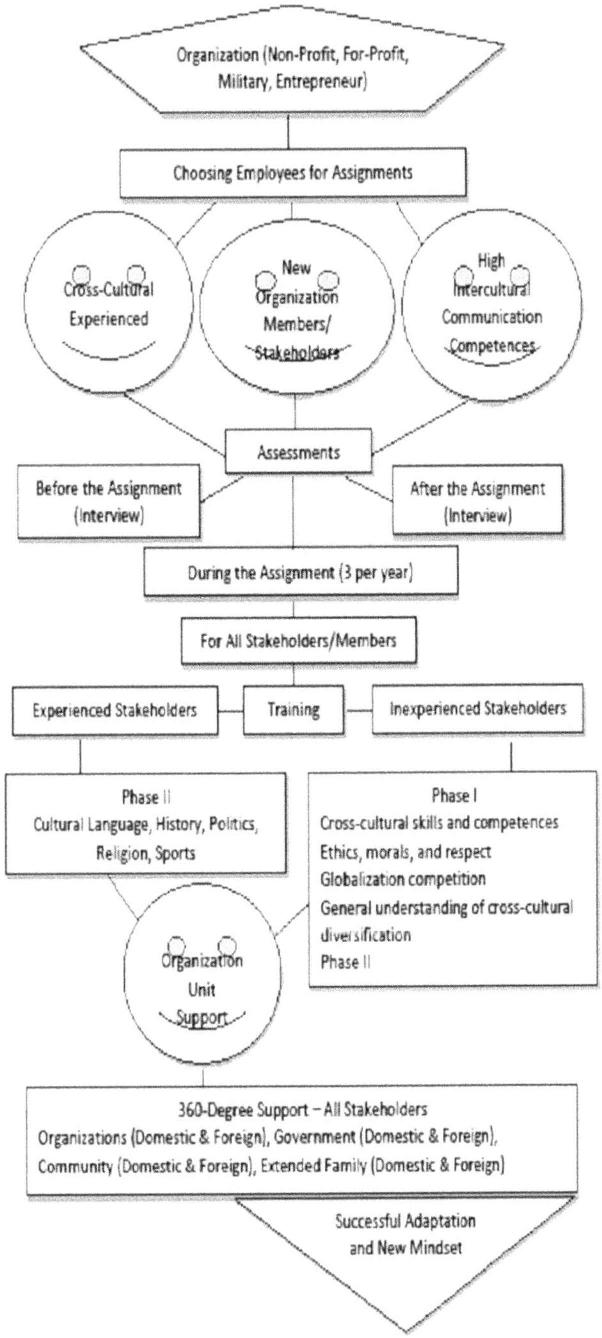


As stated by the 35th President of the United States John F. Kennedy, "Ask not what your country can do for you, ask what you can do for your country." This mindset will attract the best of the best. Do not use stereotypes. Give all stakeholders a chance to help. Provide the best creditable advice based on facts. It is also recommended to not act on emotions because emotion is not empathy. Be empathic and make solid business decisions to maintain equilibrium, promote autonomous thinking, and communicate.

*Table 1. Factors Contributing to Organisation Unit Success*

| Qualities, Traits, Attributes, Behaviors, or Characteristics | 360-Degree Support Preparation Feedback | The Power of Knowledge Education and Training | Parenting Grooming Leading Transforming | Organizational Hiring Coaching and Mentoring |
|---|---|---|---|---|
| Analyzer | | Best | | |
| Appreciative | Best | | | |
| Assertive | | | Best | |
| Confident | | | | Best |
| Collective | | Best | | |
| Committal | Best | | | |
| Communicative | Best | | | |
| Courageous | | | | Best |
| Cross-Cultural | | | Best | |
| Edifier | | | | Best |
| Effective Managerial | Best | | | |
| Empathy | | | Best | |
| Environmentalist | Best | | | |
| Ethics | Best | | | |
| Flexibility | | | Best | |
| Future Orientation | | Best | | |
| Human Orientation | | | Best | |
| Influence | | | | Best |
| Integrity | | | Best | |
| Intelligence/Globally | | Best | | |
| Knowledge | | Best | | |
| Motivator | | | | Best |
| Obligation | Best | | | |
| Open-Mindedness | Best | | | |
| Power | | | | Best |
| Researcher | | Best | | |
| Respect | | | Best | |
| Responsible | Best | | | |
| Sensitive | Best | | | |
| Sociable | Best | | | |
| Teacher | | Best | | |
| Trainer | | | | Best |
| Transformational | | | Best | |
| Trustful | Best | | | |
| Understanding | | Best | | |
| Values | | | Best | |
| Wisdom | Best | Best | Best | Best |

## FUTURE RESEARCH DIRECTIONS

"Will organizations, entrepreneurs, and private individuals get out of their comfort zone to take on the challenges of diversification or cross-cultural communications for the betterment of global businesses as well as global families?" (Bowser, 2015: 125). Many cultures suffer because leaders are confused in understanding unity equilibrium. Research is needed on how to bring about ethical behavior, equal rights, and responsibility for all stakeholders. A no-tolerance policy for disrespecting others can start with family structure and family members venturing out into the business world to promote this policy through domestic organizations, global organizations, and family systems. There will then be global transformation to the liking of what the Creator of all and everything may be pleased. The author refers to this as the "Gospel of Unity." Some bad habits must be broken, the lies must stop, and everything in our life processes must be connected through spirituality. It is challenging to unify when minds, families, communities, cities, states, and countries are not unified. Research should take in consideration family system theory, ethical behavior and responsibilities, global unification, and build on the constructs of this chapter.

Organizational managerial strategies can be developed through critical thinking with qualitative as well as quantitative grounded theory with phenomenology as a particular research approach (Bowser, 2015). Management field researchers have not fully embraced this approach (Ehrich, 2005). This approach is holistic and can provide insight of human understanding, reflection, and sensitivity (Meyer-Drawe, 1997). The author believes the norm of research literature that separates processes and concepts of social, psychosocial, psychology, philosophy, and phenomenology will change because global business management and organizational leadership are requiring a holistic approach for inductive based explanations for successful organizations.

## CONCLUSION

Emerging business models and managerial strategies in the non-profit sector are more similar if not the same as in any other organizations, including global organizations. The differences can be found in the design or footprint of the organizational unit structure. This chapter focused on bringing awareness to leaders concerning unified concepts of management, leadership, and adaptability of change or a new mindset for developing modeled global-friendly organizations, whether non-profit or for-profit.

This chapter provided background on how to consider a grounded theory approach to understanding organizational behavior by incorporating hermeneutic phenomenology to analyze the deeper meaning of actions and reactions (Bowser, 2015). Several scholars are mentioned as to how they addressed management strategies from IC (Kong, 2008), investing in intellectual property, information, experience, and knowledge (Stewart, 1997), investing in technology, skills, and customer relations (Edvinsson & Malone, 1997), identifying stereotyping non-profit vs. for-profit organizations (Aaker et al., 2010), and boundaries between non-profit organizations and for-profit organizations (Bailly & Chapelle, 2012). The lack of knowledge is the holdback in addressing growth, change, and development of new concepts and new ways of thinking. To gain knowledge, one must understand how to connect human nature and relations, spirituality, environment, and global thought of unification. One must understand how this knowledge navigates the organizational transformation process.

CLT helped in discussing issues of why an organization's adjustment and adaption to change were easy or challenging. Knowledge and awareness of cultural leadership constructs demonstrated how these constructs shape stakeholder ILT and the belief system of the organizational unit system. Therefore, the attitudes of stakeholders/members stem from the culture of that specific organization. The GLOBE project's six leadership dimensions (House & Javidan, 2004) were discussed based on cultural organizational and leadership effectiveness. It was realized that economic competition, as well as human conditions of societies, were related to the influence of behavior.

These facts led to CQ of leaders being able to understand and engage others in adjusting and adapting to a new mindset and environment. The process of perspective-taking is necessary and is influenced based upon assigned duties and responsibilities. Perspective-taking helps one to be aware of differences and similarities in a mindset, as well as helps one to make unbiased decisions. Competencies in leadership are necessary to better understand adaptability to change, which is explained in Figure 3. The Cognition Step, the Behavior Step, and the Trait Step are levels of ignorance, awareness, understanding, transitioning, appreciation, learning, adapting, and transformation. In making decisions and maintaining organizational equilibrium, leaders and managers must be knowledgeable and able to identify the challenges and stressors. In doing so, the ABCXT's concept is shown and demonstrated in Figure 4, showing how each component represents organization's stressors, resources, perception of event, and whether the organization can meet demands. For scholars or scientists to further assist organizations to investigate lived experiences with created patterns and relationships of organizational meaning, hermeneutic phenomenology is appropriate for revealing deeper insights into behavior and the condition of the organizations.

Non-profit organization awareness and understanding of a successful organizational structure and the importance of an on-going open transformation system involving all stakeholders of the organizational unit will give rise to a stronger system. The diversity and competing expectation brought to the organization will allow the organization to maintain and preserve its effectiveness. Figure 5 depicts an organizational unit structure's open transformation system, which will strengthen its foundation, as well as the stakeholders' autonomous social and transitioning behaviors. An open transformation system is ethical, unified, feasible, and stable for addressing the demands of constant change and 21$^{st}$ century's globalization concerns. Therefore, Table 1 provides a list of factors that can contribute to better understanding open transformation and support of non-profit organizations in managerial strategies. An OAP model, as in Figure 6, demonstrates the flow of managerial process strategy for recognizing the need of leadership competences, support, and training for continuous transformation. Although the author did not discuss developing policy and procedure manuals with constant updates, an OAP model can serve as an outline for such manuals. It will take deliberate efforts and actions to create an organizational culture of global diverse inclusion and cannot be created indefinitely without good ethics, spirituality, patience, and perseverance.

## REFERENCES

Aaker, J., Vohs, K. D., & Mogilner, C. (2010). Nonprofits are seen as warm and for-profits as competent: Firm stereotypes matter. *The Journal of Consumer Research*, *37*(2), 224–237. doi:10.1086/651566

Alexander, J. (2000). Adaptive strategies of non-profit human service organizations in an era of devolution and new public management. *Nonprofit Management & Leadership*, *10*(3), 287–303. doi:10.1002/nml.10305

Ang, S., van Dyne, L., Koh, C., Ng, K. Y., Templer, K. J., Tay, C., & Chandrasekar, N. A. (2007). Cultural intelligence: Its measurement and effects on cultural judgement and decision making, cultural adaptation and task performance. *Management and Organization Review*, *3*(3), 335–371. doi:10.1111/j.1740-8784.2007.00082.x

Avolio, B. J. (2007). Promoting more integrative strategies for leadership theory-building. *The American Psychologist*, *62*(1), 25–33. doi:10.1037/0003-066X.62.1.25 PMID:17209677

Bader, B., Berg, N., & Holtbrügge, D. (2013). Expatriate performance in high-risk countries: Influence of family-related stress. *Academy of Management Proceedings, 50*(1).

Bailly, F., & Chapelle, K. (2012). The training of jobseekers by non-profit organizations: An analysis based on data from the upper Normandy region of France. *Metroeconomica*, *64*(4), 645–682.

Barnard, C. I. (1938). *The functions of the executive*. Cambridge, MA: Harvard University Press.

Bauer, T. N., & Taylor, S. (2001). When managing expatriate adjustment, dont forget the spouse. *The Academy of Management Executive*, *15*(4), 135–137. doi:10.5465/AME.2001.5898750

Bell, M. P., & Harrison, D. A. (1996). Using intra-national diversity for inter-national assignments: A model of bicultural life experiences and expatriate adjustment. *Human Resource Management Review*, *6*(1), 47–74. doi:10.1016/S1053-4822(96)90004-2

Berry, J. W. (1990). Psychology of acculturation: Understanding individuals moving between cultures. In R. W. Brislin (Ed.), *Applied cross-cultural psychology* (pp. 232–253). Newbury Park, CA: Sage. doi:10.4135/9781483325392.n11

Bloomberg, L. D., & Volpe, M. (2012). *Completing your qualitative dissertation. A road map from beginning to end*. Thousand Oaks, CA: Sage.

Bowser, B. R. (2015). *A grounded theory approach to creating a new model for understanding cultural adaptation of families in international assignments*. ProQuest Dissertation UMI 3718617. Capella University, Ann Arbor, MI: ProQuest, LLC.

Bronfenbrenner, U. (1979). *The ecology of human development: Experiments by nature and design*. Cambridge, MA: Harvard University Press.

Caligiuri, P. M., Hylan, M. M., & Joshi, A. (1998). Testing a theoretical model for examining the relationship between family adjustment and expatriates work adjustment. *The Journal of Applied Psychology*, *83*(4), 598–614. doi:10.1037/0021-9010.83.4.598 PMID:9729928

Caligiuri, P. M., & Tarique, I. (2009). Predicting effectiveness in global leadership activities. *Journal of World Business*, *44*(3), 336–346. doi:10.1016/j.jwb.2008.11.005

Charmaz, K. (2006). *Constructing grounded theory: A practical guide through qualitative analysis*. Thousand Oaks, CA: Sage.

Chin, C., Gu, J., & Tubbs, S. (2001). Developing global leadership competencies. *The Journal of Leadership Studies*, *7*(3), 20–31. doi:10.1177/107179190100700402

Creed, G. S. (2006). *Families in cross-cultural transitions: Psychological adjustment, socio-cultural adaptation and acculturation strategy* (Unpublished doctoral dissertation). University of Northern Colorado, Greeley, CO.

Deutsch, K. W. (1968). Toward a cybernetic model of man and society. In W. Buckley (Ed.), *Modern systems research for the behavioral scientist*. Chicago: Aidine Publishing Company.

Dorfman, P., Javidan, M., Hanges, P., Dastmalchian, A., & House, R. (2012). GLOBE: A twenty-year journey into the intriguing world of culture and leadership. *Journal of World Business*, *540*, 1–15.

Earley, C. P., & Ang, S. (2003). *Cultural intelligence: Individual interactions across cultures*. Stanford, CA: Stanford University Press.

Edvinsson, L., & Malone, M. S. (1997). *Intellectual capital – The proven way to establish your company's real value by measuring its hidden brainpower*. New York: Harper Business.

Ehrich, L. C. (2005). *Revisiting phenomenology: Its potential for management research*. Retrieved from http://eprints.qut.edu.au/2893/1/2893.pdf

Eisenberg, P. (1997). A crisis in the non-profit sector. *National Civic Review*, *86*(4), 331–341. doi:10.1002/ncr.4100860409

Farh, C. I. C., Bartol, K. M., Shapiro, D. L., & Shin, J. (2010). Networking abroad: A process model of how expatriates form support ties to facilitate adjustment. *Academy of Management Review*, *35*(3), 434–454. doi:10.5465/AMR.2010.51142246

Firoz, N. M., & Ramin, T. (2004). Understanding cultural variables is critical to success in international business. *International Journal of Management*, *21*(3), 307–323.

Gupta, G., & Gupta, A. (2012). International assignments, expatriate adjustment and perceived impact of parent organization support. *Business & Management Review*, *3*(1), 57–65.

Harrison, D. A., Shaffer, M. A., & Bhaskar-Shrinivas, P. (2004). Going places: Roads more and less traveled in research on expatriate experiences. *Research in Personnel and Human Resources Management*, *22*, 203–252.

Hill, R. (1949). *Families under stress: Adjustment to the crises of war separation and reunion*. New York, NY: Harper.

House, R. J., & Javidan, M. (2004). Overview of GLOBE. In R. J. House, P. Hanges, M. Javidan, P. Dorfman, & V. Gupta (Eds.), *Culture, leadership, and organizations: The GLOBE study of 62 societies* (pp. 9–28). Thousand Oaks, CA: Sage.

Iida, M., Seidman, G., Shrout, P., Fujita, K., & Bolger, N. (2008). Modeling support provision in intimate relationships. *Journal of Personality and Social Psychology*, *94*(3), 460–478. doi:10.1037/0022-3514.94.3.460 PMID:18284292

Javidan, M., Dorfman, P. W., de Luque, M. S., & House, R. J. (2006). In the eye of the beholder: Cross-cultural lessons in leadership from Project GLOBE. *The Academy of Management Perspectives*, *20*(1), 67–90. doi:10.5465/AMP.2006.19873410

Kast, F. E., & Rosenzweig, J. E. (1972). General systems theory: Applications for organization and management. *Academy of Management Journal*, *15*(4), 447–465. doi:10.2307/255141

Kong, R. (2008). The development of strategic management in the non-profit context: Intellectual capital in social service non-profit organizations. *International Journal of Management Reviews*, *10*(3), 281–299. doi:10.1111/j.1468-2370.2007.00224.x

Konopaske, R., Robie, C., & Ivancevich, J. M. (2005). A preliminary model of spouse influence on managerial global assignment willingness. *International Journal of Human Resource Management*, *16*(3), 405–426. doi:10.1080/0958519042000339570

Lord, R. G., & Maher, K. J. (1991). *Leadership and information processing: Linking perceptions and performance* (Vol. 1). Cambridge, MA: Unwin Hyman.

Maslow, A. H. (1943). A theory of human motivation. *Psychological Review*, *50*(4), 370–396. doi:10.1037/h0054346

McCubbin, H. L., & Patterson, J. M. (1982). Family adaptation to crises. In H. L. McCubbin, E. Cauble, & J. M. Patterson (Eds.), *Family stress, coping, and social support* (pp. 26–47). Springfield, IL: Thomas.

McCubbin, H. L., & Patterson, J. M. (1983). The family stress process: The double ABCX model of adjustment and adaptation. In H. L. McCubbin, M. B. Sussman, & J. M. Patterson (Eds.), *Advances and developments in family stress theory and research* (pp. 7–37). New York, NY: Haworth. doi:10.1300/J002v06n01_02

Meyer-Drawe, K. (1997). Education. In L. Embree, E. A. Behnke, D. Carr, J. C. Evans, J. Huertas-Jourda, J. J. Kockelmans, & R. M. Zaner (Eds.), *Encyclopedia of phenomenology* (pp. 157–162). Dordrecht, Netherlands: Kluwer. doi:10.1007/978-94-017-5344-9_36

Minuchin, S. (1974). *Families and family therapy*. Cambridge, MA: Harvard University Press.

Nebus, J. (2006). Building collegial information networks: A theory of advice network generation. *Academy of Management Review*, *31*(3), 615–637. doi:10.5465/AMR.2006.21318921

Osula, B., & Ng, E. C. W. (2014). Toward a collaborative, transformative model of non-profit leadership: Some conceptual building blocks. *American Scientist*, *4*, 87–104.

Park, J. H., & Abbott, J. L. (2011). A new approach to expatriate effectiveness: A perspective-taking model for global assignments. *Academy of Management Review*, *91*(1), 1–6.

Sanchez, J. I., Spector, P. E., & Cooper, C. L. (2000). Adapting to a boundaryless world: A developmental expatriate model. *The Academy of Management Executive*, *14*(2), 96–106.

Searle, W., & Ward, C. (1990). The prediction of psychological and socio-cultural adjustment during cross-cultural transitions. *International Journal of Intercultural Relations*, *14*(4), 449–464. doi:10.1016/0147-1767(90)90030-Z

Shaw, J. B. (1990). A cognitive categorization model for the study of intercultural management. *Academy of Management Review*, *15*(4), 626–645.

Silvanto, S., & Ryan, J. (2014). Relocation branding: A strategic framework for attracting talent from abroad. *Journal of Global Mobility*, *2*(1), 102–120. doi:10.1108/JGM-07-2013-0046

Sternberg, R. J. (1982). *Handbook of human intelligence*. Cambridge, UK: Cambridge University Press.

Stewart, T. A. (1997). *Intellectual capital: The new wealth of organizations*. New York: Currency Doubleday.

Stoltz, P. (1997). *Adversity quotient*. New York, NY: John Wiley & Sons.

Todres, L., & Wheeler, S. (2001). The complementarity of phenomenology, hermeneutics and existentialism as a philosophical perspective for nursing research. *International Journal of Nursing Studies*, *38*(1), 1–8. doi:10.1016/S0020-7489(00)00047-X PMID:11137717

van Manen, M. (1990). *Researching lived experience: Human science for an action sensitive pedagogy*. Albany, NY: State University of New York Press.

van Manen, M. (1991). *The tact of teaching: The meaning of pedagogical thoughtfulness*. Albany, NY: State University of New York Press.

Wang, Z. (2006). *Displaced self and sense of belonging: A Chinese researcher studying Chinese expatriates working in the United States*. ProQuest Dissertation UMI 3240429. University of South Florida, Ann Arbor, MI: ProQuest, LLC.

Ward, C., & Rana-Deuba, A. (1999). Acculturation and adaptation revisited. *Journal of Cross-Cultural Psychology*, *60*(4), 422–442. doi:10.1177/0022022199030004003

White, C., Woodfield, K., & Ritchie, J. (2003). Reporting and presenting qualitative data. In J. Richie & J. Lewis (Eds.), *Qualitative research practice: A guide for social science students and researchers* (pp. 287–320). London: Sage.

## KEY TERMS AND DEFINITIONS

**Autonomous:** Having the right or power of self-government to capably exist independently and respond, react, or develop independent of the whole.

**Cultural Distance:** The differences of cultural values amongst countries, organizations, and stakeholders.

**Hermeneutic:** The use of poetic (sensitive/reflective) language put to writing to present human experience, feeling, and deep meaning, allowing for a better understanding of a phenomenon more carefully with a moral dimension.

**Intellectual Capital:** Wealth created by investments in intellect, experience, skills, information, knowledge, training, technology, spirituality, autonomism, Unitarianism, and customer relations.

**Open Transformation:** An on-going process of incoming and outgoing communications addressing new demands, increasing CQ and knowledge on organizational behavior in view of social, psychosocial, philosophical, and psychological development.

**Perspective-Taking:** A cognitive process that allows one to imagine or picture the world from someone else's viewpoint or lens.

**Phenomenology:** A methodology for exploring human experiences in management studies, as well as other disciplines.

**Spirituality:** Goodness and truth within or self-actualization.

**Tie-Formation:** A process that examines how a combination of various factors influence organizational relationships and structural transformations.

# Chapter 9
# Crowdfunding for Non-Profits: Opportunities and Challenges

**Amir Manzoor**
*Bahria University, Pakistan*

## ABSTRACT

*Crowdfunding has been applied to equity investments as well as in a preproduction consumer purchase model. Crowdfunding is projected to become a $US90-96 billion industry by 2025, and is being touted as a valuable tool for fundraising for charitable non-profits. For leading non-profits around the globe a critical question is whether charitable crowdfunding is a threat or an opportunity for them. This chapter demonstrates that charitable crowdfunding represents a powerful new fundraising tool for leading, start-ups and not for profit organisations. This discussion contributes to the financial knowledge, specifically in the online crowdfunding and non-profit organisations and concludes that non-profit organisations through crowdfunding has the potential to expand the donor base.*

## INTRODUCTION

Crowdfunding, a recent phenomenon of the contemporary not for profit marketplace, raises capital from an extensive online community of individuals, called a crowd. The funds obtained from the individual is usually small-to-medium (Ordanini, 2009). According to Mulvey, (2013), the non-profit sector can couple crowdfunding with social media to produce radical changes in the way nonprofits obtain funds. Crowdfunding has changed the dynamics of funding and has become the new avenue of fundraising for non-profits to do so social good (Hobey, 2014). Crowdfunding occurs on an information technological platform which directly links donors and requestors, resulting in a very effective fundraising method. In the contemporary marketplace environment, non-profit stakeholders should seriously analyze the potential of crowdfunding revenue raising and the financial contributions to the organization. Crowdfunding today has become so important that some researchers now consider crowdfunding for non-profit sector as important as what digital file sharing once was for in the music industry (Southin, 2013).

This chapter examines crowdfunding as a phenomenon, applications and impact of crowdfunding as an additional source of revenue for nonprofits. Following the introduction, a background of crowd-

DOI: 10.4018/978-1-5225-2537-0.ch009

Copyright © 2017, IGI Global. Copying or distributing in print or electronic forms without written permission of IGI Global is prohibited.

funding is provided. A brief summary of the non-profit sector and crowdfunding explores recent trends that have made crowdfunding a significant opportunity for non-profits. Section four explores various regulatory changes that would be needed keeping in view the trends that are occurring in the nonprofit sector. The behavior of donors, aggregated increase in funding for not for profit organizations, legislation and taxation are discussed. This chapter generates knowledge in facilitating alternative revenue opportunities and concludes with

## CROWDFUNDING PHENOMENON

Crowdfunding is an attractive alternative to traditional funding even for individuals. Crowdfunding is so popular that the campaign sponsors can achieve their funding goal in a very short period. It takes a lot of preparation before the launch of crowdfunding campaign to achieve funding goal. Sometimes, celebrity power can also help achieve funding goal. Take example of music legend Neil Young. He started his crowdfunding campaign and was able to achieve his $2.4 million funding goal in just one day (Ursery, 2014). For small businesses, crowdfunding is a great source of alternative funding. These businesses, musicians, and real estate are the major beneficiaries of crowdfunding (Hogue, 2015; Fisk et al., 2011). In 2014, more than 60% of small and medium businesses (SMBs) in USA alone were looking at alternative sources of funding including friends and family.

For not for profit organizations as well, there is enormous potential to secure financial resources and to leverage the power of the crowd to achieve organizational outcomes by using crowdfunding platforms, such as:

1. Kickstarter,
2. Fundly,
3. IndieGoGo,
4. Kiva,
5. Peerbackers,
6. Fundable.

The US Jumpstart Our Business Startups (JOBS) Act of 2011 allowed smaller investors to purchase shares of a company and some US states enacted their own legislation to allow exemption for intrastate crowdfunding. Several states (including Georgia, Michigan and Washington) were actively seeking actions to shape crowdfunding industry to suit today's needs (Ursery, 2014). The JOBS act allowed the use of small amounts of capital from a large number of individuals to finance a new business venture over the Internet.

Crowdfunding is an opportunity as well for both large and small non-profits. Specifically, crowdfunding is a powerful fundraising tool for nonprofits that can substantially increase the donor base for all nonprofits. It's easy for anyone living anywhere to set up a web page for his/her crowdfunding project and start soliciting donation from the crowd. There are however, few basic requirement that the initiator of the crowdfunding project must meet. These requirements relate to the crowdfunding platform the initiator will be using. First, the initiator must set a funding goal. A funding goal determines the amount of funds the initiator wished to receive. Second, there must be a timeline of the crowdfunding project.

A timeline determines the possible number of days in which the funding goal can be achieved. Third requirement is the project pitch. A project pitch refers to the verbal and/or visual description of the crowdfunding project. Recent technological developments, especially web 2.0, has boosted crowdfunding. Now crowdfunding project initiators and donors can easily interact with each other e.g. by using social media. One great example is the 2008 US presidential election campaign. In this campaign, Barack Obama obtained 1 total of US$ 750 million in donation. Out of this amount, more than 50% came from donations whose individual worth was less than US$ 1000 (Glaser, 2010). During last decade, many crowdfunding platforms have emerged on the scene. One of the largest of these is the kickstarter.com.

## Kickstarter

Kickstarter is a very large global community developed to support creative projects. Around the globe, more than 10 million donors have supported Kickstarter project. In July 2016, Kickstarter was running 108,651 successful projects. The successful project is the one that achieved its funding goal. These project raised approximately $2480 million worth of donations (Kickstarter, 2016). The basic model of Kickstarter is based on a reward for donation. Kickstarter solely operates in US.

## Fundly

Fundly is another large online crowdfunding platform that operates exclusively for nonprofits and charities. Fundly only services U.S-based crowdsourcing campaigners and donors. Despite this limitation, by 2013, Fundly was running more than 3000 campaigns. These campaign raised more than US$ 300 million in donations (Fundly, 2013). Fundly charges a platform fee 4.9% + credit card processing fee 2.9 percent + $.30/transaction to set up a fundraising page (Fundly, 2016).

## Indiegogo

Indiegogo (www.indiegogo.com) is one of the world's largest crowdfunding platforms. With social media integration, direct email, and announcement features users can easily spread the word, raise awareness, and increase funding. For 501c) 3) nonprofits and charities in the US IndieGoGo offers a 25 percent fee reduction (indiegogo.com, 2016). In general, this exemption is applied to not-for-profit organizations (scientific, charitable, educational, religious, etc.) that must be registered and verified by the US Government through the IRS. 501(c) (3) tax exemptions and deductions are only available in the United States. Besides these very large crowdfunding platforms, there are many other small-to-medium sized crowdfunding platforms for nonprofits such as:

1. Causes,
2. CauseVox,
3. Crowdrise,
4. Giveffect,
5. Donate Now,
6. DonorsChoose,
7. FirstGiving,
8. Fundraise,

9. FundRazr,
10. Givezooks,
11. GoFundMe,
12. Help Attack,
13. Just Give,
14. Pay It Square,
15. Razoo,
16. StayClassy, and
17. Causes.

## Causes

Causes is a crowdfunding platform for GuideStar-verified 501(c) (3) nonprofits. Users can create a cause to support a nonprofit and integrate the campaign page with social media to mobilize their network to make donation.

## CauseVox

CauseVox is an online crowdfunding platform that nonprofits can use to create customized fundraising websites for campaigns.

## Crowdrise

Crowdrise is an online crowdfunding platform that followers of nonprofits can use to create personal fundraising pages where their friends and family can donate.

## Giveffect

Giveffect is exclusively for charitable crowdfunding where donations go directly to partner nonprofits (Chung, 2013).

## Donate Now

Donate Now/Network for Good provides free and economical fundraising tools that nonprofits can use to obtain donations on their own websites and on social networks.

## DonorChoose

DonorsChoose is a platform that individuals can use to obtain donations for needy students.

## FirstGiving

FirstGiving can be used by individuals to obtain online donations.

### Fundraise.com

Fundraise.com can be used by both individuals and organizations to manage their online fundraising activities.

### FundRazr

FundRazr is a social fundraising tool for both individuals and nonprofits.

### Givezooks

Givezooks! Can be used by nonprofits to create custom online crowdfunding campaigns and integrate their campaign sites with social media to increase donor base.

### GoFundMe

GoFundMe is a do-it-yourself online fundraising service for nonprofits.

### Help Attack

Help Attack! uses social media to collect donations.

### Just Give

JustGive (www.justgive.org) is crowdfunding platform where donors can give to nonprofit organizations through e.g. fundraising registries.

### Pay It Square

Pay It Square is a crowdfunding platform to create customized fundraising pagesand collect donations online.

### Razoo

Razoo is a platform that individuals and organizations can use to create fundraising pages and accept donations.

### StayClassy

StayClassy is used by small- and medium-size nonprofits for online crowdfunding.

To evaluate how effective the crowdfunding for nonprofits can be, the hurricane Sandy is a good case example. Within days after Sandy hit USA, many affected individuals started crowdfunding campaigns on sites like GoFundMe and IndieGoGo. The response received by these campaigns was very impressive and many initiators reported that they received donations from donors completely stranger for them (Goldmark, 2012). The American Red Cross also set up two campaigns with the option of directly contributing. These campaigns raised about US$ 2 million (Goldmark, 2012).

The scope of nonprofits crowdfunding can be easily judged by noting that American Red Cross collected US$ 178 million for Hurricane Sandy (American Red Cross, 2012a). Fundly (the largest non-profit crowdfunding platform) was able to raise US$ 305 million since its inception. In comparison, The American Red Cross' was able to generate of a revenue of $3.2 billion in 2012 alone (American Red Cross, 2012b). These examples make it clear that while nonprofit crowdfunding platforms are still in their nascent stages they have garnered attention for its success and become a novel approach of fundraising.

Many nonprofits have used crowdfunding successfully. Malaria No More is a campaign run by malarianomore.org to end malaria deaths. The campaign is run on causes.com and has 20,000 supporters. Ricky Martin, a Grammy award winning singer, human rights activist, launched a campaign to help combat human trafficking. The campaign had 21,000 supporters. Maria No More auctioned shirt worn by Andy Murray during his winning Wimbledon match to raise £10,000 (News, 2016).

The An Hour of Code for Every Student was initiated in December 15, 2014 at Indiegogo and was able to raise $5 million. The objective of the project is to provide every student in every school the opportunity to learn computer science at Code.org. Kids Company is a UK nonprofit that supports vulnerable children with various kinds of support including meals and clothing.

Kids Company became UK's innovation leader in fundraising after they raised more than £100,000 in a crowdfunding campaign run on Crowdfunder (Ratty, 2015). In USA, a young woman was fighting multiple life threatening diseases. The diseases put her into a situation where she needed a full accessible home; one in which she could move freely. Website Chive was inspired to feature Smith's story and in just 14 months, over 12,000 donors helped raise $US413,000 through the Hope for a Home campaign (Kim, 2015).

## TRENDS FOR CROWDFUNDING IN NOT FOR PROFITS

### The Demographics of Donors

Very little is understood about the demographic variables about crowdfunding donors. To gain insight into the demographic variables of donors and crowdfunding trends in nonprofit organization fundraising highlights how nonprofit organizations can capitalize on the opportunities provided through the crowdfunding platforms. An exploration of these trends can reveal the current strategic position of nonprofits to benefit from crowdfunding.

Nonprofits generate most of their revenue through government grants. However, for most non-profits individual donors are still a significant portion of the charity donors (Government of Canada, 2015; Fritz, 2015). In Canada, approximately one in five individual taxpayers made an average donation of $446 in the tax year 2010. According to Charity Navigator (Charity Navigator, 2016), charitable giving continued its upward trend in 2015. In 2015, as an estimated $373 billion was donated for charity. For the second year in a row, total giving reached record levels. During 2014 to 2015, donations for charity increased by more than 10%. In Canada, individual donors contributed 50% of the total amount of charitable donation in 2010.

More than two-third of charitable donations came from individuals aged 45 years and more. In 2010, the United Kingdom was the eighth most charitable nation in the world while the world's fastest growing major economies - China and India - rank among the least altruistic (Ramesh, 2010). Few notable characteristics of top donors included: aged 75 and over, widowers and widows, university graduates, and people with household income of at least $120,000. A glance over the demographic trends of donors reveals that most contributions come from same group of older and wealthy donors (Snipes & Oswald, 2010; Guy & Patton, 2013; Marx & Carter, 2014). This can be a problem for nonprofits of all sizes. With increase in population, the donor base remains stagnant. One particular demographic group of donors can be key for success in fundraising campaigns.

Crowdfunding for nonprofits can provide a distinctive solution to this problem. Since crowdfunding platforms to not release the demographic information of their donors, it is difficult to model demographic profile of crowdfunding donors. However, there is increased possibility that these users are technologically sophisticated and do not belong to the same old and wealthy demographic group of conventional donors (Gore & DiGiammarino, 2014; Belleflamme, Lambert, & Schwienbacher, 2013). Crowdfunding appears to be attracting newer donors. These are people who haven't given philanthropically before. However, in the early days of crowdfunding, it's not yet clear what demographics the fundraising method appeals to (The Canadian Press, 2012).

While there exist no clear picture of demographic profile of crowdfunding donors, one piece of information available is their average contribution amount. In 2012, the average amount of donation made at IndieGoGo was $76 (Indiegogo, 2012). It is probably safe to assume crowdfunding campaigns can attract smaller donations from a large group of donors. If this trend increases substantially, it can encourage nonprofits of all sizes to leverage this large base of online donors capable of making small donations. These donors would be the individuals who most probably would never have been accessed through traditional fundraising methods. Non-profits already tapping the conventional group of donors can tap this additional group of donors to add another revenue stream.

## Behavioral Motivations of Donors and Non-Donors

The understanding of behavioral motivations of donors can supplement the nonprofit crowdfunding efforts. Nonprofits of all sizes can equally benefit from crowdfunding. A review of studies on behavioral motivations of donors suggests that many factors are responsible for people's decision to donate for charity including self-esteem, public recognition, satisfaction of expressing gratitude for one's own wellbeing, and relief from feelings of guilt and obligation (Hibbert & Horne, 1996; (Bennett, 2003; White, 2001; Wojciechowski, 2009; Gore & DiGiammarino, 2014; Belleflamme, Lambert, & Schwienbacher, 2013). Self-esteem and public recognition are two main behavioral motivations for donors to donate. That means nonprofit crowdfunding is in a unique position to capitalize on these two factors. Nonprofits can harness self-esteem by narrowing the cause of their crowdfunding campaigns and by making modest funding goals. To harness public recognition of the donor, nonprofits should link their crowdfunding campaign with social media platforms such as Facebook.

Bendapudi, Singh, and Bendapudi (1996) developed a model that explains the donors' behaviors towards charity. This framework outlines multiple factors divided into categories that influence donors' behavior towards charity. A nonprofit can shape the factors of source (i.e. the overall image conveyed by the nonprofit in their crowdfunding campaign), message (i.e. all the elements in the message used to convince the donor to donate), and request (i.e. the amount of help solicited for) to modify the frequency and volume of donors' behavior in their favor. In a study based on the analysis of data obtained from IndieGoGo, Evers, Lourenço, and Beije (2012) applied these drivers and found that most important success factors were setting an achievable funding goal and the number of comments on the page of crowdfunding campaign.

To achieve greater success, fundraising campaign should have a short and positive pitch. Evers, Lourenço and Beije, (2012) found that the fundraising campaigns were able to gain more generous donations and achieve a large fundraising goal when they used campaign messages which praised potential donor's compassion and generosity. It appears that donors have a self-esteem motivation with a philanthropic drive and want to feel that their contribution made some significant difference in the lives of people who need help. This apparent donors' preference was reflected in the findings of Statistics Canada. Statistics Canada (Statistics Canada, 2010) found that donors felt most motivated to donate when they felt compassion towards people in need. Nonprofits focusing their pitches on a narrow cause can leverage this preference of donors. Nonprofits, such as World Vision, are already using this approach by running Adopt a Child program. Nonprofit crowdfunding campaigns can harness public recognition of donors though interconnectedness with Facebook and other social media platforms.

Smith, Windmeijer, and Wright (2012) analyzed a large dataset of donations made on behalf individual fundraisers. The donations were made through two websites (Justgiving and Virgin Money Giving) that both worked the same way. Fundraisers set up a web page on behalf of a nonprofit and then used social media to appeal to people for donation. Smith et al. also found that, on average, a £10 increase in the mean of past donations lead new donations of £3.60 more. Findings indicate that this crowding in occurs in nonprofit crowdfunding because the crowdfunding platform can be linked with social media so that a donor's network sees when they make a donation. Established charities like the International Red Cross and Red Crescent Movement capitalized on this and were able to get more than 129,000 likes on Facebook. This supporter base can also notify other people in their network when they donate. This social currency can quickly transform into charitable currency via crowdfunding (Southin, 2013).

## Understanding Non-Donor Behavior

A survey of Statistics Canada (Statistics Canada, 2010) revealed that the most common reason for donors not giving more was that they could not afford to give more. Two other popular reason were that they were happy with what they had already given and that they had given money directly to people in need rather than to organizations. Another study found that Americans donated twice as much as individuals in other rich nations but many donors did not donate more because of various reasons such as they felt they had already given too much, they needed savings for themselves and family, they thought their donation was not large enough to make an impact, they poverty is inevitable, that their donation don't get to people in need, that eradicating poverty is the job of government only, people should solve their problems themselves, and that giving donation can lead to overpopulation (The Life You Can Save, 2016).

To appeal to non-donors, nonprofit crowdfunding campaigns should be narrow and personalized. One more issues is these non-donors negative perception of how organizations used their money. This negative perception can increase with age. This concern over efficiency of fund use is particularly relevant to crowdfunding. To overcome this concern, nonprofits should ensure that they get themselves registered with the relevant tax authorities and highlight it in their crowdfunding campaigns. When donors know that a nonprofit is registered, they know the risk of fraud is minimum because authorities know where a donation is going. In this aspect, established nonprofits are in a better position to take advantage of crowdfunding than the newly started nonprofits.

## MISSAPPROPRIATIONS OF CROWDFUNDING

Since crowdfunding has become a new and attractive source of financing, more and more stories are surfacing about the misuse of crowdfunding. On crowdfunding platforms, many campaigns are started with a story to appeal potential donors to donate. These stories may range from saving a cancer patient to help an infertile couple have a baby. Truth of such stories is difficult to prove. Several U.S. states have issued warnings for immense potential misuse of crowdfunding. One example is a crowdfunding campaign that was initiated by a women to raise funds for her breast cancer treatment. It appeared that this women used the funds generated for her breast augmentation that could have been done free of cost at some breast implant service providers (DocCheck News, 2012).

In another case, the Europe's biggest Kickstarter project, the Zano mini-drone ended up nothing. The project had 12,000 backers and raised £2.3m in funding. The project was started by Torquing Group, a business started by a self-taught engineer Ivan Reedman to build a marketable drone. The Zano project was cleverly marketed and a video was released that showed a drone was already developed but its performance was poorer than expected. This video excited so much interest in the project. Later it was discovered that video showed features of drone that were not operational at the time it was shot.

The Torquing's directors managed their business poorly and spent the Kickstarter money too freely. Kickstarter chose Zano as a "staff pick". The Zono project was one of the projects shortlisted by the tech news site Engadget for their best of CES 2015 award. All this happened even though the Torquing team could not demonstrate the drone flying at the show. The creators of the "Smarty Ring" raised about $US400,000 on Indiegogo without having to provide any background information on the team or the production company. They missed delivery dates but occasionally provided terse updates saying that they would deliver at some point. The most important lesson to be learnt is for crowdfunding platform providers. These crowdfunding platforms need to reconsider the way they deal with projects involving complex hardware, massive overfunding, or large sums of money (Cellan-Jones, 2016).

The current crowdfunding mechanisms provide little consumer protection. While crowdfunding platforms claim to use complex algorithms and automated tools to identify and investigate suspicious activity on projects it is caveat civitas. The platforms get bigger and delve into equity crowdfunding and crowdfunding audience is getting larger and more money is flowing to projects and sponsors with relatively limited information about them. For example, Altrius Management, a company that raised $25,000 on Kickstarter for a playing card game called Asylum designed by a Serbian artist. The company missed delivery dates and provided no updates. The company was sued by the state of Washington and sought restitution for donors and penalties for violating the state's consumer protection statutes.

In another case, Federal Trade Commission (FTC) charged Erik Chevalier for misuse of $122,874 he raised on Kickstarter for a board game called, "The Doom That Came to Atlantic City". The game was never delivered and Erik promised to refund the money but he never did. The FTC settled the matter with Erik by refraining him from future misrepresentations about crowdfunding and penalized him $111,000, though the penalty was suspended due to Chevalier's inability to pay. The FTC has launched a program called FinTech aimed at protecting consumers in crowdfunding projects. Still with no objective third party review/validation of the investment details presented, investing on equity crowdfunding platforms can be a very risky business (Cohen, 2015).

## REGULATORY REGIME

### Tax Credit

Current tax incentives are limited to those taxpayers itemizing deductions or designating bequests. This structure leads to lost opportunities in higher levels of donations. A recent study indicates that tax deductibility encourages charitable giving at all levels of income (Enders, 2016). The regulatory regime needs many changes to support crowdfunding for nonprofits. In Canada, Imagine Canada (a large Canadian charitable organization) proposed 'stretch tax credit' to address the issue of limited number of conventional donors and encourage new and less wealthy donors to become philanthropists.

The Stretch Tax Credit is a proposal to increase the federal charitable tax credit on giving that exceeds a donor's previous highest giving level. The tax credit would increase from 15% to 25% for eligible amounts below $200, and from 29% to 39% for eligible amounts above $200. The broad objective of this proposed tax credit was to provide Canadians with an extra incentive to stretch their giving, as the proportion of Canadian tax filers claiming charitable donations is declining and the amount they collectively donate has gone down.

Research shows that more than half of donors would increase their giving if there were better tax incentives (Imagine Canada, 2016). The Canada's House of Commons Standing Committee on Finance endorsed this proposal (Imagine Canada, 2015) and submitted it for further consideration by the Finance Minister due to its potential to expand the donor base and the overwhelming support it had received from nonprofits and charities. Offering similar incentives worldwide to first time and small donors would assist crowdfunding's ability to increase donor base. All donors may not value tax incentive the same but we saw earlier that one major reason cited for not donating was the unaffordability. This reason, coupled with non-trust on nonprofits for their ability to utilize donations, tax credit can ensure charitable crowdfunding could significantly increase overall because donors can feel positively about their finances (Southin, 2013).

### Crowdsourced Policing

The herding behavior can be encouraged by crowdfunding and there is inherent chances of fraud in crowdfunding projects (Hazen, 2012). To address the threat of fraudulent use of crowdsourced funds, it is important that tax authorities should initiate programs where citizens could inform them of any tax violations. In Canada, the Revenue Agency implemented an expended online crowdsourced Informant Leads program. This is an online system that citizens can use to report suspected income tax violations by organizations (Government of Canada, 2012).

Expansion of systems like these can enable citizens to report suspected fraudulent crowdfunding campaigns by individuals or nonprofits. Tax authorities could run campaigns to guide independent investigations conducted by people who find any suspect of fraudulent use of the funds. To extend their crowdsourced policing mechanism, tax authorities can provide online crowdsourced investigation of nonprofits to assure future donors that their funds will be used as promised. Use of social media can ensure getting prompt response from people and ensure the funds raised in response to onetime events such as disasters are administered properly (Schneider & Trottier, 2012).

## Crowdfunding Legislation

In many parts of the world, crowdfunding is effectively banned due to the extensive registration and disclosure requirements imposed on parties seeking to raise capital from the public. Some accredited investors (i.e. those who meet certain requirements for income and net worth) are exempted from these registration requirements. The growing crowdfunding industry has also highlighted a need for establishing frameworks through which can invest in a company's shares without being subject to traditional rules of publicly traded securities. These frameworks, such as US JOBS act, will permanently allow crowdfunding and shrink the regulatory burden for companies seeking to go public. At the same time, these frameworks will have broad implications for the capital markets and their participants, particularly CFOs.

The US SEC amended the Regulation A of the Securities Act of 1933 to provide tiers of crowdfunded businesses. Smaller businesses made up the first tier and had to fulfill specific documentation requirements, such as disclosures to the SEC staff prior to the offering as well as periodic disclosures. The larger companies were placed in second tier, were required to provide audited financial statements and subjected to stringent conditions with respect to the amount of company stock that investors who are not accredited can purchase. However, opponents of these favorable legislations for crowdfunding argue that the Internet-enabled fund raising brings so many risks. For example, the crowdfunding platform can be closed, failed or hacked. In these cases, there will be a significant loss of data and investment losses for crowdfunding investors. Another concern is that decreased transparency can greater risk of fraud and malfeasance.

The regulatory authorities may not have the resources or the time to effectively police these relatively small, localized securities offerings before they are sold to the public. Governments need to enact legislation so that these crowdfunding campaigns receive appropriate regulatory scrutiny to ensure investor protection. If these legislations are not in place, there is a danger that crowdfunding investors may undervalue the good companies against companies with inferior prospects or less transparency. Governments also need legislation that ensure crowdfunding campaigns do not misguide the non-professional and less-sophisticated investors. These less sophisticated investors are more likely to trade on pro forma earnings and tend to overestimate the stability of company's earnings (Gaynor, Morse, & Pevzner, 2015). The crowdfunding legislation also needs to take into account the corporate malfeasance (such as accounting fraud) that can significantly hurt crowdfunding. When companies raising capital through crowdfunding are subject to relaxed underwriting rules and less scrutiny, there is a high risk that non-professional investors can run into financial losses. Besides legislation, one remedy for this risk is the use of online communities. These communities can various parties to monitor and provide ongoing feedback for a crowdfunding project.

# CONCLUSION

Crowdfunding is a relatively new phenomenon and at its early stages of development in the nonprofit sector. It has become an important source of revenue and fundraising for startups and nonprofit organizations. As an additional resource, crowdfunding can provide additional financial avenues for both large and small nonprofits. In the contemporary marketplace environment, non-profit stakeholders should seriously analyze the potential of crowdfunding revenue raising and the financial contributions that can be made to the organization.

However, research on crowdfunding in not for profit organizations is just beginning to emerge. This chapter provided a snapshot to understanding crowdfunding and highlighted the emerging trends and opportunities that could benefit not for profit organizations in future.

Crowdfunding also addresses the issue of limited number of conventional donors available for funding nonprofits. Nonprofits can use their enhanced understanding of the behavioral motivations of donors and non-donors to take advantage of crowdfunding. There exists a level playing field for both large and small nonprofits with respect to crowdfunding.

However, to expand use of crowdfunding for nonprofits it is important that some changes should be made in the regulatory regime including the tax credit scheme and crowdsourced policing. These changes can help extend donor base and aggregate funding by them for nonprofit crowdfunding campaigns. Future search projects could be undertaken to:

1. Explore the impact of crowdsourcing taxation on not for profit organizations globally, comparing different taxation policies across countries.
2. Conduct a comparative analysis of internal organizational crowdfunding knowledge in large and small not for profit organizations would expand existing insights on organizational capacity exploit this contemporary financial resource as an alternative fundraising mechanism.
3. Examine online behavioral characteristics of donors who provide financial support for not for profit organizations through the online crowdfunding platform could be further investigated to enhance understanding of donor-non-donor support for the not for profit organizations that seek, and access financial resources through the crowdfunding online platform.

## REFERENCES

American Red Cross. (2012a). *American Red Cross FY12 Financial Results*. Retrieved from http://www.redcross.org/images/MEDIA_CustomProductCatalog/m16040150_2012_fiscal_year_auditedFinancialSta tementDocs.pdf

American Red Cross. (2012b). *Superstorm Sandy: One Month Update*. Retrieved from http://www.redcross.ca/cmslib/general/int_news_sandy_update_monthone_2012.pdf

Belleflamme, P., Lambert, T., & Schwienbacher, A. (2013). Individual crowdfunding practices. *Venture Capital*, *15*(4), 313–333. doi:10.1080/13691066.2013.785151

Bendapudi, N., Singh, S., & Bendapudi, V. (1996). Enhancing helping behavior: An integrative framework for promotion planning. *Journal of Marketing*, *60*(3), 33–49. doi:10.2307/1251840

Bennett, R. (2003). Factors underlying the inclination to donate to particular types of charity. *International Journal of Nonprofit and Voluntary Sector Marketing*, *8*(1), 12–29. doi:10.1002/nvsm.198

Cellan-Jones, R. (2016, January 20). Zano: The rise and fall of Kickstarter's mini-drone. *BBC News*. Retrieved from http://www.bbc.com/news/technology-35356147

Charity Navigator. (2016). *Giving Statistics*. Retrieved July 8, 2016, from http://www.charitynavigator.org/index.cfm?

Chung, E. (2013, June 21). *Charity crowdfunding site launched by Toronto firm - Technology & Science - CBC News*. Retrieved July 8, 2016, from http://www.cbc.ca/news/technology/charity-crowdfunding-site-launched-by-toronto-firm-1.1337335

Cohen, R. (2015, July 2). *The Feds Take Action against Crowdfunding Fraud, and It's About Time!* Retrieved September 12, 2016, from https://nonprofitquarterly.org/2015/07/02/the-feds-take-action-against-crowdfunding-fraud-and-its-about-time/

DocCheck News. (2012, June 20). *Crowd Funding: The flock instead of public health insurance*. Retrieved September 12, 2016, from http://news.doccheck.com/en/56/crowd-funding-the-flock-instead-of-public-health-insurance/

Enders, B. (2016). *Tax Incentives: An Economic Basis for Charitable Giving | Learning to Give*. Retrieved July 8, 2016, from https://www.learningtogive.org/resources/tax-incentives-economic-basis-charitable-giving

Evers, M. W., Lourenço, C., & Beije, P. (2012). *Main drivers of crowdfunding success: a conceptual framework and empirical analysis*. Erasmus Universiteit.

Fisk, R. P., Patrício, L., Ordanini, A., Miceli, L., Pizzetti, M., & Parasuraman, A. (2011). Crowd-funding: Transforming customers into investors through innovative service platforms. *Journal of Service Management*, *22*(4), 443–470. doi:10.1108/09564231111155079

Fritz, J. (2015, December 4). *How Nonprofits Support Themselves*. Retrieved July 8, 2016, from http://nonprofit.about.com/od/fundraising/a/fundraising101.htm

Fundly. (2013, February 26). *World's Largest Crowdfunding-for-Good Platform, Fundly, Announces Campaign of the Year Winners*. Retrieved July 8, 2016, from http://www.prnewswire.com/news-releases/worlds-largest-crowdfunding-for-good-platform-fundly-announces-campaign-of-the-year-winners-193240701.html

Fundly. (2016, July 7). *Pricing*. Retrieved July 8, 2016, from http://fundly.com/pricing/

Gaynor, G., Morse, J., & Pevzner, M. (2015, October 1). *The Crowdfunding Effect*. Retrieved from http://sfmagazine.com/post-entry/october-2015-the-crowdfunding-effect/

Glaser, M. (2010, November 30). *Fundly + Facebook = Millions in Micro-Donations for Campaigns*. Retrieved July 7, 2016, from http://mediashift.org/2010/11/fundly-facebook-millions-in-micro-donations-for-campaigns334/

Goldmark, A. (2012, December 10). *Everyone Chip In, Please: Crowdfunding Sandy*. Retrieved July 8, 2016, from http://www.npr.org/2012/12/10/166742312/everyone-chip-in-please-crowdfunding-sandy

Gore, E. M., & DiGiammarino, B. (2014). *Crowdfunding for Nonprofits*. Standford Social Innovation Review.

Government of Canada. C. R. A. (2012, January 3). *Informant Leads Program*. Retrieved July 8, 2016, from http://www.cra-arc.gc.ca/leads/

Government of Canada. S. C. (2015, December 16). *Infographic: Charitable Giving in Canada*. Retrieved July 8, 2016, from http://www.statcan.gc.ca/pub/11-627-m/11-627-m2015006-eng.htm

Guy, B. S., & Patton, W. E. (2013). The marketing of altruistic causes: Understanding why people help. *Journal of Consumer Marketing*.

Hazen, T. L. (2012). Social Networks and the Law: Crowdfunding or Fraudfunding? Social Networks and the Securities Laws-Why the Specially Tailored Exemption Must Be Conditioned on Meaningful Disclosure. *North Carolina Law Review*, *90*, 1735–2162.

Hibbert, S., & Horne, S. (1996). Giving to charity: Questioning the donor decision process. *Journal of Consumer Marketing*, *13*(2), 4–13. doi:10.1108/07363769610115366

Hobey, E. (2014, July 4). *Fundly: Crowdfunding for the Greater Social Good Interview with Dennis Hu, CEO of Fundly*. Retrieved July 7, 2016, from http://www.crowdfundinsider.com/2014/07/43251-fundly-crowdfunding-greater-social-good-interview-dennis-hu-ceo-fundly/

Hogue, J. (2015, March 23). *Your Crowdfunding Questions, Answered*. Retrieved September 12, 2016, from http://www.crowd101.com/your-crowdfunding-questions-answered/

Imagine Canada. (2015, March 10). *Tax Incentives for Charitable Donations in Canada with a Focus on the Stretch Tax Credit for Charitable Giving | Imagine Canada*. Retrieved July 8, 2016, from http://www.imaginecanada.ca/sites/default/files/chief_economist_tax_incentives_discussion_paper_03102015.pdf

Imagine Canada. (2016). *Who we are | Imagine Canada*. Retrieved July 8, 2016, from http://www.imaginecanada.ca/who-we-are

Indiegogo. (2012, May 17). *Indiegogo Insight: Nearly 40% of Active Campaigns Receive Money From Multiple Countries - Indiegogo Blog*. Retrieved July 8, 2016, from https://go.indiegogo.com/blog/2012/05/indiegogo-insight-nearly-40-of-active-campaigns-receive-money-from-multiple-countries.html

indiegogo.com. (2016, July 7). *How To Raise Tax-Deductible Funds*. Retrieved July 8, 2016, from http://support.indiegogo.com/hc/en-us/articles/202444736-How-To-Raise-Tax-Deductible-Funds

Kickstarter. (2016, July 7). *Kickstarter Stats — Kickstarter*. Retrieved July 8, 2016, from https://www.kickstarter.com/help/stats

Kim, L. (2015, January 2). *Most Successful Feel-Good Crowdfunding Campaigns of the Year*. Retrieved September 12, 2016, from http://www.inc.com/larry-kim/most-successful-feel-good-crowdfunding-campaigns-of-the-year.html

Marx, J. D., & Carter, V. B. (2014). Factors influencing US charitable giving during the great recession: Implications for nonprofit administration. *American Scientist*, *4*(3), 350–372.

Mulvey, J. (2013, March 13). *Crowdfunding executive living the dream through his job | MNN - Mother Nature Network*. Retrieved July 7, 2016, from http://www.mnn.com/money/green-workplace/stories/crowdfunding-executive-living-the-dream-through-his-job

News, M. M. (2016, August 10). *Murray Wimbledon shirt raises £10,000 for Malaria No More UK*. Retrieved September 12, 2016, from http://fundraising.co.uk/2016/08/10/murray-wimbledon-shirt-raises-10000-malaria-no-uk/

Ordanini, A. (2009, March 23). *Crowd Funding: Customers as Investors - WSJ*. Retrieved July 7, 2016, from http://www.wsj.com/articles/SB123740509983775099

Ramesh, R. (2010, September 8). *Charitable giving by country: who is the most generous?* Retrieved July 8, 2016, from http://www.theguardian.com/news/datablog/2010/sep/08/charitable-giving-country

Ratty, J. (2015, May 14). *Crowdfunding Charities: 9 of the best UK charity crowdfunds*. Retrieved from http://www.crowdfunder.co.uk/blog/crowdfunding-charities-9-of-the-best-uk-charity-crowdfunds/

Schneider, C. J., & Trottier, D. (2012). The 2011 Vancouver riot and the role of Facebook in crowd-sourced policing. *BC Studies*, (175): 57.

Smith, S., Windmeijer, F., & Wright, E. (2012). *The effect of social information on charitable donations: Evidence from the (running) field1*. University of Bristol Working Paper.

Snipes, R. L., & Oswald, S. L. (2010). Charitable giving to not-for-profit organizations: Factors affecting donations to non-profit organizations. *Innovative Marketing*, *6*(1), 73–80.

Southin, T. (2013). *Harnessing the Fundraising Potential of Charitable Crowdfunding in Canada*. Retrieved from http://travissouthin.com/images/pdf/CharitableCrowdfunding-TravisSouthin.pdf

Statistics Canada. (2010). *Charitable giving by Canadians*. Retrieved July 8, 2016, from http://www.statcan.gc.ca/pub/11-008-x/2012001/article/11637-eng.htm

The Canadian Press. (2012, August 4). *Crowdfunding trend thrust into spotlight by Canadian campaigns - Toronto - CBC News*. Retrieved July 8, 2016, from http://www.cbc.ca/news/canada/toronto/crowdfunding-trend-thrust-into-spotlight-by-canadian-campaigns-1.1136447

The Life You Can Save. (2016). *Ten reasons why people don't donate to charity*. Retrieved July 8, 2016, from http://www.thelifeyoucansave.org/learn-more/common-objections-to-giving

White, D. E. (2001). Why do people donate to charity? *The Nonprofit Handbook: Fund Raising, 3*.

Wojciechowski, A. (2009). Models of charity donations and project funding in social networks. In *OTM Confederated International Conferences on the Move to Meaningful Internet Systems* (pp. 454–463). Springer. doi:10.1007/978-3-642-05290-3_58

## ADDITIONAL READING

Howe, J. (2006, June 1). The Rise of Crowdsourcing | WIRED. Retrieved July 8, 2016, from http://www.wired.com/2006/06/crowds/

Imagine Canada. (2012). Stretch tax credit for charitable giving. Retrieved from http://www.imaginecanada.ca/files/www/en/publicaffairs/stretch_tax_credit_2012.pdf

Imagine Canada. (2013, March 22). Imagine Canada Reacts to Budget 2013 | Imagine Canada. Retrieved July 8, 2016, from http://www.imaginecanada.ca/who-we-are/whats-new/news/imagine-canada-reacts-budget-2013

Imagine Canada. (2016). Stretch Tax FAQ | Imagine Canada. Retrieved July 8, 2016, from http://www.imaginecanada.ca/our-programs/public-policy/stretch-campaign/stretch-tax-faq

Lindsey, J. A. (2012, December 13). Online Fundraising Websites for Nonprofits and Donors | The PayPal Official Insider Guide to Online Fundraising: A Wealth of Fundraising Options | Peachpit. Retrieved July 8, 2016, from http://www.peachpit.com/articles/article.aspx?p=1997936&seqNum=4

Maldonado, M. (2012, August 5). Crowd-funding campaigns gaining popularity with Canadians. Retrieved July 7, 2016, from http://www.nationalpost.com/m/wp/news/blog.html?b=news.nationalpost.com/2012/08/05/crowd-funding-campaigns-gaining-popularity-with-canadians

Ursrey, L. (2014, March 18). Before You Launch Your Crowdfunding Campaign, Read This. Retrieved September 12, 2016, from http://www.forbes.com/sites/lawtonursrey/2014/03/18/before-you-launch-your-crowdfunding-campaign-read-this/

## KEY TERMS AND DEFINITIONS

**Branding:** Refers to aligning what an individual or firm want people to think about itself with what people actually do think about the individual or firm.

**Business Plan:** A business plan defines business goals, explain why they are attainable, and plans for reaching them.

**Community:** Refers to a group of people who share some common interest.

**Crowdfunding Platform:** Refers to a website used to develop and run a fundraising campaign.

**Crowdfunding:** Refers to raise funds for a venture using a large group of people.

**Donor:** Refers to a person who donates something, especially money to charity.

**Non-Profit:** Refers to an organization that uses its surplus revenues to further achieve its purpose or mission.

**Recognition:** Refers to public acknowledgement of person's status or merits.

**Social Networking:** Refers to the use of dedicated websites and applications for people interaction.

**Sponsor:** Refers to a person who pays for a specific item to be released.

# Chapter 10
# Evaluation of Theories and Information System Adoption Drivers in Government Organizations:
## Using a Systematic Literature Review Process

**Nayeth Idalid Solorzano Alcivar**
*Escuela Superior Politécnica del Litoral (ESPOL), Ecuador*

**Louis Sanzogni**
*Griffith University, Australia*

**Luke Houghton**
*Griffith University, Australia*

## ABSTRACT

*The suitability of current Information System (IS) adoption models is anachronistic when uniformly applied across regions in developing economies, including Latin American (LAT) countries where the context varies from the accepted norm. From the premise that the major ingredients of adoption studies are drivers whose relationships are encapsulated into theoretical models, this chapter present a comprehensive Systematic Literature Review (SLR) process convergent towards the critical selection of reliable scholarly sources in order to identify empirically supported drivers of IS adoption successes and assesses their applicability in public organizations situated in LAT, as not for profit environments. Participants from Public Ecuadorian Organizations were sought out as a focus case to gather opinions and scrutinize identified drivers to demonstrate the depth of this problem. The study offers an overall comprehensive rationalization of proposed drivers, and the identified need for an adapted IS adoption theory for LAT contexts.*

DOI: 10.4018/978-1-5225-2537-0.ch010

Copyright © 2017, IGI Global. Copying or distributing in print or electronic forms without written permission of IGI Global is prohibited.

## INTRODUCTION

Information Systems (IS) in government organizations of developing economies are often overlooked by those conducting studies on technology acceptance and adoption. In particular, researchers look past the context of developing economies, such as Latin America (LAT) where opportunities to carry out studies are not readily available or difficult to come by. Regardless, local governments, as not for profit organizations, often struggle with such technology because it is undeveloped, under-resourced and it often does not live up to the expectations of those who have developed it. From a research integrity viewpoint, challenges remain in terms of how such economies successfully develop and adopt technology. The authors argue that current IS theories related to technology adoption have not adequately studied this context. For the purpose of this study, public organizations in Ecuador are looked at as a case in point to illustrate the research process applied.

The objective of this chapter is to illustrate the rigorous process that is required, by starting with a thorough Systematic Literature Review (SLR) process. This is to identify and homogenize relevant drivers of IS adoption. These drivers and the related theories –in some cases viewed as models– proposing such drivers are applied in our analysis with the purpose to understand adoption in the context of local government organizations in LAT. This research was sparked by a lack of IS adoption literature concerning public government organizations in LAT regions, despite the notorious overall volume of literature in this context. It is also supported by a concern that almost no scholarship exists that explores how these developing economies adopt and use IS and Information Technology (IT) in general.

The study begins with the identification of existing theories and proposed factors as drivers of IS/IT adoption, IS success, or software usage that have been associated with the successful adoption of IS in organizations. A general explanation of the analysis and the possible applicability of existing theories used in IS adoption to LAT regions then follows (sections 1 and 2).

First, to ensure a sound critical analysis of the existing research on the topic (Hart, 1998), an SLR was conducted as the key relevant part of the current investigation. This method uses a more rigorous and well-defined approach to literature review that helps to answer well-focused research questions more effectively (Cronin, Ryan, & Coughlan, 2008) (sections 3, 4 and 5). Second, from extracted data obtained through the SLR process, a rationalized set of empirically supported drivers of systems adoption success are determined (section 6). Third, drivers identified are also organized by control characteristics as is suggested by the existing literature examined. This was done in order to compare which group of the identified drivers is considered more relevant contextually in LAT and from the existing studies that emerged from the SLR process. Fourth, the set of drivers obtained was shown to local practitioners and IS/ICT experts working in Public Ecuadorian Organizations (PEOs) and used as a focus case study, to gather opinion about the relevance given to such drivers in local LAT organizational environments (section 7). Subsequently, as part of the analysis process it was noted that, contrary to the existing literature identified during the SLR process (mostly from developed countries), local practitioners and experts give more relevance to drivers related to technological infrastructure aspects rather than to other subjective aspects (section 8).

This chapter concludes with a rationalized list of adoption drivers put forward as possible candidate drivers of Successful IS Adoption (SISA) in local public organization within an LAT context. However, the need of further research to examine particular cases of IS adoption in local LAT contexts is suggested in order to strengthen the outcomes (section 9). Overall, the dentification of a refined set of drivers obtained through the detailed SLR process undertaken and scrutinized by individuals working in PEOs, indicates to stakeholders and researchers about relevant aspects that can affect SISA in LAT environments. The relationship and the level of significance between determined drivers will help to identify IS adoption issues for boosting technology readiness, particularly in government organization of developing economies.

## Background

Despite the volume of research on IS/IT adoption, there is a lack of IS adoption literature concerning public government organizations in emerging economies such as the LAT regions. For example, numerous empirical studies explain different facets of technology acceptance and/or software or system usage at the individual and organizational level; see, for example, Davis (1989), Venkatesh and Davis (2000), Rogers (1995), Tornatzky, Fleischer, and Chakrabarti (1990), and DeLone and McLean (1992). Most IS studies center on research in countries other than LAT countries, which have been largely omitted (Gomez, 2013), and in which the need of improved technology readiness have been mainly identified (Dutta & Bilbao-Osorio, 2012). Local public institutions in developing economies may be currently using IS platforms, however successful adoption needs to be ensured in order to improve their technology readiness. It is therefore appropriate that researchers identify a suitable theory or propose an adapted theory identifying the drivers that may most affect IS adoption, in this context.

## Issues, Controversies, Problems

Existing theories, grounded in developed economies, assume a higher developed consciousness of technology than that which is present in developing economies. It is therefore appropriate that researchers identify a suitable theory and drivers of successful adoption for organizations using IS platforms in developing economies.

The main part of this study is focused on identifying existing theories and proposed factors as drivers of IS/IT adoption, IS success, or software usage that have been associated with the successful adoption of IS in organizations. An analysis of the applicability of the theories to developing economies then follows. The aims are to homogenize a set of factors on adoption studies from existing theories and determine whether any of these theories, or an adapted theory, should be applied in order to understand adoption in the context of LAT economies.

# RESEARCH PURPOSE AND THE RESEARCH QUESTIONS

In order to ensure a thorough critical analysis of the existing research on the topic (Hart, 1998), an SLR process was conducted. This method uses a rigorous and well-defined approach to literature review that will help answer well-focused research questions more effectively (Cronin et al., 2008). Using an SLR guided by a search and selection review protocol, literature from digital journal databases utilizing the major terms used in the review questions (see section 2) and titles of known IS-related studies identified from the Association of Information System (AIS) Website was retrieved. A snowballing approach was adopted, searching further for papers published by selected authors or referenced within papers initially identified as relevant to the research. Manual searches were also included in order to retrieve, from physical libraries, predetermined seminal studies of theories used to support IS adoption not available from digital sources. The ongoing, snowballing approach continued across similar studies until the final selection process was reached, before proceeding with the analysis of the data extracted.

The extracted data were then analysed using a coding approach in NVivo software, a computerized qualitative research tool, starting from open codes and moving to thematic groups formed as themes. The coded data, referred to in the selected literature as variables, determinants, factors, categories, mediators, constructs, and drivers of IS/IT adoption and system usage, was repeatedly grouped by name and similarity of meaning. A meta-analysis, undertaken to integrate the findings and summarize the results based on the SLR, then followed. The frequency that each identified theme was proposed or referenced in the literature analysed was then determined. Finally, the formed themes were organized by related characteristics in order to identify which aspects –technological, subjective and social, organizational, cultural, economic, demographic, or industry and market– enclosed the most relevant drivers that can affect IS adoption in government organizations of LAT.

The theories referenced by the selected literature, which encloses the proposed drivers that needs to be identified in relation to the current study, were closely examined to determine how they may support this study. Further, significant IS adoption and IS development research gaps within developing economies (e.g., LAT region) (Gomez, 2013; Ifinedo, 2012), and concerns regarding the applicability of existing theories in the local context (i.e., cultural influence) (Erumban & de Jong, 2006; Tang & Koveos, 2008) emerged. These concerns are analysed and briefly discussed in the latter part of the chapter.

As a result of this study, the theories mostly used in IS adoption, a set of themes representing drivers proposed by these theories, and their applicability to in LAT region were determined. The outcomes—which include the ongoing beneficial uses of IS in general (Tang & Koveos, 2008)—will be useful to researchers and practitioners willing to investigate SISA in developing economies. The findings reported in the current study are mainly oriented towards organizational adoption in LAT economies and particularly in PEOs, considering endemic concerns about the necessity of IS studies in most of these regions. For instance, in Ecuador, a lack of studies in the IS adoption field has been identified together with a growing interest in determining adoption outcomes. Ecuador's recently proposed e-Government National Plan 2014–2017 (SNAP, 2014) serves as a topical example. Therefore, PEOs were chosen as the focus case for the current study.

The reviewed literature shows that studies concerning factors affecting IS/IT adoption have been extensive in developed countries, either at the individual or organizational level. Notwithstanding, concerns exist in particular regions such as LAT, where a lack of studies and a growing interest in IS adoption outcomes has been noted. Therefore, this research addresses the following question

**RQ:** How do existing theories and their proposed drivers used in IS adoption apply to the Latin American IS adoption context?

An SLR process was used to assess the existing studies. The aim was to identify a list of the most common drivers that could empirically support SISA in a particular context. This began with the identification of the list of the most commonly used theories in IS research directly related to adoption. How frequently these theories and associated factors (drivers) have been applied to studies related to SISA in public organizations, particularly in LAT countries, was then determined. This allowed the investigation of the LAT contexts to determine cogency between established uses of adoption and success factors as drivers of adoption.

## OVERVIEW OF THE SLR AS THE ADOPTED REVIEW METHOD

### The SLR method

An SLR is a well-defined approach to assess available literature relevant to a subject (in this case IS adoption). In this study, existing SLR guidelines were adopted to develop a review protocol for the SLR process, which includes three major phases: planning, conducting, and reporting (Biolchini, Mian, Natali, & Travassos, 2005; Kitchenham, 2004; Kitchenham & Brereton, 2013).

The search and selection strategies were initially defined in order to identify relevant literature and to determine the rigor and the completeness required in the SLR method. Exclusion and inclusion criteria were considered for each of the potential studies accessed in two subsequent searches. The review protocol enabled the confirmation of the search strategy and selection validity. A quality assessment of the literature selected for the review was undertaken to refine the literature selection. Analysis of data extracted from the included studies was conducted to gather evidence related to the research and to synthesize the findings.

### The Search and Selection Protocol

A review protocol was developed using a combination of the protocols proposed by the authors (Kitchenham and Brereton (2013); Steinmacher, Graciotto Silva, Gerosa, and Redmiles (2015)); and the guide of search expressions used by Biolchini et al. (2005). The designed review protocol shown in Figure 1 illustrates the general search and selection processes, including the mechanism for the initial search in the digital libraries that justify the use of an SLR process. Two search and selection processes based on the inclusion-exclusion criteria were determined by the researchers. These were followed by a final validation process based on a quality assessment to guide a refined literature selection (see Figure 2).

### The Search and Selection Process

An initial search was conducted to identify the theories mostly used in IS adoption. Subsequently, a second search was conducted to identify related studies of IS adoption, especially in public organizations of LAT or developing countries. Both processes are illustrated in Figure 1, where "t" represents the number of studies found related to seminal theories, models, and theoretical frameworks and "s" represents the number of studies of IS adoption identified that include developing countries in their data analysis (named as local studies).

The outcomes of the 1st and 2nd search processes were validated and refined to reach a final set of selected articles for data extraction (see Figure 2). In other words to assist the selection process, an inclusion and exclusion criteria for searching related literature and a quality assessment process to validate the final search, were employed. The inclusion and exclusion criteria followed and the validation process are both explained in the following sections of this chapter.

*Figure 1. Search processes*

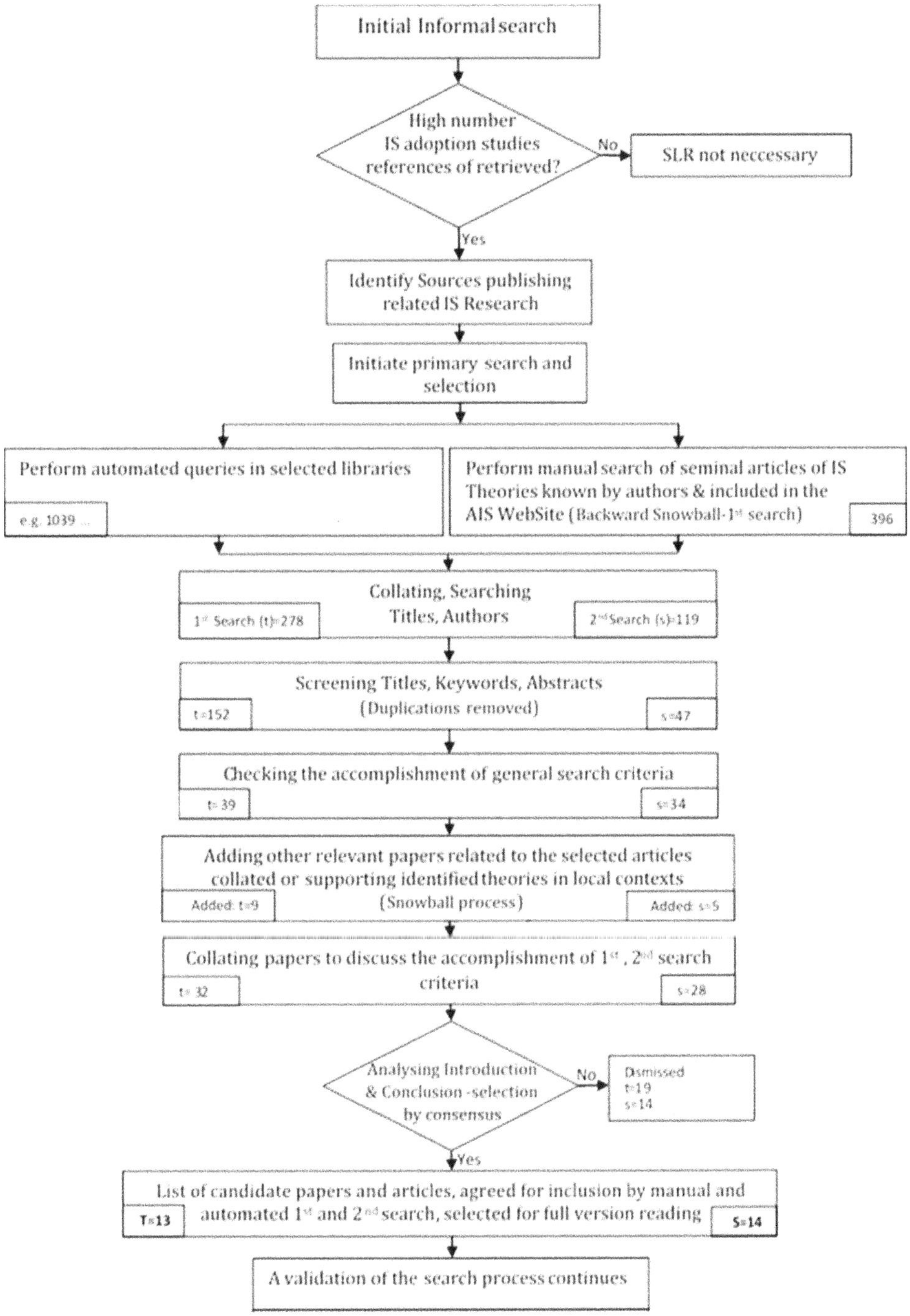

*Figure 2. Search and selection validation*

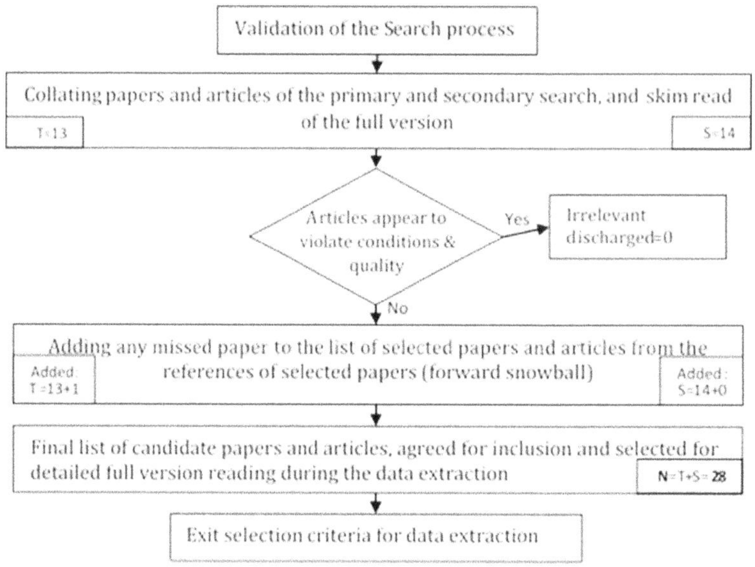


## The Digital Libraries' Search Protocol

As part of the SLR process, a common search expression approach, based on the Population, Intervention, Control, Outcome, and Application (PICOA), was structured (see Table 1) (Biolchini et al., 2005; de Almeida Biolchini, Mian, Natali, Conte, & Travassos, 2007; Steinmacher et al., 2015). This structure helps to organize the searching of articles from a variety of sources including journal papers, conference proceedings, theses, and books all of which contain studies of proposed theories most used in IS adoption. Particular attention was given to research performed in LAT countries. However, due to the

*Table 1. PICOA structure summary*

| Structure | Concept | Context | |
|---|---|---|---|
| Problem | Defines the SLR target by briefly describing the research context | Identification of candidate factors from IS theories to be used in IS research in Hispano American Regions, Developing countries | |
| **Structure** | **Concept** | **Keywords** | **Synonyms** |
| Population | What will be observed by the intervention | Successful Information System Adoption (SISA) | IS adoption, IS success, IS usage, system usage, IT adoption |
| Intervention | What is going to be observed in the planned SLR | Factors | drivers, constructs, determinants, variables, items |
| Control | Initial data set that researchers already posses | NONE | |
| Outcomes | Metric used to measure the effect | Affecting | effect, relationships, affect, affecting, influencing, measuring, effectiveness |
| Application | Roles, application areas that will benefit from the SLR results | IS Adoption research in Public Organizations of Latin America (LAT) | Hispano American regions, developing countries, emerging economies, Ecuador |

lack of studies identified in those regions, research papers from other developing economies were also considered. As studies evidencing the relationship between the use of technology and culture emerged, research articles on cultural dimensions were also included to define cultural differences, if any, between regions. The search parameters for digital libraries, the context of the research as the target problem of the SLR and the PICOA structure, are presented in Figure 1.

Using the keywords and synonyms listed in the PICOA structure, generic search expressions were defined and refined through several trials before applying them to the first and second search processes. After applying a combination of several key words and using linking Boolean expressions such as AND, and OR, three different combinations of search expressions for the different stages that produced better results on the searches were determined.

Preliminary search expression:

*("Factors" OR "Drivers") AND ("Affecting" OR "Impacting" OR "Measuring") AND ("Successful Information System Adoption" OR "IS Adoption" OR "System Usage" OR "IS Success" AND "Latin America").*

Search expression to the primary search (1st search process):

*("Information System Adoption" OR "IS adoption" OR "System Usage" OR "IS Success") AND ("Theory" OR "Model" OR "Framework").*

Search expression to the secondary search (2nd search process):

*("Factors" OR "Drivers") AND ("Affecting" OR "Impacting" OR "Measuring") AND ("Successful Information System Adoption" OR "IS adoption" OR "System Usage" OR "IS Success").*

Using a preliminary search expressions that combined the different words related to the overall focus of the current research "drivers affecting successful information system adoption in Latin America", no results were identified by browsing known electronic databases such as Scopus or Web of Science. In contrast, search engines such as Google Scholar and Griffith Browser returned a large number of hits. However, neither the Google nor Griffith browsers were considered suitable due to their inability to refine some of the inclusion and exclusion criteria determined for the selection of the studies. Nevertheless, the amount of related literature initially identified from these search engines and the variations in results were the reason for determining the need for an SLR process in the current study.

Several electronic databases were again searched using refined search expressions determined for two more search processes. The results of the 1st refined search process were based on the established inclusion and exclusion criteria and the consensus of the authors to dismiss duplicate articles and literature of seminal articles explaining theories used in IS research, but not necessarily and directly related with adoption in developing economies. For the 2nd search process, the authors decided to include in the selection related literature that was closely focused on the specific research application area –SISA– (determined in PICOA structure – Table 1) and referencing one or more of the identified theories from the first search.

### Inclusion and Exclusion Criteria

The results obtained from the search expressions were further refined using the following inclusion and exclusion criteria.

#### Inclusion Criteria

- Available as a full paper or text;
- Written in English;
- Available from open access databases (except from textbooks—referred to as seminal articles in the AIS Website);
- Published in a peer-reviewed venue, including workshops, conferences, and journals (in the case of journal and conference papers);
- Printed by a recognized published press (in the case of seminal articles identified from book chapters or theses);
- The literature of the primary search must be related to seminal studies of theories, models– or theoretical frameworks used in IS research. Particularly, studies empirically evidencing factors affecting IS/IT/ICT adoption or usage or success; and
- In the secondary search the studies should be related to IS/IT or Software adoption or usage or success in public organizations and in developing countries, or focused on LAT countries or studies that evidence relationships between cultures and factors affecting SISA.

#### Exclusion Criteria

- Remove duplicate studies;
- Exclude citation only;
- Remove similar studies published in more than one paper;
- Exclude literature related to IS but not within the scope of this research; and
- From the secondary search, remove articles published before 2001 (not older than 10 years, since we began the current study in 2012). This was in order to preferably include updated studies of local IS Adoption oriented to developing and especially LAT countries due to the rapid changes that many of these countries have been experiencing in the last ten years, based on the information presented in the Global Information Technology Report about the Technology Readiness of Society (Dutta & Bilbao-Osorio, 2012; Dutta, Dutton, & Law, 2011; Dutta & Mia, 2010).

## LITERATURE EXTRACTION, ANALYSIS, AND SELECTION

### The Initial Informal Search Process

From the initial search, a considerable number of articles were identified, but without any refined criteria (see column two of Table 2). However, this preliminary search did not yield any or a significant amount of literature from the search engines of specialized databases. A considerable number of studies were retrieved, however, using PICOA applied without the restriction of including words related to LAT regions

*Table 2. Search expression results examples*

| Primary Screening Search | Preliminary Search Expression | General Search Expression 1st Process | General Search Expression 2nd Process |
|---|---|---|---|
| Griffith Browser | 26170 | 48803 | 204577 |
| Google Scholar | 1400 | 16600 | 16800 |
| Scopus search | 0 | 1039 | 77 |
| Web of Science | 0 | 1307 | 93 |
| AIS Website references | | 396 | 300 |

(Application) and instead using a combination of synonyms more closely related to the sub-research questions 1 and 2. In this case, for example, 1039 titles were found using Scopus search and 1,307 using Web of Science browser (see column three of Table 2). These are some of the examples that justified the need for a systematic process to refine the search of IS adoption literature, and also confirming the lack of related research in LAT regions.

## The 1st Search Process: IS Adoption Theories Literature

Due to the extensive amount of general IS adoption-related literature retrieved, it was decided to begin identifying those theories used in IS adoption from which empirically validated factors originated. This was undertaken with a parallel search in a backward snowballing process, using the title and author(s)' name(s) of seminal articles mentioned in a list of theories used in IS research proposed by the Association of Information System (AIS) Website as a base reference. This process was useful in narrowing the search list. We then continued with more refined searches to obtain more pertinent articles supporting the IS theories identified and related to the research questions.

## The 2nd Search Process: Other related IS Adoption Studies

The second search phase was carried out to determine related IS adoption literature following a process similar to the one used in the first search phase. However, this second search was mainly focused on public organizations in developing countries with particular emphasis on LAT. At this point, from the readings of the 1st set of articles, in a snowballing process, other articles considered relevant to the current study emerged from the second search.

## The Search and Selection Validation Process

In order to validate the outcomes obtained from the analysis of the 1st and 2nd sets, the search process was validated in a joint session between the authors by re-checking the defined criteria and following determined quality assessments to shape the final selection of the literature to be further analysed.

The refining process was carried out following the steps noted below:

1. Articles that appeared to violate the determined criteria were dismissed and a final list of articles was identified.

2. A check for any missing articles directly related to the topic, if they were referenced by several of the selected studies, was conducted.
3. A quality assessment process was applied to all the preselected articles, and its relevance to the current research was scored.
4. After adding any missed articles, a final set of articles was established in order to proceed with the data extraction process.

## Quality Assessment

In order to strengthen the validation of the selection process, two checklists were designed, one for assessing the quality of the selected studies (see Table 3) and the second to identify the type of literature chosen for further analysis (see Table 4). For the quality checklist (see Table 3), some of the questions proposed in other SLR studies such as Kitchenham and Brereton (2013), Salleh, Mendes, and Grundy (2011), Kitchenham (2004) were used and adapted. Six questions with a corresponding score were designed to assess the quality of the chosen studies.

In the second checklist (see Table 4), four questions were then included to identify the study type, research approach, the origin of the data collected, and the existing theories mainly referenced by each of the selected studies.

## The SLR Study Selection Summary

A list of all the articles found, from the first retrieval to the final refined selection, is presented in Table 5. Web of Science and Scopus returned the largest number of hits from the selected list of electronic database sources selected (around 21% and 22%). This can be explained because these databases index literature from a number of publishers and disciplines. ProQuest and JSTOR also returned the highest hits (around 14% and 15%). It was noted that these libraries also index some venues, including international conferences and journal publications related to Software Engineering and Information Systems. We excluded Citeseer and El Compendex because they did not return any hits. More than 10% of the identified literature was also retrieved from physical libraries due to our interest in identifying the origin of theories used in IS adoption. After all duplicate references and dead-end citations were eliminated, the

*Table 3. Quality checklist*

| Question | Answer | Score |
|---|---|---|
| 1) Can it be clearly determined which other theories used in IS adoption the study is referencing? | Yes/Partially/No | 2,1,0 |
| 2) Does the literature explain in some ways a theory /model/ framework related to factors affecting IS Adoption or IS Success? | Yes/Partially/No | 2,1,0 |
| 3) Was the article refereed or is it a recognized edited text in the field? | Yes/Partially/No | 2,1,0 |
| 4) Were the goal(s) of the study clearly stated? | Yes/Partially/No | 2,1,0 |
| 5) Was the research approach clearly determined? | Yes/Partially/No | 2,1,0 |
| 6) Was the analysis procedure well conveyed? (Origin of the primary data, justification of method choice, tools, etc.) | Yes/Partially/No | 2,1,0 |

*Table 4. Type of study checklist*

| Study Type and Origin | Answer |
|---|---|
| 1) What is the type of study identified? | T = Seminal article/literature related theories used in IS/IT/ICT Adoption or Success<br>S = IS/IT/ICT Adoption or Success studies supported by existing theories to explain determined IS adoption in public organization of developing countries and/or Latin America. Comparative Developing and Developed countries studies related to the topic are included<br>C = Study analysing culture and its relationship in some ways with Technology adoption |
| 2) What is the research approach used? | EM = Empirical and Experimental<br>TH = Theoretical<br>MX = Qualitative and Mix studies (as Critical revisions, comparative, or combined studies condensed in selected books) |
| 3) Is the collected primary data empirically supported or carried out in …? | L=Latin American Countries,<br>U=Other developing countries, D=developed countries<br>Or the combination of them DU, DL, UL |
| 4) Which theories used in IS adoption are mainly referenced in the study? | e.g., TAM, TPB, DOI, D&M-ISS etc. |

selection was strengthened by choosing only sources with full text available that appeared to be relevant to the topic. Then, the search was refined using the inclusion and exclusion criteria and the quality assessment determined to score the selected studies for a final validation.

Overall, 199 hits were obtained from the 1st and the 2nd search processes once duplication and citations were eliminated. From the 1st search, 152 full text sources, including journals papers and sections from books related to theories used in IS research were retrieved. From the 2nd search, 47 hits were obtained (see Table 5), although these were more specifically related to either IS/IT/ICT adoption in general and referenced existing IS theories. The Titles and Abstracts were screened respectively, refining the selection only to include articles that appeared to be more related to theories that supported and explained factors affecting SISA at the level of individuals and organization. This reduced the total list to 73 articles (39 from the 1st search and 34 from the 2nd search). After screening the books' contents and other papers, obtained by references in a snowballing process, 14 more articles (9 retrieved from the first search and 5 from the second search) were added. Revisiting the results, extra information was sourced from books, and one more article considered relevant for inclusion was added.

More precisely, after general inclusion and exclusion criteria reasoning, a list of 60 articles (32 from the 1st process and 28 from the 2nd process) was esignated for further analysis and discussion (see Table 5). From the 32 studies identified in the 1st process, a final set of 13 studies was chosen. This set includes eight journal papers: DeLone and McLean (1992), DeLone and McLean (2003), Bandura (1982), Davis (1989), Davis, Bagozzi, and Warshaw (1989), Venkatesh and Davis (2000), Ajzen (1991), Venkatesh, Morris, Davis, and Davis (2003); one eBook, Rogers (1995); and four books, Rogers (2003), Bandura (1986), Tornatzky et al. (1990), Fishbein and Ajzen (1975). Revisiting the preliminary results, one more study was added from the validation process. This is the case of the Modernization Theory (MT) and the influence of technology adoption (McClelland, 1967) identified as highly referenced in some books related to IT/IS adoption. The MT theory is also mentioned in several other theories used in IS adoption research. The fourteen studies were selected based on how closely they matched the criteria from the

*Table 5. Process of literature retrieved*

| Source (Digital Library / Library) | Search Process 1 | Search Process 2 | Total | % Search Efficacy |
|---|---|---|---|---|
| IEEE Xplore | 4 | 2 | 6 | 1.5 |
| ACM Digital Library | 4 | 0 | 4 | 1.0 |
| INSPECT | 1 | 0 | 1 | 0.3 |
| Science Direct | 6 | 9 | 15 | 3.8 |
| Springer Link | 4 | 2 | 6 | 1.5 |
| *Scopus* | 49 | 36 | 85 | **21.4** |
| EBSCO host | 3 | 1 | 4 | 1.0 |
| *ProQuest* | 36 | 23 | 59 | **14.9** |
| SAGE full | 3 | 0 | 3 | 0.8 |
| Science | 1 | 0 | 1 | 0.3 |
| *JSTOR (MIS Quarterly)* | 52 | 8 | 60 | **15.1** |
| *Web of Science* | 62 | 27 | 89 | **22.4** |
| Emerald | 0 | 4 | 4 | 1.0 |
| Griffith Research Online Database and Others | 12 | 7 | 19 | 4.8 |
| Physical Search of Library Sources | 41 | 0 | 41 | 10.3 |
| Number of sources literature identified | 278 | 119 | 397 | |
| Excluding duplications retrieved | -119 | -69 | -188 | |
| Excluding citation only retrieved | -7 | -3 | -10 | |
| Literature initially retrieved without duplications | 152 | 47 | 199 | |
| Literature dismissed (general exclusion reasoning) | 113 | 13 | 126 | |
| Literature screened criteria reasoning | 39 | 34 | 73 | |
| Literature added (snowballing) | 9 | 5 | 14 | |
| *Literature selected for analysis and discussion* | *32* | *28* | *60* | |
| **Literature pre-selected for validation** | **13** | **14** | **27** | |
| Literature added (missed) | 1 | 0 | 1 | |
| **Final literature selected for data extraction** | **14** | **14** | **28** | |

1st search process and the quality assets score obtained by each of them as seminal studies that better explain theories used in IS adoption at either the individual or organizational level.

From the 28 studies identified in the 2nd search process,13 journal papers—Aboelmaged (2010), Al-Ghaith, Sanzogni, and Sandhu (2010), Al-Somali, Gholami, and Clegg (2009), Erumban and de Jong (2006), Huang and Palvia (2001), Ifinedo (2012), Lin, Fofanah, and Liang (2011), Rokhman (2011), Wadie (2011), Wang and Liao (2008), Van Everdingen and Waarts (2003), Borker (2012), Kowal and Roztocki (2013) and one conference proceedings article, Shajari and Ismail (2010), were also selected (see Table 5). These 14 studies proposed candidate factors affecting adoption, but mainly focused on local context in organizations in developing countries. However, the developing countries investigated were not necessarily from LAT due to lack of research in the region.

The remaining studies preselected for analysis and discussion were dismissed because they did not match some of the inclusion and exclusion criteria determined. For example, they were earlier versions of the other selected studies that lacked relevant amendments related to the latest version, or they were out of date. In the case for local studies identified from the 2nd search process, for example, only research from the 10 years prior to the period of this study was considered. Nevertheless, several of these studies not considered for data analysis were, in some cases, used as references to support some of the final selected studies. This was because, in some manner, they explained and supported the importance of the theories the authors identified as the most commonly used in IS adoption research. For instance, Oliveira and Martins (2011) highlighted the frequency of how the Diffusion of Innovation Theory (DOI) (Rogers, 1995, 2003) and The Technology Organization and Environment Framework (TOE) (Tornatzky et al., 1990) were used in different studies to measure IS/IT adoption at the organizational level. Another example of this is the study proposed by Seddon (1997), complementing and analysing the pertinence in adoption studies of the chosen studies of DeLone and McLean's model of IS Success (DeLone & McLean, 1992).

On the whole, 28 studies were selected for further analysis and data extraction to answer the research questions of the current research. This study also contributed to the discipline by giving a detailed and significant example that illustrates and summarize how a SLR process through planned protocols guiding the search processes helps to critically refine the number of studies retrieved until a final set relevant to the purpose of the study can be chosen (see Figure 1 and Figure 2, and Table 5).

## THE DATA EXTRACTION PROCESS

The current research required a broader set of mixed literature, including seminal articles to identify theories used to explain IS adoption, and studies applied in local contexts, to demonstrate how IS adoption theories have been applied in specific organizational environments, particularly in developing economies. Thus, an SLR method was applied to select appropriate articles useful for the data extraction related to the current research.

### General Data Extraction

The data extraction process began by uplifting standard information from each article, such as title, author's name, date of publication, publisher of the journal or text, type of paper, scope of the study, abstract, summary, main topic covered, and the place where the study was developed. This was done in order to identify the type of study, assess the validity, and score the quality of the literature selected for data extraction relevant to our investigation.

The score chosen for quality assessment of each study ranged from 0 to 3 = Poor quality, 4 to 6 = Fair quality, 7 to 9 = Good quality, and 10 to 12 = Very good quality (see Table 3). In order to minimize bias, one author read the selected literature and extracted the initial data. This author was also in charge of setting up, coding, and scoring the data in a spreadsheet, supported by an assistant researcher. The data was then reviewed iteratively by all of the authors until an agreement was reached on the quality of the final list of the selected literature. None of the selected 28 studies were considered poor due to the well-established inclusion and exclusion criteria followed in each search process. As shown in Figure 3, more than 67% of the literature (19 studies) scored as Very Good; around 28% (8 studies) scored as

*Figure 3. Primary studies quality scored*

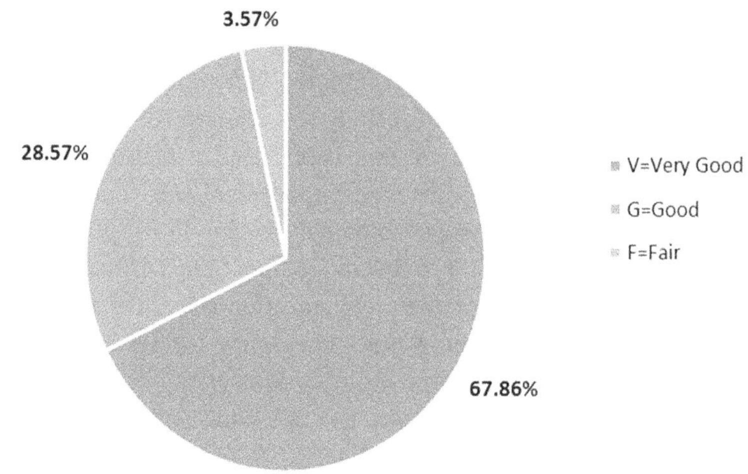


Good; and around 3% (only one study) scored as Fair. This is evidence that the quality of the studies selected was considered reliable and appropriate by the researchers.

Using the checklist indicated in Table 4, the type of literature selected, the type of study approach, the origin of each study and the origin of the data collection were also determined (see Table 6). Figure 4 shows that 50% of the literature identified is related to seminal theories studies used in IS adoption, over 35% is linked to local studies mostly focused on organizational adoption in developing and/or LAT countries, and around 14% was selected from studies demonstrating the relationship between culture and technology adoption. The latter was selected due to the necessity of understanding the connection between cultures in developing and developed countries and IS adoption. This conceivable relationship emerged from the reading of earlier seminal studies discussing the influence of culture in technology adoption and innovations such as those by T3, T4, and T14.

The selected literature mostly originated from empirical studies, including qualitative and experimental research (67%), followed by theoretical research (17%), with the remaining 14% identified as qualitative and mixed method studies, including critical revisions and comparative studies of previous research (see Figure 5). The existence of a number of mixed studies was expected, as some of the contents selected

*Figure 4. Type of study*

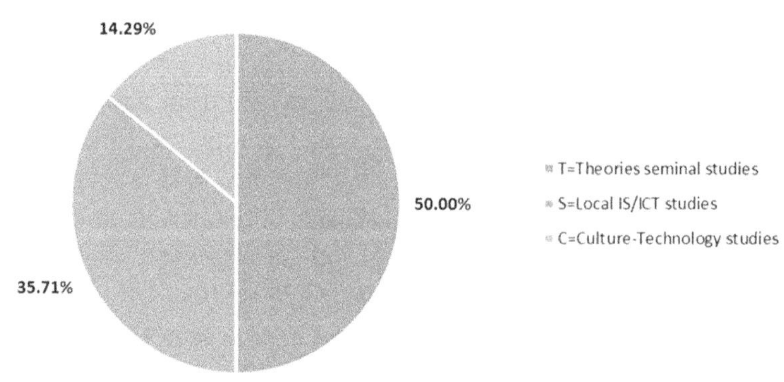

*Figure 5. Type of research approach*

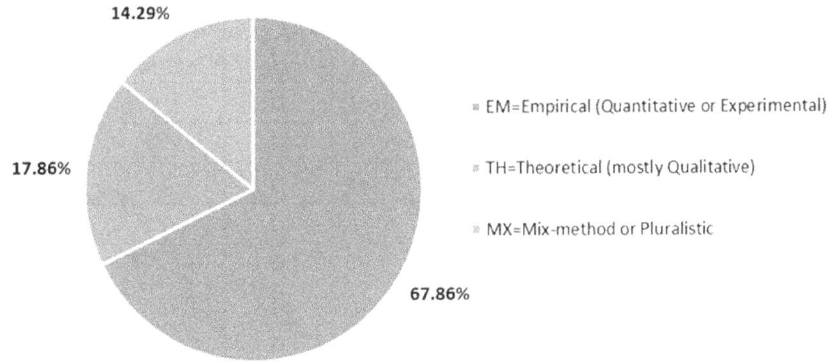


as seminal articles were collected from books in which a mix of research evidence complemented this investigation. The highest percentage, obtained from empirical studies, includes most of the local IS adoption studies in specific organizational contexts. These studies applied empirical approaches for testing their research hypotheses by using or adapting identified theories used in IS research (see also Table 6). Therefore, it can be determined that most of the identified factors from these studies have been empirically tested and so are relevant to the current research.

## Data Extraction to Identify Proposed Drivers of IS/IT Adoption

To facilitate the data extraction process the selected articles were coded with a short identifiers (see Table 6). 14 articles (mostly seminal articles) that proposed or reviewed IS adoption theories were sequentially coded from T1 to T14, and 14 articles that explained IS adoption in local contexts were sequentially coded from S1 to S14 (see Table 6).

A database was set up to extract all the items and related information mentioned by the 28 studies. From this this data a variety of names used by authors to identify drivers of IS/IT adoption such as factors, determinants, predictors, constructs, moderators, drivers, forces, contexts, dimensions, categories, and variables was also noted. Also included in the database were the study's origin, author(s)' name(s), year of the study, source of the primary data collected, theories used as a basis of the study, and the definition assigned to each item (if included).

The database was then imported into NVivo in order to begin organizing the identified proposed drivers of IS/IT adoption as open codes (in NVivo identified as child nodes) and consolidating the classification of related data extracted from the studies. Within this initial process, a total of 425 open codes were obtained from the 28 selected studies (see Table 6). Considering that the identified drivers (mentioned with different denominations) were extracted from all the articles as open codes, duplication of some of these drivers with exactly the same name was noted. Thus, the list was reduced to 289 drivers grouped as axial codes (in NVivo mentioned as parent nodes) when duplicated names were condensed in a second refined group (Table 6). From this process, items coded representing dependent variables of IS adoption studies were removed from this group, because they could not be considered as part of identified drivers of SISA. The refined analysis was resumed by regrouping the axial codes using related meanings and

*Table 6. Selected studies and number of identified themes*

| Code - Authors' Name and Year | Publication Type | Study Type | Study Origin | Data Collection Origin | Study Approach | Items Coded |
|---|---|---|---|---|---|---|
| T1 - DeLone and McLean (1992) | Journal paper | T | D | D | EM | **7** |
| T2 - DeLone and McLean (2003) | Journal paper | T | D | D | EM | **9** |
| T3 - Rogers (1995) | eBook | T | D | DL | MX | **22** |
| T4 - Rogers (2003) | Book | T | D | DL | MX | **22** |
| T5 - Bandura (1982) | Journal paper | T | D | D | MX | **6** |
| T6 - Bandura (1986) | Book | T | D | DL | TH | **6** |
| T7 - Davis (1989) | Journal paper | T | D | D | EM | **5** |
| T8 - Davis et al. (1989) | Journal paper | T | D | D | EM | **5** |
| T9 - Venkatesh and Davis (2000) | Journal paper | T | D | D | EM | **13** |
| T10 - Tornatzky et al. (1990) | Book | T | D | D | EM | **13** |
| T11 - Ajzen (1991) | Journal paper | T | D | D | EM | **5** |
| T12 - Fishbein and Ajzen (1975) | Book | T | D | D | MX | **13** |
| T13 - Venkatesh et al. (2003) | Journal paper | T | D | D | EM | **28** |
| T14 - McClelland (1967) | Book | T | D | DU | TH | **14** |
| S1 - Aboelmaged (2010) | Journal paper | S | U | U | EM | **6** |
| S2 - Al-Ghaith et al. (2010) | Journal paper | S | D | U | EM | **20** |
| S3 - Al-Somali et al. (2009) | Journal paper | S | D | U | EM | **15** |
| S4 - Erumban and de Jong (2006) | Journal paper | C | D | D | EM | **44** |
| S5 - Huang and Palvia (2001) | Journal paper | S | D | DL | TH | **51** |
| S6 - Ifinedo (2012) | Journal paper | S | D | UL | EM | **10** |
| S7 - Lin et al. (2011) | Journal paper | S | U | U | EM | **13** |
| S8 - Rokhman (2011) | Journal paper | S | D | U | EM | **6** |
| S9 - Shajari and Ismail (2010) | Conference paper | S | U | DU | EM | **12** |
| S10 - Wadie (2011) | Journal paper | S | U | U | EM | **11** |
| S11 - Wang and Liao (2008) | Journal paper | S | U | U | EM | **12** |
| S12 - Van Everdingen and Waarts (2003) | Journal paper | C | D | D | EM | **15** |
| S13 - Borker (2012) | Journal paper | C | D | DU | TH | **30** |
| S14 - Kowal and Roztocki (2013) | Journal paper | C | D | D | TH | **12** |
| Total open code (child nodes) | | | | | | **425** |
| Total axial codes (parent nodes) - drivers grouped by similar names | | | | | | **289** |
| Final set of themes (grandparent nodes) drivers regrouped by similar meaning and aspects | | | | | | **60** |

similar classifications. This iterative process continued until the minimum number of regrouped and merged axial codes (named as themes), with matching connotations, was reached. As a result, a refined set of 60 themes identified as possible candidate drivers of SISA was obtained.

## DISCUSSION OF THE OUTCOMES OBTAINED FROM THE SLR PROCESS

### The Theories Most Used in IS Research That Have Been Applied to IS Adoption or IS Success Studies

From the selected studies, existing theories most commonly used or referenced to support specific investigations that helped to answer research questions or confirm hypotheses were noted (Table 7).

From the analysis of the extracted data, 11 theories related to IS/IT were identified as the most commonly used in IS adoption studies. Six of these have been proposed at the level of individual adoption and five at the level of organizational adoption contexts (Table 8). It was noted that most of these theories were used for adapting models (e.g., T10, S1, S9), by combining them as proposed hybrid models (e.g., T9, T11, T13, S11), or at least as references to support their own proposed model (e.g., S6, S10, S14) (see Table 7).

After the data analysis, these preliminary findings led to the conclusion that the 11 theories, models, and theoretical frameworks listed in Table 8 are the most common theories used in IS adoption research or IS success studies. Nonetheless, it was noted that several local studies in developing countries proposed the use of hybrid models coming from these theories or their own frameworks, referencing some of these theories to measure SISA in determined contexts. Consequently, the necessity for further analysis to identify the applicability of either one of the identified theories or a proposed adapted theory to be tested in a specific organizational LAT environment follows.

### Themes Identified from the Selected Studies as Possible Drivers of SISA

A set of 60 drivers (determined as themes in the qualitative analysis process undertaken) was identified from the reviewed studies. In order to better visualize this initial outcome, the list of the formed themes was grouped by color and organized by similar characteristics identified between themes (See Table 9). Seven themes, related to Behavioural and Subjective Aspects, were identified as possible main constructs (predictors) of adoption: these are Intention to Use (also defined as Attitude Towards Using), Usage Behaviour, Perceived Ease of Use, Perceived Usefulness, User Satisfaction, Net Benefit, and Use (as a complementary effect of Intention to use). Four of these themes (Attitude Towards Using, Usage Behaviour, Perceived Usefulness, and Perceived Ease of Use,) were identified as main constructs of TAM (T7, T8). Intention to Use, Use, User Satisfaction, and Net Benefit were recognized as root constructs proposed in the D&M-UISS model (T1, T2). The remaining 53 themes were clustered in 6 groups by similar characteristics identified, (see Table 9). In addition, these themes were associated as possible constructs or moderators based on studies of theories such UTAUT (T13), or associated as determinants proposed for example by DOI (T3, T4). Nevertheless theses associations needs to be confirmed in further studies.

*Table 7. Theories, models and frameworks most referenced by the selected studies*

| Study Source Code | Theory Supported | Theories Mainly Referenced |
|---|---|---|
| T1 | D&M-ISS | Determined factors proposed in TAM coming from earlier studies |
| T2 | D&M-UISS | D&M-ISS |
| T3 | DOI | SCT |
| T4 | DOI | SCT |
| T5 | SCT | SCT/ Social Learning Theory (SLT) |
| T6 | SCT | DOI, TOE |
| T7 | TAM | TRA / SCT |
| T8 | TAM | TRA / SCT |
| T9 | TAM2 | (TAM) / TRA, TPB |
| T10 | TOE | DOI |
| T11 | TPB | (TRA) / SCT |
| T12 | TRA | Cognitive Dissonance Theory (CDT) |
| T13 | UTAUT | (TRA, TAM, TAM2, TPB, MM, DOI, SCT, MPCU) |
| T14 | MT | MT |
| S1 | Adapted | (TAM, TPB) / TRA,UTAUT,DOI |
| S2 | DOI | (DOI) / TAM2, UTAUT |
| S3 | TAM | (TAM) / TAM2, TRA, TPB, UTAUT, SCT |
| S4 | DOI | DOI, Hofstede, Others authors' studies |
| S5 | D&M ISS | D&M ISS, Others authors' studies |
| S6 | Own | (Own) / MT, PEST |
| S7 | TAM | (TAM) / D&M, ISS, TPB, DOI |
| S8 | DOI | (DOI) / TAM, TAM2 |
| S9 | Adapted | (Mix) / TAM, TAM2, UTAUT, DOI, TOI, Trustworthiness |
| S10 | Own | (Own) / DOI, SCT, TAM |
| S11 | D&MUISS | (D&M-UISS) / D&M-ISS |
| S12 | DOI | DOI, Hofstede/Hall cultural dimensions |
| S13 | DOI | DOI, Hofstede, Gray |
| S14 | Own | Others authors' studies |

Number of Sources referenced (NS), Number of References obtained from each source (NR), Number of References divided by the number of sources examined (FR), Frequency of References obtained from the sources analysed in the SLR process (FRs), Frequency of References obtained from the transcript of the interviews examined (FRi)

The origin of the themes linked to the theories which have proposed them as factors/construct of IT/IS adoption, also give the current study a significant reason to point out TAM and D&M-UISS as theories containing the most fundamental themes recognized as main drivers of SISA but not necessarily in LAT regions. This was follow by themes identified from UTAU and DOI. Therefore, the analysis suggest these theories as the most relevant in IS adoption studies that needs to be considered for further investigation.

*Table 8. Common theories, models and theoretical frameworks used in IS/ICT adoption studies*

| **Theories Used in IS Adoption Studies** | |
|---|---|
| **Theories and Model IS/IT Adoption by Individuals** | |
| 1 | The Theory of Reasoned Actions (TRA) (Fishbein & Ajzen, 1975) |
| 2 | Social Cognitive Theory (SCT) (Bandura, 1982, 1986) |
| 3 | The Technology Acceptance Model (TAM) (Davis, 1989; Davis et al., 1989) |
| 4 | The Extended Technology Acceptance Model (TAM2) (Venkatesh & Davis, 2000) |
| 5 | The Theory of Planned Behaviour (TPB) (Ajzen, 1991) |
| 6 | The Unified Theory of Acceptance and Use of Technology (UTAUT) (Venkatesh et al., 2003) |
| **Theories and Models of Innovation Adoption and IS Success to the Organization Level** | |
| 7 | The Achieving Society - McClelland's Modernization Theory (MT) (McClelland, 1967) |
| 8 | The Technology Organization, and Environment Framework (TOE) (Tornatzky et al., 1990) |
| 9 | The Diffusion of Innovation Theory (DOI) (Rogers, 1995, 2003) |
| 10 | The DeLone and McLean's Model of Information System Success (D&M-ISS) (DeLone & McLean, 1992) |
| 11 | The Updated DeLone and McLean's Model of Information System Success (D&M-UISS) (DeLone & McLean, 2003) |

*Table 9. Identified themes formed from the SLR process and scrutinized by PEOs*

| | **SLR = 28 Sources** | | | **INT= 38 Interviews** | | | | |
|---|---|---|---|---|---|---|---|---|
| **Control Characteristics / Theme Names** | **NS** | **NR** | **FRs = NR/ SLR** | **NS** | **NR** | **FRi = NR/ INT** | **Fri/ FRs** | **Driver Type** |
| ***Behavioural and Subjective Aspects*** | ***24*** | ***94*** | ***3.36*** | ***3*** | ***58*** | ***1.53*** | ***0.45*** | |
| Attitude Toward Using - Intention to Use (AU) | 18 | 24 | **0.86** | 4 | 15 | **0.39** | 0.46 | TAM D&M Main construct |
| Perceived Ease of Use (PE) | 12 | 15 | **0.54** | 9 | 10 | **0.26** | 0.49 | TAM Main construct |
| User Satisfaction (US) | 8 | 10 | **0.36** | 13 | 14 | **0.37** | 1.03 | D&M Main construct |
| Perceived Usefulness (PU) | 9 | 11 | **0.39** | 11 | 11 | **0.29** | 0.74 | TAM Main construct |
| Usage Behaviour (BU) | 12 | 17 | **0.61** | 2 | 2 | 0.05 | 0.09 | TAM Main construct |
| Net Benefit (NB) | 10 | 11 | **0.39** | 5 | 5 | 0.13 | 0.33 | D&M Main construct |
| Use (U) | 6 | 6 | **0.21** | 1 | 1 | 0.03 | 0.12 | D&M Main construct |
| ***Social Aspects*** | ***17*** | ***33*** | ***1.18*** | ***12*** | ***15*** | ***0.39*** | ***0.33*** | |
| Outcome Expectations (OE) | 6 | 11 | **0.39** | 5 | 6 | **0.16** | 0.40 | Construct |
| Subjective Norms (SN) | 7 | 11 | **0.39** | 5 | 5 | 0.13 | 0.33 | Construct |
| Job Relevance (JR) | 6 | 6 | **0.21** | 2 | 2 | 0.05 | 0.25 | Construct |
| Image (IM) | 5 | 5 | 0.18 | 2 | 2 | 0.05 | 0.29 | Construct |
| ***Technological Aspects*** | ***20*** | ***76*** | ***2.71*** | ***35*** | ***124*** | ***3.26*** | ***1.20*** | |
| ICT costs (PP) | 3 | 3 | 0.11 | 18 | 18 | **0.47** | 4.42 | Construct |

*continued on next page*

*Table 9. Continued*

| | SLR = 28 Sources | | | INT= 38 Interviews | | | | |
|---|---|---|---|---|---|---|---|---|
| **Control Characteristics / Theme Names** | **NS** | **NR** | **FRs = NR/ SLR** | **NS** | **NR** | **FRi = NR/ INT** | **Fri/ FRs** | **Driver Type** |
| Infrastructure Availability (IA) | 6 | 10 | **0.36** | 10 | 10 | **0.26** | 0.74 | Construct |
| Information Quality (IQ) | 6 | 7 | **0.25** | 12 | 12 | **0.32** | 1.26 | Construct |
| Systems Security (SP) | 3 | 5 | 0.18 | 12 | 12 | **0.32** | 1.77 | Construct |
| Implementation Process (IP) | 1 | 1 | 0.04 | 15 | 15 | **0.39** | 11.05 | Construct |
| System Characteristics (SY) | 7 | 10 | **0.36** | 4 | 4 | 0.11 | 0.29 | Construct |
| Internet Readiness (IR) | 5 | 5 | 0.18 | 7 | 9 | **0.24** | 1.33 | Construct |
| System Quality (SQ) | 4 | 4 | 0.14 | 10 | 10 | **0.26** | 1.84 | Construct |
| Complexity (CX) | 4 | 6 | **0.21** | 7 | 7 | **0.18** | 0.86 | Construct |
| Compatibility (CP) | 6 | 6 | **0.21** | 6 | 6 | **0.16** | 0.74 | Construct |
| Service Quality (QS) | 4 | 4 | 0.14 | 8 | 8 | **0.21** | 1.47 | Construct |
| Time (TT) | 4 | 4 | 0.14 | 7 | 8 | **0.21** | 1.47 | Construct |
| National Telecommunication Monopoly (NM) | 1 | 1 | 0.04 | 5 | 5 | 0.13 | 3.68 | Construct |
| Nature of Development (ND) | 3 | 3 | 0.11 | 0 | 0 | 0.00 | 0.00 | Construct |
| Observability (OB) | 3 | 3 | 0.11 | 0 | 0 | 0.00 | 0.00 | Construct |
| Triability (TR) | 3 | 3 | 0.11 | 0 | 0 | 0.00 | 0.00 | Construct |
| Energy (BE) | 1 | 1 | 0.04 | 0 | 0 | 0.00 | 0.00 | Construct |
| ***Organizational Aspects*** | ***22*** | ***73*** | ***2.61*** | ***23*** | ***34*** | ***0.89*** | ***0.34*** | |
| Communication Channels (CC) | 7 | 14 | **0.50** | 12 | 12 | **0.32** | 0.63 | Construct |
| Organizational Experience (EX) | 3 | 7 | **0.25** | 12 | 14 | **0.37** | 1.47 | Construct |
| Trust and Leadership (TL) | 7 | 9 | **0.32** | 10 | 10 | **0.26** | 0.82 | Construct |
| Organizational Slack (OS) | 5 | 8 | **0.29** | 5 | 5 | 0.13 | 0.46 | Construct |
| Environmental Influence (EI) | 5 | 6 | **0.21** | 2 | 2 | 0.05 | 0.25 | Construct |
| Size - Organizational Size (SZ) | 6 | 7 | **0.25** | 0 | 0 | 0.00 | 0.00 | Construct |
| Power Concentration (PC) | 4 | 4 | 0.14 | 2 | 2 | 0.05 | 0.37 | Construct |
| Organizational Income (OI) | 3 | 3 | 0.11 | 1 | 1 | 0.03 | 0.25 | Construct |
| Organizational Location (OL) | 2 | 2 | 0.07 | 1 | 1 | 0.03 | 0.37 | Construct |
| ***National and Cultural Aspects*** | ***12*** | ***55*** | ***1.96*** | ***31*** | ***67*** | ***1.76*** | ***0.90*** | |
| Cultural Dimension (CD) | 3 | 21 | **0.75** | 8 | 9 | **0.24** | 0.32 | Determinant |
| Regulations and Policies (RP) | 8 | 15 | **0.54** | 10 | 10 | **0.26** | 0.49 | Determinant |
| Technology Maturity (TM) | 3 | 6 | **0.21** | 14 | 14 | **0.37** | 1.72 | Determinant |
| Political Influence (PI) | 3 | 3 | 0.11 | 10 | 10 | **0.26** | 2.46 | Determinant |

*continued on next page*

*Table 9. Continued*

| | SLR = 28 Sources | | | INT= 38 Interviews | | | | |
|---|---|---|---|---|---|---|---|---|
| **Control Characteristics / Theme Names** | **NS** | **NR** | **FRs = NR/ SLR** | **NS** | **NR** | **FRi = NR/ INT** | **Fri/ FRs** | **Driver Type** |
| Political Stability (PS) | 2 | 2 | 007 | 10 | 10 | **0.26** | 3.68 | Determinant |
| Political Culture (PO) | 2 | 2 | 0.07 | 8 | 9 | **0.24** | 3.32 | Determinant |
| Values and Practices (VP) | 2 | 3 | 0.11 | 3 | 3 | 0.08 | 0.74 | Determinant |
| Loyalty (LY) | 2 | 2 | 0.07 | 1 | 1 | 0.03 | 0.37 | Determinant |
| Population Changes (EP) | 1 | 1 | 0.04 | 1 | 1 | 0.03 | 0.74 | Determinant |
| ***Demographic Aspects*** | ***12*** | ***34*** | ***1.21*** | ***29*** | ***53*** | ***1.39*** | ***1.15*** | |
| Education and Skills (ED) | 10 | 16 | **0.57** | 22 | 23 | **0.61** | 1.06 | Moderators |
| Age (AG) | 7 | 7 | **0.25** | 15 | 15 | **0.39** | 1.58 | Moderators |
| Language (LA) | 1 | 1 | 0.04 | 8 | 8 | **0.21** | 5.89 | Moderators |
| Gender (GE) | 6 | 6 | **0.21** | 2 | 2 | 0.05 | 0.25 | Moderators |
| Individual's Income (IC) | 3 | 3 | 0.11 | 2 | 2 | 0.05 | 0.49 | Moderators |
| Entrepreneurship (ET) | 1 | 1 | 0.04 | 3 | 3 | 0.08 | 2.21 | Moderators |
| ***National Economic Aspects*** | ***6*** | ***14*** | ***0.50*** | ***7*** | ***12*** | ***0.32*** | ***0.63*** | |
| Economic Growth (EG) | 3 | 5 | 0.18 | 6 | 4 | 0.11 | 0.59 | Determinant |
| National Income Level (NE) | 5 | 6 | **0.21** | 2 | 1 | 0.03 | 0.12 | Determinant |
| Economic Climate (EC) | 2 | 2 | 0.07 | 5 | 5 | 0.13 | 1.84 | Determinant |
| Welfare (EW) | 1 | 1 | 0.04 | 2 | 2 | 0.05 | 1.47 | Determinant |
| ***Industry and Market Aspects*** | ***3*** | ***5*** | ***0.18*** | ***5*** | ***11*** | ***0.29*** | ***1.62*** | |
| Market Structure (MK) | 1 | 1 | 0.04 | 5 | 5 | 0.13 | 3.68 | Construct |
| Market Competition (MM) | 1 | 2 | 0.07 | 3 | 3 | 0.08 | 1.11 | Construct |
| Manufacture Strengths (MS) | 1 | 1 | 0.04 | 2 | 2 | 0.05 | 1.47 | Construct |
| Labour Force (LF) | 1 | 1 | 0.04 | 1 | 1 | 0.03 | 0.74 | Construct |
| Median | | | **0.21** | | | **0.16** | | |
| Mean | | | **0.35** | | | **0.28** | | |

## Control Characteristics Groups Developing from the Selected Studies

In the analysis process, it was observed that several researchers grouped some of the data extracted by similar characteristics to form the themes. Some studies grouped proposed factors / constructs / drivers / determinants and so on under clusters named as Categories, Context, Focus, Aspects, Grouping Conditions, or Dimensions. For example, the DOI theory and the TOE framework grouped variables by characteristic to explain organizational innovativeness (T3, T4 and T10). In the case of DOI studies, certain items (variables) such as Organizational Slack, Organizational Size, Organizational Location, and some others, are classified in a group called "Internal Organizational Characteristics Context". TOE studies, for instance, create a family called "Organizational Context" in which all the items are grouped as related to organizational characteristic such as Structure, Communicational Process, Slack and Size.

Some other examples are the studies S2, S6, S10, proposing IT/IS adoption frameworks that group items (drivers) by different contexts. S10, for instance, groups the proposed items into four categories: Economic, Social, Technological, and Political. Therefore, in the current research, themes containing similar aspects were organized under the denomination of Control Characteristics groups (see Table 9). These groups are recognized as clusters containing drivers related to same aspects, family, or similar context that allows the researchers to visualize possible relationships between such drivers.

Based on this analysis, and qualitative evaluation of the data content, eight Control Characteristic groups were then formed (see Table 10). Each of these groups encloses several of the formed themes (see Table 9). This helps the researchers establish a structured view of the 60 themes formed from the identification of the most common drivers/factors/constructs or any other denomination proposed to measure IS/IT adoption in different environments.

## THE DRIVERS OF IS ADOPTION IN PEOS

The identified set of 60 themes was discussed with local practitioners and IS/ICT experts working in PEOs as part of an interview process in order to gather their opinion about successes and failures in IS adoption as experienced in their organizations, and to scrutinize the relevance of such themes as drivers of SISA. Authorities, IS/ICT heads of departments, advisors, and policy makers of PEOs were interviewed with this purpose. The guiding questions for the interviews included a list of proposed themes (Table 9). The interviewees were asked to check the list and suggest which of the themes (drivers) they considered relevant to help their organization in succeeding in the adoption of any system implemented or to be implemented. They were also asked to make comments about these themes. From the 50 experts and practitioners interviewed, 38 were willing to go through the list, analysing each of the themes. The data collected from the interviews were then interpreted using hermeneutical circle analysis and, scrutinized, and coded in NVivo software again. This helps to compare the results based on the number of references obtained from the SLR process and through the interviewees (Table 9).

*Table 10. Control Characteristics group identified and number of themes clustered*

| | Number of Themes | | SLR = 28 Sources | | |
|---|---|---|---|---|---|
| | **Control Characteristics Groups** | **SLR(60 themes)** | **NS** | **NR** | **FRs = NR/ SLR** |
| 1C | Behavioural and Subjective Aspects | 7 | 24 | 94 | 3.36 |
| 2C | Social Aspects | 4 | 17 | 33 | 1.18 |
| 3C | Technological Aspects | 17 | 20 | 76 | 2.71 |
| 4C | Organizational Aspects | 9 | 22 | 73 | 2.61 |
| 5C | National and Cultural Aspects | 9 | 12 | 55 | 1.96 |
| 6C | Demographic Aspects | 6 | 12 | 34 | 1.21 |
| 7C | National Economic Aspects | 4 | 6 | 14 | 0.50 |
| 8C | Industry and Market Aspects | 4 | 3 | 5 | 0.18 |

## Relevance of Themes Identified as Possible Drivers of SISA

Remarkable differences and some similarities between the Frequencies of References (FR), considered as the relevance given by the analysed sources from the local experts (FRi) and from existing studies (FRs) in relation to several of the identified themes, were identified. For example, themes linked to Subjective Aspects such as Attitude Towards Using – Intention to Use are considered almost half as relevant to locals in relation to the relevance identified from existing studies, but themes such as User Satisfaction were considered almost equally relevant (see Figure 6). Some themes linked to Technological Aspects such as Implementation Process are noted as highly relevant to locals but of very low relevance to existing studies. Themes clustered in Demographic Aspects such as Education and Skills equally relevant to both sources are noted. Figure 6 shows a comparison of the FR reached by each theme from the analysis

*Figure 6. Themes Frequency of Relevance from the SLR process and Interviews (INT)*

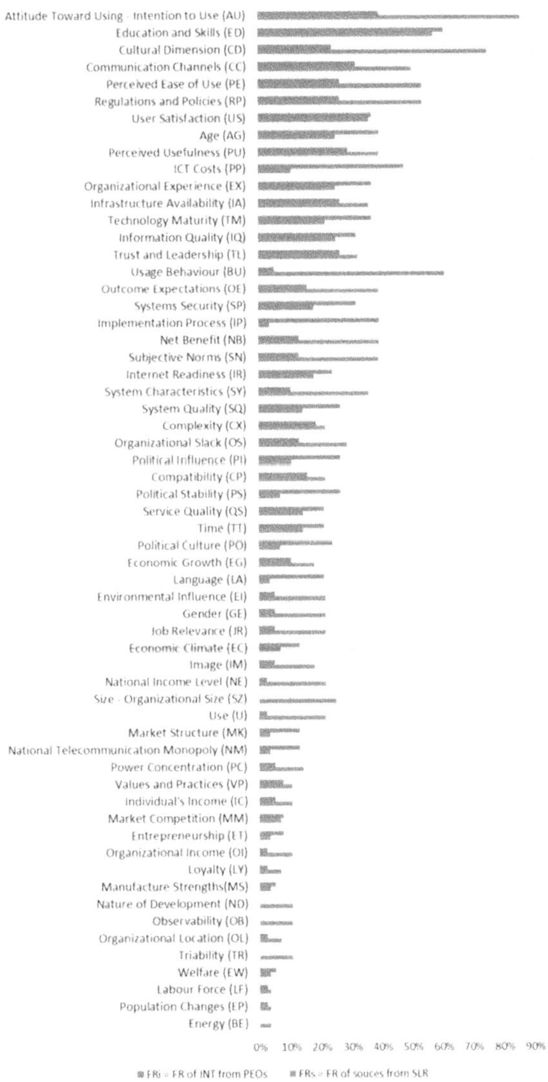

of existing literature and the transcript of the local interviews. In summary, it is noted that different aspects need to be considered to select any of the identified themes as candidate drivers affecting SISA for government organization in LAT regions such as PEOs.

## Control Characteristics Groups Redefined from the PEOs

Analysing the transcripts of the interviews and the locals' answers about the scrutinized set of themes, it was noted that some of the Control Characteristic groups determined from the SLR needed to be re-organized. Therefore, these groups were regrouped again in six clusters (see Table 11). For example, it was determined that the themes grouped in both Behavioural Aspects and Social Aspects are predominantly referring to subjective and individuals perceptions aspects; thus they were reorganized in only one set named as Subjective Aspects. Organizational Aspects and National and Cultural Aspects were also reorganized in one group named Public Aspect because the focus of local contexts in the current research is government organizations as part of the national system. Consequently, the organized Control Characteristic clusters were reduced to six groups.

*Subjective Aspects* groups all the formed themes related to subjective features of social perceptions (Social control characteristics) as well as behaviour and perceptions related to the individuals (knowing that individuals are responsible for managing the organizations and using the systems). Features such as behaviour, attitude, perceptions, subjective norms, and motivations are considered Subjective Aspects, incorporating the selected themes clustered in this group.

*Technological Aspects* groups the themes formed by a variety of characteristics related to the features of computerised systems and the infrastructure involved for developing, implementing, and using technological applications associated with the adoption of IS.

*Public Aspects* includes all themes related to national and organizational characteristics. This involves determined external environment features, such as culture, politics, polices and regulations, government orientation, and the different organization features.

*Table 11. Reorganized control characteristics groups*

| Number of Themes Over the Median | | | SLR = 28 Sources | | | INT= 38 Interviews | | | |
|---|---|---|---|---|---|---|---|---|---|
| **Control Characteristics groups** | **SLR** | **INT.** | **NS** | **NR** | **FRs = NR/ SLR** | **NS** | **NR** | **FRi = NR/ INT** | **FRi/FRs** |
| Subjective Aspects | **10** | **5** | 26 | 27 | 4.54 | 7 | 3 | 1.92 | 0.42 |
| Technological Aspects | **5** | **11** | 20 | 6 | 2.71 | 5 | 124 | 3.26 | 1.20 |
| Public Aspects | **9** | **9** | 22 | 28 | 4.57 | 0 | 101 | 2.66 | 0.58 |
| Demographic Aspects | **3** | **3** | 12 | 4 | 1.21 | 9 | 53 | 1.39 | 1.15 |
| National Economic Aspects | **1** | **0** | 6 | 4 | 0.50 | 7 | 12 | 0.32 | 0.63 |
| Industry and Market Aspects | **0** | **0** | 3 | 5 | 0.18 | 5 | 11 | 0.29 | 1.62 |
| **FR Median** | | | | | **0.21** | | | **0.16** | |

*Demographic Aspects* groups themes linked to characteristics about the target of the population researched, such as age, gender, education, and income. This helps to assemble data about specific characteristic of the population, if required.

*National Economic* Aspects groups themes involved with characteristics related to economic activities of a society such as economic growth, income level, or economic climate. This aspect, for example, is currently used as a fact determinant of the development of knowledge society (Dutta & Bilbao-Osorio, 2012).

*Industry and Market Aspects* groups the themes related to characteristics that involve a broad range of issues about environment, dynamics, and attractiveness of special markets in determined industries, such as market structure, competition, and labour force, among others.

### Comparing the Outcomes Obtained From the SLR Process and Interviews

After the reorganization of themes clustered in control characteristic groups was undertaken, the relevance of the themes per group was again examined. To identify the most relevant themes to the sources selected in the SLR process and to the local interviews (INT), the medians of references (SLR median = 0.21, INT median = 0.16) in relation to the number of sources analysed in each case were considered (see Table 10). The themes identified over the normalized medians obtained in each case were considered as the most relevant themes referenced in each analysis.

The number of themes identified over the medians obtained, which are linked to Technological Aspects and Subjective Aspects, present substantial variations between existing studies and from the opinion of local practitioners and experts working in PEO (see Table 9 and Table 10). However, the number themes over the media grouped in Public Aspects and Demographic Aspects remains of similar relevance. Themes clustered in National Economic Aspects and Industry and Market Aspects were less frequently or not at all mentioned by interviewees; therefore, they may not need to be considered relevant to be considered for further studies in LAT contexts.

It was also noted that Subjective Aspects enclosed the main number of drivers identified as the most relevant from existing literature. In this case, drivers linked to Public Aspects were followed according to relevance, and drivers related to Technological Aspects were less relevant to the existing empirical literature selected for analysis. To the contrary, Technological Aspects enclosed the main number of relevant themes from the points of view of local experts and practitioners. This was followed by drivers linked to Subjective Aspects and Public Aspects, in that order. Themes linked to Demographic Aspects were identified as low relevant in both cases. The other two Control Characteristics groups were ultimately considered less or not relevant to the sources analysed (see Table 11 and Figure 7).

## THE RESULTS: ANSWERING THE RESEARCH QUESTION

### How Do Existing Theories and Their Proposed Drivers Used in IS Adoption Apply to the Latin American IS Adoption Context?

Following the SLR process and from the analysis of the extracted data, 60 themes were formed from the selected studies as the most common candidate factors of SISA identified. Seven themes were determined as possible main constructs and 53 themes were clustered in seven groups named as Control

*Figure 7. Comparison relevant themes between SLR and INTERVIEWS*

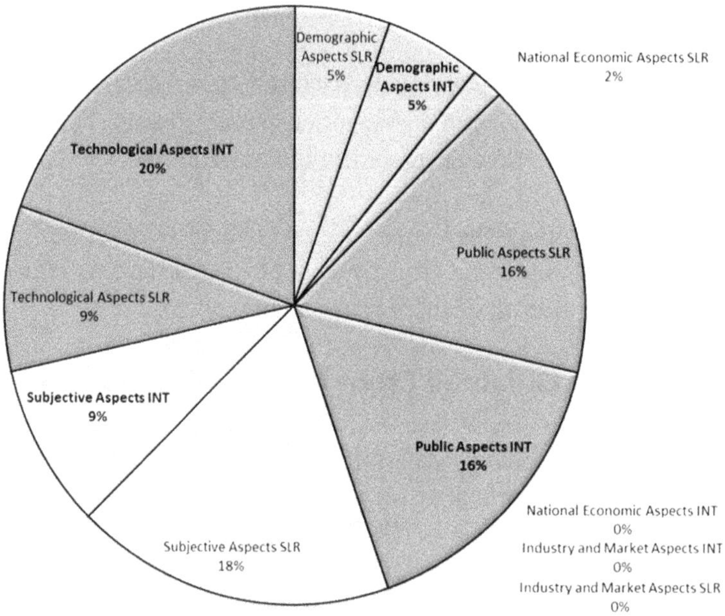


Characteristics. Within this analysis, TAM and D&M-ISS theories were noted as the theories from where the most frequently identified themes emerged, mostly determined as main constructs of IS adoption. However, demographic moderators proposed by UTAUT and determinants proposed by DOI (which group factors by similar characteristics) were also considered as highly significant in the identification of the formed themes. This leads us to suggest that the themes identified as factors proposed in TAM, D&M-ISS, UTAUT, and DOI should be reflected in IS local studies. However, not a single theory should be considered as an adequate model to investigate SISA in local LAT organizational contexts. Therefore, the researchers suggested that these two theories need to be included as a basis for the construction of an adaptive theory suitable for the LAT context.

In addition, comparable themes related to national level such as national culture and economic aspects, and the relationship of such aspects with IS/ICT readiness, were determined between LAT regions and developed societies. Encouraging cultural similarities and almost the same level of technology readiness were also identified between LAT economies. Contrary, remarkable differences, in these contexts, between LAT regions and the developed economies (from where most of the selected studies originated) were evidenced. For example, it is supports that cultural dimensions of LAT countries are considered as a separate cluster, with similar scores in most of the cultural dimensions proposed in related studies, and with remarkable differences from developed western societies (Hofstede, 2013; House et al., 2004). In addition, it was noted that developed western societies, for example, are characterized by a high individualism cultural dimension. This is suggested as a reason to explain the importance that existing studies have given to Subjective Aspects, focusing on drivers most related to attitude and individual behaviors, which is different from LAT societies evidenced as more collectivist cultures. Therefore, in LAT economies Subjective Aspects such as individualism are not a main concern. On the other hand, low indexes of Networked Readiness in Technology (NRI) are identified as common in LAT economies, which is different from western developed economies. Thus, because the similar low level of technology readiness of almost all LAT economies (Dutta & Bilbao-Osorio, 2012; Dutta, Geiger, & Lanvin, 2015) it is suggested that for local organizations in LAT environments, drivers linked to Technological Aspects can be the main focus of concern.

The researchers have identified a set of themes as feasible candidate drivers of SISA in PEOs, together with the combination of four recognized theories commonly used to support IS adoption studies. Therefore, they support the claim that these findings should be considered regarding the need for an adaptive theory of SISA particularly oriented to government organizations in the LAT contexts which share similar cultural aspects and level of technology readiness, thereby answering the stated research question.

## SUMMARY AND CONCLUSION

From an SLR process, 28 studies were chosen in order to gather justifiable evidence of the most common theories used in IS adoption research, and factors frequently proposed and empirically evidenced as drivers of adoption in different environments. This was done with the purpose of identifying a list of candidate drivers (identified as themes in the qualitative analysis undertaken) and to propose a suitable model that may be applied to measure SISA in LAT economies. All the items identified as drivers, factors, constructs, moderators or with any other denomination determined by the selected studies, were initially coded as open codes, then regrouped until a set of 60 themes was formed.

In an ongoing analysis of the data extracted, and from the analysis and scrutinization of the 60 themes considering the points of view of local practitioners and expert of PEOs, these themes were refined and re-organized in six control characteristics groups. From them, seven themes proposed as drivers of adoption were noted as conceivable main constructs, 34 as possible constructs, 13 as candidate determinants, and six as potential moderators of SISA in different environments. Most of the identified themes were empirically proposed as drivers affecting IS/IT adoption by the existing studies and ratified by locals' opinions. Even though, from this analysis, a group of themes were distinguished over the FR median, it is suggested that all the identified themes can be considered as candidate drivers of SISA for further refined studies. This is because more contextual research on organizational LAT contexts needs to be done.

Concurrently, 11 theories were identified as the most commonly referenced in adoption studies. From these, TAM and D&M-UISS were determined as the theories containing the themes identified as main constructs because all of these themes had an FR over the median. From UTAU and DOI, an important number of themes were also identified. Parallel to this analysis, some themes related to National, Culture, and Economy Characteristics also emerged as possible drivers in determining the use of IS in different economies. Therefore, cultural similarities and differences between developed and LAT societies were also analysed, obtaining an implied strong correlation between LAT cultures, and the index of Technology readiness of a country (NRI). Considerable differences between LAT and developed economies were identified in the same contexts.

These findings gave some indication that the set of the identified candidate drivers of SISA needs to be further refined, and no one specific model from the existing theories used to measure adoption, such as TAM, UTAU, or D&M-ISS, may necessarily be functionally applicable in LAT IS adoption studies by themselves. However these models should be used as a base reference to construct an adapted theory to be proposed as a hybrid model to measure adoption in government institutions as nonprofit organization of LAT regions.

## Future Work

From the outcomes obtained in the current study, a set of themes considered as a preliminary list of candidate factors of SISA was identified, as well as theories that could be used in a hybrid model to measure SISA in LAT. However, the set of themes is still too broad and mostly oriented towards developed and developing economies and not particularly toward LAT countries, apart from PEOs as a focus case in which the identified drivers were scrutinized. Therefore, continuing stages to complete an overall research should be undertaken.

A long-term study to complement the current findings based on more data collected from local government organizational context is recommended. Within this process, other candidate drivers may emerge, and some of the current drivers identified (as formed themes) in the current study could be rejected. At this point some hypotheses will also emerge. Therefore, once the results of the qualitative phase are accomplished, a further quantitative studies are recommended to be undertaken, in which proposed hypothesis will be empirically accepted or rejected, and the usefulness of the model will be explained and then generalized by suggesting its possible applicability in other organizational environments of LAT economies.

## REFERENCES

Aboelmaged, M. G. (2010). Predicting e-procurement adoption in a developing country: An empirical integration of technology acceptance model and theory of planned behaviour. *Industrial Management & Data Systems*, *110*(3), 392–414. doi:10.1108/02635571011030042

Ajzen, I. (1991). The theory of planned behavior. *Organizational Behavior and Human Decision Processes*, *50*(2), 179–211. doi:10.1016/0749-5978(91)90020-T

Al-Ghaith, W. A., Sanzogni, L., & Sandhu, K. (2010). Factors influencing the adoption and usage of online services in Saudi Arabia. *The Electronic Journal of Information Systems in Developing Countries*, *40*(1), 1–32.

Al-Somali, S. A., Gholami, R., & Clegg, B. (2009). An investigation into the acceptance of online banking in Saudi Arabia. *Technovation*, *29*(2), 130–141. doi:10.1016/j.technovation.2008.07.004

Bandura, A. (1982). Self-efficacy mechanism in human agency. *The American Psychologist*, *37*(2), 122–147. doi:10.1037/0003-066X.37.2.122

Bandura, A. (1986). Social foundations of thought and action: A social cognitive theory. Englewood Cliffs, NJ: Prentice Hall, Inc.

Biolchini, J., Mian, P. G., Natali, A. C. C., & Travassos, G. H. (2005). Systematic review in software engineering. *System Engineering and Computer Science Department COPPE/UFRJ. Technical Report ES*, *679*(05), 45.

Borker, D. R. (2012). Accounting, culture and emerging economies: IFRS in Central and Eastern Europe. *International Business & Economics Research Journal*, *11*(9), 1003–1018.

Cronin, P., Ryan, F., & Coughlan, M. (2008). Undertaking a literature review: A step-by-step approach. *British Journal of Nursing (Mark Allen Publishing)*, *17*(1), 38–43. doi:10.12968/bjon.2008.17.1.28059 PMID:18399395

Davis, F. D. (1989). Perceived Usefulness, Perceived Ease of Use, and User Acceptance of Information Technology. *Management Information Systems Quarterly*, *13*(3), 319–340. doi:10.2307/249008

Davis, F. D., Bagozzi, R. P., & Warshaw, P. R. (1989). User Acceptance of Computer Technology: A Comparison of Two Theoretical Models. *Management Science*, *35*(8), 982–1003. doi:10.1287/mnsc.35.8.982

de Almeida Biolchini, J. C., Mian, P. G., Natali, A. C. C., Conte, T. U., & Travassos, G. H. (2007). Scientific research ontology to support systematic review in software engineering. *Advanced Engineering Informatics*, *21*(2), 133–151. doi:10.1016/j.aei.2006.11.006

DeLone, W. H., & McLean, E. R. (1992). Information Systems Success: The Quest for the Dependent Variable. *Information Systems Research*, *3*(1), 60–95. doi:10.1287/isre.3.1.60

DeLone, W. H., & McLean, E. R. (2003). The DeLone and McLean model of information systems success: A ten-year update. *Journal of Management Information Systems*, *19*(4), 9–30.

Dutta, S., & Bilbao-Osorio, B. (2012). The global information technology report 2012: Living in a hyperconnected world. In I. World Economic Forum (Ed.), *The Global Information Technology Report*. Geneva, Switzerland: SRO-Kundig.

Dutta, S., Dutton, W., & Law, G. (2011). The New Internet World: A Global Perspective on Freedom of Expression, Privacy, Trust and Security Online. In I. World Economic Forum (Ed.), *The Global Information Technology Report*. World Economic Forum, INSEAD Business School.

Dutta, S., Geiger, T., & Lanvin, B. (2015). The global information technology report 2015: ICTs for Inclusive Growth. In W. E. F. Cornell University, INSEAD (Ed.), The Global Information Technology Report. Geneva, Switzerland: SRO-Kundig.

Dutta, S., & Mia, I. (2010). The global information technology report 2009–2010: ICT for Sustainability. In I. World Economic Forum (Ed.), *The Global Information Technology Report*. Geneva, Switzerland: SRO-Kuding.

Erumban, A. A., & de Jong, S. B. (2006). Cross-country differences in ICT adoption: A consequence of Culture? *Journal of World Business*, *41*(4), 302–314. doi:10.1016/j.jwb.2006.08.005

Fishbein, M., & Ajzen, I. (1975). *Belief, attitude, intention, and behavior: An introduction to theory and research*. London: Addison-Wesley.

Gomez, R. (2013). The Changing Field of ICTD: Growth and maturation of the field, 2000-2010. *The Electronic Journal of Information Systems in Developing Countries, 58.*

Hart, C. (1998). *Doing a literature review: Releasing the social science research imagination*. London: Sage Publications.

Huang, Z., & Palvia, P. (2001). ERP implementation issues in advanced and developing countries. *Business Process Management Journal*, *7*(3), 276–284. doi:10.1108/14637150110392773

Ifinedo, P. (2012). Drivers of E-Government Maturity in Two Developing Regions: Focus on Latin America and Sub-Saharan Africa. *Journal of Information Systems and Technology Management*, *9*(1), 5–22. doi:10.4301/S1807-17752012000100001

Jeyaraj, A., & Sabherwal, R. (2008). Adoption of information systems innovations by individuals: A study of processes involving contextual, adopter, and influencer actions. *Information and Organization*, *18*(3), 205–234. doi:10.1016/j.infoandorg.2008.04.001

Kitchenham, B. (2004). *Procedures for performing systematic reviews* (Vol. 33). Keele, UK: Academic Press.

Kitchenham, B., & Brereton, P. (2013). A systematic review of systematic review process research in software engineering. *Information and Software Technology*, *55*(12), 2049–2075. doi:10.1016/j.infsof.2013.07.010

Kowal, J., & Roztocki, N. (2013). Information and Communication Technology Management for Global Competitiveness and Economic Growth in Emerging Economies. *The Electronic Journal of Information Systems in Developing Countries, 57.*

Lin, F., Fofanah, S. S., & Liang, D. (2011). Assessing citizen adoption of e-Government initiatives in Gambia: A validation of the technology acceptance model in information systems success. *Government Information Quarterly*, *28*(2), 271–279. doi:10.1016/j.giq.2010.09.004

McClelland, D. C. (1967). The Achieving Society. New York, NY: Free Press.

Oliveira, T., & Martins, M. F. (2011). Literature review of information technology adoption models at firm level. *The Electronic Journal Information Systems Evaluation*, *14*(1), 110–121.

Rogers, E. M. (1995). *Diffusion of Innovations* (4th ed.). New York, NY: Free Press.

Rogers, E. M. (2003). *Diffusion of Innovations* (5th ed.). New York, NY: Free Press.

Rokhman, A. (2011). E-Government Adoption in Developing Countries; The Case of Indonesia. *Journal of Emerging Trends in Computing and Information Sciences*, *2*(5), 228–236.

Salleh, N., Mendes, E., & Grundy, J. (2011). Empirical Studies of Pair Programming for CS/SE Teaching in Higher Education: A Systematic Literature Review. *IEEE Transactions on Software Engineering*, *37*(4), 509–525. doi:10.1109/TSE.2010.59

Seddon, P. B. (1997). A respecification and extension of the DeLone and McLean model of IS success. *Information Systems Research*, *8*(3), 240–253. doi:10.1287/isre.8.3.240

Shajari, M., & Ismail, Z. (2010). *A comprehensive adoption model of e-government services in developing countries.* Paper presented at the Advanced Management Science (ICAMS), 2010 IEEE International Conference on, Chengdu, China. doi:10.1109/ICAMS.2010.5552982

SNAP. (2014). *E-Government National Plan 2014-2017, Summary (Resumen del Plan de Gobierno Electrónico 2014-2017).* Ecuadorian National Government (GNE) - National Secretary of Public Administration (SNAP). Retrieved from http://www.gobiernoelectronico.gob.ec/wp-content/uploads/2015/02/Resumen-Ingl%C3%A9s-PNGE.pdf

Steinmacher, I., Graciotto Silva, M. A., Gerosa, M. A., & Redmiles, D. F. (2015). A systematic literature review on the barriers faced by newcomers to open source software projects. *Information and Software Technology*, *59*, 67–85. doi:10.1016/j.infsof.2014.11.001

Tang, L., & Koveos, P. E. (2008). A framework to update Hofstedes cultural value indices: Economic dynamics and institutional stability. *Journal of International Business Studies*, *39*(6), 1045–1063. doi:10.1057/palgrave.jibs.8400399

Toland, J., & Yoong, P. (2013). Envisaging the "Big Picture": Information systems researchers. *Australasian Journal of Information Systems*, *18*(1).

Tornatzky, L. G., Fleischer, M., & Chakrabarti, A. K. (1990). *The processes of technological innovation*. Lexington, MA: Lexington Books.

Van Everdingen, Y. M., & Waarts, E. (2003). The effect of national culture on the adoption of innovations. *Marketing Letters*, *14*(3), 217–232. doi:10.1023/A:1027452919403

Venkatesh, V., & Davis, F. D. (2000). A Theoretical Extension of the Technology Acceptance Model. *Management Science*, *46*(2), 186–204. doi:10.1287/mnsc.46.2.186.11926

Venkatesh, V., Morris, M. G., Davis, G. B., & Davis, F. D. (2003). User Acceptance of Information Technology: Toward a Unified View. *Management Information Systems Quarterly*, *27*(3), 425–478.

Wadie, N. (2011). Factors Influencing the Adoption of Internet Banking in Tunisia. *International Journal of Business and Management*, *6*(8), 143. doi:10.5539/ijbm.v6n8p143

Wang, Y.-S., & Liao, Y.-W. (2008). Assessing eGovernment systems success: A validation of the DeLone and McLean model of information systems success. *Government Information Quarterly*, *25*(4), 717–733. doi:10.1016/j.giq.2007.06.002

## KEY TERMS AND DEFINITIONS

**Adapted Theory:** Combined or redefined theory that can be viewed as a model. It describes, explains, and represents a phenomenon under study but adjusted to the determined reality.

**Control Characteristics:** Clusters named as Categories, Context, Focus, Aspects, Grouping Conditions, or Dimensions, aimed to better organize a set of the drivers linked by similar aspects.

**Drivers:** Identified as factors, constructs, determinants, mediators, or moderators as influencers of IS adoption. The drivers are tested in a variety of contexts at the level of individuals or organizations.

**Frequency of References:** Identify the number of times that significant statements (grouped in corresponding themes) are highlighted and coded from the examined sources. These frequencies are calculated to identify the relevance given to each of the formed themes from the data sources.

**Information System (IS):** A set of interconnected components (human interaction, technology, features, and processes) that collect, operate, store, and distribute data, and disseminate information to meet an objective; they act as a feedback mechanism that helps organizations to achieve their goals (Toland & Yoong, 2013).

**IS Adoption:** A developing process linking actions between potential adopters, individuals who might influence the adopters, and actions within the adopter's context, in which all potential adopters (stakeholders) expect progressive results (Jeyaraj & Sabherwal, 2008).

**IS Theories:** Determined theories, models, and theoretical frameworks linked to technology adoption, IS/ICT adoption, and/or IS success studies.

**Public Ecuadorian Organizations (PEOs):** Government institutions investigated as focus case of nonprofit organizations in LAT economies.

**Successful Information System Adoption (SISA):** Defined as the linking action process that measures the impacts of drivers influencing the use of implemented systems in an organization. In other words, SISA will explain how well a system is adopted, and how it fits the required specification and fulfils the expectations of the stakeholders in an organization, including the ongoing benefit of using a system over extended periods of time.

# Chapter 11
# Investigating Factors Influencing Third Sector Social Enterprise Managers' Career Orientations:
## A Conceptual Framework

**Chi Maher**
*St. Mary's University Twickenham, London, UK*

## ABSTRACT

*This chapter proposes conceptual framework that explores factors that influence managerial career orientations (self-perceived talents and abilities, basic values and the evolved sense of motives and needs that influences a person's career-related decisions. The argument put forward is that demographic (age, gender, social class, marital status, ethnicity, professional and educational qualifications); societal and organisational factors (government policies, labour market conditions, diversification of income streams, organisation size, structure and culture) will influence small third sector manager's career orientations. Identifying and understanding the career orientations of managers provide organisations with greater awareness of employee career needs and the ability to target career management effectively. The results indicate positive outcomes in organisational commitment, improved productivity and staff retention. This chapter concludes with a summary of finding, implications and future research directions.*

## INTRODUCTION

Asserted by various authors (Schein, 1990; Feldman and Bolino, 1996; Coetzee and Schreuder, 2008; Guan, Wen, Xiaohua, Haiyang, Wei, L., Liu, Wang, Zhang, and Dong; 2013) organisational ability to enhance career management efficiently can be improved by identifying and understanding the career orientations of managers and to provide organisations with greater awareness of employee career needs. Targeting career management efficiently has been a challenge across all organisational sectors and is

DOI: 10.4018/978-1-5225-2537-0.ch011

Copyright © 2017, IGI Global. Copying or distributing in print or electronic forms without written permission of IGI Global is prohibited.

particularly interesting in the contemporary context of the small third sector social enterprise. Third sector social enterprise development began in the nineteenth century in the evaluation of social economy and incorporated organizations such as, mutual benefits societies, and co-operatives (Dart, 2004; Hines, 2005). Social enterprises are defined as enterprises that trade to meet social/environmental goals (Department of Trade and Industry, 2002). The concept of social enterprise has achieved policy recognition in many countries. These types of social businesses became more prominent in the United States during the late 1970s and 1980s in response to the economic downturn and major cutbacks in government spending (Kerlin, 2006; Young, 2006).

Social enterprises in Europe also gained momentum during the economic downturn in the 1970. As the downturn led to cuts in government budgets across Europe, reducing the states' ability to provide unemployment assistance and job reintegration (Crimmins & Keil, 1983; Eikenberry and Kluver, 2004). This paved the way for the emergence of social enterprise as a widely accepted concept of addressing socio-economic problems due to a necessity resulting out of state reduction in funding. Moreover, social enterprises are an integral part of the third sector and contribute to the modernization and delivery of public services in the UK. The sector mission is to achieve social goals (for example, improving the community, environment, economic well-being, health and social care) (National Council for Voluntary Organisations, 2009; 2015). The sector organizations operate within a range of institutional, legal and financial constraints. The sector is self-governing which allows stakeholders such as, service users, volunteers, workers and managerial staff to have a say in policy development and service delivery procedures (Kendall, 2003; Anheier, 2005).

Several authors view the sector organizations as effective, because they target the unmet needs of local people and make a positive contribution to the regeneration of deprived areas by addressing gaps in public services, combating socio-economic exclusion and facilitating and local democratic structures based on empowering individuals to make decisions at the local level (Morphet, 2008). They help to build citizenship (participation and membership in the community) by engaging citizens in the development of their communities (Steinberg, 2003).

Steinberg (2003) and later Morphet (2008) offer a unique way of social organizing, based on the values of independence which includes freedom of association, altruism that entails concern for others and community collective action (Kendall and Knapp, 1995; Kendall, 2003). The advocacy role of the sector organizations has helped enhance social exclusion. Social inclusion involves building shared values, reducing disparities in wealth and income and enabling local communities to have sense that they are facing shared challenges and finding mutually satisfactory solutions (Kendall, 2003; Harris, 2010). The sector organizations encourage citizen participation in the delivery of community services and plays a role in generating social capital (Kendall. 2003; Knight and Robson, 2007; Damm, 2012). Academic interest in the sector has increased in the last four decades as the understanding of the benefits and the contributions of the sector to the economy increases (Lowe and Butcher, 1994; Borzaga and Defourny, 2001; Vickers, 2010).

The state has failed to fulfill the demand for public services, and therefore, the sector organizations emerge to fill the gaps (Halfpenny and Reid, 2002; Peattie and Morley, 2008; Jenner, 2016). The explicit inclusion of the third sector in the UK government social enterprise policy document was to encourage third sector organizations to diversify their income generation streams. This policy agenda opened up new 'developmental' funding streams for the sector organizations to build capacity and to develop new services to enable them to sustain a social enterprise 'business model'. New funding streams from which organizations benefited includes: Future Builders, Capacity Builders Funds, Adventure Capital Fund,

Social Enterprise Investment Fund, the Social Impact Bond (Amin, Cameron, and Hudson;1999; Millar and Hall, 2013; Ridley-Duff and Bull, 2015).

The government believes that the sector adopting a social enterprise 'business model' allows the sector organizations to be more sustainable and financially independent. The limited contracts that government award to the sector organizations do not only affect their ability to expand in a competitive market (The Kings Fund, 2011; Maher, 2016); it also influences their ability to manage their key assets such as, their governance structures, employees, volunteers and limits the developments of managerial careers in these organizations. Furthermore, it constraints these organization's ability to develop long term career management systems for managers, that will enable them to retain managers (Cunningham, 2009; Maher, 2009; NVCO, 2015).

The literature suggests that these organizations are continuously expanding their income generating activities to cope with the shortage of government contracts awarded to them and to reduce their dependence on a single funding body (the government) (NVCO, 2014; Maher, 2015b; Jenner, 2016). Often volunteers are recruited to contribute to service delivery so that managers have the capacity to reach greater numbers; extending hours of operation; or diversifying the types of services offered by the organization (Denhardt, Denhardt and Aristigueta, 2015). Volunteers often support and complement the existing skills of salaried managers and help the organization be more effective in achieving its objectives (Royce, 2007; Doherty, Haugh and Lyon; 2014).

The reduction in third sector government contracts has led to an increasing number of organization's to generate income from a multiple sources in order to reduce their dependence on government and short-term contracts (Aiken, 2007; Di Domenico, Tracey, and Haugh; 2009; Maher, 2015b). Seeking multiple income sources is not without its constraints. There is the unpredictability of income from national and local businesses. Often organizations have found themselves serving multiple funders each with slightly differing priorities and administrative practices. Several researchers have found that the short-term nature of government funding to the sector has restricted organizations from implementing long term career strategies that takes into account manager's career needs (Cunningham, 2009; Maher, 2016).

However, the literature search for career management in the small third sector organizations found that these organizations are primarily concerned with ensuring that they spend funding awarded on delivering client services as directed by the funders (Bennett and Savani, 2011; Achleitner, Spiess-Knafl, and Volk; 2014; Ridley-Duff and Bull, 2015).In most cases the funding awarded does not include funding to build management capacity or to develop managerial career management systems. Thus, the organizations often relegate managerial career management to the background.

Developing appropriate career management systems in an organization is a difficult task for any organization, especially when it is taking place against the backdrop of the financial uncertainties facing the sector organizations. Hirsh (2005) suggests that the three main difficulties with implementing career management systems in an organization are:

1. It relies on a variety of people management practices such as training and performance management.
2. It has to deal with tensions between individuals and the organization's need and;
3. It requires persistent and consistent attention over long periods of time.

These issues can be challenging, particularly, for small third sector social enterprises as they do not always have systems in place to identify and support managers' individual career needs (Maher, 2009; 2015a). Therefore, the chapter aim is to identify factors that could influence managerial career orientations in small third sector social enterprises. The objectives are to specifically identify societal, demographic and organizational factors that influence the career orientations of managers.

The chapter consist of four sections which are outlined below. Section one has outlined the background to third sector social enterprises and how government polices impacts on these organisations. Section two discusses the concept of a career, identifies and evaluates the traditional and new career models differing career perspectives (Hall, 1976; Kanter, 1987; DeFillippi and Arthur, 1994). Section three concentrates on examining Schein's (1978) career anchor/orientations model and section four presents and discusses the conceptual model as the general framework to conduct the research to understand factors influencing small social enterprises managerial career orientations.

## METHODOLGOY

Articles selected for inclusion in this chapter were selected through citation search in academic conferences, per-reviewed journals and working papers and using the abstracting and on-line services such as, ProQuest and Google Scholar (Maher, 2013). The search was limited to articles published in English, reviewed article are listed in the chapter's reference section. The search was completed in September 2016.

Articles were reviewed based on the framework used by Ellram (1995) which classifies research as primarily descriptive or prescriptive and empirically or conceptually based. This was very helpful not only in developing a literature review with a critical perspective, but also in assessing gaps in theories and empirical findings of studies.

## LITERATURE REVIEW

The concept of a career has been examined by several disciplines such as, sociology, psychology, counselling, labour economics and business management studies. Each of these disciplines has their own, language, discourse and concept of a career (Herr, 1990).As a result the literature on the concept of a career has been described as "multidisciplinary, multi-level and difficult to distil" (Millward, 2005:163). On the one hand, the concept of a career is not strictly an academic discipline; often it is a term which individuals use to construct their daily lives (e.g. a teacher, house wife, baker, doctor, and lawyer). Therefore, the concept of a career is fairly ambitious, which makes it inherently challenging to study. For these reasons, this chapter reviews models as defined by a number of scholars (Super, 1957; Hall, 1976; Schein, 1978; Kanter, 1987; DeFillippi and Arthur, 1994). The following section introduces a range of career models and considers these career models' applications to examining the career orientations of social enterprise managers.

Scholars such as Kanter, (1989) (bureaucratic and professional career models); DeFillippi and Arthur, (1994), (boundaryless career model); Hall (1996) (The protean career mode); Schein, (1978) (career anchor/orientations model) have developed different career models and ways of understanding the complexity of careers. Each of these model are discussed followed by considering its applicability to understanding the career orientations of small third sector social enterprise managers.

## Traditional Career Model

Traditional career models, such as the bureaucratic and professional career models, conceptualise careers as a series of upward progression of individuals within an organisation hierarchy with increasing income, status, power and security within a single organisation or a professional grouping (Kanter, 1989). The bureaucratic and professional career models were developed from studies by Erickson (1968) and Levinson, (1978).They suggests that careers are bounded by the organisational career structure (organisational career model) or by a profession's career structure (professional career model).

## Bureaucratic Career Model

The bureaucratic career model was developed with the notion that a career involves upward progression within an organisation. In such an organisation, the organisation defines the individual's career management. According to Kanter, (1989) one builds one's bureaucratic career on the basis of advancement and growth. In this context, advancement means progression within the organisational hierarchy (determined by the organisation). Growth means promotion to a higher position; within an organisation. Furthermore, Kanter (1989) suggests the following assumptions are behind the bureaucratic career model:

1. A limited pool of competitors for high positions, with the 'losers' accepting their place, thus permitting a pyramidal distribution of people and maintenance of legitimacy of hierarchy;
2. Continuing organisational growth, so that the organisation can offer opportunity through expanding the width of the pyramid; and
3. Continuing employment security, so that eventually, employees would receive rewards foregone now later, at higher ranks (Kanter 1989: 510).

Kanter (1989) suggests that in bureaucratic careers, all the elements of career opportunity (such as responsibilities, challenges and constrains) are related to the ranks within the organisation which provides a clear chain of command. This implies that the higher an individual progresses through the organisational hierarchy, the more power and opportunities the individual will expect. Kanter (1989) argues that the basis of the bureaucratic career is that it discourages strong attachment to tasks or work groups, while encouraging strong attachment to the organisation, "since ultimate financial and political rewards will only come with striking it out longer" (Kanter, 1989: 509).

Kanter (1989) associates the bureaucratic career with large twentieth century bureaucratic organisations which operated in stable and predictable economic markets. Adams (1991) contends that the bureaucratic career model provides individuals with specialised knowledge, facilitates the development of expertise and attachment to the organisation. Adams (1991) further suggests that the main advantage of the bureaucratic career model from the employee's perspective is that they understand the effort required to achieve progression through the organisational hierarchy. Traditionally, scholars have also associated the concept of a career with the idea of advancement from a humble beginning to more senior positions in a profession.

## Professional Career Model

Kanter (1989) suggests conceptualising the professional career as progressing through a predictable regular sequence, from one position to another, within an individual's profession. This implies membership of a professional body that is independent of the employing organisation, and meeting the requirement of the professional body's own codes of practice (Pearson, 1991).Therefore, different types of occupations have a sequential advancement structure (such as the accounting, medical and legal professions). Any job within an occupational grouping (e.g. medicine, accountancy and law) which does not offer individuals the opportunity for further advancement does not constitute a career. Dalton, Thompson and Price (1977) suggest four different stages that guide professional career advancement:

1. **Apprentice:** In this stage, the individual learns how to cope with organisational life, assigned to work under an experience senior colleague in order to be guided and supported.
2. **Independent Specialists:** In this stage, the individual acquires competence and is in a good position to make solid and justifiable contributions to organisation work.
3. **Mentor:** In this stage the individual manages the work and development of newcomers to the organisation by acting as a facilitator.
4. **Sponsor:** In this stage, the individual becomes involved with the goals of the organisation, the activities and the development of junior members of staff.

These developmental stages enable professionals, to grow, develop and practice their skills and to have the opportunity later in their career to be involved in more important and demanding activities, which challenges their skills and ability (Kanter 1989). Kanter (1989) argues that for professionals, career growth involves the opportunity to practice their skills and to have the opportunity to engage in more important and demanding activities, which challenges their skills and ability. Therefore, the reward for a good job is the opportunity to undertake more jobs in order to gain rewards. Kanter (1989) contends that for professionals; 'upward mobility' involves reputation for greater skills. This implies that as professionals get involved in more demanding and important work, their reputation grows due to the skills and knowledge they possess and the reputation they acquire over the years.

Kanter (1989) affirms that the main difference between the bureaucratic career and professional career models is that the bureaucratic career model as opposed to the organisational career model does not depend on other people retiring or moving to other positions for the individual to move to the next occupational hierarchical level. Increasingly, many career management researchers are challenging the traditional career models. They argue that the traditional career models neglect the interrelationship between the individual's career values, motivations social structures and organisational factors that can influence the careers of the individual concerned (Volcour and Tolbert, 2003, Vos et al.; 2008, Cabrear, 2009).

In addition, the tradition career models fail to take into account, organisational size and non-hierarchical management structures which may limit an individual manager's chances of a steady step-by-step upward career progression. Including demographic factors such as gender, ethnicity and educational qualifications which may influence individuals' careers (Gunz et al., 2000; Omair, 2010). In the context of the third sector, the size of small social enterprises and the short-term nature of their funding and income streams suggest that the traditional career model conceptualisation of a career are difficult for several small social enterprises to implement. Careers in these organisations are often influenced by the organisation's funding contract specification and income duration (Maher, 2015b; 2016).

Furthermore, other researchers are challenging the traditional career models (DeFillippi and Arthur, 1994; Arthur and Rousseau, 1996; Hall, 2004; Baruch, 2006). These researchers argue that the traditional careers have disappeared due to:

1. Organisational restructuring (downsizing and de-layering) has led to the reduction of the workforce and the number of hierarchical tiers within the organisational structure.
2. Technological advances in communication and information technology have led to changes in organisational structures, as well as flexible forms or working, for example, individuals can work part-time or from home with hours to suit their needs.
3. Demographic and labour market changing; the population is aging; individuals are staying on at work longer even after they have reached the state retirement age and this is impacting on the labour market (Arthur and Rousseau, 1994; Arnold, 2011).

DeFillippi and Arthur, (1994) and Arthur and Rousseau, (1996) contend that the concept of a career is clearly changing in line with labour market trends; therefore, we should accept that new career models are developing within the context of the changes taking place in the employment market.

## New Career Model

There is a growing consensus that careers are changing from the traditional career model to careers based on employees taking more responsibility for their own career management. Several scholars suggest that individuals are developing and accumulating skills in order to further their careers across occupational areas, organisations, specialties or disciplines during their working life (DeFillippi and Arthur, 1994; Arthur and Rousseau, 1996).This implies that individuals are self-directing their careers, by focusing on the acquisition of skills and knowledge that they can gain at any point in time to enable them to move to the next job. Individuals can apply the acquired skills in other jobs or organisational contexts as the opportunity arises. DeFillippi and Arthur (1994) named the emergence of the changes in career opportunities that go beyond the boundaries of a single organisation 'boundaryless career'.

## Boundaryless Career Model

DeFillippi and Arthur (1994) were one of the first writers to use the term 'boundaryless career' to describe the career structures that are emerging due to the economic, technological and social realms transcending organisational systems and boundaries. Careers were becoming more diverse and less structured by employers. The concept of the boundaryless career is seen as an alternative to the traditional career models. Arthur and Rousseau (1996: 214) define the boundaryless career as within the general meaning of boundaryless careers (as being opposite of organisational careers) lie in several specific meanings, or emphasis. The most prominent of these are:

1. The case of where a career, like the stereotypical Silicon Valley career, moves across the boundaries of separate employers;

2. Meaning occurs when a career, like that of an academic or a carpenter, draws validation – and marketability – from outside the present employer;
3. Third meaning is involved when a career, like that of a real-estate agent, is sustained by external networks or information;
4. Meaning occurs when traditional organisational career boundaries, notably those involving hierarchical reporting and advancement principles, are broken;
5. Meaning occurs when a person rejects existing career opportunities for personal or family reasons; and
6. Meaning depends on the interpretation of the career actor, who many perceive a boundaryless future regardless of structural constraints. Source: Arthur and Rousseau (1996)

A common factor in the occurrence of all these meaning is one of independence from, rather than dependence on, traditional organisational career arrangement.

Arthur and Rousseau (1996) contend that due to changes taking place in the economy and labour market in the 1990s such as, organisations downsizing and de-layering that careers based on a hierarchical, vertical progression in one organisation is not applicable in most organisations. They posited that careers are no longer determined by the organisation. As a result, individuals are taking responsibility for accumulating and developing marketable skills and competencies in order to determine their careers within and across organisations during their working life (DeFillippi and Arthur, 1994; Arthur and Rousseau, 1996). Arthur and Rousseau (1996) suggest that in order for an individual to pursue a successful boundaryless career, it is crucial that the individual acquires the skills and competencies to know why, whom and how to develop their careers. Arthur and Rousseau (1996) described three 'ways of knowing' as:

1. **Knowing-Why:** Knowing why competencies relate to an individual's personal values and motivation. These competencies provide the individual with a sense of purpose, career clarity, identification with the world of work and enable the individual to decouple their identity from their current organisation in order remain alert for new career opportunities.
2. **Knowing-Whom:** Knowing whom competencies are the network relationships that individuals have inside and outside organisational boundaries in order to develop contacts and a reputation which can enable them to progress their careers.
3. **Knowing-How:** Knowing how competencies encompass the skills and knowledge individuals accumulate over time through their work, which are transferable across organisational and occupational boundaries (Arthur and Rousseau, 1996).

The boundaryless career model can be advantageous to individuals with the right competencies and skills to draw upon when the opportunity arises (Lichtenstein and Mendenhall, 2002; Sullivan and Arthur, 2006). Mirvis and Hall (1994) argue that the boundaryless career model involves the individual developing his or her own career without the support of the organisation. This will create too much uncertainty about the future for the individuals concerned. Several authors suggest that the boundaryless career model has underestimated institutional effects on individual careers and how contextual factors and social structures impact on career needs of individuals (Zeitz et al., 2009). They argue that there will always be boundaries. In relation to small social enterprises, boundaries can occur due to the organisational size, structure and the funding regime (Maher, 2015b). However, Hall (1996) in support of the boundaryless model declared that the traditional career model is 'dead'. Hall (1996) posited careers as 'protean'.

## Protean Career Model

The term 'protean' comes from the Greek god Proteus, who could change shape at will, suggesting that individuals are able to change their career to suit their needs. This career model places greater emphasis on the individual needs as a major factor that influences the careers of individuals. Hall (1996) defines the protean career as:

*A process which the person, not the organisation, is managing. It consists of all the persons' varied experiences in education, training, work in several organisations, changes in occupational field, etc. The protean career is not what happens to the person in any organisation (Hall, 1976: 201).*

The protean career model does not view careers as hierarchical or tied into an organisation. A protean career is self-managed by the individual according to their own personal needs and values, rather than organisational needs (Hall, 1976, 2004; Baruch, 2006; Arnold, 2011). It acknowledges work and non-work roles overlap to shape a person's career. It defines a career as a series of experiences in work, education and lifelong on-going learning processes that provide individual self-fulfilment.

Both the boundaryless and the protean career models do not mention how the education system or labour market conditions might influence an individual's career needs. Instead they suggest that every aspect of a career is left to the individual to manage, develop and control without considering how societal factors influences the individual's career. These new career models fail to acknowledge that organisations have a role to play in individuals' careers, for example, most organisations provide training, mentoring, coaching and support for staff and managers lacking specific skills required to fulfil their career needs.

Zeitz, G., Blau, G., and Fertig, J. (2009) suggest that careers have not become 'totally boundaryless'. They argue that there will always be boundaries to a career. In certain situations, boundaries can be in terms of the organisational size or structure. In the case of small social enterprises size and structure of the organisation could limit an individual's career progression (Maher, 2015a). Furthermore, the traditional and new career models do not explicitly explain how contextual factors such as, public policies, organisational culture or structure influences individual career orientations.

A particular useful career model for understanding the different career orientations which individuals hold, entitled career anchor/orientations model (Schein, 1978) is discussed next. Schein's (1978) career anchor/orientations model incorporates both the influence of the individual's career needs and motives and the individuals' working environment) view of a career.

## Career Anchor/Orientation Model

The career anchor/orientations model facilitates an understanding of individuals' internal career needs and career orientations. Understanding an individual's career orientations are important because it influences career choices and influences the individual's selection of specific occupations and work settings (Schein, 1978). Delong (1982) supports this view and contends that the career orientations model has a wide range of applications for organisations seeking to find a match between the individual and the organisational needs in order to develop career management systems suited to the individual and the organisation. The career anchor/orientations model was developed by Schein from a 10-12 year longitudinal study of 44 managers who graduated from Massachusetts Institute of Technology (MIT). Schein (1978) used in-depth interviews to examine individual career motivations, educational and job histories, values, work attitudes, ambitions and future plans. Schein describes career anchor/orientations as consisting of three important components: Perceived talents and abilities based self-assessment on actual successes in a variety of work settings;

1. Perceived motives and needs based on opportunities and experiences gained through self-diagnosis from undertaking a variety of job assignments or projects; and feedback from others; and
2. Perceived attitudes and values based on actual encounters between an individual and the norms and values of the employing organisation and work settings (Schein, 1978).Schein (1978) claims that through a process of the three components (perceived talents, motives and attitudes); most people develop an understanding of their work life and their own role within it. Schein (1978) suggests that there are five types of career anchor/orientations: technical, general management, security, entrepreneurial, autonomy. Some years later, Schein (1990) added three more career anchors: service and dedication to a cause, challenge and lifestyle.

The eight anchor/orientations are summarised below.

1. **Technical:** The individual seeks the opportunity to apply his/her skills in a technical or functional area of competence and continues to develop those skills. He/she values his/her expertise and seeks the opportunity to advance in the functional and specialist area of their job. The individual is not averse to management roles, but general management roles that take him/her away from his/her area of expertise would not be of interest. These individuals place value in getting opportunities for learning and development, as they are keen to continuously improve their skills. The technical-orientated individual values the formal recognition of being identified to colleagues as a specialist in their area of work.
2. **General Management:** The individual seeks the opportunity to move upwards into a general management position in an organisation and opportunities for leadership. The individual want high levels of responsibility, varied and integrative work. This career orientation involves: analytical competence, the ability to identify and solve problems; interpersonal competence: the ability to lead, manage and supervise others and emotional resilience: the capacity to bear high levels of responsibility and the ability to exercise power and facilitate the decision-making processes and implementation.
3. **Security:** The individual is motivated by long-term employment security, attachment to one organisation; he/she is willing to conform and to be fully socialised into an organisation's values and norms; that he/she feels this will guarantee security. The hierarchical promotion level that the individual achieves is less important than the stability that the organisation can offer. The security-orientated individual wants to be recognised and that his/her loyalty makes a contribution to the organisation's performance.
4. **Entrepreneurial:** The individual seeks the opportunity to create projects or enterprises and is motivated by the need to develop or create a project or enterprise that is entirely his/her own idea. The individual is motivated by the need to generate ideas and develop projects with which to identify; rather than managing the existing organisation's projects. He/she is constantly looking for ways to improve the organisation and project activities.
5. **Autonomy:** The individual seeks the opportunity to work in organisations where he/she can set his/her own work schedules and pursue particular area of specialism. The individual is likely to agree

to organisational set targets but once the targets are set, he/she wants to be left alone to get on with the tasks without close supervision. He/she is willing to trade off opportunities for promotion to have more freedom in defining the pace of their work. The autonomy-orientated individuals are self-reliant and independence of judgement.

6. **Challenge:** The individual seeks to work on solutions to seemingly unsolved problem. He/she is loyal to organisations that give adequate opportunities for developing new projects. The individual defines his/her career in terms of daily competition in which winning is everything and he/she is very single-minded and intolerant of those with less comparable aspirations.
7. **Lifestyle:** This concerns individuals seeking the opportunity that allows them to integrate personal needs, family needs and a balanced work and career lifestyle. He/she seek flexibility in an employment relationship and is happy to work for a long period within an organisation that offers flexibility and understanding of the kind to which they aspire.
8. **Service/Dedication:** The individual seeks the opportunity to pursue work that achieves personal value such as helping others and contributing to causes which meets his/her values and skills. The individual seeks recognition and support both from his/her professional peers and higher levels of management. The service/dedication-orientated individual, value work that permits him/her to be instrumental in realising their values and to have clout in getting things done. Source: Schein (1990).

The main attribute at the centre of Schein's (1978) career anchor/orientations model is congruence. Schein's (1978, 1990) empirical evidence suggests that when individuals achieve congruence between their career orientations and work environment, they are more likely to achieve positive organisational outcomes, which may include organisational commitment and intention to stay. On the other hand, incongruence can lead to job dissatisfaction, role conflict, reduce organisational commitment and result in an intention to leave the organisation.

Schein (1978) has been criticised because he conducted his original research with highly educated men in their late 20s and early 30s in the USA. Therefore, the transferability to women and less educated groups is questionable. Schein (1978) acknowledges this sample bias, but stated that in his opinion, career anchor/orientations have broader applicability to a range of managerial and non-managerial occupations.

Despite these criticisms of Schein (1978, 1990), several managerial career studies (Beck and Lopa, 2001; Kniveton 2003; Suutari and Taka, 2004; Wong, 2007; Rasdi, Ismaila, Uli, Noah, (2009) have utilised Schein's (1978) career anchor/orientations model to identify career orientations of managers. Career anchor/orientations studies (Kniveton, 2003; Wong, 2007; Gubler, Biemann, Tschopp & Grote (2015) contend that organisational benefits of identifying and recognising the career orientations of managerial staff include: understanding an individual's (internal) career needs, tailoring career management interventions appropriately and a reduction in managerial staff turnover. Several studies using the model to understand the career orientations managers found that individual's career orientations are influenced by demographic factors such as gender Garavan, O'Brien, and O'Hanlon (2006) age (Kniveton, 2004) and educational qualifications (Allen and Katz, 1996; Erdogmus, 2003).

To date, no research in small third sector social enterprises has examined the relationship between demographic differences and the career orientations of social enterprise managers. With increased changes in the characteristics and diversity in third sector social enterprise organisations, an examination of the influence of gender, age, availability of training opportunities, ethnicity, marital status, professional qualifications, educational system and qualifications, on managers' career orientations; is required to improve our knowledge and understanding of small third sector social enterprises managerial career needs.

The identification of the factors influencing the career orientations of managers could be useful for small third sector social enterprise organisations seeking to develop career management strategies congruent with the career orientations of managers.

## CONCEPTUAL MODEL DEVELOPMENT

The theoretical and empirical studies discussed in this chapter have contributed to the general body of knowledge of factors that scholars have identified to influence managerial careers. The literature review has discussed societal factors, demographic factors organisational factors; the traditional and new career models perspectives. Schein (1978) has eight career anchor/orientations namely which includes: technical, managerial, security, autonomy, challenge, lifestyle, entrepreneurial, service and dedication. Based on the review of third sector and career models literature, the author has developed a conceptual framework that will contribute to our understanding of factors that influence managerial career orientations in small social enterprises.

The first part of the conceptual framework suggests that societal factors such as, government policies, the education system, labour market conditions and availability of jobs will influence managerial career orientations. The time limited funding contracts the government award to the sector organisations limit the developments of managerial careers in these organisations (Maher, 2015b; Maher, 2016). Furthermore, it limits organisation's ability to develop long term career management systems for managers (Cunningham, 2009; NVCO, 2015; Maher, 2015b).

The second part suggest that demographic factors such as, age, ethnicity, marital status, professional and educational qualifications will influence the career orientations of individual managers. Previous

*Figure 1. Conceptual framework*
*Source Maher (2016) 1*

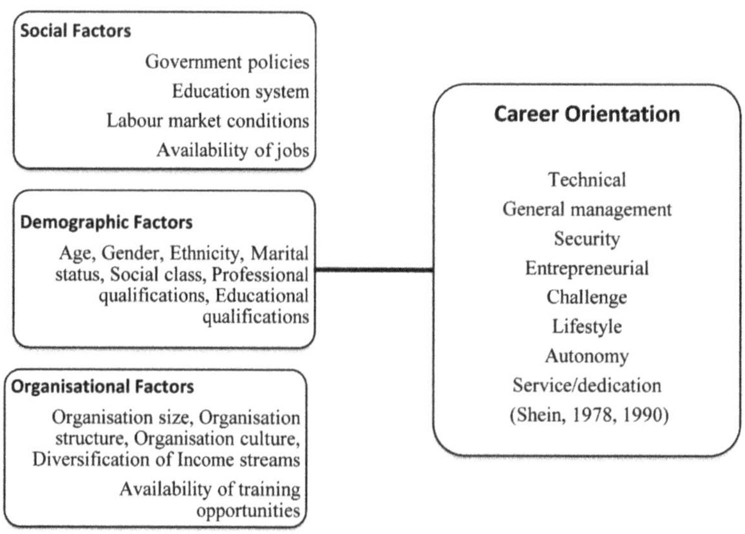

public and private sector career orientations studies have examined the influence of demographic factors (such as, age and educational qualification) on career orientations. For instance, Kniveton (2004) contends that age influences managerial career orientations. Igbaria et al.'s (1995) study of MIS professionals/managers in South Africa, found a significant relationship between education qualification and the participants' identified career orientations. The author also expects there will be meaningful differences in the types of career orientations held by social enterprise male and female managers.

The third part suggests that organisational size, structure, culture and diversification of income sources (Lee, 2003; The King's Fund, 2011; NVCO, 2012) will influence managerial career orientations. These factors are important contextual influences on managerial careers in the sector (Alatrista and Arrowsmith, 2003; Cunningham, 2010; Kelliher and Parry, 2011, Maher, 2015b; Nicolás and Rubio, 2016). Furthermore, reduction in government funding to the third sector has led to small social enterprises seeking funding from a diversification of sources (such as, crowd funding, national and local businesses). In some cases, organisations receive funding from these sources for as little as a few months (Lee, 2003; Milligan, 2001; McKinney and Kahn, 2004; NVCO, 2013, 2014) which impacts on the careers of managers. Also the literature suggest that the short-term nature of the sector funding streams makes it particularly difficult for small organisations to provide management training that will enable individuals to pursue managerial careers in these organisations (Parry et al., 2005; Cunningham, 2008; Hunter and Renwick, 2009).

The fourth part of the conceptual framework relates to Schein's (1978, 1990) career anchor/orientation model. Several researchers suggest that understanding managerial career orientations is the key to developing effective organisational career management strategies that will enable organisations to identify managerial career needs (Pemberton and Herriot, 1994; Mignonac, 2002; Garavan, O'Brien, and O'Hanlon, D. (2006; Wong, 2007). Yarnall (1978) suggest that organisational benefits in understanding employees' career orientations include:

1. Tailors career interventions appropriately;
2. Offer opportunities congruent with an individual's anchor;
3. Design appropriate reward and promotion systems;
4. Increase understanding as to what drives employees' career satisfaction;
5. Understand the overriding career culture in the organisation; and
6. Structure meaningful career discussions and exit interviews.

Identifying the career orientations of employees also provides the organisation with greater awareness of employees' career needs resulting in positive outcomes such as, job role planning, organisational commitment, improved productivity and low staff turnover (Schein, 1990; Lambert et al., 2016; Schein & Van Maanen, 2016). Other career orientations researchers have suggested that understanding manager's career orientations is the key to developing an effective organisational career management strategy that will help organisations to retain managers (Beck & Lopa, 2001; Mignonac, 2002; Kniveton, 2004; Maher, 2016).

The next step is to empirically test the conceptual framework to determine factors influencing the career orientations of small social enterprise managers. These tests will help validate the conceptual framework model or lead to amendments according to research findings.

## CONCLUSION AND FUTURE RESEARCH

This chapter introduced the career concept and five career models' perspectives. The traditional career models (organisational and professional career models), the new career models (boundaryless and protean career models) and Schein (1978, 1990) career anchor/orientation model. The chapter explains the rational for the selection of Schein's (1978) career anchor/orientations model as the career model proposed to identify small social enterprise managers' career orientations. The popularity of the career orientation model Schein (1978, 1990) in academic literature and its potential for supporting the development of small third sector social enterprise managers' career orientations that benefit the individual and the organisation has been discussed.

The integration of the review of third sector theoretical and empirical studies and career orientation studies have contributed to the general body of knowledge on societal, demographic and organisational factors that are likely to influence the career orientations of social enterprise managers contributed to the development of the conceptual framework. The conceptual framework does not purport to be an explanation of all factors that influence the career orientations of small third sector social enterprise managers. However, every effort has been made to include all identified contextual and demographic factors that could influence managerial career orientations. The exclusion of other plausible factors may be justified, given the research environment and time limitations inherent in any research project.

Subsequent research could then be conducted to verify whether these factors identified apply across organisations, using methods that allow results to be generalised to larger populations. New research in this area may also be able to identify emerging factors that influence the career orientations of managers that have not been documented in the literature thus far. Empirical studies should provide important tests and insights for the next stage of theory construction.

Future work could improve this framework by taking a closer look at particular sub-bodies of publications, for example, from a research methodology perspective. This may allow specific features to be identified in greater detail. In-depth investigative methods such as case studies and longitudinal studies could be used to discover the nuances of the career management systems within specific organisational settings. Such studies would also be able to identify factors that influence managers' career orientations. Further comparative research could be conducted to enable us to understand how factors influencing small social enterprises manager's career orientations compare with small commercial enterprises manager's career orientations.

## REFERENCES

Achleitner, A. K., Spiess-Knafl, W., & Volk, S. (2014). The financing structure of social enterprises: Conflicts and implications. *International Journal of Entrepreneurial Venturing*, *6*(1), 85–99. doi:10.1504/IJEV.2014.059404

Adams, J. (1991). Issues in the management of careers. Contemporary Career Development Issues, 1-24.

Aiken, M. (2007). What is the role of social enterprise in finding, creating and maintaining employment for disadvantaged groups. Social Enterprise Think Piece for the Office of the Third Sector, Cabinet Office, London.

Allen, T. J., & Katz, R. (1986). The dual ladder: Motivational solution or managerial delusion? *R & D Management, 16*(2), 185–197. doi:10.1111/j.1467-9310.1986.tb01171.x

Amin, A., Cameron, A., & Hudson, R. (1999). Welfare as work? The potential of the UK social economy. *Environment & Planning A, 31*(11), 2033–2051. doi:10.1068/a312033

Anheier, H. K. (2005). *A Dictionary of Civil Society, Philanthropy and the Third Sector*. Routledge.

Arnold, J. (2011). *Career concepts in the 21st century*. British Psychological Society.

Arthur, M. B., & Rousseau, D. M. (1996). A career lexicon for the 21st century. *The Academy of Management Executive, 10*(4), 28–39.

Baruch, Y. (2006). Career development in organisations and beyond: Balancing traditional and contemporary viewpoints. *Human Resource Management Review, 16*(2), 125–138. doi:10.1016/j.hrmr.2006.03.002

Baruch, Y., & Reis, C. (2016). How Global Are Boundaryless Careers and How Boundaryless Are Global Careers? Challenges and a Theoretical Perspective. *Thunderbird International Business Review, 58*(1), 13–27. doi:10.1002/tie.21712

Beck, J., & La Lopa, J. M. (2001). An exploratory application of Scheins career anchors inventory to hotel executive operating committee members. *International Journal of Hospitality Management, 20*(1), 15–28. doi:10.1016/S0278-4319(00)00035-9

Bennett, R., & Savani, S. (2011). Surviving mission drift: How charities can turn dependence on government contract funding to their own advantage. *Nonprofit Management & Leadership, 22*(2), 217–231. doi:10.1002/nml.20050

Borzaga, C., & Defourny, J. (2001). Conclusions: Social enterprises in Europe: A diversity of initiatives and prospects. The Emergence of Social Enterprise, 350-370.

Cabrera, E. F. (2009). Protean organizations: Reshaping work and careers to retain female talent. *Career Development International, 14*(2), 186–201. doi:10.1108/13620430910950773

Carbery, R., Garavan, T. N., OBrien, F., & McDonnell, J. (2003). Predicting hotel managers turnover cognitions. *Journal of Managerial Psychology, 18*(7), 649–679. doi:10.1108/02683940310502377

Carroll, K. M., & Rounsaville, B. J. (2007). A vision of the next generation of behavioural therapies research in the addictions. *Addiction (Abingdon, England), 102*(6), 850–862. doi:10.1111/j.1360-0443.2007.01798.x PMID:17523974

Chapman, J. R. (2015). Fostering career management using career anchor theory in Handbook of career intervention: Vol. 2. *Application*. Washington, DC: American Psychological Association.

Coetzee, M. (2008). Psychological career resources of working adults. *Journal of Individual Psychology, 34*(2), 10–20.

Coetzee, M., & Schreuder, D. (2009). using the Career Orientations Inventory (COI) for internal career orientations in the South African Organisational Context. *South African Journal of Industrial Psychology, 35*(1), 1–14.

Coetzee, M., Schreuder, D., & Tladinyane, R. (2007). Organisational commitment and its relation to career anchors. *Southern African Business Review*, *11*(1), 65–86.

Cunningham, I. (2008). A race to the bottom? Exploring variations in employment conditions in the voluntary sector. *Public Administration*, *86*(4), 1033–1053. doi:10.1111/j.1467-9299.2008.00752.x

Cunningham, I. (2010). The HR function in purchaser-provider relationships: Insights from the UK voluntary sector. *Human Resource Management Journal*, *20*(2), 189–205. doi:10.1111/j.1748-8583.2009.00112.x

Cunningham, I., & Nickson, D. (2011). A gathering storm: Re-tendering and the voluntary sector workforce. *International Journal of Public Sector Management*, *24*(7), 662–672. doi:10.1108/09513551111172486

Dalton, G., Thompson, P., & Price, R. (1977). The four stages of professional careers: A new look at performance by professionals. *Organizational Dynamics*, *5*(1), 19–42. doi:10.1016/0090-2616(77)90033-X

Damm, C. (2012). *The third sector delivering employment services: an evidence review*. Academic Press.

Dart, R. (2004). The legitimacy of social enterprise. *Nonprofit Management & Leadership*, *14*(4), 411–424. doi:10.1002/nml.43

De Vos, A., Dewettinck, K., & Buyens, D. (2008). To move or not to move? The relationship between career management and preferred career moves. *Employee Relations*, *30*(2), 156–175. doi:10.1108/01425450810843348

DeFillippi, R. J., & Arthur, M. B. (1994). The boundaryless career: A competency-based perspective. *Journal of Organizational Behavior*, *15*(4), 307–324. doi:10.1002/job.4030150403

Defourny, J., & Nyssens, M. (2008). Social enterprise in Europe: Recent trends and developments. *Social Enterprise Journal*, *4*(3), 202–228. doi:10.1108/17508610810922703

Delong, T. J. (1982). Re-examining the career anchor model. *Personnel*, *59*(3), 50–61.

Denhardt, R. B., Denhardt, J. V., & Aristigueta, M. P. (2015). *Managing human behaviour in public and nonprofit organizations*. Sage Publication.

Di Domenico, M., Tracey, P., & Haugh, H. (2009). Social economy involvement in public service delivery: Community engagement and accountability. *Regional Studies*, *43*(7), 981–992. doi:10.1080/00343400701874180

Doherty, B., Haugh, H., & Lyon, F. (2014). Social enterprises as hybrid organizations: A review and research agenda. *International Journal of Management Reviews*, *16*(4), 417–436. doi:10.1111/ijmr.12028

Eby, L. T., Burk, H., & Maher, C. P. (2010). How serious of a problem is staff turnover in substance abuse treatment? A longitudinal study of actual turnover. *Journal of Substance Abuse Treatment*, *39*(3), 264–271. doi:10.1016/j.jsat.2010.06.009 PMID:20675097

Ellram, L.M. (1995). Total Cost of Ownership: An Analysis Approach for Purchasing. *International Journal of Physical Distribution and Logistics Management, 25*(8), 4-23.

Enterprise, D. T. (2002). *I 'Social. "A strategy for success*. London: DTI.

Erdogmus, N. (2004). Career orientations of salaried professionals: The case of Turkey. *Career Development International*, *9*(2), 153–175. doi:10.1108/13620430410526193

Erikson, E. (1968). Youth: Identity and crisis. New York, NY: WW.

Feldman, D. C., & Bolino, M. C. (1996). Career within careers: Reconceptualising the nature of career anchors and their consequences. *Human Resource Management Review*, *6*(2), 89–112. doi:10.1016/S1053-4822(96)90014-5

Garavan, T., OBrien, F., & OHanlon, D. (2006). Career Advancement of Hotel Mangers Since Graduation: A Comparative Study. *Personnel Review*, *35*(3), 252–280. doi:10.1108/00483480610656685

Garrett, D. F., & Pavan, A. (2012). Managerial turnover in a changing world. *Journal of Political Economy*, *120*(5), 879–925. doi:10.1086/668836

Guan, Y., Wen, Y., Xiaohua, S., Haiyang, C., Wei, L., Liu, Y., & Dong, Z. et al. (2013). The role of perceived organizational career management and career anchor. *European Journal of Work and Organizational Psychology*.

Gubler, M., Biemann, T., Tschopp, C., & Grote, G. (2015). How Career Anchors Differentiate Managerial Career Trajectories A Sequence Analysis Perspective. *Journal of Career Development*, *42*(5), 412–430. doi:10.1177/0894845315572891

Gunz, H., Evans, M., & Jalland, M. (2000). Career boundaries in a 'boundaryless' world. *Career frontiers: New conceptions of working lives*, 24-53.

Halfpenny, P., & Reid, M. (2002). Research on the voluntary sector: An overview. *Policy and Politics*, *30*(4), 533–550. doi:10.1332/030557302760590369

Hall, D. T. (1996). Protean careers of the 21st century. *The Academy of Management Executive*, *10*, 8. doi:10. 5465/AME.1996.3145315

Hall, D. T. (2004). The protean career: A quarter-century journey. *Journal of Vocational Behavior*, *65*(1), 1–13. doi:10.1016/j.jvb.2003.10.006

Harris, B. (2010). Voluntary action and the state in historical perspective. *Voluntary Sector Review*, *1*(1), 25–40. doi:10.1332/204080510X496993

Harrow, J., & Mole, V. (2005). I want to move once I have got things straight: Voluntary sector chief executives career accounts. *Nonprofit Management & Leadership*, *16*(1), 79–100. doi:10.1002/nml.91

Herr, E. L. (1990). Issues in career research. Methodological approaches to the study of career, 3-21.

Hines, F. (2005). Viable social enterprise: An evaluation of business support to social enterprises. *Social Enterprise Journal*, *1*(1), 13–28. doi:10.1108/17508610580000704

Hirsch, F. (2005). *Social limits to growth*. Routledge.

Hopkins, K. M., Cohen-Callow, A., Kim, H. J., & Hwang, J. (2010). Beyond intent to leave: Using multiple outcome measures for assessing turnover in child welfare. *Children and Youth Services Review*, *32*(10), 1380–1387. doi:10.1016/j.childyouth.2010.06.006

Igbaria, M., Meredith, G., & Smith, D. C. (1995). Career orientations of information systems employees in South Africa. *The Journal of Strategic Information Systems*, *4*(4), 319–340. doi:10.1016/0963-8687(95)80002-8

Inkson, K., Gunz, H., Ganesh, S., & Roper, J. (2012). Boundaryless careers: Bringing back boundaries. *Organization Studies*, *33*(3), 323–340. doi:10.1177/0170840611435600

Jager, U., Hover, H., & Schroer, A., & Strauch, M. (2012). Experience of Solidarity: Why Executive Directors Work for Market Driven Nonprofits. *Nonprofit and Voluntary Sector Quarterly*.

Jenner, P. (2016). Social enterprise sustainability revisited: An international perspective. *Social Enterprise Journal*, *12*(1), 42–60. doi:10.1108/SEJ-12-2014-0042

Kanter, R. M. (1987). *Careers and the wealth of nations: A macro-perspective on the structure and implications of career forms*. Division of Research, Harvard Business School.

Kendall, J. (2003). *The voluntary sector: Comparative perspectives in the UK*. Psychology Press. doi:10.4324/9780203400128

Kendall, J., & Knapp, M. (1995). A loose and baggy monster. An introduction to the voluntary sector, 66-95.

Kerlin, J. A. (2006). Social enterprise in the United States and Europe: Understanding and learning from the differences. *Voluntas*, *17*(3), 246–262. doi:10.1007/s11266-006-9016-2

Kim, S. E., & Lee, J. W.Seok Eun Kim; Jung Wook Lee. (2007). Is mission attachment an effective management tool for employee retention? An empirical analysis of a non-profit human services agency. *Review of Public Personnel Administration*, *27*(3), 227–248. doi:10.1177/0734371X06295791

Knight, B., Robson, S., & House, C. (2007). The value and independence of the voluntary sector. Newcastle, UK: CENTRIS. UK.

Knight, D. K., Broome, K. M., Edwards, J. R., & Flynn, P. M. (2011). Supervisory Turnover in Outpatient Substance Abuse Treatment. *The Journal of Behavioral Health Services & Research*, *38*(1), 80–90. doi:10.1007/s11414-009-9198-7 PMID:19949883

Kniveton, B. H. (2004). Managerial career anchors in a changing business environment. *Journal of European Industrial Training*, *28*(6/7), 564–573. doi:10.1108/03090590410549984

Lambert, S., Rothwell, A., & Herbert, I. (2016). Exploring Career Anchors in Shared Service Centres. In *International Workshop on Global Sourcing of Information Technology and Business Processes* (pp. 51-76). Springer International Publishing. doi:10.1007/978-3-319-47009-2_4

Lee, S. (2003). The regulation of fundraising: In search of the public good or an intractable problem of vested interest? *International Journal of Nonprofit and Voluntary Sector Marketing*, *8*(4), 307–314. doi:10.1002/nvsm.221

Levinson, D. J. (1978). *The seasons of a man's life*. Random House Digital, Inc.

Lichtenstein, B. M. B., & Mendenhall, M. (2002). Non-linearity and response-ability: Emergent order in 21st-century careers. *Human Relations*, *55*(1), 5–32. doi:10.1177/0018726702055001604

Lowe, R., & Butcher, T. (1994). The welfare state in Britain since 1945. *Public Administration-London, 72*(1), 137–137.

Maher, C. (2009). Managing Career Development in the Not for Profit Sector. Business Leadership Review, 6(4).

Maher, C. (2013). A Qualitative Case Study Approach to Understanding Third Sector Managers' Career Orientations. Work Based Learning e-Journal International, 3(2).

Maher, C. (2015a). Social enterprise managers career path preferences. *International Journal of Globalisation and Small Business*, *7*(1), 59–72. doi:10.1504/IJGSB.2015.069032

Maher, C. (2015b). Public Policies Impact on Third Sector Social Enterprises in UK Regions. Handbook of Research on Entrepreneurial Success and its Impact on Regional Development, 246-266.

Maher, C. (2016 September). *Managerial Careers in Small Social Enterprise: Contextual Issues*. Paper presented at the 9th Annual Conference of the EuroMed Academy of Business, Warsaw, Poland.

McKinney, R., & Kahn, H. (2004). Lottery funding and changing organizational identity in the UK voluntary sector. *Voluntas*, *15*(1), 1–19. doi:10.1023/B:VOLU.0000023631.74069.d7

Mignonac, K. (2002). Understanding willingness to accept domestic relocation: The example of French managers. *Career Development International*, *7*(6), 359–370. doi:10.1108/13620430210444385

Milbourne, L., & Cushman, M. (2013) From the third sector to the big society: how changing UK government policies have eroded third sector trust. *VOLUNTAS: International Journal of Voluntary and Nonprofit Organisations*, 1-24.

Millar, R., & Hall, K. (2013). Social return on investment (SROI) and performance measurement: The opportunities and barriers for social enterprises in health and social care. *Public Management Review*, *15*(6), 923–941. doi:10.1080/14719037.2012.698857

Milligan, C. (2001). *Geographies of Care: space and the voluntary sector*. Ashgate.

Millward, L. (2005). *Understanding Occupational & Organisational Psychology*. London: Sage Publications.

Morphet, J. (2008). Modern Local Government. *Local Government Studies, 34*(4).

Nicolás, C., & Rubio, A. (2016). Social enterprise: Gender gap and economic development. *European Journal of Management and Business Economics*, *25*(2), 56–62. doi:10.1016/j.redeen.2015.11.001

NVCO. (2012). *The UK Civil Society Almanac*. London: NVCO Publication.

NVCO. (2013). *The UK Civil Society Almanac*. London: NVCO Publication.

NVCO. (2014). *The UK Civil Society Almanac*. London: NVCO Publication.

NVCO. (2015). *The UK Civil Society Almanac*. London: NVCO Publication.

Omair, K. (2010). Typology of career development for Arab women managers in the United Arab Emirates. *Career Development International*, *15*(2), 121–143. doi:10.1108/13620431011040932

Onyx, J., & Maclean, M. (1996). Careers in the Third Sector. *Nonprofit Management & Leadership*, *6*(4), 333–345. doi:10.1002/nml.4130060404

Pearson, R. (1991). *The human resource: managing people and work in the 1990s*. McGraw-Hill Book Co Ltd.

Peattie, K., & Morley, A. (2008). Eight paradoxes of the social enterprise research agenda. *Social Enterprise Journal*, *4*(2), 91–107. doi:10.1108/17508610810901995

Pemberton, C., Herriot, P., & Bates, T. (1994). Career orientations of senior executives and their implications for careers guidance. *British Journal of Guidance & Counselling*, *22*(2), 233–245. doi:10.1080/03069889408260317

Ramakrishna, H. V., & Potosky, D. (2003). Conceptualisation and exploration of Composite career anchors: An analysis of Information Systems Personnel. *Human Resource Development Quarterly*, *14*(2), 199–214. doi:10.1002/hrdq.1060

Rasdi, R.M., Ismaila, M., Uli, J., & Noah, S.M. (2009). Career aspirations and career success among managers in the Malaysian public sector. *Research Journal of International Studies*, (9), 21-35.

Ridley-Duff, R., & Bull, M. (2015). Understanding social enterprise: Theory and practice. *Sage (Atlanta, Ga.)*.

Royce, M. (2007). Using human resource management tools to support social enterprise: Emerging themes from the sector. *Social Enterprise Journal*, *3*(1), 10–19. doi:10.1108/17508610780000718

Schein, E. H. (1978). *Career Dynamics: Matching Individual and Organisational Needs*. Reading, MA: Addison-Wesley.

Schein, E. H. (1990). *Career anchors and job/role planning: the links between career pathing and career development*. Academic Press.

Schein, E. H., & Van Maanen, J. (2016). Career anchors and job/role planning: Tools for career and talent management. *Organizational Dynamics*, *45*(3), 165–173. doi:10.1016/j.orgdyn.2016.07.002

Skagert, K., Dellve, L., & Ahlborg, G. Jr. (2012). A prospective study of managers turnover and health in a healthcare organization. *Journal of Nursing Management*, *20*(7), 889–899. doi:10.1111/j.1365-2834.2011.01347.x PMID:23050622

Steinberg, R. 2003. Economic theories of nonprofit organizations. In The study of the nonprofit enterprise (pp. 277-309). Springer US. doi:10.1007/978-1-4615-0131-2_16

Sullivan, S. E., & Baruch, Y. (2009). Advances in career theory and research: A critical review and agenda for future exploration. *Journal of Management*, *35*(6), 1542–1571. doi:10.1177/0149206309350082

Super, D. E. (1957). *The psychology of careers; an introduction to vocational development*. Academic Press.

Suutari, V., & Taka, M. (2004). Career anchors of managers with global careers. *Journal of Management Development*, *23*(9), 833–847. doi:10.1108/02621710410558440

The King's Fund. (2011). *Social Care Funding and NHS: An Impending Crisis?* London: King's Fund.

Valcour, P. M., & Tolbert, P. (2003). Gender, family and career in the era of boundarylessness: Determinants and effects of intra-and inter-organizational mobility. *International Journal of Human Resource Management*, *14*(5), 768–787. doi:10.1080/0958519032000080794

Vickers, I. (2010). *Social enterprise and the environment: a review of the literature*. Third Sector Research Centre Working Paper 22. Universities of Birmingham and Southampton Birmingham.

Wong, A. L. Y. (2007). Making career choice: A study of Chinese managers. *Human Relations*, *60*(8), 1211–1233. doi:10.1177/0018726707081661

Yarnall, J. (1998). Career anchors: Results of an organisational study in the UK. *Career Development International*, *3*(2), 56–61. doi:10.1108/13620439810207536

Young, D. R. (2006). Social enterprise in community and economic development in the USA: Theory, corporate form and purpose. *International Journal of Entrepreneurship and Innovation Management*, *6*(3), 241–255. doi:10.1504/IJEIM.2006.009877

Zeitz, G., Blau, G., & Fertig, J. (2009). Boundaryless careers and institutional resources. *International Journal of Human Resource Management*, *20*(2), 372–398. doi:10.1080/09585190802670763

## KEY TERMS AND DEFINITIONS

**Career:** An occupation, profession or all the roles you undertake throughout your life, including education, training, paid and unpaid work.

**Career Management:** The process that plans and shapes the progression of individuals within an organisation in accordance with the organisational needs and employees' needs.

**Career Orientation:** The constellation of self-perceived attitudes, talents and values that form the core of a person's occupational self-concept. It guides and influences the individual's selection of specific occupations and work settings (Schein, 1978, 1990).

**Conceptual Framework:** An analytical tool used to make conceptual distinctions and organise ideas concepts, assumptions, expectations, beliefs, and theories that supports and informs your research.

**Manager:** A person responsible for managing, controlling or administering tasks or a certain subset of a company or group of staff.

**Social Enterprise:** Social enterprises are defined as enterprises that trade to meet social/environmental goals (Department of Trade and Industry, 2002).

**Third Sector:** The third sector includes a very diverse range of organisations comprising non-governmental and non-profit-making organisations or associations, including charities, voluntary and community groups, cooperatives and mutual benefits societies.

# Chapter 12
# Online Disclosure of Social Responsibility Strategies:
## Perceptions and Reality Among Nonprofit Organisations

**Juana Alonso-Cañadas**
*University of Almería, Spain*

**María Del Carmen Caba-Pérez**
*University of Almería, Spain*

**María Del Mar Gálvez-Rodríguez**
*University of Almería, Spain*

**Laura Saraite**
*University of Almería, Spain*

## ABSTRACT

*Nonprofit organisations should be at the forefront in implementing corporate social responsibility in their actions and in disclosing these practices, not only to improve their image but also to enable access to corporate social responsibility information to be used as an effective instrument for continuous improvement. This chapter analyses perceptions of online transparency and web-usage as a means of online corporate social responsibility disclosure practices. Data is obtained from nonprofit case study analysis of Spanish Verdiblanca. The results reveal a contradiction between the corporate social responsibility information that is considered most important and actual practices of information disclosure. In particular, the information disclosure that is most highly valued concerns the social impact made by the organisation, compared to information on economics which is the most visible on the organisational webpage.*

DOI: 10.4018/978-1-5225-2537-0.ch012

Copyright © 2017, IGI Global. Copying or distributing in print or electronic forms without written permission of IGI Global is prohibited.

## INTRODUCTION

Non-profit organisations (NPOs) are of public interest due to the social, political and economic impact of their activities. In relation to their social impact, NPOs fill gaps in the public welfare network (García-Mainar & Marcuello, 2007; Baur & Schmitz, 2012) and enhance corporate social responsibility (Laasonen, Fougere, & Kourula, 2012). With respect to their political impact, they are one of the main agents that exert pressure in favour of democracy (Jordan, 2005). With regard to their economic impact, many NPOs make a considerable contribution to the national GDP, mainly through the number of persons employed (Salamon, Sokolowski, Megan, & Tice, 2012).

In general, NPOs function on the basis of public and private funding received and thanks to the altruistic help of volunteers (Burger & Owens, 2010; Gugerty, 2010; Taylor & Doerfel, 2011). In the current economic crisis, NPOs often undertake additional responsibilities, despite the increased difficulties being faced in fundraising (Clark, 2011). Hence, NPOs need to highlight the added value they provide to society in order to ensure their continuing existence and thus to benefit society.

Fundamentally, NPOs need to disclose information in order to satisfy the demands of their stakeholders in this respect, to demonstrate a professional image and to reinforce their legitimacy as agents that serve society (Burger & Owens, 2010; Gandía, 2011; Campos, Andion, Serva, Rossetto, & Assumpção, 2011).

Regarding the need for greater provision of and access to information, in academic and business sectors there is increasing interest in the question of corporate social responsibility (CSR) in organisations, including NPOs (Degli Antoni, & Portale, 2011). CSR can be defined as the procedures and actions that organisations adopt in order to apply best practices in the management of the economic, social and environmental impact of their actions. According to De la Torre (2009), this ethical behaviour is voluntary and has a permanent effect on the organisation's structure and on its relationship with stakeholders.

Moneva (2007) emphasised that one of the basic principles of CSR is transparency is the full and accurate information that an organisation provides regarding its behaviour in society and with respect to social expectations. In this respect, the implementation of effective communication systems is of vital importance. Among the different channels of communication that are available, information and communications technology (ICTs) are of proven excellence and constitute one of the main drivers of recent social change (Saxton & Guo, 2012; Kim, Chun, Kwak, & Nam, 2014).

ICTs have enabled NPOs to improve their administrative and financial management. Thus, the internet in general, and web pages in particular, provide a strategic means of providing society with information of interest quickly and easily. Accordingly, NPOs are recommended to apply a proactive communication strategy, disclosing CSR information via their web pages (Saxton & Guo 2011; Tremblay-Boire & Prakash, 2015), thus underlining their social responsibility credentials and heightening transparency.

Although CSR and online transparency arouse considerable interest among NPOs, little is known as to whether, in fact, they apply best practices in this regard. Previous studies in this field have mainly focused on the role played by NPOs in enhancing the social practices of the private sector (Grosser, 2015) or on the information provided by the corporate sector with respect to CSR (Herbohn, Walker, & Loo, 2014).

In view of the above considerations, a discussion on the perceptions of the importance granted by NPOs to online transparency regarding CSR is further explored in the case study of Spanish NPO *Verdiblanca*. Data were obtained by questionnaire and by examining the web pages posted by this NPO. Following the introduction, CSR is defined and its main advantages for NPOs are highlighted. Mechanisms of accountability, particularly the Global Reporting Initiative (GRI) reporting model is explored followed by the case study analysis.

## SOCIAL RESPONSIBILITY OF NONPROFIT ORGANISATIONS

Currently, there is no consensus on the definition of CSR (McWilliams, Siegel, & Wright, 2006; Godfrey & Hatch, 2007; Crespo, 2010), although there are areas of agreement in terms of the commitment it represents to the development of society in general (Mercado & García, 2007), which is characterised by volunteerism, integration, consistency and information transparency (Albareda & Balaguer, 2007).

The origin of CSR dates back to the eighteenth century, when concerns for the common good, apart from that of the individual, began to arise (Vélez, 2011). Its conceptualisation has continually evolved and been adapted to changing times, up to the present wide-ranging definition given by the European Commission (2011: 7) as "the responsibility of enterprises for their impacts on society". The aim of CSR is held to be to "maximise the creation of shared value for owners/shareholders and other stakeholders and for society at large and to identify, prevent and mitigate possible adverse consequences".

As regards NPOs, Canyelles (2009: 136) defines an organisation that acts in a socially responsible way as one that seeks to create and maximise value for its stakeholders through ethical behaviour, responsiveness to social concerns and co-responsibility in working for sustainability and human development.

The question of CSR has been addressed in numerous recent studies (Wirl, 2014), although these are characterised by a high level of specialisation and fragmentation (Aguinis & Glavas, 2012). In the business world, CSR is often considered a source of competitive advantage (Alvarado & Schlesinger, 2008), as it can: a) contribute to enhancing financial results (Fulop, Hisrich, & Szegedi, 2000; Orlitzky, 2005); b) raise the value of the company (Elkington, 2007); c) have a positive impact on consumption (Lii & Lee, 2012); d) confer greater legitimacy on the organisation (Stanaland, Lwin, & Murphy, 2011).

However, in the context of NPOs, little attention has been paid to this field (Lin-Hi, Hörisch, & Blumberg, 2015). In recent years, studies have shown that there is significantly less discussion of social responsibility-related issues in the field of NPOs than in the business sector (Kearns, 1994; Rothschild & Milofsky, 2006; Jegers, 2009; Weerawardena, McDonald, & Mort, 2010), despite the fact that CSR provides an opportunity to strengthen legitimacy, manage social excellence and supply new channels of dialogue with stakeholders (Canyelles, 2012).

Focusing on previous studies that have analysed socially responsible management by NPOs, we can identify researches in different temporal and geographic contexts (Bouckaert & Vandenhove, 1998; Hogan, 2008; Weidenbaum, 2009; Sarstedt & Schloderer, 2010; Costa, Ramus, & Andreaus, 2011; Andreini, Pedeliento, & Signori, 2012; Tschirhart & Bielefeld, 2012; Lin-Hi et al., 2015; Skouloudis, Evangelinos, & Malesios, 2015; Kourula & Delalieux, 2016).However, the disclosure of CSR by NPOs (Puentes, Mozas, Bernal, & Chaves, 2012) or the important role played in general by NPOs in the field of CSR (Arenas, Lozano & Albarando, 2009) has been analysed in a lesser extent.

In view of the particularities of the sector, NPOs need to address their management of CSR by adopting their own forms of model rather than reproducing models used in business (Canyelles, 2012). In this regard, Vidal, Torres, Guix, & Peña (2005) identified a number of key elements in the development of an effective model of CSR for an NPO, such as its personnel, stakeholders, mission and values, together with the environmental, economic and social management of its activities, in terms of the impact made in these respects, and finally, the transparency and communication of these actions (Vidal et al., 2005). Transparency is a question that should be of prime concern to NPOs, as it constitutes one of the main assets of such organisations (Bekkers, 2003; Weidenbaum, 2009; Drevs, Tscheulin, & Lindenmeier, 2014), enabling them to build up valuable relationships with their stakeholders (Harrison, Bosse, & Phillips, 2010).

## BENEFITS OF CORPORATE SOCIAL RESPONSIBILITY

NPOs have experienced continuous global growth (Gibelman & Gelman, 2004) and have played an increasingly important role in implementing major social and economic initiatives, both domestically and internationally (Jordan, 2003). However, since the mid-1980, a number of scandal have negatively impacted non-profit organisations. Non-profit efforts to improve transparency on CSR have strengthened consistently since the mid-1980s (Ebrahim, 2003).

Moreover, these entities are under pressure to act in the public interest, and therefore they should accept responsibility for their public statements and for positions adopted in carrying out their social and economic initiatives (Marschall, 2002). Furthermore, non-profits are especially impacted by public scrutiny and in this sense; it is worth noting that Transparency on CSR contributes to strengthening non-profit legitimacy (Crespy & Miller, 2011). Reporting on NPOs' actions regarding social responsibility is one contributing activity that could positively influence non-profit image, reputation and contribute to strengthening trust (Puentes, et al., 2012). Although the promotion of greater transparency regarding CSR helps minimise the scepticism of stakeholders (Du, Bhattacharya, & Sen, 2010) and promotes positive associations between the organisation and its stakeholders (Morsing & Schultz, 2006) still is scarce the research that address this issue.

Transparency, defined as the information provided by each organisation to its stakeholders (Vaccaro, 2006), is considered to be an important ethical practice that generates confidence among stakeholders (Vaccaro, 2006; Vaccaro & Madsen, 2006). Business managers and academics have embraced the concept of transparency by organisations in discussions concerning the ethics of information and CSR (Capurro, 2005).

Theories that explain why companies disclose information about their CSR practices include the well-research theories of stakeholder theory (Ullmann, 1985; Gray, Kouhy, & Lavers, 1995; Gray, Owen, & Adams, 1996; Ruiz, Rios, & Tirado, 1994; Donaldson & Preston, 1995; Mitchel, Agle, & Wood, 1997; Roberts, 1992; Argandoña, 1998) and legitimacy theory (Shocker & Sethi, 1974; Gray, et al., 1996). Regarding, Stakeholder Theory, the organisation must serve the interests of its stakeholders because its success or failure depends on them while legitimacy theory focuses on the pressure received from external organisations (Brown & Deegan, 1999; Buhr, 1998; Cho, 2009; Deegan & Rankin, 1996, in Deegan, 2007; Patten, 1991; Tilling & Tilt, 2010).

### Models of CSR Accountability and of Online Communication

Transparency then, plays a crucial role in CRS as non-profit organisations are accountable to their internal and external stakeholders (Spiro, 2001; Keohane, 2002). This requires the disclosure of information that meets the demands of external stakeholders which in the case of NPOs includes the state and the sources of their funds (Ebrahim, 2009). Internally, it consists of meeting the information needs of stakeholders within the NPO, such as managers, paid staff and volunteers (Unerman & O'Dwyer & 2010).

Ebrahim (2003) supports the view that different accountability reporting and disclosure measures include statements, assessments and evaluations of performance and participation, as well as areas such as self-regulation and social audits. One of the more interesting mechanisms for communicating CSR is the guide to prepare sustainability reports prepared by the Global Reporting Initiative (GRI). This entity incorporates recommendations on accountability and governance, and that the contribution of volunteers is a fundamental part of such an organisation's human capital (Gálvez, Caba, & López, 2012).

GRI has created a global framework for the reporting of the economic, environmental and social impacts of corporate and then other organisations (White, 2005). GRI guidelines are increasingly used by NPOs as well as corporations who use the GRI reporting mechanism to prepare CSR, thus facilitating the long-term comparability of information (Marcuello, Bellostas, Marcuello, & Moneva, 2007; Moneva & Bellostas, 2007; Gelbmann, 2010). Furthemore, it has been established on the principles of the Triple Bottom Line, business model which incorporates three dimensions of reporting: economic, social and environmental.

## Economic Dimension

Economic dimension concerns the organisation's impact on the economic conditions of stakeholders and on local, national and global economic systems. The GRI identifies and analyses the financial performance information which is fundamental to understanding the organisation and its sustainability. The economic dimension focuses on socially responsible investments and to implement best practices in the management of its resources through the ethical fundraising and the appropriate allocation of resources (Gálvez et al., 2012).

## Environmental Dimension

Environmental dimension refers to the impact made by an organisation on living and nonliving natural systems, including ecosystems, soil, air and water. It also reflects performance related to biodiversity, compliance with environmental legislation, and other relevant information such as environmental spending and the impacts of an organisation'

## Social Dimension

Social dimension is concerned with the products and service delivery. Social dimension describes the impacts of an organisation's activities on the social systems in which it operates. The GRI indicators of social performance identify the main aspects of performance in relation to labour issues, human rights, society and product responsibility (GRI, 2010). GRI provides a supplement for the non-profit sector NPOs calls for information to be provided regarding the usefulness of their activities and the affinity of these activities with the organisation's stated mission.

The GRI guidelines also stress that it is not sufficient to merely compile information; it must be transmitted to the organisation's stakeholders. To this end, ICTs can provide a valuable platform for enhancing corporate transparency (Tapscott & Ticoll, 2003; Vaccaro & Madsen, 2006). The internet is a strategic element of communication with stakeholders (Pérez & Mateos, 2006; Ingenhoff & Koelling, 2007) due to its speed, accessibility, availability, interaction capability and low cost. Moreover, it enables information to be segmented according to the information needs of each stakeholder (Castelo & Lima, 2008).

The web pages of NPOs can give them a competitive advantage, in areas such as obtaining donors, recruiting volunteers and paid staff and satisfying the information needs of stakeholders (Lee, Chen, & Zhang, 2001). In this line, Burger (2005) observed that NPOs should use web pages as a mechanism for transparency about their CSR practices. Internet-based technologies can help organisations increase the information made available about their business practices, enabling them to create direct relationships with geographically dispersed individuals. Nevertheless, most NPOs currently make only limited use of the internet as a channel for disclosing their social responsibility-related actions to stakeholders (Puentes et al., 2012).

## CASE STUDY: VERDIBLANCA

The *Verdiblanca* Association of Persons with Disabilities was created on 23 March 1979, since when this organisation has worked with one fundamental aim: the integration of persons with disabilities, whatever their condition, and the normalisation of their lives. This association, based in Almeria, southern Spain, and the oldest of its type in the region of Andalusia, is dedicated to improving the welfare of local persons with disabilities. For this purpose, it organises and implements numerous programmes and projects aimed at bringing this group out of passivity and at strengthening awareness within society of the special needs of this population.

Verdiblanca's activities constitute an integrative, normalising process in the fields of education, labour issues, social affairs, family and health, addressing questions that may affect the reference population, and assisting them to develop and function capably in society. Verdiblanca operates at a regional scale, with 390 employees, 3,200 end-users and 36 work centres, serving private and public companies and government administrations. The organisational objectives are to:

1. Contribute to the integration and normalisation of persons with disabilities.
2. Raise awareness of the problems and aspirations of this population.
3. Promote and call for the enforcement of legislation on disability and equality.
4. Promote and defend the participation of persons with disabilities in all spheres of public administration.
5. Achieve the gradual elimination of architectural, urban, communication and social barriers.
6. Report on disability, on the means of preventing it and on overcoming barriers.
7. Promote, prepare and report on social volunteerism.
8. Seek the promotion and integration of women with disabilities and to strive for their equality of opportunity.
9. Promote, inform and develop the participation, whether direct or indirect, of this population in plans and programmes relating to health in this sector.
10. Promote, inform of and develop issues related to culture and sport for persons with disabilities.
11. Work in favour of environmental interests.
12. Achieve the full integration and socio-labour normalisation of persons with disabilities, through career guidance, vocational training and job creation.

Verdiblanca, in particular, was chosen as an object of study due to the leading role this NPO plays in the sector in the province of Almeria. This organisation is outstanding in the job opportunities it provides to the disabled, and in the numerous activities it conducts, such as workshops on the treatment of persons with disabilities, emergency programmes for dependent people in their homes and occupational therapy. Moreover, it has received many awards and official recognition of its work to combat the exclusion of women and to achieve the integration of persons with disabilities.

## METHOD

The research was conducted using a case study method, which is considered appropriate for the analysis of a given phenomenon or topic (Parker, 2012). In the present case, this approach facilitated an in-depth analysis of the degree of coherence between perceptions of the importance of online transparency regarding SR and actual disclosure practices in this regard. The study, thus, addresses two fundamental questions, and the method in each case is presented below.

Perceptions of the importance of transparency on SR were analysed by means of a survey addressed to 14 paid staff members of Verdiblanca in their workplace. These administrative and management staff are directly involved in creating and applying the organisation's communication policy, and so are directly involved in our area of research (Qu & Dumay, 2011). Therefore, although the number of respondents may appear to be small, compared to the total workforce, the information obtained is sufficient and relevant, as it is obtained from those primarily responsible for the management of the organisation, and for the decisions taken on transparency.

The respondents included ten women and four men, aged between 36 and 45 years. Most of them held middle management positions, although one was employed at a basic administration level and one was a senior official. All of these respondents had a university degree. The survey was conducted face-to-face, with all respondents, during April 2016. At the outset, all of the respondents were asked to attend a group discussion in a meeting room at the organisation's headquarters, after the questionnaire forms were handed out. This meeting lasted for two hours, during which the purpose of the study was explained and questions answered. The event took place in a calm and focused atmosphere.

The survey had a total of 25 questions divided into three main blocks related to the importance of online transparency on the economic, social and environmental impact of the organisation. Of the 25 questions, four corresponded to the economic impact, six to the environmental impact and the remaining 15 to the social impact. In addition, the respondents were asked to give an overall weighting of the importance of online transparency for each of the above three impacts. The survey questions were based on the current GRI model, selecting those considered most suitable for this study; accordingly, not all of the GRI items were included. Each question/statement was answered on a scale from 1 to 5 according to the degree of importance granted to the online disclosure of CSR information offered, in response to stakeholders' demands for information transparency.

To determine whether Verdiblanca, the NPO examined in this study, is transparent in its online provision of SR information, an exhaustive survey was conducted during May 2016 of its official website, to see if the GRI items related to the organisation's economic, social and environmental impact were sufficiently disclosed online.

The results indicated an absence of the profit motivation and the social nature of their activities underpin the view that NPOs are inherently socially responsible (Andreini et al., 2012). However, there is evidence of irresponsible behaviour in this sector (Cordery & Baskerville 2011; Fassin, 2009; Smith & Richmond, 2007; Gibelman & Gelman, 2004), It is Taking into account the increasingly mercantile nature of the practices of NPOs (Ponte, 2008), the disclosure of issues related to their socially responsible performance in the three areas of economic, social and environmental dimensions, it is of fundamental importance to legitimise NPOs' actions to their stakeholders.

Respondents assigned a weighting to the aspects of each of the CSR dimensions that they, as the persons responsible for the organisation's communication policies, considered important to disclose online. Thus, each respondent awarded a percentage rating to each of the three aspects, such that their sum was 100% (see Table 1). The data obtained show that greatest importance was awarded to disclosing the organisation's social impact (44%). Environmental questions were considered least necessary to disclose (24%), and economic aspects occupied an intermediate position (32%). The dispersion among the opinions expressed was not significant.

## Economic Dimension

Considered the most important to disclose online (mean score: 4.29), was that of the economic impact produced on the area in which it operated, while the minimum rating in this respect was 2. The aspect that was least highly considered, with a mean value of 3.5 and a minimum of 1, was the online publication of information about the organisation's sources of funding. The standard deviations obtained show that there is little dispersion in these opinions, i.e., the respondents present a reasonable degree of consensus.

## Social Dimension

Most value on the online disclosure of information about the social benefit produced by the NPO's activities in the community in which it operated, with a mean rating of 4.57. In the ranking, this was followed by the online disclosure of information about the organisation's participation in institutions that defended a just cause. By contrast, the least appreciated aspect was the online disclosure of information about suppliers, with a mean score of 3.57 and a minimum of 2. The second least highly rated aspect concerned the online disclosure of information about systems for staff recruitment, evaluation, retention or dismissal, with a mean score of 3.64. Unlike the other impacts (economic and environmental), the degree of dispersion with respect to the social impact was considerable among the respondents, reflecting a greater discrepancy of opinions.

## Environment Dimension

The highest scores to the online disclosure of information on compliance with environmental regulations (mean rating: 4.43) and the lowest ones (mean rating: 4.00) to the online disclosure of information on water consumption and savings. In both cases, the minimum score awarded was 2. The spread among opinions was not significant, since there was little difference between the standard deviations for the

*Table 1. Weighting impact of CRS dimensions*

| | Economic Impact | Environmental Impact | Social Impact |
|---|---|---|---|
| **Mean** | 32% | 24% | 44% |
| **Std Dev** | 0.06 | 0.11 | 0.13 |
| **Max** | 40% | 50% | 70% |
| **Min** | 20% | 0% | 20% |

Source 1 Prepared by the authors

items, meaning that the respondents were in general agreement on these questions. Table 2 details the priorities assigned by the respondents to each of the three aspects (economic, environmental and social).

## Results Obtained for the Online Disclosure of Social Responsibility Information

Analysis of the Verdiblanca website shows that it provides most information about the economic impact made, publishing 100% of the items included in the GRI items considered. Regarding the social impact, more than half of these items analysed are published. By contrast, little information (16.66%) is revealed on the environmental impact. These findings are consistent with the respondents' views on the importance of the SR items that should be disclosed online. The overall level of disclosure results was economic (100%), social (60%) and environmental (16.6%).

## Online Disclosure of the Economic Dimension

Disclosure results of the economic impact in the case of Verdiblanca are in line with those of previous research, which has defined this area as being most thoroughly reported online, both among non-profits (Galvez et al., 2011) and in the corporate sector (Gallego-Álvarex & Quina-Custodio, 2013) The findings indicate that Verdiblanca publishes website information on economics, social and the environment. Transparency highlighted in this area responds to the requirements of the organisation's major funders (Ebrahim, 2005), as well as facilitating access to external finance, which is vital for its survival (De Castro, 2005). Findings also suggest that a clear social purpose does not make NPO's indifferent to profit (Hansmann, 1980) but in line with previous research, NPO's operationalize surpluses to perform the social mission (Anheier, 2005; Lee, Johnson, & Prakash, 2012).

## Online Disclosure of the Environmental Dimension

Online disclosure of environmental dimension, the only significant information provided by Verdiblanca is that compliance with environmental regulations which could be attributed to the environment dimension not being a priority for this organisation. This conclusion is consistent with the views of Brammer & Pavelin (2008), who point out that organisations whose products or services do not produce a direct environmental impact do not have transparency in the area of environment as a priority. Therefore, although NPOs are considered an influential pressure group in the reporting of corporate environmental sustainability (O'Dwyer, 2005), the one in our study, Verdiblanca, like the vast majority of its counterparts, does not show publish information online about its responsible attitude in this area (Skouloudis et al., 2015).

## Online Disclosure on the Social Dimension

Verdiblanca's disclosure of its social dimension published online most of the items (60%) including training programmes for volunteers and paid staff, its programme for safety in the workplace, and compliance with regulations. However, there was no transparency regarding monitoring of the volunteers or the provision of health programmes for paid staff and volunteers. Neither was any information published about reports on suppliers, mechanisms to combat corruption, interventions in social conflicts or participation in institutions that defend a just cause.

*Table 2. Assessment of importance of disclosure by item and dimension*

| | Mean | Std.Dev. | Max. | Min. |
|---|---|---|---|---|
| ***2.1 Online Transparency Concerning the NPO's Economic Impact*** | | | | |
| 2.1.1 Online disclosure of information about the use made of resources | 3.93 | 0.83 | 5.00 | 2.00 |
| 2.1.2 Online disclosure of information about the organisation's sources of funding | 3.50 | 1.22 | 5.00 | 1.00 |
| 2.1.3 Online disclosure of information about the organisation's economic policies | 3.57 | 1.09 | 5.00 | 1.00 |
| 2.1.4 Online disclosure of information about the impact made on the geographic area in which it operates | 4.29 | 0.91 | 5.00 | 2.00 |
| ***2.2 Online Transparency Concerning the NPO's Environmental Impact*** | | | | |
| 2.2.1 Online disclosure of information about the use made of recycled materials | 4.21 | 0.97 | 5.00 | 2.00 |
| 2.2.2 Online disclosure of information about energy consumption and savings | 4.14 | 1.10 | 5.00 | 2.00 |
| 2.2.3 Online disclosure of information about water consumption and savings | 4.00 | 1.11 | 5.00 | 2.00 |
| 2.2.4 Online disclosure of information about initiatives to reduce the environmental impacts of its activities, products and services | 4.29 | 0.91 | 5.00 | 2.00 |
| 2.2.5 Online disclosure of information about compliance with environmental regulations | 4.43 | 0.94 | 5.00 | 2.00 |
| 2.2.6 Online disclosure of information about significant environmental impacts of the transport of products and other goods and materials used by the organisation to conduct its activities | 4.14 | 0.95 | 5.00 | 2.00 |
| ***2.3 Online Transparency Concerning the NPO's Social Impact*** | | | | |
| 2.3.1 Online disclosure of information about the effectiveness of the organisation's programmes | 4.36 | 0.74 | 5.00 | 3.00 |
| 2.3.2 Online disclosure of information about the annual report of its activities | 4.43 | 0.76 | 5.00 | 3.00 |
| 2.3.3 Online disclosure of information about systems for personnel hiring, evaluation, retention and dismissal | 3.64 | 1.08 | 5.00 | 2.00 |
| 2.3.4 Online disclosure of information about the monitoring of volunteers; awareness and evaluation of volunteers' activities, from their recruitment until their departure from the organisation | 4.07 | 0.83 | 5.00 | 3.00 |
| 2.3.5 Online disclosure of information about training programmes for volunteers and paid staff | 4.36 | 0.74 | 5.00 | 3.00 |
| 2.3.6 Online disclosure of information about healthcare programmes for volunteers and paid staff | 4.14 | 0.95 | 5.00 | 2.00 |
| 2.3.7 Online disclosure of information about programmes to promote safety in the workplace | 3.93 | 1.14 | 5.00 | 2.00 |
| 2.3.8 Online disclosure of information about equality of opportunities for women and/or marginal groups | 4.43 | 0.76 | 5.00 | 3.00 |
| 2.3.9 Online disclosure of information about suppliers; compliance with contracts for the purchase of goods, materials and services | 3.57 | 1.02 | 5.00 | 2.00 |
| 2.3.10 Online disclosure of information about programmes to achieve a good working environment, in areas such as work hours and the provision of crèche facilities | 4.14 | 1.03 | 5.00 | 2.00 |
| 2.3.11 Online disclosure of information about the social benefit produced to the community in which it operates | 4.57 | 0.65 | 5.00 | 3.00 |
| 2.3.12 Online disclosure of information about mechanisms to combat corruption among the organisation's staff or managers | 4.21 | 0.97 | 5.00 | 2.00 |
| 2.3.13 Online disclosure of information about the organisation's intervention in social conflicts, acting as a pressure group | 4.43 | 0.85 | 5.00 | 3.00 |
| 2.3.14 Online disclosure of information about the organisation's participation in institutions that defend just causes | 4.50 | 0.76 | 5.00 | 3.00 |
| 2.3.15 Online disclosure of information about the organisation's compliance with applicable regulations in the country in which it operates | 4.21 | 0.70 | 5.00 | 3.00 |

Source 2 Prepared by the authors

The online transparency highlighted that reporting in the social dimension is in line with that presented by other Spanish NPOs (Gálvez et al., 2012), which is generally low level of disclosure. It is interesting to note that although volunteers make up a fundamental part of the human capital of the organisation, that that area was not reflected in the online publishing data (Gálvez et al., 2012).

In summary, an average level of online transparency highlights the importance of three dimensions of corporate social responsibility. The online information revealed interesting aspects of two of the three dimensions of CRS. The overall results highlighted that although stakeholders tend to trust NPOs more than profit-motivated companies (Handy et al., 2010; Witesman & Fernández, 2012; Drevs et al., 2014; Schlesinger, Mitchell & Gray, 2004), (Cordery & Baskerville, 2011), more attention should be paid to non-profit CRS dimensions, transparency and online reporting. However, there is opportunity for improvement and the use of the internet to communicate the non-profit sector CSR practices (Puentes et al., 2012).

## CONCLUSION

A sustainable future must necessarily be based on the application of corporate socially responsible practices. NPOs have the opportunity to be leaders in corporate social responsibility (CSR) and in reporting their performance online. Such transparency is essential not only to improve their image but also so that access to this information can be used for feedback and as an organisational learning tool. ICT contributes particularly in the use of the internet as a mechanism for disclosure.

Given the importance of this issue and the scant body of previous research, on methods and mechanisms of disclosure of non-profit sector CSR reporting, this chapter has contributed to highlight the need for further research in this area. At a practical level the information provided here inform NPOs of the extent to which their decisions are consistent global CRS guidelines. From a research point of view, the factors most importance are not always those about which most information is reported. In general, in planning the CSR information to be provided, greatest weight must be placed on publicising the organisation's social impact, followed by the economic impact of its activities, while environmental aspects are least considered. In practice, the non-profit appears to be more inclined to publish economic data, followed by social information, and pays little attention to reporting its policies in the field of environmental protection.

Verdiblanca's website in line with stakeholder theory and legitimacy theory, seek to meet the information needs of their key stakeholders in order to underpin their image as agents benefiting society, and their actions, hence, are subordinated to society's demands, rather than their own values and beliefs. This understanding is corroborated by the contradiction between what Verdiblanca's policy makers consider should be reported, and the information that is actually provided on the organisation's website.

The results obtained led us to conclude that non-profits disclose information on the economic aspects of its activities as a mechanism to eliminate prejudice. In other words, its transparency acts as a mechanism of accountability that is geared exclusively to cater to its main external stakeholders, fund providers and is a reliable source of information regarding the management of the resources entrusted to the organisation. Future research directions could consider:

1. Research in the area of non-profit organisations strengthening the reporting on the three dimensions of corporate social responsibility, but in particular, the environmental dimension.
2. Research could also explore the nature of non-profit organisations and online disclosure of the social aspects of their activities is a means of maintaining and strengthening their legitimacy to stakeholders.
3. A comparative analysis of the economic, social and environmental impact of non-profit organisations could be explored in terms of corporate social responsibility, transparency and accountability.
4. The gap between what non-profit managers consider as important to be disclosed on their website and what actually takes place, reflecting the strong influence of external stakeholders in NPO decision making would provide further insights into the corporate social responsibility of non-profit organisations and managerial decision-making.
5. Research on the use of the internet as a mechanism for information disclosure would provide greater understanding on how managers of non-profit organisations communication policies.
6. Research on whether a 360º approach to accountability on economic, social and environmental issues would improve online accountability would generate knowledge in a relatively new area of non-profit organisations.
7. It would be valuable to conduct a longitudinal study to analyse developments in this area over an extended time.

## REFERENCES


Aguinis, H., & Glavas, A. (2012). What we know and dont know about corporate social responsibility: A review and research agenda. *Journal of Management*, *38*(4), 932–968. doi:10.1177/0149206311436079

Albareda, L., & Balaguer, M. R. (2007). La responsabilidad social de la empresa y los resultados financieros. Contabilidad y dirección, Barcelona.

Alvarado, A., & Schlesinger, M. (2008). Dimesionalidad de la responsabilidad social empresarial percibida y sus efectos sobre la imagen y la reputación: Una aproximación desde el modelo de Carroll. *Estudios Gerenciales*, *24*(108), 37–59. doi:10.1016/S0123-5923(08)70043-3

Andreini, D., Pedeliento, G., & Signori, S. (2012). *The customer satisfaction in a nonprofit context: The role of social responsibility and its communication*. Papers of the 37th Annual Macromarketing Conference, Berlin, Germany. Retrieved from http:// macromarketing.org/wp-ontent/uploads/2011/08/Macromarketing2012Proceedings.pdf

Anheier, H. K. (2005). *Nonprofit organizations: Theory, management, policy*. London: Routledge.

Arenas, D., Lozano, J. M., & Albareda, L. (2009). The role of NGOs in CSR: Mutual perceptions among stakeholders. *Journal of Business Ethics*, *88*(1), 175–197. doi:10.1007/s10551-009-0109-x

Argandoña, A., (1998). *La teoría de los stakeholders y el bien común*. División de investigación IESE. Universidad De Navarra. Documento de Investigación nº. 355, Enero.

Baur, D., & Schmitz, H. P. (2012). Corporations y NGOs: When Accountability Leads to Co-optation. *Journal of Business Ethics*, *106*(1), 9–21. doi:10.1007/s10551-011-1057-9

Bekkers, R. (2003). Trust, accreditation, and philanthropy in the Netherlands. *Nonprofit and Voluntary Sector Quarterly*, *32*(4), 596–615. doi:10.1177/0899764003258102

Bouckaert, L., & Vandenhove, J. (1998). Business ethics and the management of non-profit institutions. *Journal of Business Ethics*, *17*(9/10), 1073–1081. doi:10.1023/A:1006071416514

Brammer, S., & Pavelin, S. (2008). Factors influencing the quality of corporate environmental disclosure. *Business Strategy and the Environment*, *17*(2), 120–136. doi:10.1002/bse.506

Brown, N., & Deegan, C. (1999). The public disclosure of environmental performance information – a dual test of media agenda setting theory and legitimacy theory. *Accounting and Business Review*, *9*, 21–41.

Buhr, N. (1998). Environmental performance, legislation and annual report disclosure: The case of acid rain and Falconbridge. *Accounting, Auditing & Accountability Journal*, *11*(2), 163–190. doi:10.1108/09513579810215455

Burger, R. (2005). What we have learnt from post-1994 innovations in pro-poor service delivery in South Africa: A case study-based analysis. *Development Southern Africa*, *22*(4), 483–500. doi:10.1080/03768350500322966

Burger, R., & Owens, T. (2010). Promoting Transparency in the NGO Sector: Examining the Availability and Reliability of Self-Reported Data. *World Development*, *38*(9), 1263–1277. doi:10.1016/j.worlddev.2009.12.018

Campos, L., Andion, C., Serva, M., Rossetto, A., & Assumpção, J. (2011). Performance evaluation in non-governmental organizations (NGOs): An analysis of evaluation models and their applications in Brazil. *Voluntas*, *22*(2), 238–258. doi:10.1007/s11266-010-9145-5

Canyelles, J. M. (2009). *Per un territori socialment responsable. Promovent la Responsabilitat Social dels Ajuntaments*. Fundació Pro Penedès. Vilafranca del Penedès.

Canyelles, J. M. (2012). La responsabilidad social de las organizaciones no lucrativas. *Revista de Contabilidad y Dirección*, *14*, 129–156.

Capurro, R. (2005). Privacy. An intercultural perspective. *Ethics and Information Technology*, *7*(1), 37–47. doi:10.1007/s10676-005-4407-4

Castelo, M., & Lima, L. (2008). Factors Influencing Social Responsibility Disclosure by Portuguese Companies. *Journal of Business Ethics*, *83*(4), 685–701. doi:10.1007/s10551-007-9658-z

Cho, C. H. (2009). Legitimation strategies used in response to environmental disaster: A French case study of Total SAs Erika and AZF incidents. *European Accounting Review*, *18*(1), 33–62. doi:10.1080/09638180802579616

Clark, J. (2011). Civil Society in the Age of Crisis. *Journal of Civil Society*, *7*(3), 241–263. doi:10.1080/17448689.2011.604986

Cordery, C. J., & Baskerville, R. F. (2011). Charity transgressions, trust and accountability. *Voluntas: International Journal of Voluntary and Nonprofit Organizations*, *22*(2), 197–213. doi:10.1007/s11266-010-9132-x

Costa, E., Ramus, T., & Andreaus, M. (2011). Accountability as a managerial tool in non-profit organizations: Evidence from Italian CSVs. *Voluntas: International Journal of Voluntary and Nonprofit Organizations*, *22*(3), 470–493. doi:10.1007/s11266-011-9183-7

Crespo, F. (2010). Entre el concepto y la práctica: Responsabilidad social. *Estudios Gerenciales*, *26*(117), 119–130. doi:10.1016/S0123-5923(10)70137-6

Crespy, C. T., & Miller, V. V. (2011). Sustainability reporting: A comparative study of NGOs and MNCs. *Corporate Social Responsibility and Environmental Management*, *18*(5), 275–284. doi:10.1002/csr.248

De Castro, M. (2005). La Responsabilidad Social de las Empresas, o un nuevo concepto de empresa. CIRIEC-España. *Revista de Economía Pública. Social y Cooperativa*, *53*, 137–161.

De la Torre, I. (2009). Fundamentos de la responsabilidad social de la empresa. *Revista de Responsabilidad Social de la Empresa*, *1*, 71–86.

Deegan, C. (2007). Organizational legitimacy as a motive for sustainability. In Sustainability Accounting and Accountability. Routledge.

Deegan, C., & Rankin, M. (1996). Do Australian Companies Report Environmental News Objectively? An Analysis of Environmental Disclosures by Firms Prosecuted Successfully by the Environmental Protection Authority. *Accounting, Auditing & Accountability Journal*, *9*(2), 50–67. doi:10.1108/09513579610116358

Degli Antoni, G., & Portale, E. (2011). The effect of Corporate Social Responsibility on Social Capital Creation in Social Cooperatives. *Nonprofit and Voluntary Sector Quarterly*, *40*(3), 566–582. doi:10.1177/0899764010362568

Donaldson, T., & Preston, L. E. (1995). The stakeholder's theory of the corporation: Concepts, evidence and implications. *Academy of Management Review*, *20*(1), 65–91.

Drevs, F., Tscheulin, D. K., & Lindenmeier, J. (2014). Do patient perceptions vary with ownership status? A study of nonprofit, for-profit, and public hospital patients. *Nonprofit and Voluntary Sector Quarterly*, *43*(1), 164–184. doi:10.1177/0899764012458179

Du, S., Bhattacharya, C. B., & Sen, S. (2010). Maximizing Business Returns to Corporate Social Responsibility (CSR): The Role of CSR Communication. *International Journal of Management Reviews*, *12*(5), 8–19. doi:10.1111/j.1468-2370.2009.00276.x

Ebrahim, A. (2003). Accountability in practice: Mechanisms for NGOs. *World Development*, *31*(5), 813–829. doi:10.1016/S0305-750X(03)00014-7

Ebrahim, A. (2005). Accountability Myopia: Losing Sight of Organizational Learning. *Nonprofit and Voluntary Sector Quarterly*, *34*(1), 56–87. doi:10.1177/0899764004269430

Ebrahim, A. (2009). Placing the Normative Logics of Accountability in Thick Perspective. *The American Behavioral Scientist*, *52*(6), 885–904. doi:10.1177/0002764208327664

Elkington, J. (1997). *Cannibals with Forks. The triple bottom line of 21st century business.* Oxford, UK: Inglaterra.

Fassin, Y. (2009). Inconsistencies in activists behaviours and the ethics of NGOs. *Journal of Business Ethics*, *90*(4), 503–521. doi:10.1007/s10551-009-0056-6

Fulop, G., Hisrich, R., & Szegedi, K. (2000). Business ethics and social responsibility in transition economies. *Journal of Management Development*, *19*(1), 5–31. doi:10.1108/02621710010308135

Gallego-Álvarez, I., & Quina-Custodio, I. A. (2016). Disclosure of corporate social responsibility information and explanatory factors. *Online Information Review*, *40*(2), 218–238. doi:10.1108/OIR-04-2015-0116

Gálvez, M. M., Caba, M. C., & López, M. (2012). Responsabilidad social y transparencia on-line de las ONG: Análisis del caso español. *CIRIEC-España, Revista de Economía Pública. Social y Cooperativa*, *74*, 207–238.

Gandía, J. L. (2011). Internet disclosure by nonprofit organizations: Empirical evidence of nongovernmental organizations for development in Spain. *Nonprofit and Voluntary Sector Quarterly*, *40*(1), 57–58. doi:10.1177/0899764009343782

García-Mainar, I., & Marcuello, C. (2007). Members, Volunteers, and Donors in Non-profit Organizations in Spain. *Nonprofit and Voluntary Sector Quarterly*, *36*(1), 100–120. doi:10.1177/0899764006293179

Gelbmann, U. (2010). Establishing Strategic CSR: An Austrian CSR Quality Seal to Sub-stantiate the Strategic CSR Performance of SMEs. *Sustainable Development*, *18*(2), 90–98. doi:10.1002/sd.448

Gibelman, M., & Gelman, S. R. (2004). A Loss of Credibility: Patterns of Wrongdoing among Nongovernmental Organizations. *Voluntas*, *15*(4), 355–381. doi:10.1007/s11266-004-1237-7

Global Reporting Initiative. (2011). *Guía Para La Elaboración De Memorias De Sostenibilidad*. Amsterdam.

Godfrey, P. C., & Hatch, N. W. (2007). Researching corporate social responsibility: An agenda for the 21st century. *Journal of Business Ethics*, *70*(1), 87–98. doi:10.1007/s10551-006-9080-y

Gray, R., Kouhy, R., & Lavers, S. (1995). Corporate Social and Environmental Reporting: A Review of the Literature and a Longitudinal Study of UK Disclosure. *Accounting, Auditing & Accountability Journal*, *8*(2), 47–77. doi:10.1108/09513579510146996

Gray, R. H., Owen, D. L., & Adams, C. (1996). *Accounting and accountability, changes and challenges in corporate social and environmental reporting*. Hemel Hempstead, UK: Prentice Hall.

Grosser, K. (2015). Corporate Social Responsibility and Multi-Stakeholder Governance: Pluralism, Feminist Perspectives and Women's NGOs. *Journal of Business Ethics*, 1–15.

Gugerty, M. K. (2010). The Emergence of Non-profit Self-Regulation in Africa. *Nonprofit and Voluntary Sector Quarterly*, *39*(6), 1087–1112. doi:10.1177/0899764010372972

Handy, F., Seto, S., Wakaruk, A., Mersey, B., Mejia, A., & Copeland, L. (2010). The discerning consumer: Is nonprofit status a factor? *Nonprofit and Voluntary Sector Quarterly*, *39*(5), 866–883. doi:10.1177/0899764010362113

Hansmann, H. B. (1980). The role of nonprofit enterprise. *The Yale Law Journal*, *89*(5), 835–901. doi:10.2307/796089

Harrison, J. S., Bosse, D. A., & Phillips, R. A. (2010). Managing for stakeholders, stakeholder utility functions, and competitive advantage. *Strategic Management Journal*, *31*(1), 58–74. doi:10.1002/smj.801

Herbohn, K., Walker, J., & Loo, H. Y. M. (2014). Corporate Social Responsibility: The Link Between Sustainability Disclosure and Sustainability Performance. *Abacus*, *50*(4), 422–459. doi:10.1111/abac.12036

Hogan, E. (2008). Does 'corporate' responsibility apply to not-for-profit organizations? In S. O. Idowu & W. L. Filho (Eds.), *Professionals' perspectives on corporate social responsibility* (pp. 271–288). Berlin: Springer.

Ingenhoff, D., & Koelling, A. M. (2007). The potential of Web sites as a relationship building tool for charitable fundraising NPOs. *Public Relations Review*, *1*(35), 66–73.

Jegers, M. (2009). Corporate Governance in nonprofit organizations: A nontechnical review of the economic literature. *Nonprofit Management & Leadership*, *20*(2), 143–164. doi:10.1002/nml.246

Jordan, L. (2003). *Mechanisms for NGO Accountability*. GPPI Research Paper Series No.3. Global Public Policy Institute.

Jordan, L. (2005). *Mechanisms for NGO Accountability*. GPPI Research Paper Series 3. Global Public Policy Institute.

Kearns, K. P. (1994). The strategic management of accountability in nonprofit organizations: An analytical framework. *Public Administration Review*, *54*(2), 185–192. doi:10.2307/976528

Keohane, R. O. (2002, May). Political accountability. In *Conference on Delegation to International Organizations* (p. 8).

Kim, D., Chun, H., Kwak, Y., & Nam, Y. (2014). The Employment of Dialogic Principles in Website, Facebook, and Twitter Platforms of Environmental Nonprofit Organizations. *Social Science Computer Review*. Available at: http://ssc.sagepub.com/content/early/2014/01/30/0894439314525752

Kourula, A., & Delalieux, G. (2016). The micro-level foundations and dynamics of political corporate social responsibility: Hegemony and passive revolution through civil society. *Journal of Business Ethics*, 1–17.

Laasonen, S., Fougere, M., & Kourula, A. (2012). A Dominant Articulations in Academic Business y Society Discourse on NGO-Business relations: A critical Assessment. *Journal of Business Ethics*, *109*(4), 521–545. doi:10.1007/s10551-011-1143-z

Lee, T., Johnson, E., & Prakash, A. (2012). Media independence and trust in NGOs: The case of postcommunist countries. *Nonprofit and Voluntary Sector Quarterly*, *41*(1), 8–35. doi:10.1177/0899764010384444

Lee, T. E., Chen, J. Q., & Zhang, R. (2001). Utilizing the Internet as a competitive tool for non-profit organizations. *Journal of Computer Information Systems*, *41*(3), 26–31.

Lii, Y. S., & Lee, M. (2012). Doing right leads to doing well: When the type of CSR and reputation interact to affect consumer evaluations of the firm. *Journal of Business Ethics*, *105*(1), 69–81. doi:10.1007/s10551-011-0948-0

Lin-Hi, N., Hörisch, J., & Blumberg, I. (2015). Does CSR Matter for Nonprofit Organizations? Testing the Link Between CSR Performance and Trust worthiness in the Nonprofit Versus For-Profit Domain. *Voluntas*, *26*(5), 1944–1974. doi:10.1007/s11266-014-9506-6

Marcuello, C., Bellostas, A., Marcuello, Ch., & Moneva, J. M. (2007). Transparencia y rendición de cuentas en las empresas de inserción. *CIRIEC-España, Revista de Economía Pública. Social y Cooperativa*, *59*, 91–122.

Marschall, M. (2002). *Legitimacy and effectiveness: civil society organizations' role in good governance*. Paper presented at the poverty reduction strategies forum, Baden, Austria.

Mcwilliams, A., Siegel, D., & Wright, P. (2006). Corporate social responsibility: Strategic implications. *Journal of Management Studies*, *43*(1), 1–18. doi:10.1111/j.1467-6486.2006.00580.x

Mercado, P., & Garcia, P. (2007). La responsabilidad social en empresas del valle de Toluca (México): Un estudio exploratorio. *Estudios Gerenciales*, *23*(102), 119–135. doi:10.1016/S0123-5923(07)70005-0

Mitchell, R., Agle, B., & Wood, D. (1997). Toward a theory of stakeholder identification and salience: Defining the principle of who and what really counts. *Academy of Management Review*, *22*(4), 853–886.

Moneva, J. M. (2007). El marco de la información sobre la responsabilidad social de las organizaciones. *Ekonomíaz*, *65*, 284–317.

Moneva, J. M., & Bellostas, A. (2007). *Accountability en las Entidades sin Fines Lucrativos*. Centros de Investigación de Economía y Sociedad.

Orlitzky, M. (2005). Social responsibility and financial performance: Trade-off or virtuous circle. *University of Auckland Business Review*, *7*(1), 37–43.

Parker, L. D. (2012). Qualitative management accounting research, Assessing deliverables and relevance. *Critical Perspectives on Accounting*, *23*(1), 54–70. doi:10.1016/j.cpa.2011.06.002

Patten, D. M. (1991). Exposure, Legitimacy, and Social Disclosure. *Journal of Accounting and Public Policy*, *10*(4), 297–308. doi:10.1016/0278-4254(91)90003-3

Pérez, V., & Mateos, C. (2006). ONG, Internet y Comunicación Alternativa en las ONG dedicadas a la inmigración en España. *Razón y Palabra*, *29*, 49.

Ponte, S. (2008). Greener than thou: The political economy of fish ecolabeling and its local manifestations in South Africa. *World Development*, *36*(1), 159–175. doi:10.1016/j.worlddev.2007.02.014

Puentes, R., Mozas, A., Bernal, E., & Chaves, R. (2012). E-corporate social responsibility in small non-profit organisations: The case of Spanish Non Government Organisations. *Service Industries Journal*, *32*(15), 2379–2398. doi:10.1080/02642069.2012.677831

Qu, S. Q., & Dumay, J. (2011). The qualitative research interview. *Qualitative Research in Accounting and Management*, *8*(3), 238–264. doi:10.1108/11766091111162070

Roberts, R. W. (1992). Determinants of Corporate Social Responsibility Disclosure: An Application of Stakeholder Theory. *Accounting, Organizations and Society*, *17*(6), 595–612. doi:10.1016/0361-3682(92)90015-K

Rothschild, J., & Milofsky, C. (2006). The centrality of values, passions, and ethics in the nonprofit sector. Special issue introduction. *Nonprofit Management & Leadership*, *17*(2), 137–143. doi:10.1002/nml.139

Ruiz, M., Ríos, A., & Tirado, P. (2009). La responsabilidad social y la crisis económica. ¿Responden las entidades financieras españolas a los grupos de interés? *Revista de Economía Pública. Social y Cooperativa*, *65*, 33–58.

Salamon, L., Sokolowski, S. W., Haddock, M. A., & Tice, H. S. (2012). *The State of Global Civil Societyand Volunteering: Latest findings from the implementation of the UN Non-profit Handbook*. Working Paper No. 49. Baltimore, MD: Johns Hopkins Center for Civil Society Studies.

Sarstedt, M., & Schloderer, M. P. (2010). Developing a measurement approach for reputation of nonprofit organizations. *International Journal of Nonprofit and Voluntary Sector Marketing*, *15*(3), 276–299.

Saxton, G. D., & Guo, C. (2011). Accountability online: Understanding the web-based accountability practices of nonprofit organizations. *Nonprofit and Voluntary Sector Quarterly*, *40*(2), 270–295. doi:10.1177/0899764009341086

Saxton, G. D., & Guo, C. (2012). Conceptualizing Web-Based Stakeholder Communication: The Organizational Website as a Stakeholder Relations Tool. *Communication & Science Journal*. Available at: http://www.galileoco.com/comSciJliterature/saxtonGuo12.pdf

Schlesinger, M., Mitchell, S., & Gray, B. H. (2004). Public expectations of nonprofit and for–profit ownership in American medicine: Clarifications and implications. *Health Affairs*, *23*(6), 181–191. doi:10.1377/hlthaff.23.6.181 PMID:15537597

Shocker, A. D., & Sethi, S. P. (1974). An approach to incorporating social preferences in developing corporate action strategies. In The Unstable Ground: Corporate Social Policy in a Dynamic Society (pp. 76-80). Melville.

Skouloudis, A., Evangelinos, K., & Malesios, C. (2015). Priorities and perceptions for corporate social responsibility: An NGO perspective. *Corporate Social Responsibility and Environmental Management*, *22*(2), 95–112. doi:10.1002/csr.1332

Smith, P. C., & Richmond, K. A. (2007). Call for greater accountability within the U.S. nonprofit sector. *Academy of Accounting & Financial Studies Journal*, *11*(2), 75–87.

Spiro, R. J. (2001). Principled pluralism for adaptative flexibility in teaching and learning to read. In R. F. Flippo (Ed.), *Reading researchers in search of common ground* (pp. 92–97). Newark, DE: International Reading Association.

Stanaland, A. J., Lwin, M. O., & Murphy, P. E. (2011). Consumer perceptions of the antecedents and consequences of corporate social responsibility. *Journal of Business Ethics*, *102*(1), 47–55. doi:10.1007/s10551-011-0904-z

Tapscott, D., & Ticoll, D. (2003). *The naked corporation*. New York: Free Press.

Taylor, M., & Doerfel, M. L. (2011). Evolving network roles in international aid efforts: Evidence from Croatias post-war transition. *Voluntas: International Journal of Voluntary and Non Profit Organizations*, *22*(2), 311–334. doi:10.1007/s11266-010-9155-3

Tilling, M. W., & Tilt, C. A. (2010). The Edge of legitimacy Voluntary social and environmental reporting in Rothmans´19561999 annual reports. *Accounting, Auditing & Accountability Journal*, *23*(1), 55–81. doi:10.1108/09513571011010600

Tremblay-Boire, J., & Prakash, A. (2015). Accountability.org: Online Disclosures by U.S. Nonprofits. *Voluntas. Voluntas*, *26*(2), 693–719. doi:10.1007/s11266-014-9452-3

Tschirhart, M., & Bielefeld, W. (2012). *Managing nonprofit organizations*. San Francisco, CA: Jossey-Bass. doi:10.1002/9781119051626

Ullmann, A. A. (1985). Data in search of a theory: A critical examination of the relationship among social performance, social disclosure, and economic performance of U.S. Firms. *Academy of Management Review*, *10*(3), 540–557.

Unerman, J., & O Dwyer, B. (2010). NGO accountability and sustainability issues in the changing global environment. *Public Management Review*, *12*(4), 475–486. doi:10.1080/14719037.2010.496258

Vaccaro, A. (2006). Privacy, security and transparency: ICT-related ethical perspectives and contrasts in contemporary firms. In D. Howcroft, E. Trauth, & J. DeGross (Eds.), *Social inclusion: Societal and organizational implications for information systems*. New York: Springer. doi:10.1007/0-387-34588-4_17

Vaccaro, A., & Madsen, P. (2006). Firms' information transparency: Ethical questions in the information age. In J. Berleur (Ed.), *Social informatics: An information society for all?* New York: Springer. doi:10.1007/978-0-387-37876-3_12

Vélez, A. M. (2011). Un recorrido hacia la responsabilidad social corporativa. *Revista Ciencias Estratégicas*, *19*(25), 55–74.

Vidal, P., Torres, D., Guix, B., & Peña, M. (2005). *La responsabilidad social de las organizaciones no lucrativas*. Centro de recursos del observatorio del tercer Sector. Available at: http://www.galileoco.com/comSciJliterature/saxtonGuo12.pdf

Weerawardena, J., McDonald, R. E., & Mort, G. S. (2010). Sustainability of nonprofit organizations: An empirical investigation. *Journal of World Business*, *45*(4), 346–356. doi:10.1016/j.jwb.2009.08.004

Weidenbaum, M. (2009). Who will Guard the Guardians? The Social Responsibility of NGOs. *Journal of Business Ethics*, *87*(1), 147–155. doi:10.1007/s10551-008-9813-1

White, G. (2005). How to report a company's sustainability activities. *Management Accounting Quarterly*, *7*(1), 36–43.

Wirl, F. (2014). Dynamic corporate social responsibility (CSR) strategies in oligopoly. *OR-Spektrum*, *36*(1), 229–250. doi:10.1007/s00291-013-0319-6

Witesman, E. M., & Fernandez, S. (2012). Government contracts with private organizations: Are there differences between nonprofits and for-profits? *Nonprofit and Voluntary Sector Quarterly*, *42*(4), 689–715. doi:10.1177/0899764012442592

## KEY TERMS AND DEFINITIONS

**Accountability:** The action to inform stakeholders on management of the organization in order to justify the behavior and activities carried out.

**Corporate Social Responsibility:** Procedures and actions that organisations adopt in order to apply best practices in the management of the economic, social and environmental impact of their actions.

**Legitimacy:** Image or perception that society has on an organization. In NPOs context, this image should be as agents that serve society.

**Nonprofit Organization:** An independent organization that serves the public interest with a non-profitable purpose.

**Online Disclosure:** Dissemination of information through a website.

**Stakeholders:** A person, group or organization such as volunteers, donors, beneficiaries that are affected, in a greater or lesser extent, by the decisions made by the NPO.

**Transparency:** The commitment of an organization to let stakeholders access information on demanded.

# Chapter 13
# Social Media Use by Chambers of Commerce and Industry (TCCI) in Turkey

**Ali Acilar**
*Bilecik Şeyh Edebali University, Turkey*

**Muzaffer Aydemir**
*Yıldız Technical University, Turkey*

## ABSTRACT

*This chapter empirically investigates the Turkish chambers of commerce and industry's social media usage. Specifically, the research explores the prevalence, types, frequency, reasons, and the most importantly effectiveness of social media usage among the Turkish Chambers of Commerce and Industry (TCCI). A web based survey conducted to gather data from the TCCI. The chapter consists of five main parts: Introduction, social media as a modern business imperative, survey about social media usage in Turkish chambers of commerce and industry, and conclusion.*

## INTRODUCTION

Information and communication technologies have become an important part of our life. Especially the Internet and the Web together have deeply affected our lives from education to communication, from business to entertainment for the past decades. But that was not the case at the beginning of the Internet. In the early years of the Internet, web sites were static, according to Tim Berners-Lee "read-only" websites (Shivalingaiah & Naik, 2008), did not have interactive content and allowed its users to have unilateral communication (Acılar, 2015; Acılar & Mersin, 2015). This first phase of the World Wide Web (WWW) is called as "Web 1.0". The earliest Web sites provided little opportunity for two-way communication, presumably at best providing contact information such as mailing address, e-mail, or phone number (Andzulis, Panagopoulos, & Rapp, 2012).

Since it was invented in 1989, the WWW has evolved greatly through the years and it continues to grow and evolve. Today, in addition to static content, Web sites enable people to collaborate, share

DOI: 10.4018/978-1-5225-2537-0.ch013

Copyright © 2017, IGI Global. Copying or distributing in print or electronic forms without written permission of IGI Global is prohibited.

information, and create new services and content online (Laudon & Laudon, 2012: 272). This stage of WWW is called as "Web 2.0". Web 2.0, also known as read-write web, is defined by O'Reilly (2007) as "the network as platform, spanning all connected devices; Web 2.0 applications are those that make the most of the intrinsic advantages of that platform: delivering software as a continually-updated service that gets better the more people use it, consuming and remixing data from multiple sources, including individual users, while providing their own data and services in a form that allows remixing by others, creating network effects through an "architecture of participation," and going beyond the page metaphor of Web 1.0 to deliver rich user experiences." Unlike Web 1.0, Web 2.0 allows more interaction with less control (Aghaei, Nematbakhsh & Farsani, 2012). Web 2.0 can be defined as a collection of second generation online technologies and services that enable users to communicate create content and share it with each other via communities, social networks and virtual worlds more easily than before (Jussila, Kärkkäinen & Aramo-Immonen, 2014). The concept of "Web 2.0" was born with a conference brainstorming session between O'Reilly and MediaLive International (O'Reilly, 2005) according to a common acceptance in the literature. Web 2.0 has four characteristic features: interactivity, real-time user control, social participation, and user-generated content (Laudon and Laudon, 2012, p. 272). Web 2.0 includes technologies and services such as blogs, really simple syndication (RSS), wikis, mashups, tags, folksonomy, and tag clouds (Aghaei, Nematbakhsh & Farsani, 2012).

## Social Media

According to Kaplan and Haenlein (2010) Web 2.0 can be considered as the platform for the evolution of social media. Social media can be defined as "a group of Internet-based applications that build on the ideological and technological foundations of Web 2.0, and that allow the creation and exchange of User Generated Content" (Kaplan & Haenlein, 2010). Social media consists of a wide range of a new generation of Internet applications and encompasses tools that allow individual and collective publishing; sharing of multimedia such as images, audio and video; and the creation and maintenance of online social networks (Constantinides & Stagno, 2011; Bennett et al., 2012). Social media describes online platforms that allow for user-generated content, interaction and collaboration. It is a relatively new phenomenon, linked to the emergence of 'web 2.0' and the move from a static to an interactive internet (Dormey, 2016). The broad term, social media, have been used to apply to a variety of technologies, such as wikis, blogs, microblogs, social networking sites, virtual worlds, and video-sharing sites (Kane, Alavi, Labianca, & Borgatti, 2014). In other words, social media are a group of Internet-based applications which allow the creation and exchange of user generated content through online social networks (Kaplan & Haenlein, 2010; Constantinides & Stagno, 2011; Bennett et al., 2012). Social media help to convert monologue into dialogue, gives free access to almost all types of available information, to transform Internet users from mere readers to creators of online content and to interact in the online world so as to form new personal or business relationships (Holotescu and Grosseck, 2013).

Rapid developments on mobile devices such as smart phones, tablets and notebooks have also opened new avenues for social media. Today's mobile devices and the use of social media presented new opportunities for interaction, provided opportunities for collaboration, allowed users to engage in content creation and communication using social media and Web 2.0 tools with the assistance of constant connectivity (Gikas & Grant, 2013). Today, social media applications in the Internet have been integrated into the daily practices of many users worldwide, supported by different websites, tools, and networks (Oberer & Erkollar, 2012). As the penetration of smart mobile devices and Internet increase, so does the use of social media application in these devices. Smart mobile devices provide the opportunity for people to post and share anywhere and anytime.

Accordingly, today "social networking" has become very popular and occupied an important role in most people's lives (Zaidieh, 2012). "Social Network" can be defined as "a network of relationships between different information processing entities such as people, groups, and organizations" (Hosny & Fatima, 2012). According to Boyd and Ellison (2008) social network sites are "web-based services that allow individuals to (1) construct a public or semi-public profile within a bounded system, (2) articulate a list of other users with whom they share a connection, and (3) view and traverse their list of connections and those made by others within the system." With providing tools on the Internet for posting messages, sharing photos, creating personal pages and groups, social networking sites, such as Facebook, Twitter, Instagram, LinkedIn, etc., bring people together and allow them to communicate by making new friends, exchanging ideas and engaging in similar interests (Hosny & Fatima, 2012).

The emergence of social media has brought numerous opportunities for interpersonal and organizational communication (Lovejoy & Saxton, 2012). The rapid diffusion of social media all around the world is creating new era of possibilities for organizations to communicate with their stakeholders such as stockholders, employees, customers, suppliers and the general public (Lovejoy & Saxton, 2012). Since most of the internet users have at least one social media account and social media use is widespread worldwide, it is natural for the companies to use it as a marketing channel too (Kovacs & Wensley, 2015). However, it is often a painful process for organizations to adopt and use of new technologies, social media also create some obstacles for organizations (Kuikka, M. & Äkkinen, M. 2011).

Technological developments such as social media are gaining popularity and are increasingly used for personal and business purposes. However, the study of social media use in organizations is in its infancy. (Treem & Leonardi, 2012).

## SOCIAL MEDIA AS A MODERN BUSINESS IMPERATIVE

In today's rapidly changing business environment social media are indispensible. In other words, social media are modern business imperative for many organizations, including start-ups, small, medium-sized, and large private organizations as well as public and nongovernmental organizations. In this part, social media usage of organizations is discussed throughly. Namely "social media usage in organizations", "factors affecting acceptance and adoption of social media", "social media plans / policies", "social media professionals, training and development of social media users", "potential benefits of social media usage for organizations", "risks of social media usage for organizations", "barriers of social media usage", "performance evaluation of social media usage", and finally "recommendation for effective social media usage."

### Social Media Usage in Organizations

Social media are suitable for all kinds of companies from public to private sectors, from service to manufacturing industries, and all can gain something from their use. However, they are probably more useful for SMEs, since these companies have greater difficulties in reaching the market. 61% of the SMEs are making formal use of social media. In terms of SMEs' social media usage, the leading countries are United Kingdom (90%), Netherlands (79%) and Latvia (75%). (Batikas & Bavel, 2013).

The use of social media has grown exponentially in the last decade. Currently around one employer in two makes use of a social media tool. Use of social media is largely focused externally on marketing and engaging with customers. Fewer employers – only around one in six – use an enterprise social network internally to engage with employees and promote employee voice. Larger organizations and certain sectors such as information and communication are more likely to use social media in this way. Whereas three in four employees use social media in their personal life, just one in three do so as part of their work. Nevertheless, the high levels of personal usage might be driving the organizational take-up of social media in the form of enterprise social networks (Dormey, 2016).

There has been an explosion in the popularity of social media sites such as Facebook, MySpace, Twitter, and LinkedIn in recent years. Their popularity has transcended languages, borders and cultures, and it is probably no exaggeration to say that we are witnessing a social media revolution. Facebook alone currently has over 500 million users, equating to roughly 1 in every 13 people on this planet. It is estimated that over 50 per cent of these users log on to Facebook every day. By anyone's standards, these are staggering figures and yet they relate only to one social media site. It is therefore no surprise that social media are beginning to permeate almost every aspect of our lives, whether it be on a personal, social or professional level. Many businesses have been adept at harnessing the power of social media to their advantage. Others have been less so, but they are catching on (Abate et al., 2011).

Perhaps the defining characteristic of social media is the speed at which they develop. It is therefore difficult to predict the future of any given tool – in five years' time, the sites which are currently household names may have been supplanted by media that have yet to be invented. One thing that seems likely, however, is that an increasing amount of social media traffic will go through mobile devices such as smartphones and tablets. Overall, it is clear that the use of social media for recruitment purposes is increasing, as companies experiment with new tools like LinkedIn, Facebook, Twitter and the rest (Broughton et al., 2013).

Nowadays, consumers prefer to use companies' Facebook and Twitter accounts instead of official websites. Social media platforms are especially creating good sales opportunities for companies in fast consumptions products and services sectors (Ying, 2012).

Several studies investigated social media use in Turkish organizations. Yılmazel (2011) conducted a research with 233 charitable foundations in Turkey to analyze how these foundations use Web and Web 2.0 technologies in terms of public relations realm. Research has focused on 124 charitable foundations that have Web pages. Web pages and social media (Facebook and Twitter) web pages of these foundations were examined by the help of content analysis technique. Research findings showed that Turkish charitable foundations do not use Web pages effectively enough. Furthermore, only a bunch of foundations use Web 2.0 technologies. Only a few foundations have Facebook and Twitter accounts. Specifically, 11 foundations have Facebook account; 4 foundations have Twitter account and 2 foundations have blogs. Only 26% of these foundations communicate with their members through Facebook and only 9% of these foundations communicate with their members through Twitter. Besides most of the charitable foundations have not yet completed their Web pages integration with Web 2.0 technologies such as RSS, blog, Facebook and Twitter.

Aslan (2014) conducted a research with 12 labor unions and three labor union confederations (TÜRK-İŞ, DİSK, and HAK-İŞ) in Turkey. Aslan has classified these labor unions into three different groups according to their attitudes and behaviors towards social media usage: Avid, reluctant, and forced. First group consists of big and well organized labor unions. Management teams of these labor unions are very eager to use modern technologies. These labor unions are using social media very effectively to communicate with their members and other stakeholders as well. Second group of labor unions who are reluctant about using social media do not believe the benefits of social media. Furthermore, they do not have necessary technological infrastructure and human talents to use social media. The most importantly this group of the labor unions have old fashion management styles; bureaucratic, centralized and less democratic. Therefore management teams of these labor unions are not eager to use social media and do not encourage others for using social media. This group has some reservation about the drawback of social media such as cyber-attacks. The last group of labor unions which is called "forced to use social media" has some management and organization problems. Therefore they feel that they have to use modern technologies like social media to overcome those problems. They believe that they can attract more members and supporters by the help of social media. In addition, they favor social media to lessen budget problems. This group do not hire specialist for social media operations. Instead they use current personnel for these purposes too. Overall, most of the labor unions have problems developing quality content for social media platforms.

Onan (2010) analyzed 5 well known environmentalist nongovernmental organizations' social media practices in Turkey. Those organizations are TEMA (The Turkish Foundations for Combating Soil Erosion for Reforestation and the Protection of Natural Habitats), WWF - Türkiye (World Wildlife Fund), Greenpeace Akdeniz, Doğa Derneği (Doğa is the partner of BirdLife International), ÇEKÜL (The Foundation for the Protection and Promotion of the Environment and Cultural Heritage). According to the research findings, these organizations have got most of the benefits of social media usage such as creating awareness about nature, gaining recognition from society, increasing communication channels and quality of communication between the organizations and their stakeholders, increasing the amount of donations from public etc.

Uzunoğlu and Kip (2014) analyzed the Turkish environmental non-profit organizations' Websites to determine dialogic potential, including social media adoption. However, 23 of 50 websites examined failed to meet half the criteria for building relationships. Of 19 sites with connections to social media, 16 used new media potentialities, however only four met all social media adoption criteria. In other words, environmentalist NPO websites in Turkey fail to fully meet the dialogic communication features, particularly with regard to providing direct social media links.

## Factors Affecting the Acceptance and Adoption of Social Media

Organizations' technology competence, pressure from clients, and characteristics of the mobile environment significantly affect the acceptance of social media usage (Schaupp and Belanger, 2014). Organizations with defined public relations departments are more likely to adopt social media technologies and use them to achieve their organizational goals. In addition, public relations practitioners are more likely to use social media tools if they find them credible. Social media techniques will become more abundant as public relations practitioners become mindful of their effectiveness in regards to reaching target audiences, promoting a specific cause, and further developing communication strategies (Curtis, at all, 2010).

Social media applications, however, are slowly diffusing across all levels of government. The organizational dynamics underlying adoption and use decisions follow a process similar to that for previous waves of new information and communication technologies. First, agencies experiment informally with social media outside of accepted technology use policies. Next, order evolves from the first chaotic stage as organizations recognize the need to draft norms and regulations. Finally, organizational institutions evolve that clearly outline appropriate behavior, types of interactions, and new modes of communication that subsequently are formalized in social media strategies and policies (Mergel and Bretschneider, 2013).

Support from employers and top level managers are also important factors for usage of social media in organizations. Survey evidence illustrates that use of social networking sites by employees has grown significantly in recent years. However, some small-scale survey evidence shows that among higher skilled workers, only slightly fewer than 15 per cent have access to social networking sites at work. This may indicate that employers are prohibiting use of such internet sites to avoid having to manage any negative consequences. Especially younger generations who are more conversant with social networking sites are more prone to use them less careful. Inattentive employees may easily post something inappropriate on a social networking site and it can create serious problems (Broughton et al., 2009).

Business organizations can only leave and prosper by the help of their customers, employees, shareholders etc. Likewise nonprofit organizations survive through grants and donations. As society progresses into the technology age, it is important for nonprofit organizations to follow suit and become more technologically adept. The days in which donations were obtained through direct mailings, phone calls, and emails are fading. In order to stay current with the most donors, nonprofit organizations need to have a presence on social media websites, and should explore the use of social media and text-to-give campaigns for the solicitation of donations. Therefore, reaching supporters, volunteers and members and persuade them to contribute to the organization is very important reason for the adoption of social media. According to Schwedel (2013) research all organizations that participated in his research have a significant presence on social media websites and most of them have experience with receiving donations through mobile applications (Schwedel, 2013).

Social media are also used for recruitment. There is a wide variety of practice in the use of social media tools for recruitment. Use depends on factors such as company size and sector as well as the type of employee whom the employer is trying to reach. Many organizations are experimenting with these tools, which, being relatively new, are moving forward on a trial and error basis. Triggers for using social media for recruitment include: operating within an environment in which competitors are using these tools (e.g. retail); wanting to target particular groups of people, particularly in the case of senior jobs; and linking the use of social media to brand and awareness-building. Social media tools are usually used in combination with more traditional recruitment strategies rather than substituting for these (Broughton et al., 2013)

According to Zincir (2014) socialization, information gathering and dissemination, personal brand creation, business network development and collaboration are five common purposes for Turkish managers' social media usage.

## Social Media Plans / Policies

There is an increased use of social media and social networking sites by organizations. Organizations social media usage approaches can be classified as passive or active, proactive or reactive, and tactical or strategic uses (Sinclaire and Vogus, 2011).

Strategic approach to the social media usage brings fruitful results for organizations. In a survey conducted by Batikas and Bravel (2013) 61% of the users claimed to have a planned strategy for their social media use. A greater percentage of those who had a formal strategy considered that their financial situation has improved, compared to those who did not have a formal strategy. However, none of the participants interviewed used metrics or incorporated externally collected data to their strategy. The main reasons given were lack of time and lack of human or financial resources (Batikas & Bavel, 2013).

In addition to the strategic approach to social media use, having a social media policy is also very important. However many organizations are missing critical social media use policies and implementation strategies. At best, they are not leveraging the potential power of social media, at worst, they are exposed to social media related risks and inappropriate use by their members (Barkan, 2011). Despite strong interest in social media, the lack of strategy, policies, guidelines for employees, training, monitoring, and evaluation in relation to social media are decreasing the effectiveness of these tools (Macnamara & Zerfass, 2012).

A good and clear policy on what constitutes an unacceptable use of social media will help both the employer and the employee to understand where the boundaries between acceptable and non-acceptable use lie. It is advisable to carry out some type of research beforehand, involve all stakeholders. This will make the policy much stronger and more widely accepted. The joint development of a policy may also enable the parties to strike a balance between individual freedom of speech and actions that could have a negative effect on the employer (Broughton et al., 2009).

Well prepared social media usage policy will guide all the related parties. Especially younger generations who are more conversant with social networking sites are more prone to use them less careful. Inattentive employees may easly post something unappropriate on a social networking site and it can create serious problems. Education and reminders to staff on these types of issues should therefore be a key part of any policy on the use of social media. Social networking sites tend to blur the boundaries between public and private life. Therefore employers should make clear to all the employees what is acceptable and what is unacceptable on social networking sites. Employees should be informed about posting sensitive information on social networking sites such as personal and financial information etc. (Broughton et al., 2009).

Social media plans, policies and strategies should also be regularly reviewed and developed. Because the world of social networking and online media are moving at a fast pace (Broughton et al., 2009). Ethical and legal sides of social media usage should be updated properly.

## Social Media Professionals, Training, and Development of Social Media Users

Social media usage requires expertise about information and communication technologies, social media platforms, ethical and legal issues related to the social media usage etc. Therefore organization should hire social media professionals and / or train and develop current personnel responsible from organization's social media operations.

Usage of social media effectively requires more skills and resources. Especially managing the organization's presence in different channels effectively necessitates abilities of coordination and control (Batikas & Bavel, 2013). Training and education of PR and corporate communication practitioners in social media practices, not simply the technologies, is an important step towards achieving that balance in organizational social media engagement (Macnamara and Zerfass, 2012).

In the vast majority of organizations, no one person is being made responsible for social media which creates lack of accountability. Social media is being assigned to staff without removing any existing responsibilities because of personnel shortages. In 90% of the organizations surveyed the social media effort has no dedicated budget or staff resources. ROI and objectives are either not defined, or are not being measured which results from lack of a coherent strategy. Nevertheless organizations are struggling to both measure and to grow engagement in their social media communities (Barkan, 2011).

Many employers have been quick to use social media to recruit staff. Others have been adept at allowing employees to use social media in the workplace to develop business and commercial relationships. Some employers have simply been keen to use social media as a better way of engaging with its staff and fostering a more collegiate environment. However this casual approach to social media is not ideal one. Therefore many organizations will be familiar with the news stories of employees misusing social media at or outside of work to the disadvantage of their employer (Abate et al., 2011).

## Potential Benefits of Social Media Usage for Organizations

Social media are business imperative for modern organizations. Organizations in private, public and nongovernmental sectors use social media for marketing, advertising, employee recruitment, and overall communications with their employees, clients, and partners. Organizations utilize social media to create brand image, recruit new employees, and obtain information about people, products and services in the marketplace (Schultz et al., 2015). Social media are seen as a cost effective tool to enhance understanding about markets, customers, and competitors (DiStaso et al., 2011). Social media are not only a communication platform; it is a huge marketplace too. Plenty of organizations use social media to market organizational activities, remain relevant to key constituencies, and enhance community awareness (Campbell, et al., 2014).

The most important perceived benefit of social media for SMEs is their effectiveness for marketing. SMEs who have a planned strategy appreciate the benefits of social media more than those who do not have a planned strategy (Batikas & Bavel, 2013).

Social media have the potential to change a wide variety of management practices in nonprofit and public organizations too. Technological developments such as mobile devices and social media are causing an ongoing transformation in the nonprofit sector as well as in private sector. Aforementioned developments change the nonprofit organizations from the way supporters engage with their favorite nonprofits to the way organizations fundraise, market, and manage information. Tremendous opportunities exist for nonprofit organizations using the technology to deliver their messages and accomplish their goals and objectives effectively.Social networks such as Facebook, LinkedIn, and Twitterprovide access to networks of potential donors, volunteers, members, alumni, patrons, and supporters (Westmoreland, 2014). In other words, social media become important channels to communicate between non-profit organizations and community (Attouni and Mustaffa, 2014).

The social media explosion has significantly impacted how organizations communicate with their various publics through sites such as Facebook and Twitter. However, research has found that most nonprofits are not taking full advantage of social media. Moreover, the organizations that did use social media typically employed one-way communication strategies primarily on information dissemination (Sisco and McCorkindale, 2013). According to Waters et al., (2009) although nonprofits are open and transparent with their Facebook profiles, they are not using the sites to their full potential to inform others and get them involved with organizational activities. Nonprofit organizations overwhelmingly prefer to use their website to cultivate relationships with their stakeholders. The results of Waters and Feneley' study (2013) demonstrated that the organizations' websites were used significantly more often than their organizations' official Facebook pages for these efforts. After analyzing 4655 tweets, Lovejoy et al., (2012) found that the United States' largest nonprofits are not using Twitter to maximize stakeholder involvement. Instead, they continue to use social media as a one-way communication channel. Findings indicate that the use of social media is scarce, particularly pertaining to content related to fostering stakeholder involvement. Moreover, the factors "network activity", "internationalization" and "experience in social media" are significant predictors of the use of this tool as a channel for communication and dialogue (Galvez-Radriguez et al., 2014). Campbell et al., (2014) examined social media use among nonprofit organizations and country departments involved in the delivery of human services in a six-county area in South-central New York State. The study found that a modest number of non-profit organizations were using Facebook, and few were using other forms of social media.

Although YouTube is just one of many social media tools a nonprofit can use to expand its audience, it is an important one for any organizations to consider given its popularity and its ability to strengthen an organization's identity and brand. According to the research of Waters, and Jones (2011) nonprofit organizations primarily use their YouTube videos to inform and educate viewers about their missions, programs, and services. While the videos also occasionally discuss the organizations' advocacy, volunteering, and fundraising efforts, nonprofit organizations were not living up to their potential in terms of engagement through direct appeals for involvement.

Social media and social networking sites can have specific benefits in the employment relations context. For example, by allowing employees to blog organizations can have a chance to present the human face of a company, allowing employees the freedom to use social networking sites can therefore be a positive step towards goo employer-employee relationships (Broughton et al., 2009). In other words, social media may help to create more human business environment and help to create close touch with employees and customers. Social media can enhance trust among employees too. In return trust may enhance knowledge exchange in the workplace. Specifically, according to Cao et al., (2012) social media enhance knowledge transfer by fostering trust among employees, thus leading to better work performance. According to Barkan's study (2011) people from all age groups are using social media to a high degree to meet a portion of their professional networking, information sharing and professional development needs today (Barkan, 2011).

There are a range of benefits available to employers using social media for recruitment purposes, centering on cost and time savings. Organizations that use tools such as LinkedIn for recruiting to senior and strategic positions instead of using agencies or head-hunters are finding that this results in significant cost savings. Furthermore, social media can help organizations to target their recruitment more accurately, present a realistic picture of their workplace, and reach a wider range of potential candidates. This combination of reach that is at the same time wider and more targeted is very interesting for recruiting organizations. Social media can also help companies to increase brand-awareness and two-way communication with potential candidates, fostering realistic expectations on the part of potential candidates. It can also mean that some individuals can be deterred from applying at an earlier stage, as they are able to gain a realistic impression of an organization before starting the application process. This saves time and money for both the individual and the company (Broughton et al., 2013). Social media are widely used for job searching in Turkey. %64 of people who search job use social media. LinkedIn is the most used (%53) social media for job searching (Adecco Group, 2014).

Organizations can enrich their communication channels and instruments with social media platforms. Social media are an important element of an overall communications mix. However they are not yet in a position to replace traditional communications channels. Email remains a prime communication tool and should be used in tandem with your social media campaigns. Search Engine Optimization (SEO) is another critical element that should be reflected in organizations' overall communications planning and activities (Barkan, 2011). Treem and Leonardi (2012) uncovered four relatively consistent affordances enabled by social media for organizations: visibility, persistence, editability, and association.

Some employers are making use of social media to promote and access employee voice. Use of social media is largely focused externally on marketing and engaging with customers. Fewer employers – only around one in six – use an enterprise social network internally to engage with employees and promote employee voice. Larger organizations and certain sectors such as information and communication are more likely to use social media to promote employee voice. Enterprise social networks are potentially a very powerful tool for employee voice. There is certainly evidence that more needs to be done to promote voice, with just one UK employee in three saying their managers are good at allowing them to influence decision-making. Some types of enterprise social networks can potentially help to promote a richer employee voice, allowing organizations to go beyond monologue and one-way communication to two-way and indeed multi-directional communication. Using such networks for employee voice provides the opportunity for organizations to drive insight and innovation. It also has immense potential to support collaboration, allowing employers to access 'the wisdom of crowds' – where, rather than an individual, groups of people work together to reach a solution or an outcome (Dormey, 2016).

## Risks and Barriers of Social Media Usage for Organizations

Using social media may create some rewards as well as risks. Therefore organizations should develop policies and strategies to minimize risks related to social media usage in the workplace. Given the growing use of social media in the workplace and the associated risks, organizations should consider a proactive approach to ensure that social media use does not damage the organizations. To accomplish this, employers should stay informed and current about evolving laws and rules affecting social media use in the workplace. Clear social media policies and procedures are required to effectively manage the issues emerging from social media usage (Schultz et al., 2015).

Using social media professionally requires some amount of costs. There is the actual cost of dedicating resources to social media sites, as traffic can be significant and unpredictable. There are also issues surrounding the accuracy of the information gained by the use of social media tools – there is no guarantee that the information that individuals, or others, post on their SNSs is accurate. There are also issues around the depth of the applicant pool that social media tools can access, giving rise to potential problems around diversity and discrimination, particularly in terms of reaching older candidates and those who are not as comfortable with using computers. This means that there are a number of legal aspects that employers should consider when thinking about using social media tools for recruitment. These include difficulties arising from HR decisions based on inaccurate information, issues related to employee privacy, equality and diversity and the use of standardized information about candidates. Furthermore, given the diversity of information about individuals available on social networking sites, it is difficult to see how this can be fairly compared (Broughton et al., 2013).

Misusing social media by employees is another risk for organizations. It is now clear that employers and employees both need to consider how social media sites may affect employment. Many organizations will soon be all too familiar with the news stories of employees misusing social media at or outside of work to the disadvantage of their employer. Some stories have featured employees who have been dismissed after posting inappropriate comments about colleagues or their employer. Quite often, the legal issues that lie beneath these stories are overlooked. For example, is it lawful to vet job applicants using social media sites? What legal risks arise when permitting employees to use social media at work? How can an employer manage the risks that arise. Although the risks that arise from the use of social media sometimes vary, the solutions that have been recommended to manage these risks are more or less the same (Abate et al., 2011). Having a social media usage policy, monitoring the usage of social media regularly and giving training and education to all related parties are the common solutions.

Potential risks and barriers block to collect all the benefits from social media in organizations. In other words, employers are far from exploiting the full potential of enterprise social networks and social media. Some of these barriers are as follow: Many employers and employees do not yet see the relevance of enterprise social networks in the workplace. In addition to this, many managers are concerned that using these networks at work could lead to time-wasting and impact on productivity negatively. There are big concerns around the potential misuse of social media at work. The perception of a fear of loss of control seems to be a concern to employers, as enterprise social networks allow for interaction between staff and fewer opportunities to control the conversation. Some employers are also skeptical about the demand for enterprise social networks within organizations and the extent to which it would be used (Dormey, 2016).

Contrary to the general expectation, the lack of financial resources is not a barrier to adopting social media. Users who are in a better financial situation do not think that lack of financial resources, lack of control and risk of inappropriate posting by employees are barriers (Batikas & Bavel, 2013).

## Performance Evaluation of Social Media

Organizations from government departments and corporations to small businesses are increasingly adopting social media for strategic corporate and organizational communication and public relations. This is seen by many as a positive development because the openness of the Web 2.0 environment potentially democratizes voice and affords participation, dialogue, and community-building. However, optimistic views of the benefits of organizational social media communication fail to adequately take account of potential conflict between the philosophy of openness that characterizes Web 2.0 and organizational strategy and management processes. However, organizational social media communication is most often undertaken without clear objectives and it is not integrated with other organizational communication, and not evaluated against objectives and Key Performance Indicators. This is most likely a result of the relative newness of social media (Macnamara and Zerfass, 2012).

Companies should take certain steps to harvest the fruits of social media. Authentic and trustworthy leaders should help those people develop social media skills. Leaders should support to build social media communities that emphasize authenticity, pride, attachment and fun. In other words, leaders should build emotional capital. Without developing emotional capital in organization, it is not realistic to expect instrumental benefits such as improved information exchange, motivation, morale, reduced turnover etc. The role of social media in building emotional capital became apparent. Executives whose social media initiatives had increased emotional capital for their company reported that social media made it easier to communicate both across hierarchical levels (vertical communication) and functional units (horizontal communication). However, companies where social media had not increased emotional capital found that social media had little impact on the ease of communication in the company and in some cases even aggravated existing problems (Huy and Shipilov, 2012).

The use of social media enhances business capabilities and business performance. The impact is not due to one social media tools only, but due to successfully combining the several social media tools into one effective social media ecosystem that enables coordination between internal and external business processes.A combination of inter-linked social media forms a social media ecosystem that enhances business capabilities. In other words, Empirical evidence supports that the use of social media enhances business capabilities and enhanced business capabilities lead to improved business process performance (Smits and Mogos, 2013).

## Recommendation for Effective Social Media Usage

Harvesting the benefits and limiting the relevant risks of social media require certain precautions to be taken. Following are worth to be mentioned:

Organizations should have an internet / social media use policy that sets out clearly and explicitly the organization's expectations of and definitions of acceptable and unacceptable behavior. Policies should advise employees to assume that everything they say on the internet could at some point be made public and to think about whether, for example, the comment they are about to post on a social networking site is something that they would want a colleague, their boss or a senior manager to read. The policy on internet/social media use should be drawn up in consultation with staff, either through their representatives, if present, or directly, if no representatives are present. A prior survey of employee awareness of issues can help to achieve buy-in to future policy. Consultation with staff on the actual policy will help to ensure that it is fair. This participative process will help to build employee commitment to the policy and raise awareness of the fact that a policy is being formulated, which may be important for dissemination. A policy on internet use needs to be communicated. Managers need to ensure that individuals understand the policy and may need to think carefully about how they explain and justify it, which may need to vary between staff groups (Broughton et al., 2009).

Organizations should explain acceptable and unacceptable behavior, as well as the consequences of violation. (Broughton et al., 2009) Social media policy should underline disciplinary actions (Abate et al., 2011). This means being open to a loss of some control, trusting staff and resisting the temptation to restrict the conversation. Senior leaders play an essential role in helping to create the culture of employee voice, by promoting the tools, encouraging employees to use them, and by using them themselves. Having champions across the organization that encourage others to use the technology can also be effective. Using an enterprise social network is most effective when its goals are explicit and it is clearly seen as a tool for work related discussions. For this to happen it needs to be designed to improve organizational performance and working life. However, permitting some non-work usage can be helpful in encouraging use and building a sense of community (Dormey, 2016).

Organizations should make sure that there are adequate mechanisms for employees to raise formal and informal grievances (Broughton et al., 2009).

Employees and customers should be encouraged to involve social media interactions. Employees may write blogs etc. (Broughton et al., 2009). Employees should be encouraged to speak up and their views should be listened to and, where possible, acted on (Dormey, 2016).

Employers should keep up to date in developments in employment law relating to social media such as privacy. It is advisable to consider potential legal issues, particularly those surrounding data protection and privacy, even if these have not as yet been an issue to contend with (Broughton et al., 2009). it is recommended that social media policies be put in place, appropriate training be provided to employees and appropriate confidentiality clauses and post-termination restrictive covenants be incorporated into contracts of employment (Abate et al., 2011). Cyber-bullying is something that is linked to the rise of social networking tools, although the evidence in terms of workplace cyber-bullying is scant. Nevertheless, employers should work on developing strong anti-bullying policies that are updated in the light of new kinds of technology, and need to bear in mind the fact that that cyber-bullying can occur outside the workplace to a much greater extent than conventional bullying, making it harder for employers to deal with easily. It will probably be the case that cyber-bullying will largely be covered by existing policies on bullying, and so policies or guidance on the use of social networking sites just need to refer employees back to the organization's bullying policy. (Broughton et al., 2009).

Employers need to consider reviewing policies on internet use/social media on a regular basis. Regular policy reviews involving all key stakeholders will ensure that policies address the organization's main concerns. (Broughton et al., 2009)

If you are using social media for recruitment practices, it is necessary to verify information on applicants' SNSs through other means. It should be borne in mind that the information there may not be accurate – at the least, it may be a site created by the applicant for job application purposes etc. (Broughton et al., 2013).

Do not over-invest in social media tools It is wise to adopt a fairly cautious approach in terms of investment in social media tools, as it is difficult to predict which tools will become popular and which will become obsolete. Close monitoring of trends is advisable. Social networking tools cannot entirely replace face-to-face contact. (Broughton et al., 2013).

Always search cost effective approaches to social media usage. Social media creates financial and personnel costs etc. (Broughton et al., 2013).

Provide training and information for those involved in using social media applications and technologies. (Broughton et al., 2013).

Do not lose control of the security of SNSs It is easy for organizations to lose control of media such as Twitter – it is possible for individual employees to hold access codes that no other company representative has. It is therefore advisable to put into place protocols relating to passwords and accounts so that individual employees are not the sole guardians of security information. Organizations should remember that social media are an informal medium and its use is relatively relaxed. In this context, innovation and an open mind are crucial –organizations wishing to use social media should not be afraid to engage (Broughton et al., 2013).

In order for enterprise social networks to be effective, there needs to be an organizational culture that supports employee voice. An enterprise social network will not change the culture of an organization on its own, but it does need a supportive environment to work effectively. Organizations should go with the grain of the technology (Dormey, 2016).

Organizations should have a robust social media policy – developed with staff involvement – which sets expectations for use. This should be based on common sense, clearly communicating to staff that the same rules apply online as offline. Such policies can help prevent misuse and protect employers in rare cases where this does happen. An enterprise social network should be integrated with other voice platforms rather than being used to replace them. Having a variety of voice channels will suit different circumstances and different personal preferences. Enterprise social networks are very promising tools which offer huge potential for employee voice. They could help transform how organizations communicate with staff and access their voice, how they involve them, how they collaborate and innovate. But this potential seems to be largely under-used. Few employers are using social media internally – in the form of an enterprise social network -for voice, and where they are, success has been limited. There are strong signs that where employers are using enterprise social networks, they are doing so in a way which doesn't go with the grain of the technology. They are using a modern tool, designed for networking and open-communication, bottom-up, user-generated content, in a more traditional way, which is top-down and controlled. If employers wish to get the best out of social media and unleash its potential, they should use it in a way that matches the technology's capabilities, and ensure it is part of a wider approach to supporting voice at work. (Dormey, 2016).

In the coming part, social media usage practices and habits of Turkish Chambers of Commerce and Industry will be discussed. Turkish Chambers of Commerce and Industry is a semi-public institution. There is no empirical study about the social media usage of Turkish Chambers of Commerce and Industry in the literature. Therefore this research is first in this area.

## METHODOLOGY

An online survey was conducted with members of the Union of Chambers and Commodity Exchanges of Turkey using the Bilecik Seyh Edebali University's online survey system. The Union of Chambers and Commodity Exchanges of Turkey (In Turkish is TOBB) is the highest legal entity in Turkey representing the private sector and today, it has 365 members in the form of local chambers of commerce, industry, commerce and industry, maritime commerce and commodity exchanges, operating in 81 provinces and 160 districts in Turkey (TOBB, 2016). There are 181 chambers of commerce and industry, 57 chambers of commerce, 12 chambers of industry, 2 chambers of maritime commerce and 113 commodity exchanges connected to TOBB in Turkey. This study includes only 252 chambers, excluding commodity exchanges.

An online survey was conducted between March 31, 2016 and May 31, 2016. An email with the link to the online survey was sent to total of 238 chambers. Since we could not find e-mail address of 14 chambers, they are excluded from the study. During this period, a reminder e-mail was sent three times to participants who had not responded to the initial request. We received 61 completed and 72 uncompleted survey questionnaires.

Questionnaire items related to perception of benefits and barriers are adopted from Batikas & Bavel (2013) and items related to reasons for not using social media are adopted from Rhoads (2012).

## DATA ANALYSIS

### Respondent Characteristics

The distribution of respondents by gender and education reported in Table 1 reveals that 19.7% of the respondents were female and 80.3% male. As for the education level, majority of the respondents (83.6%) has a university degree (associate or bachelor degree), 8.2% of the respondents have a secondary education (high school) and 6.6% of the respondents stated having a postgraduate degree.

### Characteristics of Participant Chambers

Characteristics of participant Chambers are provided in Table 2. Most of the participant chambers (55.7%) established after the year of 1950. Participant Chambers are distributed according to the number of their members as follow: 14.8 percent of the participant Chambers have less than 500 members, 27.9 percent has between 501 and 1000, 21.3 percent has between 1001 and 1500, and remaining has

*Table 1. Respondent characteristics*

| | n | % |
|---|---|---|
| | **Gender** | |
| Female | 12 | 19.7 |
| Male | 49 | 80.3 |
| | **Education** | |
| High school | 5 | 8.2 |
| University | 51 | 83.6 |
| Postgraduate degree | 4 | 6.6 |
| Missing value | 1 | 1.6 |

more than 1500 members. Turkish Chambers Accreditation System was introduced by TOBB in 2001. Majority of the participant Chambers are accredited. There are only eight Chambers reported that they are not accredited by TOBB. 24.6 percent of the participant Chambers accredited as "A" class, 32.8 percent accredited as "B" and 29.5 percent accredited as "C" class. Number of personnel employed in Chambers varies. Majority of the participant Chambers (72.1%) employ between 1 and 10 personnel, 16.4 percent employ between 11 and 20 personnel, 4.9 percent employ between 21 and 30 personnel and only 6.6 percent employ more than 30 personnel.

## Website and Social Media Use by Chambers

Vast majority of the participant Chambers own a website (98.4%) and use social media officially (95.1%). There is only one Chamber reported to not have a website and three Chambers reported that they were not represented in social media officially.

## The Reasons for Not Using Social Media Officially

In the questionnaire, we asked the reasons for not using social media officially to not users. Two answered this question as "Fear of liability or malpractice concerns" and one answered as "Too much work". (Table 4)

## Social Media Platforms Used by Participant Chambers and Frequency

Facebook and Twitter are the most popular platforms. All the Chambers using social media use Facebook (58 Chambers), 42 Chambers use Twitter and 13 Chambers use YouTube. Two Chambers reported that they use six social media platforms listed in Table 5, one Chamber reported one, two Chambers reported two social media platforms and 15 Chambers reported that they use only one social media platform which is Facebook listed in Table 5.

*Table 2. Characteristics of participant chambers*

| Establishment Year of Participant Chambers | n | % |
|---|---|---|
| < 1900 | 7 | 11.5 |
| 1901-1925 | 13 | 21.3 |
| 1926-1950 | 7 | 11.5 |
| 1951-1975 | 18 | 29.5 |
| 1976- 2000 | 16 | 26.2 |
| >2000 | 0 | 0.0 |
| **Number of Members** | **n** | **%** |
| < 500 | 9 | 14.8 |
| 501-1000 | 17 | 27.9 |
| 1001-1500 | 13 | 21.3 |
| 1501-2000 | 4 | 6.6 |
| 2001-2500 | 3 | 4.9 |
| 2501-3000 | 3 | 4.9 |
| 3001-3500 | 4 | 6.6 |
| >3500 | 8 | 13.1 |
| **TOBB Accreditation Level** | **n** | **%** |
| No accredited | 8 | 13.1 |
| A | 15 | 24.6 |
| B | 20 | 32.8 |
| C | 18 | 29.5 |
| **Have a Public Relations Department** | **n** | **%** |
| Yes | 27 | 44.3 |
| No | 34 | 55.7 |
| **Number of Personnel** | **n** | **%** |
| 1-10 | 44 | 72.1 |
| 11-20 | 10 | 16.4 |
| 21-30 | 3 | 4.9 |
| >30 | 4 | 6.6 |
| **Total** | **61** | **100.0** |

*Table 3. Website and social media use by chambers*

| Own a website | n | % |
|---|---|---|
| Yes | 60 | 98.4 |
| No | 1 | 1.6 |
| **Represented in Social Media Officially** | **n** | **%** |
| Yes | 58 | 95.1 |
| No | 3 | 4.9 |

*Table 4. The Reasons for not using social media officially**

| Reasons | n |
|---|---|
| Social media is just a fad; it's not worth bothering with | 0 |
| Fear of liability or malpractice concerns | 2 |
| Concern that users will post negative comments about your organization | 0 |
| Too much work | 1 |
| Lack social media expertise | 0 |

*Respondents were allowed to choose more than one option.

*Table 5. Social media platforms used by participant chambers**

| Social Media Platforms | n | % |
|---|---|---|
| Facebook | 58 | 100 |
| Twitter | 42 | 72.4 |
| YouTube | 13 | 22.4 |
| LinkedIn | 5 | 8.6 |
| Blogs | 0 | 0.0 |
| Pinterest | 2 | 3.4 |
| Instagram | 7 | 12.4 |
| Other | 3 | 5.2 |

* Respondents were allowed to choose more than one option.

*Table 6. Which of the following social media platforms does your chamber use the most?*

| | n | % |
|---|---|---|
| Facebook | 52 | 89.7 |
| Twitter | 5 | 8.6 |
| YouTube | 0 | 0 |
| LinkedIn | 0 | 0 |
| Blogs | 0 | 0 |
| Pinterest | 0 | 0 |
| Instagram | 0 | 0 |
| Other | 1 | 1.7 |
| Total | 58 | 100.0 |

*Table 7. How long have your Chamber been using social media officially?*

| | n | % |
|---|---|---|
| Less than 4 months | 1 | 1.7 |
| Between 4-8 months | 0 | 0.0 |
| Between 8-12 months | 2 | 3.4 |
| Between 1-2 years | 13 | 22.4 |
| Between 2-3 years | 10 | 17.2 |
| Between 3-4 years | 14 | 24.1 |
| Between 4-5 years | 6 | 10.3 |
| More than 5 years | 12 | 20.7 |
| **Total** | **58** | **100.0** |

## Duration of Social Media Usage

Vast majority of the participant Chambers (94.9%) reported that they have been using social media officially for more than one year. Only three Chambers reported that they have been using social media officially for one year or less (Table 7)

### Availability of Social Media Usage Plan and Responsible Department

32 participant Chambers (55.2%) reported that they have a clear official social media use policy/plan (Table 8) and 38 participant Chambers (65.5%) reported that they have a department responsible for social media (Table 9).

*Table 8. Does your Chamber have a clear official social media use policy/plan?*

| | n | % |
|---|---|---|
| Yes | 32 | 55.2 |
| No | 26 | 44.8 |
| **Total** | **58** | **100.0** |

*Table 9. Does your chamber have a department responsible for social media?*

| | n | % |
|---|---|---|
| Yes | 38 | 65.5 |
| No | 20 | 34.5 |
| **Total** | **58** | **100.0** |

## Availability of Social Media Experts / Specialists

36 participant Chambers (62.1%) reported that there is only one personnel responsible for social media in the Chamber, 13 Chambers (22.4%) reported two personnel and 5 Chambers (8.6%) reported more than two personnel responsible for social media in the Chamber. 4 Chambers reported that there is no personnel responsible for social media.

## Possible Outcomes of Social Media Experiences

We asked to participants that overall, how you would rate your Chamber's experience with social media. The Chambers we surveyed generally rated positive. 36 Chambers (62.1%) rated as positive, 20 Chambers (34.5%) rated as average and only one rated as negative.

## Overall Usefulness of Social Media Usage

We asked to participant that how you rate how useful social media for the Chamber. Most of the participants agree that social media is useful for the Chamber. 30 Chambers (51.7%) rated as "Very useful", 16 Chambers (27.6%) rated as "Very much useful". Only one rated as "Not at all useful".

## Necessity of a Training Program for Social Media Usage

36 participants (62.1%) think that the Chamber does not need training for social media (Table 13). It seems that most of the participants underestimate social media and they do not believe that social media usage requires special training.

*Table 10. How many personnel have responsible for social media in the Chamber?*

| | n | % |
|---|---|---|
| 0 | 4 | 6.9 |
| 1 | 36 | 62.1 |
| 2 | 13 | 22.4 |
| >2 | 5 | 8.6 |
| **Total** | **58** | **100.0** |

*Table 11. Overall, how would you rate your Chamber's experience with social media?*

| | n | % |
|---|---|---|
| Too early to evaluate | 1 | 1.7 |
| Negative | 1 | 1.7 |
| Average | 20 | 34.5 |
| Positive | 36 | 62.1 |
| **Total** | **58** | **100.0** |

*Table 12. How useful is social media for the Chamber*

| | n | % |
|---|---|---|
| Not at all useful | 1 | 1.7 |
| Very little useful | 2 | 3.4 |
| Slightly useful | 9 | 15.5 |
| Very useful | 30 | 51.7 |
| Very much useful | 16 | 27.6 |
| **Total** | **58** | **100.0** |

*Table 13. Do you think that your Chamber needs training for social media?*

| | n | % |
|---|---|---|
| Yes | 22 | 37.9 |
| No | 36 | 62.1 |
| **Total** | **58** | **100.0** |

## Recommendation of Social Media Usage to Other Chambers

All of the social media user Chambers recommend the use of social media to the other Chambers and institutions (Table 14).

## Evaluation and Control of Social Media Usage

We asked whether you assess the official use of social media for the Chamber. Most of the participants (65.5%) answered as "Yes".

## Problems Faced by Chambers in the Use of Social Media

We asked a non-compulsory open-ended question "What are the problems your Chamber face in the use of social media?". 12 responses are received for this question. Responses to this question by the participants are listed in Table 16. Main problems faced by Chamber in the use of social media are as follows; negative comments or inappropriate posts, the use of social media among members and lack of personnel.

## Perception About the Benefits of Social Media Usage

Both social media users and non-users participants were asked about the perception of benefits of the use of social media. The question was asked as follows: "To what extent do you agree with each of the following statements about the benefits of using Social Media for business purposes". The questions and the distribution of responses to them are presented in Table 17.

*Table 14. Would you recommend the use of social media to the other Chambers and institutions?*

| | n | % |
|---|---|---|
| Yes | 58 | 100.0 |
| No | 0 | 0.0 |
| **Total** | **58** | **100.0** |

*Table 15. Do you assess the official use of social media for the Chamber?*

| | n | % |
|---|---|---|
| Yes | 38 | 65.5 |
| No | 20 | 34.5 |
| **Total** | **58** | **100.0** |

*Table 16. What are the problems your Chamber face in the use of social media?*

| |
|---|
| Not well-intentioned comments to posts. |
| Since we are a trade body, we have to be careful in communication. Therefore, it can be difficult to prepare content |
| Political or offensive negative personal comments leading to argument and spam users comments |
| Invitation from fake accounts and inappropriate comments. |
| Members cannot be accessed enough because some members do not use social media. |
| In my opinion, social media is not very useful and it may be used for out of institutional objectives. |
| Lack of attention for the posts from audience. |
| Members sometimes show no interest towards posts. Their performance in the using social media is poor. |
| Lack of social media usage habits among members except Facebook. In particular, the use of Twitter in our city is very rare. |
| There are some members who do not have social media habits. |
| Reaching smaller number of audience. |
| Because of personnel shortages, we cannot assign personnel solely for social media. |

Vast majority of the participants agree (agree and strongly agree) with "Social media increases effectiveness of communication and public relations of the Chamber." (100.0%), "Social media increases the speed of accessing knowledge, (It increases speed to access knowledge)" (95.1%), "Social media reduces communication costs." (90.2%) and "Social media reduces communication and public relations costs of the Chamber." (90.2%) as the benefits of using social media. These participants disagree (disagree and strongly disagree) on "Social media is better than any other type of media for the purposes of the Chamber." (19.7%) and "Social media reduces communication costs." (9.8%) as the benefits of using social media.

*Table 17. Perception of benefits of the use of social media*

| | | Strongly Disagree | | Disagree | | Neither Agree Nor Disagree | | Agree | | Strongly Agree | |
|---|---|---|---|---|---|---|---|---|---|---|---|
| | | n | % | n | % | n | % | n | % | n | % |
| 1 | Social media increases the speed of accessing information. | 0 | 0.0 | 2 | 3.3 | 1 | 1.6 | 25 | 41.0 | 33 | 54.1 |
| 2 | Social media reduces communication costs. | 1 | 1.6 | 5 | 8.2 | 0 | 0.0 | 20 | 32.8 | 35 | 57.4 |
| 3 | Social media increases effectiveness of communication and public relations of the Chamber. | 0 | 0.0 | 0 | 0.0 | 0 | 0.0 | 24 | 39.3 | 37 | 60.7 |
| 4 | Social media increases the Chamber's member satisfaction. | 0 | 0.0 | 3 | 4.9 | 5 | 8.2 | 28 | 45.9 | 25 | 41.0 |
| 5 | Social media reduces communication and public relations costs of the Chamber. | 0 | 0.0 | 5 | 8.2 | 1 | 1.6 | 28 | 45.9 | 27 | 44.3 |
| 6 | Social media increases speed to access external experts when needed by the Chamber. | 0 | 0.0 | 4 | 6.6 | 7 | 11.5 | 29 | 47.5 | 21 | 34.4 |
| 7 | Social media is great for engaging with members of the Chamber. | 0 | 0.0 | 3 | 4.9 | 8 | 13.1 | 29 | 47.5 | 21 | 34.4 |
| 8 | Social media is better than any other type of media for the purposes of the Chamber. | 2 | 3.3 | 10 | 16.4 | 10 | 16.4 | 28 | 45.9 | 11 | 18.0 |

## Barriers of the Social Media Usage

Both social media users and non-users participants were asked about the barriers of the use of social media. The question was asked as follows: "To what extent do you agree with each of the following statements as being a barrier (or risk) for the use of social media for business purposes". The questions and the distribution of responses to them are presented in Table 18.

Approximately half of the respondents agree (agree and strongly agree) with "Legal issues that may arise related to social media." (50.8%); "Concerns about employees gets distracted by social media." (45.9%); "Lack of strategy for the use of social media." (45.9%) and "Lack of demand and willingness to use social media in the Chamber by members of the Chamber." (42.6%) as being barriers of the use of social media. On the contrary, these participants disagree (disagree and strongly disagree) on "Lack of incentives to use social media for employees." (62.3%), "No strong business case to use social media because of the nature of our business." (60.7%), "Lack of financial resources for social media" (59%) and "Costs of the software applications in using social media." (57.4%) as being barriers of the use of social media.

*Table 18. Barriers of the use of social media*

| | | Strongly Disagree | | Disagree | | Neither Agree Nor Disagree | | Agree | | Strongly Agree | |
|---|---|---|---|---|---|---|---|---|---|---|---|
| | | n | % | n | % | n | % | n | % | n | % |
| 1 | Lack of financial resources for social media | 12 | 19.7 | 24 | 39.3 | 8 | 13.1 | 13 | 21.3 | 4 | 6.6 |
| 2 | Lack of control of social media / risk of inappropriate posting by employees. | 4 | 6.6 | 21 | 34.4 | 13 | 21.3 | 20 | 32.8 | 3 | 4.9 |
| 3 | Concerns about employees get distracted by social media. | 3 | 4.9 | 18 | 29.5 | 12 | 19.7 | 23 | 37.7 | 5 | 8.2 |
| 4 | No strong business case to use social media because of the nature of our business. | 9 | 14.8 | 28 | 45.9 | 11 | 18.0 | 10 | 16.4 | 3 | 4.9 |
| 5 | Lack of incentives to use social media for employees. | 5 | 8.2 | 33 | 54.1 | 14 | 23.0 | 9 | 14.8 | 0 | 0.0 |
| 6 | Concerns on loss of data, privacy in social media | 3 | 4.9 | 17 | 27.9 | 17 | 27.9 | 19 | 31.1 | 5 | 8.2 |
| 7 | Costs of human resources implementing/using social media. | 7 | 11.5 | 21 | 34.4 | 14 | 23.0 | 16 | 26.2 | 3 | 4.9 |
| 8 | Costs of the software applications in using social media. | 7 | 11.5 | 28 | 45.9 | 13 | 21.3 | 11 | 18.0 | 2 | 3.3 |
| 9 | Lack of skills for the use of social media. | 5 | 8.2 | 24 | 39.3 | 14 | 23.0 | 16 | 26.2 | 2 | 3.3 |
| 10 | Lack of strategy for the use of social media. | 5 | 8.2 | 18 | 29.5 | 10 | 16.4 | 25 | 41.0 | 3 | 4.9 |
| 11 | Lack of demand and willingness to use social media in the Chamber by members of the Chamber. | 6 | 9.8 | 20 | 32.8 | 9 | 14.8 | 18 | 29.5 | 8 | 13.1 |
| 12 | Legal issues that may arise related to social media. | 4 | 6.6 | 13 | 21.3 | 13 | 21.3 | 23 | 37.7 | 8 | 13.1 |

## CONCLUSION AND DISCUSSION

An online survey was conducted with 238 members of The Union of Chambers and Commodity Exchanges of Turkey. Only 133 members answered the questionnaire. Following findings are noteworthy to be underlined:

- Most of the participant chambers (55.7%) established after the year of 1950. Majority of the participant chambers are accredited. Majority of those (72.1%) employ between 1 and 10 personnel.
- Vast majority of the participant chambers own a website (98.4%) and use social media officially (95.1%).
- Facebook and Twitter are the most popular platforms. 58 chambers use Facebook; 42 chambers use Twitter and 13 Chambers use YouTube.
- Vast majority of the participant chambers (94.9%) reported that they have been using social media officially for more than one year.
- 32 chambers (55.2%) reported that they have a clear official social media use policy / plan and 38 chambers (65.5%) reported that they have a department responsible for social media.
- 36 chambers (62.1%) reported that there is only one personnel responsible for social media in the chamber.
- The chambers surveyed generally (%62.1) rated positive their social media usage experience. 34.5% of chambers rated as average and only one rated as negative.
- Most of the participants (79.3%) agree that social media is useful for the chamber.
- 36 Participant chambers (62.1%) think that the chamber does not need a training program for social media usage.
- All of the chambers which use social media recommend to the other chambers and institutions to use social media.
- Most of the participants (65.5%) evaluate and control the social media usage / performance.
- Most of the problems related to the social media usage seem to be reparable in nature with proper training programs.
- Vast majority of the participants believe that 1) Social media increases effectiveness of communication and public relations of the chamber. 2) Social media helps to increase the speed of accessing necessary information. 3) Social media reduces communication and public relations costs of the chamber. 4) Social media increases the chamber's member satisfaction. 5) Social media helps to increase the speed to access external experts when needed by the chamber. 6) Social media is great for engaging with members of the chamber.
- Major barriers that block the usage of social media for business purposes are as follow: 1) Legal issues that may arise related to social media. 2) Lack of strategy for the use of social media. 3) Concerns about employees may get distracted by social media. 4) Lack of demand and willingness to use social media in the chamber by members of the chamber. 5) Concerns on loss of data, privacy in social media. 6) Lack of control of social media / risk of inappropriate posting by employees.

In conclusion, as semi-public professional organizations the Turkish Chambers of Commerce and Industry has a good performance about social media usage. Almost all the participant chambers use one or several social media platforms. However, there are some skeptics about the necessity and the usefulness of social media. The Turkish Chambers of Commerce and Industry should hire professional social media experts and keep them up to date with appropriate training programs.

## REFERENCES


Abate, D., Hoffman, D., Robertson, N., Rogers, A., & Zeppenfeld, G. (2011). *The Use of Social Media in the Workplace*. Mayer-Brown. Retrieved from https://www.mayerbrown.com/public_docs/TheUseofSocialMediainTheWorkplace.pdf

Acılar, A. (2015). The Use of Social Media in the Higher Education Institutions in Turkey: A Case of the Higher Education Institutions in Istanbul. In Strategic Customer Relationship Management in the Age of Social Media (pp. 95-107). Hershey, PA: Business Science Reference. DOI: doi:10.4018/978-1-4666-8586-4.ch006

Acılar, A., & Mersin, S. (2015). Undergraduate Students' Attitudes Toward Facebook Use. *CKS 2015 – Challenges of the Knowledge Society*. Retrieved from http://cks.univnt.ro/download/138_cks_2015.pdf

Adecco Group. (2014). *GlobalRecruiting – A Global Study*. Rapor 2014 Türkiye. Author.

Aghaei, S., Nematbakhsh, M. A., & Farsani, H. K. (2012). Evolution of the World Wide Web: From Web 1 to Web 4. *International Journal of Web & Semantic Technology*, *3*(1), 1–10. doi:10.5121/ijwest.2012.3101

Andzulis, J., Panagopoulos, N. G., & Rapp, A. (2012). A review of social media and implications for the sales process. *Journal of Personal Selling & Sales Management*, *32*(3), 305–316. doi:10.2753/PSS0885-3134320302

Arslan, G. (2014). *The Use of Social Media By Labour Unions in Turkey* (Master Thesis). Pamukkale University, Graduate School of Social Sciences, Labour Economics and Industrial Relations Department, Denizli.

Attouni, M. A. K., & Mustaffa, C. S. (2014). How do Non-profit Organizations in Libya Adopt and Use Social Media to Communicate with The Society, The International Conference on Communications and Media 2014 (i-COME14), 1820 October 2014, Langkawi, Malaysia. *Procedia: Social and Behavioral Sciences*, *155*, 92–97. doi:10.1016/j.sbspro.2014.10.262

Barkan, T. (2011). *Special Report: How are the members of associations using social media today?* SOCIALSTRAT, Professional Social Media Strategy.

Batikas, M., & Bavel, R. (2013). *Assessing the Benefits of Social Networks for Organizations*. Report on the Second Phase of the SEA-SoNS Project, Publications Office. Retrieved from ftp://s-jrcsvqpx102p.jrc.es/pub/EURdoc/EURdoc/JRC85669.pdf

Bennett, S., Bishop, A., Dalgarno, B., Waycott, J., & Kennedy, G. (2012). Implementing Web 2.0 technologies in higher education: A collective case study. *Computers & Education*, *59*(2), 524–534. doi:10.1016/j.compedu.2011.12.022

Boyd, D. M., & Ellison, N. B. (2008). Social network sites: Definition, history, and scholarship. *Journal of Computer-Mediated Communication*, *13*(1), 210–230. doi:10.1111/j.1083-6101.2007.00393.x

Broughton, A., Foley, B., & Cox, A. (2013). *The Use of Social Media in the Recruitment Process*. Institute for Employment Studies. Retrieved from www.acas.org.uk/researchpapers

Broughton, A., Higgins, T., Hicks, B., & Cox, A. (2009). *Workplaces and Social Networking – The Implications for Employment Relations*. Institute for Employment Studies. Retrieved from www.acas.org.uk/researchpapers

Campbell, D. A., Lambright, K. T., & Wells, C. J. (2014). Looking for Friends, Fans, and Followers? Social Media Use in Public and Nonprofit Human Services. *Public Administration Review*, *74*(September-October), 655–663. doi:10.1111/puar.12261

Cao, X., Vogel, D. R., Guo, X., Liu, H., & Gu, J. (2012). Understanding the Influence of Social Media in the Workplace: An Integration of Synchronicity and Social Capital Theories. *45th Hawaii International Conference on System Sciences*, 3938-3947. doi:10.1109/HICSS.2012.618

Constantinides, E., & Stagno, M. C. Z. (2011). Potential of the social media as instruments of higher education marketing: A segmentation study. *Journal of Marketing for Higher Education*, *21*(1), 7–24. doi:10.1080/08841241.2011.573593

Curtis, L., Edwards, C., Fraser, K. L., Gudelsky, S., Holmquist, J., Thornton, K., & Sweetser, K. D. (2010). Adoption of social media for public relations by nonprofit organizations. *Public Relations Review*, *36*(1), 90–92. doi:10.1016/j.pubrev.2009.10.003

DiStaso, M. W., McCorkindale, T., & Wright, D. K. (2011). How Public Relations Executives Perceive and Measure the Impact of Social Media in Their Organizations. *Public Relations*, *37*(3), 325–328. doi:10.1016/j.pubrev.2011.06.005

Dormey, J. (2016). *Going Digital? Harnessing Social Media for Emloyee Voice*. The Involvement and Participation Association.

Gálvez-Rodriguez, M. D. M., Caba-Perez, C., & López-Godoy, M. (2014). Facebook: A new communication strategy for non-profit organisations In Colombia. *Public Relations Review*, *40*(5), 868–870. doi:10.1016/j.pubrev.2014.10.002

Gikas, J., & Grant, M. M. (2013). Mobile computing devices in higher education: Student perspectives on learning with cellphones, smartphones & social media. *The Internet and Higher Education*, *19*, 18–26. doi:10.1016/j.iheduc.2013.06.002

Holotescu, C., & Grosseck, G. (2013). An Empirical Analysis Of The Educational Effects Of Social Media In Universities And Colleges. *Internet Learning*, *2*(1), 21–32.

Hosny, M. I., & Fatima, S. (2012). Facebok in education: Students, teachers, and library perspectives. *Journal of Computing*, *4*(6), 78–86.

Huy, Q., & Shipilov, A. (2012). The key to social media success within organizations. *MIT Sloan Management Review*, *54*(1), 72–81.

Jussila, J., Kärkkäinen, H., & Aramo-Immonen, H. (2014). Social media utilization in business-to-business relationships of technology industry firms. *Computers in Human Behavior*, *30*, 606–613. doi:10.1016/j.chb.2013.07.047

Kane, G. C., Alavi, M., Labianca, G., & Borgatti, S. P. (2014). What's different about social media networks? A framework and research agenda. *MIS Querterly*, *38*(1), 274–304.

Kaplan, A. M., & Haenlein, M. (2010). Users of the world, unite! The challenges and opportunities of social media. *Business Horizons*, *53*(1), 59–68. doi:10.1016/j.bushor.2009.09.003

Kovacs, N. O., & Wensley, A. (2015). Social media in organizations: Leveraging knowledge sharing. Pannon Management Review, 4(1), 35-65.

Kuikka, M., & Äkkinen, M. (2011). Determining the Challenges of Organizational Social Media Adoption and Use. *ECIS 2011 Proceedings*. Retrieved 22 February, 2016, from http://aisel.aisnet.org/ecis2011/248

Laudon, K., & Loudon, J. (2012). *Management information systems: Managing the digital firm* (12th ed.). Prentice Hall.

Lovejoy, K., & Saxton, G. D. (2012). Information, Community, and Action: How Nonprofit Organizations Use Social Media. *Journal of Computer-Mediated Communication*, *17*(3), 337–353. doi:10.1111/j.1083-6101.2012.01576.x

Lovejoy, K., Waters, R. D., & Saxton, G. D. (2012). Engaging stakeholders through Twitter: How nonprofit organizations are getting more out of 140 characters or less. *Public Relations Review*, *38*(2), 313–318. doi:10.1016/j.pubrev.2012.01.005

Macnamara, J., & Zerfass, A. (2012). Social media communication in organizations: The challenges of balancing openness, strategy, and management. *International Journal of Strategic Communication*, *6*(4), 287–308. doi:10.1080/1553118X.2012.711402

Mergel, I., & Bretschneider, S. I. (2013). A three-stage adoption process for social media use in government. *Public Administration Review*, *73*(3), 390–400. doi:10.1111/puar.12021

O'Reilly, T. (2005). *What is Web 2.0: Design patterns and business models for the next generation of software*. Retrieved 26 February, 2016, from http://www.oreillynet.com/pub/a/oreilly/tim/news/2005/09/30/what-is-web-20.html

O'Reilly, T. (2007). *What Is Web 2.0: Design Patterns and Business Models for the Next Generationof Software*. MPRA Paper No. 4578. Retrieved 23 February, 2016, from http://mpra.ub.uni-muenchen.de/4578/

Oberer, B., & Erkollar, A. (2012). Social media integration in higher education. cross-course google plus integration sown in the example of a masters degree course in management. *Procedia: Social and Behavioral Sciences*, *47*, 1888–1893. doi:10.1016/j.sbspro.2012.06.918

Onat, F. (2010). *Social Media Practices as a Public Relations Application Field: An Analysis About NonGovernmental Organizations. İletişim Kuram ve Araştırma Dergisi*, *31*, 103–122.

Rhoads, J. (2012). *Ready to Interact: Social Media Use by U.S. Hospitals and Health Systems*. CSC. Retrieved from http://assets1.csc.com/health_services/downloads/CSC_Survey_Social_Media_Use_by_U.S._Hospitals_and_Health_Systems.pdf

Schaupp, L. C., & Bélanger, F. (2013). The value of social media for small businesses. *Journal of Information Systems*, *28*(1), 187–207. doi:10.2308/isys-50674

Schultz, M. D., Koehler, J. W., Philippe, T. W., & Coronel, R. S. (2015). Managing the effects of social media in organizations. *SAM Advanced Management Journal*, *80*(2), 42–47.

Schwedel, M. (2013). *Nonprofit Organizations, Social Media, and Mobile Applications*. (Master's Thesis). Southern Illinois University.

Shivalingaiah, D., & Naik, U. (2008). Comparative Study of Web 1.0, Web 2.0 and Web 3.0. Proceedings of the International Convention on Automation of Libraries in Education and Research Institutions (pp. 499–507). Allahabad, India: CALIBER. Retrieved from http://ir.inflibnet.ac.in/bitstream/1944/1285/1/54.pdf

Sinclaire, J. K., & Vogus, C. E. (2011). Adoption of social networking sites: An exploratory adaptive structuration perspective for global organizations. *Information Technology Management*, *12*(4), 293–314. doi:10.1007/s10799-011-0086-5

Sisco, H. F., & McCorkindale, T. (2013). Communicating pink: An analysis of the communication strategies, transparency, and credibility of breast cancer social media sites. *International Journal of Nonprofit and Voluntary Sector Marketing*, *18*(4), 287–301. doi:10.1002/nvsm.1474

Smits, M., & Mogos, S. (2013). The Impact of Social Media on Business Performance. *Proceedings of the 21st European Conference on Information Systems*, 1-12.

TOBB (The Union of Chambers and Commodity Exchanges of Turkey). (n.d.). *History*. Retrieved from http://www.tobb.org.tr/Sayfalar/Eng/Tarihce.php

Treem, J. W., & Leonardi, P. M. (2013). Social media use in organizations: Exploring the affordances of visibility, editability, persistence, and association. *Annals of the International Communication Association*, *36*(1), 143–189. doi:10.1080/23808985.2013.11679130

Uzunoğlu, E., & Kip, S. M. (2014). Building relationships through websites: A content analysis of Turkish environmental non-profit organizations (NPO) websites. *Public Relations Review*, *40*(1), 113–115. doi:10.1016/j.pubrev.2013.06.001

Waters, R. D., Burnett, E., Lamm, A., & Lucas, J. (2009). Engaging stakeholders through social networking: How nonprofit organizations are using Facebook. *Public Relations Review*, *35*(2), 102–106. doi:10.1016/j.pubrev.2009.01.006

Waters, R. D., & Feneley, K. L. (2013). Virtual stewardship in the age of new media: Have nonprofit organizations moved beyond Web 1.0 strategies? *International Journal of Nonprofit and Voluntary Sector Marketing*, *18*(3), 216–230. doi:10.1002/nvsm.1469

Waters, R. D., & Jones, P. M. (2011). Using video to build an organizations identity and brand: A content analysis of nonprofit organizations YouTube videos. *Journal of Nonprofit & Public Sector Marketing*, *23*(3), 248–268. doi:10.1080/10495142.2011.594779

Westmoreland, M. B. (2014). *Five Ways Technology Will Shape the Nonprofit Sector in 2014*. Blackbaud. Retrieved from www.blackbaud.com

Yılmazel, M. (2011). *A Content Analysis About Social Media Usage of Charitable Funds Which Activate in Turkey* (Master Thesis). Anadolu University, Graduate School of Social Sciences, Department of Public Relations and Advertising, Eskişehir.

Ying, M. (2012). *Marketing From Social Media Platforms and the Firms That Use These Platforms Effectively* (Master's Thesis). Kadir Has University, Social Sciences Institute.

Zaidieh, A. J. Y. (2012). The use of social networking in education: Challenges and opportunities. *World of Computer Science and Information Technology Journal*, *2*(1), 18–21.

Zincir, O. (2014). *For What Purposes Do Managers Use Social Media? A Conceptual Framework Development Effort* (Master Thesis). Istanbul University, Graduate School of Social Sciences, Business Administration Department, İstanbul, Turkey.

# Chapter 14
# New Perspectives:
## Not-for-Profit Organizations in the Advent of the 4th Industrial Revolution

**Albena Antonova**
*Sofia University, Bulgaria*

## ABSTRACT

*As social and environmental struggles intensify, the raising economic and social role of not for profits will continue to expand globally. Not for profit organizations have the potential to mobilize digitally-enabled communities and to work on various global challenges, overcoming the limitations of governmental institutions, local and short-term perspectives of public administration and private interests of business organizations. The present research aims to reassess the business models and value creation behind NFP operational models, their role for social innovation, the impact of the new technologies and the characteristics of the emerging digital communities. Further, there will be discussed the new perspectives for NFP development as innovative instruments, protecting social interests between government and private organizations, and contributing to solve increasing social problems.*

## INTRODUCTION

Not for profit – NFP or referred as well as non-government organizations expand globally and have become an important source of economic activity. While NFP organizations have long traditions both in developed and developing countries a recent economic phenomenon is their rising importance as providers of public goods and services (Aldashev, Jaimovich & Verdier, 2016). In the Organization of Economic Co-operation and Development (OECD) countries NFP have become the main public goods and services providers especially in sectors such as healthcare, media, education, arts and poverty relief (Bilodeau & Steinberg, 2006). Quite remarkably, NFPs employ about 7.5 percent of economically active population in OECD countries and even in Belgium, Netherlands, Canada, U.K., USA and Ireland their share exceeds 10 percent (Salamon, 2010). The NFPs sector contributes for 5.3 percent of the USA GDP, employing about 10.1 percent of the USA workforce (Salamon, Sokolowsky & Geller, 2012).

DOI: 10.4018/978-1-5225-2537-0.ch014

Copyright © 2017, IGI Global. Copying or distributing in print or electronic forms without written permission of IGI Global is prohibited.

At a time when public debt is rising and government funding for social services is decreasing globally the activity of NFP organizations and social entrepreneurship is assumed as an instrument to complement governments' financing of social welfare (Dey, Schneider & Maier, 2016). Thus, even in countries where welfare services are mainly delivered by the public sector, the initially auxiliary or complimentary role of private NFP organizations and social entrepreneurship augment. This trend comes along with the increasing attacks against the public sector and the rhetoric that public services in a whole are inefficient, costly and ultimately useless (Archibugi & Filippetti, 2016). Social entrepreneurship emerges as a promise to both generate commercial income and to solve social problems while becoming financially self-sufficient (Dey et al, 2016).

Social entrepreneurship nurtures further public expectation toward NFP's role, promoting social entrepreneurship as more efficient solution for social services procurement and wealth distribution. NFPs are therefore popularized as alternative providers of welfare services, managing deepening social and environmental problems. Moreover, the research in the field of NFPs is largely dominated by enthusiasts who restraint to make critique, over-emphasizing the political arguments and potentials or failing to analyze NFPs efficiency and impact (Chell, Spence, Perrini & Harris, 2016; Dey et al, 2016). Different reports highlight the real controversies and problems with NFP mode of operation, accountability and efficiency, both on local and on international level. For example, in the paper Small is Beautiful (Aldashev, Jaimovich and Verdier, 2016) discussed different problems that NFP organizations experience in the areas as resource allocation and efficiency when coping with environmental disasters.

Aldashev, Jaimovich and Verdier (2016) summarized findings of the humanitarian campaigns evaluations after the tsunami disaster in 2004 in Indonesia and Sri Lanka, comparing them with NFPs campaigns after the earthquake in Haiti in 2010. They concluded that even sufficiently financed humanitarian campaigns manifested numerous problems in relief activities, leading to inefficiencies in the distribution of funds, unsatisfactory plans, cost escalations and many coordination failures, leading to even more weak and inefficient national institutions and devastated local social systems. Several reasons for these fails were outlined, of which one is the rush of too many NGOs to carry out short-term but highly visible (for the donors) activities in disaster-prone areas. Aldashev et al. (2016) derived at a model proving that rent-seeking and ego-utility seeking motives can attract selfish individuals and organizations in the NFP sector, which in turn may end up crowding out and displacing intrinsically motivated agents. Furthermore, selfish motives and motivational crowding out can become increasingly severe as economies get richer and give more generously to the non-profit sector, as in the case of disaster attacks and many international donors. The findings indicate that as NFPs play an increasing role for state-aid allocation of funding, the efficiency and long-term effects on the operations of NFPs could benefit from further exploration.

Not for profit organizations, whatever their scope of operation is, have the responsibility and the commitment to justify their efficiency and capacity to implement development projects. Moreover, new technologies and Internet, social media and virtual communities, NFPs could further transform their financial and operational models for the benefit of all – donors, beneficiaries, public and private entities. Thus the increasing role of internet technologies and platform-oriented business models can additionally help to attain better social effect. Therefore operation of non-for-profit internet organizations and foundations like World Wide Web Foundation, Open-Source software movement, Wikimedia and others can serve as role-models proposing sustainable models for global collaboration and cooperation in a non-profit manner beneficial for all. Internet-based NFPss are global actors, work in international environment and promote global cooperation and services, improving access to knowledge, international cooperation, providing meaningful services to all. As NFPs business models can be successfully applied in Internet and IT sector, these technology innovations can enable further scenarios for activating users, developers, customers and partners to solve local, national and international problems.

The present chapter aims to analyze the nature of the NFP organizations and to discuss some of the operational models used by the sector. More specifically how NFP can adopt technology-enabled and networked business models, involving and better collaborating with different stakeholders and communities to provide better value on local, national and global level drive this discussion. The analysis of the platform business models will serve as a matrix for problem solving and value creation from NFP perspective. Providing insights into some of the issues of NFP organizations, are two main problems:

- How new technologies can enhance development of new business models and mode of operations for Non-profit organizations.
- How open business models of Internet-based organizations can be exploited in NFPs perspective.

While private organizations gain more instruments and resources to cope with the new coming economic revolution and to adapt to organizational change, many NFPs and public organizations often work under increasing financial and social pressure. This is due both on the raising expectations from the public and donors, and demand for better Return-on-Investments schemes. But moreover, as developed in Sedlarski (2013), public organizations and NFP work in more rigid institutional framework, slowly adapting to the environment due to many institutional settings (such as lock-in costs, path-dependencies, special-interest-groups pressure and lobbying). Thus providing theoretical research on NFPs business models innovations and analyzing in more details the value-formation mechanisms can help to better conceptualize NFP value-providing network and to reassess their strategies for development. Holistic thinking and a new approach to evaluate the instruments, policies and models could help to manage and to survive the coming challenges.

The chapter first provide a theoretical overview of the main definitions and terms, mode of financing and mode of control specific to not for profit organizations and then discusses business models concepts, value creation and key considerations for service-dominant logic, service provision and welfare services. Key business model characteristics and components which explain the main considerations that have to be taken into account for the NFP business model implementation. An overview of Internet business models used in some NFP organizations and the problems associated with such models will be outlined with a focus on value creation and mechanisms for value formation for NFPs organizations to conclude with emerging and innovative models of NFP financing. This chapter contributes to the understanding that NFPs as institutions, protecting interests of the social community and finally how adoption of emerging technologies can further empower NFPs and increase its perspectives.

## BACKGROUND

### Defining Not for Profit Organisations

Nongovernmental organizations (NGO) were established in 1945 as a legal form by United Nations (UN). They are any type of organization from non-profit sector that is actively engaged in international cooperation (Willetts, 2009). More specifically, NGOs were designated as group of players who are active in the efforts of international development and increasing the welfare of poor people in poor countries.

NGOs work both independently and alongside bilateral aid agencies from developed countries, private-sector infrastructure operators, self-help associations, and local governments (Werker & Ahmed, 2008). However, today term NGO become interchangeable with NFP.

According to the UN, any kind of private organization that is independent from government control can be called NGO, provided that it is not-for-profit, non-prevention, and not simply an opposition political party. Not for profit organizations can be largely defined as any form of organization that is banned from distributing net earnings or profits to individuals who exercise control over it, such as members, officers, directors or trustees (Hansmann, 1980). The net earnings should be retained and devoted in their entirety to finance further production of the services that the organization was formed to provide. This basic characteristic of the NFPs is called nondistribution constraint and it is the main factor for differentiation from any other type of business or social organization (Hansmann, 1980). While most of the nonprofits are incorporated and act upon specific legislation framework, not for profit organizations, under the NGO umbrella term, include various forms of cooperatives, spin-offs, private or public organizations that acts under the clause of non-distribution constrain".

Policy-oriented UN defined the term non-profit institution (NPIs) to designate organizations that can be legal or social entities, related for the purpose of producing goods and services whose status does not permit them to be a source of income, profit or other financial gain for the units that establish, control or finance them (UN, 2003). Further non-governmental organizations (NGOs) are defined as private organizations characterized primarily by humanitarian or cooperative, rather than commercial, objectives. Under this definition, NFP pursue activities to relieve suffering, promote the interests of the poor, protect the environment, provide basic social services, or undertake community development (Werker & Ahmed, 2008).

Social enterprise (SE) and social entrepreneurship have emerged recently as alternative organizations in nonprofit sector (Nicholls, 2006). The global popularity of 'social entrepreneurship' is directly connected to 2006 Nobel Prize winner Muhammad Yunus and Garmeen Bank (Dey et al., 2016). As defined by (Dey et al., 2016), social enterprises are businesses with primarily social objectives whose surpluses are principally reinvested for that purpose in the business or community, rather than being driven by the need to maximize profit for shareholders and owners.

The main difference between social enterprises and other NFPs/NGOs is that SE addresses social or environmental problems by employing business strategies and innovative approaches, looking for innovative opportunities to raise funds. SEs are open for innovation and appropriate risk taking (Granados, Hlupic, Coakes & Mohamed, 2011). This means that the ultimate aim of the social entrepreneur is to reinvest revenues into their mission and in the same time to reduce their dependence on external sources of funding and becoming self-sustaining (Kerlin, 2013). The potential of social entrepreneurship become an increasing topic of research and consideration (Aziz & El Ebrashi, 2016).

## Mode of Financing and Mode of Operation

As the mission of NFPs/NGOs is by definition to do good things (Werker & Ahmed, 2008), it could be hard to identify hidden inefficiencies or incongruities in the NFP official statements and charters. However, the models of financing and control behind NFPs largely determine their operation. Financing schemes predefine the models of interaction, the models of dependencies and the models of governance behind NFPs. Finally, the models of financing affects the mix of products and services, their quality and the efficiency of the invested resources (return on investment) transferred to social impact and social transformation (Aziz & El Ebrashi, 2016). Analyzing the basic models of financing for NFPs/NGOs Hansmann (1980) identify three basic forms:

1. Donative or grant-depending NFPs, receiving most of their incomes as grants or donations, mostly by individuals, other organizations or state. NFPs act as intermediaries who distribute products and services to beneficiaries, in behalf of donors. This is the main model of operation and sustenance for many international foundations and institutions, like Salvation Army, Red Cross, CARE and other working to provide relief of the needy
2. Commercial NFPs receive the bulk of their incomes from prices and fees, charged for specific services. Here NFP organizations are self-sustaining and support their activities by the incomes that they collect from members or customers, who pay a tax for the obtained services, like nursing homes, hospitals, member clubs and others. The main difference in this case is that the donors are in fact the main beneficiaries or end-users
3. Mixed type NFPs, or a combination of funding from donations and commercial services. Here the income comes both from donations and from paid services and fees. Usually this is the type of financing behind universities' NFPs, where part of the funding is paid by donations and alumni support programs, and another part is paid by the fees of the actual students.

To further discuss these approaches, the agency theory is explored. Both commercial and mixed models of NFPs can be highly competitive, outperforming successfully in many cases for-profit companies. However, the mode of financing and control largely depends from the main NFPs sources of income (or the big donors) whose will shall predefine and shape the NFPs policy and agenda. Hansmann (1980) determined that in specific cases people could have intrinsic reasons to prefer different social services (as education, healthcare, social support and others) to be provided by NFPs or public organizations. This can be explained by the contract failure theory of Hansmann (1980) that views NFP organizations as a response to agency problems between consumers and for-profit firms.

Contract failure arises when consumers face an informational disadvantage and are unable to evaluate accurately the quantity or quality of certain goods and services. In such circumstances, for-profit organizations have both the incentive and opportunity to take advantage of consumers by exerting less effort, producing lower quality, or delivering less than the promised quantity (Hansmann, 1980). However, it's not clear if NFPs can overcome these problems, as they are in fact "private" agents, but acting "outside" the main market forces. For example, according to data of US National Center of Educational Statistics available on (http://nces.ed.gov/fastfacts/display.asp?id=76) for the 2013–14 academic year, annual current dollar prices for undergraduate tuition, fees, room, and board were estimated to be $US15, 640 at public institutions, $US40, 614 at private nonprofit institutions, and $US23, 135 at private for-profit institutions. Thus taxes for universities and colleges in USA show how NFPs can act opportunistically.

Furthermore, grant-based NFPs meet other types of problems coming mainly from the intermediary character of the NFPs' activities and the indirect relationship between the donors and beneficiaries. The logistics of transferring donor's payment to final goods and services on behalf of beneficiaries can be very complex, involving various international organizations, environmental conditions, institutional pre-conditions and public authorities' approval. Usually these NFPs have to overcome various dependences and limitations, transferring money and support to the needy (Aldashev, Jaimovich, & Verdier,

2016). To enhance the understanding of the complex issues, some of the main problems in financing structure and support and agency theory, public funding and government grants, support organizations are further discussed.

## Agency Theory Funding and Operations

The agency relationship is defined as one, in which one person (the principal) engage another person (the agent) to perform some service on his behalf which involves delegating some decision-making authority to the agent (Hill & Jones, 1992). From methodological point of view, the principal-agent relation is closely related to risk sharing, hidden efforts, monitoring, hidden characteristics, screening, and self-selection (Spremann, 1987). The agency theory is well studied in the for-profit companies and private relationships (as problems between shareholder-manager, employer-employee and investor-investee). Further there are well investigated interrelationships due to hierarchy and information asymmetry (Spremann, 1987). The main assumption of the Agency theory is that the interests of the principal and the agent diverge. Thus the agent will try to maximize its utility function on the expense of the principal. This can lead not only to direct loss for the principal, but as well to not-realized potential gain. Thus the agency problem become a corner-stone for organizations and the agency cost occurring in these relationships is identified such as: residual loss, monitoring expenditures and agent bonding expenditures; Moreover it's worth to mention that agency theory asserts that natural selection processes favor governance structures that economize on agency costs (Hill & Jones, 1992).

Recent research on agency theory reflects the operation of NFPs/NGOs (Van Puyvelde, Caers, Du Bois & Jegers, 2012). While there can be classified six categories of principal-agent relationships in NFPs (Van Puyvelde et al., 2012), the most important issue remain the relationship between the donors and the NFPs principal activities. As authors further summarize some of the main problems for the nonprofit organizations include the lack of shareholders who are legally entitled to financially control their agents (in this case all the decision-making is in the hands of the NFPs/NGOs executives), the nature of the work projects that can be hard to control as they are complex, hard-to-define by objective functions; the difficulty to measure accurately the NFPs output and investments in operations, the lack of financial measurement of the managerial performance and the lack of effective control mechanisms. All issues can lead to significant agency problems.

Even if Steinberg (2010) concludes that the presence of multiple principals with different objectives hinders the potential of agency theory to resolve questions of nonprofit accountability, in many cases due to the Agency costs, donors can pre-define NFPs services and products provisions. Mainly by donating to a nonprofit organization, private and corporate donors become principals who delegate decision-making authority to the organization and thus can further effectuate control partly or fully on its activities. Therefore the agency costs will apply mainly to donor-NFPs management relationships. Thus agency costs, such as monitoring costs, bonding costs, and residual loss will increase the transaction costs, but in the same time these additional fees will predefine the donor's interests to support the NFPs/NGOs activity. Especially in the case of public/government funding, organizational funding or substantial private funding, donors will require specific clauses and contractual relationships that can control NFPs/NGOs activities. Some of the main agency costs for NFPs/NGOs are (Van Puyvelde et al., 2012):

1. First, to improve the access of information, the principal may require additional efforts from the agent on providing evidences - information, monitoring and reporting, increasing paperwork and reducing capacity of the NFPs to perform its main work.
2. Second, there could be identified different ways to replace the compensation schemes from effort-based pay (for example – per hour) to outcome-based pay (paying for final product or outcome, as in many service or project-based contracts). But this can be difficult in the nonprofit context due to the problems of accurately measuring the performance and difficulty to define the final outcomes.
3. Another approach is by improving accounting and financial information from NPFs financial reports. Thus nonprofit financial reports can be divided into four categories: (a) efficiency variables that represent the degree to which the organization allocates resources to its mission, (b) financial stability variables that refer to the ability of the organization to continue operations if faced with a decrease in resources, (c) fundraising variables that serve as proxies for the amount of information available to donors, and (d) variables that represent the reputation of the nonprofit organization, such as the size or age of the organization.
4. Finally, from a signaling perspective, donors are willing to finance nonprofit organizations audited by a high-quality auditor, which further increase NFPs/NGOs transaction costs.

The findings suggest that in the case of NFPs agency costs can represent substantial transaction costs and can provide further problems for organizing the activity. Looking for overcoming this problem (for example, by orienting to one or two main donors) can be a question of long-term survival. This fact can further explain why NFPs are much more reluctant to provide short-term evidences and information reports to their donors, than to work for effective and long-term solutions for their beneficiaries (Aldashev, Jaimovich & Verdier, 2016). The nature of the relationships between NFPs/NGOs and their donors can further determine some additional and substantial limitations and obstacles for finding the best possible solutions for the needy.

In addition to agency theory Van Puyvelde et al. (2012) conceptualize the stewardship-based approach that stipulates that nonprofit organizations are motivated to act in the interests of their donors. Kelly (2001) proposed four stewardship strategies that nonprofit organizations can use to develop a favorable fundraising relationship with their donors: reciprocity, responsibility, reporting, and relationship nurturing.

1. Reciprocity requires that NFPs demonstrate gratitude toward their donors, like thank cards, note of appreciation or offering them a tax-deductible receipt.
2. Responsibility means that nonprofit organizations act in a socially responsible manner to their donors, for example, by considering them when deciding how to use their donations or by telling them which project their donations will fund so that they feel confident that their donations will be used wisely.
3. Reporting means that nonprofit organizations should inform donors about how they have used their donations by providing them with accurate financial information.
4. Relationship nurturing refers to continued relationship building with donors outside the fundraising context, for example, by inviting them to special events.

To mitigate the risk, NFP need adopt different tools, such as monitoring mechanisms, trust-building relationships, reputation, open-doors incentives, and sanctions in contract relationships to achieve goal alignment between the parties to the contract and reassess the Agency costs. Further, as Werker and

Ahmed (2008) comment, the increasing professionalization of NFPs and the increasing management competences and abilities of the NFPs management boards allow them to develop their own professionalized class, better negotiating contracts and terms and conditions with the donor organizations.

However, the question from the Agency theory is about the relationships between donors and the efficiency of their operations and the quality of the goods and services provided to final beneficiaries. In this sense, it is worth highlighting the findings of Werker & Ahmed (2008). Werker and Ahmed (2008) argues that the strengths of the NGO model produces corresponding weaknesses in agenda-setting, decision-making, and resource allocation, further leading to the debate whether NFPs provide the best alternative for resource allocation and problem-solving.

## State Aid, State Financing, and Public Funding

Global numbers show that public financing for both grant-based and commercial NFPs is increasing, and thus various NFPs can be subsidized through different public schemes. However, the policy efforts for *small government*, public service outsourcing and government aids can have further implications both for NFPs, for beneficiaries and for the efficiency of the services, financed by public sources. On one hand redistribution of public funds and outsourcing of public activities through different competitive systems for state procurements make it possible for more NGOs to find competitive and more stable sources of income. On the other hand, the reduction in communication and transaction costs and better access to information has made it easier and cheaper for social entrepreneurs and NFPs to organize and to compete for public financing and procurement contracts on a global scale (Aldashev, Jaimovich, & Verdier, 2016). This combination has provided the fodder and catalyst for many NGOs to take off with a momentum of their own.

However, as discussed above, due to Agency-based theory, government funding can directly affect the work of the NFPs/NGOs in different ways as for example through undermining the independence of nonprofits (and their course of action) or pushing them to change their approach to client service or staffing. Moreover, as summarized by Marwell & Calabrese (2015) government funding creates inefficiencies and increases transaction costs for nonprofits and this can push away the private donors. Obtaining subsidies or state contracts can result in less fundraising efforts and costs, and thus many NFPs/NGOs prefer to work with public funds. However, as different authors outline, subsidizing authority can impose increasing requirements for monitoring and paper work and explicit restrictions on other fundraising expenses and thus can make NFP/NGO increasingly dependable, leading even to hidden subsidizing for public services, as proved further in the work of (Marwell & Calabrese, 2015).

State funding to NFPs can have some important political and social characteristics. As Salamon (1997) underline, in case of public/state funding, it's very important to make the difference between charity and provision of social rights. Thus, when nonprofits use government funds to assist individuals, nonprofits are not providing "charity" services but rather then they are securing specific "rights of citizenship". Therefore social rights, as distinguished from both civil rights and political rights are affirmative government guarantees of conditions of well-being for their citizens.

Marwell and Calabrese (2015) further open the debate about how government's provision of social rights for citizens can be secured by private non-profit organizations using public funds and whereas the state can properly be considered as a guarantor of social rights when nonprofit organizations have to fit this bill. Therefore, in their research they illustrate that poor mechanisms of state/public funding of NFP/NGOs further undermine their capacity to provide quality services and to guarantee the social rights to citizens. Moreover, government funding generates significant transaction costs for nonprofits in terms of additional personnel, required to manage the contracts and additional financial costs, caused by the delays in contract payments, requiring additional funding (obtained by private loans, bank financing, donors' funds and others).

Another problem comes from the fact that more government services are allocating state funding and policy provision to NFPs/NGOs organizations. Thus different public services tend to outsource aid delivery to NGOs, following the concept amongst all organizations to outsource their non-core functions (Werker & Ahmed, 2008). This initiative comes as well from the effects of devolution and privatization on government service provision. In part this is driven by market and political ideologies that have their roots in perceptions about greater efficiencies and innovations arising from the private sector and broader support for smaller government (Van Puyvelde et al., 2012). All these initiatives for further "outsourcing" public services, paid with tax funding, can both generate inefficiencies due to agency costs, and moreover, can artificially drive to "competition" among social/subsidized service providers, who will additionally compromise the interests of the final beneficiaries, especially in areas of complex services provision, where the quality and the amount of work is hard to be proven.

## International Financing and State Aid Distribution

When discussing state financing, it becomes especially important to mention the rising role of the NFPs in international support, grants schemes and aid distribution. This is explained by the fact that state aid and international organizations support is increasingly provided through the form of NFPs project-based funding. Thus many international NFPs structures are extensively financed by state funds, replacing or substituting other forms of state aid. As explained by Aldashev et al. (2016), international NFPs started to act as large state aid intermediaries, becoming part of international public relations and inter-government policy.

This trend is to a large extent the result of the growing disillusionment in government-to-government project aid, often considered to be politicized and easily corruptible (Alesina & Dollar, 2000; Kuziemko & Werker, 2006). Therefore, the rise of the NGOs intermediation in international aid provision and support has meant an increasing emphasis of project ownership, decentralization, and participatory development. Thus, the largest single financial contributor to non-governmental organizations is often contribution from national government (Werker & Ahmed, 2008). This can generate additional agency costs, as NFPs/NGOs have to increasingly conform not only to the best practices of delivering services to beneficiaries, overcoming day-to-day struggles in international environment, but should further respond on other policy implications both in donor countries, in government policy and abroad.

## Raising Role of NFPs Support Ecosystem and Intermediary Organizations

In many cases, NFPs are financed and supported through more complex structured networks of intermediary organizations that can lead to substantial effect on their operations (Dey et al., 2016). More specifically, NFPs intermediary organizations provide not only funding, but different forms of support and environment, that can further stimulate social innovations, social entrepreneurship and forms of profit/not-profit/public and pro-bono cooperation. Especially in recent years, there are promoted different public-funded schemes that not only facilitate the access to resources, but allow more organizations and professionals to enter to NFPs and to develop social innovations projects.

Intermediaries and NFPs support organizations can be further identified as organizations whose main purposes are to provide various forms of services and environmental support for NFPs and social innovations. Some of the activities can be structured as: raising awareness, organizing social innovation competitions and public events, distributing awards and promoting best practices, providing trainings, distributing various forms of loans and debt financing, establishing and lending subsidized workspaces, providing incubation services or networking and business services, designated for social entrepreneurship and NFPs. Intermediary organizations can provide as well more traditional forms of services and support, such as legal help, business planning, money or legitimacy promotion agencies, incubators or field building actors– as pre-eminent actors in defining the meaning of SE (Dey et al., 2016). This ecosystem shift toward more "social innovations" and social entrepreneurship leads to the consequence for the rising number of social entrepreneurships funding, and in a whole as raising the role of SE as suppliers of social initiatives.

However, many of these support initiatives and intermediaries programs are transferred from the vibrant technology innovation start-up ecosystem, successfully fueled by business angels, venture capital funds, private investors, university programs, science conferences and research initiatives, government support schemes and others. As current literature further insist, some of the critiques of social entrepreneurship is that "social change" is not specified whether it should be incremental (i.e., addressing market failures through innovative products and services), institutional (readjusting existing market structures) or disruptive activity (aiming at systems change, (Nicholls & Murdock, 2012) quoted in (Dey et al., 2016). Thus when discussing the raising role of social innovations intermediaries, more specific attention should be paid on their ways of directions for promoting specific social innovations and NFP activities.

Another aspect of the agency theory and the raising role of the NFPs can be further derived by the special forms of governance, control and public treatment of the NFPs. As defined in Hansmann (1980) the crucial factor of the NFPs/NGOs governance is the patron, or the person who constitutes the ultimate source of a non-profit income. While in the most cases the patrons for small NFPs are many donors (for donative NFPs) or customers (for commercial NFPs), the largest foundations and charity organizations depend more substantially from single-source private donors. In the previous paragraphs we discussed how government and public funding can increase the agency costs of the NFPs/NGOs and this can lead to further diminishing the quality of the services provided to the beneficiaries.

In the case of private-owned NFPs governed by wealthy individuals or patrons, it is evident that NFPs activities and programs for beneficiaries cannot hurt the interests of the patrons. The emerging agency problems in this situation come from the fact that sometimes the interests of the beneficiaries (and the society as a whole) and the private interests of the wealthy individuals (NFPs/ patrons) can differ substantially. Thus in many areas, where NFPs gain increasing impact as for example in the field of breakthrough research, new technologies and health care, education and others, private interests can be divergent from the public ones. Moreover, the increasing role of the NFPs both on national and international scene can further extend and reshape political and economic processes, hindering the role of the state to assure the democratic rights and promoting private-dominating practices.

As the legal form of NFP brings many in-kind, financial and social benefits to donors and patrons, they can be successfully used as tax haven for personal fortunes or as instruments for hidden political and economic dominance. As NFPs are subject of special legal and tax treatment upon specific conditions as for example favorable corporate income taxation, better rules for social security, unemployment insurance, minimum wage, securities regulation, bankruptcy, antitrust, unfair competition, copyright, postal rates and others (Hansmann, 1980). All this can further attract "selfish" individuals and profit-seeking agents that can try to exploit NFPs/ for private interests. More specifically different examples suggest that NFPs can accumulate and distribute significant amount of funds that can be further employed for economic and politic pressure on international and local actors and economic processes. For example, one recent investigation in press (Rossell, 2015) show up how two large foundations invested more than 196 Millions USD to "push Internet regulations". Moreover, the NFPs sources of political and economic influence can be invisible through different forms of networking support and hidden subventions that can be hardly followed.

## BUSINESS MODELS, SERVICE PROVISION, AND VALUE CREATION

Business model describe the internal logic and the processes of organizing an activity for delivering value for end-user. The business model is the conceptual model of business functions, structure and systems that constitutes company´s operational and physical form (Osterwalder, Pigneur & Tucci, 2005). The business model is centered on the value provided to the customer and how it is produced and financed. The research on business models expands recently, both for profit companies and for non-profit organizations (Wirtz, Pistoia, Ullrich, & Göttel, 2016). The increasing interest to business models is due to ICT and Internet technologies that are considered as main source of differentiation (Ostenwalder et al. 2005). Thus both for profit and not-for-profit organizations can improve and enhance further the way they conceive business with adopting innovative and technology-based approach for connecting with clients, suppliers and value-defining network.

Lindgardt, Reeves, Stalk and Deimler (2009) states that business models consist of two main elements: value proposition and operating model. The value proposition stands for what is offered to whom, and it covers three main dimensions – target segment, product/service offering and revenue model (financial model). Therefore, the model of value proposition for NFPs/NGOs should strongly correspond to the interests of the beneficiaries. More specifically, as Aziz and El Ebrashi (2016) suggest, the main mission and value proposition for social enterprises (and for all NFPs as well) is to create "transformational impact", and their success should be measured by the magnitude of the provided social impact. Thus "value proposition" in the context of NFPs/NGOs should be understood as general transformation of the context, leading to meaningful, long-term impact and improvement of the situation.

On the other hand the operating model describes how to efficiently deliver the offering and include business choices of value chain, cost model and organization of value-delivering network. Thus the operating model of NFPs should discuss more specifically how to optimize the efficiency of the offering and how to extend services, involving communities and potential networks of interested suppliers.

While the research literature in the field of business models for social entrepreneurship is recently exploding (Wirtz, Pistoia, Ullrich, & Göttel (2016), we will further concentrate more specifically on new technologies and Internet and how they can extended business models of the NFPs/NGOs in order to optimize their value proposition (for beneficiaries) and their value offering (or efficiency of service provision). Therefore, more attention will be put on two main approaches – pipeline view of the business models (connected with traditional organizations) and the emerging platform view of the business, becoming popular recently after UBER (Van Alstyne, Parker, Choudary, 2016). NFPs offer value for customers and beneficiaries and the specific characteristics of value requires further discussion.

## Traditional Model

Historically, non-profits and particularly commercial non-profits emerged mainly as providers of services. Some of the reasons include the limitation to raise capital (due to non-distribution constraint) and the limitations to secure additional debt, in order to set more capital-intensive organizations (as for example manufacturing or industry organizations). NFP organizations operate primarily directly in the field of service provision (as in the case of education, healthcare, social care…) or in resource allocation (charity distribution), providing additional services for collecting goods (money, food, clothes and other) and distributing them to the needy.

As Van Slyke (2007) maintains, NFPs are usually specialized in social services that can be characterized as complex services, requiring substantial expertise and capacity to provide. He underlines a number of challenges for providing social services (Van Slyke, 2007). First, social services are more complex to evaluate than the industrial goods and their quality and efficiency may vary by both external and internal factors. Furthermore, it's more difficult to mitigate the risk in the service sector (especially in social services) and to measure directly or to evaluate indirectly the quality of the obtained services, as services are personal and labor-intensive and their reach cannot be assured. The main issue is that neither the efforts nor the quality of the service provider can guarantee the successful outcomes of the service systems and its final results (as for example – a scientific breakthrough in university research, or successful healing of every disease). Thus within the service-system focus should be put on improving the processes of service delivery and not the attainment of final assessments or results.

## Service-Dominant Logic and Value Creation

Recently, many scholars contributed to the evolution of service science, clarifying some of the basic concepts behind the fast-developing service sector (Vargo & Lusch, 2004, 2016). In general, services can be defined as intangible, non-material transactional configurations that cannot result in ownership (Beltagui, Riedel & Pawar, 2008). While traditional definitions of services describe them as "activities, deeds and performance", the evolving understanding of services is the application of competences (skills and knowledge) for the benefit of another party. The benefit provided through service is value, that is, an increase in the viability of the system (individual, family, firm, customer) under consideration, which arises as actors in an exchange integrate their varied resources (Barrett, Davidson, Prabhu & Vargo, 2015).

The competencies to provide a service can be manifested in a complex combination of goods, money, activities and institutions within a complex and social service system (Ng & Maull, 2009, Vargo & Lusch 2004). The key characteristic that differentiates a service system model from the traditional economic transaction model is the interaction with the customers as active participants in the service process (Fitzsimmons & Fitzsimmons, 2006). It is important to note that the most important feature of the service system structure consists of institutions and institutional arrangements (Vargo & Lusch, 2016). Furthermore, based on the evolved S-D model, Vargo and Lusch (2016) defined 11 Foundation Premises (FP) that constitute the basic foundations of the service science. Three general perceptions of services which are:

1. Value is co-created by multiple actors, always including the beneficiary (FP6)

2. Actors cannot deliver value but can participate in the creation and offering of value propositions (FP7)
3. Value co-creation is coordinated through actor-generated institutions and institutional arrangements (FP11).

## Value System Model

Value is generally considered to describe either the importance of something or its worth (Yusof, 2010). In traditional literature, leaded by Good-dominant (G-D) logic, value is understood as intrinsic or exchange-based. The intrinsic value is constant and do not depends on circumstances or time, while the exchange value reflects the price variations at the time of the exchange (Yusof, 2010). Thus the intrinsic value is usually attributed to the product's costs and alternatives, while the exchange value reflects the market dynamics (Supply-Demand processes) and the prices of the competitive/complimentary goods and goods elasticity.

### Goods Dominator

While within Goods-dominant (G-D) logic the producer is conceptualized as creator of value and the customer is a final user or destroyer of value, in Service-dominant (S-D) logic, the both parties are resource integrators (FP 9), actors in an "A2A" (actor-to-actor) relationship, who jointly co-create value (FP 6). However, resources are valuable only within particular social context and the respective social system. Moreover, as (Edvardsson, Tronvoll & Gruber, 2011) highlight service provision can lead to power and information asymmetries, including such phenomena as opportunism, deception, persuasion and seduction. Additional research have to focus on how power relationships influence service exchange and value co-creation, and how various actors perceive the value being created in the service exchange.

### Service Dominator

Thus within the service-dominant logic the value is no longer characterized as value-in-exchange, even neither as value-in-use (Ng & Maull, 2009), but more specifically as "value-in-social-context" (Edvardsson et al., 2011). This means that an individual's value perceptions are, at least in part, dependent on the relative positions of the individual within the wider social context, depending on much larger extend to its social environment and its social role. Moreover as Vargo & Lusch (2016) underline, the most important features of the social structure consists of institutions "rules, norms, meanings, symbols, practices, and similar aides to collaboration" and, more generally, institutional arrangements and interdependent assemblages of institutions. Therefore the concept of value-in-social-context (Edvardsson et al., 2011) can extend our understanding about service-provision, as the value is due not only on the possession/exchange/use – but more specifically on the social context, defined largely by institutional premises;

Focusing more specifically on customer value, in traditional for-profit firm, it can be simply defined as what customers get (benefits, quality, worth, utility) versus what it costs him (price, costs, sacrifices) (Yusof, 2010). More specifically, to identify the term "customer value" Zeithaml (1988) explored the concepts of perceived price, perceived quality and perceived value and found out that customers thought of value in four ways: "value is low price; value is whatever I want in a product; value is the quality I get for the price I pay; value is what I get for what I give. Extending these findings to the case of NFPs/

there can be made the following observations. The NFP customer -the final beneficiary is not expected to contribute substantially to the costs (as they do not have to pay the (full) price, or their costs are substantially lower than in the market situations). However, from theoretical point of view, there should be a balance between what the beneficiary gets: "quality, worth, utility, benefits, anything that I get and what they give. As literature suggest, this equality will generally depend from more complex social and institutional context.

### Institution Dominator

Thus, in the case of NFPs beneficiaries, the price of getting products and services could be much more socially-determined and linked to social elements and human standing in the social structure. Therefore becoming "beneficiary" of the NFPs services can have a specific social price as it can designate a person in a weak social status (illness, aging, poverty, need to be supported, addiction, social exclusion, ignorance, family problems, loneliness, lack of support etc.). This means that the status of beneficiary" of the NFPs can hurt person's social standing and social position, including his/her dignity, self-confidence and self-respect, social networks and motivation for improvement and change. Therefore, when considering beneficiaries and actual receivers of NFPs/ products and services qualified as charity, we have to admit the social and emotional price that they have to pay. That is largely influenced by social context and institutions (rules, norms, social practices and others). Thus the perception of value-in-social-context should lead to better understanding of the real social costs and social values associated with the work of NFP organizations.

Many NFPs provide public services that cannot be attributed to specific target users or where the impact could be evaluated only as long-term and for the benefit to all. Based on the taxonomy proposed by Simmons (1998) the not for profit activities can range in the fields such as: advocacy; information gathering and analysis; information dissemination; generation of ideas and recommendations; monitoring and watchdog role; service delivery; meditation/facilitation. There, the final impact of activities cannot be measured with terms such as value-in-context, as the results from activities as research, raising awareness, improving the social rights and environmental protection can lead to more general institutional change that can make a better life for all. Good examples of organizations that strive for institutional change can be Amnesty International, The World Conservation Union, Reporters without Borders and others.

Simmons (1998) maintained that in the early 1800s, the British and Foreign Anti-Slavery Society were the driving forces behind government action on the slave trade, and Anglo-Oriental Society for the Suppression of the Opium Trade were leading influential antidrug movement, that culminated in the 1912 Hague Opium Convention. Therefore, the work of the not for profit organizations should be defined as crucial for the institutional paradigm shift, in the way that NFPs organizations can actually change the institutional settings, overcoming the institutional dependencies and provoking new legislation frameworks, better understanding of social and environmental problems, breaking cultural norms and leading to more substantial transformational changes.

## Operational Model of Business

To evaluate the operating models and how not for profit organizations mobilize resources to provide value for the beneficiaries and the society, the concept of Hansmann (1980), is discussed. Hansmann (1980) explored 5 specific situations, where NFPs can play specific role to:

1. Act as intermediary organization, collecting and distributing goods and services from donors and delivering them to different recipients and end-use
2. Work for the procurement of "public goods" that would be difficult to be enjoyed by a single person, but can contribute for everybody (for example environmental protection, social rights, health research and others)
3. Finance NFPs working in the narrow fields of expertise or interest and operating in terms of price discrimination. In this case, it is observed the problem of subsidies (donations) and collected ticket prices for specific art events, museums and performances, where the final price is distributed on several groups of persons
4. Work in situations of implicit financing (as alternative for loans/debt financing), where the alumni donations actually represent additional payments to the reduced costs of the received services – as in the case of university education
5. Coordinate complex services that require better coordination of various contributing organizations and fields of expertise.

As many scholars have shown (Dey et al., 2016, Chell et al., 2016, Aldashev et al., 2016 to name a few) it is very difficult to set specific standards for measuring and determining the social value or the mechanisms by which NFPs operate for accomplishing their mission. Thus, the final goal is that invested money and efforts by NFPs organizations lead to more substantial transformational change and long-term impact for the beneficiaries and for the future development. One of the main problems, as recognized by Simmons (1998) is that NGOs become source of pressure and influence since they get increasingly financed by national governments, organizations and private interests. Thus NGOs, governments and multilateral institutions need to ensure public participation that draw on expertise and resources of NGOs, innovation, sense of purpose, commitment and freedom from bureaucratic constraints (Simmons, 1998).

## Controversies With Business Models

There is abundant economic literature that discuss the controversies of NFPs organizations, their benefits and limitations. For example, one of the widely-discussed controversies comes from the fact that NFPs work largely with voluntary work, with non-competitive HR policies and staff incentives. Different studies pointed out that NFPs could use other forms of compensation of their staff as reduced labor service, non-material stimulus and others (Marwell & Calabrese, 2015, Aldashev et al., 2016). Moreover, as there lacks profit or financial results that can motivate the management body, different researchers pointed out that it would be difficult to attract competent experts in the field. However, empirical data prove that NFPs attract many professional employees and provide competitive salaries that are close to the public sector, but less than the private companies. Further, instead of working less, some in-house inspections of time schedules show that even the permanent staff of NFPs works voluntary and provide more services. Even the research of (Marwell & Calabrese, 2015) demonstrated how private NFPs subsidized in fact public funded services as social care. As Aldashev, Jaimovich, & Verdier (2016) state, NFPs work have to be primary intrinsic motivated, leaded by internal and altruistic intentions and mission-driven. Furthermore, in specific cases, the market dynamics and the easy access to (public) funding can attract some profit-oriented organizations and rent-looking entrepreneurs;

A major controversy is that non-governmental organizations, especially working as distributors of charities delivers goods and services to a population that provides little feedback on the range or quality of the delivered products. This comes primary by the consequence that NFPs are more interested to guarantee donor satisfaction than beneficiary welfare. For instance, if donors expect that charity products or services should be with inferior quality than market-traded products/services, then NFPs should provide evidences about the wisely use of the donations. Indeed, donations are the only "market force" in the non-government sector industry, where donors can be viewed as desiring to improve the quantity and quality of the product of the NGO without having their donation expropriated. In this instance, the donor and funding base of NGOs will reveal the primary set of interests that a NGO is forced to manage (Figure 1).

Some other problems of NFPs operations come with the fact that it is in neither the interests of the NGOs nor the official donor agency, complicit as a funder, to publicize less-than-stellar results (Riddell & Robinson, 1995). In addition, public opinion of non-government organizations is is generally high in rich countries and poor countries alike, so the demand for rigorous and critique evaluation is correspondingly low (Barr & Fafchamps, 2006). Too many actors, lack of coordination to achieve efficient result, too many stakeholders separating fund-raising to actual work by subcontracting it to local NFPs where there can arise some agency problems and too many missions without clear understanding of NFPs efficiency impede improved operations of NFPs. Furthermore, fund and resource allocation and how these pass through multiple channels, from the taxpayer (public funding) to a bilateral aid agency, to an intergovernmental organization, to an international and finally to a local organizations before being finally spent on goods or services is increasingly a problem. Additionally, whether NFPs collectively are better at development than public or private-sector institutions is increasingly questioned. Moreover, as evaluations that allow for causal inference are rarer, substantiating the quality and effectiveness in NFP organizations, although increasing, remains a challenge.

*Figure 1. Traditional (pipeline) model of financing, control and operation*
*Source 1 Antonova (2016)*

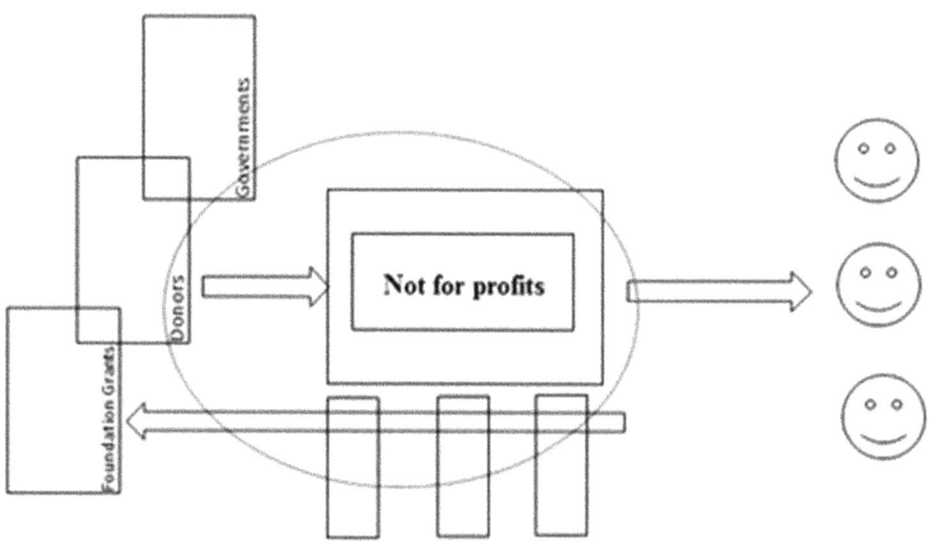

## BUSINESS MODELS

Successful business models have in common that they are designed in a way to reduce the upfront investments, to accelerate the revenue/receivables and cash inflow and to obtain reliable customer feedback often and earlier. Chen (2009) pointed out that business model in the twenty-first century has to combine the capabilities of Web 2.0 as collective intelligence, network effects, user generated content, and the possibility of self-improving systems. He emphasized that Business Model 2.0 should include not just technology but also the networking and open business effect. Thus in coherence with Web 2.0 movement it is identified Open Business models. For the NFPs/NGOs, open business model mean business models that do not restrict the results of the innovation to the rest of humanity, open business models cannot be based on restrictive forms of intellectual property.

### Open Business Model

Open business is in general the concept of doing business in a transparent way by intimately integrating an ecosystem of stake holders and abiding by a model of transparency. Often, small minorities harness the business benefits away at the cost of other stakeholders and the market. Open Business structures seek to rectify this. They activate personal productivity like no other organization can by simply redirecting the returns to those that produced them, and by their nature, the individuals themselves play a central role.

A more strict definition is inspired by free software movement, open standards, open source and open content, which implies that an open business, is a business whose business model is run on open standards, "free software" and "open source" software and open content principles, and focuses on creating `open´ products and services. This approach would guarantee that the business is run for the benefit of all, and not just for one group or stakeholders, whether shareholders, personnel, government etc. Also the strict application of open principles will guarantee that bankruptcy of a specific open business will not result in the loss of the fruits of its knowledge. Some of the basic characteristics of an Open Business Model are:

1. Transparent business exchanges and production of products or services, with transparent processes.
2. Majority-oriented as a commitment for the majority of involved people:
    a. Sustainable by caring for a sustainable local and global system.
    b. Wellbeing-oriented, giving the health and wellbeing of people the highest preference.
    c. Flexible, opening up space for people to grow, communicate, build trust and relationship.
    d. Flat, taking measures to devolve power over decision making in different ways.
3. Wealth-sharing, offering shared revenue.
4. Location-independent, encouraging distributive production.

Furthermore, it is important to state that open business models generated the momentum and paved the way to the emergence of more complex platform business models. As stated in (Van Alstyne, Parker & Choudary, 2016) the platforms businesses have existed for years, like malls that link consumers and merchants. However, the difference emerged with the ICT and the reduced needs to possess physical infrastructure and assets, as IT makes building and scaling up platforms vastly simpler and cheaper. This allows nearly frictionless participation that strengthens network effects, enhances the ability to capture, analyze, and exchange huge amounts of data that increase the platform's value to all. This can further explained the examples of platform businesses, from Apple iPhone, to Uber, whose spectacular growth abruptly upended their industries.

As Van Alstyne, Parker & Choudary (2016) further reveals, platforms have an ecosystem with the same basic structure, comprising main four types of players. *The owners of* the platforms control their intellectual property and governance, setting the main rules and interaction models. Providers serve as the platforms interface with users. Producers create their offerings, and consumers use those offerings. Thus the platform value-adding is based on the evolving networks interactions, where creating fruitful ecosystem become crucial factor for success. Main characteristics of platform organizations are listed below (Van Alstyne, Parker & Choudary, 2016):

1. Resource orchestration, instead of resource control.
2. External interaction, instead of internal optimization.
3. Ecosystem value, instead of customer value.

The main asset for the platform organizations is the community and the resources its members own and contribute, be they rooms or cars or ideas and information (as in the case of AIRBNB, Uber or Wikipedia).The main efforts for the platform organizations are to create value by facilitating interactions between external producers and consumers. Because of this external orientation they have to organize and master good ecosystem governance or setting appropriate rules and mechanisms for interaction inside the ecosystem. Finally, the platforms seek to maximize the total value of an expanding ecosystem in a circular, iterative, feedback-driven process. Sometimes that requires subsidizing one type of consumer in order to attract another type. Although researchers have attempted to reveal how external factors and institutions influence and have a leading impact on the performance of the NFPs (Aziz & Ebrashi, 2016; Muñoz & Kibler, 2015), it is crucial to highlight the opposite process – or what is the capacity of the NFPs to transform the environment, including existing social systems and institutions.

Institutions shape the social realm as they pre-define the social framework or complex set of rules, norms, meanings, symbols, practices, and similar aides to collaboration. Therefore, institutions form socially-determined understandings of what is good and what is bad, what is right and what is wrong and what is acceptable and unacceptable. Thus institutional transformation and social development is a difficult and complex process, involving substantial efforts and reassessment of evident" and well-proved traditional understandings. However governance of the ecosystem as a complex social mechanism. To this end, ecosystem governance, institutional change and platform model of operation require further vision development.

## Social Entrepreneurship Model

It is anticipated that the role of not for profit organizations in the sphere of social entrepreneurship will continue to increase as not for profit organizations continue to adapt the operation of social systems and institutions. As the main mission for not for profit organizations and social enterprises are to create transformational impact on social or environmental ecosystems (Werker & Ahmed, 2008), its further success will largely depend on their mode of operation. Therefore, better understanding of the transformational impact that not for profit organizations have on social systems and institutional transformation is important. Successful business models for non-for-profit organizations need to orchestrate elements:

1. Good ecosystem governance.
2. Proper technology mastering.
3. Appropriate financing mechanisms.
4. Outperforming the agency problems.

Historically, NFPs played substantial role for institutional and social transformation. As described in Simmons (1998), different social movements and forms of social associations played substantial role for the abolishment of slavery, for drug control, for rising human rights, for introducing environmental protection and many others. If working for the interests of their beneficiaries and for their causes, NFPs can lead to large institutional changes, playing substantial role for shaping better "rules of the game". Thus in the advent of major economic transformations such as the 4th industrial revolution, where many new social issues will further emerge, NFPs can provide many incentives, knowledge and perspectives for shaping better rules in society. That is why there should be investigated more specifically the mechanisms by which NGOs/NFPs can assist the social transformation, successfully overcoming some of the rising problems such as agency dependency and private/narrow shaped interests of specific groups of donors, national/institutional funders, private interests and other funders and donors.

## Platform Model

Analyzing the platform models for organizing NFPs activities provides a more successful way to mobilize resources, to deliver better value-in-social-context, and to set more transparent rules of interaction and governance. Communities, end-users, companies and for-profit organizations, public organizations and institutions can work together for delivering better services and better social perspectives for all. This comes to show that we need to change our thinking for NGOs/NFPs from pipeline (Figure 1) to platform-oriented (Figure 2) organizational models. As reveal (Van Alstyne, Parker, Choudary, 2016), discussing the uberization effect on the economy, when a platform enters a pipeline organization's market, the platform almost always wins.

*Figure 2. Platform oriented model of operation multiple interactions between various partners*
*Source 2 Antonova (2016)*

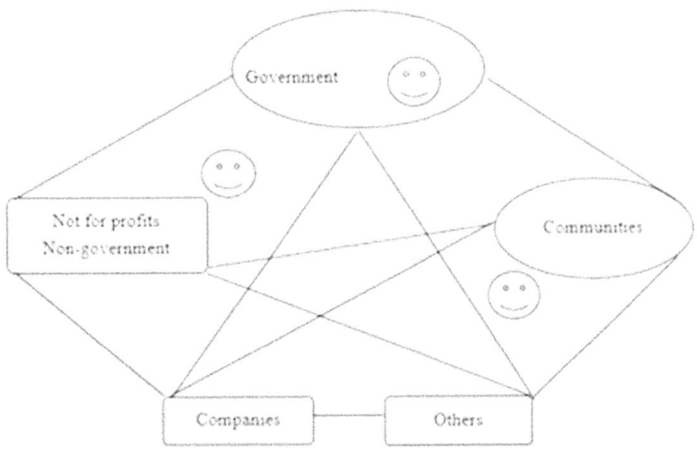

As George & Reeds (2016) emphasize NFPs should try to build strong social networks and connections with partners, communities and stakeholders with broader power and decision-making abilities. It is important to highlight that ecosystem design and involvement of different stakeholders, as for example state and public institutions and civil society communities will largely differ from state to state, as historically the social institutions emerged differently and thus there are not available "one-fit-all" solution (Aziz & Ebrashi, 2016). Furthermore, defining the social design of a platform-based organizational model consists of making appropriate rules and architecture.

An *open architecture* allows players to access platform resources and to create new sources of value for them. *Open governance* allows players other than the owner to shape the rules of trade and reward sharing on the platform. Regardless of who sets the rules, a fair and transparent reward/motivation system is a key. If platform have an open architecture but do not share the some valuable compensation or rewards, potential platform participants will have the ability to engage but no incentives. On opposite, if rules are open but the architecture (the way of interaction is relatively closed), potential participants could have incentives to engage but not the ability (Van Alstyne, Parker, Choudary, 2016).

The critical strategic aim of the platform organization is the strong up-front design of the processes that will attract the desired participants, enable the right interactions (so-called core interactions), and encourage ever-more-powerful network effects. To that end, platform must define the access (whom to let onto the platform) and governance (or "control"—what consumers, producers, providers, and even competitors are allowed to do), fostering further interactions and the associated network effects as the ultimate source of competitive advantage.

## Technology Factors and Internet Models

In order to design better organizational models for NFPs it is important to outline the important features of the Internet technologies that can further contribute for better communication, networking and communities' collaboration for the non-for-profit. As Rheingold (1993) states one of the surprising properties of the computing is that it is a social activity.

The driving force behind the rising internet economy is the demand-side economies of scale or the network effect (Van Alstyne, Parker, Choudary, 2016). These are enhanced by technologies that create efficiencies in social networking, demand aggregation and other phenomena that help social networks to expand. In the internet economy, platforms that achieve higher "volume" than competitors (or that attract more participants) offer a higher average value (value-in-social-context) per transaction. That's because the larger the network, the better the matches between supply and demand and the richer the data that can be used to find matches. Greater scale generates more value, which attracts more participants, which creates more value, and thus forming another virtuous feedback loop that produces monopolies (Van Alstyne, Parker, Choudary, 2016).

Furthermore, the wider application of ICT technologies and Internet contributed to the decrease of the transaction costs (Masanell & Ricart, 2007). Thus, Internet improved largely the information asymmetries and made the information accessible globally, decreasing communication costs, along with remote business operations, and transforming tremendously the global NGOs/NFPs realms. But more importantly Internet brought enormous leverage to ordinary citizens at relatively little cost, including intellectual leverage, social leverage, commercial leverage, and most important, political leverage (Rheingold, 1993). As the public sphere depends on free communication and discussion of ideas, the Internet can enhance NGOs/NFPs efforts for leading to institutional transformation by bringing open access, voluntary participation, generation of public opinion through assemblies of citizens who engage in rational argument, freedom to express opinions, and freedom to discuss matters of the state and criticize the way state power is organized.

## Alternative Internet-Based Funding Models

One of the crucial factors for NFPs modes of operations are the ways for NFPs financing. As discussed above, the main transaction costs that occur in NFPs are purely related to agency costs – or the costs of getting funding, including communication and negotiation between the donors and the management of the NFPs. This is explained by the fact that many non-for profits invest considerable resources to collect donations, to develop fundraising programs or to apply for specific grant programs.

Some of the alternatives to reduce the agency costs and fundraising efforts for some NFPs can be to stick on some public financing programs (specializing in specific areas) or to attract investments and funding from wealthy individuals, but both of these models can lead to governance and management problems, hindering the ultimate goal – helping the end-users and leading social transformations. Thus we will discuss another funding alternative or crowdfunding that emerged largely as platform activity. Some popular web-platforms for crowdfunding are Kickstarter.com and Indiegogo.com, presenting many financing opportunities both for investors and for (social) entrepreneurs.

More specifically, crowd-funding is a peculiar form of funding with customers (or final users) acting as direct investors (Belleflame, Lambert & Schwienbacher, 2010). The data reveals that a large share of crowdfunding initiatives are based on passive investments, or investments with a promise of compensation but no direct involvement in the decision-making process, or provision of time or expertise for the initiative. But more importantly, crowdfunding is for sharing information and finding partnership, communities and networking. Furthermore, it is important to note that non-profit organizations tend to be more successful in finding and attracting crowd-funding financing (Belleflame, Lambert & Schwienbacher, 2010). Further, Wojciechowski (2009) discusses that donations via crowdfunding platforms increase and that social networks can become a worthwhile model for money collection for many charity organizations and NGOs.

Thus, using crowdfunding can improve not only fundraising for NFPs, but it can help to improve visibility and participation opportunities, including better options for transparency, evidences, credibility; inserting ratings and others, and leading to better organization and operation. All this will further decrease the agency and transaction costs for NFPs operations, providing better opportunities for organizations to increase their activities and to lead to substantial ecosystem transformations.

# CONCLUSION

Recently the interest and funding for not for profit organizations largely increased in a global perspective and further augmented their possibility to exercise power both on political and economic processes. Thus, as not for profit organizations continue to become active players for social transformation and their share of social services providers raised not only on regional, but as well on national and international context. However, a small critical literature exists questioning whether NFPs are effective in improving lives or providing goods and services for their beneficiaries. Moreover, there is a lack of evidences and proper understanding of service providers and alternative public organizations or for-profit private organizations which has resulted in a number of controversies about governance and management capacity of not for profit organizations. Some of the issues, reported by different researchers state that nobody has the interest to measure and report negative outcomes of the not for profit activities and it is very difficult to identify quantified approach and measures to assess the quality of the work of non-profits in large.

Even if social organizations can play increasing role for the institutional transformation and social development, this model of development of not for profit is not without challenges. Many researches prove that decentralized and multi-layered decision-making can lead to inefficiencies and furthermore – can create additional burden for public and social services funding. Thus, new technologies and emerging business models for not for profit operations can help the organizations to improve coordination, to reduce transaction costs and to increase visibility of services, increasing the focus on beneficiaries and end-users. Therefore not for profits must be considered as service integrators or platforms, connecting different actors, communities and stakeholders.

Further research is needed to identify how not for profit organizations interact with public organizations and how they actually influence political and institutional decisions. More specifically, it's important to investigate how not for profit organizations are financed by public funds or large private donors can undermine the social development, supporting status-quo or just defending the interests of the donors and not of the beneficiaries. Adopting more flexible, open and platform-based business model can enhance not for profit main goal, the potentials for social and institutional transformation.

## REFERENCES


Aldashev, G., Jaimovich, E., & Verdier, T. (2016). *Small is Beautiful: Motivational Allocation in the Non-Profit Sector.* ECARES Working Papers.

Alesina, A., & Dollar, D. (2000). Who gives foreign aid to whom and why? *Journal of Economic Growth*, *5*(1), 33–63. doi:10.1023/A:1009874203400

Archibugi, D., & Filippetti, A. (2016). *The Retreat of Public Research and its Adverse Consequences on Innovation*. CIMR Research Working Paper Series, Working paper 31. Retrieved from http://www.bbk.ac.uk/innovation/publications/docs/WP31.pdf

Aziz, H. A., & El Ebrashi, R. (2016). A Business Model Design Process for Social Enterprises: The Critical Role of the Environment. *World Academy of Science, Engineering and Technology, International Journal of Social, Behavioral, Educational, Economic. Business and Industrial Engineering*, *10*(5), 1377–1383.

Barr, A., & Fafchamps, M. (2006). A client-community assessment of the NGO sector in Uganda. *The Journal of Development Studies*, *42*(4), 611–639. doi:10.1080/00220380600682009

Barrett, M., Davidson, E., Prabhu, J., & Vargo, S. L. (2015). Service innovation in the digital age: Key contributions and future directions. *Management Information Systems Quarterly*, *39*(1), 135–154.

Belleflamme, P., Lambert, T., & Schwienbacher, A. (2010, June). Crowdfunding: An industrial organization perspective. In *Workshop Digital Business Models: Understanding Strategies* (pp. 25-26).

Beltagui, A., Riedel, J. C., & Pawar, K. S. (2008, June). Product—Service transition: Research questions. In *2008 IEEE International Technology Management Conference (ICE)* (pp. 1-8). IEEE.

Bilodeau, M., & Steinberg, R. (2006). Donative nonprofit organizations. Handbook of the Economics of Giving, Altruism and Reciprocity, 2, 1271-1333.

Chell, E., Spence, L. J., Perrini, F., & Harris, J. D. (2016). Social entrepreneurship and business ethics: Does social equal ethical? *Journal of Business Ethics*, *133*(4), 619–625. doi:10.1007/s10551-014-2439-6

Chen, T. F. (2009). Building a platform of Business Model 2.0 to creating real business value with Web 2.0 for web information services industry. *International Journal of Electronic Business Management*, *7*(3), 168–180.

Chesbrough, H., & Rosenbloom, R. S. (2002). The role of the business model in capturing value from innovation: Evidence from Xerox Corporations technology spin-off companies. *Industrial and Corporate Change*, *11*(3), 529–555. doi:10.1093/icc/11.3.529

Dey, P., Schneider, H., & Maier, F. (2016). Intermediary Organisations and the Hegemonisation of Social Entrepreneurship: Fantasmatic Articulations, Constitutive Quiescences, and Moments of Indeterminacy. *Organization Studies*, 1–22.

Edvardsson, B., Tronvoll, B., & Gruber, T. (2011). Expanding understanding of service exchange and value co-creation: A social construction approach. *Journal of the Academy of Marketing Science*, *39*(2), 327–339. doi:10.1007/s11747-010-0200-y

Fitzsimmons, J. A., & Fitzsimmons, M. J. (2006). *Service management: operations, strategy and information technology* (5th ed.). London: McGraw -Hill.

Foster, W. L., Kim, P., & Christiansen, B. (2009). Ten nonprofit funding models. *Stanford Social Innovation Review*, *7*(2), 32–39.

George, C., & Reed, M. G. (2016). Building institutional capacity for environmental governance through social entrepreneurship: Lessons from Canadian biosphere reserves. *Ecology and Society*, *21*(1), 18. doi:10.5751/ES-08229-210118

Granados, M. L., Hlupic, V., Coakes, E., & Mohamed, S. (2011). Social enterprise and social entrepreneurship research and theory: A bibliometric analysis from 1991 to 2010. *Social Enterprise Journal*, *7*(3), 198–218. doi:10.1108/17508611111182368

Greer, C. R., Lusch, R. F., & Vargo, S. L. (2016). A service perspective. *Organizational Dynamics*, *1*(45), 28–38. doi:10.1016/j.orgdyn.2015.12.004

Hansmann, H. B. (1980). The role of nonprofit enterprise. *The Yale Law Journal*, *89*(5), 835–901. doi:10.2307/796089

Healey, P. (1998). Building institutional capacity through collaborative approaches to urban planning. *Environment & Planning A*, *30*(9), 1531–1546. doi:10.1068/a301531

Hill, C. W., & Jones, T. M. (1992). Stakeholder -agency theory. *Journal of Management Studies*, *29*(2), 131–154. doi:10.1111/j.1467-6486.1992.tb00657.x

Kelly, K. S. (2001). Stewardship: The fifth step in the public relations process. In R. L. Heath (Ed.), *Handbook of public relations* (pp. 279–290). Thousand Oaks, CA: SAGE. doi:10.4135/9781452220727.n21

Kerlin, J. A. (2013). The 501(c)(3) Nonprofit social enterprise. In T. S. Lyons (Ed.), *Social entrepreneurship: how businesses can transform society* (Vol. 1, pp. 27–46). Santa Barbara, CA: Praeger.

Kuziemko, I., & Werker, E. (2006). How much is a seat on the Security Council worth? Foreign aid and bribery at the United Nations. *Journal of Political Economy*, *114*(5), 905–930. doi:10.1086/507155

Lindgardt, Z., Reeves, M., Stalk, G., & Deimler, M. (2009). *Business Model innovation*. The Boston Consulting Group.

Marwell, N. P., & Calabrese, T. (2015). A deficit model of collaborative governance: Government–nonprofit fiscal relations in the provision of child welfare services. *Journal of Public Administration: Research and Theory*, *25*(4), 1031–1058. doi:10.1093/jopart/muu047

Masanell, R., & Ricart, J. (2007). *Competing through business models*. Working paper no 713, University of Navarra.

MIT-Brynjolfsson, McAfee, et al. (2015). *Open Letter on the Digital Economy, A group of leading technologists, economists, and investors propose a new approach to help us adapt to new technologies*. Available on: https://www.technologyreview.com/s/538091/open-letter-on-the-digital-economy/

Muñoz, P., & Kibler, E. (2015). Institutional Complexity and Social Entrepreneurship: A Fuzzy-Set Approach. *Journal of Business Research*.

Ng, I. C., & Maull, R. (2009, July). Embedding the new discipline of service science: A service science research agenda. In *Service Operations, Logistics and Informatics, 2009. SOLI'09. IEEE/INFORMS International Conference on* (pp. 68-73). IEEE. doi:10.1109/SOLI.2009.5203906

Nicholls, A. (Ed.). (2006). *Social entrepreneurship: new models of sustainable social change*. New York, NY: Oxford University Press. doi:10.4135/9781452218557.n489

Nicholls, A., & Murdock, A. (2012). The nature of social innovation. In Social innovation (pp. 1-30). Palgrave Macmillan UK. doi:10.1057/9780230367098_1

Osterwalder, A., Pigneur, Y., & Tucci, C. L. (2005). Clarifying business models: Origins, present, and future of the concept. *Communications of the Association for Information Systems*, *16*(1), 1.

Rheingold, H. (1993). *The Virtual Community: Homesteading on the Electronic Frontier*. New York: Addison-Wesley.

Robinson, M., & Riddell, R. C. (1995). *Non-governmental organizations and rural poverty alleviation*. OUP Catalogue.

Russel, J. S. (2015). *Ford Foundations 'Lavish' $196 Million to Push Internet Regulations*. Available on: http://newsbusters.org/blogs/joseph-rossell/2015/02/25/soros-ford-foundations-lavish-196-million-push-internet-regulations

Salamon, L. M. (1987). Of market failure, voluntary failure, and third-party government: Toward a theory of government-nonprofit relations in the modern welfare state. *Nonprofit and Voluntary Sector Quarterly*, *16*(1-2), 29–49. doi:10.1177/089976408701600104

Salamon, L. M. (2010). Putting the civil society sector on the economic map of the world. *Annals of Public and Cooperative Economics*, *81*(2), 167–210. doi:10.1111/j.1467-8292.2010.00409.x

Salamon, L. M., Sokolowski, S., & Geller, S. (2012). *Holding the Fort: Nonprofit Employment during a Decade of Turmoil*. Nonprofit Economic Data Bulletin #39. Johns Hopkins University. Available on: http://ccss.jhu.edu/wp-content/uploads/downloads/2012/01/NED_National_2012.pdf

Sedlarski, T. (2013). New Institutional Economy. Sofia University Press. (in Bulgarian)

Simmons, P. J. (1998). Learning to live with NGOs. *Foreign Policy*, (112): 82–96. doi:10.2307/1149037

Spremann, K. (1987). Agent and principal. In *Agency theory, information, and incentives* (pp. 3–37). Springer Berlin Heidelberg. doi:10.1007/978-3-642-75060-1_2

Steinberg, R. (2010). Principal–agent theory and nonprofit accountability. In K. J. Hopt & T. Von Hippel (Eds.), *Comparative corporate governance of non-profit organizations* (pp. 73–125). Cambridge, UK: Cambridge University Press. doi:10.1017/CBO9780511712128.006

Tapscott, D., Lowy, A., & Ticoll, D. (2000). *Digital capital: Harnessing the power of business webs*. Harvard Business Press.

United Nations. (2003). *Handbook on Non-Profit Institutions in the System of National Accounts, Studies in Methods, Series F., No. 91*. Retrieved from http://unstats.un.org/unsd/publication/seriesf/seriesf_91e.pdf

Van Alstyne, M., Parker, G., & Choudary, S. (2016). Pipelines, Platforms and the new rules of strategy. *Harvard Business Review*. Retrieved from https://hbr.org/2016/04/pipelines-platforms-and-the-new-rules-of-strategy

Van Puyvelde, S., Caers, R., Du Bois, C., & Jegers, M. (2012). The governance of nonprofit organizations integrating agency theory with stakeholder and stewardship theories. *Nonprofit and Voluntary Sector Quarterly*, *41*(3), 431–451. doi:10.1177/0899764011409757

Van Slyke, D. M. (2007). Agents or stewards: Using theory to understand the government-nonprofit social service contracting relationship. *Journal of Public Administration: Research and Theory*, *17*(2), 157–187. doi:10.1093/jopart/mul012

Vargo, S. L., & Luch, R. F. (2004). Evolving to a new dominant logic for marketing. *Journal of Marketing*, *68*(January), 1–17. doi:10.1509/jmkg.68.1.1.24036

Vargo, S. L., & Lusch, R. F. (2016). Institutions and axioms: An extension and update of service-dominant logic. *Journal of the Academy of Marketing Science*, *44*(1), 5–23. doi:10.1007/s11747-015-0456-3

WB. (2014). *FY 15 World Bank Budget*. Available on: http://www-wds.worldbank.org/external/default/WDSContentServer/WDSP/IB/2014/10/24/000350881_20141024085127/Rendered/PDF/918340BR0R201400disclosed0100230140.pdf

Werker, E., & Ahmed, F. Z. (2008). What do nongovernmental organizations do? *The Journal of Economic Perspectives*, *22*(2), 73–92. doi:10.1257/jep.22.2.73

Willetts, P. (2009). Non-governmental organizations. Conventions, Treaties and other Responses to Global Issues. London, UK: Encyclopedia of Life Support Systems, 229-248.

Wirtz, B. W., Pistoia, A., Ullrich, S., & Göttel, V. (2016). Business models: Origin, development and future research perspectives. *Long Range Planning*, *49*(1), 36–54. doi:10.1016/j.lrp.2015.04.001

Wojciechowski, A. (2009, November). Models of charity donations and project funding in social networks. In *OTM Confederated International Conferences "On the Move to Meaningful Internet Systems"* (pp. 454-463). Springer Berlin Heidelberg doi:10.1007/978-3-642-05290-3_58

World Economic Forum. (2016). *The future of jobs: employment, skills and workforce strategy for the fourth industrial revolution.* World Economic Forum, Geneva, Switzerland.

Yusof, S. W. M. (2010). *Developing Strategy for Customer Value Creation Towards a Professional Services. Academic Press.*

Zeithaml, V. A. (1988). Consumer perceptions of price, quality, and value: A means-end model and synthesis of evidence. *Journal of Marketing*, *52*(3), 2–22. doi:10.2307/1251446

## KEY TERMS AND DEFINITIONS

**Institutional Transformation:** New technologies and new business models for not for profit operations can help the organizations to improve coordination, to reduce transaction costs and to increase visibility of services, increasing the focus on beneficiaries and end-users. Thus institutional transformation should put not-for-profits as service integrators or platforms, connecting different actors, communities and stakeholders.

**Platform model:** it is enhanced by technologies that create efficiencies in social networking and demand aggregation that help social networks to expand. Platforms offer a higher average value when attracting more participants. The larger the network, greater scale generates more value, which attracts more participants, which creates more value, and thus forming another virtuous feedback loop that produces monopolies.

**NFP Impact:** Historically, NFPs played substantial role for institutional and social transformation, as for example - forms of social associations played substantial role for the abolishment of slavery, for drug control, for rising human rights, for introducing environmental protection and many others. If working for the interests of their beneficiaries and for their causes, NFPs can lead to large institutional changes, playing substantial role for shaping better "rules of the game".

# Chapter 15
# Re-Inventing the Social Business Model:
## New Opportunities for the Third Sector Organizations in Italy

**Dario Cavenago**
*University Milano-Bicocca, Italy*

**Laura Mariani**
*University of Bologna – Alma Mater Studiorum, Italy*

## ABSTRACT

*The recent global economic crises and the decline of the traditional welfare state are challenging the development of third sector organisations involved in the provision of public services. With the support of the Italian case and the experiences of different Italian third sector organisations, this contribution highlights how organisational survival and growth require reinvention of the business model, commencing with the concept of social, economic and environmental sustainability. The scope of third sector organisations depends on the type of government, the stage of economic development, the model of civil society, the existence of philanthropic traditions and the law and regulation. All these variables affect the business model of third sector organisations. This chapter contributes to the third sector knowledge in Italy and concludes with a discussion on solutions that are able to incentivize the use of entrepreneurial principles, stimulate networking, cooperation and growth while maintaining the relationship with the territories.*

## INTRODUCTION

The global economic crises, and the decline of the traditional welfare state, are two important challenges that third sector organizations (TSO) are facing. In particular, the survival and the growth of these organizations require the re-invention of their business model, starting from the concept of social, economic and environmental sustainability.

DOI: 10.4018/978-1-5225-2537-0.ch015

Copyright © 2017, IGI Global. Copying or distributing in print or electronic forms without written permission of IGI Global is prohibited.

The Italian Third Sector has some peculiarities that make this case emblematic (Borzaga & Fazzi, 2011; Mariani & Cavenago, 2013; Ranci, 2015). On one hand, the institutional context, characterized in the past by a farraginous regulatory framework, is now evolving toward a model in which the barriers between nonprofit and for profit sector are reducing progressively. On the other hand, the Italian TSO have to reduce their structural dependence from the public sector.

The theoretical framework aims at defining the task environment of TSO operating in regulated institutional contexts. Welfare societies, in fact, rely on a complex mix of different providers (state, markets, family, and TSO). At the same time, changing welfare discourses have opened up space for new partnerships, divisions of labour, and responsibilities between these actors.

In particular, the development of Third Sector depends on several institutional conditions. The type of Government (Kerlin, 2013; Lee, 2010), the stage of Economic development (Kerlin, 2013; Lee, 2010), the model of civil society (Salamon & Anheier, 1998), the existence of philanthropic traditions (Wang & Morgan, 2011), and the regulation – legal frames, tax reduction, transparency, accountability - (Wang & Morgan, 2011), can affect the governance structure and the business model of TSO.

According to Lecy and Van Skyle (2012), many of the theories of nonprofit sector size are descriptive and reactive, while the understanding of the drivers of opportunity for TSO are still unexplored. Consequently, scholars need to empirically address a set of questions about how TSO develop adaptive and responsive strategies to turbulence, opportunity, stability, and growth. This chapter aims at contributing to fill this gap.

Combining the literature on the density of Third Sector at system level, with those on the strategic management of individual TSO, several emerging issues for the development of sustainable social business models are identified.

The results can be significant for similar contexts, characterized by the presence of a "Welfare Partnership model" with both a civil society strongly involved in the provision of welfare services, and a strong dependence of TSO from public funding. In particular, a relationship between regulation features, and growth of Third Sector emerges, and such relationship is mediated by the ways in which TSO design and re-invent their own business models.

## BACKGROUND AND LITERATURE OVERVIEW

This study builds a framework to investigate the current trends emerging in TSO institutional and social context, and its main consequences on the development of renewed business models. In this context, the definition of nonprofit proposed by Salamon and Anheier (1997) is adopted. The authors identify the five core structural or operational features – namely:

- Formal constitution;
- Non-governmental basic structure;
- Self-governing;
- Non-profit-distributing;
- Presence of voluntary activities or resources.

These features distinguish TSO from other types of social institutions. More specifically, this contribution focuses on TSO that – providing welfare services – have a more or less important relationship with the public administrations.

In order to support the framework development, the background of this work aims at explaining the effect of the social-institutional context on the development of Third Sector, and the effect of such conditions on the implementation of their business models.

The observed variation in TSO across countries and regions suggests the importance of social and institutional context in their development. Contextual conditions define the dimension and the characteristic of the Third Sector in each country. In particular, given specific institutional and societal boundaries, TSO have a potential environment in which they can fulfil the organizational mission through the offer of their own Value Proposition. The formation and growth of TSO in a particular country are likely to be influenced by the characteristics of its civil society, its economic situation, and they are defined by its legal and regulatory framework. As a consequence, changes in the institutional environment – due to reforms and public policies - affect the growth (or reduction) of the Third Sector (Figure 1).

With a specific focus on welfare characteristics, the density and development of Third Sector depend on the characteristics of civil society (Salamon & Sokolowski, 2010): the larger is the contribution of civil society, the larger is the Third Sector dimension. Furthermore, according to dimension of the welfare states, the services provided by TSO can vary. Salamon and Sokolowski (2010) describe five models: Liberal, Welfare Partnership, Social Democratic, Deferred Democratization, and Traditional.

- **Liberal Model:** The civil society is large because of greater reliance on private services in the face of a relatively small welfare state. Government funding is limited and there is a sizeable reliance on private support.
- **Welfare Partnership:** Civil society is still large and involved in the provision of welfare services, however funding is characterized by a large share of government revenue, rather than private resources.

*Figure 1. Institutional context and Third Sector evolution*
*Source 1: Cavenago, D & Mariani, L (2016)*

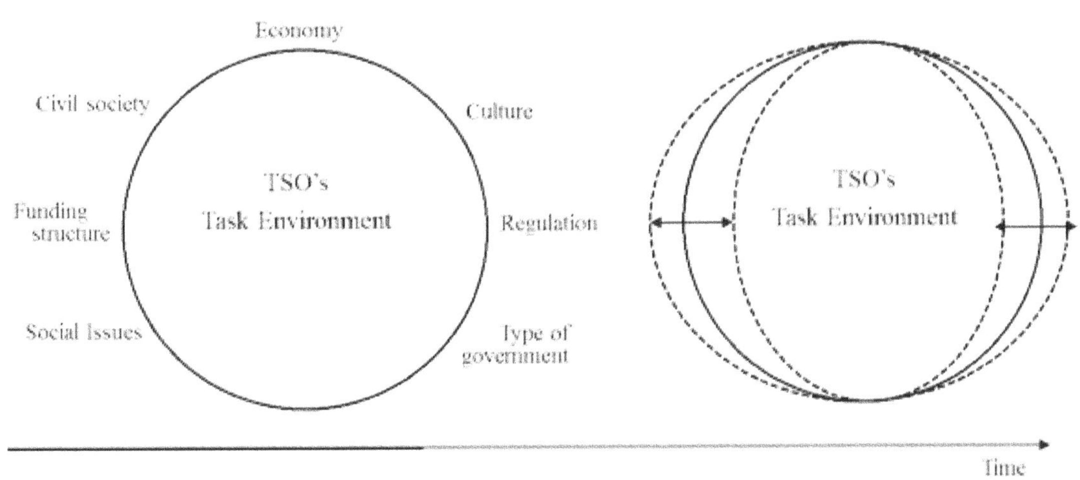

- **Social Democratic:** Civil society can be large but limited to expressive roles in the advocacy, sports and culture industries. This is due to a sizable welfare state that both funds and delivers social services.
- **Traditional Countries:** The civil society is small and it is characterized by the persistence of traditional forms of helping. With the government providing little support even for welfare services, TSO focuses on antipoverty services, through the financing of international aid.
- **Deferred Democratization:** Civil society remains small due to repressive and neglectful policies of a State. With little government support, therefore, the Third Sector relies on both fees where it provides services for the upper class, and international aid where it serves the poor.

Other contributions highlight the relationship between the dimension of Third Sector and societal characteristics such as diversity and the structure of social capital.

- **Diversity:** The relationship between society diversity and Third Sector development can be explained through the government failure theory (Weisbron, 1977, 1986, 1988). According to this theory, when a society is diverse the median voter preferences are not be sufficient to satisfy the demand of different groups for different social services. Preferences that result from diversity in a society are referred to as heterogeneous demand, that can be faced by specialized TSO. The features of diversity that have been considered include variables of racial diversity (Corbin, 1999; Matsunaga & Yamauchi, 2004), immigrant populations (Paarlberg & Gen, 2009), and religious diversity (Salamon, Hems, & Chinnock, 2000; Brooks &Wilson, 2007).
- **Social Capital:** The development of social capital and Third Sector development seems to be positively related. Social capital refers to connections among individuals, social networks and the norms of reciprocity and trustworthiness that arise from them (Putnam, 2000). Social capital is a variety of different entities consisting of some aspect of social structure, and facilitating certain actions of individuals who are within the structure (Coleman, 1990). The extent of social capital depends on citizens engagement in public affairs, community volunteerism, community organizational life, informal sociability, and social trust (Putnam, 2000).

Finally, nonprofit laws and regulation are among the most important factors in determining the size and scope of Third Sector in many countries (Salamon & Flaherty, 1996). In particular, the regulatory framework that defines the sector and the agenda of governments for the sector are central factors (Borzaga & Fazzi, 2011; Haddad, 2011; Schneider, 2013; Wang & Morgan, 2011; Heurlin, 2010).

Changes in the institutional environment and societal structure do not affect exclusively the density of TSO in a specific context, but they also affect the behaviours of these organizations. According to the neo-institutional theory, organizations are influenced by the society in which they work and they have to change and adopt the norms of this society to conform to external expectations about what forms or structures are acceptable (DiMaggio & Powell, 1983; Meyer & Rowan, 1977). Therefore, individual TSO preserve their legitimacy by incorporating (or appearing to incorporate), the new practices, norms and values: if the organization is not viewed as legitimate, its survival is thought to be at stake (Dowling & Pfeffer, 1975).

However, under a strategic perspective, TSO do not suffer passively the external pressure; rather, they interact with their own environment determining the conditions of their development and growth, which are strictly related to a balanced and positive relationship with the external conditions. In particular, each TSO selects a certain segment of the external environment, defined by institutional and social contexts, and it carries out certain types of transaction with it (Normann, 1977). Within a wider regulated environment, TSO select a specific task environment, and they also choice the type of transactions to undertake there. Therefore, on one hand, the complex environment of the TSO is characterized by different actors and interdependencies whose effects are (partially) inevitable, but, at the same time, these interdependencies are the result of their choices. With reference to the changes of regulation in Japan, the reforms favorited the growth of TSO number, but they also incentivized new approaches of business, and TSO became more active in their relationship with public agencies. They have started identifying community problems, crafting policy solutions to those problems, and participating actively in implementing solutions in the perspective of public-private cooperation (Haddad, 2011).

Within a potential environment – bounded by institutional context and societal characteristics – the TSO can develop their own social business idea, actualized into a specific social business model. In defining the business idea, TSO have to maintain the coherence between three different components (Normann, 1977): the external environment and its needs, the offering of the organization – or Value Proposition –, and the internal factors (organizational structure, resources, knowledge and capabilities, systems, values). This concept of business idea is systemic in nature and the relation to the external environment depends on the offering, which in turn is dependent upon firm-internal factors.

The implementation of a social business idea by TSO, can be represented through the components of their business model. The concept of business model has attracted the researchers' attention in the last years and, although there is no consensus as to its definition, literature uses to distinguishing its three major components: the product/service proposed to customers, the way the company is organized so as to deliver this product and service to its customers, and the revenue model (Chesbrough & Rosenbloom, 2002; Zott & Amit, 2008)

In this work, the definition of business model adopted is those proposed by Yunus, Moingeon and Lehmann-Ortega (2010) that, focusing on the experience of Greeman Bank, emphasizes the role social value, which is particularly significant for TSO (Figure 2).

According to this model, the components of business model are the Value Proposition, the Value Constellation, and the Profit Equation, composed of social and economic profit equations.

*Figure 2. Environment task and business model*
*Source 2: Cavenago, D & Mariani, L (2016)*

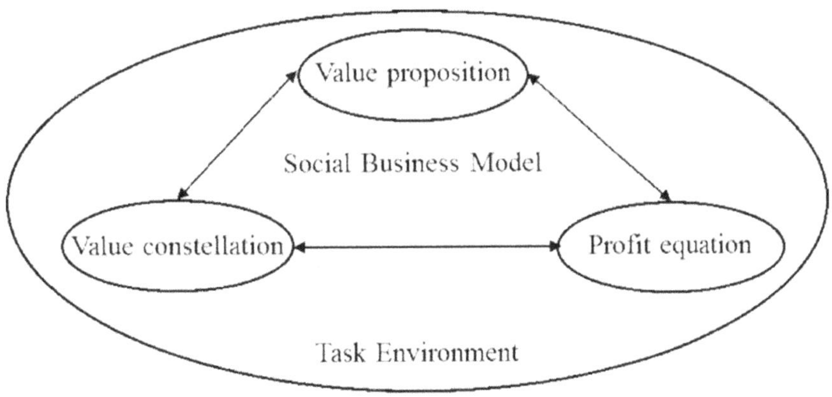

- **Value Proposition:** It includes the identification of TSO' users, and it summarizes the characteristics of the value provided, as well as the relationships with the users. The Value Proposition of each TSO focus, alternatively or simultaneously, on the provision of services aimed at facing the needs of different categories of users, the development of social innovation, and the accomplishing of representational activities (Salamon et al., 2000).
- **Value Constellation:** It includes the way in which services are provided through both the internal value chain and external partners support. With a specific focus on the role of services provision, the Value Constellation of TSO can be presented through the description of the services' content, and the main phases of the provision process of a welfare service: (1) access; (2) screening; (3) intervention planning and implementation; (4) monitoring in progress; and (5) follow up (Mariani & Cavenago, 2013). The access phase represents the first contact between the TSO and the user, where the organization provides information on the service and reduces any barriers which could compromise the overall service supply. Organizations are then involved in the screening phase, which allows the evaluation of individual needs. The planning and implementation phase consists in formulating objectives, identifying the necessary resources, defining the timing and implementing the intervention, while in-progress monitoring is carried out so as to keep the objectives fixed during planning. Finally, follow-up procedures consist of periodical check-ups in the post-service stage. In all the phases, the role of the client/user is crucial. In the provision of welfare services, in fact, the co-production process is essential for service effectiveness, and the clients' behaviour has a significant impact on the final quality of the supply process (Pestoff & Brandsen, 2013; Prahalad & Ramaswamy, 2004). All the phases of service provision process are not necessary implemented by an individual TSO. Frequently, in fact, TSO act toward an embedded networking approach, based on stable and intense connections among different institutions, sharing reciprocal trust. The network model is adopted by many TSO with the aim to tackle with greater efficiency the needs of their users through institutionalized ties with social services, public administration, hospitals, advice bureaus, primary care bureau and other actors through formal and informal connections (Mariani & Cavenago, 2013).
- **Profit Equation:** It is the financial translation of the other two – Value Proposition and Value Constellation –, including the value captured from the revenues, and costs structure. Profit Equation can be furthered decomposed into Social Equation, which summarizes the desired social profits through a comprehensive eco-system view, and the Economic Equation, which targets the full recovery of both costs, and capital. The expenses of TSO are directly related to the structure of the offer – personnel cost, depreciation of equipment, supplies, financial expenses and so on –, while the revenues of TSO are strongly related to the overall institutional context that determined the weight of public financing on the overall revenues. A general criterion usable in order to assess the sustainability of Profit Equation is considering if it has been managed in a balanced manner. The need to fulfil the social mission still maintaining a financial and economic balancing is a precondition for the sustainable development of TSO. In particular, TSO are called to maintain a clear identity and focus tied to social mission with better means of measuring nonprofit performance in order to reconcile financial and mission-related performance (Young, 2005).

## THIRD SECTOR IN ITALY: TOWARD THE RE-DESIGN OF BUSINESS MODELS

To assess of the effect of the task environment on the business models of TSO, the evolution of nonprofit sector in Italy is proposed.

### Methodology

In order to build the Italian case study, a documental analysis has been conducted. In particular, the case draws upon content analysis of the relevant regulation and the literature on the Third Sector and welfare system in Italy, combined with the assessment of demographical and economic trends. Table 1 includes the description of the sources used for the development of the case study.

Furthermore, the study draws from research actions and field investigations conducted over the last years by the authors in several Italian TSO belonging to different regional welfare systems.

The information has been assessed by two researchers, who selected, separately, the emerging themes affecting the business model of TSO, classifying them under the business model component: value proposition, value constellation, and profit equation. Discrepancies on both themes' selection and themes' classification have been discussed, with the aim to concord a common judgement. To align the information, and gain other perspectives some control interviews with a selection of academics and professionals of the Italian Third Sector have been conducted.

### Historical Context of Italian TSO

Characterized by a progressive reduction of public spending for welfare services, as well as by the introduction of recent reform that should simplify the overall fragmented regulatory framework, the Italian TSO has to face different new challenges. Toward the description of the evolution of Third Sector in

*Table 1. Specific Italian TSO research*

| Source | Description |
|---|---|
| **Census of Italian Third Sector** | The data warehouse of the 9th Industry and Services Census 2011 contains a wealth of detailed information on the main features of businesses, non-profit institutions and public institutions, disaggregated at local. The census reference date is 31 December 2011. |
| **Literature on the Italian Third Sector** | Defourny and Borzaga (2001); Borzaga and Fazzi (2011); Mariani and Cavenago (2013); Colombo (2008); Ranci (1994, Ranci 2015, Salamon and Anheier (1998). |
| **Grey literature and Sectorial Newspapers** | *Unicredit Bank - Report on Third Sector, 2011,* Vita nonprofit, nonprofit Online (il portale del terzo settore). |
| **Law and other Regulation before the reform** | Civil Code; Law 49/1987 on social cooperation and NGO repealed by Law 125/2014 on Governing International Development Cooperation; Law 381/91 on social cooperatives; Law 266/91 on voluntary associations; Legislative Decree 153/1999 on foundation banks; Legislative Decree 460/1997 on Socially Oriented Not-for-Profit Organizations (ONLUS); Law 328/2000 on integrated system of interventions and social services; Law 383/2000 on association of social promotion; Legislative Decree 155/2006 on social enterprise; Legislative Decree 77/2002 on voluntary service |
| **Reform of Third Sector** | Law 106/2016 |

Source 3: Cavenago, D & Mariani, L (2016)

Italy, as well as the presentation of TSO task environment, this contribution highlights today and future challenges for these organizations.

In Italy, until the end of the Eighteenth Century, social protection was provided by private TSO, financed by private citizens and local authorities. The most important TSO were the *Opere Pie*, a form of Charities owned and managed by different congregations of the Catholic Church. *Opere Pie* were present in the country even prior to unification, providing benefits to the poor, as well as social and health services. In 1861 there were about 18.000 of them. These organizations were private charitable institutions with estate consisting mainly of legacies and donations acquired over the course of the century.

Between 1866 and 1890, the Italian state passed laws aimed at confiscating the estate of various religious orders and congregations also forcing the *Opere Pie* to submit to state control. In 1866, in a first attempt to reduce Catholic influence over public life, the Parliament passed the act suppressing 1.800 religious orders and congregations and confiscating their property. The buildings expropriated were allocated to local authorities for use as schools, hospital and other welfare institutions. Consequently, the Italian state assumed regulatory responsibility for private social welfare for the first time in its history. The autonomy of TSO both in the choice of objectives and activities, as well as their management were drastically reduced (Defourny & Borzaga, 2001).

At the beginning of Twentieth Century the construction of the Italian public welfare continued. The expansion of the state's functions in the field of welfare strengthened during the Fascist period, with the introduction of compulsory insurance against invalidity, public pensions and maternity. At the same time, Fascism eliminated any form of self-organization by new organizations, included TSO, in the context of welfare services. The regime also attacked workers movement and second level organizations, replacing them with a single body closely controlled by the Fascist Party. The Civil Code, approved in 1942, confirmed the residual role of TSO.

The end of Fascism and the approval of the Constitution (1948) marked a change in the conception of TSO and welfare state through the introduction of a Universalist type of welfare, and the recognition of the role of civil society and TSO as important actors of the social welfare.

Three phases characterize the evolution of Third Sector in Italy from 1980 to 2005: pioneering, expansion, and institutionalization (Borzaga & Fazzi, 2011).

- **Pioneering Phase:** It stated with the development of the new Third Sector in 1980s. A renewed sector of nonprofit organizations emerged, characterized by voluntary associations. Due to lack of regulation able to envisage a regulatory framework consistent with the activities of the new types TSO, some promoters adopted the cooperative form in order to promote 'social-purpose cooperatives' (Borzaga & Fazzi, 2011). Until the beginning of the 1990s, the new TSO had been developed with a high degree of autonomy in their choice of what services to furnish and what needs to satisfy, focused mainly on the assistance and support for persons in need who were inadequately served by public policies. During this first phase, in 1987, the Italian Parliament also approved the regulation of NGOs (Law 49/1987).
- **Expansion Phase:** It started at the beginning of 1991s, when law 381/91 on social cooperatives and law 266/91 on voluntary associations were enacted. These laws recognized, for the first time, both the social and public function of TSO engaged in the production of welfare services and the work integration of disadvantaged people. Since 1991, the amount of public expenditure on social services increased and the number of TSO underwent impressive growth. Public financing rapidly became the principal source of funding for TSO, and the issue of a more efficient allocation of

public resources became more pressing: public authorities started applying for more competitive selection criteria. During the Expansion Phase, the regulation for foundation banks (Legislative Decree 153/1999), and Socially Oriented Not-for-Profit Organizations - ONLUS – (Legislative Decree 460/1997) have been introduced. With the attempt to provide a clear legal context in which place the activities of TSO, the introduction of ONLUS regulation was aimed at giving a sharper definition to the characteristics of TSO and to guarantee them support, above all fiscal benefits. The main characteristics of the Legislative Decree 460/1997 was the introduction of a list of sector/services in which TSO have to operate in order to obtain fiscal benefits.

- **Institutionalization Phase:** It started in 2000, through the approval of a new national law on social services (L. 328/00) aimed at recasting the Italian system of social services on the basis of the principle of greater equity and on more precise planning procedures. Contracts between TSO and public authorities became more formalized, and new rules and more prescriptive organizational criteria were widely employed to manage the social services system. In particular, greater use was made of competitive procedures for service contract, the intention being to select the cheapest suppliers. During this phase, the Italian Parliament also approved the law n.383/2000 aimed at introducing the Association of social promotion: TSO promoting solidarity services as well as social aggregation through the pursuit of social and cultural activities.

In 2005, the introduction of the regulatory framework for social enterprises (D.lgs 155/2006) represented, for the first time in the Italian history, the attempt to rationalize the Italian regulation of nonprofit organization. The process for the introduction of the Social Enterprise figure has been recently closed with the approval, by the Italian Parliament of the Third Sector reform, as described in the next section.

## The Task Environment of TSO in Italy

The first dimension of Italian TSO that affect their business models is the relationship with the Government. Similar to other West European countries, Italy has a strong welfare state, and the Italian civil society sector is considered to be a Welfare Partnership model in which TSO are involved in the provision of public services (Kerlin, 2013; Salamon & Sokolowski, 2010). The relationship between TSO and Government is characterized by a weak cooperation with regard to objectives and planning, but there is a strong functional interdependence between the two sectors and consequently each supports the other (Ranci, 1994). Central and local governments depend on Third Sector for the provision of public services and TSO depend on the public sector for financing their activities. The strong relationship with the governments have determined a Third Sector characterized by a significant number of TSO providing welfare services. Table 2 includes some highlights on the structure of Third Sector in Italy, with a specific focus on education, healthcare, and social services.

In Italy, there are about 301,000 TSOs (Istat 2011). The welfare sector, with a smaller number of units (17.1% of the total TSO), has the higher inflows of cash (29.7 million) equal to 46,5% of the total inflows of Italian TSO, and it also employs the majority of paid workers (74.2%). Looking at the income statement revenues (Table 3), the private sources account for 66% while the public sources represent 34%, demonstrating a significant contribution from the public. Public funding is significant, especially in welfare sectors: healthcare (68%), social assistance (56%) and education and research (42%). For almost a third of TSO operating in the welfare, public funding is over 50% of total revenue. Despite the financial dependence of the Third Sector from the public sector is still significant, the recent economic

*Table 2. Italian TSO and welfare services*

| TSO Industry | No. Volunteers (th) | No. Employees (th) | No. TSO | Cash Inflows (Mil Euros) |
|---|---|---|---|---|
| **Welfare services** | 1.114<br>23,4% | 505<br>74,3% | 51.532<br>17,1% | 29.731<br>46,5% |
| ***Education/Research*** | 177<br>3,7% | 121<br>17,8% | 15.519<br>5,2% | 8.123<br>12,7% |
| ***Healthcare*** | 338<br>7,1% | 159<br>23,4% | 10.969<br>3,6% | 11.378<br>17,8% |
| ***Social Assistance*** | 599<br>12,6% | 225<br>33,1% | 25.044<br>8,3% | 10.230<br>16,0% |
| **Other industries** | 3.645<br>76,6% | 175<br>25,7% | 249.659<br>82,9% | 34.209<br>53,5% |
| **TOTAL** | 4.759 | 680 | 301.191 | 63.940 |

Source 1 Instat TSO Census (2011)

crisis has marked the reduction of the welfare state, and this reduction is also translated into a gradual downsizing of the state contribution for TSO. Table 3, provides a composition of TSO revenue.

The evolution of the cash inflows from 2008 to 2011 (Table 4) show the public budget cuts to TSOs. In particular, a reduction of revenue arising from the public contracts funded with local and central government grants.

Together with a strong relationship with central and local governments, the second dimension of the task environment that affect more strongly Italian TSO' business models is the regulatory framework that is characterized by the existence of laws overlaps, on one hand, and an activity-centred approach in producing regulation, on the other hand. Modern TSO are based on the Italian Constitution approved in 1948 that promotes and protect the citizens self-organizations. More recently, in 2001, the role of Third

*Table 3. TSO revenue composition*

| Type of TSO | Public Funding (Mil Euros) | | | Private Funding (Mil Euros) | | | | | (%) Public Funding |
|---|---|---|---|---|---|---|---|---|---|
| | Public Grants | Public Contracts | Total Public | Associates' Fees | Commercial Activities | Donations | Other | Total Private | |
| **Education / research** | 886 | 2.511 | 3.397 | 1.003 | 2.303 | 554 | 866 | 4.726 | 42 |
| **Healthcare services** | 314 | 7.457 | 7.771 | 373 | 2.283 | 403 | 549 | 3.608 | 68 |
| **Social assistance services** | 419 | 5.360 | 5.780 | 767 | 2.328 | 678 | 677 | 4.450 | 56 |
| **Total welfare services** | 1.619 | 15.329 | 16.947 | 2.143 | 6.914 | 1.635 | 2.092 | 12.784 | 57 |
| **Other services** | 1.641 | 3.317 | 4.958 | 14.667 | 5.021 | 2.951 | 6.612 | 29.252 | 15 |
| **Total TSO** | 3.260 | 18.646 | 21.906 | 16.810 | 11.936 | 4.585 | 8.704 | 42.036 | 34 |

Source 2 Istat TSO Census (2011)

*Table 4. Changes in public contracts and public grants (2008-2011)*

| | Associations (%) | (Social) Cooperatives (%) | Foundations (%) |
|---|---|---|---|
| Timeline | 2008 – 2011 | | |
| Public Contracts | -4,3 | +3,5 | -13,1 |
| Public Grants | -9,1 | -15,5 | -24,1 |

Source 3 UniCredit Bank Report (2011)

Sector in Italy has been strengthen through the incorporation, in the Italian Constitution, of the principle of subsidiary, together with the increase of regional autonomy, stating that public institutions at different levels of government should favour initiatives by individuals and civil society organizations aimed at addressing public needs (Colombo, 2008). Italian Constitution coexists with the antecedent regulation of the Civil Code of 1942 including the laws that define the general framework of TSO. From the Expansion Phase, the Italian law evolution has been characterized by the progressive introduction of special regulation, aimed at filling the gap in the Civil Code regulation in order to answer to societal changes. In particular, the Civil Code defines the main figures of TSO: Association, Foundations and Co-operatives.

Associations represent the most common form that the civil society can assume when self-organizing for a certain purpose. Foundations are furthered characterized by the disposability of assets devoted to a specific social aim, finally, cooperatives are firms owned, controlled, and operated by a group of users for their own benefit. Indeed, the special regulation introduces the frameworks for NGOs, voluntary organizations, Sports clubs, social cooperatives for the provision of welfare services (type A) or for integration of disabled people in the labour market (Type B), Banking foundations, corporate foundations. Associations for social promotion, and nonprofit organizations of Social Utility (ONLUS). ONLUS regulation, in particular, aims at defining the enabling characteristics of TSO for the access to preferential taxation as well as to public founding. In this context, the regulation of Italian Third Sector highlights different levels of overlaps: the first one between Civil Code and special regulation figures, and the second one among special regulation.

Crossing the Civil Code framework with the special regulation, different configurations of TSO emerge, in particular, in order to provide specific services, or operating in a specific area, a certain combination of Civil Code framework and special regulation is required (Table 5).

Furthermore, special regulation tends to list the services that can be provided under a specific legal form determining an activity-centred approach in the definition of TSO that is reinforced by the ONLUS

*Table 5. Civil code framework and special regulation intersection*

| Type of Organisation | Associations | Foundations | Cooperatives |
|---|---|---|---|
| Voluntary organizations | Solidarity activities | | |
| NGOs | International cooperation in developing Countries | | |
| Association for social promotion | Promotion of social aims | | |
| Social cooperatives | | | Provision of Healthcare, Social and Educational services (type A), and Services favouring the access to labour market for disabled (type B). |

Source 4: Cavemago, D & Mariani, L (2016)

regulation which includes a list of services that can be provided in order to access tax reductions and public financing.

Finally, a third level of overlap concerns, finally, the coexistence of Civil Code, special laws, and specific industry regulation: TSO work often in public regulated industries (i.e. healthcare, social services, labour market, education) in which the government regulation adds an extra layer of formalities to be completed. This also adds the need to coordinate the instances of various actors and bodies (for example, the juvenile court, the social workers, school districts), as well as the need to fulfil additional law enforcements, at different levels.

Focusing on the limitations to non-voluntary employment and commercial activities, governance models, and earning distribution, Table 6 offers a further representation of the complexity of Italian TSO framework of regulation. In particular, it is highlighted, here, how the provision of a wider range of services could be difficult under a unique legal form.

## The Effect of the Task Environment on Italian TSO' Business Models

The complex regulatory framework – joined with the strong dependence of Third Sector from public financing – affects the traditional business model of Italian TSO. Table 7 summarizes the major challenges that the TSO have to face in order to design and implement their business models in Italy, with reference to the Value Proposition, Value Constellation, and Profit Equation.

*Table 6. Limitations of special regulation*

| Type of Organisation | Employees | Volunteers | Commercial | Governance | ONLUS | Dividends Distribution |
|---|---|---|---|---|---|---|
| **Voluntary organizations** | Paid work is excluded (art. 2, L. 266/91). | No Limitation | Revenues from commercial activities lower than 66% of total expenses. | Democratic governance model | Onlus by operation of law | Excluded |
| NGO | Conditions regulated by the law for overseas staff (L. 125/2014) | Conditions regulated by the law for overseas staff (L. 125/2014) as well as by the regulation of Community service (Voluntary Service). Decree 77/2002 | No Limitation | No Limitation | Debated: Onlus by operation of law (according to L.49/1987) or On request (according to L. 125/2014) | Excluded |
| **Association for social promotion** | Prevalence of Volunteers on Employees | No Limitation | Commercial activities has to be ancillary, subsidiary, and related to the fulfilment of the institutional aims. | Democratic governance model | On request | Excluded |
| **Social cooperatives** | No Limitation | Max 50% of the associated | No Limitation | Democratic governance model | Onlus by operation of law | Max equal to the legal interest |

Source 5: Cavemago, D & Mariani, L (2016)

*Table 7. Challenges for Italian TSO business models*

| | Dependence on Public Financing | Activities Centred Approach and Regulations' Overlaps |
|---|---|---|
| **Value Proposition** | Effect of goal displacement | Limitation of potential clients/users |
| **Value Constellation** | Public sector as the most important external relationship | Growth through nonprofit group |
| **Profit Equation** | Low diversification of revenues | Increase of cost of coordination due to: the management of the group; different legal fulfilments |

Source 6: Cavemago, D & Mariani, L (2016)

As regards the effect of the prevalence of public financing on overall revenue sources, the first consequence on the business model, evidently, concerns the economic Profit Equation composition, which is characterized by a limited diversification of sources. The concentration of revenues implies a substantial lack of autonomy, as well as the increase in the risks for organizations whose development depend on the tenure for a relationship with the public administration.

Literature suggests that the dependence on any one type of income, including private contributions, commercial activity, or government funding can produce a goal displacement (Eikenberry & Kluver, 2004; Froelich 1999; Salamon & Anheier, 1998) affecting the Value proposition itself. The need of public administration for equitable treatment of the public, accountability, and standardization can limit the TSO responsiveness to the needs of user, and service variety, inducing TSO to take on functions that are not central to their initial purpose and, consequently, to modify the characteristics of services delivered.

The effect of goal displacement on the TSO Value constellation can imply changes in the operating activities in order to answer the government pressure for higher professionalization and bureaucratization. In this context, TSO business model has to be designed with the aim to reduce the risk to lose their administrative autonomy, still maintaining their unique character, avoiding to mirror the structure and behaviour of government agencies. With regard to the effect of the regulatory framework on the business model of Italian TSO, the main challenges concern the need to manage different legal forms, simultaneously, in order to both fulfil legal requirements, and operate, at the same time, in different fields. The activities centred approach implies that the scope of services able to be supplied under a specific regulatory frameworks, defined in advance and this reduces the niches of potential clients/users.

In order to avoid these barriers, Italian TSOs have traditionally resorted to the implementation of nonprofit organizations' groups. Since the operating activities of Italian TSOs are significantly reduced by the relevant regulation,-strategies of service differentiation cannot be applied within a specific legal form. Rather, it is necessary to resort to combinations of different legal forms. The consequence is the emergence of nonprofit organizations groups that - under both a common label, and same leadership-carry out various activities in different sectors.

The effect of activities centred approach and regulations overlapping on the Profit equation of TSO is a general rise of coordination costs. Coordination costs, also referred to as organization costs (Masten, Meehan, & Snyder, 1991) or management costs (Demsetz, 1988) are the implicit costs of managing resources within organizations (Alston & Gillespie, 1989). Examples of coordination costs include administrative overhead, the costs of monitoring employees, and bureaucratic inefficiency (Anderson, 1985; Masten et al., 1991).

In the case of Italian TSOs, the increase of coordination costs relates to the need to lead and manage the group of nonprofit organizations that, under different legal labels, have to fulfil the same end goal. With increasing complexity due to both the need to manage a group, on the one hand, and the need to face the multilevel requests of public administration, on the other hand, the requirement of integration and coordination increase. In particular, when complexity is low, hierarchy and organizational routines are enough to manage coordination, while when complexity rises, coordination requires additional tools such as working groups, ad-hoc task forces, and staff members specifically dedicated. The final effect is the overall increase of coordination costs.

## SOLUTION AND RECOMMENDATIONS

At the end of May 2016, the Italian Parliament has approved the reform of the Third Sector (hereafter "the Reform") under the law 106/2016, in order to face the limitation of the fragmented framework, as described in previous paragraph. The opportunities provided by the Reform are here discussed with the aim to identify potential solutions and recommendations for the development of sustainable business models in Italian TSOs.

A crucial step will take place within 12 months from the Reform, the period after which the Government is required to issue decrees that will implement the Reform. In the meantime, several initiatives that could affect the business model of Italian TSO can be identified.

These changes can be summarized into: (1) simplification of the overall framework, (2) revision of TSO' activities list, (3) opening to a participatory governance model of public services, (4) and re-design of Social Enterprise's framework (Table 8).

With reference to the first point, the Reform lists some initiatives aimed at simplifying the TSO' regulatory framework. These includes the reorganization and revision of the rules relating to Third Sector through the Unified Code of nonprofit organization, which is going to collect and coordinate all existing provisions. Furthermore, the Reform involves the reorganization of both the registration of TSO, and other bureaucratic fulfilments, through simplified procedures. The collection of existing legislation into the Unified Code - which coordinates the rules of the Civil Code with that special laws, as well as special regulations among themselves - can lead to a reduction of the overlaps mentioned above. Therefore the

*Table 8. Reform effects on TSOs*

| | Simplification | Scope Enlargement | Participatory Governance | Social Enterprise |
|---|---|---|---|---|
| **Value Proposition** | | Access to new forms of responsible business<br>new categories of users | | New categories of clients |
| **Value Constellation** | | Review of core processes | Public Administration as a partner. | Introduction of new managerial competences<br>Reduction of the use of nonprofit group |
| **Profit Equation** | Coordination costs reduction | New source of revenues | | Coordination costs reduction<br>New source of revenues |

Source 7: Cavemago, D & Mariani, L (2016)

effects of simplification could have a positive impact on TSO business model through the reduction of coordination costs and, consequently, through the improvement of Profit Equation balancing.

Referring to the second point, although the Reform still maintains the "activities centred" approach of the entire regulatory framework, this also opens to a more flexible definition of the sectors. The Government is asked to identify the list of activities of general interest, civic purpose, and solidarity that the TSO have to play in order to access to different benefits. However, the Reform mentions the need to perform periodic updates to the list. In this way, it enables the TSO to take into account emerging social needs previously not considered, through the provision of innovative services in new industries (i.e. social housing and the fair trade). The increasing trend of nonprofit activities can lead to an even more significant impact on the business model of the TSO, for all three dimensions. In terms of Value Proposition, the greater scope can lead TSO to invest in new forms of social responsible business facing, in this way, the needs of new categories of service users. The effect of this expansion on the Value Constellation could involve changes in the phases of service provision, which influences the revenue composition of the Profit Equation.

As for the opening of participatory governance models, the Reform calls for greater involvement of TSO in policies. In particular, it envisages the enhancement of the role of TSO in the programming phase, at the local level, for both social services, and the protection and enhancement of cultural heritage, landscape and environment. In particular, the Reform recognizes and incentivizes the networks of TSO in order to increase their representation with the public administration.

According to the perspective of the participatory governance models, TSO are engaged in policies' definition, the consequence is the shift from the direct provision of solutions to public issues by local administrations, to a situation where the solutions are reached through mobilization of a variety of actors. Such involvement implies a renewed role of TSO whose behaviour is oriented by the national or local policies of the public administration, which, in turn, receives stimulation from a Third Sector that is particularly receptive to its territory's needs. The implication on the TSO' business model concerns, primary, the Value Constellation, with specific focus on the characteristics of TSO external relationship. Public administration has the opportunity to change its role from end-payer for public services, to those of peer-partner: the relationship between TSO and Government can turn from buyer-contractor to co-producers, and the way that the TSO relate with the public administration would be inspired by criterion of collaboration and mutual trust.

Finally, the Reform aims at modifying and implementing the previous – not compelling – regulations of the social enterprise. Approved in 2005, previous legislation had a marginal impact on the Italian Third Sector, probably because of the substantial lack of specific incentives. The approved reform integrates the regulation defining the social enterprise as a private organization that carries out business activities for the typical purpose of the nonprofit. The social enterprise may resort to legal forms for businesses, but allocates its profits primarily to achieve the social purpose.

Furthermore, it has to adopt procedures for responsible and transparent management by promoting greater involvement of stakeholders. The initiative that will be implemented in order to promote the diffusion of social enterprises in Italy will be a strategic opportunity both for existing TSO looking for alternative private resources, and for new social start-ups whose growth may be favoured by more flexible regulatory frameworks.

The existing TSO moving toward the new framework of social enterprise could expand their Value Proposition through the identification of new categories of receivers. In particular, in a more entrepreneurial perspective, social enterprises have the opportunity to expand the scope of traditional TSO by targeting, in addition to the users of welfare services, also to customers in the market environments. For example, supporting the development of alternative forms of welfare - such as corporate employee welfare services - the TSO may offer assistance services to for-profit organizations. Corporate employees welfare services, in fact, often includes services typically provided by TSO such as personal services connected with sickness, bereavement, domestic problems, elderly and retired employees, or group services consist of sports and other social activities.

The use of social enterprise form by the TSO also leads to potential changes in the Value Constellation. First, whenever the conditions for the transition from the previous regulatory framework to those of the social enterprise would be accessible, the TSO, from a theoretical point of view, could simplify its governance model, by reducing the appeal of the nonprofit group, and the direct consequence would be the reduction of coordination costs. The social enterprise's regulatory frame provides that social business can be carried out regardless of the legal category, also drawing the shapes of the Civil Code specifically provided for for-profit organizations.

The second effect on Value Constellation regards, indeed, the need to introduce within organizational boundaries, new managerial skills that typically do not belong to the Third Sector, but whose development is needed as a pre-condition to successfully compete in free markets. Apparently, the shift to social enterprise is not an obvious choice for TSO, however this is an opportunity that would allow them to get an effect of diversification of revenues, with positive effects on the Profit Equation and, more generally, on the organizational autonomy of the medium-long term.

## CONCLUSION

The literature highlights how TSOs in the Italian context are defined by the social and institutional contexts. Social and institutional contexts affect the business model development of TSOs. In particular, the effect of the task environment on TSOs is in contrast to the neo-institutional theory. A resilient Third Sector that, throughout history have survived in less favourable periods have grown over time through public financing, albeit in the presence of a fragmented legislation.

TSOs, however, are facing contraction of welfare expenditure and they are compelled to review their traditional business models. The transition of traditional TSO toward forms of social entrepreneurship can be a viable solution. In such a hybridization process, TSO business models must reflect organizational solutions incentivizing the use of entrepreneurial principles to organize, mobilize and manage for the creation of economic and social value. At the same time, through networking and cooperation, TSO can improve partnership building with other TSOs, for-profit organizations, and public sectors, shifting from the contractor-supplier approach to the co-production.

To cope the activities centred approach that characterizes the Italian TSO should move towards the growth and new opportunities approach and the identification and measurement of social impact. TSOs should develop internal managerial skills and measurement of impacts to grant the alignment of different stakeholder aims and to improve partnership and networking. At the system level, the shift from the welfare state model to an entrepreneurship social welfare model should be seriously reflected upon.

## REFERENCES

Alston, L. J., & Gillespie, W. (1989). Resource coordination and transaction costs: A framework for analyzing the firm/market boundary. *Journal of Economic Behavior & Organization*, *11*(2), 191–212. doi:10.1016/0167-2681(89)90013-9

Anderson, E. (1985). The salesperson as outside agent or employee: A transaction cost analysis. *Marketing Science*, *4*(3), 234–254. doi:10.1287/mksc.4.3.234

Borzaga, C., & Fazzi, L. (2011). Processes of institutionalization and differentiation in the Italian Third Sector. *Voluntas*, *22*(3), 409–427. doi:10.1007/s11266-010-9159-z

Brooks, A. C., & Wilson, J. Q. (2007). *Who really cares: The surprising truth about compassionate conservatism--america's charity divide--who gives, who doesn't, and why it matters*. New York: Basic Books.

Chesbrough, H., & Rosenbloom, R. S. (2002). The role of the business model in capturing value from innovation: Evidence from Xerox Corporations technology spin-off companies. *Industrial and Corporate Change*, *11*(3), 529–555. doi:10.1093/icc/11.3.529

Coleman, J. S. (1990). *Foundations of social capital theory*. Cambridge, UK: Belknap.

Colombo, A. (2008). The Lombardy Model: Subsidiarity-informed Regional Governance. *Social Policy and Administration*, *42*(2), 177–196. doi:10.1111/j.1467-9515.2008.00602.x

Corbin, J. J. (1999). A study of factors influencing the growth of nonprofits in social services. *Nonprofit and Voluntary Sector Quarterly*, *28*(3), 296–314. doi:10.1177/0899764099283004

Defourny, J., & Borzaga, C. (2001). *From third sector to social enterprise*. London: Routledge.

Demsetz, H. (1988). The theory of the firm revisited. *Journal of Law Economics and Organization*, *4*(1), 141–161.

DiMaggio, P. J., & Powell, W. W. (1983). The iron cage revisited: Institutional isomorphism and collective rationality in organizational fields. *American Sociological Review*, *48*(2), 147–160. doi:10.2307/2095101

Dowling, J., & Pfeffer, J. (1975). Organizational legitimacy: Social values and organizational behavior. *Pacific Sociological Review*, *18*(1), 122–136. doi:10.2307/1388226

Eikenberry, A., & Kluver, J. (2004). The marketization of the nonprofit sector: Civil society at risk? *Public Administration Review*, *64*(2), 132–140. doi:10.1111/j.1540-6210.2004.00355.x

Froelich, K. A. (1999). Diversification of revenue strategies: Evolving resource dependence in nonprofit organizations. *Nonprofit and Voluntary Sector Quarterly*, *28*(3), 246–268. doi:10.1177/0899764099283002

Haddad, M. A. (2011). A state-in-society approach to the nonprofit sector: Welfare services in Japan. *VOLUNTAS: International Journal of Voluntary and Nonprofit Organizations*, *22*(1), 26–47. doi:10.1007/s11266-010-9135-7

Heurlin, C. (2010). Governing civil society: The political logic of NGO–state relations under dictatorship. *VOLUNTAS: International Journal of Voluntary and Nonprofit Organizations*, *21*(2), 220–239. doi:10.1007/s11266-009-9103-2

Kerlin, J. A. (2013). Defining Social Enterprise Across Different Contexts A Conceptual Framework Based on Institutional Factors. *Nonprofit and Voluntary Sector Quarterly*, *42*(1), 84–108. doi:10.1177/0899764011433040

Lecy, J. D., & Van Slyke, D. M. (2012). Nonprofit sector growth and density: Testing theories of government support. *Journal of Public Administration: Research and Theory*, *23*(1), 189–214. doi:10.1093/jopart/mus010

Lee, T. (2010). The rise of international nongovernmental organizations: A top-down or bottom-up explanation? *VOLUNTAS: International Journal of Voluntary and Nonprofit Organizations*, *21*(3), 393–416. doi:10.1007/s11266-010-9137-5

Mariani, L., & Cavenago, D. (2013). Redesigning Welfare Services for Policies Effectiveness: The nonprofit organizations (NPOs) perspective. *Public Management Review*, *15*(7), 1011–1039. doi:10.1080/14719037.2012.758307

Masten, S. E., Meehan, J. W., & Snyder, E. A. (1991). The costs of organization. *Journal of Law Economics and Organization*, *7*(1), 1–25.

Matsunaga, Y., & Yamauchi, N. (2004). Is the government failure theory still relevant? A panel analysis using US state level data. *Annals of Public and Cooperative Economics*, *75*(2), 227–263. doi:10.1111/j.1467-8292.2004.00251.x

Meyer, J. W., & Rowan, B. (1977). Institutionalized Organizations: Formal Structure as Myth and Ceremony. *American Journal of Sociology*, *83*(2), 340–363. doi:10.1086/226550

Normann, R. (1977). *Management for growth*. London: John Wiley & Sons.

Paarlberg, L. E., & Gen, S. (2009). Exploring the Determinants of nonprofit Coproduction of Public Service Delivery The Case of k-12 Public Education. *American Review of Public Administration*, *39*(4), 391–408. doi:10.1177/0275074008320711

Pestoff, V., & Brandsen, T. (2013). *Co-production: The Third Sector and the Delivery of Public Services*. New York: Routledge.

Prahalad, C. K., & Ramaswamy, V. (2004). Co-creation Experiences: The Next Practice in Value Creation. *Journal of Interactive Marketing*, *18*(3), 5–14. doi:10.1002/dir.20015

Putnam, R. D. (2000). Bowling alone: America's declining social capital. In *Culture and Politics* (pp. 223–234). New York: Palgrave Macmillan US.

Ranci, C. (1994). The Third Sector in welfare policies in Italy: The contradictions of a protected market. *VOLUNTAS: International Journal of Voluntary and Nonprofit Organizations*, *5*(3), 247–271. doi:10.1007/BF02354035

Ranci, C. (2015). The Long-Term Evolution of the Government–Third Sector Partnership in Italy: Old Wine in a New Bottle? *VOLUNTAS: International Journal of Voluntary and Nonprofit Organizations*, *26*(6), 2311–2329. doi:10.1007/s11266-015-9650-7

Salamon, L., & Sokolowski, S. (2010, July). *The social origins of civil society: Explaining variations in the size and structure of the global civil society sector.* Paper presented at the 9th International Conference of the International Society for Third Sector Research, Istanbul, Turkey.

Salamon, L. M., & Anheier, H. K. (1997). *Defining the nonprofit sector: A cross-national analysis.* Manchester, UK: University Press.

Salamon, L. M., & Anheier, H. K. (1998). Social origins of civil society: Explaining the nonprofit sector cross-nationally. *VOLUNTAS: International Journal of Voluntary and Nonprofit Organizations*, *9*(3), 213–248. doi:10.1023/A:1022058200985

Salamon, L. M., & Flaherty, S. L. (1996). *Nonprofit law: Ten issues in search of resolution.* Baltimore, MD: Johns Hopkins University Press.

Salamon, L. M., Hems, L. C., & Chinnock, K. (2000). *The Nonprofit Sector: For What and For Whom?* Baltimore, MD: Johns Hopkins University Press.

Schneider, J. A. (2013). Comparing Stewardship Across Faith-Based Organizations. *Nonprofit and Voluntary Sector Quarterly*, *42*(3), 517–539. doi:10.1177/0899764012461399

Wang, L., Graddy, E., & Morgan, D. (2011). The development of community-based foundations in East Asia. *Public Management Review*, *13*(8), 1155–1178. doi:10.1080/14719037.2011.619068

Weisbrod, B. A. (1977). *The voluntary nonprofit sector.* Lexington, MA: Lexington Books.

Weisbrod, B. A. (1986). Toward a theory of the voluntary nonprofit sector in a three-sector economy. In S. Rose-Ackerman (Ed.), *The economics of nonprofit institutions: Studies in structure and policy* (pp. 1–44). New York: Oxford University Press.

Weisbrod, B. A. (1988). *The nonprofit economy.* Cambridge, MA: Harvard University Press.

Young, D. (2005). *Mission-market tension in managing nonprofit organizations.* Atlanta, GA: Andrew Young School of Policy Studies, Research Paper Series.

Yunus, M., Moingeon, B., & Lehmann-Ortega, L. (2010). Building social business models: Lessons from the Grameen experience. *Long Range Planning*, *43*(2), 308–325. doi:10.1016/j.lrp.2009.12.005

Zott, C., & Amit, R. (2008). The fit between product market strategy and business model: Implications for firm performance. *Strategic Management Journal*, *29*(1), 1–26. doi:10.1002/smj.642

## KEY TERMS AND DEFINITIONS

**Institutional Context:** System of bodies, rules, regulation, policies, procedures and processes that characterize the task environment of a third sector organization.

**Profit Equation:** Translation of the Value Proposition and Value constellation in terms of benefits and costs. It can be furthered decomposed into Social Equation and Economic Equation.

**Social Business Idea:** Outcome of an entrepreneurial sensitivity in identifying an emerging social need and the related sustainable answers.

**Social Business Model:** Actualization of a social business idea through the identification of the value proposition, value constellation and a sustainable profit equation.

**Social Context:** Combination of demographical, religious, racial diversities, and social capital peculiarities that characterize the task environment of a third sector organization.

**Task Environment:** Setting in which third sector organizations develop their business idea through a business model. The boundaries of this setting are defined by the institutional and social contexts.

**Value Constellation:** Ways in which third sector organizations provide their services through both the internal value chain and external partners support.

**Value Proposition:** Summaries of the characteristics of the value provided by the organization, as well as the relationships with the users.

# Chapter 16
# Exploring Philanthropic Foundations' Motivations and Managerial Model of Strategic Change from Grant-Making to Impact Investing

**Lijun He**
*Pace University, USA*

**Jessika C. Graterol Alfronzo**
*Pace University, USA*

**Kilian Tep**
*Pace University, USA*

## ABSTRACT

*Little scholarly research has systematically examined impact investing in the nonprofit realm. In the overview, the paper presents a case study of a U.S.-based private foundation that has transformed itself from a grant-maker to an impact investor, and the associated challenges of institutional entrepreneurial motivations, successful strategy for institutional adaptation, and the ensuing lessons for the field of impacting investing. The paper has two main objectives: to identify the motivation and enabling environment for such strategic change, and to analyze the issues and changes of the managerial model when evolving from traditional grant-making to impact investing. We argue that organizations that are mission-driven, entrepreneurial in spirit and structure, with embedded business/philanthropy principles acting as a source of change in the institutional field. However, it faces technical and legitimacy problems resulting from the new practice's lack of institutional saturation in the field.*

DOI: 10.4018/978-1-5225-2537-0.ch016

Copyright © 2017, IGI Global. Copying or distributing in print or electronic forms without written permission of IGI Global is prohibited.

## INTRODUCTION

The current philanthropy and nonprofit organizations environment demands an entrepreneurial spirit to tackle the ever-increasing social problems effectively. Some nonprofit organizations now increasingly resort to a business approach to address social problems; and some traditional private grant-making foundations are experimenting with mission-related investing, program-related investing and responsible investing. An umbrella term for the aforementioned investment activities that intend to generate both positive social and financial returns is impact investing. There is a growing interest among foundations in allocating more resources towards the achievement of their mission. Therefore, impact investment has emerged as a financial tool that allows foundations to achieve their mission through the use of endowments, and to generate social impact. Such activity also allows foundations to tackle social issues and generate social changes in a more sustainable way than is possible through grant allocation.

Private foundations have traditionally been the engines to fuel the nonprofit sector and social change since the early 20th century; and they are comprised of experts chiefly from the public sector. The shift from a purely charitable model to an enterprise model confronts many challenges from legal, cultural, and managerial perspectives. Clarifying the enabling environment/motivations and approaches to such strategic change(s) by philanthropic foundations would allow us to have a better understanding of how and why, as well as the keys to, successful organization change (Armenakis & Bedeian, 1999). The results of the study aim to provide a greater understanding of the strategic change processes carried out by an exemplary private foundation, which will broaden the theory related to strategic change. The practical implication consists of accelerating the implementation by foundations that intend to adopt impact investing as a new strategy.

Little scholarly research has systematically examined impact investing in the nonprofit realm. Based on an in-depth qualitative case study of the ABC Foundation (a pseudo name) in New York, a pioneering American grant-making foundation that has shifted its strategic focus to impact investing, this chapter has two main objectives: to identify the motivation and enabling environment of the strategic change; and to analyze the issues and changes confronting the managerial model when evolving from traditional grant-making to impact investing. This chapter consists of four sections, including an introduction, background and literature review, case description and analysis, and a conclusion.

## BACKGROUND AND LITERATURE REVIEW

The term, *impact investing*, was coined by the Rockefeller Foundation in 2007. The Global Impact Investing Network (GIIN) defines impact investing as investments made into companies, organizations, and funds with the intention to generate social and environmental impact alongside a financial return (GIIN, 2016). The notion of a financial return in addition to social and environmental impact is key because of the implied strategic consequence associated with such investment, which we will discuss below. The current size for this market amounts to $60 billion and is expected to grow in the next two decades (Etzel, 2015).

Long before the term *impact investment* became popular, some organizations could arguably be identified as prototypes for impact investors. The most renowned example is most likely Ashoka. Since its establishment in 1980 by Bill Drayton, a former McKinsey Consultant, Ashoka has been involved in identifying and incubating leading social entrepreneurs associated with traditional nonprofits, which hold social mission as its central focus. More recently, an increasing number of organizations have extended support, through provision of financial capital for social enterprises, consisting of both nonprofit and for-profit organizations that aim to mitigate, through business ventures, a social problem or market failure (Atler, 2016).

The Acumen Fund is one of such organization. Not only does it seek social impact similar to a traditional grant-making foundation, but it also pursues financial returns like a traditional investment fund. To a certain extent, an impact investor is to a social enterprise what a grant-maker is to a nonprofit organization. Both provide financial support for organizations with social missions; however, a grant-maker's financial support to a nonprofit is usually considered as a 'gift" based on the assessment of nonprofit's social impact. In contrast, an impact investor assesses both business operations and social impact. Financial institutions, family offices, philanthropic foundations, and wealthy individuals are the major players in the field (Drexler, Noble, & Bryce, 2013).

This chapter focuses on the evolution of the impact investing strategy by philanthropic foundations. Philanthropic foundations, a subtype of 501 (c) (3) not-for-profit organisations under the tax code of U.S. Internal Revenue Service, are specifically engaged in impact investing through two major approaches:

1. Program-related investments (PRIs), and
2. Mission-related investments (MRIs).

## Program Related Investments

PRIs are investments made by foundation to "support one or more of the foundation's charitable, religious, scientific, education, or other exempt purposes described in section 170(c) (2) (B) of the federal tax code" (Lilly Family School of Philanthropy, 2013, p. 6). For example, a foundation makes a high-risk investment in a nonprofit's low-income housing project. Unlike a grant, a foundation's PRI expects a repayment from the nonprofit, allowing fund recycling.

## Mission Related Investment

MRIs refer to investments made by a foundation to support its mission in order to achieve market-rate financial return on a risk-adjusted basis plus social and /or environmental return related to the mission of the organization (Bernholz & Richter, 2009, p. 42). The fund for MRIs usually comes from a foundation's investment asset, while the fund for PRIs comes from a foundation's program and is counted toward the 5% legally mandated payout.

According to the Foundation Center's database, a broad range of foundations were engaged in impact investing between 2000 and 2010. The reasons foundation are engaged in impact investing are categorized as follows:

1. Recycle and increase financial return through PRIs, because PRIs, unlike grants, are expected to be repaid (Lilly Family School of Philanthropy, 2013; Cooch & Kramer, 2007; Hoque, 2016).
2. Maximize mission achievement (Hoque, 2016; Snider, 2015; Lilly Family School of Philanthropy, 2013).

3. Driven by leadership/ Accompanied by organization transformation (Lilly Family School of Philanthropy, 2013).
4. Peer learning (Lilly Family School of Philanthropy, 2013).
5. Forced to adapt to an economic downturn (Lilly Family School of Philanthropy, 2013).
6. Enhancement of legal environment regarding impact investing, especially PRIs (Lilly Family School of Philanthropy, 2013).
7. Competitive advantage for a public foundation (Hoque, 2016).
8. Accountability (Rubaltelli, Ritov & Rumiati (2015).

Despite growing interests among foundations, especially family and independent foundations, studies of foundation's program-related investment and mission-related investment (Lilly Family School of Philanthropy at Indiana University, 2013; Center for Effective Philanthropy, 2015; Snider, 2015; Drexler, Noble & Bryce 2013) have identified the following barriers to engage in impact investing:

1. Not convinced by the theory.
2. Lack of information.
3. Lack of expertise.
4. Potential transaction cost associated with impact investing.
5. **Lack of Appropriate Opportunities:** Many nonprofits do not generate sufficient return to underwrite a foundation's investment.
6. Prioritizing the focus on the financial return of their assets.
7. Complex measurement requirements.

Despite the above-mentioned challenges associated with impact investing, there was a raise in the total number of PRIs from mid-1990s (fewer than 200) to mid-2000s (more than 400) (Lilly Family School of Philanthropy, 2013). Moreover, investors are increasingly armed with better data and improved portfolio construction techniques that make it easier to integrate impact into the investment process; investors and fund managers are thus better able to incorporate robust quantitative and factor research analysis into their investment decision processes in order to build a portfolio with positive impact and return (Snider, 2015). It is predicted that impact investing will evolve into a $500 billion market by 2020, which attests to the fast evolution of this movement (Drexler, Noble, & Bryce, 2013).

Except for a handful of researchers, little scholarly research has systematically examined impact investing in the nonprofit realm. Glanzel and Scheuerle (2016) studied the impediments to social impact investing in Germany from the conflicting institutional logics perspective. Richter (2013) examined the history of impact investing and how it is applied in health and community development through a public-private partnership lens. Research on the evolving process of a private foundation shifting from grant-making to impact investing is virtually nonexistent.

Based on an in-depth qualitative case study of the ABC Foundation in New York, a pioneering American grant-making foundation that has shifted its strategic focus to impact investing, this case study will use institutional entrepreneurship theory to examine the motivation/conditions of strategic change and the process of change.

## INSTITUTIONAL ENTREPRENEURSHIP THEORY

The defining character of institutional entrepreneurs is duality, namely *structure* and *agency* (Sewell, 1992). That is to say, institutional entrepreneurs are confined or constrained by the structure or the preexisting institutional environment (structure), yet they generate entrepreneurial activities (agency) based on an attempt to break through the old structure and modify or create a new structure. Through the interplay of habits, reflection, and judgment, the institutional entrepreneurs reproduce and transform those structures in interactive response to the problems posed by the changing historical situations (Garud, Hardy, Maguire, 2007, p.10). Innovative institutional entrepreneurs create externalities outside of the organization. In this case study, ABC is an institutional entrepreneur that deviates from private foundations' traditional grant-making by designing a new institution among private foundations, namely, impact investing.

The choice of a qualitative case study methodology is consistent with the theory-building focus of this study, as well as our emphasis on the process of change. Information was gathered from multiple sources to allow for triangulation of data, including key informant interviews, multi-year annual reports, news releases, organizational reports and publications, and websites.

## CASE DESCRIPTION AND ANALYSIS

### Organizational Background

ABC Foundation is a New York-based private foundation created in 1992. Its mission is to assist people and communities seeking to help themselves out of poverty. Over time, its programs have evolved to focus on asset building and wealth creation opportunities as a means of helping its clients make decisions that allow them to take control of their lives and their families.

The Foundation started as a grant maker aimed at supporting community-based organizations seeking to promote and implement wealth-creation strategies for low income communities, emphasizing a range of diverse areas such as home ownership, enterprise development, access to capital, child care, homelessness prevention, education and training, and job and workforce development. Four years after its establishment in 1992, the Foundation added mission–related investing to its grant-making agenda. In 2006, the Foundation re-evaluated its strategy and narrowed its mission to four major areas: home ownership, enterprise development, child care, and access to capital. Due to the decision to deepen impact investing strategies, the Foundation eliminated the child care program and emphasized the importance of wealth preservation over wealth creation (ABC Annual report, 2006). Over the years, the Foundation allocated an increasing portion of its assets in alignment with its revised mission by investing in both qualified nonprofit and for-profit organizations.

Currently, the Foundation's assets total approximately about $300 million. As of the end of 2014, the annual expenditures amounted to $14,766,543. The typical average grant ranges from $25,000 to $125,000, and the program-related investment ranges from $250,000 to $1,000,000. The market rate deposits amount to $100,000 per depository institution and the market rate mission-related investment is up to $2.5 million per investment.

In 1996, ABC started to expand its programmatic support to include impact investing due to the myriad of challenges accompanying effective grant-making and managing a growing endowment. The impact investing approach to philanthropy represented uncharted territory at that time. U.S. foundations traditionally allocate 5% of their endowment to charitable organizations every year. Now a decade on from its strategic decision, the Foundation has set a goal for 100% of its giving to be based on impact investing (by 2017). In order to achieve this goal, the foundation adopts an investment policy that takes both social and financial performance into consideration and invests in enterprises regardless of tax status. Most uniquely, the Foundation blends the functions of its program and investment departments, allowing a single team to work as one to deploy the Foundation's assets through a variety of financial vehicles. This is a dramatic and fundamental change from traditional grant-making among private foundations.

## Major Organizational Changes

Prior to 1996, the Foundation took a traditional approach to grant-making and tackled poverty through supporting "proven, effective programs that promote self-sufficiency, and that engender economic independence in individuals, families, and communities" (ABC Annual report, 1995, p. 2). The Foundation committed itself to high-quality community-based organizations to achieve its mission. Grants made by the Foundation were in the form of general support, specific programs or projects, and scholarships.

Starting from 1996, the Foundation added program-related investments as its major method for achieving its mission, and has been increasing the proportion of impact investing tools in its portfolios. Specifically, the Foundation seeks impact investing through the following methods:

1. **Program-Related Investment:** It provides loans or equity-like investment to both nonprofit and for-profit organizations whose work closely aligns with the Foundation's programmatic focus.
2. **Market-Rate Insured Deposits:** It provides private equity and fixed income securities in low-income designated credit unions or community development banks with substantial social benefits to low-income families and communities.

As shown in Figure 1 the share of Mission-Related Investments (MRIs) within ABC's portfolio has been increasing and is now the primary type of philanthropic commitment by the Foundation.

## Program Changes

Since its establishment, the Foundation functioned as a traditional grant-maker, prioritizing broader program categories, such as strengthening individuals and families, strengthening communities, and special initiatives. Figure 2 illustrates the Foundation's program areas in the year of 1995, a typical year in the early stages of grant-maker activities. Grants during the 1990s chiefly supported community organizations to fight poverty, grappling primarily with the major issues that contributed to individual, family, and community poverty; child care; homeless prevention; education and training; access to capital; job and workforce development; and small business development.

The addition of mission-related investment, starting from 1996, has been dedicated to accessing capital, job and work force development, and small business development. Figure 3 and 4 provide a snapshot of the Foundation's program focus on the aforementioned areas. As is shown, the commitment to child care,

*Figure 1. Evolution of the share of MRIs within ABC's asset portfolio*
*Source: Created according to ABC Foundation's annul report, 2003-2014*

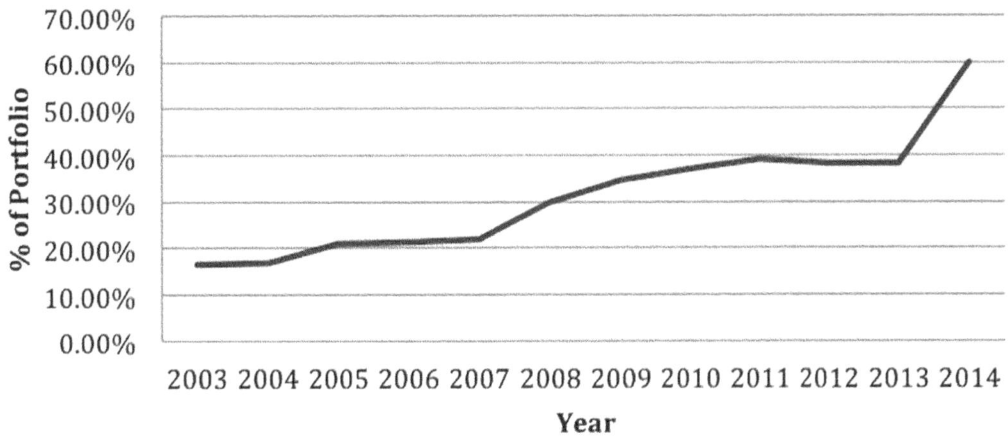


*Figure 2. Grant allocation by program area in 1995*
*Source: Adapted from ABC's Annual Report (1995)*

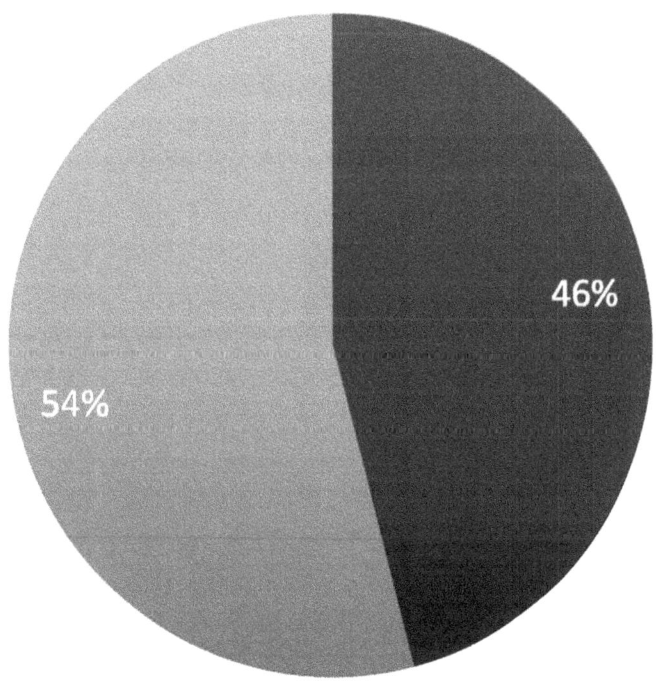

*Figure 3. Grants by program areas from 1997-2000*
*Source: Created according to data from ABC's Annual Report 1997-2000*
*Note: FI: financial independence; PI: personal independence*

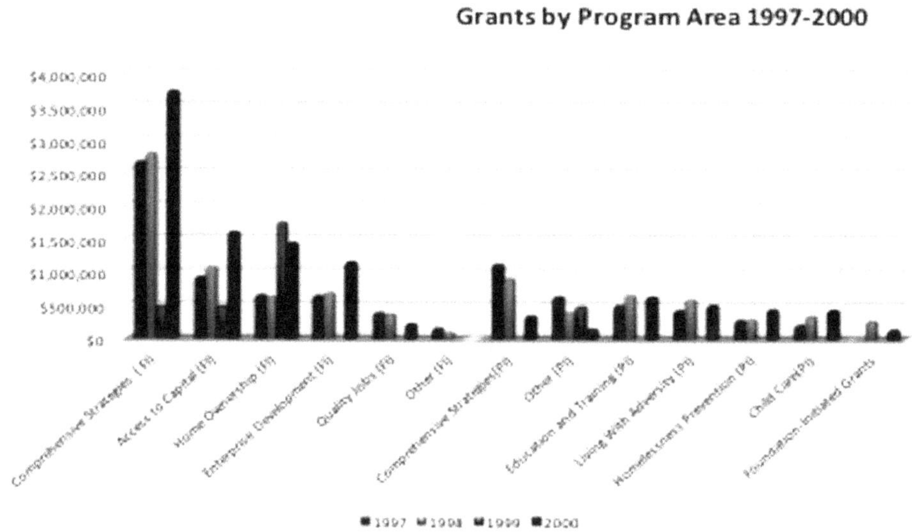


*Figure 4. Grants by program areas 2001- 2007*
*Source: Created according to data from ABC Annual Report 2000-2007*

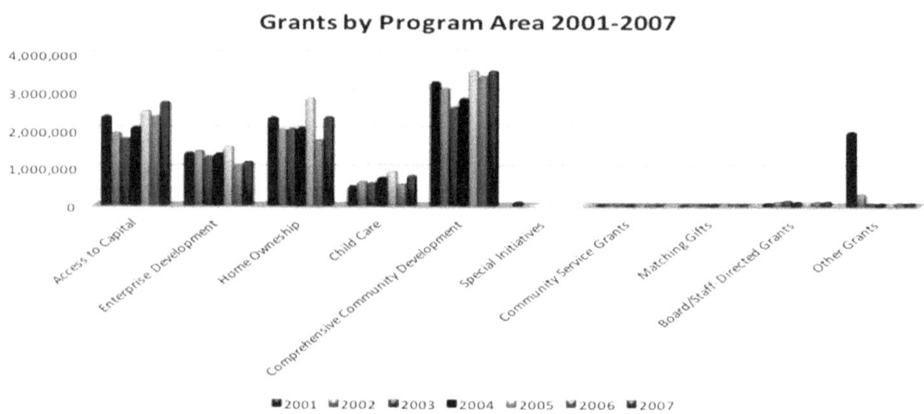


education and training, and homeless prevention was gradually phased out. In 2006, childcare programs were officially removed from its program areas. The organization, therefore, moved to a stage mainly as "mission investor" from 1997-2010.

Following the Foundation's trajectory of impact investing, ABC altered its strategy to primarily invest in enterprises capable of creating reliable incomes stream for people striving to get out of poverty as well as rewarding enterprise(s) that produce both positive financial and social impact. Its proportion of mission investment has witnessed a significant rise, from less than 6% to 37%. Subsequently, the Foundation continued to reshape its vision, shifting to ABC as an enterprise (2011-2016).

## Organizational Structural Changes

Accordingly, the Foundation's organizational structure has undergone major changes as it shifts from a grant-maker to mission investor and then to an enterprise over the time. Figures 5, 6, 7 represent the Foundation's organizational structure changes prior to the adoption of impact investing, partial adoption of impact investing, and full adoption of impact investing. As seen in the organization chart portrayed in these figures, the organizational structure changes include: expansion of board members from 2 to 6 and additional positions for investment; on the other hand, the program officer position, a typical position at a traditional foundations, has been eliminated.

*Figure 5. ABC Grant Maker Organisational Structure (1995-6)*
*Source: Created according to data from Annual Report (1995)*

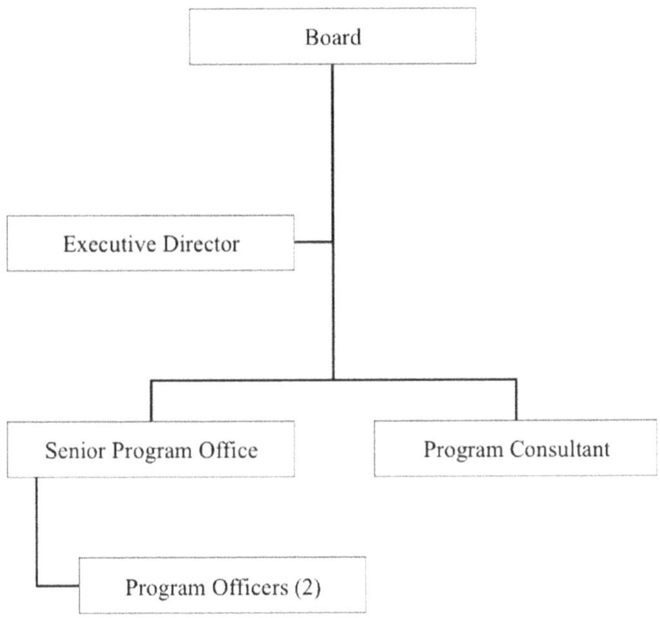


*Figure 6. ABC's organization structure in 2002 as a mission investor*
*Source: Created according to data from Annual Report (2002)*

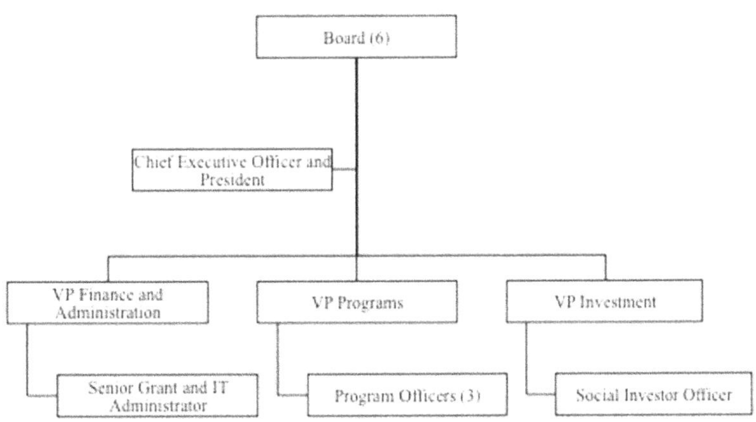

*Figure 7. ABC's organization structure in 2016 as an enterprise*
*Source: Created according to ABC's website*

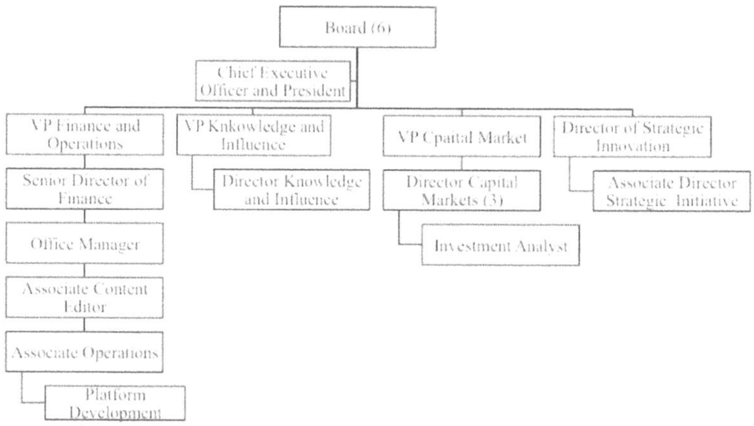


## Exploring the Player and Reasons for Change

Under institutional entrepreneurship theoretical framework, the key question arises: under what conditions does institutional entrepreneurship occur? Multiple players and reasons can account for a foundation's strategic shift from grant-making to impact investing. In short, it can be explained through organization's both external and internal perspectives. Externally, a foundation's "old" approach to philanthropy cannot meet the ever-changing needs of a dynamic social and economic environment. Poor performance of the grant-making approach produces a contradiction between institutional conformity and functional efficiency as the operating environment changes, increasing the motivation to adopt alternative possibilities. As noted in the Foundation's Annual Report,

*Much has changed in the world since we got started. A partial list of issues barely on the radar screen in 1992 includes: globalization; dynamic patterns of immigration; access to health care; new technology and telecommunication; gentrification with attendant displacement; climate change; escalating energy costs; churning in the financial service sector, predatory lending, and recent record foreclosure rates (ABC Annual Report FY 2007, p. 1)*

During the last 15 years, the global economy has been affected by three interrelated long-term trends: geography has become less critical for business location decisions, disintermediation, and globalization; each has been promoted by increased use of information technology. These trends, accompanied by the global financial crash in 2008 and the following the Great Recession, completely changed the environment in which the Foundation operated, altering its mission, vision and business model, and negatively affecting society as a whole. In a word, poverty took on increasingly structural characteristics. There was no assurance of life employment for individuals, and the complex skills needed to make a living continued to evolve. Although the programs the Foundation funded for years were important and necessary, they were not enough to address poverty in a meaningful way. The opportunities that the Foundation offered through its endowment were available only to a relatively small group; in short, the gap that the ABC Foundation had been trying to fill became larger and occurred more frequently, and the problems it sought to solve became more complex and intertwined.

Such changes in the cultural, political, social, and legal context generates pressures to create new understandings of the need for institutional change (Oliver, 1992). The macro-level environmental changes provide legitimacy or building blocks for new institutional fields; however, how the building blocks are used to construct a field depends upon the local actor's choices (Lawrence & Phllips, 2004). Thus, ABC Foundation's responses to the environment it operates in, as an institutional entrepreneur, are worthy of further analysis.

Internally, we can observe that the Foundation's chairman of the board and its CEOs embraced different views on the root problems of poverty. At the establishment of the Foundation, the mainstream belief found in American philanthropic thinking and reflected by ABC Foundation Board leadership was that poverty was a marginal phenomenon. In other words, poor people were left at the bottom of the economic and social scale because poverty either resulted from a long American history of ethnic discrimination or was due to failures of markets and social policies, a point noted by the current President in one of her essays. People were not capable of enriching themselves and joining the middle class because they were left at the margin, and could not fully participate in the economy and seize the opportunities at their disposal. With this initial paradigm in mind, ABC initially implemented programs explicitly stating the following goals:

1. Increasing access to capital;
2. Supporting enterprise development;
3. Advancing home ownership;
4. Reducing the barriers to full participation in the economy by providing quality child care;
5. Employing comprehensive community development approaches with a strong focus on the wealth-creation strategies noted above.

Each of these programs was aimed at producing wealth creation. Yet, these policies relied on a fundamental assumption in order to be truly effective: the economy and the labor market have to constantly create jobs, which will enable poor households to accumulate wealth. Structural changes in the economy since establishment have urged the ABC to review its approach to solving poverty. In its President' words:

*Industrial and technological advances now lead as often to reductions in employment as to increases. Loyalty, diligence, and a history of regular promotions no longer inoculate most workers from the risk of sudden, enduring unemployment that raises the odds of lasting poverty. Employment at a living wage is neither reliable nor commonplace.*

Indeed, the recent trends in the economy have now led to an increasing amount of job automation, affecting millions of unskilled workers. As the number of these unemployed workers increases, more and more people are at risk of being exposed to poverty. This realization instigated a fundamental paradigm shift within ABC and its Board leadership. The Foundation no longer considered poor people to be at the margins of society, concluding that poverty is caused by the structure of society itself. As a result of this paradigm shift, ABC has made the decision to strive to create a philanthropic portfolio made up of impact investments at the level of one hundred percent. By doing so, its goal is to re-shape the structure of the economy by investing in companies that create the conditions for a fair, inclusive, and environment-friendly system for every willing member of society. This approach is really about utilizing the foundations of capitalism: providing capital that will not only promote entrepreneurship and seek profit, but will also be fair and inclusive for all.

The evolving role of the chairman of the board and the Foundation's CEOs contributes to our understanding of the process of strategic business model. Motivated to carry on mission stewardship that could be measured in terms of impact, the board of directors concluded that the ratio of effort and time directed to investment performance and on programs made the private foundation into an entity that more resembles an investment firm. Since the legally mandated 5 percent payout is far from adequate to realize the Foundation's philanthropic goals, the remaining 95 percent corpus could be conceived as a boarder philanthropic toolbox.

From its early stage to the present, each of the Foundation's Board chairs has embraced an entrepreneurial and risk-taking spirit to mission fulfillment, striving to put resources to their highest and best use. Risk taking is considered one of the key elements necessary for successful mission stewardship in a resource-constrained environment. The current chairman of the board is an entrepreneur in the nonprofit field; he established a reputable national rating agency for nonprofits and encourages more partnership between foundations and companies.

Indeed, almost all of ABC's chair of board are prominent philanthropic leaders and have extensive leadership experience in grant-making foundations. The new president of the foundation, moreover, has a strong finance background and has been a recognized leader known for her enterprising approach to nonprofit leadership and management. The "centrality' role of these philanthropic leaders makes them less likely to only conform to professional norms; instead, they seek alternatives. Based on their extensive knowledge and experience in the field, their leadership position challenges the limited thinking found at a majority of grant-making foundations, e.g., narrow focus on programs, modest in size, short term funding, and lack of flexibility.

## Process of Change

ABC's shift from grant-making to impact investing is an incremental one. It started with grant-making, then shifted to mission investment and now strives for 100% impact investing. In the previous section, we have laid out the external and internal factors that account for the Foundation's strategic shift. The Foundation's impact investing strategy represents a significant deviation from traditional grant-making and identifies the organization as a pioneer of impact investing in the realm of philanthropy. In the paragraphs to follow we will explore the institutional entrepreneurship theory to understand how the "agent" (the Foundation) pursued change.

Institutional entrepreneurs typically construct a new system based on the embedded context of the organization in which they are situated. Institutional entrepreneurship theory emphasizes the process of constructing new practices prior to their popular adoption and diffusion. Institutionalization is not a simple, systematic, linear process; rather, it results from recognition of an institutional problem that needs fixing. This process reflects the relative power of organized interests and actors who mobilize them. Institutional entrepreneurship usually start with deinstitutionalization of a dysfunctional institution and reconstruction of a new institution, which is followed by institution diffusion and institutionalization after theorization and legitimation (Greenwood, Suddaby, & Hinings, 2002). Hargrave and Van de Ven (2006, p.866) define *institutional change* as a difference in form, quality, or state over time in an institution.

As observed by Hargrave and Van de Ven (2006), institutional change can be determined by observing the arrangement at two or more points in time on a set of dimensions (frames, norms, rules) and then calculating the differences over time in these dimensions. An institutional change can be viewed from four dimensions:

1. Institutional design,
2. Institutional adaptation,
3. Institutional diffusion,
4. Collective action.

The institutional adaptation and institutional diffusion models focus on the conformity of individual organizations and organization fields due to the regulative and normative environment. In contrast, the *institutional design* dimension focuses on the intentional behaviors of an individual entrepreneur in the creation or revision of an existing institution to achieve one's desired goals. As pointed out by Hargrave and Van de Ven (2006, p. 867), the institutional arrangement reflects the pursuit of collective and conscious choices. Hargrave and Van de Ven (2006) provides an institutional circular perspective to report organisational transformation through collective action of institutional innovation which are briefly discussed below.

## Institutional Design

As discussed above, the Foundation changed its operational model from grant-making to impact investing. It started from a decision to incorporate an impact investing structure to the organization in addition to grant-making programs, proceeding to fully blending of the grant and investment departments. Its goal is to realize impact investing at the level of 100%.

## Institutional Adaptation Theorization and Legitimation

Traditionally, U.S. foundations focus on wealth preservation; grant-making and investment are kept separate. The first step in building a new institution is to deinstitutionalize the old strategy. In the case of the ABC Foundation, the process started with foundation-wide reflection and program reviews. The Foundation board invited all the current grantees and investee clients as well as outside experts to provide feedback and recommendations. Such feedback, along with several review reports, were placed transparently on the website; subsequently, internal meetings were held among staff to analyse each program area, key funding priorities, and geographic areas.

The next step was to propose a new strategy in support of the longstanding Foundation goal of effectively implementing its mission stewardship through publicizing the logic of the new strategy through newsletters and various board, staff, and grantee meetings. These publications and speeches served as a "theorizing" mechanism. As noted by Dacin, Goodsten and Scott (2002, p. 48), theorization involves both the specification of the failings of existing norms and practices and justification of new norms and practices in terms of moral or pragmatic considerations.

As the Foundation shifted from grant-maker to the mission investor stage, the Chair of Board argued that effective stewardship entails the deployment of assets to their highest and best use. In this view, preservation of the "assets to fund" ratio should not be the only focus of the board's fiduciary duty. Mission stewardship challenges board members to do more than protect Foundation assets from jeopardy; it requires the board to govern in a way that maximizes the Foundation's overall effectiveness. As the Foundation moves forward to the "enterprise stage", it relied on the analogy of a traditional foundations' funding model as a terrarium. The majority of its resources were contained inside in order to guarantee its survival, and only a small portion of its energy (grants) went outside of the glass. Therefore, the Foundation's contribution to the issues it was created to solve was marginal and not consistent with the challenges society was facing.

In terms of the Foundation's finance distribution structure, it should be noted that the investing side was focused traditionally on profitability with little or no regard for the mission. In other words, the financial investment was aimed at protecting the Foundation assets (which is comparable with a terrarium), investing 95% for financial returns to ensure the Foundation's ability to fund grants and cover its operating expenses. Based on this framework, the investment side invested millions of dollars in various enterprises in order to ensure a financial return that kept the Foundation moving forward. However, little or no scrutiny was made in terms of the effects of those enterprises on society. On the other hand, the program side allocated the Foundation's grants, which represented 5% of the endowment, with little or no regard for financial investment. The Foundation's operations were guided by the docket model of philanthropy, which posits that the market demand for grants is reliable, and that success will be guaranteed through a detailed scrutiny of grantees and restrictions of funds.

## Diffusion

After the Foundation successfully theorized its strategic change, its operations have been continuously modified consistent with the new direction adopted. For example, it has curtailed the number of supporting programs: the child care program no longer exist as a mission area; wealth creation is promoted, concentrating resources on enterprise development and access to capital; and geographic areas receiving major funding have been reduced from twelve to five. In addition, the Foundation has also expanded the staff and management team in the finance department, leading to elimination of the grants or program department. Finally, the whole organization now has a staff comprised of personnel with intensive business and finance backgrounds.

Consistent with its new mission, the Foundation now incrementally cultivates a risk-taking culture. The board chair has been outspoken in encouraging the entrepreneurial spirit of philanthropy. For example, in one of the Foundation's newsletters, he admiringly comments that major philanthropists such as Bill Gates, Warren Buffet and Pierre Omidyar are challenging philanthropy conventions, and their questioning posture is worth following. Such statements confirm the degree of cultural and philosophical change found within the Foundation, extending to its personnel changes as well. The new view posits that all investing is impact investing. By focusing on those investments that generate a positive effect on society, expanding the Foundation's influence and reaching new allies from different industries, it is possible to address poverty in a more meaningful and effective way as well as attempt to educating the organization and stakeholders on the nature of impact investing in terms of both program-related investments (PRIs) and mission-related investments (MRIs).

Although ABC initiatives are path breaking, according to the Director of Communication, it has had little problem finding talented people to join the organization. The type of individuals the Foundation hires are characterized as being very flexible in mindset and approach, open to the change, experimentation and challenges. For ABC, specific skills are not as important as temperament and judgment. ABC's team promotes discussion through regular meetings. These discussions encompass different topics such as the economy, poverty, new ways to make the Foundation more efficient, and conversations about those practices that are not meeting expectations. These ongoing conversations build staff cohesion.

It should be noted, in summary, that ABC unified the investment side and program side under the same mission, which consisted of utilizing the breadth of the Foundation in service to its mission. This change promoted learning and exchange of ideas, since the members of each team had different levels of expertise, skills, and knowledge. At the same time, it represented a change in the way the members of the different teams had been working, and the way they perceived how philanthropy should operate. According to ABC's perspective, this change was aspiring aimed at creating a perfect mix between efficient-oriented bankers on the investment side, and passionate mission-oriented members on the program side. With regard to the challenges associated with the changing process implied, it is important to mention that those who preferred a more traditional program officer role eventually found opportunities outside the Foundation.

## Institution Saturation

The Foundation's leaders have been transparent in communicating its new logic. The new CEO wrote essays calling for an impact-investing approach to philanthropy for 21st century foundations as well as graciously entertaining interviews with major financial and philanthropy newspapers about the new strategy. The current chairman of the board is also optimistic and strongly advocates the new approach. In short, the Foundation's leaders are engaged in public knowledge dissemination. Following the successful internal transformation, ABC actively diffuses/reproduces the knowledge and insights gained to multiple actors in the field. It is part of ABC's blueprint that it needs to build influence and spread knowledge among various actors—private companies, other philanthropic actors, NGOs, the world of politics, etc. ABC has recently created an Influence and Knowledge division that aims to: 1) have other influential stakeholders embrace this paradigm shift; and 2) create an ecosystem where knowledge and findings on poverty alleviation is shared. In other words, ABC is an active advocate for change within the economic system it operates.

The Foundation places high importance on the collaboration of co-investors and trusted partners to achieve its goal. ABC is developing a data infrastructure with other institutions, comparable performance analyses, and certification protocols; these efforts promote its influence and co-investment, which, at the same time, reduce associated transactional costs. This type of collaboration is reflected by the partnership that ABC established with the Sustainability Accounting Standard Boards (SASB) to standardize and enhance Expert Global Solution (EGS) data for public equities. The hope is that all public companies start presenting their financial reports using SASB metrics, which would result in comparable data, allowing investors to make better decisions based on this information. To sum up, institutional changes occur as the result of an interaction between the contextual factors and intra-organizational dynamics (such as interest, values, power dependencies, and capacity for action) (Greenwood & Hinings, 1996).

## Slow Field Saturation

The current chairman of the board revealed that few foundations follow ABC's lead in impact investing. A recent report from the Center for Effective Philanthropy found that median percentage of endowments going toward impact investing is only two percent (Center for Effective Philanthropy, 2015). According to ABC's vice president of Capital Market, private foundations face three major challenges to adopt the impact investing practices: lack of uniformity in describing and defining the nascent concept of impact investing, difficulty of accessing to "deal" in private market and products, and managerial challenges for board governance (Coutts Million Dollar Donors Report, 2014).

Furthermore, peer foundations often questioned the board chair and the CEO regarding how much of its financial return was discounted by its mission investment strategy. Such question mirrors the peer foundations' concern for financial returns and, more generally, a conventional foundation's strategy for wealth preservation.

### Impact of ABC Assets

ABC's new strategy also comprises an examination of its holdings at the enterprise level. According to ABC, the key to its strategy is to track the impact of the assets allocation on society and make decisions based on that information. Due to data availability limitations, ABC has found it difficult to gauge the impact of its strategy. Nonetheless, the Foundation is in the process of examining all the enterprises contained in its portfolio in order to gain deepened understanding. Such analysis includes the asset class level or intermediary level as well as the enterprise level, allowing for the Foundation to make the most of its investments and ensure high performance in terms of both the social and financial level metrics.

ABC's approach also aims to support social and financial performance across enterprises and assets classes over time. Nevertheless, the lack of data in the field constitutes one of the biggest challenges in benchmarking the performance of different businesses and comparing them. The availability of such data helps to keep organizations accountable. Proxies sometimes are used as a replacement but can be misleading. In past years, it was common to use a company's corporate philanthropy as an indicator of whether they are good corporate citizens, but in some cases such measures created a false positive.

However, without sufficient data, it is hard to know whether the enterprises the Foundation is investing in are producing a positive or negative effect on society. Although much work is needed, the ABC Foundation is continuously investing in those enterprises aimed at improving data transparency and promoting standardization. For its direct investments, ABC reports to an external data warehouse that collects information directly from their records and enabling enterprises to report social performance metrics through the system. For indirect investments, ABC Foundation relies on Bloomberg Data to track social and financial performance data.

## ORGANISATIONAL OPTIONS AND SOLUTIONS

Based on the findings, one probable solution to ABC's challenges is rooted in better understanding how the philanthropic field of impact investing now matures, in combination with charting the extent to which impact investing practices have begun to diffuse. This finding is one that calls for additional resources and the further development of power to influence its philanthropic foundations network. Recommendations suggested to target further data collection on impact measurement and on theorization of impact investing's saturation of the field include:

1. Continue to educate and clarify the new concept.
2. Use the Foundation's existing power and influence over its own "investees" to look for benchmark performance in one or two focus areas.
3. Use existing well accepted standard in the field, such as B Lab's impact access tools. B Lab is a nonprofit organization that certifies corporations that are dedicated to creating shared value for corporations, society and environment.
4. Set up, at an organization level, a measurement /assessment team to gauge the desired impact goals that the organization is seeking. This step recognizes two needs: that when the field is not mature, actions can be taken regarding its own success and failure that will benefit the field generally; and that the existing organizational structure has yet to create a performance measurement department. By taking these steps, positions of responsibility are created. In short, positions need to be created for program evaluations to gain legitimacy among the internal stakeholder.
5. Document and share the experience of the changing process associated with the impact investment, allowing others to emulate. Peer learning networks are usually effective contributors to diffusion of new practices. Furthermore, the more foundations start adopting impact investing, the more resources will be likely to be devoted to finding solutions for the organizational challenges associated with impact assessment and data availability.
6. Collaboration can play a role in the production of new institutions/norms by facilitating their creation and making them available inter-organizationally, but the level of collaboration between the peer foundations and their investees needs to be deepened. The level of involvement among collaborating organizations and the level of embeddedness of a collaboration in the institution field significantly affects the degree to which the collaboration is likely to initiate the production of institution establishment (Lawrence, Hardy, & Philips, 2002). The Foundation should seek out in-depth and meaningful ways to be engaged with its investees other than through merely deploying funds. Through such deeper level collaboration and engagement, the Foundation could initiate data collection through its observation, reflection, and story-telling to showcase the impact of its fund(s) allocation.
7. As the Foundation still needs to accommodate the existing institutional logic(s) (impact investing may not be the whole solution to challenges facing philanthropy), it follows that it will be hard for other foundations to emulate its approach.

It will be important to be selective about whom to target for diffusion purposes. The adoption of a revised form or practice is variously affected by organizational attributes, linkages and population characteristics (Dolfsma &Verburg, 2008). ABC can primarily engage with foundations with similar mission areas and similar values to help diffuse knowledge about impact investing.

## CONCLUSION

This chapter examined a US-based private foundation case study that has transformed from a grant-maker to an impact investor. Associated challenges of institutional entrepreneurial motivations, successful strategy for institutional adaption, and the lessons for the field of impacting investing, we analysed. Examined through the lens of an institutional entrepreneurship theoretical perspective, this chapter identified the major motivations that account for the Foundation's strategic change from a grant-maker to an impact investor and the process of such change. We have argued that impact investor organizations are mission-driven, entrepreneurial in spirit and structure, embedded business/philanthropy principles; and their leaders plays a central role in the field.

These internal factors serve as a source of change, along with organizational transformation and economic downturn, as attested by other literature (Hoque, 2016; Snider, 2015; Lilly Family School of Philanthropy, 2013). Additionally, the process of change within the organization is found to be relatively smooth, adapting successfully to new institutional design, theorization, and legitimization; however, the organization faces technical and legitimacy problems resulting from the new practice's lack of institutional saturation in the field.

Recommendations made to support organizations saturate or institutionalize entrepreneurial practices underline the continuous improvement of the infrastructure building (data collection and measurement) through the internal organizations capacity building and benchmarking and collaborations within and across industries. The results of the study provide a greater understanding of the strategic change processes carried out by an exemplary private foundation, thereby broadening the theory related to strategic change. The practical implication is to accelerate the implementation by foundations that intend to adopt impact investing as a new strategy.

This case study presents an opportunity for future research to enrich institutional entrepreneurship theory. To advance institutional entrepreneurs and strategies for institutional change future research studies may explore:

1. A private organization that strives for mission accountability/stewardship will tend to garner legitimacy from the domain or field.
2. An organization with an embedded or mixed structure is more likely to be an institutional entrepreneur.
3. Leaders with entrepreneurial propensity are more likely to be an institutional entrepreneur

## ACKNOWLEDGMENT

This chapter is made possible by generous support of the Helene & Grant Wilson Center for Social Entrepreneurship at Pace University, New York, USA

## REFERENCES

Armenakis, A., & Bedeian, A. (1999). Organizational change: A review of theory research in the 1990s. *Journal of Management*, *25*(3), 293–315. doi:10.1177/014920639902500303

Atler, K. (2016). *Social enterprise typology*. Retrieved May 20, 2016, from http://www.4lenses.org/setypology

Bernholz, L., & Richter, L. (2009). *Equity advancing equity: How community philanthropy can build racial and social equity through mission investing*. San Francisco, CA: Blueprint Research & Design and GPS Capital Partners.

Center for Effective Philanthropy. (2015). *Investing and social impact: Practices of private foundations.* Retrieved March 18, 2016, from http://www.effectivephilanthropy.org/wp-content/uploads/2015/05/Investing-and-Social-Impact-2015.pdf

Cooch, S., & Kramer, M. (2007). *Compunding impact: Mission investing by US foundations.* Boston, MA: FSG Social Impact Advisors.

Coutts, M. D. R. (2014). *Case study: ABC Foundation.* Retrieved Oct.12, 2016, from http://philanthropy.coutts.com/en/reports/2014/united-states/case-studies/dana-pancrazi.html

Dacin, M., Goodstein, J., & Scott, W. (2002). Institutional theory and institutional change: Introduction to the special research forum. *Academy of Management Journal, 45*(1), 45–57. doi:10.5465/AMJ.2002.6283388

Dolfsma, W., & Verburg, R. (2008). Structure, agency and the role of values in processes of institutional change. *Journal of Economic Issues, XLII*(4), 1031–1053. doi:10.1080/00213624.2008.11507201

Drexler, M., Noble, A., & Bryce, J. (2013). *From the margins to the mainstream: Assessment of the impact investment sector and opportunities to engage mainstream investors.* Geneva, Switzerland: World Economic Forum.

Etzel, M. (2015). Philanthropy's new frontier – impact investing. *Stanford Social Innovation Review.* Retrieved June 1, 2016, from http://ssir.org/articles/entry/philanthropys_new_frontierimpact_investing

ABC Foundation (1995-2014). *Annual Reports 1995-2014.* New York, NY: Author.

Garud, R., Hardy, C., & Maguire, S. (2007). Institutional entreprenuership as embedded agency: An introduction to the special issue. *Organization Science, 28*(7), 957–969. doi:10.1177/0170840607078958

GIIN. (2016). *What is impact investing?* Retrieved April 05, 2016, from https://thegiin.org/impact-investing/need-to-know/#s1

Glanzel, G., & Scheuerle, T. (2016). Social impact invesitng in Germany: Current impediments from investors and social entrepreneurs perspectives. *Voluntas: International Journal of Voluntary &Nonprofit Organizations, 27*(4), 1638–1668. doi:10.1007/s11266-015-9621-z

Greenwood, R., & Hinings, C. R. (1996). Understanding radical organizational change: Bringing together the old and new institutionalism. *Academy of Management Review, 21*, 1022–1054.

Greenwood, R., Suddaby, R., & Hinings, C. R. (2002). Theorizing change: The role of professional association in the transformation of institutionalized fields. *Academy of Management Journal, 45*(1), 58–80. doi:10.2307/3069285

Hargrave, T., & Van de Ven, A. (2006). A collective action model of insitutional innovation. *Academy of Management Review, 31*(4), 864–888. doi:10.5465/AMR.2006.22527458

Hoque, F. (2016). *Family offices and investing for impact: How to manage wealth, expand legacies and make a difference in the world*. Retrieved June 5, 2016, from http://www.ussif.org/files/Publications/Family_Offices.pdf

Lawrence, T., Hardy, C., & Phillips, N. (2002). Institutional effects of interorganizational collaboration: The emergence of proto-institutions. *Academy of Management Journal*, *45*(1), 281–290. doi:10.2307/3069297

Lawrence, T., & Phllips, N. (2004). From Moby Dick to Free Willy: Micro-culture discourse and institutional entrepreneurship in emerging institutional fields. *Organization Science*, *11*(5), 689–711. doi:10.1177/1350508404046457

Lilly Family School of Philanthropy at Indiana University. (2013). *Leveraging the power of foundations: An analysis of program-related investing*. Retrieved March 20, 2016, from https://philanthropy.iupui.edu/files/research/complete_report_final_51713.pdf

Oliver, C. (1992). Strategic response to institutional process. *Academy of Management Journal*, *16*, 145–179.

Richter, L. (2013). Social impact investing at the intersection of health and community development. *National Civic Review*, *102*(4), 67–71. doi:10.1002/ncr.21160

Rubaltelli, E., Lotto, L., Ritov, I., & Rumiati, R. (2015). Moral investing: Psychological motivations and implications. *Judgment and Decision Making*, *10*(1), 64.

Sewell, W. H. Jr. (1992). A theory of structure: Duality, agency, and transformation. *American Journal of Sociology*, *98*(1), 1–29. doi:10.1086/229967

Sherer, L., & Lee, K. (2002). Institutional change in large law firms: A resource dependency and institutional perspective. *Academy of Management Journal*, *45*(1), 102–119. doi:10.2307/3069287

Snider, A. (2015). *Impact investing: The performance realities*. Wealth Management Institute.

## KEY TERMS AND DEFINITIONS

**Grant-Making:** Foundations make grants to qualified nonprofit organizations to carry out its mission.

**Impact Investing:** Direct investments made into companies, organizations, and funds with the intention to generate social and environmental impact alongside a financial return. The investment can be made in the form of loans, equity, debts, cash and cash equivalents.

**Institution Diffusion:** An act of reproducing an established norm, value or practice.

**Institutional Entrepreneurship:** A behavior carried by an agent embedded in a preexisting institutional environment to break through the old structure and create a new structure through its resource mobilization.

**Institutionalization:** A process that reinforces an established social norm, value, belief, or practice.

**Mission-Related Investing (MRI):** Financial investments with the intention of advancing a foundation's mission and recovering the principal invested or earning financial returns across all asset classes with both market rate and below market rate.

**Private Foundation:** A type of U.S. 501(c)3 nonprofit organization that is voluntarily established by wealthy private individuals, corporations, or families to primarily pursue the public good. It is a tax-exempt nonprofit organization that does not raise money from general public and is required to pay out a mandatory 5 percent of its annual assets.

**Program-Related Investing (PRI):** An investment created or carried by private foundations with the primary purpose of accomplishing charitable, religious, scientific, literary, educational or other tax-exempt purposes. For example, low-interest or interest-free loans to needy students or nonprofits.

# Chapter 17
# The Regulatory Environment of Non-Profit Higher Education and Research Institutions and Its Implications for Managerial Strategy:
## The Case of Medical Education and Research

**Marian Mahat**
*The University of Melbourne, Australia*

**Alan Pettigrew**
*The University of Melbourne, Australia*

## ABSTRACT

*The concept of strategy in non-profit higher education is a contested issue. It is argued that strategy, in the business sense, does not apply to a substantially public and more institutionalized sector such as higher education and is not achievable in complex, loosely coupled organizations such as universities. Additionally, strategy does not sit easily with organizations operating in regulated contexts limiting competitive market pressures. This chapter discusses the regulatory environment of non-profit higher education by focusing on one of the most highly regulated disciplines: medical education and research. The chapter will begin by developing a context for discussion by firstly mapping the landscape of Australian medical education and research. Subsequently, the chapter argues that medical schools and research institutes need to exercise as much discretion as they can in the area under their control, develop sound strategies to deal with their changed circumstances, and develop a coherent and defensible basis for decision making through assessing their environment.*

DOI: 10.4018/978-1-5225-2537-0.ch017

Copyright © 2017, IGI Global. Copying or distributing in print or electronic forms without written permission of IGI Global is prohibited.

## INTRODUCTION

Every not-for-profit organization needs a strategy—a set of unified actions undertaken to advance a not-for profit organization's mission by leveraging its competitive advantage (La Piana, 2008). In higher education and research, key issues shaping the competitive landscape compel not-for-profit institutions to make strategic choices in order to make use of their resources effectively and efficiently. However, the concept of strategy in non-profit higher education in particular is a contested issue. It is argued that strategy, in the business sense, does not apply to a substantially public and more institutionalised sector such as higher education (Amaral, Jones, & Karseth, 2002; Gumport, 2001) and is not achievable in complex, loosely coupled organisations such as universities (Leslie, 1996; Musselin, 2007). Additionally, strategy does not sit easily with organisations operating in regulated contexts limiting competitive market pressures (Mahon & Murray, 1980, 1981; Smith & Grimm, 1987). Managing higher education and research institutions is a task complicated by complex, multistage regulatory processes. Many organizations, including governments, professional bodies, funding and accreditation agencies play important roles and provide various levels of input or control.

Operating within higher education systems is a task made complex by frequent reviews of performance, standards and funding arrangements, the compartmentalised nature of the regulatory environment, and uncertainty resulting from changes in legislation. Regulation in higher education is common across countries although the extent of regulation intervention varies among systems. In most cases, and Australia is no exception, institutions globally are being granted more autonomy by governments. But it is fair to say that governments have sometimes been hesitant to grant institutional autonomy in all areas (Esterman & Nokkola, 2009). Moreover, governments have often exchanged a priori control (through regulation) with ex post controls (through evaluation) (Neave, 2012). In the Australian context, regulation of higher education can be summarised as follows:

*Australia's change in funding regime and its subsequent battles over risk-based regulation, institutional profiles and standards provides for further evidence of the dual dynamic of growing marketization and competition that is coupled with growing hierarchical oversight and reduced discretionary professional judgement (Black et al., 2015, p. 7).*

Although the Australian higher education sector has witnessed substantial growth over the years, concerns have been raised about the quality of Australian higher education generally and its competitiveness within the global market (see, for example, Coaldrake & Stedman, 2013). Moreover, significant and diverse forces, such as globalisation and the growing use of technology, have driven further changes in the higher education landscape. The question then arises, can higher education institutions, especially universities with a long history of academia and scholarship, navigate such a regulated context, to make strategic decisions about their positions with the system?

This chapter discusses the regulatory environment of non-profit higher education by focusing on one of the most highly regulated disciplines in the field: medical education and research. In Australia, some faculties of medicine have annual revenues larger than some universities, or larger than all faculties put together within their university. Additionally, medical education is an intensely evidence-driven professional field that operates in an increasingly regulated environment as compared to other fields within universities, which can have an impact on the role and character of an institution's strategy. Many universities and their faculties of medicine are closely aligned with Medical Research Institutes (MRIs), be they part of the university itself or independent entities with varying levels of support from governments or philanthropy. The activities of these institutions, through the nature of their work in science, health and medicine, are also subject to regulation that influences the implementation of strategy.

The chapter begins by developing a context for discussion by firstly mapping the landscape of Australian medical education, training and research, including its regulatory contexts. Subsequently, it discusses strategy formulation in non-profit medical schools and research institutions. The chapter concludes by providing future research directions and implications for managerial strategies in medical education and health and medical research.

## BACKGROUND

### Australian Medical Education, Training, and Research

There are four main phases in Australian medical education and training—basic medical education, prevocational training, vocational training and continuing professional development. Different organizations and agencies have responsibility for the different phases. The first phase is the responsibility of the medical schools. The Deans of these schools form the council of the Medical Deans Australia and New Zealand (MDANZ), which represents professional entry-level medical education, training and research in Australia and New Zealand.

There are currently 18 medical schools in Australia (MDANZ, 2015a) that provide professional qualifications over a range of medical specialisations and foci, and have alliance(s) with or operate a hospital, hospital service, medical centre, or several of these. These medical schools are located within Australia's universities, of which there are 40 (TEQSA, 2015). There are also 17 rural clinical schools with multiple training locations, managed by 16 universities (Commonwealth of Australia, 2013). Table 1 shows the 18 medical schools chronologically listed by their commencement dates. Since 2008, the University of New England has a joint medical program affiliated with the University of Newcastle. At the time of the current study, one new medical school at Curtin University in Western Australia was approved by the Federal Government for commencement in 2017.

The profile of Australian university medical students has evolved. In 2004, there were 2,120 commencing undergraduate and graduate student enrolments in Australia's 18 medical schools, of which approximately 20 percent were international students (MDANZ, 2015d). Since 2004, medical schools have been enrolling domestic full-fee paying students in addition to Commonwealth-funded ones, although this ceased in 2009 following changes in legislation (which applies to the whole higher education sector, not just medical education). A decade later, in 2014, Australia had 3,737 commencing medical students, including 552 (approximately 15 percent) international students (MDANZ, 2015d), a 76 percent increase in overall enrolments.

The second phase (prevocational training) consists of a compulsory intern year for new graduates and several subsequent years of informal training as junior doctors. Prevocational training is the responsibility of the Postgraduate Medical Councils (PMCs) in each state and territory, under the approval and authority of the Medical Board of Australia. The Board is also responsible for granting general registration to Australian and New Zealand medical graduates who have completed an intern year. Although structural models vary widely between the states and territories, the eight PMCs have responsibility for developing the education and training requirements in prevocational clinical training of medical schools' graduates

*Table 1. Australian medical schools*

| No. | Institution | Year Commenced |
|---|---|---|
| 1 | The University of Melbourne | 1862 |
| 2 | The University of Sydney | 1883 |
| 3 | University of Adelaide | 1885 |
| 4 | The University of Queensland | 1936 |
| 5 | The University of Western Australia | 1957 |
| 6 | Monash University | 1961 |
| 7 | The University of New South Wales | 1961 |
| 8 | The University of Tasmania | 1965 |
| 9 | Flinders University of South Australia | 1974 |
| 10 | The University of Newcastle* | 1978 |
| 11 | James Cook University | 2000 |
| 12 | The Australian National University | 2004 |
| 13 | Griffith University | 2005 |
| 14 | The University of Notre Dame Australia (Fremantle/Sydney) | 2005/2008 |
| 15 | Bond University | 2006 |
| 16 | The University of Western Sydney | 2007 |
| 17 | The University of Wollongong | 2007 |
| 18 | Deakin University | 2008 |
|  | The University of New England* | 2008 |
|  | Curtin University | 2017 |

Source: Various medical schools' websites

working in public hospitals. Despite the fragmented administration across eight jurisdictions and the lack of any legislative authority, the Confederation of Postgraduate Medical Councils (CPMEC), the peak body representing all the councils, developed the Australian Curriculum Framework for Junior Doctors in 2010 (Geffen, 2014). The framework outlines the knowledge, skills and behaviours required of junior doctors, particularly in the domains of clinical management, professionalism and communication (CPMEC, 2008).

The number of internships and funding for clinical placements is broadly controlled by the Department of Health or Human Services in each state and territory, and reflects the service needs of the intern training institutions and the number of graduates in each state who are Australian citizens or who have permanent resident status. Each state varies as to whether applications for internships are made to the Health Department, a Postgraduate Medical Council or individual hospitals. The audit of internship applications in 2014 identified 3,676 applicants for internships in 2015, of which 3,004 were domestic medical graduates, 480 were international full fee paying medical graduates of Australian universities. There were 192 other applicants (AMSA, 2015). As at June 2014, there were approximately 3,210 state and territory intern positions available for 2015 (AMSA, 2015).

The medical colleges, as providers of specialist medical training, are responsible for the third and fourth phases of vocational training and continuing professional development. There are currently 24 medical colleges, such as the Royal Australian College of General Practitioners and the Royal Australasian College of Surgeons. The Colleges are responsible for 24 vocational training programs that expand into 64 sub-specialty programs (Australian Medical Council, 2012a, 2012b). Vocational training varies between programs and colleges—from funding to admissions criteria to curricula, format and assessments.

The Australian Medical Council (AMC) assesses courses, including those offered by specialist medical colleges, and accredits medical schools and recently acquired oversight of prevocational training. Commissioned by the Medical Board of Australia, the AMC has developed a national framework for the intern year, which includes development of global outcome statements, national standards for intern training and draft guidelines for rotations (Australian Medical Council & Medical Board of Australia, 2013). In 2014, the AMC began to oversee the national framework, including periodic review of the intern training accreditation bodies.

Medical Research Institutes (MRIs) are institutes that conduct research on a broad spectrum of human health issues, and can either be mission-based charities that operate independently from a university or hospital, independent institutes established under state legislation, university-based institutes, part of a hospital or health provider, or institutes arising from alliances between a hospital and university. They are primarily co-located with major teaching hospitals and provide a unique interface between research and healthcare delivery. Through affiliations with universities, MRIs also provide a cohesive training environment, attracting medical and science graduates for training of the next generation of researchers and scientists. Independent MRIs train higher degree research students through affiliations with one or more universities.

As non-profit organizations, MRIs receive the majority of their funding through competitive grants for research projects—primarily through the Australian Government's National Health and Medical Research Council (NHMRC). The remaining funding comes largely through state government support for infrastructure and operating costs, competitive grants from foundations and trusts, commercialisation collaborations and contracts, and community donations. Australia's MRIs vary in size from 20 to over 1,000 staff and students, and together they employ more than 10,000 staff and higher degree students (AAMRI, 2015).

In recent years, there has been substantial interest in the role Academic Health Science Centres (AHSC) can play in promoting health and economic development in Australia. An AHSC is established when a leading university joins with a major tertiary health care provider in a tripartite mission of excellence in clinical service, research and education (Fisk et al., 2011). It is believed that AHSCs have the capability and the collective responsibility to transform medicine, improve health, and reduce healthcare disparities locally and globally. In 2015, four Australian centres were recognised as being of top quality internationally and have been recognised as Advanced Health Research and Translation Centres (National Health and Medical Research Council (NHMRC), 2015).

## Regulation in Australian Medical Education, Training, and Research

Medical education, training and research comprise a complex, multistage process in which many organizations, including the Australian and state and territory governments, universities, specialist colleges, funding and other health agencies play important roles and provide various levels of input. Although the combined efforts of organizations have produced a medical education and training system that is highly regarded, the relationships within the systems have developed, in some cases, in an implicit and fragmented way and the entire system is devoid of coordinated governance (Dowton, Stokes, Rawstron,

Pogson, & Brown, 2005). In an effort to reduce bureaucracy, the government, in 2014, closed three agencies - Health Workforce Australia, General Practice Education and Training Ltd (GPET), and Australian National Preventative Health Agency (ANPHA) - and transferred their functions to the Department of Health (The Honorable Peter Dutton, Member of Parliament (Minister for Health and Sport), 2014). This further highlights the transient and dynamic nature of regulation in Australian medical education.

Australia's Federal Department of Education has the primary responsibility for policy relating to, and the funding of, university education of medical students. In 2008, this funding comprised approximately $100,000 per student for a six-year course (Commonwealth of Australia, 2008). In conjunction with the Department of Health, the Department of Education also determines the number of university places available each year in medicine. The Government's commitment to medical education includes provision of funding, in part, of the clinical training component. The universities in turn contract with teaching hospitals for the use of facilities for training purposes (Australian Institute of Health and Welfare, 2007). The Federal Department of Health also provides support and funding through health and hospital infrastructure and regional and rural health (Commonwealth of Australia, 2012). For instance, the regional and rural health program supports facilities for training medical students and registrars in rural and remote communities.

On the other hand, state and territory governments and departments of health manage and jointly fund, with the Australian Federal government, public hospitals, where the bulk of pre-vocational and vocational training for medical students is provided. The state and territory governments' contributions to medical education deliver important components of hospital infrastructure and on-the-job staff trainers in hospital environments, as part of the Australian Healthcare Agreements. The state and territory governments and departments also develop the policy frameworks for operating healthcare systems, including education and training components. This split responsibility—federal funding for undergraduate/graduate medical education and state funding for clinical training in hospitals—leads to some tension and confusion. For example, changes in the delivery of healthcare (state responsibility) has led to unanticipated consequences for clinical training (Dowton et al., 2005) with little coordination and collaboration with their federal counterparts. The 'acrimonious negotiations' over the Australian Healthcare Agreements in 2003 is another example of the tensions and generally uncooperative relationships between the federal government and the states that have been reported (Humphreys & Gregory, 2012).

Health sector organizations and agencies play key roles in the education and training of medical practitioners, and have a direct and indirect impact on the strategic management of medical schools. These include the Postgraduate Medical Councils, Medical Board of Australia, Medical Training Review Panel, National Rural Health Alliance, and the Australian Health Practitioner Regulation Agency, as well as local health systems and public and private hospitals. The Australian Medical Council (AMC) is responsible for the accreditation process for all phases of medical education, and sets the requirements, standards and learning outcomes of medical graduates.

Research in medical and health sciences is undertaken in 39 of Australia's 40 universities, though not all universities offer medical degrees. Medical and health sciences is also the most highly funded research discipline in the Australian university sector (Australian Research Council, 2016). Together with the MRIs, Australian universities have a long standing reputation for international excellence in medical and health research. The volume of this activity has increased over the decade 2001-2010 (and beyond) along with significantly increased government funding through the NHMRC over that decade. In addition to providing many forms of relatively short-term financial support for research, the NHMRC requires strict adherence of research institutions with rules and reporting requirements governing the application process for funding, management of funding awarded, ethical approval for research involving humans or animals, and regulation of sensitive areas such as the use of human embryos. In addition, the NHMRC and the Australian Research Council (ARC), as government funding agencies, have a unified approach in the provision of guidelines and reporting requirements on research integrity. Thus, the medical and health research environment is complex and requires deft management of resources, both physical and human.

There are many types of stakeholders in medical education and, given the importance of health to society, the interests of some may be in conflict with those of others. Many have argued that there is a lack of coherent coordination in all aspects of medical education and training and that these tensions need to be resolved (Dowton et al., 2005; McGrath, Graham, Crotty, & Jolly, 2006). Figure 1 shows the interactions between different stakeholders in the regulatory architecture of Australian medical education, training and research. Depending on where one is located within the medical school environment, the interactions between stakeholders and medical schools will have an impact on the strategic management of the school.

In summary, medical education, training and research in Australia would appear to be one of the most diverse and dynamic medical environments in the world (Brooks, Doherty, & Donald, 2001). The number of medical schools has more than doubled in the last fifty years. There have been significant changes to admission criteria, programs, curricula, and assessments. However, the lack of cohesion, across health and education systems and across national and state jurisdictions (McGrath et al., 2006) remains, and to some extent has been exacerbated with the more recent introduction, and demise, of related agencies, organizations, and systems. While government funding for education has increased in absolute terms,

*Figure 1. Regulatory architecture of Australian medical education, training and research*

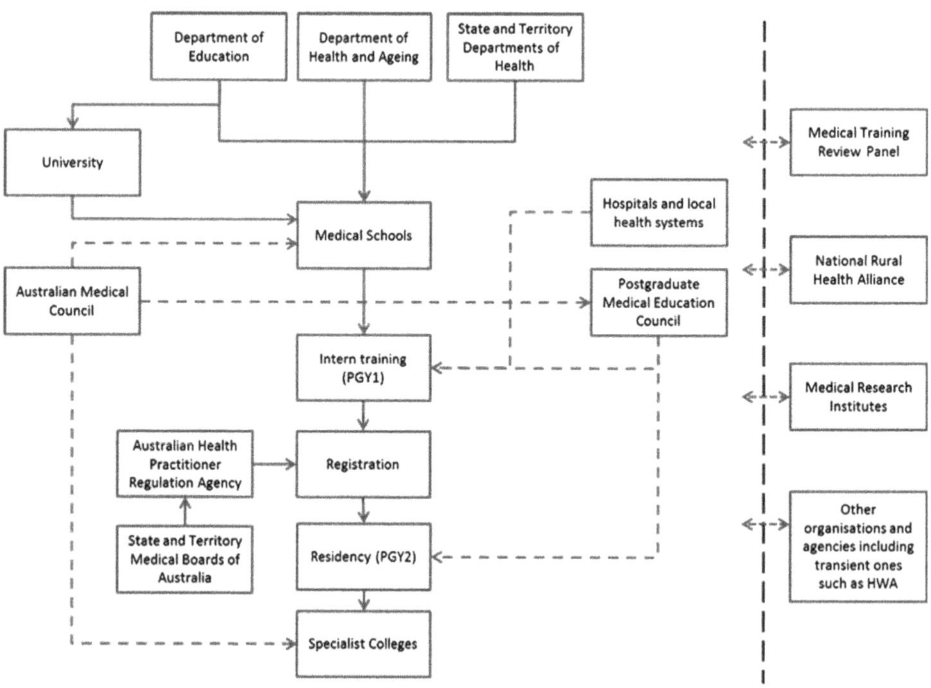

there is now less funding available on a per student basis. Furthermore, the student mix has diversified, as have the modes of student learning. As a result, the medical workforce continues to change, especially with the growing number of international students studying for medical qualifications.

## STRATEGY IN MEDICAL EDUCATION, TRAINING, AND RESEARCH

The environments of public and non-profit medical education and research organizations have changed dramatically in the last few decades. Flexner's 1910 report changed the face of American medical education (Bonner, 2002; Cooke, Irby, Sullivan, & Ludmerer, 2006; Hamilton, 2010; Lagemann, 1983), and had an impact on the situation in Europe and the United Kingdom (Leinster, 2011) and Australia (Hamilton & Vandewerdt, 1990; Hamilton, 2010). Medical education and research has been peppered with myriad reviews and recommendations, followed by reforms. As a result, there have been significant changes, in relation to medical education, to admission criteria, programs, curricula, and assessments, as well as funding at various levels. Three major reviews since 1998 of government support for medical and health research have led to progressive changes in governance, strategy, priority setting and funding of the NHMRC (Grant, 2004; McKeon, 2013; Wills, 1998).

Strategic thought and action are increasingly important to the continued viability and effectiveness of public and non-profit organizations of all sorts. Without considered strategic formulation it is unlikely that these organizations will be able to successfully meet the numerous challenges that face them. To cope with these various pressures, Bryson (1988) recommends a pragmatic approach for strategy formulation in public and non-profit organizations. Medical education and research non-profit organizations must do at least three things: (1) exercise as much discretion as they can in the areas under their control, (2) develop good strategies to deal with their changed circumstances, and (3) develop a coherent and defensible basis for decision making (Bryson, 1988).

First, these organizations need to exercise discretion in order to ensure responsiveness to their stakeholders. Within the highly regulated environment, medical schools need to deal with the operational or technical aspects of regulation (Tan & Litschert, 1994) such as responding to accountability frameworks set up by the government, and managing their interactions with external entities such as regulatory agencies (Post & Mahon, 1980). It has been argued that a more focused strategy is not feasible in regulated environments that are deterministic (Smith & Grimm, 1987). Indeed, strategies for organizations in such regulated situations would seem to be negotiated (Murray & Isenman, 1978).

Despite operating in a regulated environment, several studies have shown that medical schools are not all the same (Brosnan, 2010; Lawson, Chew, & Van Der Weyden, 2004; Mahat & Coates, 2016; Mahat, 2016). They diverge in terms of their core functions of teaching and learning, research and knowledge exchange as well as have varying historics, locations, size, student profile and international orientation. Non-profit medical schools have demonstrated their ability to exercise discretion to ensure that they position themselves distinctively in areas in which they have control.

The discretion available to MRIs on the other hand appears to be broader than in medical schools where expertise is required in the full range of pre-clinical and clinical disciplines. MRIs are better able to establish priority areas or disciplines within medical and health research that will be fostered. Many MRIs therefore exhibit specialist and high performing profiles in restricted areas, such as cancer, diabetes, mental health, or cardiovascular disease, for which they become widely known.

Second, these organizations need to develop sound strategies to deal with their changed circumstances. Non-profit organizations in general are established to further cultural, educational, religious, professional, or public service objectives. In economic terms, a non-profit organization uses its surplus revenues to further achieve its purpose or mission, rather than distributing its surplus income to the organization's shareholders as profit or dividends. Accordingly, achieving a surplus can be an objective or strategy for non-profit organisations, but not in the traditional business sense of making a profit.

Good strategies come in different shapes and forms (Chaffee, 1985; Mintzberg, 1973). Porter (1980) describes three general types of strategies that are commonly used by organizations. They are cost leadership, differentiation, and market segmentation (or focus). Market segmentation is narrow in scope while both cost leadership and differentiation are relatively broad in market scope. In medical education, it has been found that Australian medical schools have used student market segmentation to gain a foothold in a particular niche or differentiation strategies to emphasise specific research focus areas (Mahat & Coates, 2016). In medical and health research, it is discipline specialisation that provides opportunities for broad market segmentation.

Cost leadership and (price) differentiation are less prominent in defining strategies because unit costs per research discipline can be relatively constant across institutions. The exception here is where size and scale of an institution can lead to efficiencies in, for example, the purchase, maintenance and use of expensive infrastructure. In the cases where MRIs are within or closely affiliated with host universities, such scale is more easily achieved. For other independent MRIs supported by state government funding, opportunities can arise for step improvements in their research environment. For those MRIs dependent almost solely on philanthropic and competitive grant funding, differentiation based on scale is far more difficult, hence they are usually highly specialised in a restricted range of research disciplines. It is out of these constraints, together with the desire and requirement for all medical research institutions to achieve advances in research outcomes, that collaboration and partnerships between institutions have become more prominent in recent years.

Third, institutions conducting medical education and/or research need to develop a coherent and defensible basis for decision making. Previous research and conceptualisations of strategy have long stressed the need to scan and assess the environment for matching opportunities with organizational capabilities and managerial desires. There is a basic agreement that organizations that align their strategies with the requirements of their environment outperform organizations that fail such alignment (Chaganti & Mahajan, 1989; Venkatraman & Prescott, 1990). Past research has attributed the successes of organizations to their strategic responses to meet the environmental challenges facing them (Ansoff & Brandenburg, 1971; Beal, 2000; Clark, 1971; Lindsay & Rue, 1976; Manu & Sriram, 1996; Venkatraman & Prescott, 1990).

There is considerable value in assessing the Australian higher education system through the lens of Porter's five forces framework (Collis, 1999, 2000; King, 2008; Martinez & Wolverton, 2009a, 2009b; Mathooko & Ogutu, 2015; Pringle & Huisman, 2011). From an analysis of medical education (Mahat & Goedegebuure, 2016), it is possible to determine that industry rivalry in medical education is *dimension and context specific*, and can range from *limited* to *very strong*. The barriers to entry, such as government and accrediting agencies, and high teaching and capital cost, are quite *high*. These provide the strongest protecting forces for the medical education industry. Supplier power, in the form of academic research staff, is *high* as they offer products that are differentiated and for which there is limited substitution. This also applies to medical research conducted by MRIs both inside and outside universities. On the other hand, buyer power in medical education is *weak* as there are many more suitable candidates than there are places and students cannot compete on price. By the same token, the threat of substitution can also be considered *low*.

Factors such as policies set by governments and regulatory bodies, technology, economic fluctuations, and demographic changes, can potentially shift the five forces over time. For instance, the use of simulation in medical education is increasing in an attempt to reduce the number of safety concerns (Issenberg, Gordon, Gordon, Safford, & Hart, 2001). As well, simulated scenarios are realistic enough to engage the students emotionally, thus providing a unique learning experience, where the high fidelity simulator 'patient' actually talks, breathes, blinks, and moves like a real patient; and are being adapted to accommodate the needs of various medical specialties such as anesthesia, emergency medicine and trauma, intensive care medicine, obstetrics, pediatrics, and radiology (Khan, Pattison, & Sherwood, 2011). Consequently, technology has the potential to replicate much of the education experience at marginally lower cost, and hence reduce entry barriers. For MRIs, the research environment is also changing, both socially (in terms of vastly increased emphasis on national and international collaboration) and technically through greatly improved computing power and capacity, intelligent manipulation of 'big data', and increased sophistication, and cost, of instrumentation. Furthermore, both medical education and research are increasingly competitive environments – for the best students and staff, for available funding, and for the most productive and innovative researchers.

The resulting changes in the environment may force a reconfiguration of the medical education industry. Indeed, as described briefly above, medical schools and research institutes function in an increasingly complex environment. As a result, they require more reflective and evidence-based strategic leadership and management.

## FUTURE RESEARCH DIRECTIONS

Most studies on management strategy have presented theoretical perspectives and empirical research centred on the commercial business environment. There is limited research on management strategy in the context of higher education, and much less in medical education and research. This chapter begins a discussion on these issues by arguing that medical schools and research institutes exercise as much discretion as they can in limited areas under their control and strive to develop strategies to deal with externally driven changes in their circumstances. Above all, these institutions must develop coherent and defensible bases for decision making through thorough assessment of their complex and changing environment.

An important consideration for these institutions is the 'moment in time' nature of most analytical approaches to management strategy. The example of Porter's five forces framework described earlier is based on a snapshot of the environment of medical schools and research institutes at a particular time. It by no means provides insights into the strategic orienting that medical schools and research institutions must go through in order to navigate the longer-term dynamics and uncertainties of the higher education and research landscape that are influenced by national and international developments in standards and intellectual insights. A time series reporting on the changing profiles of the environment and the responses of institutions to those changes can provide useful information on the developmental dynamics of strategy formulation in medical education and research. Ideally, such longitudinal studies of strategic development should also examine performance outcomes in the short- and long-run in order to understand the level of coherence between strategies and intended outcomes.

At the same time, regulated environments such as those operating in medical education and research, impose certain conditions and consequently can be relatively static. Additionally, it is highly likely that any regulatory changes in the environmental have a strong propensity to affect medical schools' strategic formulation. Consequently, future inquiry could focus on time-linked environmental variability (degree of change), complexity (heterogeneity and range) and illiberality (degree of threat from external competition) (Child, 1972) in the regulatory environment and the responses of institutions to those changes. Such a study could illuminate the different types of organizational strategy that medical schools and research institutes have adopted in order to achieve high levels of performance.

## CONCLUSION

Strategic thought and action are increasingly important to the continued viability and effectiveness of public and not-for-profit organizations (Bryson, 1988). Without strategic thought and action, it is unlikely that these organizations will be able to successfully meet the numerous challenges that face them. This paper has argued that despite the regulatory context, not-for-profit medical schools and research institutions can and should develop a set of coherent strategies to leverage their competitive advantage.

The importance of strategy in non-profit higher education is gaining momentum as the sector continues to undergo rapid transformation. Increasingly, universities and academic departments within them, operate in a more turbulent and dynamic environment, where the growth of global competition and related functions of marketization are evident. These changes require universities to understand the competitive forces in their environment and the key activities within their range of activities that will help them develop strategies to meet their overall objectives. Examples of dynamic change that influence competitive positioning in medical education programs include the introduction of new technologies in teaching and the rapid adoption of new scientific approaches (especially, for example, in genetics, biotechnology and imaging) and clinical practices emerging from publications in international scholarly journals.

At the system level, part of the difficulty in strategic planning currently faced by many universities in Australia and internationally is uncertainty in the political approach to future public funding for higher education. The uncertainty centres on political indecision concerning the appropriate sharing of costs between national governments and their local students, together with the role played by full-fee local and international students. These and other related factors make analysis of the current and future competitive landscape for non-profit higher education in Australia particularly difficult.

For non-profit MRIs, and particularly those that stand alone outside universities, the competitive environment is perhaps somewhat more stable, *except* for the major uncertainty they face in continuity of funding, be that either government-based or philanthropic. It is with this focus in mind that MRIs regularly adopt and review corporate strategies that, foremost, aim to ensure high productivity in impactful research. It is an institution's reputation in achieving these outcomes that underpins their capacity and credibility to seek some security in funding from governments and donors. A significant added challenge for stand-alone MRIs in this context is the competition they face from large university-based faculties and institutes (where funding capacity is often larger and hence more flexible in its application) in attracting and retaining top flight researchers. As with all organisations in for-profit and non-profit settings, these complex competitive requirements raise significant responsibilities for leaders, managers and governing bodies in higher education institutions and medical research institutes.

## REFERENCES

Amaral, A., Jones, G., & Karseth, B. (2002). Governing Higher Education: National Perspectives on Institutional Governance (Vol. 1). Dordrecht: Springer Science & Business Media.

Ansoff, H. I., & Brandenburg, R. G. (1971). A language for organization design: Part I. *Management Science*, *17*(12), B705–B716. doi:10.1287/mnsc.17.12.B705

Association of Australian Medical Research Institutes (AAMRI). (2015). *Association of Australian Medical Research Institutes*. AAMRI.

Australian Institute of Health and Welfare. (2007). Health expenditure Australia 2005–06. Health and Welfare Expenditure Series no. 30. Cat. no. HWE 37. Canberra: Author.

Australian Medical Council. (2012a). *List of Australian Recognised Medical Specialties*. Retrieved from http://www.amc.org.au/images/Recognition/AMC-list-of-specialties.pdf

Australian Medical Council. (2012b). *Specialist Medical Colleges*. Retrieved from http://www.amc.org.au/index.php/ass/apo/spp/smc

Australian Medical Council & Medical Board of Australia. (2013). *The National Internship Framework - Newsletter 1*. Retrieved from http://www.medicalboard.gov.au/News/2013-05-31-joint-newsletter.aspx

Australian Medical Students' Association (AMSA). (2015). National Internship Crisis.

Beal, R. M. (2000). Competing effectively: Environmental scanning, competitive strategy, and organizational performance in small manufacturing firms. *Journal of Small Business Management*, *38*(1), 27–47. Retrieved from http://ezproxy.library.capella.edu/login?url=http://search.epnet.com/login.aspx?direct=true&db=buh&an=2716872

Black, J., Boggs, A. M., Fry, H., Jackson, S., King, R., Lodge, M., … Black, J. (2015). *The regulation of higher education*. Academic Press.

Bonner, T. N. (2002). *Iconoclast: Abraham Flexner and a Life in Learning*. Baltimore, MD: John Hopkins University Press.

Brooks, P. M., Doherty, R. L., & Donald, K. J. (2001). Expansion and diversification of medical education in Australia, 1951-2000. *The Medical Journal of Australia*, *174*(1), 25–28. PMID:11219787

Brosnan, C. (2010). Making sense of differences between medical schools through Bourdieus concept of field. *Medical Education*, *44*(7), 645–652. doi:10.1111/j.1365-2923.2010.03680.x PMID:20636583

Bryson, J. M. (1988). A Strategic Planning Process for Public and Non-profit Organizations. *Long Range Planning*, *21*(1), 73–81. doi:10.1016/0024-6301(88)90061-1

Chaffee, E. E. (1985). Three models of strategy. *Academy of Management Review*, *10*(1), 85–98.

Chaganti, R., & Mahajan, V. (1989). Profitable small business strategies under different types of competition. *Entrepreneurship. Theory into Practice*, *13*, 21–35.

Child, J. (1972). Organizational structure, environment and performance: The role of strategic choice. *Sociology*, *6*(1), 1–22. doi:10.1177/003803857200600101

Clark, B. R. (1971). Belief and loyalty in college organization. *The Journal of Higher Education*, *42*(6), 499–515. doi:10.2307/1979081

Coaldrake, P., & Stedman, L. (2013). *Raising the Stakes: Gambling with the future of universities*. Brisbane: University of Queensland Press.

Collis, D. (1999). When Industries Change: Scenarios for Higher Education. In D. Collis (Ed.), *Exploring the Future of Higher Education* (pp. 47–70). New York: Forum for the Future of Higher Eucation.

Collis, D. (2000). When industries change revisited: New scenarios for higher education. In Forum futures: Exploring the future of higher education (pp. 103–126).

Commonwealth of Australia. (2008). *What Makes for Success in Medical Education: Synthesis Report*. Author.

Commonwealth of Australia. (2012). *Department of Health and Ageing Annual Report 2011-2012*. Canberra: Department of Health and Ageing.

Commonwealth of Australia. (2013). *List of Rural Clinical Schools*. Retrieved from http://www.health.gov.au/clinicalschools

Confederation of Postgraduate Medical Education Councils (CPMEC). (2008). *Australian Curriculum Framework for Junior Doctors*. Melbourne: Confederation of Postgraduate Medical Education Councils.

Cooke, M., Irby, D. M., Sullivan, W., & Ludmerer, K. M. (2006). American Medical Education 100 years after the Flexner Report. *The New England Journal of Medicine*, *355*(13), 1339–1344. doi:10.1056/NEJMra055445 PMID:17005951

Dowton, S. B., Stokes, M.-L., Rawstron, E., Pogson, P. R., & Brown, M. A. (2005). Postgraduate medical education: Rethinking and intergrating a complex landscape. *The Medical Journal of Australia*, *182*(4), 177–180. PMID:15720174

Esterman, T., & Nokkola, T. (2009). *University Autonomy in Europe I Exploratory Study*. Brussels: European University Association.

Fisk, N. M., Wesselingh, S. L., Beilby, J. J., Glasgow, N. J., Puddey, I. B., Robinson, B. G., & Smith, P. J. et al. (2011). Academic health science centres in Australia: Let's get competitive. *The Medical Journal of Australia*, *194*(2), 59–60. PMID:21241215

Geffen, L. (2014). A brief history of medical education and training in Australia. *The Medical Journal of Australia*, *201*(1Suppl), 19–22. doi:10.5694/mja14.00118 PMID:25047770

Grant, J. (2004). *Investment Review of Health and Medical Research*. Canberra: Academic Pressa.

Gumport, P. J. (2001). Restructuring: Imperatives and opportunities for academic leaders. *Innovative Higher Education*, *25*(4), 239–251. doi:10.1023/A:1011042522978

Hamilton, J. (2010). *Medical Education Today: What would Flexner think of it?* Australian and New Zealand Association for Medical Educators (ANZAME).

Hamilton, J., & Vandewerdt, J. M. (1990). The accreditation of undergraduate medical education in Australia. *The Medical Journal of Australia, 153*, 541–545. PMID:2233477

Humphreys, J. S., & Gregory, G. (2012). Celebrating another decade of progress in rural health: What is the current state of play? *The Australian Journal of Rural Health, 20*(3), 156–163. doi:10.1111/j.1440-1584.2012.01276.x PMID:22620481

Issenberg, S. B., Gordon, M. S., Gordon, D., Safford, R. E., & Hart, I. R. (2001). Simulation and new learning technologies. *Medical Teacher, 23*(1), 16–23. doi:10.1080/01421590020007324 PMID:11260734

Khan, K., Pattison, T., & Sherwood, M. (2011). Simulation in medical education. *Medical Teacher, 33*(1), 1–3. doi:10.3109/0142159X.2010.519412 PMID:21182376

King, M. A. (2008). A strategic assessment of the higher education industry: applying the Porter's five forces for industry analysis. In *Southeastern Decision Sciences Institute Annual Conference*. Blacksburg, VA: Pamplin College of Business, Virginia Polytechnic Institute and State University.

La Piana, D. (2008). *The nonprofit strategy revolution: real-time strategic planning in a rapid-response world*. Fieldstone Alliance.

Lagemann, E. C. (1983). *Private Power for the Public Good: A History of the Carnegie Foundation for the Advancement of Teaching*. Middletown, CT: Wesleyan University Press.

Lawson, K. A., Chew, M., & Van Der Weyden, M. B. (2004). The new Australian medical schools: Daring to be different. *The Medical Journal of Australia, 181*(11/12), 662–666. PMID:15588204

Leinster, S. J. (2011). The history of change in the UK. In P. Cavenagh, S. J. Leinster, & S. Miles (Eds.), *The Changing Face of Medical Education*. Oxford, UK: Radcliffe Publishing Ltd.

Leslie, D. W. (1996). Strategic governance: The wrong questions? *The Review of Higher Education, 20*(1), 101–112. doi:10.1353/rhe.1996.0004

Lindsay, W. M., & Rue, L. W. (1976). *Environmental Complexity in Long-Range Planning*. Oxford, UK: Planning Executives Institute.

Mahat, M. (2016). Strategic positioning in Australian higher education: The case of medical schools. In C. Sarrico, P. Teixeira, A. Magalhães, A. Veiga, M. J. Rosa, & T. Carvalho (Eds.), *Global Challenges, National Initiatives, and Institutional Response. The Transformation of Higher Education* (pp. 119–141). Rotterdam: Sense. doi:10.1007/978-94-6300-675-0_7

Mahat, M., & Coates, H. (2016). Strategic positioning of medical schools: An Australian perspective. *Medical Teacher*, 1–6. PMID:27111532

Mahat, M., & Goedegebuure, L. C. J. (2016). Strategic positioning in higher education: Reshaping perspectives. In J. Huisman & M. Tight (Eds.), *Theory And Method In Higher Education Research*. Bingley: Emerald. doi:10.1108/S2056-375220160000002011

Mahon, J. F., & Murray, E. A. (1980). Deregulation and strategic transformation. *Journal of Contemporary Business*, *9*(2), 123–138.

Mahon, J. F., & Murray, E. A. (1981). Strategic planning for regulated companies. *Strategic Management Journal*, *2*(3), 251–262. doi:10.1002/smj.4250020304

Manu, F., & Sriram, V. (1996). Innovation, marketing strategy, environment, and performance. *Journal of Business Research*, *35*(1), 79–91. doi:10.1016/0148-2963(95)00056-9

Martinez, M., & Wolverton, M. (2009a). Analyzing higher education as an industry. In M. Martinez & M. Wolverton (Eds.), *Innovative Strategy Making in HIgher Education* (pp. 45–62). Charlotte, NC: Information Age Publishing.

Martinez, M., & Wolverton, M. (2009b). Enriching planning through industry analysis. *Planning for Higher Education*, *38*(1), 23–30.

Mathooko, F. M., & Ogutu, M. (2015). Porters five competitive forces framework and other factors that influence the choice of response strategies adopted by public universities in Kenya. *International Journal of Educational Management*, *29*(3), 334–354. doi:10.1108/IJEM-12-2013-0187

McGrath, B. P., Graham, I. S., Crotty, B. J., & Jolly, B. C. (2006). Lack of integration of medical education in Australia: The need for change. *The Medical Journal of Australia*, *184*(7), 346–348. PMID:16584370

McKeon, S. (2013). Strategic Review of Health and Medical Research in Australia – Better Health Through Research. Canberra: Academic Press.

Medical Deans Australia and New Zealand (MDANZ). (2015a). *MDANZ Membership*. MDANZ.

Medical Deans Australia and New Zealand (MDANZ). (2015b). Table 3 (a): Commencing Medical Students 2002-2014 (Australia). MDANZ.

Mintzberg, H. (1973). Strategy-making in three modes. *California Management Review (Pre-1986)*, *16*(2), 44–53.

Murray, E. A., & Isenman, A. W. (1978, August). *The concept of strategy formulation as a negotiation process*. Academy of Management Meeting.

Musselin, C. (2007). Transformation of academic work: Facts and analysis. In M. Kogan & U. Teichler (Eds.), *Key Challenges to the Academic Profession* (pp. 175–190). Kassel: UNESCO Forum on Higher Education, Research and Knowledge/International Centre for Higher Education Research Kassel.

*National Health and Medical Research Council (NHMRC)*. (2015). NHMRC Advanced Health Research and Translation Centres.

Neave, G. (2012). *The evaluative state, institutional autonomy and re-engineering higher education in Western Europe. The prince and his pleasure*. Basingstoke, UK: Palgrave Macmillan. doi:10.1057/9780230370227

Porter, M. E. (1980). *Competitive Strategy: Techniques for Analysing Industries and Competitors*. New York: Free Press.

Post, J. E., & Mahon, J. F. (1980). Articulated turbulence: The effect of regulatory agencies on corporate responses to social change. *Academy of Management Review*, *5*(3), 399–407.

Pringle, J., & Huisman, J. (2011). Understanding universities in Ontario, Canada: An industry analysis using Porter's Five Forces Framework. *Canadian Journal of Higher Education*, *41*(3), 58.

Smith, K. G., & Grimm, C. M. (1987). Environmental variation, strategic change and firm performance: A study of railroad deregulation. *Strategic Management Journal*, *8*(4), 363–376. doi:10.1002/smj.4250080406

Tan, J., & Litschert, R. J. (1994). Environment-strategy relationship and its performance implications: An empirical study of Chinese electronics industry. *Strategic Management Journal*, *15*(1), 1–20. doi:10.1002/smj.4250150102

Tertiary Education Quality and Standards Agency (TEQSA). (2015). *National Register of higher education providers. National Register breakdown as at August 2015*. TEQSA.

The Honorable Peter Dutton Member of Parliament (Minister for Health and Sport). (2014). *Media release: Rebuilding General Practice Training*. Author.

Venkatraman, N., & Prescott, J. E. (1990). Environment-strategy coalignment: An empirical test of its performance implications. *Strategic Management Journal*, *11*(1), 1–23. doi:10.1002/smj.4250110102

Wills, P. (1998). *Health and Medical Research Strategic Review*. Canberra: Academic Press.

# Chapter 18
# Operational Challenges in Hybrid Organizations:
## Insights for Future Research

**Liliana Ávila**
*University of Aveiro, Portugal*

**Marlene Amorim**
*University of Aveiro, Portugal*

## ABSTRACT

*The last few years have witnessed the emergence of hybrid business models, in particular, social enterprises, which combine social and economic concerns in the same extent. Social enterprises are ambidextrous organizations that conduct activities to meet the social needs of their target beneficiaries simultaneously with income generating activities. This hybrid operational nature raises new questions about the definition and identification of an effective operations management strategy. The present chapter aims to identify the main operational challenges faced by hybrid organization in order to open avenues for future research. Drawing on current literature, the main concepts, the definition of an operations strategy and the social enterprises as hybrid organizations, are discussed. Findings suggest that the main operational challenges arise from hybridity. This chapter contributes to the theory and practices of social enterprises and concludes by identifying some opportunities for future research.*

## INTRODUCTION

In recent years, there has been a proliferation of hybrid organizations and a diversification of the organizational and competitive landscape (Walker, 2015). Social enterprises as hybrid organizations are attracting a growing interest among academics and practitioners (Doherty, Haugh, & Lyon, 2014). The emergence of these organizations with a hybrid nature has been explained to a great extent by the economic context that has been fueled by the economic crisis, especially in the European context. This has resulted in substantial shortenings in the financial support provided by the State to nonprofit organizations, who typically address social needs (e.g. elderly care, support and social inclusion of disadvantaged individuals,

DOI: 10.4018/978-1-5225-2537-0.ch018

Copyright © 2017, IGI Global. Copying or distributing in print or electronic forms without written permission of IGI Global is prohibited.

etc.). In the current context, the financial sustainability of organizations addressing such beneficiaries is put at risk, and they are forced to find alternative ways to generate revenues while pursuing their social mission (Battilana & Lee, 2014; Smith, Gonin, & Besharov, 2013).

Social enterprises face many challenges once they try to conciliate social and economic concerns under a common organizational and operational system. To be successful they need to do a great job managing limited resources, therefore the attainment of effective operations management must be at the core of their priorities. Nevertheless, and unlike traditional for-profit organizations, social enterprises are not necessarily targeting the pursuit of a competitive advantage in order to overcome their competition. Glavas and Mish (2014) suggest that those organizations, aiming to become more responsive socially and ecologically while prospering economically, they focus on assuring a collaborative advantage more than a competitive advantage, since most of them strive to have sustainable resources, which are imitable, easy to find and substitutable. This is important to ensure that it is possible to scale their organizational and operational models in order to implement them in different contexts.

Whereas the topic of operations strategy is, to this date, largely unaddressed for the specific context of social enterprises, it is an exhaustively explored and mature topic in operations management literature. The definition of an operations strategy involves a set of managerial decisions concerning the structure and functioning of the production system. A company can choose between many operations strategy configuration models, according to what is perceived, in a specific moment and decision making context, as the best alternative to improve production effectiveness, in order to meet market requirements and achieve the expected performance. Several authors have mentioned in their studies the important role of operations strategy in performance (Díaz Garrido, Martín-Peña, & García-Muiña, 2007; Espino-Rodriguez & Gil-Padilla, 2014; Martín-Peña & Díaz-Garrido, 2008). According to McDermott, Markman and Balkin (2003), if entrepreneurs successfully identify opportunities but fail in their implementation at the operational level, their ability to sustain a competitive advantage will also fail.

The emergence of hybrid organizational structures such as social enterprises is challenging the prevalent knowledge on operations management and more specifically on operations strategy. It raises a set of interrogations regarding the goals to which the operations function must respond, as well as the nature of the operations decisions involved. Most of the studies addressing the management of social enterprises published to this date have focused on the definition and characterization of their goals and activities, the identification of their specificities when compared with traditional nonprofit and for-profit organizations, while the development of new managerial knowledge in this domain remains largely unexplored.

However, there are enough arguments to sustain that it is important to develop knowledge about the operational organization of the activities of these enterprises, notably from the perspective of their operations management. The ambidexterity that characterizes the operations of these organizations, i.e. conducting income generating activities simultaneously with other activities for the generation of social impact, raises questions about how to typify the operations strategies adopted by social enterprises. Building on the literature and on the rationale derived from the practices of social enterprises acting in field (that are geographically closed to the authors and, therefore, they were better known by them), this chapter aims to:

1. Present the main concepts behind the definition of an operations strategy and the main reasons why social enterprises are labelled as hybrid organizations, as well as the tensions emerging from their hybridity.

2. Identify key operational challenges faced by social enterprises motivated by the ambidexterity of their activities.
3. Put forward directions for future research derived from the specificities of operations management in social enterprises, for which there are no answers in the literature yet.

The chapter is organized as follows: the next section reviews the main principles and concepts that support the development of an operations strategy and presents social enterprises as hybrid organizations, identifying the main tensions arising from that hybridity. After that, a section is devoted to the discussion of the operational challenges, building on the literature and the practices of social enterprises. Finally, some directions for future research are put forward, emerging from the identification of some specificities of social enterprises, notably as regards the organization of the operations in an ambidextrous context, whose answers would be useful for supporting managerial decision. A conclusion section is also offered.

## BACKGROUND

### Operations Strategy

The topic of operations strategy is one of key importance within the operations management literature, ranking among the top five research foci, according to an exhaustive historical analysis of survey research articles published between 1980 and 2000 in Operations Management, acknowledging the importance of this domain (Rungtusanatham, Choi, Hollingworth, Wu, & Forza, 2003). Slack, Chambers and Johnston (2001) define operations strategy as "the pattern of strategic decisions and actions which set the role, objectives and activities of operations". On the other hand, Lowson (2001) provides a more elaborate definition, arguing that "an operations strategy aims to perform key operational management activities better than rivals so as to provide support for the overall strategy of a firm as well as serving as a firm´s distinctive competence." According to the same author, individual activities can be quickly imitated by other companies, but not the way they are combined to form a unique operations strategy.

The literature on operations strategy has focused and discussed essentially two aspects: the process and the content. The process refers to how an organization develops an appropriate operations strategy following a certain perspective and addressing selected priorities, whereas the content refers to the identification and characterization of key decision areas that need to be addressed for developing an operations strategy. The ultimate goal of an operations strategy is to contribute to achieve a competitive advantage which will allow the company to overcome its competitors. Thus, the effectiveness of an operations strategy can be measured by assessing to which extent the competitive advantages and corresponding operational decisions are consistent among themselves (Leong, Snyder, & Ward, 1990). In what follows, a brief discussion is offered concerning the outlines of the process and the content for the definition of an operations strategy.

#### Process

As aforementioned, within the operations strategy field, the term "process" is used to refer the way an enterprise develops its operations strategy by subscribing to a specific perspective. Overall, managers may choose among four alternative perspectives that differ in what concerns the importance attributed to external or internal aspects. Each one of these perspectives puts different questions to managers (Figure 1). In the top-down perspective the operations strategy is derived from the organization's business strategy. In the market requirements perspective the operations strategy is developed from the requirements of the organization's market position. A third perspective is labelled the bottom-up perspective. In this case, the operations strategy emerges from the day-to-day experience, the actions and decisions taken within operations. Finally, an operations resources perspective suggests the definition of an operations strategy based in the operations resources available (Slack et al., 2001).

## Content

The content of an operations strategy involves a set of decisions that materialize how the enterprise makes use of its resources to reach a sustainable competitive advantage in its sector (Lowson, 2002), that will allow the company to overcome its competitors, and to obtain the expected performance. The literature on operations management emphasizes cost, quality, flexibility and delivery as the main competitive advantages commonly pursued by firms (Espino-Rodriguez & Gil-Padilla 2014; Díaz Garrido et al. 2007; Martín-Peña & Díaz-Garrido 2008). However, in addition to these, other dimensions of competitive advantages are emerging, such as innovation (Nair & Boulton, 2008; Samarrokhi, Jenab, Arumugam, & Weinsier, 2015) or environmental and social sustainability (Longoni & Cagliano, 2015), as the concerns related with the use of natural resources, the quality of life and the welfare of communities become central for businesses.

Different types of operations decisions have been identified. A common classification distinguishes structural and infrastructural decisions. Structural decisions are characterized by having strategic implications, requiring significant investment and having a long-term impact. These decisions include choices regarding aspects such as the production process technology, the degree of vertical integration, as well as elements related to the facilities and plant location. Infrastructural decisions, in turn, have a short-term impact, typically require smaller investments and are related to operational practices and decisions, for example, in terms of planning and control systems, organizational structure, workforce or quality management (Díaz Garrido et al., 2007; Espino-Rodriguez & Gil-Padilla, 2014). Figure 1 illustrates the relationship between operations decisions, competitive advantages and the organization's performance.

In the last decades, many typologies and taxonomies have been proposed that identify different configuration models in operations strategy.

One of the most cited in the literature is the taxonomy proposed by Miller and Roth (1994) which identifies three manufacturing strategy types observed in several industries (Caretakers, Marketers and Innovators) depending on the relative importance attached to a set of competitive advantages. A literature review conducted by Martín-Peña and Díaz-Garrido (2008) on typologies and taxonomies of operations strategy identifies three generic operations strategies for industrial companies that are commonly accepted in the literature: strategies aiming to minimize costs; strategies focusing on the highest quality products and also trying to adapt to customer's needs; and strategies adopted by organizations which implement new technologies and new operations processes with great flexibility as a way to differentiate. The same authors also identify an additional operations strategy in which organizations combine more than one operations competitive priority in order to obtain competitive advantages.

Whereas it is possible for companies to engage in the pursuit of multiple directions for competitive advantage, it is recommended to focus on only a strategic priority at a time, since different strategic priorities require different strategic decisions. An enterprise focused on low cost priorities will probably

*Figure 1. Overview of operations strategy*
*Source 1 Elaborated upon and Adapted from Slacks et al. (2001)*

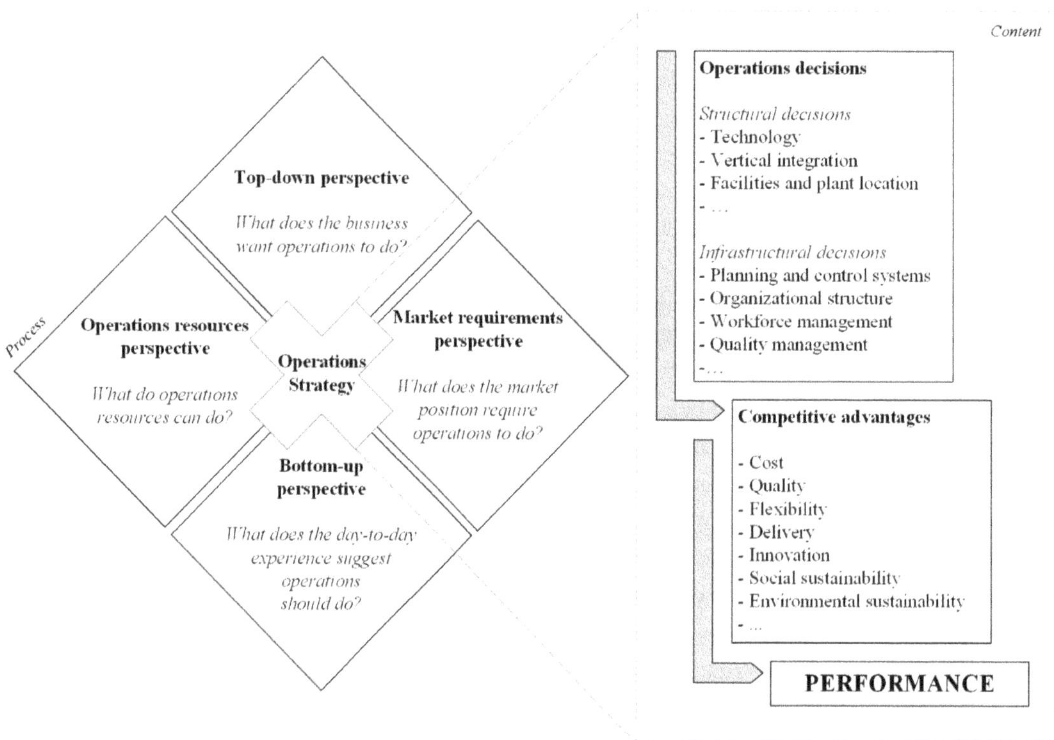


struggle to deliver high quality or distinctive products and services, meeting all the requirements of their customers (Boyer & Lewis, 2002). According to the competitive advantage pursued by an organization, structural and infrastructural decisions assume different degrees of importance. For example, an organization competing by cost and delivery should pay special attention to location decisions. Vertical integration decisions are important to organizations competing in the market by flexibility, and supply chain management is more important to those aiming to provide high quality products and services (McDermott et al., 2003).

An enterprise pursuing several competitive advantages, probably is a world class organization and has the resources needed to successfully compete in more than one front, otherwise it does not have a clearly defined strategy (Boyer & Pagell, 2000). In young or smaller enterprises, the successful alignment among strategic objectives and operations decisions would lead to a more effective and efficient use of scarce resources. On the other hand, the lack of alignment would lead to wasted resources, missed opportunities and loss of competitiveness (McDermott et al., 2003).

Operational decisions and competitive advantages pointed on the literature in the manufacturing field also apply to a great extent to service firms, although they present some specificities (Espino-Rodriguez & Gil-Padilla, 2014; Roth & Menor, 2003). In the context of services, structural decisions may also include those related to the touch points with clients as the relative allocation of service tasks to the front- and back-office or the number and types of distribution channels (Roth & Menor, 2003). In the same extent, service firms may pursue additional competitive advantages due to their distinct characteristics, such as service provision instead the delivery considered for manufacturing firms, the customer focus and know-how (Ibrahim, 2010; Phusavat & Kanchana, 2008).

### The Strategic Role of Operations Over Time

Operations tend to assume different strategic roles over time according to the maturity level of the enterprise. A four-stage model was proposed by Hayes and Wheelwright in 1984 to explain the development of the strategic impact of operations over time. This model is commonly accepted in the literature and has been used as a reference both in manufacturing and services (Lillis & Sweeney, 2013; Slack et al., 2001). It suggests that the operations function evolves from an initial stage where it is internally neutral, passing through intermediate stages, to the last stage where it is labelled as externally supportive.

In a first instance, the operations function is internally focused, mainly reactive, working to correct the worst problems. In the second stage, during the implementation of the strategy, efforts are conducted to adopt the best practices and the company aims to be as good as its competitors. The third stage sees the operations function seeking to support the organization's business strategy in order to become the best in its industry (Slack et al., 2001). In the second stage, the company strives to improve through the imitation of its competitors, whereas in the third stage it is more successful in their improvement efforts by exploring potential new resources and practices for consistency with its operations strategy (Wu, Melnyk, & Flynn, 2010). Ideally, in the fourth and ultimate stage, operations are the basis for ensuring a competitive advantage for the organization, enabling it to redefine industry expectations and to set new standards (Slack et al., 2001).

## Social Enterprises as Hybrid Organizations

Social enterprises are organizations that combine social and economic concerns, i.e. organizations pursuing a social mission, often involving activities that do not generate income, while engaging in commercial activities (Battilana & Lee, 2014; Pache & Santos, 2012). In the organizational landscape, social enterprises are positioned between traditional nonprofit and traditional for-profit organizations (Neck, Brush, & Allen, 2009; Wilson & Post, 2011). For this reason they are considered hybrid organizations since they often incorporate characteristics from the private and social sector (Ebrahim, Battilana, & Mair, 2014; Jäger & Schröer, 2013; Pache & Santos, 2012; Smith et al., 2013; Wilson & Post, 2011). A wide range of business models can fit into such spectrum. Some authors argue that social enterprises may also incorporate characteristics from the public sector and civil society (Brandsen & Karré, 2011; Doherty et al., 2014).

Social enterprises may adopt different legal forms according to the existing legal framework in the context in which they operate. In some countries, social enterprises are not recognized legally as such, a circumstance that leads those organizations to develop their activities as associations, cooperatives or even as commercial enterprises. Regardless of the legal form they adopt, what distinguishes social enterprises from other organizations are the principles they follow, and the way they shape the nature of their activities. Social enterprises are different from socially responsible businesses. The latter incorporate the generation of profits and its distribution among shareholders as a core objective. Social enterprises also differ from nonprofit organizations that run commercial activities as a way of get additional funds. Figure 2 shows the positioning of social enterprises in the organizational landscape. According to the

*Figure 2. Positioning social enterprises in the organizational landscape*
*Source 2 Adapted from Teasedale (2012)*

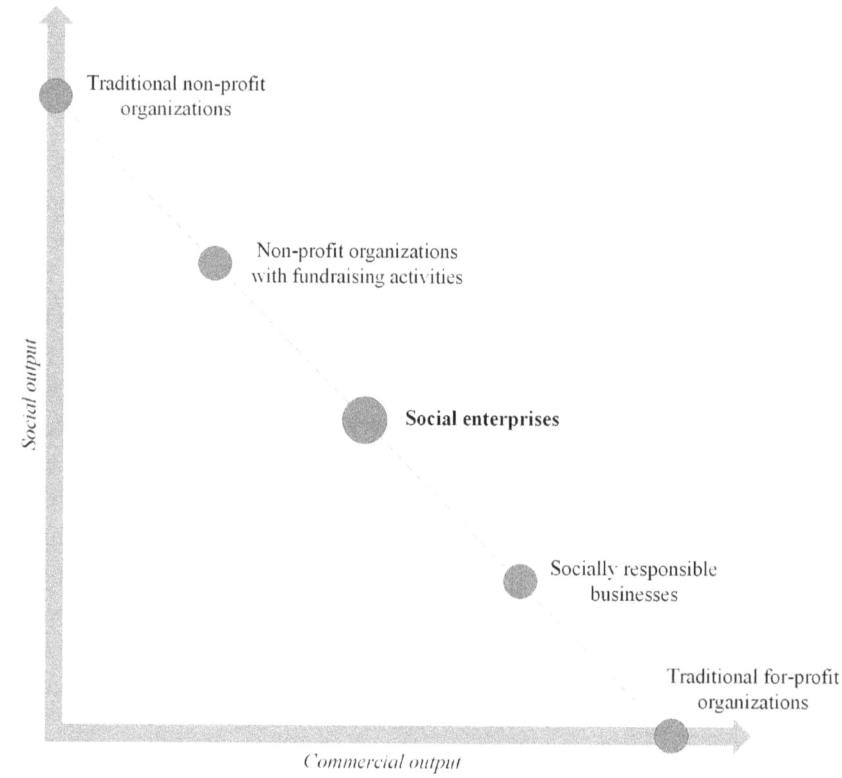


authors' understanding, a social enterprise has a social mission clearly defined and should conduct commercial activities that allow the organization to generate a great part of their revenues and thus ensure its financial sustainability. Profits, if they exist, must be reinvested to scale the social impact.

Battilana, Lee, Walker and Dorsey (2012) define the hybrid ideal as a fully integrated organization. Everything the enterprise does produces both social value and commercial revenue. Mission and profit aims are integrated in the same strategy. The case of ColorADD offers a good example of a social enterprise following an integrated approach. ColorADD is a colour identification system developed by a Portuguese designer which aim is to make the communication for colour-blind more efficient and inclusive through a licensing system available to any organization wanting to incorporate and display the code in its products and services. As the number of organizations using the code increases, more colour-blind people will have access to it. ColorADD also promotes some activities for children in schools to make them aware of colour-blindness and teach how they can use the code that is already available in several products and services through the licensing system. Both activities are important to the fulfilment of the social mission *"integrate without discriminate"*, and, at the same time, the first one contributes for the generation of revenues that ensure the financial sustainability of the enterprise.

However, for many organizations it is difficult to follow a fully integrated approach, as they serve disadvantaged groups who are not able to pay for their products and services as common customers. This fact may force these organizations to follow less integrated approaches, performing other activities that may be or not related with their mission, but which are also important for the organization because they enable the generation of revenues. An illustrative example of this is SPEAK. It is a linguistic and cultural service offer, provided by a nonprofit organization, aiming to get together people from different cultures as a way to include migrants in the cities where they are living and fight against their social exclusion. Any person interested in participating can apply to learn or teach a language or culture including local people. Teachers are volunteers. On the other hand, this nonprofit organization created the SPEAK PRO program which provides specialized services to individuals and other organizations. Revenues generated through this program are used to ensure the financial sustainability and the pursuit of social impact of SPEAK. In this case, social and income generating activities are run separately, they are independent from each other.

In their recent work, Santos, Pache and Birkholz (2015) propose a typology of hybrid models using the concept of business model as the central unit of analysis to understand the functioning of hybrid organizations. The typology consisting of four social business hybrid models – Market hybrid, Bridging hybrid, Blending hybrid and Coupling hybrid – is derived from two dimensions: the level of contingent value spillovers (automatic value spillovers vs contingent value spillovers) and the degree of overlap between clients and beneficiaries (beneficiaries are the clients that pay for services/products vs beneficiaries are different from clients). The authors explore differences between these social business models taking into consideration four aspects dealing with specific challenges experienced by hybrid organizations: managerial structure, governance, human resources and performance management.

In fact, the hybrid nature of social enterprises forces them to deal with several tensions, whose understanding is important since it is believed that they are the basis of many operational challenges faced by these organizations. In the next section will be presented the main tensions that have been identified in the literature.

## Tensions Emerging From Social Enterprise's Hybridity

Despite the evidence that social enterprises generate great social impact, their hybrid nature make them fragile organizations that run the risk of internal tensions and mission drift (Ebrahim et al., 2014; Santos et al., 2015).This is particularly true if their social impact and revenue generating activities are not integrated and are performed separately. In recent years, some authors have dedicated their work identifying some domains where tensions arising from the hybrid nature of social enterprises are reported, i.e. the desire to pursue social and economic goals simultaneously.

Wilson and Post (2011) suggest that these tensions are mostly at the operational than strategic level. According to Doherty et al. (2014), they impact operationally on goals and acquisition of resources. The way each social enterprise chooses to deal with them depends on a great extent in the degree of integration of their activities and the diversity of stakeholders with whom it interacts (Battilana & Lee, 2014). Doherty et al. (2014) suggest two operational mechanisms to manage these tensions. The first is to use the social mission as a force for strategic direction and the second mechanism consists in finding the optimum conditions to successfully link the generation of revenues to the creation of social value.

In the same article where Battilana et al. (2012) define the hybrid ideal, they also identify four main challenges with which social enterprises struggle when they try to find a suitable place between for-profit and nonprofit sectors, even when they manage to integrate social and income generating activities in a sustainable manner. First, they point the legal structure. Social enterprises may choose register as a for-profit, a nonprofit or alternatively create two separate legal entities to get access to the benefits of both legal structures, for example, in terms of financing, which is the second challenge identified by the authors. In this matter, hybrid organizations may adopt a differentiated funding strategy, searching for different sources of financing for social and income generating activities, or choose a mixed structuring of funding. For instance, getting funding from public authorities in an early-stage and then trying to attract venture capital in a more advanced stage of development.

The third challenge concerns the recipients of the solution the social enterprise is providing. Customers and beneficiaries can be the same or represent different populations. The last challenge refers the organizational structure and talent development. Once it is hard to find people with a "hybrid" profile, social enterprises may opt between hiring people who have work experience in the social or private sector and hiring people from both sectors.

Smith et al. (2013) present other perspective regarding the tensions within social enterprises, classifying them into four categories:

1. Performing,
2. Organizing,
3. Belonging,
4. Learning tensions.

Performing tensions are related to the metrics used for performance measurement. Metrics used to evaluate the financial performance are very different from those used to measure social performance. The first tend to be clear, quantitative and short-term, whereas the last tend to be ambiguous, qualitative and long-term. Because of their distinct nature, social enterprises run the risk of giving prevalence to business metrics or social mission metrics, since it becomes difficult to balance both.

Organizing tensions rely on decisions such as the separation or integration of organizational structures, practices and roles associated with social and income generating activities, the inclusion of beneficiaries of the social mission as employees and the adoption of a for-profit or nonprofit structure.

Belonging tensions can arise from the difficulty in the alignment of all the organization with profit and social mission motives, without favoring one of those goals. Moreover, other source of tensions between social and commercial goals may be hiring individuals with distinct professional backgrounds. According to the authors, an alternative to this may be hiring individuals with no background in order to train them to be employees with a "hybrid" profile. They also mention tensions inherent to the adoption of different approaches to communicate with each stakeholders group or the creation of a consistent message that will be understood by all stakeholders.

Learning tensions derive from the desire to create a business model that balances revenues with excess social mission costs. It is always challenging for social entrepreneurs remain committed to their social mission while becoming more efficient and also growing the organization. More recent work, have emphasized some of the tensions listed by Battilana et al. (2012) and Smith et al. (2013). They are most frequently referred tensions related to the integration of social and income generating activities, the legal forms chosen by social enterprises, their sources of financing, the way they manage their relationships with several groups of stakeholders, as well as tensions regarding the management of human resources, the potential need to balance staff with both commercial and social knowledge (Battilana & Lee, 2014; Cornforth, 2014; Doherty et al., 2014).

As mentioned previously, many social enterprises face resources constraints and sometimes they rely on the resources of others to be able to perform their activities. Cornforth (2014) refers the resource dependency perspective as one of the causes on mission drift, not only regarding financing but other aspects such as equipment, raw materials or labor. According to Cornforth (2014), the more an organization is dependent on the resources of others, more the amount of power they have to influence the decisions made in the organization. This issue is more critical for social enterprises once it is hard for them ensure all the resources they need to achieve their social and financial goals. The degree of dependence on other actors, i.e. the risk of rely on the resources of others and become dependent, can be affected by the importance of the resources to the organization, how much control those that provide the resource have over their deployment and to what extent the provider has the monopoly of the resource or there are other sources to obtain the same resource.

Despite the existing literature exploring the main tensions faced by social enterprises, little is known concerning the strategies adopted by social enterprises from the point-of-view of operations management, although there are some evidences from the observation of social enterprises acting in the field that point to the existence of differences between them. The next section will be devoted to the identification of the main operational challenges in hybrid organizations in light of what are the main concepts discussed in the literature on operations management and operations strategy, in an attempt to combine these two knowledge domains and subsequently identify opportunities for future research.

## OPERATIONAL CHALLENGES IN HYBRID ORGANIZATIONS

Operations management can be generically defined as the process of converting inputs into outputs. Hybrid organizations, in particular social enterprises, convert a set of resources (inputs) in order to deliver products and/or services that will contribute to solve a social need or problem (the main desired outcome) to their beneficiaries (Figure 3). However, as mentioned previously, most social enterprises need to manage limited resources and it is difficult to them integrate social and income generating activities once they aim to serve disadvantaged groups.

A key challenge for such organizations is precisely how to conciliate the management of operations associated to the activities that aim to fulfill the social mission, which may not generate (enough) revenues, with other income generating activities. This ambidexterity in the domain of operations management may affect the way they get the resources needed to run the activities sustainably as well as the way they define and implement an effective operations strategy. In the following sections will be explored in greater detail these two topics based on the literature and perceptions derived from the practices of social enterprises acting in the field.

*Figure 3. Converting inputs into outcomes in hybrid organizations*
*Source 3 Figure elaborated by the authors*

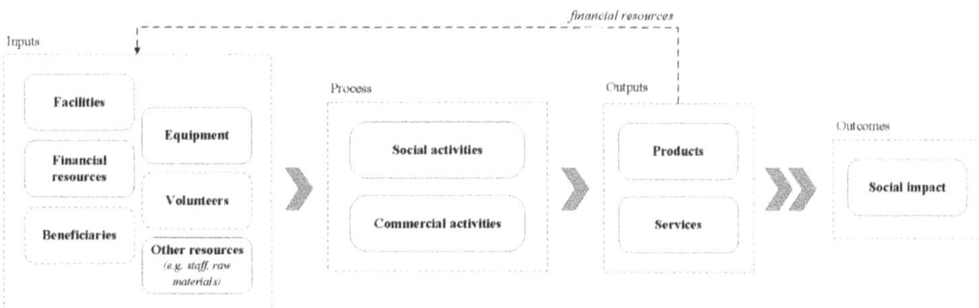

## Gathering the Necessary Resources

In order to produce the desired outcome, i.e. achieve the desired social impact, social enterprises have to gather the resources needed. In the best case scenario, activities that generate social impact also generate enough revenues to support the operation of the enterprise in an autonomous way. The case of ColorADD already described in this chapter is a good example of an enterprise adopting this integrated approach. Otherwise, there are social enterprises that run activities producing social impact separately from income generating activities. In this case, income generating activities are run with the purpose of supporting the pursuit of social aims. However, as mentioned before, these social enterprises adopting a less integrated approach run a higher risk of mission drift and usually they cannot afford all necessary resources by themselves. Therefore, they have to find other ways to get these resources to balance the ratio between inputs and outputs and ensure that the proposed solution is sustainable in the long-term.

On the one hand, they can establish partnerships with external entities to get access to their resources. For instance, it is frequent to find social enterprises that are running their activities in facilities owned, for example, by the city council, which allows them to reduce their fixed costs. On the other hand, regarding possible constraints in terms of human resources, a common practice is the recruitment of volunteers for their workforce in order to reduce costs with staff (Doherty et al., 2014; Fazzi, 2012) or even design a solution where the beneficiaries are involved as co-creators or co-producers of that solution. In practice, social enterprises struggling to get their own resources try to find the most adequate mix of owned and external resources, combining some of the alternatives presented in order to be more sustainable economically as possible. Examples of organizations that have adopted some of these strategies include Vintage For A Cause and Projeto Rios.

Vintage For A Cause is a sewing club, where women with over 50 years without professional occupation transform used clothes - mainly donated by others - into vintage inspired clothes, with an exclusive design and supported by professional stylists. The mission statement of Vintage For A Cause is *"promotion of an active ageing, personal development, interpersonal relationship and social inclusion through occupation"*. The clothes produced by these women are sold in the online shop as well as in some stores and the revenues are reinvested in the organization. However, they are still not enough to ensure the operation of ateliers where clothes are transformed. In order to face these constraints in terms of resources, the organization is supported by the city council who rents the space where Vintage For A Cause runs its activities at a lower cost. In this case, social goals are achieved through the direct involvement of beneficiaries (the women over 50 years who transform the clothes) in operations as part of the organizational structure.

Projeto Rios is a project of environmental education which contributes to the implementation of sustained solutions for problems in river ecosystems in Portugal. The project aims to improve the environmental awareness through voluntary and citizen participation, creating a network for the adoption and monitoring of river sections by organized local groups. As happens with Vintage For A Cause, Projeto Rios generates some revenues through the provision of services such as training programs, but they are not enough to ensure all necessary resources, since this is an organization acting at the national level. Therefore, partnerships are crucial to sustain its operation.

The space where Projeto Rios is based (the Water Pavilion owned by the city council) has been ceded in exchange for some services. Projeto Rios is responsible by opening the Water Pavilion the last Saturday each month, promoting some activities and helping to disseminate the work of this entity. This way, it does not have to pay for renting the space or bills of internet, light and water. Moreover, the organizational structure was conceived to be supported in volunteer work. After ten years of activity, more than 330 groups of volunteers have been created in more than 100 different municipalities, whose activities improved the quality of 170 km of rivers all over the country. It would be impossible for the organization do that work with their own staff.

Having access to the resources is important but not enough.Organizations need to have an operations strategy which sets up how to use those resources in the most effective way. The next section explores the operational challenges arising from the definition and implementation of an effective operations strategy in hybrid organizations.

## Defining and Implementing an Effective Operations Management Strategy

Nowadays, exists a wide variety of configurations for hybrid organizations, and, for this reason, there are significant differences among them in the way they organize their operations, as well as in relation to other types of organizations, once they propose solutions in many different domains (e.g. environment, health, poverty, etc.) and aim to achieve different levels of social impact. For instance, Smith and Stevens (2010) suggest the existence of three types of social entrepreneurship. The first one takes into account concerns at the local level and focuses on the development of solutions that are often rather small in scale and scope.

The second type of social entrepreneurship identified deals with issues relevant to local concerns but the developed solution can be replicable in other different contexts. The last type of social entrepreneurship focuses on large-scale issues. In this case, social entrepreneurs aim to create social enterprises providing solutions that have the potential to replace those currently provided by the existing institutions. For example, SPEAK, Vintage For A Cause and Projeto Rios propose solutions that can be replicable in other contexts (what already happened for SPEAK and Projeto Rios), representing the second type of social entrepreneurship described above, while ColorADD is a worldwide solution, which can be classified in the third type.

### One or More Operations Strategies

Social enterprises, likewise any organization, should make some strategic design choices when defining their operations management strategy. It is expected that they must adopt distinct approaches according to the level of integration between social impact and income generating activities. Unlike the hybrid ideal, as described by Battilana et al. (2012), empirical evidences point to the fact that social enterprises adopting a less integrated approach may define different operations strategies for the different domains where they act (i.e. the social and commercial). Once again, the case of SPEAK can be used to illustrate this. It is possible to distinguish two independent structures – SPEAK and SPEAK PRO – both important for the mission accomplishment.

The first one represents the operationalization of the mission, the second one is vital for the financial sustainability of the organization. The same is valid for ColorADD. Although its activities are more integrated (the licensing system and educational activities), most probably they require different strategies due to their distinct nature and target-groups they serve (on the one side are companies and in the other side are children and youth). Examples like SPEAK and ColorADD make believe that some social enterprises are adopting more than one operations strategy, with different goals, operations decisions and perhaps using different resources, in order to ensure that they have an effective action and that nor social concerns neither commercial concerns are undervalued.

## What Goals to Pursue

In the organizational context, operations decisions are a mean to achieve a competitive advantage that should be aligned with organizational goals. The literature on social enterprises emphasizes their focus on proposing a solution to a social problem or need that is at least economically sustainable and that can be replicable. In this sense, they aim to increase their social impact and even try to mitigate the social problem or need they are addressing, instead of having the highest market share or to overcome the competition (Trivedi & Stokols, 2011). Therefore, the idea that social enterprises are competing in the market by low costs or quality is limiting towards the much more ambitious goals they have from the "social" point-of-view.

Competitive advantages reported in the literature of operations management probably do not fit all social enterprises. Perhaps, in some cases, they can be used to characterize commercial activities, when they are not integrated with social activities. For instance, Doctor Gummy is a startup that sells sweets gluten and lactose-free, without artificial colorings or preservatives. A chemical engineer had the idea of adding the active principle of medicines to sweets in order to facilitate the administration of medication to children, since children usually do not like medicines but love sweets. Although the pharmaceutical industry was the main target of Doctor Gummy, the idea quickly attracted the interest of important food distribution chains that started selling the product even before reaching the pharmaceutical industry. When Doctor Gummy is dealing with food distribution companies, it is competing with others by the quality of its products which have distinctive characteristics.

The same is applicable to the SPEAK PRO program that is sold as a high-quality service, provided by specialized staff. However, the mission of SPEAK is help to solve the problem of social exclusion of migrants and contribute to their integration in the cities where they live through a program of linguistic and cultural knowledge sharing. It aims to break language barriers and bring people from different backgrounds together. In this case, it would make more sense to talk about the building or reinforcement of the sense of community as a goal to pursue. It was already mentioned by Luke, Barraket and Eversole (2013) as one of the performance goals of social enterprises. This would support the idea of Glavas and Mish (2014) that these organizations pursue a collaborative advantage instead a competitive advantage.

## What Operations Decisions Must Be Made

As mentioned previously, the definition of an operations strategy comprises the definition of goals and a set of operations decisions. This includes some long-term decisions (structural decisions), often related to physical assets of the social enterprise such as facilities and points-of-contact with stakeholders (e.g. beneficiaries or clients). Social enterprises like Vintage For A Cause involve directly beneficiaries as co-producers of the solution it produces. In the same extent, they may decide to establish partnerships to incorporate external resources or even involving volunteers in the process as a way to reduce costs with staff.

On the other hand, there are decisions with a short-term impact (infrastructural decisions). These decisions are related to domains such as governance, human resources and performance measurement systems, which are in some extent connected to the tensions emerging from the hybrid nature of social enterprises aforementioned. For instance, social enterprises may adopt different strategies in terms of governance. If they are acting in more than one location, they can choose if they want to involve local actors in the decision making, as experts on local issues, or make decisions centrally (e.g. at the national level) and give to experts the legitimacy to address organizational and strategic challenges of the social enterprise (Pache & Santos, 2012).

As SPEAK acts at the community level, probably some local actors are included in its governance model and involved in decisions at the local level, in addition to their involvement in the delivery of the solution. Regarding human resources and performance measurement, decisions may focus on issues such as the professional background of staff and the balance between social and financial metrics for performance monitoring and identification of opportunities to the continuous improvement of operations, since they have distinct characteristics. Table 1 compares structural and infrastructural decisions in for-profit and hybrid organizations, putting forward some of the questions managers face when they are defining and implementing an operations strategy.

## FUTURE RESEARCH DIRECTIONS

As mentioned at the beginning of the chapter, currently new business models are emerging combining characteristics from different sectors mainly due to contextual pressures which are forcing organizations, especially those from the nonprofit sector, to become more financially sustainable. Along the chapter, some of the challenges faced by hybrid organizations were presented as well as a discussion about how they can benefit from the prevalent literature on operations management, in particular, the literature on

*Table 1. Structural and Infrastructural Decisions in for-profit and hybrid organizations*

| | For-Profit Organizations | Hybrid Organizations |
|---|---|---|
| Structural decisions | What is the right mix of permanent versus temporary workers? | What is the right mix of employees versus volunteers? |
| | Does the organization prefer to have a great variety of products for different segments or a great level of homogeneous products? | Does the organization prefer to have an impact at the individual's level or to have an impact in the society as a whole? |
| | Does the organization prefer to increase their existent plants or to build other new ones in different places? | Does the organization use their own resources or rely on resources of others (e.g. public entities)? |
| | What are the customer contact touch points and the number and types of distribution channels? | Are the beneficiaries involved in the process as co-producers or co-creators or are they not involved in the delivery of the solution to the social problem? |
| Infrastructural decisions | What is the preferred decision system: centralization or decentralization to middle managers? | What is the level of involvement of local actors in the governance of the social enterprise? |
| | What are the recruitment, selection, and formation processes, and how is the person-to-job assignment? | Does the social enterprise prefer to have human resources with a commercial or a social background or both? |
| | How will service/ product standards be set? | Will the social enterprise give preference to social or financial indicators? |

operations strategy. Several questions remain unanswered, claiming for future research efforts. Future research would add value in a number of areas.

First, more research is needed in order to investigate to what extent social enterprises define different operations strategies for different activities, to what extent it makes sense to set up different operations strategies, to investigate if social enterprises adopting separated social and commercial operations are more successful than those with more integrated approaches and how they avoid the risk of mission drift. Understand more deeply how social enterprises organize their operations facing this ambidexterity will be important to advance the knowledge in the field and help practitioners to deal with it, supporting them in the decision-making process.

Second, research opportunities are also linked to the need to identify what are the most common goals of social enterprises when they define their operations strategy, as well as the operational decisions made in order to reach those goals. Do social enterprises tend to adopt a competitive or a collaborative approach as suggested by Glavas and Mish (2014)? How do they manage heterogeneous human resources and define adequate performance measurement metrics? These are just some of the questions that remain without answer.

Finally, there is potential to explore the role of operations over time. The organizational needs change over time as companies go through different stages of their life cycle, and social enterprises are not an exception. New empirical research should be conducted in order to collect evidence on the roles that the operations function assumes in social enterprises according to the stage of development where they are and evaluate to which extent the model proposed by Hayes and Wheelwright in 1984 should be rethought and adapted to hybrid business models.

In order to get answers to these questions, and since this is a relatively unexplored field, in a first instance it is suggested conducting some exploratory work using qualitative data (e.g. case studies). In-depth studies can be a good way to support the definition of a typology of operations strategies in hybrid organizations, as there are some typologies of operations strategies in the literature for manufacturing companies. However, due to the great variety of social enterprises, it is believed that future research will evolve to quantitative data collection methods which allow the study of larger samples and the generalization of results.

## CONCLUSION

In the forthcoming years, it is expected that all organizations, regardless of the sector they belong, will incorporate social, economic and environmental concerns in their activities, evolving to more hybrid models of organizing. This is already happening mainly in the nonprofit sector and is attracting a growing interest among academics and practitioners in hybrid organizations. Taking into consideration this trend, the present chapter aimed to identify the main operational challenges of hybrid organizations in order to provide insights for the conduction of future research.

Social enterprises are a particular case of hybrid organizations that pursue social objectives while conducting income generating activities. When compared with pure for-profit organizations, social enterprises face many challenges arising from their hybrid nature that should be reflected in their operations strategy, notably in terms of goals, decisions and ambidexterity of operations. The wide variety of social enterprises in terms of the social problems addressed, the level of integration between social and income generating activities, and the need to deal with resource constraints make believe that there are many opportunities in this field to translate and adapt what is the existing knowledge in the operations management literature to these new hybrid models that are emerging in the organizational landscape.

The chapter focused on two main aspects considered especially challenging in this context. On the one hand, the way social enterprises face resource constraints and get the necessary resources to build a sustainable solution and, on the other hand, how they define and implement an effective operations strategy, the goals and the structural and infrastructural decisions that are more critical to the organization.

It is urgent to draw theoretical contributions from what is being done in the field in order to inform practitioners and help them in the development of new solutions that are sustainable in the long-term, contributing to solve social problems or needs and creating more social impact.

## REFERENCES

Battilana, J., & Lee, M. (2014). Advancing Research on Hybrid Organizing – Insights from the Study of Social Enterprises. *The Academy of Management Annals*, *8*(1), 397–441. doi:10.1080/19416520.2014.893615

Battilana, J., Lee, M., Walker, J., & Dorsey, C. (2012). In Search of the Hybrid Ideal. Stanford Social Innovation Review, 10, 51–55.

Boyer, K. K., & Lewis, M. W. L. (2002). Competitive Priorities: Investigating the Need for Trade-Offs in Operations Strategy. *Production and Operations Management Society, 11*(1), 9–20. Retrieved from http://doi.wiley.com/10.1111/j.1937-5956.2002.tb00181.x

Boyer, K. K., & Pagell, M. (2000). Measurement issues in empirical research: Improving measures of operations strategy and advanced manufacturing technology. *Journal of Operations Management*, *18*(1), 361–374. doi:10.1016/S0272-6963(99)00029-7

Brandsen, T., & Karré, P. M. (2011). Hybrid Organizations: No Cause for Concern? *International Journal of Public Administration*, *34*(13), 827–836. doi:10.1080/01900692.2011.605090

Cornforth, C. (2014). Understanding and combating mission drift in social enterprises. *Social Enterprise Journal*, *10*(1), 3–20. doi:10.1108/SEJ-09-2013-0036

Díaz Garrido, E., Martín-Peña, M. L., & García-Muiña, F. (2007). Structural and infrastructural practices as elements of content operations strategy. The effect on a firms competitiveness. *International Journal of Production Research*, *45*(9), 2119–2140. doi:10.1080/00207540600735480

Doherty, B., Haugh, H., & Lyon, F. (2014). Social Enterprises as Hybrid Organizations: A Review and Research Agenda. *International Journal of Management Reviews*, *16*(4), 417–436. doi:10.1111/ijmr.12028

Ebrahim, A., Battilana, J., & Mair, J. (2014). The governance of social enterprises: Mission drift and accountability challenges in hybrid organizations. *Research in Organizational Behavior*, *34*, 81–100. doi:10.1016/j.riob.2014.09.001

Espino-Rodriguez, T. F., & Gil-Padilla, M. (2014). The structural and infrastructural decisions of operations management in the hotel sector and their impact on organizational performance. *Tourism and Hospitality Research*, *15*(1), 3–18. doi:10.1177/1467358414553866

Fazzi, L. (2012). Social Enterprises, Models of Governance and the Production of Welfare Services. *Public Management Review*, *14*(3), 359–376. doi:10.1080/14719037.2011.637409

Glavas, A., & Mish, J. (2014). Resources and Capabilities of Triple Bottom Line Firms: Going Over Old or Breaking New Ground? *Journal of Business Ethics*, *127*(3), 623–642. doi:10.1007/s10551-014-2067-1

Ibrahim, S. E. (2010). An alternative methodology for formulating an operations strategy: The case of BTC-Egypt. *Management Decision*, *48*(6), 868–893. doi:10.1108/00251741011053442

Jäger, U. P., & Schröer, A. (2013). Integrated Organizational Identity: A Definition of Hybrid Organizations and a Research Agenda. *VOLUNTAS: International Journal of Voluntary and Nonprofit Organizations*, *25*(5), 1281–1306. doi:10.1007/s11266-013-9386-1

Leong, G. K., Snyder, D. L., & Ward, P. T. (1990). Research in the process and content of manufacturing strategy. *Omega*, *18*(2), 109–122. doi:10.1016/0305-0483(90)90058-H

Lillis, B., & Sweeney, M. (2013). Managing the fit between the views of competitive strategy and the strategic role of service operations. *European Management Journal*, *31*(6), 564–590. doi:10.1016/j.emj.2012.10.001

Longoni, A., & Cagliano, R. (2015). Environmental and social sustainability priorities: Their integration in operations strategies. *International Journal of Operations & Production Management*, *35*(2), 216–245. doi:10.1108/IJOPM-04-2013-0182

Lowson, R. H. (2001). Retail Operational Strategies in Complex Supply Chains. *The International Journal of Logistics Management*, *12*(1), 97–111. doi:10.1108/09574090110806253

Lowson, R. H. (2002). Operations strategy: Genealogy, classification and anatomy. *International Journal of Operations & Production Management*, *22*(10), 1112–1129. doi:10.1108/01443570210446333

Luke, B., Barraket, J., & Eversole, R. (2013). Measurement as legitimacy versus legitimacy of measures: Performance evaluation of social enterprise. *Qualitative Research in Accounting and Management*, *10*(3/4), 234–258. doi:10.1108/QRAM-08-2012-0034

Martín-Peña, M. L., & Díaz-Garrido, E. (2008). Typologies and taxonomies of operations strategy: A literature review. *Management Research News*, *31*(3), 200–218. doi:10.1108/01409170810851294

McDermott, C. M., Markman, G. D., & Balkin, D. B. (2003). Operations strategy and new venture formation. *Management Research*, *1*(2), 195–205.

Miller, J. G., & Roth, A. V. (1994). A Taxonomy of Manufacturing Strategies. *Management Science*, *40*(3), 285–304. doi:10.1287/mnsc.40.3.285

Nair, A., & Boulton, W. R. (2008). Innovation-oriented operations strategy typology and stage-based model. *International Journal of Operations & Production Management*, *28*(8), 748–771. doi:10.1108/01443570810888599

Neck, H., Brush, C., & Allen, E. (2009). The landscape of social entrepreneurship. *Business Horizons*, *52*(1), 13–19. doi:10.1016/j.bushor.2008.09.002

Pache, A.-C., & Santos, F. (2012). Inside the Hybrid Organization: Selective Coupling as a Response to Competing Institutional Logics. *Academy of Management Journal*, *56*(4), 972–1001. doi:10.5465/amj.2011.0405

Phusavat, K., & Kanchana, R. (2008). Competitive priorities for service providers: Perspectives from Thailand. *Industrial Management & Data Systems*, *108*(1), 5–21. doi:10.1108/02635570810844052

Roth, A. V., & Menor, L. J. (2003). Insights into service operations management: a research agenda. *Production & Operations Management, 12*(2), 145–164. Retrieved from http://search.ebscohost.com/login.aspx?direct=true&db=bth&AN=12334481&site=ehost-live

Rungtusanatham, M. J., Choi, T. Y., Hollingworth, D. G., Wu, Z., & Forza, C. (2003). Survey research in operations management: Historical analyses. *Journal of Operations Management*, *21*(4), 475–488. doi:10.1016/S0272-6963(03)00020-2

Samarrokhi, A., Jenab, K., Arumugam, V. C., & Weinsier, P. D. (2015). Analysis of the effects of operations strategies on sustainable competitive advantage in manufacturing systems. *International Journal of Industrial and Systems Engineering*, *19*(1), 34–49. doi:10.1504/IJISE.2015.065944

Santos, F. M., Pache, A.-C., & Birkholz, C. (2015). Making Hybrids Work: Aligning business models and organizational design for social enterprises. *California Management Review, 57*(3), 36–58. 10.1525/cmr.2015.57.3.36

Slack, N., Chambers, S., & Johnston, R. (2001). *Operations management* (3rd ed.). Harlow, UK: Financial Times Prentice Hall.

Smith, B. R., & Stevens, C. E. (2010). Different types of social entrepreneurship: The role of geography and embeddedness on the measurement and scaling of social value. *Entrepreneurship & Regional Development*, *22*(6), 575–598. doi:10.1080/08985626.2010.488405

Smith, W. K., Gonin, M., & Besharov, M. L. (2013). Managing Social-Business Tensions. *Business Ethics Quarterly*, *23*(3), 407–442. doi:10.5840/beq201323327

Trivedi, C., & Stokols, D. (2011). Social Enterprises and Corporate Enterprises: Fundamental Differences and Defining Features. *Journal of Entrepreneurship*, *20*(1), 1–32. doi:10.1177/097135571002000101

Walker, J. (2015). Hybrid Organizations: Origins, Strategies, Impacts and Implications. *California Management Review*, *57*(3), 5–13. doi:10.1525/cmr.2015.57.3.5

Wilson, F., & Post, J. E. (2011). Business models for people, planet (& profits): Exploring the phenomena of social business, a market-based approach to social value creation. *Small Business Economics*, *40*(3), 715–737. doi:10.1007/s11187-011-9401-0

Wu, S. J., Melnyk, S., & Flynn, B. B. (2010). Operational Capabilities: The Secret Ingredient. *Decision Sciences Journal of Innovative Education*, *41*(4), 721–754. doi:10.1111/j.1540-5915.2010.00294.x

## KEY TERMS AND DEFINITIONS

**Beneficiary:** The main target group that a social enterprise intends to serve (e.g. a disadvantaged group such as elderly, children and youth, victims of abuse, refugees, etc.).

**Competitive Advantage:** A characteristic of an organization which allows it to differentiate from the competition (e.g. cost of products, quality, etc.).

**Hybrid Organization:** An organization that combines characteristics from different sectors.

**Income Generating Activity:** An activity carried out in order to generate revenues used to ensure the financial sustainability of the organization.

**Operations Strategy:** A set of decisions made at the operational level in order to achieve a competitive advantage.

**Operations Decision:** A decision regarding an operational aspect such as the location of a plant, the technology to use, the workforce management or the quality management.

**Social Activity:** An activity which main purpose is to solve a social problem or need and, therefore, generate social impact.

**Social Enterprise:** An organization that combines social and economic goals, performing social and income generating activities simultaneously.

# Chapter 19
# Social Impact Measurement and Management:
## Between Theory and Practice

**Tomaso Amati**
*Politecnico di Milano, Italy*

**Irene Bengo**
*Politecnico di Milano, Italy*

**Marika Arena**
*Politecnico di Milano, Italy*

**Debora Caloni**
*Politecnico di Milano, Italy*

## ABSTRACT

*This chapter aims to contribute to the debate about performance measurement and management in the social business sector through the analysis of the critical issues that arise in the implementation of impact assessment models in social business organizations. To this aim, the social impact measurement approaches, which are suggested in the literature, are analyzed and the strengths and weaknesses of different frameworks are highlighted. Then, the critical issues that could emerge in the implementation of social impact assessment practices are identified and discussed base on the case of an Italian social enterprise working in the education field, Cometa. Finally, the paper provides some guidelines and recommendations aimed to mitigate these critical issues.*

## INTRODUCTION

In the last decade, relevant social problems started to afflict our communities and the worldwide financial crisis has restrained the world economy, generating problems of financial sustainability to private and public organizations (Organisation for Economic Co-operation and Development, 2014). This situation has led the need of cutting social programs (like education, health care, work benefits) to preserve financial sustainability (Karanikolos, M., Mladovsky, P., Cylus, J., Thomson, S., Basu, S., Stuckler, D., Mackenbach, & J.P. McKee, M., 2013). One of the solution that have been developed to meet these challenges is represented by social business, that has been defined as a market based arrangement whose primarily focus is on the pursuit of social and environmental objectives, however, ensuring the economic sustainability (Yunus, M., Moingeon, B., & Lehmann - Ortega, L., 2010). In this respect, social busi-

DOI: 10.4018/978-1-5225-2537-0.ch019

Copyright © 2017, IGI Global. Copying or distributing in print or electronic forms without written permission of IGI Global is prohibited.

ness is conceived as a new form of entrepreneurial initiative that joins the social purpose traditionally associated to the not for profit sector with the creation of economic value traditionally associated to for profit organizations (Wilson & Post, 2013; Alter, 2006).

This idea has attracted the attention of many different players in the economic system since there is some preliminary evidence that's social business initiatives can actually pay off, socially and financially (Wilson and Post, 2013). On the one hand, new forms of organizations with the specific aim of developing social business - i.e. the so called Social Enterprises (SEs) - emerged and grew rapidly in numbers (European Commission, 2013). On the other hand, also profit and not for profit organizations started to find a potential role in social business. The profit sector, in fact, saw the opportunity to invest in social business, as a possible way to exploit new synergies between financial and social performances and to redefine their corporate social responsibility strategies (Sinkovics, N., Sinkovics, R. R., & Yamin, M., 2014). The not for profit organizations recognized the ability of social business of dealing effectively with the social problems, being more sustainable in financial terms (Santos, 2012).

Despite the enthusiasm raised by its origin, social business initiatives still struggle to survive and grow, because they have to deal with a progressive reconfiguration that is taking place in the social business ecosystem that requires a change of mindset from the operators as well as the adoption of new managerial tools (Bengo, I., Arena, M., Azzone, G., & Calderini, M., 2016). Concerning this issue, different authors identified the poor understanding of value generated amongst the stakeholders and the rise of tensions and conflicts in meeting both the financial and the social bottom line as critical barriers to the growth of the social business sector (Nicholls, 2010a).

In order to capture this value and demonstrate the impact of social business organizations, proper performance measurement and management systems are needed (Bengo et al., 2016). Over the last two decades, several authors, have proposed different models and instruments to address this issue resulting in a considerable variety of practices that could potentially been used (Pearce & Kay, 2008). However, despite the existence of different models and despite the calls of external stakeholders for the introduction of adequate social impact measurement, most of the organizations that operate in the social business sector tend to resist to the adoption of formalized systems. The main reasons of such resistances are that social enterprises have limited human and financial resources and time constrains (Arena, M., G. Azzone, & Bengo, I., 2015), whilst the development of a performance measurement system is potentially expensive in terms of data and resources invested (Thomas, 2004). In addition, in some cases, they do not perceive the relevance and the usefulness of these instruments.

With this background, this chapter aims to contribute to the debate about performance measurement and management in the social business sector through the analysis of the critical issues that arise in the implementation of impact assessment models in social business organizations. To this aim, we first analyse the approaches that are suggested in the literature to measure performance with specific reference to social impact in social business organizations, highlighting the strengths and weaknesses of different approaches related to their implementation. Then, we present the case of an Italian social business organization, Cometa, that operates in the field of education and we outline its paths in connection to social impact measurement. Based on the case evidence, we highlight the key problems emerged in the implementation of social impact assessment practices and we discuss how these problems could be solved.

## BACKGROUND

The literature review draws a picture of different approaches proposed by scholars and practitioners' organizations to measure performance in social business organization. Proposed approaches can be clustered into three main families of models. The first category includes synthetic indicators, aimed to measure social value creation such as Social Return On Investment (New Economics Foundation, 2007), Local Multiplier 3 (Sacks, 2002) and Gamma Model (Grabenwarter and Liechtenstein, 2011). The second group of models includes process based approaches that focus on the social value chain (inputs-outputs-outcomes and impacts) to measure performance in social business organizations. These are for instance the contingency framework proposed by Ebrahim and Rangan (2010), or the multidimensional control system of Bagnoli and Megali (2011), the Methodology for Impact Analysis and Assessment (MIAA) proposed by Hornsby (2012), the Social Impact Assessment (Global Social Venture Competition, 2012), the stepwise method for social enterprises (Arena et al., 2015). Finally, the third group includes dashboards and scorecards (Kaplan, 2001; Somers, 2005; Bull 2007). This group considers also models based on the stakeholders perspective (Simmons, 2003; Bassi, 2011) and the guidelines to support the identification of the performance dimensions and the related KPIs, as The Fit for Purpose model (DTA, 2008) or Social Impact for Local Economy model (McLoughlin et al., 2009).

For each category, some selected instruments will be discussed as follows to explain the capacity of these models of answering to the informative needs of social business organizations and highlight what problems they could entail for these organizations and their stakeholders. The first group of models leads to a definition of a synthetic indicator that summarizes the impacts create by an organization. The most famous among these models is the social return on investment (SROI). This instrument was first developed by the Roberts Enterprise Development Fund (REDF, 2000) to financially calculate the unreported benefits of the work's activities. In 2007, the methodology was extended through the work of the New Economics Foundation (NEF) (Nicholls, 2004b). Nowadays, the framework is used to capture and monetize the social value created by the activities of an organization in many different sectors. According to this approach, the first thing to do is identify the key stakeholders and define the key social objectives. Second, an 'impact map' based on input-output-outcome-impact model should be drawn (Cupitt, 2009). In particular, inputs are the total costs in the project, outputs are the quantitative effects, outcomes the direct and indirect changes in stakeholders and communities and impacts are outcomes discounted by what would have happened without any activities of organization. Finally, it is necessary to define indicators and financial proxies for monetizing social value created (Nicholls, 2009). The SROI is then calculated dividing the social benefits that an organization creates by the relative cost of achieving those benefits and it is defined by the following formula (Millar and Hall, 2013). SROI = Net Present Value of Benefits/ Net Present Value of Investment.

The literature reports a number of cases documenting the use of this indicator (Ryan and Lyne, 2008). The application of the SROI is associated to several positive effects that range from the involvement of external stakeholders, support to internal decision-making processes; the demonstration of the financial return generated by an organization (Millar and Hall, 2013). The implementation of this instrument can support the improvement of the organization itself (New Philanthropy Capital, 2010) and the reinforcement of the legitimacy with stakeholders, in particular investors (Bengo et al., 2016). Despite these positive effects, the SROI presents some limitations. The most relevant limitations consist in the difficulty of attributing a financial dimension to soft, qualitative and subjective outcomes (Sheridan, 2011) and the trouble of compare SROI ratios across different activities (Arvidson et al., 2010) and across social ventures with different objectives (Pathak and Dattani, 2014). Moreover, often there are problems of getting complete and reliable data (New Philanthropy Capital, 2010) and to the difficulty of calculating the effects of deadweight and attributions (Millar and Hall, 2013). Finally, the implementation and the measurement of the SROI is costly in terms of time and specialist skills (Gair, 2009).

A further synthetic indicator is the Local Multiplier 3 (LM3). At the beginning, the idea of a multiplier as a macroeconomic indicator was developed by the economist John Maynard Keynes (Březina, 2013). The local multiplier indicates to what extent the money spent by an organization circulates within the region before it leaves the area and to what extent it represents an income for other local organisations (e.g. suppliers) and individuals (e.g. employees) (Meter, 2010). To deal with the complexity of the calculation the economic multipliers, Sacks (2002) developed a dedicated tool, named LM3, for the New Economy Foundation (NEF) (Thatcher and Sharp, 2008). The calculation of the LM3 is based on three steps (1) Determining the initial income; (2) Identifying how much of this is spent locally; (3) Understanding how much of this is re-spend within the defined geographic area (Sacks, 2002). The advantage of the use of the LM3 is that it can be used for quantifying the effectiveness of expenditures invested in regional areas. Thus, organizations may demonstrate how much they support the local economy by choosing local suppliers and hiring employees from the region (Březina, 2013). On the other hand, the limitations of this models are related to the difficulties in the data collection process, which entails the administration of questionnaires to suppliers that in turn could be reluctant to disclose actual and punctual figures (Meter, 2010).

The second group of models is based on an analysis of the process of social impact's generation. In particular, the process-based approaches identify guidelines to develop a set of indicators for measuring social impact, starting from the construction of the social value chain. Among these approaches, we mention the social impact assessment (SIA) that is an increasingly popular model (Mahmoudi, H., Renn, O., Vanclay, F., Hoffmann, V., & Karami, E., 2013). The concept of impact assessment has origin within the environmental impact assessment (EIA) (Grieco, C., Michelini, L., & Iasevoli, G., 2015). Only later, this methodology has been further developed and broadened, leading to the emergence of social impact assessment frameworks. In particular, Vanclay (2003) defines social impact assessment as "the processes of analysing, monitoring and managing the intended and unintended social consequences, both positive and negative, of planned interventions and any social change processes invoked by those interventions".

Moving from these premises, in 2012, the Global Social Value Competition (GSVC) developed the SIA model as an instrument for identifying, measuring and reporting the social impacts generated by social enterprises, limiting the analysis to the three priority results that the organization wants to achieve. According to this approach, there are three steps to follow (GSVC, 2014; Bengo, at al., 2016): 1. The definition of the organization's social value proposition; 2. The identification of the calculation methodology of the three most relevant and measurable social impact indicators; 3. The explanation of a feasible plan for impact evaluation and monitoring. Accordingly, first of all, the social value is defined starting from the stakeholders' involvement and the impact value chain construction that describes how and why the organization's activities will lead to the desired results. Then, the indicators are identified as the most strongly correlated with the desired social outcomes and they refer to the Impact Reporting and Investment Standards (IRIS) and international proxy. Finally, the measuring plan includes the monitoring of unintended and/or negative consequences of the business.

SIA is a widely used model due to its applying' simplicity and flexibility. Its strengths are related to the possibility of identifying the needs and the aspirations of the stakeholders, the development of a participatory process (Esteves, A. M., Franks, D., & Vanclay, F., 2012) and the possibility of tailoring it on the specific characteristics, activities and objectives of the organization (Grieco et al., 2015). Furthermore, it provides clear steps (Nicholls, 2009), supporting the identification of the outputs, the outcomes and the impacts generated by the organization (GSVC, 2014). However, the U.K. Interorganizational Committee on Guidelines and Principles for Social Impact Assessment (1994) underlines some weaknesses of the framework. One the one hand, they pinpoint the necessity to find qualitative and quantitative measures according to SIA model, but often KPIs are influenced by personal judgment. On the other hand, they point out the need to collect reliable data that should be done by professional social scientists that too often are not involved due to economic resource limitation.

Another process-based framework is the Methodology for Impact Analysis and Assessment. MIAA has been developed by Investing for Good and it has been explained in the publication "The Good Analyst". The framework is thought in response to a business need: providing the investors the information necessary to take decisions on investments in social propose organizations. To do this, the method focuses on both social and financial evaluations, which are kept together in an integrated system that mutually informs each section. According to Hornsby (2012), the measurement process includes two parts: confidence and impact. Confidence is related to financial stability and risk of the organization; impact looks at the social and environmental benefits that the organization generate. In addition to the two analytical parts, another non-evaluative step is the mapping of the organization and the drawing of the profile of the enterprise in order to construct potentially comparison. In particular, to map the activities, the outputs and the outcomes of the organization, MIAA relies on the theory of change (GSVC, 2012). Finally, the framework offers a detailed series of indicators that reflect the peculiarities of the social enterprise and provides an impact analysis report that enables to communicate the results to the stakeholders and investors. The advantage of this methodology is that it is linear, well defined, tested and improved. However, it requires the involvement of an external analysis team constituted by trained and experienced people and it requires to have available data about organization. In addition, another problem related to this method could be the lack of sector-specific benchmarks (Hornsby, 2012).

The third group of approaches includes dashboards and scorecards. These approaches aims to identify a set of performance indicators that are representative of the results of the social business organization. Among these models, the most famous group of contributions includes the modification and the adaptation of the traditional Balanced Scorecard that is proposed by Robert Kaplan and David Norton in 1996 to improve the results and performances of the companies. The most important aspect is that the Balanced Scorecard includes not only financial indicators but also such non-financial and qualitative measures such as employee satisfaction, corporate mission and customer loyalty (Kaplan and Norton, 2001). In particular, this framework includes four perspectives that descend from an organization vision and strategy: financial perspective; customer perspective; internal processes perspective; learning and growth perspective. In order to make the original approach more aligned with the emerging peculiarities and needs of social businesses, during the years, several authors have proposed some modifications to the original model.

In 2005, Somers adapted the model to the context of social organizations and developed the Social Enterprises' Balance Scorecard (SEBC). Somers realized three main changes. First, he introduced the social goal above the financial prospective; second he widened the financial prospective adding the financial sustainability; third, he expanded the customer prospective to include all the stakeholders (Bengo et al., 2016). In 2007, Bull made some further changes to the original balanced scorecard framework to address social enterprise's needs. In particular, Bull transformed the original perspectives into: multi-bottom line, that is concerned with social, environment and financial sustainability; stakeholders' environment, that is expanded and includes end users, funders, communities and society; internal activities, that is lightly changed and deals with structure, communication, quality; learning organization, that is related to training, knowledge management, team working; visioning, that is link to managers' engagement with business tools and communications (Bull, 2007).

Despite Somers and Bull's models provide a more comprehensive view of Social Enterprises' performances, these frameworks seem to simplify and underestimate the complexity deriving from their hybrid nature. First, they partially realized the importance of the social impact originated by the activities (McLoughlin, J., J. Kaminski, B. Sodgar, S. Khan, R. Harris, G. Arnaudo, & S. Mc Brearty., 2009). Second, despite the enlargement of the customer perspective, they do not totally answer to the informative needs of different stakeholders (Arena et al., 2015). Third, they are static models that does not consider performances' changes during social businesses' life cycle (Brignall, 2003). In addition, some of the proposed indicators are hard to be measured, such as the KPIs (Key Performance Index) related to social capital and knowledge (McLoughlin et al., 2009). Finally, the lack of managerial skills represents a problem for some organizations that has to face the social impact measurement's process (Bull, 2007).

A further dashboards and scorecards' framework is the Social Impact for Local Economy (SIMPLE) that is configured as a guideline to support the identification of the performance dimensions and the related KPIs (DTA, 2008) of social enterprises (McLoughlin et al., 2009). The SIMPLE framework is based on a five-step: 1. Scope it (the conceptualization of the impact problem and objective); 2. Map it (the identification and the prioritization of impacts); 3. Track it (the choice and the assignment of appropriate indicators to measure); 4. Tell it (the report of impacts); 5. Embed it (the integration the results in management decision making and in the culture of the organization) (McLoughlin et al., 2009). The benefits of using the SIMPLE framework include the improvement of the organisation's performance through strategically analysis, the identification of a set of indicators – Key Impact Indicators – and the stakeholders' involvement (Bengo at al., 2015). However, the tool it is partially appropriate to measure long-term social impact (Amani et al., 2015) and it is rather complex.

## THE CASE OF AN ITALIAN SOCIAL ENTERPRISE

### Setting the Case

The empirical analysis is based on a single case study (Yin, 1994). Data was collected on about a year time frame through different sources: interviews, participant observation, and documental analysis. The case setting is an Italian Social Enterprise, Cometa, founded in Como in the 1987 by a network of families committed to foster and educate children and young people in distress. Cometa has significantly grown through the years and it is now composed by seven different organizational units offering a wide range of social, health and education services to both children and their families. Since its foundation, Cometa

Formazione has faced the social needs of young people providing a tailor made professional education. In particular, in 2009, the new Oliver Twist School's headquarters were opened, offering vocational training courses on carpentry, tailoring and hospitality. Cometa Formazione's school represents an opportunity for adolescents who have learning difficulties or have dropped out school early. In 2015, Cometa's school had approximately 400 enrolled students, 75 teachers and educators, and 28 people in support of the activity of Cometa. Synthetically, the objectives that Cometa Formazione aim to address were to:

1. Provide a professional education for young people;
2. Foster young people employment, creating a contact between the school and the labour world;
3. Create social inclusion, especially for children and young people that experience some social problems (e.g. difficult family situation, drop out, learning difficulties, foster care).

In order to provide high quality professional training, Cometa Formazione has developed three different "laboratories": the carpentry, the restaurant and the coffee shop and the tailor atelier. The students attend approximately one third of their school time in the "laboratories". During the workshop's hours, students are overseen by experts and they face didactic-work experiences measuring themselves with real clients and commissions. Furthermore, every student during his educational path has to attend a curricular stage period working in a local enterprise. Cometa Formazione provides also the opportunity to organize extra-curricular stages for the students who want it. In order to provide these services, Cometa Formazione has created a network with more than 400 local enterprises during the years. In this way, the graduated students have quite often their first work experience in the enterprise in which they take the stage with the opportunity to become structured personnel. In order to foster the employment of its own graduated students, Cometa Formazione provides also a job placement service, creating a contact between the students of the school and the network of local enterprises.

Social inclusion is one of the pillar of Cometa Formazione that intervenes in situations of children dropping out of school or having learning difficulties, often caused by personal, family or social difficulties. More than one third of Cometa's students present at least one of these specific situations where negative thinking and acting is more pronounced and the downwards spiral of failures progressively reinforces the negative self-image. Then, the school offers them the possibility to regain self-confidence and education promoting young people's harmonious growth and development and encouraging the expression of each individual talent and capacity. This is made possible thanks to study, knowledge, experience and personal attention dedicated to each student's needs. In fact, 14 tutors work every day in the school providing a personalized face-to-face support to each student both in the studying sphere and in the personal one. Furthermore, the activities of Cometa Formazione include several specific prevention training courses addressed to young and adult NEETs or migrants organized every year or semester. These projects obviously contribute to the impact generation of the organization but also increase the complexity of the structure.

The outcome of the educational process shows that nearly all of them passed the final exam and almost the 70% of the young people that finished school in June 2015 found a job within the first six months. As the majority of SEs (Wilson, 2014), Cometa Formazione presents a multi objective and multi stakeholder model. In fact, the organization looks for the generation of social benefits, guaranteeing economic sustainability to its activities. Due to its multi objective nature, the social enterprise economic sustainability is based not only on public and private resources but also on the revenues of the workshops, especially the restaurant and the coffee bar. Moreover, Cometa Formazione has direct and strong connections with the local community and the territory, presenting a wide range of different stakeholders involved in its activities. All these heterogeneous stakeholders – students and their families, teachers and collaborators, local enterprises, public and private donors, clients – with different needs surely provide an added value for the organization, but also, generates more complexity in managerial and operational terms.

As shown, in its development the organization has presented a strong "demand side" approach, establishing its own strategy development to answer to the punctual needs encountered in its activities and experiences. This has brought to a continuous but not structured growth of the organization that has never "had the time" to plan a formal long period strategy. Furthermore, the organization has always recognized a great value to the research as a fundamental driver of innovation. For this reason, Cometa has developed 14 Intership PhD, working and investigating over the principal organization needs for improving its model. Indeed, besides the educational themes, one of the major observed need was connected to strategically and managerial competences in support to the development and growth of the organisation. In particular, performance and impact measurement was recognized as one of the most relevant aspects to be addressed for Cometa sustainability.

## MEASUREMENT PROCESS

### Why Measure Social Impact

The starting point for the development of Cometa's social impact measurement systems was the recognition of the need of measuring the benefits generated by its activities, considering the effects not only on the direct beneficiaries but also on the community. The motivations behind this need were associated to three main issues: enhancing funding opportunities, improving the communication and involvement of the stakeholders and enabling an internal performance management and were related to the need of assuring the economic sustainability of Cometa.

Due to their multi objective nature, funding needs are common for all social enterprises and the role of impact measurement is arising as an essential enabler. The financial inflows of Cometa Formazione are constituted for about the 15% by the revenues generated by the "laboratories", and for the remaining 85% by public and private donations. The donators themselves are increasingly asking for the adoption of some impact measurement model, and Cometa management saw it as a precondition to improve their reputation with the donors guaranteeing more funding continuity and enabling new funding opportunities with different donors.

*We are doing good, we feel it, but we want to demonstrate our results to everybody. We want to be able to do even better. One of our final goals is the production and disclosure of a sustainability report in order to meet all the information needs of the different stakeholders of our organization. (President of Cometa Formazione)*

A clear and complete communication aimed to demonstrate the value of the activities that Cometa Formazione performs could produce a positive reputational effect that could enable, in turn, a more active involvement of the stakeholders and, in the end, an economic impact for Cometa (thanks to the increase of the number of clients and donors). The rapid scaling of Cometa during the years has not allowed the formalization of a structured strategy for development, as it happens in the case of many small enterprises that experience a quick growth. The management, aware of this situation, has seen in the development of a social impact measurement model the first (and core) element of a performance measurement and management system to be developed in the medium-long term with the aim to measure different performance dimensions on which Cometa can leverage to implement its strategy (efficiency, effectiveness, impact).

## The Challenges

Despite the clear will and the strong commitment, Cometa management realized that the design and the implementation of the social impact measurement process could not be done, leveraging on internal resources only. In fact, the design and implementation of this new measurement process requires time, specific competencies and resources. These conditions clash with the daily "priorities" of Cometa employees, with limited time that could be dedicated to activities other than the core services provided by Cometa and some financial constraints that impede to hire new and dedicated human resources. Moreover, the idea of implementing this type of process encountered some resistances of the employees who raised some doubts about the long term benefits that these processes could bring.

*In the recent past we have encountered a lot of problems trying to monitor the employment rates of our former students. The educators in charge of the surveys delivery and the data collection consider this type of activity somehow as a secondary task, compared to education. They sometimes struggle to understand the importance of this measurement process. (Project Manager of Cometa Formazione)*

Indeed, one of the greatest constrains encountered was the lack of internal competences. Despite the commitment in the research field, Cometa realized that the complexity of impact measurement and the correlated subjectivity in the choice of the most appropriate model and indicators, require specific competences and expertise. For these reasons, the involvement of external experts to set up the measurement process, was recognized as a necessary support. This choice lead to the need of tackling the measurement process with a bilateral participatory approach. In fact, the experts, in order to provide an effective support, had to deeply understand the reality of the organization, its characteristics and its needs. Only with a continuous comparison and exchange during meetings between the experts and the management and the staff of Cometa, the measurement process could be defined. Moreover, the participatory approach allowed the planning of training moments for the Cometa management on the theoretical and practical impact measurements theory and models. In this way, the knowledge transfer enabled a more active participation of the management itself that is fundamental for their ability to effectively "appropriate" of the model. At the same time, the importance of involving Cometa employees and collaborators was clearly recognized.

*There is a great necessity to involve even the educators, the tutors and all the Cometa Formazione's employees. (International relationships and research manager)*

To answer to this request, some "awareness seminars" were organized for the personnel in order to foster a cultural change and make them aware of the importance of impact measuring. More than half of Cometa employees attended the awareness seminars who left extremely positive feedbacks.

*Moments of comparison like this should be organized more often because they allow us to understand the interconnection existent between our different works that in reality aim to the same final goal. (Educator)*

The participation of the external experts further legitimated the process that was under development, presenting different existing approaches and providing some explanations about the methodological choices that had been performed. This continuous involvement of Cometa management, Cometa personnel and collaborators and external experts favoured the acceptance and the "appropriation" of the model by different Cometa's constituencies. In the end, thanks to the participatory approach also the needs of the main stakeholders' categories were investigated in order to recognize their informational needs and define the most appropriate measurement model and indicators. More than 800 surveys to eight different stakeholders' categories were filled out in order to involve and investigate their perspectives.

The process has brought to the development of a methodology tailored to the peculiarities of the organization and the information needs of its stakeholders. Indeed, once defined this model and the indicators to be used, several operative issues arose. First of all, the availability of existent and archived data raised some concerns. There was not a unique and comprehensive database, but several independent archives; a lot of data were only in paper format; and most relevant data were not monitored at all. In addition, due to the complexity of the organization, every structure collected and managed its own data independently and there wasn't any coordination or person in charge. The urgency of overcoming this situation emerged clearly from Cometa's personnel.

*Data collection and monitoring system are to be organized and created as soon as possible. (International relationships and research manager)*

To solve these problems, a comprehensive set of performance indicators, including outcomes and impacts have been identified for being measured every year. In addition, the allocation of responsibilities of the data collection and management was defined. Actually, during the process of definition and implementation of the ad hoc methodology for the social impact measurement, the organization itself understood that for calculating impact it is necessary to develop a model that has to be scalable and replicable and managed autonomously through an operative activities plan and data collection definition. In this way, even the initial investment, in terms of time, economic and human resources, could be rewarded, and the social value generated by the organization could be communicated to all the stakeholders.

## Conceptualization of the Theory-Practice Gap

The case analysis allows to highlight the critical issues that emerge in connection to the implementation of a social impact measurement system pinpointing the existence of a theory-practice gap. Actually, on one hand, from the literature review it emerges that the social impact measurement models can work well only if it occurs some conditions (e.g. the availability of complete and reliable data; the availability of resources; the participation of the employees and the management) in the implementation of the framework (Hornsby, 2012; Meter, 2010; Gair, 2009; Bull 2007). On the other hand, the application of the measurement process in the case study shows that the tensions related to the measurement dynamics have resulted in a number of problematic factors that have had a direct impact on the effective outcome of the process.

The first problematic issue consists in the lack of resources and competences that is often inherent in the organizational structure of these entities (Venturi & Zandonai, 2012). More in details, the lack of resources is connected not only with the time to spend on measuring but also on data collection and monitoring. Moreover, the lack of time and money dedicated to the training of people and the financial need to invest on reinforcement of competencies, and from acquiring external support (such as consultants). Finally, the difficulty to invest resources for activities that are perceived not strictly connected to the core business and more as a burden, rather than a source of competitive advantage (Bull, 2007).

The second problem relates to the subjectivity of the choice of models and metrics that can be used to measure social impact. The available models, being general in scope, do not provide an operational guidance for supporting the selection of metrics (Darby & Jenkins, 2006) leaving this up to the single organization. This discretion could be positive because it allows organisations to formulate their own evaluation template, but it also represents a blank space where social business organizations could get lost. Obviously, this problem is also connected to the lack of internal competencies.

Finally, the third problem consists in the cultural resistance and discomfort of the organizations to be controlled by external stakeholders, who could call for the adoption of a specific model or demand for information concerning how the organisation is operating and what it is achieving (Arvidson & Lyon, 2014). These discomfort and resistance can cause tensions both with the external stakeholders and within the organisation itself, if the measurement process is not shared among the different parts of

*Table 1. Conceptualisation of critical issues of the impact measurement process*

| General Difficulties | Specific Difficulties | Case Declination |
|---|---|---|
| Scarce resources and competences | Time | People are saturated and can't spent time on measuring social impact.<br>Data are not structured and organized; there are few reports; most of the data are on paper format; there is a lack of communication between different subjects and areas. |
| | Money | The economic sustainability of the social enterprise is due to commercial activities and grants. It is not the easy for the organization to immobilize funds for activities with long-term returns. |
| | Human | Nobody is the person in charge of measuring and monitoring social benefits and impacts. Few people in the social enterprise have the managerial competencies. |
| Subjectivity of the choice of models and metrics | Complexity and heterogeneity of existing tools | There are many models and nobody in the organization has the specific ability and competences to choose and implement the best approach for measuring the value and impact created by the social enterprise. |
| | Different organizational structures | The organization offers an innovative business model, so it necessary but not sufficient to show the as-is. It is important for the organization to have a measuring system that is dynamic and responsive as the organization itself is. |
| | Difficulty in identifying performance indicators | The choice of the indicators is often subjective and complex and it could not be made by the organization itself. |
| Cultural resistance | Difficulty in understanding the importance of performance measurement | The management of the social enterprise believes that impact measurement is fundamental to grow, instead the employees and the staff show some resistance. |
| | Difficulty in identifying and involving all stakeholders | The social enterprise is part of a larger organization and has many partners. Moreover, many people, that are part of a larger network, influence and are influenced by the decision of social enterprise.<br>It is not easy for the social enterprise to involve all the stakeholders in the measuring process. |

the organization. For example, the managers of the organization believes that impact measurement is fundamental to grow, instead the employees and the staff do not recognise this importance. Table 1shows the specific problems encountered in the case study.

## SOLUTIONS AND RECOMMENDATIONS

The critical issues, which have been analysed in the literature review and then later emerged in the case study (e.g. the scarce resources and competences, the subjectivity of the choice of models and metrics and the cultural resistance) could be partially mitigated with some recommendations as shown in Table 2. As discussed above, the literature provides several impact measurement models, which are characterised by strengths, weaknesses and different levels of complexities. The strengths are, for instance, the opportunity to demonstrate the financial return (Millar and Hall, 2013) and the possibility of tailoring the model on the organization's specific peculiarities (Grieco et al, 2015). While the weaknesses are demonstrated in, for example, the difficulty of attributing a financial dimension to soft, qualitative and subjective outcomes (Sheridan, 2011) and the lack of sector-specific benchmarks (Hornsby, 2012).

A common issue between all the above models is the incomplete development and existence of the standard indicators and calculation methodologies across all different fields in which social enterprises operate (Pathak and Dattani, 2014). For example, when an organization works in the educational sector, indicators to measure certain outcomes are needed, such as, the number of students who have improved their personal and professional skills; the number of adolescents who find a job after graduation. While for a SE operates in the healthcare field, different evaluation metrics are required, as for instance, the percentage of recovered people and the public expenditure savings which are generated by the organization itself. Thus, the peculiarities of the sector and the social enterprise have both influenced the choice of the social impact measurement model and the adopted methodology.

The involvement of experts is expected to assist the organizations by providing them with a map to disentangle the measurement process path. Actually, the external professionals, thanks to their previous expertise, could help to identify the most appropriate model to apply in addition to recognize the indicators, which have been already developed and could suit an organization's measurement need. Thus, the involved experts fill the lack of internal human competences in the measurement field (Hornsby, 2012). Moreover, involving a third part would guarantee the transparency and the impartiality of the measurement process (Zappalà, G., & Lyons, M., 2009). As shown in the case study, both Cometa's employees and external stakeholders recognized more legitimacy in the measurement process implementation, thanks to the involvement of external experts. Indeed, defining a process that suits the needs of a certain SE's stakeholders should be the final goal of this SE and any involved experts; this definition has to express the selected measurement tools which are adapted at the organization's reality and are able to be self- replicable in the future, thanks also to the definition of the managerial and operative terms for the methodology application.

The initial investment of time and resources which is carried out to develop the measurement process could be paid back only when guaranteeing its replicability, long-term benefits and sustainability. From this point of view, a participatory approach results essential in order to set up the ad hoc methodology. The participation of all relevant stakeholders, the investigation of their needs and the involvement of the social enterprise's staff are required aspects in order to implement the measurement process (Nicholls, 2009). The significant number of surveys delivered in the case study, for example, has allowed to define the stakeholders' needs and consequently to identify relevant indicators for the measurement process. Moreover, a participatory approach could help to breach the cultural resistance concerning the utility of impact measurement (Esteves et al., 2012), which is quite common among the employees of social business organizations. For these reasons, the planning to conduct training sessions to develop the awareness among the employees and the collaborators, concerning the importance of impact measurement, could be useful to guarantee the appropriation of the process at all levels of the organization.

However, the outcomes of those awareness training sessions among SE's staff should not be underestimated; during the implementation of the Cometa measurement process, the seminars which were attended by the employees, have provided a great impulse to the project. Actually, the personnel and collaborators became an active part of the measurement process thanks to the comprehension of the importance of the work itself and the comparison with each other. Finally, delivering training sessions to the SE management could allow the necessary skills to be transferred and in turn guarantee the replicability of the process during the years.

## CONCLUSION

In the last decade, the welfare withdraw combined with the emersion of new relevant social problems, has led to the establishment of the Social Business. In particular, the Social Enterprises emerged and grew rapidly to cope with the new societal challenges. For its own nature, the SE needs to demonstrate the social value and the impact generated. Actually, the achievement of the social mission is clearly the heart of a social business initiative. From this perspective, the impact measurement is growing in importance among the social business field as an enabler of transparency and accountability, investors and resources attractiveness, performance operation management and stakeholders involvement. However, despite the existence of different indicators and metrics, most of the organizations that operate in the social business sector tend to resist to the adoption of formalized models.

*Table 2. Proposed solutions and recommendations*

| Solution | Specific Issues |
|---|---|
| Experts support | Complexity and heterogeneity of existing tools |
| | Difficulty in identifying performance indicators |
| | Human resources |
| | Time |
| Ad hoc replicable methodology | Lack of resources |
| | Complexity and heterogeneity of existing tools |
| | Different organizational structures |
| Participatory approach | Different organizational structures |
| | Difficulty in identifying and involving all stakeholders |
| Training and awareness creation | Human resources |
| | Difficulty in understanding the importance of performance measurement |
| | Difficulty in identifying and involving stakeholders |

This chapter aim to contribute to the debate analysing and highlighting the critical issues that SEs could encounter in the implementation of impact measurement process. Hence, the weaknesses and strengths of existent models proposed in literature have been critically analysed. Then, the process of development of an impact measurement system in an Italian social enterprise working in the education field has been presented, discussing the difficulties emerged. Finally, based on the evidence arisen from both theory and practice, some solutions and recommendations have been proposed in order to partially solve the key problems encountered.

In particular, the scarce resources and competences, the subjectivity of the choice of models and metrics, the cultural resistance could be mitigated by the external professional support and training process, the development of an ad hoc replicable methodology, the application of a participatory approach, the planning of training and awareness development processes.

Future research directions for consideration includes the emerging needs for impact measurement of the social enterprises and the critical issues analysed in the literature review and arisen during the implementation process in the case study, further research are required to enable and spread the impact measurement and its benefits among social enterprises. In particular, it shows the need to elaborate common guidelines and standards in order to facilitate social enterprises work in the measurement process.

Although each organization should chose and implement its own impact measurement process according to its own characteristics and stakeholders needs, common standards could make the process definition easier decreasing the complexity of the model and the subjectivity of indicator choice. Furthermore, the research in standards and guidelines on impact measurement could enable the definition of measurable policies allowing a real benchmarking between different organizations and best practice surfacing.

## REFERENCES

Alter, K. A. (2006). Social enterprise models and their mission and money relationships. In A. Nicholls (Ed.), *Social entrepreneurship: new models of sustainable social change* (pp. 205–233). Oxford, UK: Oxford University Press.

Arena, M., Azzone, G., & Bengo, I. (2015). Performance Measurement for Social Enterprises. *VOLUNTAS: International Journal of Voluntary and Nonprofit Organizations*, *26*(2), 649–672. doi:10.1007/s11266-013-9436-8

Arvidson, M., & Lyon, F. (2014). Social impact measurement and non-profit organisations: Compliance, resistance, and promotion. *VOLUNTAS: International Journal of Voluntary and Nonprofit Organizations*, *25*(4), 869–886. doi:10.1007/s11266-013-9373-6

Arvidson, M., Lyon, F., McKay, S., & Moro, D. (2010). *The ambitions and challenges of SROI*. Birmingham: TSRC.

Bagnoli, L., & Megali, C. (2011). Measuring Performance in Social Enterprises. *Nonprofit and Voluntary Sector Quarterly*, *40*(1), 149–165. doi:10.1177/0899764009351111

Bassi, A. (2011). *Il valore aggiunto sociale del terzo settore. Verso un sistema di indicatori per la misurazione della performance delle imprese sociali*. Milan: QuiEdit.

Bengo, I., Arena, M., Azzone, G., & Calderini, M. (2016). Indicators and metrics for social business: A review of current approaches. *Journal of Social Entrepreneurship*, *7*(1), 1–24. doi:10.1080/19420676.2015.1049286

Březina, D., Šafařík, D., & Hlaváčková, P. (2013). LM3–Local Multiplier in environmental economics. *Public recreation and landscape protection–with man hand in hand.*

Brignall, S. (2003). *The unbalanced scorecard: A social and environmental critique*. Retrieved from http://www.environmental-expert.com/articles/the-unbalanced-scorecard-a-socialenvironmentalcritique-2943

Bull, M. (2007). Balance: The Development of a Social Enterprise Business Performance Analysis Tool. *Social Enterprise Journal*, *3*(1), 49–66. doi:10.1108/17508610780000721

Bull, M., & Crompton, H. (2006). Business Practices in Social Enterprises. *Social Enterprise Journal*, *2*(1), 42–60. doi:10.1108/17508610680000712

Cupitt, S. (2009). *A guide to social return on investment*. Cabinet Office, Office of the Third Sector.

Darby, L., & Jenkins, H. (2006). Applying sustainability indicators to the social enterprise business model: The development and application of an indicator set for Newport Wastesavers, Wales. *International Journal of Social Economics*, *33*(5/6), 411–431. doi:10.1108/03068290610660689

Development Trusts Association (DTA). (2008). *Fit for purpose: The Development Trusts Association healthcheck for community enterprise organisations.* Accessed February 6, 2016. http://locality.org.uk/wp-content/uploads/Fit-for-Purpose.pdf

Ebrahim, A., & Rangan, K. (2010). *The Limits of Nonprofit Impact: A Contingency Framework for Measuring Social Performance.* Harvard Business School Working Paper.

Esteves, A. M., Franks, D., & Vanclay, F. (2012). Social impact assessment: The state of the art. *Impact Assessment and Project Appraisal*, *30*(1), 34–42. doi:10.1080/14615517.2012.660356

European Commission (EC). (2013). *Social economy and social entrepreneurship*. Social Europe guide, Volume 4. Directorate-General for Employment, Social Affairs and Inclusion, March 2013. Accessed November 10, 2015. http://www.sofisam.se/download/18.3453fc5214836a9a472a0430/1411643786917/EU+kommissionen,+Social+Economy+and+Social+Entreprenreurship.pdf

Gair, C. (2009). *SROI act II: A call to action for next generation SROI.* San Francisco: REDF.

Global Social Venture Competition (GSVC). (2012). *Social Impact Assessment Guidelines*. Accessed February 19, 2014. http://www.iedu.org.cn/gsvc/download/2011_GSVC_SIA_Guidelines.pdf

Grabenwarter, U., & Liechtenstein, H. (2011). *Search of Gamma---An Unconventional Perspective on Impact Investing*. IESE Business School, University of Navarra.

Grieco, C., Michelini, L., & Iasevoli, G. (2015). Measuring value creation in social enterprises a cluster analysis of social impact assessment models. *Nonprofit and Voluntary Sector Quarterly*, *44*(6), 1173–1193. doi:10.1177/0899764014555986

Hornsby, A. (2012). *The good analyst, Impact Measurement and Analysis in the Social-Purpose Universe*. Investing for Good.

Kaplan, R. S., & Norton, D. P. (2001). The strategy-focused organization. *Strategy and Leadership*, *29*(3), 41–42. doi:10.1108/sl.2001.26129cab.002

Kaplan, R. S., & Norton, D. P. (2001). Transforming the Balanced Scorecard from Performance Measurement to Strategic Management. Part II. *Accounting Horizons*, *15*(2), 147–160. doi:10.2308/acch.2001.15.2.147

Karanikolos, M., Mladovsky, P., Cylus, J., Thomson, S., Basu, S., Stuckler, D., & McKee, M. et al. (2013). Financial crisis, austerity, and health in Europe. *Lancet*, *381*(9874), 1323–1331. doi:10.1016/S0140-6736(13)60102-6 PMID:23541059

Mahmoudi, H., Renn, O., Vanclay, F., Hoffmann, V., & Karami, E. (2013). A framework for combining social impact assessment and risk assessment. *Environmental Impact Assessment Review*, *43*, 1–8. doi:10.1016/j.eiar.2013.05.003

McLoughlin, J., Kaminski, J., Sodgar, B., Khan, S., Harris, R., Arnaudo, G., & Mc Brearty, S. (2009). A Strategic Approach to Social Impact Measurement of Social Enterprises. The SIMPLE Methodology. *Social Enterprise Journal*, *5*(2), 154–178. doi:10.1108/17508610910981734

Meter, K. (2010). Learning how to multiply. *Journal of Agriculture, Food Systems, and Community Development*, *1*(2).

Millar, R., & Hall, K. (2013). Social return on investment (SROI) and performance measurement. *Public Management Review*, *15*(6), 923–941. doi:10.1080/14719037.2012.698857

New Economics Foundation (NEF). (2007). *Measuring Real Value: A DIY Guide to Social Return on Investment*. Accessed November 3, 2015. http://www.neweconomics.org/

New Philanthropy Capital. (2010). *Social Return on Investment.* Position Paper, April 2010. Author.

Nicholls, A. (2009). We do good things, dont we?: 'Blended Value Accountingin social entrepreneurship. *Accounting, Organizations and Society*, *34*(6), 755–769. doi:10.1016/j.aos.2009.04.008

Nicholls, A. (2010). Institutionalizing social entrepreneurship in regulatory space: Reporting and disclosure by community interest companies. *Accounting, Organizations and Society*, *35*(4), 394–415. doi:10.1016/j.aos.2009.08.001

Nicholls, J. (2004b). *Social return on investment: Valuing what matters*. London: New Economics Foundation.

Organisation for Economic Co-operation and Development (OECD). (2014). *General assessment of the macroeconomic situation.* Economic Outlook, no. 2. Accessed October 6, 2015. http://www.oecd.org/eco/outlook/General-assessment-of-the-macroeconomic-situation.pdf

Pathak, P., & Dattani, P. (2014). Social return on investment: Three technical challenges. *Social Enterprise Journal*, *10*(2), 91–104. doi:10.1108/SEJ-06-2012-0019

Roberts Enterprise Development Fund (REDF). (2000). *Social Return on Investment (SROI)*. Collection.

Ryan, P.W., & Lyne, I. (2008). Social Enterprise and the Measurement of Social Value: Methodological Issues with the Calculation and Application of the Social Return on Investment. *Education, Knowledge and Economy*, *2*(3), 223–37.

Sacks, J. (2002). *The Money Trail: Measuring your impact on the local economy using LM3*. London: New Economics Foundation.

Santos, F. M. (2012). A Positive Theory of Social Entrepreneurship. *Journal of Business Ethics, 111*(3), 335-351.

Sheridan, K. (2011) Measuring the Impact of Social Enterprise. *British Journal of Healthcare Management*, *17*(4), 152–56.

Simmons, J. (2003). Balancing Performance, Accountability and Equity in Stakeholder Relationships: Towards More Socially Responsible HR Practice. *Corporate Social Responsibility and Environmental Management*, *10*(3), 129–140. doi:10.1002/csr.40

Sinkovics, N., Sinkovics, R. R., & Yamin, M. (2014). The role of social value creation in business model formulation at the bottom of the pyramid–Implications for MNEs? *International Business Review*, *23*(4), 692–707. doi:10.1016/j.ibusrev.2013.12.004

Somers, A. B. (2005). Shaping the Balanced Scorecard for Use in UK Social Enterprises. *Social Enterprise Journal*, *1*(1), 43–57. doi:10.1108/17508610580000706

Thatcher, J., & Sharp, L. (2008). Measuring the local economic impact of National Health Service procurement in the UK: An evaluation of the Cornwall Food Programme and LM3. *Local Environment*, *13*(3), 253–270. doi:10.1080/13549830701669005

The Interorganizational Committee on Guidelines and Principles for Social Impact Assessment. (1994). Guidelines and principles for social impact assessment. *Environmental Impact Assessment Review*, *15*(1), 11–43.

Thomas, A. (2004). The rise of social cooperatives in Italy. *Voluntas*, *15*(30), 243–264. doi:10.1023/B:VOLU.0000046280.06580.d8

Vanclay, F. (2003). International principles for social impact assessment. *Impact Assessment and Project Appraisal*, *21*(1), 5-12.

Venturi, P., & Zandonai, F. (2012). *L'impresa sociale in Italia. Pluralità di modelli e contributo alla ripresa*. Milano: AltraEconomia.

Wilson, F., & Post, E. J. (2013). Business models for people, planet & profits: Exploring the phenomena of Social business, a market-based approach to social value creation. *Small Business Economics*, *40*(3), 715–737. doi:10.1007/s11187-011-9401-0

Wilson, K. E. (2014). *New Investment Approaches for Addressing Social and Economic Challenges. OECD Science, Technology and Industry Policy, Papers No. 15*. OECD. doi:10.1787/23074957

Yin, R. K. (1994). *Case study research: design and methods* (2nd ed.). Thousand Oaks, CA: Sage.

Yunus, M., Moingeon, B., & Lehmann-Ortega, L. (2010). Building Social Business Models: Lessons from the Grameen Experience. *Long Range Planning*, *43*(2–3), 308–325. doi:10.1016/j.lrp.2009.12.005

Zamagni, S., Venturi, P., & Rago, S. (2015). Valutare l'impatto sociale. La questione della misurazione nelle imprese sociali. *Impresa Soc, 6*.

Zappalà, G., & Lyons, M. (2009). *Recent approaches to measuring social impact in the Third sector: An overview*. Sydney: Centre for Social Impact.

## KEY TERMS AND DEFINITIONS

**Impact:** The impact of an organization is the outcome discounted by what would have happened anyway and by the contribution of others.

**Indicator:** An indicator is a number or a ratio (a value on a scale of measurement) derived from a series of observed facts. It can reveal relative changes as a function of time.

**Measurement Approach:** The measurement approach is the method that is used to evaluate the impact generated by an organization.

**Model:** A model is a simplification of the reality. It allow to better understand the organization.

**Outcome:** The outcome is the change resulting from an organization's activity. The main types of change from the perspective of stakeholders are direct and indirect, unexpected and expected, positive and negative change.

**Social Business:** A social business is an organization that provides a framework for tackling social issues by combining economic sustainability and business know-how with the generation of social benefits.

**Social Impact Measurement:** The social impact measurement is the set of procedures that an organization implement in order to identify the changes produced by the activities of the organization itself.

# Chapter 20
# Business Model Development for Stability, Sustainability, and Resilience

**Beata Maria Staszewska**
*Kozminski University, Poland*

## ABSTRACT

*Innovative business model development, understood as a static phenomenon neglects the dynamic influences on both for-profit and not for profit sectors. Business model development is a complex process which has been well researched in corporations, but predominantly remained under-researched in not for-profit organisations. An exploratory study during 2011-2015 is undertaken to examine business development process in the areas of stability, sustainability and resistance in a local not for profit public enterprise. Findings suggest that a balanced approach to economic, ecological and social characteristics, organisational coping capabilities during volatile phases of business model development and organisational capability to manage during times of instability contributes to the type of business model development process.*

## INTRODUCTION

There is an increasing consensus that innovative business model development is crucial to organisational performance (Markides, 2013) and an innovative business model often reshapes not only the organisation (Drakulevski & Nakov, 2014) but also entire industry sectors (Johnson, Christensen, and Kagermann, 2008). New technological innovations, provide modern day organisations with innovative ways of doing business. Leading business model development practitioners (Priem, Butler & Li, 2013) provide insights into the opportunities for business development.

Bellostas, López-Arceiz, and Mateos (2016) also, through their balanced approach to innovative business development processes, argued that it is possible to develop socially responsible and financially viable entrepreneurial business activities. The authors suggested a strong correlation between social value and

DOI: 10.4018/978-1-5225-2537-0.ch020

Copyright © 2017, IGI Global. Copying or distributing in print or electronic forms without written permission of IGI Global is prohibited.

economic value. Bassi and Vincenti (2015), support this view by arguing that enterprises with a social mission have the ability to generate different outcomes at each of the micro, meso and macro dimensions.

Innovative business model development in non-profit organisations, unlike their for-profit counterparts, is highly neglected in current business research and management literature. While it is the case that profit is not always the most important indicator outcomes of success, particularly for non-profit organisations, the focus on financial outcomes as indicators of success is often misleading or at worse, incomplete information. As Maguire (2009) puts it, such an organisation can hardly be expected to exist for a long time.

Traditionally, the term non-profit organisations inferred that organisations are exempt from income generating that results in a profit. Traditionally also, the financial and non-financial performance of non-profit organization was costly and difficult to measure due to the diverse purposes, programs, diverse requirements from multiple stakeholders, social and business environments. Traditionally too, the non-profit business model has been referred to the way in which the organisation does business at a specific moment in time. As have become clearer over time, organisations fail because of the rigidity of the business model (Doz & Kosonen, 2010).

Doz and Kosonen (2010) argued that business models change, and that that change is increasingly becoming more rapid. In other words, business models in the fast changing technological environment, business models change quickly and frequently. While corporations use the business model development to evolve from a specific phase of the business model to a designed and desired new business model, for non-profit organisations, it is a challenges. For example, a non-profit organization cannot use government funding, donor funding or any other privately appropriated benefits as criteria for success. This makes the selection mechanism for non-profit organisations allocating resources toward innovative business model development complex and highly misunderstood.

As stated by Doz and Kosonen (2010), organisational existence and survival have become shorter and traditional multi-dimensional complicated business models need to transform rapidly, frequently and innovatively. The emergence of technology, business intelligence and virtual markets open new sources of innovative business model development (Amit and Zott, 2001). These new forms of innovative thinking require a parallel shift in thinking about an integrative, dynamic, adaptive and entrepreneurial organisational business models (Amit and Zott, 2001).

Drakulevski and Nakov (2014) argued that innovative business model development is a process that is transformational and value-based compared to a business model as a static phenomenon which neglects the dynamic influences on organisational change. The question is not whether organizations make the strategic change towards sustainability, but how quickly, how frequently and how well they can make such changes, find and use new opportunities from the market environment. The timing of the decisions that concern innovative business model development, modification and utilisation of resource play a fundamental role in business model development but is often relegated to the not important organisational decision-making.

Innovative business model development is as important to non-profit organisations as it is to for-profit corporations. Two possible obstacles to research on innovative business model development in the non-profit enterprise sector are the assumption that there is little need to understand the non-profit business development model and that non-profit organisations lack the level of financial performance that for-profit corporations achieve.

Exploring stability, sustainability and resilience during innovative business model development in a non-profit enterprise aims to address that research gap. This study contributes to the knowledge generation in the area of innovative business model development particularly in non-profit enterprise organisations, business model development practitioners and academic researchers. Following this introduction, a definition of the business model is discussed leading to business model development in non-profit organisations. The research approach and case study is analysed to conclude with findings on stability, sustainability and resilience in innovative business model development processes in non-profit organisations.

## BACKGROUND

### Business Model Definition

Osterwalder and Pigneur (2013) have argued that the business model can be seen as the conceptual link between organisational business, system and strategy. Casadesus-Masanell and Ricart (2010), suggested that the business model is the direct result of organisational strategy. From their point of view, organisational strategic choice shapes the business model. The business model is characteristic of the organisational strategic intent so that even an external observer can identify the organisational strategy through observing business model. The business model therefore becomes an identified characteristic of the organisational strategy. If organisational strategy is the foundation for the business model development, understanding the term business model is important.

Business model development is based in the economic value-add theory and defined as the logic of the firm, the way it operates, creates and captures value for its shareholders (Linder and Cantrell, 2000; Magretta 2002; Baden-Fuller and Haefliger, 2013; Casadesus-Masanell and Ricart, 2010). It is also defined as the content, structure, and governance of transactions designed to create value through the exploitation of business opportunities (Amit and Zott, 2010). Another definition is that the business model is defined as an analytical framework that translates business structure, business processes and business infrastructure into concrete outcomes (Chesbrough and Rosenbloom, 2002, Johnson, Christensen, and Kagermann, 2008, Osterwalder and Pigneur, 2013).

Chesbrough and Rosenbloom (2002) established three core parts of the business model as:

1. Value offering.
2. Value creation architecture (containing core competencies and resources, main activities, and value creation partners).
3. Revenue model.

Johnson, Christensen, and Kagermann, (2008) identified that the business model is created by four essential components:

1. Customer value proposition.
2. Key resources.
3. Key processes.
4. Profit formula.

Osterwalder and Pigneur (2013) argued that contemporary enterprise business model should be viewed as a holistic concept that embraces all organisational parts relevant to its environment:

1. Complex system.
2. Holistic concept with many organisational parts.
3. Operating in a dynamic business environment.

George and Bock (2011) has argued that an organisational business model is characterized by internal and external coherency, especially internal coherency that drives the business model through opportunities that leads to organisational success. Supporting this view, Brege, Stehn, and Nord (2014) contend that a business model must have congruence with the environment and with different design parameters presenting a good organisational fit with the only problem the organisational focus on innovative business model development evaluation and efficiency.

Concurring with the notion that the business model is the basis for economic value-adding (Linder and Cantrell, 2000; Magretta, 2002; Baden-Fuller and Haefliger, 2013; Casadesus-Masanell and Ricart, 2010), Ronen (2014) argued that the value added is reflected in combining inputs into a desirable output. The role of business models is to facilitate quantifications of outputs by applying universal recognition and measurement principles (Ronen, 2014). Kim and Mauborgne (2000), confirms that successful business model can be identified by capturing value-adding organisational decisions. For example as Casadesus-Masanell and Ricart (2010) suggest, that slight differences in the governance of assets and policies can have dramatic effects on value creation and value capture.

Value is created due to relationships between business model components. Coherency, integration, and synergy among business model components are significant factors for value creation. The value creation process allows for transforming material value into intangible values and vice versa. Furthermore, the components of the model reinforce each other. In the basic business model framework, there are two main dimensions of value proposition: value proposition for customers and value proposition for stakeholders.

For the purposes of this discussion, a business model can be defined as an interactive system of internal and external components of the business focused on value creation. While each business model differs, this definition contains three assumptions about attributes of:

1. A business model describes a system.
2. A business model is composed of internal and external elements.
3. A business model is value creation organisational outcomes.

## Non-Profit Organizations

A non-profit organization is an independent organization with a primary purpose other than earning a profit (Salamon, 1997). This purpose is often dedicated to a valuable social cause. A non-profit organization is formed for serving a public benefit rather than the pursuit or accumulation of profits for owners or investors, and usually has a socially oriented and ethically based mission (Ebrahim, 2003). Non-profit organizations are focused on providing services to the community in general, either locally or globally (Young, Koenig, Najam, & Fisher,1999; Zatepilina-Monacell, 2012). Non-profit organizations include hospitals, schools, political parties, labor unions, volunteer organizations, museums, professional associations, research institutes, and legal aid societies.

Many local organizations like associations, cooperatives delivering programs or projects, education, and health, cultural or sports services as non-profit. Non-profit organizations are slotted into public and private categories. Non-profit organizations may obtain their financial support through donations they receive from the general public or financial support from private sources, such as a dedicated donor or investment income. Operating as a non-for-profit, the organisation cannot distribute surplus revenue but is obligated to, and must use any surplus revenue to achieve its mission (Hansmann, 1980).

Although non-profits are not permitted to generate surplus revenues, any surplus raised should be retained for its self-preservation, expansion, development or investment plans. Young (2007) claims that non-profits provide value to the society. Precisely because they provide valuable services to the public, financial performance and resource scarcity do not necessarily reflect non-profit successes or failures. Instead the degree of mission accomplishment should be used as an indicator of organizational success or failure.

However, financial performance and survival have gained in importance as indicators of non-profit success because of increasing commercialization and competition in the non-profit sector (Helmig, Ingerfurth, and Pinz, 2014). Non-profits nowadays are operating in a constrained environment, where maintaining their economic viability and growth has become a critical issue (Weerawardena, McDonald, and Mort, 2010). Therefore, a non-profit organization needs a business model to gain the required level of stability, sustainability and resilience to survive in a changing and unstable environment.

## NON-PROFIT BUSINESS MODEL DEVELOPMENT

### Stability, Sustainability, and Resilience

Three main systemic concerns that are related to the business model development:

1. Non-balance system (increasing financial stability is an important goal for financially non-balanced organizations).
2. Limited system both in terms of scope and time (sustainability is the main goal).
3. Rigid system (resilience is an important goal for the system).

Stability in organisations, but particularly in non-profit organisations are associated with risks, uncertainty and organisational capacity to manage through instability and uncertainty. Successful non-profit business model describes a set of strategies and tactical moves that creates balanced, sustainable and resilience system. Organisational capabilities which facilitate stability, sustainability and resilience of the system are particularly important for non-profit organizations. Measuring value resulting from risk is complicated and requires advanced skills (Krysiak, 2011). Risk-taking in service firms can be categorized into three types:

1. Financial risks.
2. Reputation risks.
3. Strategic risks.

Sources of the risk include both financial and non-financial determinants of risks. Financial risks are connected with external or internal events that have the potential to affect different financial outcomes, such as the ability to collect debts owed to the firm, to exchange assets for cash quickly, or to sell assets at a desired rate of return. These risks can typically be hedged with financial instruments. All other risks are non-financial risks. These include operational or business risks resulting from the failure of internal processes or systems, or from external events, as well as reputational risk and strategic risk (Rogers, 2010).

Reputation risk is defined as a risk of loss resulting from damages to a firm's reputation. This risk might expose the institution to litigation, financial loss, or a decline in its customer base and consequence leading to the destruction of shareholder value. Reputation risk has the current and prospective influence on earnings and capital from negative public opinion. This affects the ability to establish new relationships or services or continue servicing existing relationships. Reputation arises out of external observers' impressions or awareness of the organization (Gatzert, Schmit and Kolb, 2016), and is a company resource which is sensitive and can be damaged easily. The risk of loss of good reputation among stakeholders refers to the extent of the gap between their expectations and actions of an organization to fulfill that expectation. This gap can be bridged by proper management of relations with stakeholders (Szwajca, 2016). For most institutions, it takes years to acquire reputation and recognition, but it can take a single adverse event to destroy a firm's reputation completely and put the institution out of business. A good reputation is one of the most valuable assets and one of the most difficult to protect (Sobehart, 2014).

Strategic risk is a possible source of loss that arises from the pursuit of unsuccessful business strategies and plans. This risk is a function of the coherence of the firm's strategic goals, and the business strategy developed to reach those goals, the resources deployed against these goals, and the quality of implementation. The perception of strategic risk is influenced by the individual's past experiences related to the opportunities, their cognitive style for gathering and analysing information and their tolerance for ambiguous situations and outcomes (Acedo, and Florin, 2007). McConnell (2016) identified two major sets of strategic risk: strategic positioning risks (occur before and during the strategy development process, and usually before the strategy is set in motion) and strategic execution risks (occur during the execution of the strategy).

## Business Model Managed for Stability

The financial system of the firm is considered stable if it meets two fundamental requirements: it can lead to improved economic performance, and allows the elimination of distortions of endogenous factors and unanticipated or adverse events (Popa, 2015). Financial stability is critical for not-for-profit organisations. Financial stability, in particular, reflects the firm's ability to determine an efficient allocation of resources and manage financial risk through its own mechanisms. Financial stability is dynamic because the financial system changes over time; it degrades due to various external or internal shocks. Thus, the discounted cash flows measure would be derived from projections based on the expected outcomes of the plans envisaged in the business model.

The system itself tends to recover under the action of specific self-regulatory mechanisms. System stability stands for the system's ability to overcome the effects of disturbances and attain an equilibrium state, in an input-process-output system. The system response to an input can become stable, unstable or critically unstable depending on the control parameter setting. The important control parameters for financial ratios are for example: liquidity ratio, coefficient with its insurance, and solvency coefficient (Popa, 2015). Liquidity is improved with higher levels of diversification, foreign credibility, and risk management. Additionally, when competition in the market was more heated, liquidity was increased for preventive purposes and economic expansion occurred (Ji-Yong, 2014). Managers have responded to the hypercompetitive environment by not seeking a single sustained competitive advantage, but rather creating a series of short advantages that can be concatenated into the competitive advantage over time (Wiggins and Ruefli, 2005). However, the lack of strategic planning and a focus on short-term benefits during the decision-making process can severely limit resilience and the ability to respond effectively (Antony, Kumar, and Labib, 2008).

## Business Model Managed for Sustainability

Sustainable business models incorporate a value proposition that reflects a balance between economic, ecological and social needs (Boons and Lüdeke-Freund, 2013). Organizations practicing such models deliver economic, social and environmental benefit through core business activities. Sustainable development is defined as development that meets the needs of the present without compromising the ability of future generations to meet their needs. Socially driven and environmentally oriented companies are becoming strong competitors as well as appealing acquisition targets for many multinationals nowadays (Santos, 2015). A sustainable business creates, delivers and captures values in a truly balanced way by providing products within established environmental limits.

A sustainable business model comprises short and long term objectives. Short term objectives as a profit is transformed in the mechanism that allows for the long term survival through the investment in resources that are significant for the future. Therefore, a sustainable business model is a model focused on the long-term perspective of activities and activities that are oriented on a strong business ecosystem. However, a sustainable business model depends on anticipating and therefore, reacting to sequences of voluntary and emerging changes, giving the dynamic consistency to the firm's capability to build and sustain its performance while changing its business model (Demil and Lacocq, 2010). Strategic innovation capability that consists of dimensions of new idea enhancement, risk-taking circumstance acceptance, proactive activity support, market driving encouragement, and dynamic adaptation commitment have an important positive effect on firm sustainability (Sriboonlue, Ussahawanitchakit, and Raksong, 2016).

## Business Model Managed for Resilience

Business resilience is a term used to describe a company's capability to adapt and cope with environmental disturbance. Sutcliffe and Vogus (2003) argued that organizational resilience is related to a positive adjustment in the face of challenging conditions through a strengthening of the current and future entity. Carmeli and Markman (2011) suggested that resilience involves neither crisis management nor turn around programs, but rather an on-going bundling of innovation strategies. According to Lengnick-Hall, Beck and Lengnick-Hall (2011), resilience capacity is composed of cognitive abilities, behavioural characteristics and contextually related variables in the product innovation context. Product innovativeness gives the firm the necessary order and continuity of those resilience variables as reflexive domains, acts as a higher level of organizer for resilience variables and allows us to consider resilience variables as a system rather than some random practice in the organization (Sullivan-Taylor and Branicki, 2011). Linnenluecke and Griffiths (2010) pointed out that resilience is related to the organization's capacities to learn, adapt and self-organise. Management can improve a firm's resilience capacity to leverage the firm's product innovativeness and performance and to cope with environmental turbulence. Operational flexibility enables resilience through allowing the organization to respond quickly and effectively to disruptions (Sheffi, 2007). Flexibility requires the availability of resources and effective synchronization of these variables to benefit from a new opportunity. This requisite translates into the need for a firm to have the required competencies. The competencies that have been acquired have to be assimilated and strengthened (Nair, Paulose, Palacios, and Tafur, 2013).

According to Hatum and Pettigrew (2006), a resilient response required decentralization in decision making, low levels of formalization, a high degree of permeability between organizational boundaries, a low degree of embeddedness to a firm's macro culture, and establishing collaborative partnerships. Management can therefore develop values that lead to routines of collaboration and traditions of flexibility, create open communication channels and interpersonal ties as well as informal and face-to-face dialogues, seek multiple sources of information, encourage unlearning of obsolete information or dysfunctional heuristics, and promote creativity. Management can establish a clear sense of purpose and identity throughout the organization, create a mind-set that questions fundamental assumptions and positive perceptions of experiences, foster a psychologically safe environment where people can take interpersonal risks, and impose individual and group accountability (Akgün and Keskin, 2014).

## Business Model Development and Innovation

The business model concept refers to the articulation between different areas of activities. In response to the ongoing change occurring in the environment, companies are continuously seeking new opportunities and advantages to create new models and evaluate these against the business context to find a fit with the external environment. While business model development emphasizes the status quo of a firm's current business model and focuses on adjustments and incremental innovations within the established business model framework, business model innovation removes itself from the status quo and focuses on opportunities within the external environment of a firm.

The innovation of the business model requires an organization to focus its attention on the exploration and potential exploitation of arising opportunities within the environment (Schneider and Spieth, 2014). Innovation is often described as fitting three categories: product, process, and business systems. Much research has been conducted in recent years on product and process innovation, but much less has focused on business systems innovation (Kajanus, Iire, Eskelinen, Heinonen, and Hansen, 2014).

According to Girotra and Netessine (2014), any business model is essentially a set of decisions that determine how a business earns its revenue, incurs its costs, and manages its risks. Therefore, innovations of the model are changes to those decisions. It is useful to make a distinction between a business model innovation and a normal business change. Innovation can be the adoption of minor changes to the way something is done, or it can be expressed on the level of firm-wide strategic initiatives; in this case it is equal with the business model innovation. For example, oriented service innovation that changes the way value is delivered to the customer by way of customer segmentation, delivery channel, and customer relationships and allocating new resources and forging new partnerships and new activities, can be considered a business model innovation. Minor changes that do not affect the value propositions are just minor business changes (Nair, Paulose, Palacios, and Tafur, 2013).

Business model innovation goes beyond pure product or service innovation and requires the modification of an extant system. Business model innovation affects the entire organization (Amit and Zott, 2001) unlike normal business changes, which are intended to improve the operational efficiency of the firm. Companies commercialize new ideas and technologies through their business models (Baden-Fuller and Haefliger, 2013) while they are coherent with the whole system. While firms may have extensive investments and processes for exploring new ideas and technologies, at the same time, they are often limited in making critical strategic decisions. Barriers to business model innovation, which academic research has identified as including conflicts with existing assets and business models, as well as cognition in understanding these barriers.

Business model innovation activities over time can range from incremental changes in individual components of business models, the extension of the existing business model, introduction, and disruption of the business model, which may potentially necessitate replacing the existing model with a fundamentally different one (Khanagha, Volberda, and Oshri, 2014). When the organization reaches high levels of complexity, or when its environment becomes unpredictable, operations no longer follow mechanistic rules. Innovation is therefore a business model that is focused on improving the operational process of the complex system that makes up an organization rather than what it does or produces.

Sosna, Trevinyo-Rodriguez, and Velamuri (2010) provides some methods that facilitate business model innovation from the trial and error learning process in designing business models to the experimentation phases. An innovative business model focuses on experimentation, and the generation of many unique and diverse concepts can result in greater possibilities for future innovation and sustained competitive advantage (Wrigley and Straker, 2016). Learning from experimentation is fundamental to solving problems for which solutions are uncertain, or when critical information sources are inexistent or not available. Launching a series of small experiments helps minimize risk and maximize a firm's rate of learning, making it possible to identify a strategy's potential for success. Organizations may adopt a proper attitude toward business model experimentation. Some experiments will fail, but so long as failure informs new understanding within the constraints of affordable loss with discovery-driven planning, enterprises can model the uncertainties, and update their projections. Effectuation creates actions based on the initial results of experiments, generating new data which may point towards previously latent opportunity (Chesbrough, 2010).

According to (Ahokangas and Myllykoski, 2014) the business model creation process composes a dynamic learning process including visioning, strategizing, assessing, and performing. Particularly valuable is the lean start-up method, which is based on testing business hypotheses, product iteration, and validated learning which can shorten the product development cycle and reduce market risks before moving into the next stages of business development. That kind of experiment provides firms with the necessary information as to when is the most appropriate time to shift resources from established business models into new ones. Product market strategy follows the business model design or vice versa. To develop a valuable business model, firms need to manage the system to encourage upward spirals and avoid downward spirals (Kohler, 2015).

Zott and Amit (2008) suggest that product market strategy is a pattern of managerial actions that explains how an organization achieves and maintains competitive advantage through positioning in product markets. Product market strategy relates to product differentiation and cost leadership. The business model, as a source of values, could help explain why some firms outperform others. It provides a rationale for value creation and appropriation that is distinct from the firm's product market strategy (Zott and Amit, 2008). The business model is a complex system, full of interdependencies and side effects, therefore changing any part of it is likely to ripple through the entire system.

## Process of the Business Model Development

Business model changes never occur in isolation and require interactions and initiatives from a range of players, including customers, suppliers, competitors, and regulatory bodies. One business model may appear superior to others analysed in isolation but create less value when interactions are considered. Appreciating models in a stand-alone fashion leads to faulty assessments of their strengths and weaknesses and bad decision making (Nisa, 2015). Partners, employees, funders, customers do not play a stable role but work together with some sort of platform organization to create a product or service completely customized for different market niches (Pisano, Pironti, and Rieple, 2015).

Teece (2010) argues that the dynamic design of business models is a key micro foundation of dynamic capabilities. Sensing, seizing and reconfiguring skills that the business enterprise needs if it is to stay in synchronization with changing markets and which enables, not just staying alive, but to adapt to and shape the business environment. Founders created their original business models by their deeply personal experiences or gaining information from the time-absorbing and comprehensive interviews with clients. The chances for good design of the business model is a deep understanding of user needs. Put differently; a business model reflects the management's hypothesis about what customers want and how an enterprise can organize itself to best meet customer needs.

Khanagha, Volberda, and Oshri, (2014) reveal strategy formation to be a collective experimental learning process revolving around some alternative strategic intentions ranging from incremental evolution and transformation to complete replacement of the existing business model. Iterations between different modes and differing combinations are crucial in enabling the organization to make the transition to the new business model. Consideration of a resource-based and dynamic capabilities perspective is suitable to analyse both business model development and innovation; strategic entrepreneurship appears to provide additional insights to enhance our understanding of business model innovation (Schneider and Spieth, 2014). An understanding of the concept of business models, employing the right core competencies, organizing them, and creating the business model around the competencies that are gained and assimilated, can result in enhanced business performance and thus have implications for firms that want to innovate their business models (Nair, Nisar, Palacios, and Ruiz, 2012).

Doz and Kosonen (2010) claim which successful business model renewal and transformation are the main outcomes of strategic agility. Strategic agility management contains three meta-capabilities: strategic sensitivity (the sharpness of perception, awareness, and attention to strategic developments); leadership (the ability of management to make fast decisions); and resources fluidity (the capability to reconfigure capabilities and redeploy resources). Companies that manage to create value over extended periods of time successfully shape, adapt and renew their business models to fuel such valuable creation. Dixon, Meyer, and Day, (2014) indicate two distinct types of dynamic capabilities that are necessary for organizational transformation: adaptation and innovation. Adaptation relates to routines of resource exploitation supported by acquisition, internalization and dissemination of extant knowledge, as well as resource reconfiguration and integration. Dynamic capabilities relate to the creation of entirely new capabilities through exploration and path-creation processes that are supported by search, experimentation and risk taking.

Achtenhagen, Melin, and Naldi, (2013) argue that there are four critical factors: orientation towards experimenting, exploitation of the new business opportunities, a balanced use of resources, and coherence between leadership, culture and employee commitment, together shaping key strategizing actions. Business model renewal may contribute to improving adaptation to the environment, enhance competitive advantage and facilitate entrepreneurship. Particular dynamic capabilities are likely to succeed in changing their business models for entrepreneurial purposes (Roaldsen, 2014). Strategy making in complex settings involves tasks such as decision making, problem solving, explanation, learning, design and experimentation, and thus requires the combination and adaptation of different kinds of intelligence (Farjoun, 2008).

Managers, like other human beings, rarely see the full range of possibilities and have a tendency to delete information that they do not like or which does not fit the cognitive schemas. Strategic schemas enable managers to make holistic abstractions out of complex interactions. A strategic schema refers to the knowledge structures that top manager's use in making strategic decisions. Firms in high-clock-speed industries need to develop complex schemas that promote strategic flexibility to achieve higher performance. Therefore, firms need to constitute a complex schema collectively for achieving success (Nadkarni and Narayanan, 2007). The business model is a heuristic logic which might act as a mental map that mediates the way business ideas are perceived by filtering information as valuable or not. This filtering process within a successfully established organization is likely to preclude the identification of models that differ substantially from the current business model (Markides, 2013).

## RESEARCH APPROACH

The research approach includes a holistic case study analysis to explore and improve understanding of business model development in a local non-profit entrepreneurial organisation. According to Yin (2013), performing a holistic case study means, that global characteristics of an organization or program is analysed. Case study analysis is particularly recommended when the aim of the research is to understand complex interrelations between the phenomena studied (business model development) and their context (Stake, 2000). This chapter presents the analysis and findings of an exploratory research approach which is part of a longitudinal single case study (2011 to 2015).

The longitudinal single case study was considered to be the adequate empirical approach to study phenomenon of the business model development. A longitudinal case study approach not only provides us with the opportunity to look at different stages of business model innovation but also allows us to explore the sequence of events and to understand better what role members of the organization play in each decision (Hutzschenreuter and Kleindienst, 2006). For achieving validation in a research project with case study methodology, it is necessary to make use of multiple sources of evidence in order to substantiate the information. The case study research allows for the use of a huge variety of data, such as documentation, archival records, interviews, direct observation, participant observation and physical evidence for achieving validation and reliability (Masanet-Llodra, 2006).

The sources of information includes organisational documents, reports, strategy and plans, websites, press releases and surveys. Study data consists of both secondary sources (annual reports of the firm for the period from 2011 to 2015) and primary sources (surveys and focus group session). Data was collected from April 2016 to June 2016. The first type of data consists of detailed financial data, which enabled the enterprise to establish specific problems with financial stability and sustainability of the system and how the business model evolved over time. By breaking down the data allowed for an analysis in greater detail and to better understand the impact of the creation and implementation of the new business model.

The second type of primary source is surveys with open questions and supplementary interviews during a focus group session that provides additional information to the research questions. Qualitative research articles, which are produced as a result of long-term projects and engagement, bring more insight and authenticity to the topic as compared to articles which are done as a one-off exercise (Mukhopadhyay and Gupta, 2014).

Qualitative methodology is appropriate as it provides rich knowledge about the phenomenon and explains why some patterns are observed or expected (Shah and Corley, 2006). The case study protocol concerning qualitative data contained sections describing conditions of different business model strategies as well as the content of the implementation strategies. Every sentence from the survey was analysed and then allocated to appropriate sections of the protocol.

A descriptive analysis of the interview data was performed describing specific contextual factors. When the initial descriptive analyses was completed, research carried out a procedure pattern matching analysis to identify linking contexts for the holistic business model. Interpretation of qualitative data was explained during a focus group meeting and the additional interviews with management team. This analysis found the main categories describing how choices of strategies were aligned to the business model development of the organization. The sample research group for survey, focus group and additional interviews included nine persons from the management and professional team.

Data collection conducted during the research was prepared carefully to ensure security and comfortable participation. Attendance in the survey research was anonymous. Interviews were conducted during a meeting according to focus group technique (Hutt, 1979; Krueger, 1988; Morgan,1993). The findings prepared a new business model for the organization, therefore the time devoted to the research can be purposefully used by the participants for the business model development. Financial information was open to the public because the subject of the research is a local public enterprise. The company name was changed to restrict identification of the organization and to protect to its good reputation. The research questions for the survey were:

1. What is the current level of stability of the organization?
2. What positive and negative factors have influenced the level of stability?
3. How do you estimate the sustainability of the organization during the next five years?
4. What positive and negative factors influence the level of the sustainability?
5. How do you estimate the resilience capabilities of the organization?
6. What factors influence the level of resilience capabilities in a positive or negative way?

## CASE STUDY

ZN Recreation Park was founded by the local government in 2011 with the main purpose of the new communal leisure complex management (communal funds with contribution from European Regional Fund) as a non-profit project. Other non-profits enterprises are permitted to generate surplus revenues, but they must be retained for its self-preservation, development or investment plans according to social purpose. In the following five years, the public enterprise grew into a regional leader in the field of interactive education and outdoor recreation with a healthy balanced budget. The founder is a small community with limited co-finance possibilities, so financial independence from the communal budget was the main assumption for the enterprise business model.

The business offer contains products like educational laboratories (Main Laboratory, Recycling and Energy Laboratory, Laboratory of Avifauna and Troposphere, Undergrowth Laboratory), rope course, and water track, creative park for children, coffee bar, accommodation complex, and memorabilia shop. Moreover, the recreational area of the 10 ha is public, and everybody may benefit from the beach with secure bathing places, gardens, observation tower, outdoor gym, pathways and a central square with fountains (free offer). Values for the local community include new development opportunities for the local tourism sector, employment places, network of local suppliers, and promotion of local tourist brand. ZN Recreation Park offer combines many fields: education, ecology, innovation, active recreation, and represents a varied value proposition based on experience.

## Business Model Description Through Financial Date

According to Turco, (2014) the balanced scorecard framework provides information about the business model as an analysis instrument which has the aptitude to measure the performance according to a multidimensional and coordinated logic, as well as to represent the causal links between strategic goals and assumed measuring indicators. Basic financial data organized in a long time frame may create the picture of the business model logic and allow for observation strategic assumptions about profit, growth, stability, or sustainability. A dynamic approach to the financial data of the organisation shows the tendency to maximize the revenues not profit and limitation of the investments efforts for the sake of remaining some financial stability.

## Business Model Description Through Product Market

The tendency to increase revenues was able to be achieved because of the coexistence of the many types of products under the brand. The system consisting of profitable, and non-profitable or free services is an example of how many of the local business enterprises create their complex value proposition in congruence with requirements of the many groups of the stakeholders.

*Figure 1. Organisational basic financial data, 2011-2016*
*Source 1 Documents- Financial Annual Reports 2011-2015*

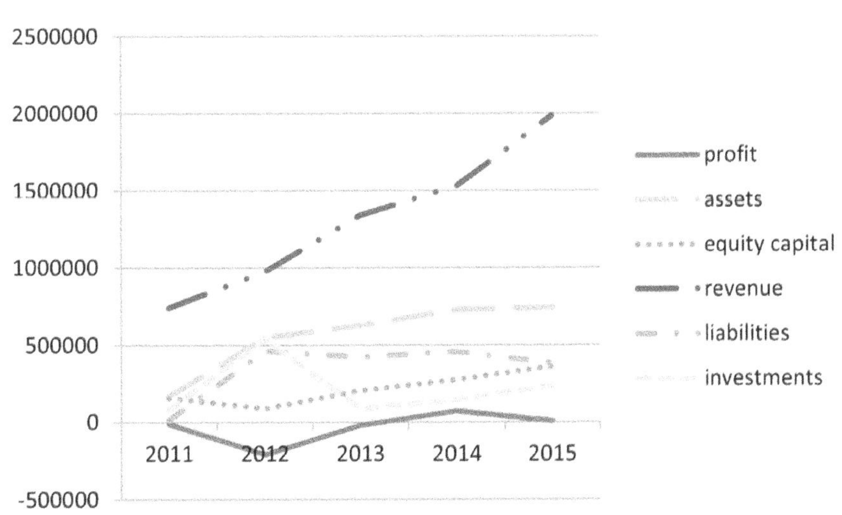

*Figure 2. Organisational main products and service revenues, 2011-2015*
*Source 2 Documents- Fnancial Annual Reports and Presentations 2011-2015*

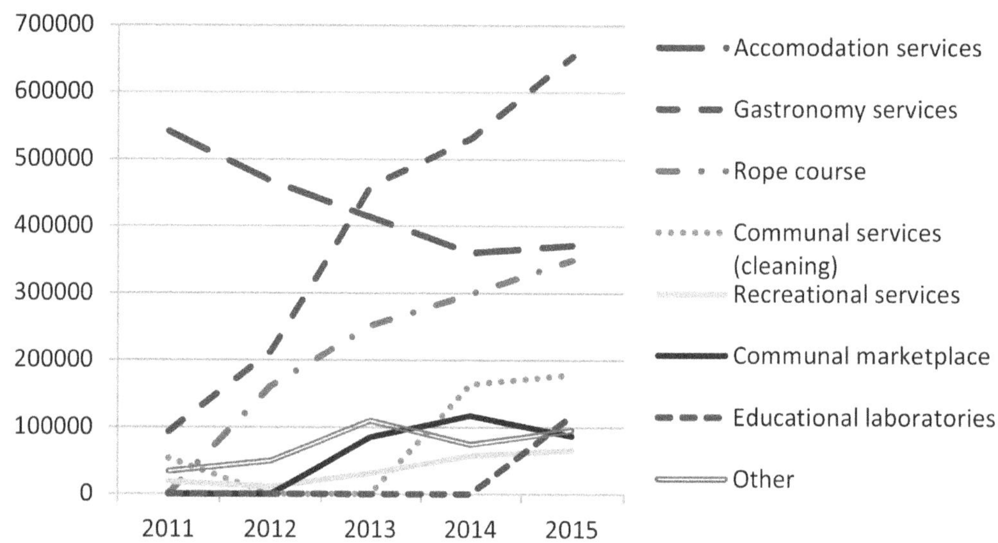


## Business Model Description Through Strategic Choices

According to Casadesus-Masanell and Ricart, (2010) an organization's business model describes an objective entity with the choices made in the organization, which have some consequences. The ZN Recreation Park business model contains basic strategic choices: services and product diversification, the no-profit approach allows for investments in new products, on-going experimentation and innovation to enable new product creation and verification.

*Table 1. Organisational business model choices*

| Choices | Consequences and Explanations |
|---|---|
| Services and products diversification | Value proposition contains a broad scope of product and services, diversification eliminated risk. |
| No profit - investments in new offers | Revenues allow for investments in new products and create possibilities for self-funding. |
| Experimentation and innovation | Experimentation and innovation enable product creation and verification. |
| Free offers and average prices | Free offers and average prices consequently trigger mechanism of large volume. |
| Product bundle bound by strong brand | Products and services are mainly focused on the brand. |
| Concentration on two customer segments | Activities are focused on two segments: children and families. |
| Little advertisement expenses - buzz marketing strategy | Strong bundle of products and personnel allow for limitation of advertisement expenses. |
| Flat structure and strong personnel strategy | Flat structure and strong personnel enable experimentation and product innovation. |
| Large volume | Large volume of customers and products are the basis for increasing revenues. |

Source 3 Survey, Focus Group and Interviews (2016)

*Figure 3. ZN recreation park - simplified business model visual representation*

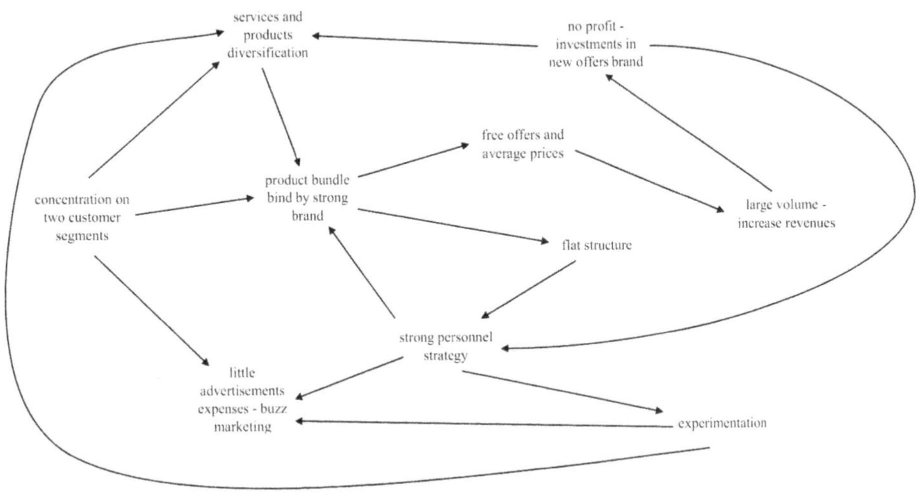


Many of the ZN Recreation Park products and services constitutes a product bundle bound by the strong brand, free offers and average prices which consequently trigger mechanism of the large volume and enable revenue increasing. A flat structure and strong personnel strategy allow for experimentation, new product development and verification assumptions about the market value of new products.

The visual presentation of the relations between core business model assumptions describes many interrelated elements of the system that trigger the upward spirals. To develop a valuable business model, firms need to manage the system to encourage upward spirals and avoid downward spirals to reach the set targets.

## Business Model Description Through Factors for Stability, Sustainability and Resilience

See Table 2.

*Table 2. Organisational stability, sustainability and resilience factors*

| Stability Factors | |
|---|---|
| Negative factors | Positive factors |
| Leaking financial control system | Tight financial control system |
| unjustified expenses | Expenses focused on important investments |
| Unstable and narrow customer group | Stable and broad customers group |
| Personnel fluctuation | Stable personel |
| Shortage of knowledge | Accumulation of experience and knowledge |
| Low value products | Valuable products with strong market value |
| Seasonal fluctuation | Stable revenue regardless of the season. |
| Unstable and inconsistent law | Stable law system. |
| Old and demage infrastructure | Valuable infrastructure. |
| Miserable creditworthiness | High lending capacity |
| **Sustainability Factors** | |
| Negative factors | Positive factors |
| Narrow activities | Product diversification |
| Old products | New and innovative products |
| Fixed, narrow product | Offer development |
| Weak brand | Strong, valuable brand |
| Decreasing sales forecast | Increasing sales forecast |
| Weak realations with customers | Strong relations with key customers. |
| Goverment changes | Strong relations with local government |
| Lack of liquidity | Financial reserves |
| **Resilience Factors** | |
| Negative factors | Positive factors |
| Weak personnel without motivation | Strong human resources potential |
| Low personnel commitment | Good team |
| Limited willingness to development | Knowledge from practice. |
| Limited dynamic capabilities | Strong dynamic capabilities |
| Slow reactions to the changes | Fast reaction |
| Inability to see opportunities | Capability to see new opportunities |
| Inability to create new product | Ability to create new product |
| Lack of creativity | Creativness |
| Activities fixation | Activities flexibility |
| Product fixation | Product flexibility |
| Product incompatibility | Products compability |

Source 5 Survey (2016)

## SOLUTIONS AND RECOMMENDATIONS

A key objective of this study was to gain understanding of the stability, sustainability and resilience of the organisation. The findings reveal interesting and valuable information but particularly, four points of interest are worth mentioning:

1. Findings indicate that the same factors appeared across stability, sustainability and resilience.
2. Stability factors are described as internal or external phenomena characterized by stability or fluctuation of resources, control system efficiency, and infrastructure value.
3. Sustainability factors showed the value of development and differentiation, necessary to building strong relations with stakeholders, partners, and customers and brand and financial potential that enable sales growth forecast.
4. Resilience factors are connected with dynamic capabilities, personnel potential and flexibility of the activities and products bundle.

The results shows that the business model description requires a holistic and systemic approach to business development. It also revealed that to enable interconnection analysis among many external and internal business model components, a comprehensive analysis is necessary. While on the one hand, business model description information about the financial system, product strategy is useful, on the other hand, for a comprehensive diagnosis of the business model, a deeper level of understanding the changes in organisation is important. The business model theory allows for the comprehensive understanding of stability, sustainability and resilience capabilities of the organisation.

Stability in business model development refers to an organisational capacity to overcome the effects of disturbances and attain an equilibrium state (Popa, 2015). In this case, stability factors are described as internal or external phenomena characterized by stability or fluctuation of resources, control system efficiency, and infrastructure value. Level of stability might be influenced by negative factors that decrease stability and positive factors that increase system stability. This study reveals that the negative influences on stability were: leaking financial control system, unjustified expenses, unstable and narrow customer group, personnel fluctuation, shortage of knowledge, low value products, seasonal sale fluctuation, unstable and inconsistent law, old and damaged infrastructure, and miserable enterprise creditworthiness. The positive influences on stability were: a tight financial control system, expenses focused on important investments, stable and broad customers group, and stable personnel, accumulation of experience and knowledge, valuable products with strong market value, stable revenues regardless of the season, stable law system, valuable infrastructure, valuable infrastructure, and high lending capacity.

Sustainability in business model development reflects a balance among economic, ecological and social needs as well as a balance between short and long term objectives. Sustainability was estimated as a potential for realizing the short and long term objectives in the same time and differentiated goals connected with the broad group of stakeholders. Short term objectives as a profit is transformed in the mechanism that allows for the long term survival through the investment in resources that are significant for the future. The negative influences on sustainability were: narrow activities, old, fixed, or narrow products, weak brand, decreasing sales forecast, weak relations with customers, government changes, and lack of liquidity. The positive influences on sustainability were: product diversification, new and innovative products, offer development, a strong and valuable brand, increasing sales forecast, strong relations with key customers, strong relations with local government and financial reserves. Sustainability factors showed the value of development and differentiation, necessary to build strong relations with stakeholders, partners, and customers; brand and financial potential that enable sales growth forecast. For the realization of long term objectives in the next five years, the organisation intends to reduce negative factors and increase positive factors in order to be sustainable.

Resilience in business model development refers to as the organisational capability to adapt and cope with environmental disturbance was estimated in connection with dynamic capabilities, personnel potential, and flexibility of the activities and products bundle. The negative influences on resilience were: limited dynamic capabilities, slow reactions to the changes, inability to see opportunities and create new products, a lack of creativity, activities fixation, product fixation and incompatibility, weak personnel potential, team without motivation, low commitment and limited willingness to development. The positive influences on resilience were: strong dynamic capabilities, the capability to see new opportunities and fast reaction, creativeness, especially the capability to create new products, activities flexibility, product flexibility and products compatibility, strong human resources potential, and good team, knowledge from practice.

The qualitative analysis allowed for the analysis of an appropriate description business model system and especially core factors that influence business model development. According to Schneider and Spieth (2014), to achieve a significant change in a business model, at least one of the basic business model dimensions (value offering, value architecture, revenue model) needs to be innovated. Ghezzi, Cavallaro, Rangone, and Balocco, (2015) contended that an innovation acts first on the business model parameters of value proposition and financial configuration three distinct basic types of business model innovation:

1. Value offering innovation.
2. Architectural innovation.
3. Revenue model innovation.

Concurring with Casadesus-Masanell and Ricard (2010) theory and methods for business model development requires business logic to achieve the set of organisational objectives. Casadesus-Masanell and Ricart, (2010) describes the choices made in the organisation which have some strategic consequences. In this case, designation of main strategic choices consequently allows them to establish a business model dynamic framework, and its visual presentation. This framework includes the relations between core business model assumptions and describes many interrelated elements of the system that trigger the upward spirals. Analysis of the business model focused on stability, sustainability and resilience show that some universal processes characterized the business model in these three dimensions. However, the findings also indicated that the financial system is inseparable with product market strategy, and these results are consistent with Zott and Amit (2008).

Zott and Amit (2008) contend that product market strategy follows business model design, or vice versa. Business model development requires systemic changes in every subsystem: financial - revenue innovation and product strategy innovation. Accordingly, the organisation then aligns its key resources, key activities, key partners and key dynamic capabilities to the emerging context. According to Zott and Amit (2008), business models can be characterized by design themes novelty and efficiency, which describe the holistic picture of a firm's business model, and they enable its conceptualization and measurement.

## FUTURE RESEARCH DIRECTIONS

There are some potential limitations of the study. The methodology that was employed has its limitation, and do not allow for the generalization of findings to a bigger population. The most common disadvantage of the case method research approach concerns the inter-related issues of methodological rigor, researcher subjectivity, and external validity. Future studies could examine factors that influence business model development in other organizational contexts. In these ways, future studies should examine the generalizability of the findings. Although the current sample is not expected to be typical and should be representative of organizations in general, future studies might be conducted to examine this phenomenon more comprehensively and within other functional and industry environment.

## CONCLUSION

This chapter outlined various business model and theoretical definitions and the development of a local not-for-profit business enterprise to gain a clearer understanding of organisational stability, sustainability and resilience.

The discussion highlighted that every business model is a representation of the organisational business strategy but that the development of the financial system, product strategy progress and latent factors that shape the business model is a complex reality for any organisation but specifically, for non-profit organisations.

Limitations of the qualitative analysis do not allow for statistical interpretation, formulation and verification of the theoretical assumptions. However, the exploratory and descriptive research, which was the focus of this chapter, contributes to an emerging phenomenon and is beneficial for future research.

## REFERENCES

Acedo, F. J., & Florin, J. (2007). Understanding the risk perception of strategic opportunities: A tripartite model. *Strategic Change*, *16*(3), 97–116. doi:10.1002/jsc.787

Achtenhagen, L., Melin, L., & Naldi, L. (2013). Dynamics of business models – strategizing, critical capabilities and activities for sustained value creation. *Long Range Planning*, *46*(6), 427–442. doi:10.1016/j.lrp.2013.04.002

Ahokangas, P., & Myllykoski, J. (2014). The practice of creating and transforming a business model. *Journal Business Models*, *2*, 6–18.

Akgün, A. E., & Keskin, H. (2014). Organisational resilience capacity and firm product innovativeness and performance. *International Journal of Production Research*, *52*(23), 6918–6937. doi:10.1080/00207543.2014.910624

Amit, R., & Zott, C. (2001). Value creation in E-business. *Strategic Management Journal*, *22*(6/7), 493–520. doi:10.1002/smj.187

Antony, J., Kumar, M., & Labib, A. (2008). Gearing six sigma into UK manufacturing SMEs: An empirical assessment of critical success factors, impediments, and viewpoints of six sigma implementation in SMEs. *The Journal of the Operational Research Society*, *59*(4), 482–493. doi:10.1057/palgrave.jors.2602437

Baden-Fuller, C., & Haefliger, S. (2013). Business models and technological innovation. *Long Range Planning*, *46*(6), 419–426. doi:10.1016/j.lrp.2013.08.023

Bassi, A., & Vincenti, G. (2015). Toward a new metrics for the evaluation of the social added value of social enterprises. *CIRIEC - España, Revista de Economía Pública. Social Cooperativa*, *83*, 9–42.

Bellostas, A., López-Arceiz, F., & Mateos, L. (2016). Social value and economic value in social enterprises: Value creation model of Spanish sheltered workshops. *Voluntas*, *27*(1), 367–391. doi:10.1007/s11266-015-9554-6

Boons, F., & Lüdeke-Freund, F. (2013). Business models for sustainable innovation: State of the art and steps towards a research agenda. *Journal of Cleaner Production*, *45*, 9–19. doi:10.1016/j.jclepro.2012.07.007

Brege, S., Stehn, L., & Nord, T. (2014). Business models in industrialized building of multi-storey houses. *Construction Management and Economics*, *32*(1/2), 208–226. doi:10.1080/01446193.2013.840734

Carmeli, A., & Markman, G. D. (2011). Capture, governance, and resilience: Strategy implications from the history of Rome. *Strategic Management Journal*, *32*(3), 322–341. doi:10.1002/smj.880

Casadesus-Masanell, R., & Ricart, J. (2010). From strategy to business models and onto tactics. *Long Range Planning*, *43*(2/3), 195–215. doi:10.1016/j.lrp.2010.01.004

Chesbrough, H. (2010). Business model innovation: Opportunities and barriers. *Long Range Planning*, *43*(2/3), 354–363. doi:10.1016/j.lrp.2009.07.010

Chesbrough, H., & Rosenbloom, R. (2002). The role of the business model in capturing value from innovation: Evidence from Xerox Corporations technology spin-off companies. *Industrial and Corporate Change*, *11*(3), 529–555. doi:10.1093/icc/11.3.529

Demil, B., & Lecocq, X. (2010). Business model evolution: In search of dynamic consistency. *Long Range Planning*, *43*(2/3), 227–246. doi:10.1016/j.lrp.2010.02.004

Dixon, S., Meyer, K., & Day, M. (2014). Building dynamic capabilities of adaptation and innovation: A study of micro-foundations in a transition economy. *Long Range Planning*, *47*(4), 186–205. doi:10.1016/j.lrp.2013.08.011

Doz, Y. L., & Kosonen, M. (2010). Embedding strategic agility: A leadership agenda for accelerating business model renewal. *Long Range Planning*, *43*(2-3), 370–382. doi:10.1016/j.lrp.2009.07.006

Drakulevski, L., & Nakov, L. (2014). Managing business model as function of organizational dynamism. *International Symposium,* 37-44. doi:10.7595/management.fon.2014.0025

Ebrahim, A. (2003). Making sense of accountability: Conceptual perspectives for northern and southern nonprofits. *Nonprofit Management & Leadership*, *14*(2), 191–212. doi:10.1002/nml.29

Farjoun, M. (2008). Strategy making, novelty and analogical reasoning — commentary on Gavetti, Levinthal, and Rivkin (2005). *Strategic Management Journal*, *29*(9), 1001–1016. doi:10.1002/smj.690

Gatzert, N., Schmit, J. T., & Kolb, A. (2016). Assessing the risks of insuring reputation risk. *The Journal of Risk and Insurance*, *83*(3), 641–679. doi:10.1111/jori.12065

George, G., & Bock, A. J. (2011). The business model in practice and its implications for entrepreneurship research. *Entrepreneurship: Theory & Practice*, *35*(1), 83–111.

Ghezzi, A., Cavallaro, A., Rangone, A., & Balocco, R. (2015). On business models, resources and exogenous (dis)continuous innovation: Evidences from the mobile applications industry. *International Journal of Technology Management*, *68*(1/2), 21–48. doi:10.1504/IJTM.2015.068777

Girotra, K., & Netessine, S. (2014). Four paths to business model innovation. *Harvard Business Review*, *92*(7/8), 96–103. PMID:24956873

Hansmann, R. B. (1980). The role of non-profit enterprise. *The Yale Law Journal*, *89*(5), 835–901. doi:10.2307/796089

Hatum, A., & Pettigrew, A. M. (2006). Determinants of organizational flexibility: A study in an emerging economy. *British Journal of Management*, *17*(2), 115–137. doi:10.1111/j.1467-8551.2005.00469.x

Helmig, B., Ingerfurth, S., & Pinz, A. (2014). Success and failure of non-profit organizations: Theoretical foundations, empirical evidence, and future research. *Voluntas: International Journal Of Voluntary & Nonprofit Organizations*, *25*(6), 1509–1538. doi:10.1007/s11266-013-9402-5

Hutt, R. (1979). The focus group interview: A technique for counselling small business clients. *Journal of Small Business Management*, *17*(1), 15–19.

Hutzschenreuter, T., & Kleindienst, I. (2006). Strategy-process research: What have we learned and what is still to be explored. *Journal of Management*, *32*(5), 673–720. doi:10.1177/0149206306291485

Ji-Yong, S. (2014). A study on the determinants of business stability in credit card firms: Evidence from Korea. *Asian Academy of Management Journal*, *19*(2), 105–122.

Johnson, M., Christensen, C., & Kagermann, H. (2008). Reinventing your business model. *Harvard Business Review*, *86*(12), 50–59. PMID:18681297

Kajanus, M., Iire, A., Eskelinen, T., Heinonen, M., & Hansen, E. (2014). Business model design: New tools for business systems innovation. *Scandinavian Journal of Forest Research*, *29*(6), 603-614.

Khanagha, S., Volberda, H., & Oshri, I. (2014). Business model renewal and ambidexterity: Structural alteration and strategy formation process during transition to a cloud business model. *R & D Management*, *44*(3), 322–340. doi:10.1111/radm.12070

Kim, W. C., & Mauborgne, R. (2000). Knowing a winning business idea when you see one. *Harvard Business Review*, *78*(5), 129–138. PMID:11143149

Kohler, T. (2015). Crowdsourcing-based business models: How to create and capture value. *California Management Review*, *57*(4), 63–84. doi:10.1525/cmr.2015.57.4.63

Krueger, R. A. (1988). *Focus groups: A practical guide for applied research*. Newbury Park, CA: Sage Publications.

Krysiak, Z. (2011). Achieving enterprise stability based on economic capital. *Graziadio Business Review, 14*(4).

Lengnick-Hall, C. A., Beck, T. E., & Lengnick-Hall, M. L. (2011). Developing a capacity for organizational resilience through strategic human resource management. *Human Resource Management Review, 21*(3), 243–255. doi:10.1016/j.hrmr.2010.07.001

Linder, J. C., & Cantrell, S. (2000). *Changing business models: Surveying the landscape*. Cambridge, MA: Accenture Institute for Strategic Change.

Linnenluecke, M., & Griffiths, A. (2010). Beyond adaptation: Resilience for business in light of climate change and weather extremes. *Business & Society, 49*(3), 477–511. doi:10.1177/0007650310368814

Magretta, J. (2002). Why Business Models Matter. *Harvard Business Review, 80*, 86–92. PMID:12024761

Maguire, M. (2009). The non-profit business model: Empirical evidence from the magazine industry. *Journal of Media Economics, 22*(3), 119–133. doi:10.1080/08997760903129333

Markides, C. C. (2013). Business model innovation: What can the ambidexterity literature teach us? *The Academy of Management Perspectives, 27*(4), 313–323. doi:10.5465/amp.2012.0172

Masanet-Llodra, M. (2006). Environmental management accounting: A case study research on innovative strategy. *Journal of Business Ethics, 68*(4), 393–408. doi:10.1007/s10551-006-9029-1

McConnell, P. J. (2016). Strategic risk management: The failure of HBOS and its regulators. *Journal of Risk Management in Financial Institutions, 9*(2), 147–162.

Morgan, D. L. (1993). *Successful focus groups: Advancing the state of the art*. Newbury Park, CA: SAGE Publications. doi:10.4135/9781483349008

Mukhopadhyay, S., & Gupta, R. K. (2014). Survey of qualitative research methodology in strategy research and implication for Indian researchers. *Vision, 18*(2), 109–123.

Nadkarni, S., & Narayanan, V. K. (2007). Strategic schemas, strategic flexibility, and firm performance: The moderating role of industry clockspeed. *Strategic Management Journal, 28*(3), 243–270. doi:10.1002/smj.576

Nair, S., Nisar, A., Palacios, M., & Ruiz, F. (2012). Impact of knowledge brokering on performance heterogeneity among business models. *Management Decision, 50*(9), 1649–1660. doi:10.1108/00251741211266732

Nair, S., Paulose, H., Palacios, M., & Tafur, J. (2013). Service orientation: Effectuating business model innovation. *Service Industries Journal, 33*(9/10), 958–975. doi:10.1080/02642069.2013.746670

Nisa, S. (2015). Inter-firm differences in the sustainability business model: A study on select firms from agri-food and IT companies. *IUP Journal of Business Strategy, 12*(4), 35–55.

Osterwalder, A., & Pigneur, Y. (2013). Designing business models and similar strategic objects: The contribution of IS. *Journal of the Association for Information Systems, 14*, 237–244.

Pisano, P., Pironti, M., & Rieple, A. (2015). Identify innovative business models: Can innovative business models enable players to react to on-going or unpredictable trends? *Entrepreneurship Research Journal*, *5*(3), 181–199. doi:10.1515/erj-2014-0032

Popa, A. (2015). Analysis methods procedures for assessing the stability of business entity. *Economy Transdisciplinarity Cognition*, *18*(1), 124–132.

Priem, R. L., Butler, J. E., & Li, S. (2013). Toward reimagining strategy research: Retrospection and prospection on the 2011 Amr decade award article. *Academy of Management Review*, *38*(4), 471–489. doi:10.5465/amr.2013.0097

Roaldsen, I. (2014). Dynamic capabilities as drivers of business model innovation - from the perspective of SMEs in mature industries. *International Journal of Entrepreneurship and Innovation Management*, *18*(4), 349–364. doi:10.1504/IJEIM.2014.064212

Rogers, D. A. (2010). *Managing financial risk and its interaction with enterprise risk management*. Wiley.

Ronen, J. (2014). On the invariance of accounting principles to business models: A discussion of the Singleton-Green and Page articles. *Journal of Management & Governance*, *18*(3), 707–716. doi:10.1007/s10997-012-9241-6

Salamon, L. M., & Anheier, H. K. (1997). *Defining the nonprofit sector: A crossnational analysis*. Manchester, UK: Manchester University Press.

Santos, F. M., Pache, A., & Birkholz, C. (2015). Making hybrids work: Aligning business models and organizational design for social enterprises. *California Management Review*, *57*(3), 36–58. doi:10.1525/cmr.2015.57.3.36

Schneider, S., & Spieth, P. (2014). Business model innovation and strategic flexibility: Insights from an experimental research deign. *International Journal of Innovation Management*, *18*(6), 1–21. doi:10.1142/S136391961440009X

Shah, S., & Corley, K. (2006). Building better theory by bridging the quantitative–qualitative divide. *Journal of Management Studies*, *43*(8), 1821–1835. doi:10.1111/j.1467-6486.2006.00662.x

Sheffi, Y. (2007). *The resilient enterprise: Overcoming vulnerability for competitive advantage*. Boston, MA: The MIT Press.

Sobehart, J. R. (2014). Rumour has it: Modelling credibility, reputation and franchise risk. *Journal of Risk Management in Financial Institutions*, *7*(2), 161–173.

Sosna, M., Trevinyo-Rodriguez, R., & Velamuri, S. (2010). Business model innovation through trial-and-error learning: The Naturhouse case. *Long Range Planning*, *43*(2-3), 387–407. doi:10.1016/j.lrp.2010.02.003

Sriboonlue, P., Ussahawanitchakit, P., & Raksong, S. (2016). Strategic innovation capability and firm sustainability: Evidence from auto parts businesses in Thailand. *Journal of Business & Retail Management Research*, *10*(2), 11–29.

Stake, R. E. (2000). Case studies. In N. K. Denzin & Y. S. Lincoln (Eds.), *Handbook of Qualitative Research* (2nd ed.; pp. 435–454). Thousand Oaks, CA: Sage.

Sullivan-Taylor, B., & Branicki, L. (2011). Creating resilient SMEs: Why one size might not fit all. *International Journal of Production Research*, *49*(18), 5565–5579. doi:10.1080/00207543.2011.563837

Sutcliffe, K. M., & Vogus, T. J. (2003). Organizing for Resilience. In K. S. Cameron, J. E. Dutton, & R. E. Quinn (Eds.), *Positive Organizational Scholarship. Foundations of a New Discipline* (pp. 94–110). San Francisco, CA: Berrett-Koehler.

Szwajca, D. (2016). Strategie zarządzania relacjami z interesariuszami w kontekście ograniczania ryzyka, pogorszenia lub utraty reputacji przedsiębiorstwa. *Research Papers of The Wroclaw University of Economics*, *420*, 324–336.

Teece, D. (2010). Business models, business strategy and innovation. *Long Range Planning*, *43*(2-3), 172–194. doi:10.1016/j.lrp.2009.07.003

Turco, M. (2014). The multidimensional value measurement: The balanced scorecard and its perspectives of development. *Annual International Conference on Accounting & Finance*, 155-165. doi:10.5176/2251-1997_AF14.65

Weerawardena, J., McDonald, R. E., & Mort, G. S. (2010). Sustainability of non-profit organizations: An empirical investigation. *Journal of World Business*, *45*(4), 346–356. doi:10.1016/j.jwb.2009.08.004

Wiggins, R. R., & Ruefli, T. W. (2005). Schumpeters ghost: Is hypercompetition making the best of times shorter? *Strategic Management Journal*, *26*(10), 887–911. doi:10.1002/smj.492

Wrigley, C., & Straker, K. (2016). Designing innovative business models with a framework that promotes experimentation. *Strategy and Leadership*, *44*(1), 11–19. doi:10.1108/SL-06-2015-0048

Yin, R. K. (2013). *Case study research: Design and methods (Applied social research methods)*. Sage Publications, Inc.

Young, D. R. (2007). *Financing non-profits: Putting theory into practice*. Lanham, MD: Alta Mira.

Young, D. R., Koenig, B. L., Najam, A., & Fisher, J. (1999). Strategy and structure in managing global associations. *Voluntas: International Journal Of Voluntary & Nonprofit Organizations*, *10*(4), 323–343. doi:10.1023/A:1021434424549

Young, D. R., Koenig, B. L., Najam, A., & Fisher, J. (1999). Strategy and structure in managing global associations. *Voluntas: International Journal Of Voluntary & Nonprofit Organizations*, *10*(4), 323–343. doi:10.1023/A:1021434424549

Zatepilina-Monacell, O. (2012). High stakes: U.S. nonprofit organizations and the U.S. standing abroad. *Public Relations Review*, *38*(3), 471–476. doi:10.1016/j.pubrev.2012.02.003

Zott, C., & Amit, R. (2008). The fit between product market strategy and business model: Implications for firm performance. *Strategic Management Journal*, *29*(1), 1–26. doi:10.1002/smj.642

Zott, C., & Amit, R. (2010). Business model design: An activity system perspective. *Long Range Planning*, *43*(2/3), 216–226. doi:10.1016/j.lrp.2009.07.004

## KEY TERMS AND DEFINITIONS

**Business Model:** An interactive system of internal and external components of the business focused on value creation.

**Financial Risk:** A risk connected with external or internal events that have the potential to affect different financial outcomes.

**Non-For-Profit Organization:** An independent organization with a primary purpose other than earning a profit.

**Reputation Risk:** A risk of loss resulting from damages to a firm's reputation.

**Resilience:** A company's capability to adapt and cope with environmental disturbance.

**Stability:** A system's ability to overcome the effects of disturbances and attain an equilibrium state.

**Strategic Risk:** A possible source of loss that arises from the pursuit of unsuccessful business strategies and plans.

**Sustainability:** A balance among economic, ecological and social needs as well as a balance between short and long term objectives.

# Chapter 21

# A Business-Like Strategic Model That Works?

## Lessons Learned From Non-Profit Incubator in China

**Xunyu Xiang**
*The University of Hong Kong, Hong Kong*

**Lucy Porter Jordan**
*The University of Hong Kong, Hong Kong*

**Cheryl Hiu-Kwan Chui**
*The University of Hong Kong, Hong Kong*

**Min-Hsiu Chiang**
*National Chengchi University, Taiwan*

## ABSTRACT

*The application of the business-like strategic model in the nonprofit sector has attracted increasing attention from scholars and practitioners in both western countries and Asian countries like China. In order to assess how the business-like strategic model can be applied successfully in an authoritarian regime, this Chapter concentrates on a single case in China's context, the Nonprofit Incubator (NPI), to identify the contributing factors to its success in applying the business-like strategic model. Drawing from two theoretical frameworks of policy window and balanced scorecard, this chapter examines the internal and external management of NPI to investigate how, and to what extent, a business-like strategic model is adopted in the context of China. Findings indicate that organizational needs to be very sensitive to both internal and external managerial environment so as to achieve its success. This chapter argues that the business-like strategic model is feasible in China without any obvious disparity compared with its implication in Western countries.*

## INTRODUCTION

The eroded boundary between the non-profit sector and the business sector has created opportunities for the implementation of business-like strategic models in the Chinese non-profit sector. Business-like strategic model refers to strategies that are widely used in the business sector, such as venture capital, and platform model (Dart, 2004). As an alternative to innovative organizational operation, business-like

DOI: 10.4018/978-1-5225-2537-0.ch021

Copyright © 2017, IGI Global. Copying or distributing in print or electronic forms without written permission of IGI Global is prohibited.

strategic models have been reasonably well received by scholars and practitioners in both Western context and countries like China. This chapter focuses on a single case in China's context—the Non-profit Incubator—to assess how a business-like strategic model can be applied successfully in an authoritarian regime. Drawing from the two theoretical frameworks of policy windows and balanced scorecard, this chapter uses the case of a Chinese non-profit support organization (NSO), the Non-Profit Incubator (NPI), to examine how, and to what extent, business-like strategic model is adopted. In addition to examining documents relevant to the NPI such as annual reports and mission statements, interviews were conducted in order to add further richness to the case study.

This chapter is structured as follows. First, an introduction of current trends regarding the convergence of business-like strategies and the non-profit sector are presented, followed by an overview of non-profit support organizations (NSOs) ranging from the definition to service delivery over the past few decades is provided. Second, we will explore the development of NSOs in contemporary China relying on statistical data. The discussion of findings resulting from statistical analysis is followed by an introduction of the emergence of business model in China, including a brief introduction of the NPI, and an exploration of business-like strategic model in the current stage. An analysis on the managerial system, strategic planning, and discussion on how the NPI executes business-like strategies follows. The final section provides a summary of the arguments made in this chapter and suggests further research recommendations.

## The Convergence of Business Strategies and the Non-Profit Sector

Thus far, studies have shown that the adoption of business-like strategic models have contributed to the success of the non-profit sector (Kearns, 2000). Non-profit organizations (NPOs), like Ashoka, and Robert Foundation Homeless Economic Development Fund, have adopted the business-like strategic model in their daily operation. The utilization of business model in the non-profit sector is spurred by its potential benefits to improve organizational performance, and resolve social issues. Securing resource is a crucial element to survival in society. Business models tend to integrate numerous resources from different stakeholders (Maier, Myer, & Steinbereithner, 2016) so as to diversify NPOs resource base. Also, intangible resources have been purveyed through business model to NPOs. For example, substantial, new and innovative knowledge (Hvenmark, 2013), influential powers in social development (Keevers, Treleaven, Sykes, & Darcy, 2012), and legitimacies (Kuosmanen, 2014) have been injected into NPOs. With the increase in business-like strategic model implementation, social welfare provisions have improved in face of complex social issues (Guo & Bielefeld, 2014). Despite its popularity and significance, both scholarly and practitioners' attitudes toward this initiative diverge: a plethora of studies recommend NPOs to be more socially entrepreneurial (Emerson & Twersky, 1996, Kearns, 2000).

In contrast, opponents opined that adopting business model may erode organizational missions or even result in a loss of idealism (Maier et al., 2016). Theoretically, becoming a business-like organization enables NPOs to capture the complexity and difficulty of the environment to meet the needs of society in a more efficient way, but balancing the business strategy and NPOs' mission and value can be challenging. It is apparent that further assessments of applying the business-like strategic model are needed for guiding future research and practice. Yet, business model has made some progress in the Western context. For instance, the US Federal government has established an office to foster these initiatives; public and non-profit sector have attempted to shift into business-like strategic model with the goal of enhancing operation effectiveness as well. While most research has originated in the Western context, the study of how non-profits can adopt business-like models is noticeably limited in developing countries, especially ones that are characterized by authoritarian regimes. There is also a dearth of knowledge with regards to how the business model and strategies can be applied to NPOs of different natures.

In authoritarian regimes, the state is depicted as the overarching ruler and regulator whereas society is perceived as passive and conforming. NPOs operating under such political contexts have limited space and are often seen as being extension of the state (Unger, 1991). However, the success of the Non-profit Incubator (NPI) in China suggests otherwise. Is the business-like strategic model suitable for the Chinese non-profit setting? Does the business model reflect distinctive characteristics in China's context? How are business strategies achieved under an authoritarian regime, and under what circumstance do they succeed? These are still some unanswered questions that warrant further examination.

In this chapter we draw on two analytical frameworks, the policy window (Kingdon, 1984) and the balanced scorecard (Niven, 2003) to explore the internal and external contexts relevant to these questions. In the following sections we examine the growth of NSOs and the non-profit sector specifically within China and more broadly before turning to the analysis.

## LITERATURE REVIEW

### Uncovering New Opportunities in China

Due to the reform of public services, the fierce competition among NPOs as well as the gradual decreased resources in non-profit sector, the business strategic model has been applied in non-profit sector around the world from 1980s onwards (Zhang, 2013). The gradual adoption of the business model in China coincided with the country's welfare reforms in the 1990s where the government decreased social spending substantially (Zhang, 2013). In addition, the involvement of International NPOs in Chinese civil society also influence the perspective of Chinese NPOs (Chen, 2012). As a result, Chinese NPOs attempted to diversify their funding sources via the adoption of business strategic model. On the other hand, more and more managerial issues (like human resources, professionalization) gradually presented themselves to NPOs, in turn requiring NPOs to find localized solutions to overcome these developmental barriers (Chen, 2012).

The emergence of NSOs marks the beginning of the adoption of business strategies in the Chinese non-profit sector (NGOCN, 2015). In order to respond to the central government's new developmental model of 'Innovating in social governance', NSOs have taken up the responsibilities to adjust prevailing organizational developmental models to improve the stability and sustainability of NPOs' organizational operations as well as support NPOs to build their competitive advantages.

In this chapter we use the case study of NPI, one of the earliest and leading NSO in China, which has already extended its operation across China with branches in cities such as Beijing, Chengdu, Shenzhen, and Nanjing. Since its inception in 2006, the organization has been assisting social innovation and cultivating social entrepreneurs in China by providing crucial supports to some newly established or small-sized grassroots NPOs. NPI has formed extensive connections with the local government, business sector and other foundations to converge a diversified resource like policies supports, funding, and technical supports from potential stakeholders. NPI, therefore, is esteemed as a resource pool containing enormous wealth to NPOs in China. Currently, around 500 grassroots organizations have received support from NPI. Most of these incubated NPOs in turn play leading roles in Chinese civil society and have become reputable in their own right.

The success of NPI has attracted considerable attention from the Chinese government, NPOs, and scholars, particularly the concept 'incubation' which is regarded as one of the most innovative reform of the Chinese non-profit sector (Xu, 2014). The non-profit incubator model has been replicated and promoted throughout China. Different types of non-profit incubators (e.g. government organized, grassroots incubator) are being set up. To date, unofficial statistics estimated that hundreds of non-profit incubators have been established. Local governments have encouraged the establishment of non-profit incubators through formulating related policies, offering office spaces and providing funding. The involvement of government made the implementation of non-profit incubator model widespread in China.

Arguably, the non-profit incubator model has contributed to the improvements of the Chinese non-profit sector. The professionalization of organizations has been enhanced as well as public legitimacy and accountability (NPO Development centre, 2014; Xu, 2014), and show that business strategies can be viable in the non-profit setting. On the other hand, the relationship between government and NPOs has become more intimate to a certain extent under an authoritarian regime (Xu, Lu, & Cao, 2014).

However, every coin has two sides; not every NSO can achieve long-term success like the NPI. Lacking professional managerial systems and thoughtful consideration of the organizational environment, some non-profit incubators were shut down within a few years. In spite of these unsuccessful cases, the case of NPI shows that business-like strategic model can significantly contribute to China's non-profit sector by ameliorating existing limitations of organizational management. Application of the business-like strategic model has the potential to provide continual support for the Chinese non-profit sector as organizations attempt to grapple with increasingly complex social issues. Nevertheless, the discourse on applying business-like strategic model in China's non-profit sector still attracts considerable debate. While, NPI is continuously introducing new business concepts to the Chinese non-profit sector along with innovations in its services planning.

## The Growth of Non-Profit Support Organization

Civil society is a multidimensional concept, including diverse organizations. Existing literature has categorized them based on a series of criteria (Pardon, 1987, Edwards & Hulme, 1992, Vakil, 1997). In this chapter, we adopt a simplified way that divides NPOs into two categories: 'Practical NPOs' and 'Support NPOs' (Zeng, 2012). Practical NPOs (NPOs, thereafter) refer to NPOs that provide social services. In other words, NPOs are service delivery non-profit organizations. Supportive NPOs, on the other hand, provide a series of distinctive services and programs which conventional NPOs (or practical NPOs) would not include in their daily operations (Sanyal, 2006), including NPO incubation, and NPOs alliances formation. 'Support Organizations' was first adopted by Brown and Kalegaokar (1999) to solve challenges like amateurism, material scarcity, paternalism and relationship with state or market, in civil society. This new type of organizations gained widespread acceptance (Mosley, 2014). The distinct features of support organizations aforementioned make it possible to converge the appropriate amount of resources for sustainable and large-scale social impact. They also have the potential to form a close connection among NPOs (Brown & Kalegaokar, 1999; 2002). Nowadays, support organizations play a vital role in strengthening NPOs (Shea, 2011).

Previous research defines NSO with different terminologies, such as support organization, umbrella organization, intermediary organization, non-profit management support organization, mediating organizations, and development NGOs (Brown & Kalegaokar, 1999, Carroll, 1992, Sanyal, 2006). Despite considerable literature, scholars have not achieved a general agreement on the definition of NSOs. In this chapter, we add the word—'non-profit'—to emphasize its organizational nature, and distinguish it from support organizations in other sectors or fields. We propose a new definition to NSOs in China's context based on existing literatures (Carroll, 1992; Osborne & Tricker, 1994; Fowler, 1997, Brown & Kalegaokar, 1999, 2002). For this purpose, Non-profit Support Organizations are a type of NPOs that are value-based, functional organizations that aim to strengthen NPOs through delivering services and supports comprising:

1. Associations, alliances and network buildings.
2. Human resources and organization development.
3. Financial resources.
4. Organizational incubation.
5. Organizational capacity building.
6. Research and information that can guide NPOs operations and/or their sustainable development.

China's NSOs have undergone significant development over the past few decades. As of 2014, an estimated 300 NSOs have been established. Generally, NSOs are classified based on its services nature, their relationship with the government and the composition of their founders (Xu, 2010; Wang, 2012, Wang, 2015). NSOs can be grouped into two types:

1. Government-led NSOs are NSOs founded and managed by the government (intermediary organization, industrial association).
2. Grassroots NSOs are established by volunteers or private parties, like our target organization NPI.

Both types of NSOs have a main objective, which is to provide support for NPO development, for instance: organization incubation, financial services and evaluation. Despite the seemingly large number of NSO, compared with other types of NPOs, the number of NSOs is scarce. Nevertheless, they have made an undeniable impact on the development of China's civil society. NSOs are considered to be of significant importance to the development of China's philanthropic ecosystem (Xu, 2010).

In the late 1990s, the first NSO the 'Chinese Foundation and NPOs Centre' was established in China for improving the sector's self-regulation. In the next few years, the number of NSOs grew rapidly in China. In 2006, the NPI was established and marked the tipping point of the development of NSOs. The number of NSOs decreased afterward. NPI has led to a trend of promoting the establishment of NSOs. The development of NSOs has experienced its embryo stage and nascent stage (NPO Development Centre, 2014). Currently, it is in a high speed developmental stage. Since 2015, various local governments such as the Guangzhou provincial government have also implemented a series of policy directives that promoted the development of civil society, for instance the *Recommendations on developing and regulating social organizations in Guangzhou* (NGOCN, 2015).

As illustrated in Figure 1, NSOs provide a wide range of services. Apart from capacity building, NSOs in China are also engaged in service provision including volunteer management, philanthropic propagation, and public relations planning. By 2014, service provision of NSOs has extended nationwide to include NPOs operating at national level, provincial level, city, county and township levels (Figure 2).

*Figure 1. Types of Services provided by NSO*
*Source 1 NPO Development Centre (2014)*

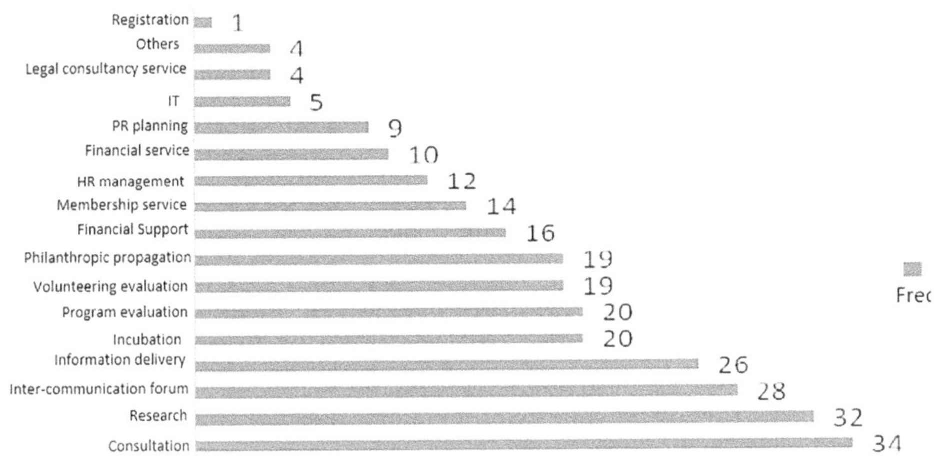


*Figure 2. Range of services*
*Source 2 NPO Development Centre (2014)*

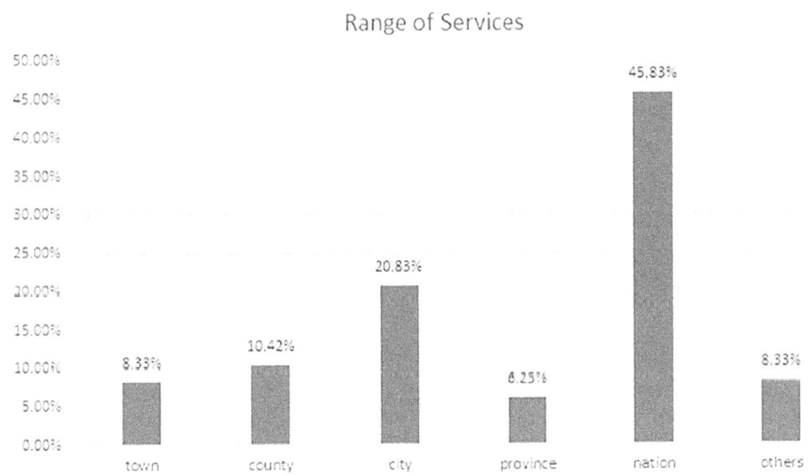


According to our observation, around 70% of NSOs are located in well-developed cities (NPO Development Centre, 2014), like Shanghai, Beijing, and Guangzhou

Recently, the relationship between NSOs and the Chinese government is becoming more interactive. These noteworthy efforts, as one of the causes, have encouraged the Chinese government to become further involved in NSOs development. A series of policies have been promulgated on the local level as well (Wang, 2015). The government's increasing financial support to NSOs has contributed to growth of these organizations. Relying on the case study approach, this chapter will investigate the success experienced by NPI to illustrate how the business strategic model has been applied in Chinese non-profit sector.

## SUPPORTING THEORETICAL FRAMEWORK

### Balanced Scorecard

To a large extent, good organizational performance depends on well-planned strategic management. However, due to rapid changes in the non-profit sector environment, a clear sense of the environment is essential for an organization to form and implement relevant strategies (Wheelan & Hunger, 2008).

The Balanced Scorecard, introduced by Kaplan and Norton (1992), has been well developed and widely applied in the business sector, as well as the public and non-profit sectors. It aims to identify, design, evaluate and measure the potential elements that are related to organization performance. The design of a balanced scorecard is based on "the cause-and-effect relationship of the financial and nonfinancial measures derived from the organization's strategy" (Martello, Waston, & Fischer, 2008: 68), and provides managers with an effective approach in grasping the trends and behaviours of organizational performance. The balanced scorecard consists of four components (Figure 3): financial perspective, customer perspective, internal process perspective, and learning and growth perspective (Niven, 2003).

Financial perspective refers how organizations assess their own capital, and economic value through multiple stakeholders' perspectives. Customer perspective not only includes clients, but also donors and volunteers whose opinions have to be taken into account by organizations to satisfy the demands of multiple stakeholders and to evaluate the level of their satisfaction. Internal process perspective refers to the general operational situation of an organization. Concerns regarding the internal managerial process,

*Figure 3. Balanced scorecard*
*Source Niven (2003) 1*

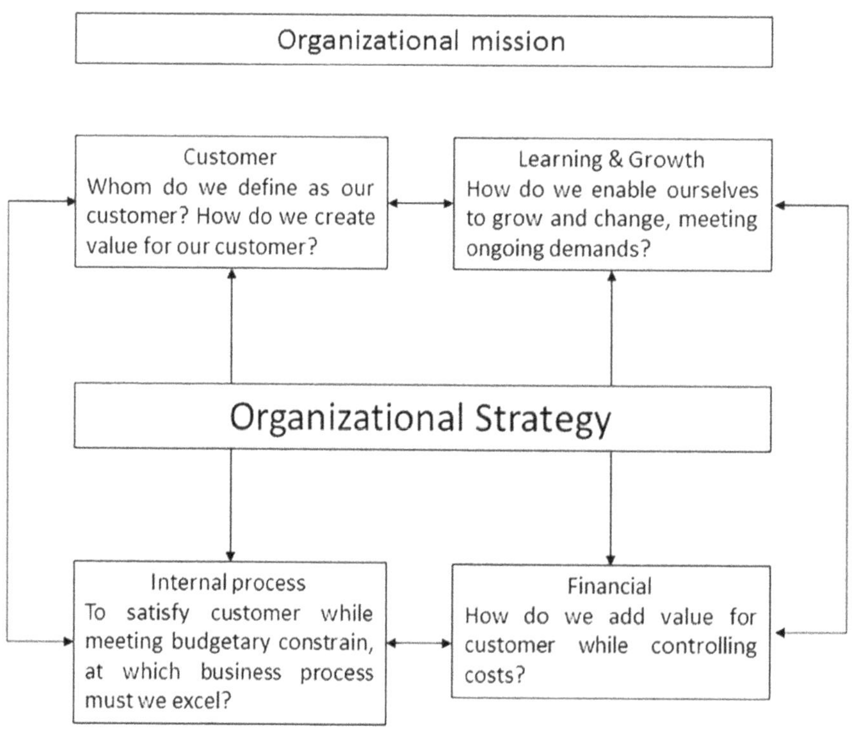

such as program and services provision, and connection with clients affect the improvement of operations, the financial supports and even the satisfaction of clients (Hartnerr & Matan, 2011). Learning and growth perspective is about human resources management. The professionalization of the staff and other human resources can influence the ability of an organization.

## Policy Window

Obviously, managers cannot allocate the same amount of time and resources to every issue. This means that issues need to be prioritized according to their order of importance. The policy window is an opportunity to call to attention particular issues. Once a window opens, opportunities appear. Policy window is a model depicting the process of agenda-setting. It first appeared in Kingdon's (1984) seminal work on the U.S. legislative system. Recently, scholars have attempted to employ this framework to study the collaboration among non-profit organizations and its governance dynamic (Takahashi & Smutny, 2002; Cornforth, Hayes & Vange, 2015)

The policy window approach focuses on the policy entrepreneur who identifies an opportunity—a policy window—and maximizes the advantage of the opportunity to push the issues from 'the government agenda' to 'the decision agenda' (Kingdon, 1984). The policy window has a limited opening, so policy entrepreneurs need to take timely action when the window opened.

In theory, the opening and closing of the windows are determined by three independent factors: the problem stream, the politics stream and the policy stream. The problem stream refers to the characteristics of the problem: what situation is defined as a problem by policy makers and needs to be addressed by the government. The politics stream refers to the inducement which stems from political institutions (governments in different levels and their branches). The policy stream refers to technical knowledge and expertise consensus from which solutions are developed. Where these three streams converge, the policy window will be opened. This marks a golden opportunity for a particular problem to be pushed forward toward the formal agenda.

This chapter integrates the balanced scorecard and policy window frameworks to critically examine NPI's strategic planning and the reasons behind its success. The balanced scored card highlights the structure of NPI's internal management process, while the policy window framework demonstrates how external situation influence organizational operation. In the following section, we present a brief introduction of NPI, from its historical background to the changes in its services.

# METHODOLOGY

## Data Collection

The case study approach has been employed in this study (Berg, 2009). A deeper exploration on a specific organization is necessary and helpful in order to obtain a comprehensive understanding on the operational dynamics of the organization. NPI is one of the success cases of utilizing the business strategic model in Chinese non-profit sector. In-depth study on its operational and managerial dynamics can contribute to the understanding of the application of business strategic model under the non-profit sector, particularly in Chinese context.

Within our case study, data was collected through in-depth interview with mid-level managers, documentary analysis, and participatory observation. With regards to interviews, a total of four interviews were conducted with one manager of a local branch of NPI, and three NPOs that partnered with NPI. Participants were asked their interactive experience with NPI. The collected data have been analysed thematically. We also collected a series of documents including annual reports and organizational pamphlets for further analysis. Lastly, because one of the authors was involved in NPI's daily operation as a program intern, participant observation was conducted via taking extensive field notes. Data collection took place in the headquarters of NPI as well as one of its branches in other city.

## Case Study: Professional Managerial System to Innovative Services Plan

The success of the NPI in the Chinese non-profit sector can be attributed to the well-planned design of the managerial system as well as innovative service planning. NPI was established by some volunteers with business background in 2006, all staffs are recruited by NPI itself without the involvement of the local government. With regards to the internal managerial structure, NPI has experienced its second developmental stage and is now approaching maturation. It has a clear and careful arrangement of its current and future working plan. The council is composed of eight individuals with diverse backgrounds, and it is the council that makes the most important decisions and plans, especially in the start-up stage.

A group of mid-level executives is in charge of daily operations. They mediate the working arrangement among different departments, lead the discussion on service models and working fields, and perform administrative management. The NPI adopts and emphasizes the use of business methods and an outcome-oriented managerial model to manage staffs. Staffs are required to have the capacity to respond to predictable and unpredictable challenges accurately and quickly. Furthermore, advice and feedback on daily operations are welcome. NPI often organizes team-building activities to build trust and cooperation among staffs. NPI even build its scientific evaluation system to evaluate staffs' performance.

Externally, the NPI continues to build and maintain connections with different sectors and actors, and tries to maximize the potential benefits among them. NPI seeks to collaborate with the local government and its branches, which in turn enables them to acquire more support from the local government in terms of resources provision, policy advocacy and information sharing. Moreover, Business sector, schools and mess media are partners of NPI. There are even foreign institutions that have engaged NPI in some capacities.

Currently, NPI has gone through its most important strategic adjustment. NPI has expanded its service fields with a more localized arrangement. All types of NPOs, including Government-organized Non-Governmental Organizations (GONGOs), are eligible to apply the supports from NPI. At the initial stage, the service plan of NPI has been inspired and influenced by the business sector. Its first program 'Non-profit Incubator' was launched in 2006. Shortly after its implementation, the non-profit incubator model has become popular and has been applied across China in order to satisfy the needs of NPOs in different developmental stages and with various characteristics.

A continuous capacity building program has been implemented to help NPOs solve their operational limitations. NPOs having financial constraints could apply for funding through a fund-raising program and a venture philanthropy program. NPO projects *Exhibition* and *Social Entrepreneur Magazine* programs provide a channel to philanthropic promotion and advocacy. Impact investment and community services concentrated on service provision for disadvantaged groups as well as residents in the local community. Taking organization X as an example, X, which was incubated by NPI in 2006, is an environmental protection NPO in Guangdong province. X has received continuous support from NPI, including the working space provision, basic capacity building training, and program funding from its early stage. Moreover, it has a long-term partnership with NPI till now. Currently, its services not only focus on Guangdong, but other provinces of China. X has earned recognition from the public for its outstanding performance in environmental protection.

To accelerate NPOs' evolution and sustainability, NPI started to shift its present services models into three major service platforms. Combining the previous designs with the new initiations, these new service mechanisms became more dynamic. The core idea of Social Entrepreneurship Platform (SEP) is to invite NPOs to get involved in a platform, in order to improve their capacity and seek resources. By partnering with the government, practical NPOs, community development representatives and residents, the LIREN Platform for community building (LP) program intended to build the community with a more interactive method. NPI Philanthropy Consultation Group (NCG) focuses on NPOs sustainable development, and promoting the frequent communication among NPOs. NCG intends to build a national network itself to achieve these goals. Concurrently, professional consultation on strategic planning as well as program evaluation demonstrate NCG's ability to support NPOs development.

## ANALYSIS AND FINDINGS

Organizational strategic planning relies on the internal arrangement and external environment (Scott & Davis, 2006), which frequently changes. As such, organizations need to respond to external changes appropriately to ensure their survival. NPI's decision-making process is influenced by the changes in both internal and external environments. The balanced view from four different aspects can provide NPI with a general view on its current status of performance with the purpose to facilitate the organizational mission making and the organizational strategic planning procedure. It will ensure NPI's short or even long-term success.

### Organizational Internal Analysis

The mission and vision of NPI were clearly stated at the early stage of its business. In particular, NPI aims to advance social innovation and to promote social entrepreneurship in China. Additionally, NPI aims to empower Chinese social entrepreneurs and NPO practitioners providing professional service and transmitting public opinions to NPOs. NPI is pragmatic and advocates for the interests of NPOs through these actions. Besides, NPI also focuses on increasing the number of NPOs and social enterprises with the greatest potential, and continues to serve NPOs professionally. Last but not least, NPI is trying its best to avoid overstepping the boundary of a NSO. Once the goals of solving a specific problem are achieved, NPI would shift its focus to other challenges.

### Customer Perspective

NSO has two main objectives. One is enhancing organizational capacities, while the other is assisting organizations to solve social issues effectively. In the early stage of NPI, start-up NPOs were the primary customer of NPI because of their potential contributions to Chinese non-profit sector. Various supports like resources, training and working spaces are provided by NPI. During the past few years, an increasing number of NPOs appeared in China. While some of these NPOs are resourceful, others lack professional skills and essential resources.

However, these two types of NPOs faced some similar issues in their operational process as well as some distinctive issues within their organizations. All of them sought support from NPI. It is unfeasible that NPI merely concentrates on the newly-established NPOs. Broadening the customer base is strategically important to maintain NPI's business. Furthermore, the previous service plan limited the support allocated to NPOs to only one year. Obviously, a limited timeframe is insufficient to meet organizational needs. As a result, many incubated organizations still do not have the ability to survive independently based on the feedbacks from staffs in NPI. It is necessary to provide services and supports to all involved NPOs to ensure they build the capability of independent operation. Values like creating opportunities to communicate and collaborate with other key stakeholders have been delivered via this method to customers.

## Financial Perspective

In order to ensure financial viability, stability and autonomy, NPI has attempted to build a diverse donor base. Previous financial strategies allowed NPI mainly to receive substantial funding from the government. Despite the stability of this funding source, relying solely on the government for funding came with many constraints as well. Even though NPI tried to obtain resources from other sectors, government funding still constitutes the largest income source. This dependency impedes NPI's ability to execute its functions in the non-profit sector to some extent. In an attempt to satisfy the needs of all kinds of NPOs, NPI started to come up with other solutions to broaden its service scope and service availability. The engagement of different actors like those from the business sector and foundations is of critical importance to NPI. This solution permits NPI to build a healthier financial system to support its operations.

## Internal Process Perspective

Adopting an internal process perspective can help organizations meet customer demands and organizational financial goals. In support of this perspective, NPI needed to set up various goals within this perspective. In the early stage, NPI paid serious attention to the relationship with the government, for maintaining a sustainable relationship was crucial for NPI. More recently, NPI has begun diversifying its stakeholder group by actively promoting and advocating its values and missions not only to the government, but also to companies, foundations, and other NPOs. Stakeholders do not merely donate money to NPI, they have the opportunities to participate in related programs as well. As a result, permanent and temporary collaborations have been built between NPI and other key stakeholders. It leverages more stakeholders to drive change and achieve its goals.

On the operational level, NPI has a good arrangement of the organizational structure and human resources. Each department and staff have their specific work focusing on different fields. For example, high levels of specialization have enabled the organization to respond effectively to both internal and external environments. According to the arrangement, organization could have a quick and accurately respond to the changes of the organizational environment. Concerning the program implementation, NPI did a lot for improving the situation. NPI has made efforts in identifying organizational needs and satisfying these local and specific needs. Programs have been enhanced so that NPOs in different stages of their life cycle could benefit from NPI's program. The coverage of program has been expended geographically as well. In order to ensure the effectiveness of these implemented programs, NPI monitors and executes each program via various ways, such as holding regular meetings, and demanding periodic progress reports.

## Learning and Growth Perspective

In order to continuously improve the capacity and professionalization of NPI staff, employees of NPI are required to attend regular training seminars. In addition, NPI also focus on engendering a positive working environment. The intent is to create a positive working culture among staffs that will foster open communication and attitudes between staffs and NPI. A policy is an opportunity window. The policy window assists mangers to identify potential opportunities that exist around the organization and then grasp the chance to address the issue in the manager's agenda (Ren & Guo, 2011). Three components of the window could help managers to identify the opportunity. They exist in parallel to and independent of one another in the organizational environment. When three streams converge, the possibility of putting the proposed issue on the current plan would increase. NPI's success could be considered as a response of the opening of the opportunity window.

# ORGANIZATIONAL EXTERNAL ANALYSIS

## Problem Stream

The rapid growth of society leads to a burgeoning demand on social services. The limited service providers and their low effectiveness in service delivery cannot meet growing demands. Improvements in service effectiveness are therefore crucial. Even though some measures have been taken to overcome the service dilemma, little progress has been made. Seeking an alternative to enhance the traditional method in order to cultivate the qualified NPOs has attracted managers' serious attention.

## Political Stream

In 2013 Xi Jinping replaced Hu Jintao in the highest government office. Tensions continue to exist between the Chinese government and NPOs. In recent months, The Charity Law, Overseas NGO management Law have been issued. More recently drafts of regulations for the registration of foundations and social services organizations, reflecting an increasingly restrictive political environment. According to our observation, those regulations temporarily did not generate any negative impact on NSOs. However, it remains to be seen in the future.

In contrast, the government's positive shift in attitude towards NPOs promotes the development of NPOs and improves NSO's capacity. NPOs are becoming increasingly critical service partners as they shoulder some of the government's responsibility in service provision. Furthermore, the Chinese government in different layers have continued to support the establishment of NSOs to promote the development of NPOs. In 2013, The Ministry of Civil affairs also highlighted the development of NSO in one of its official document called 'The ministry of civil affairs notices on the activity of building the national social services organizational innovation demonstration region'. Significant progress in terms of NSOs' development have been made in Jiangsu province, Shanghai and other coastal cities in the past few years (Ma & Liao, 2015).

NPI's successful implementation of non-profit incubator project has demonstrated that this project can be a viable alternative to remedy the previous model. The government also acknowledged the feasibility of this model, and has since invested tangible and intangible resources in this project. Recently, numerous non-profit incubators have been established by the government or NPOs. The government's strategic shift in attitudes towards NPOs provides additional opportunities to promote this model on a wider scale. These interrelated phenomena are indicative of the opening of the opportunity window.

## Policy Stream

Both scholars and practitioners have tried to enhance the effectiveness and capacity of NPOs via different methods. Limitations have been identified during the implementation period. The integration of the cross-sector and within sector collaboration that NPI adopts has some obvious advantages. Most stakeholders are involved and monitor the whole process, and all participants can obtain benefits through the collaborations. Technically, the applied business-like strategic model highlights resource and information sharing and collaboration among NPOs with other stakeholders. The goal of this model is to foster self-sufficiency in the non-profit sector. The feasibility and effectiveness of this business model convinced different interest groups and achieved consensus among interest groups to a certain extent.

## Policy Entrepreneur

As the initiator and advocator of this model, NPI had a better understanding on the current organizational development status, and identified the opportunity to apply this innovative model in solving urgent issues at the right time. Derived from the business sector, NPI adopts the platform model and applies it in advancing the development of the Chinese non-profit sector. The different and distinctive needs of each organization have been accounted for during the exploration of platform model in NPI. Each sub-project using the platform model focuses on a specific organizational management issue, which aims to resolve urgent issues extant in the Chinese non-profit sector. NPI has conceived context-relevant strategies to account for unique geographic characteristic when implementing the platform model in a specific location. The localization of the model fits with both local contexts and non-profit contexts.

Since NPI operates in an authoritarian regime, NPI needs to pay close attention to the influences of the government. NPI made substantial efforts to involve the government in platform model from the early stage. Issues were solved via NPI's efforts, which invited the government to be involved in this platform continuously. Additionally, the gradual changes of government attitudes toward the non-profit sector also promoted the development of platform model. The first success of the model in Shanghai marked the turning point for the implementation and expansion of this platform resulting in the increased willingness of the government to embrace this model. The participation of business sector, foundations and other key actors in the current model also contributed to the success of the platform model in the Chinese non-profit sector.

Furthermore, NPI has continuously diversified its revenue sources to sustain the operation of the platform. An evidence-based planning on the working arrangement has enabled the model to respond to different organizational needs in a timely manner. The success of the platform model is also a result of effective human resources management. The current service platform is an extension of non-profit incubator. In the early stage, NPI focused more narrowly on a particular group: newly established NPOs. NPI was more concerned with ensuring the sustainable development of these new and young organizations in China.

However, along with the development of non-profit sector and the increased needs of NPOs, the focus on new and young NPOs is not enough to solve the developmental issues in the Chinese non-profit sector. As NPOs mature, they are no longer eager to be incubated by a professional NSO. Instead, they need more support in other fields which could ensure their continued professionalization and maintain their competitive advantages. What's more, a large number of non-profit incubators have been established in China, in order to achieve organizational sustainability. NPI has adapted, for example, in its service clients scope and diversify service field. Since then, NPI started to reform this model, which aims at integrating and expanding existing services to provide long-term and continuous services to the participating NPO who are at different organizational life cycle stages, and have various needs.

## DISCUSSION

Thus far this chapter has explored the implication of business strategic model in China and how is it being achieved under the authoritarian regime through the description and analysis of NPI and its strategic plan rearrangement. In this section, we will attempt to explain how the authoritarian regime shapes the success of NPI, then take a deeper look at the platform model and draw out its implication for NPOs, particularly in China. Lastly, we focus attention on the debate about the business orientation of NPOs in China.

### Platform Model

Originating from the business sector, the use of the platform model enables companies to maximize their benefits through their interaction with other companies or organizations. The business sector has continuously used this model in recent years, with positive results. The platform model aims to facilitate interactions between two or more organizations, to encourage organizations to share and learn new knowledge from each other, and meet their own demands via the platform. Besides, organizations that adopt the platform model will strategically seek more potential opportunities. The platform model tends to have a win-win situation among the involved organizations.

Furthermore, the core idea of the platform model is to cultivate a better, and strong enough ecosystem within the particular sector (Xu & Yu, 2014) so as to accelerate the development of the sector. Thus building a platform does not simply mean providing a channel or some mediatory services to organizations. Rather, building a platform necessitates a comprehensive understanding of a specific sector and responding appropriately. The platform model challenges the traditional development path of relying on a single power to advance the social development. The platform strives to connect potential organizations, so as to achieve a network effects (network externality) (Katz & Shapiro, 1985) via cross-sector collaboration.

The platform model is a dynamic process. Organizations would experience a long-term developmental process to accomplish the planned tasks. Organizations who intend to apply this model are required to set up an accurate statement of organizational missions and values which is important for attracting potential clients. The number of involved organizations cannot be lower than the threshold. Technically, the threshold could be determined by organization itself: how many participants could ensure the fundamental operation of the platform. Otherwise the platform would fail.

However, once the potential clients trust that the organization would benefit them, the bandwagon effect would start to affect the platform that an increasing number of NPOs willing to participate in the platform. This would be a gradual accumulative process. When the number of involved organizations reach the tipping point, the benefits are maximized (Figure 4). The key to sustainability is ensuring the platform can maintain a stable number of organizations.

NPI was a leader in introducing the business concept of the platform model, and adapted it for the Chinese non-profit sector. The platform has achieved some progress in advancing the Chinese non-profit sector's development. At present, more and more NPOs started to build the non-profit platform in China. Even though the non-profit sector and business sector have their own distinctive characteristics and values, the implementation of platform model in non-profit sector reflects a similar path with the implementation in the business sector based on our observations.

Theoretically, organizational theories have emphasized the advantage of collective actions or collaboration (Pfeffer & Salancik, 1978; Granovetter, 1985; Williamson, 1991; Meyer & Scott, 1992). The platform model has combined the advantages of these theories. One of the core values of the platform model is to emphasize the involvement of the government, business sector and other key stakeholders. In other words, the platform model can be considered as a collaborative strategy. Apart from the exploration and practice of collaboration, the platform model expands collaborative mechanism as well. Regarding the new public management (NPM) reform (Kaboolian, 1998), the platform model is a persuasive practice to support the main argument of NPM that encourages more collaborations among different sectors, and promotes the application of the argument of NPM to the non-profit sector.

*Figure 4. Developmental path of platform model*

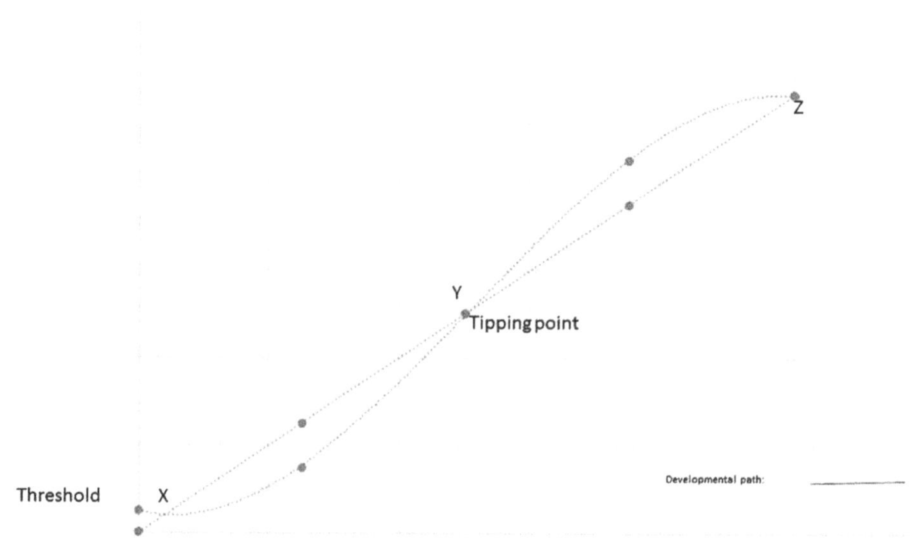

There is a consensus among scholars and practitioners that the fierce competition among NPOs is the result of varied reasons, such as limited resources, decreased government funding, unstable human resources. A single power may not easily handle the wicked problems in society (Levin, Cashore, Bernstein, & Auld, 2012). Hence, a collaborative perspective often has been promoted in the non-profit sector. The platform model provides an alternative for NPOs to explore the practice of collaboration.

The platform model has a high degree of openness, allowing for NPOs working in the same filed or at the same location to join the platform voluntarily, which could reinforce the relationship and stimulate frequent communication and resource-sharing among involved NPOs. On the other hand, the platform model is also an effective method to mobilize resources within this sector as well as resources deriving from other sectors. The greater number of NPOs involve in the platform, the more information related to their customers could be obtained. Such information help NPOs improve their performance in service delivery. Evidently, the platform model is one of the strategies that harmonizes the developmental trend of NPOs and the advancement of the non-profit sector.

Although many NPOs in China face similar challenges, they still have discrepancy in difficulties based on different developmental characteristics during their daily operation. Adopting the platform model could be a good option. However, it should be cautioned that different dynamics exist in the Chinese non-profit sector compared to non-profit sectors typically found in the West. Firstly, the Chinese government regards NPOs as a possible threat to maintaining social stability, the status quo. In the past few decades, the Chinese government has closely monitored the activities of NPOs. The dual registration system and other regulations have significantly restricted the development of NPOs. Not until the recent reform of philanthropic laws were NPOs allowed to register directly with the Ministry of Civil Affairs. Even so, it is unlikely that this is an indication of a 'relaxing' political environment.

The emergence of the platform model and its adaptation in the Chinese non-profit sector has led to possible solutions to deal with the local government in recent years. The platform model provides opportunities to the local government, so that the local government could have a better understanding on NPOs and build trust between them through direct experience with civil society. The local government, as a result, has partnered with NPOs and has changed the related regulations. These changes in the government are a result of 'a process of authoritarian learning' whereby the direct experience with civil society and observation act as feedback leading these 'endogenous institutional change' (Teets, 2014: 6). Concurrently, limited capacities hinder Chinese NPOs to evolve into professional service deliverers. In addition, the unbalanced resource and funding distribution is a common situation in the Chinese non-profit sector.

NPOs who have had an intimate relationship with government have the priority to receive most of resources and funding. The adoption of the platform model has (re)balanced the resource and funding distribution mechanisms. Through this way, the intensified competition among NPOs could be relieved to some extent. With regards to NPOs capacity, the platform model is a catalyst for innovation for NPOs. The platform model aims at professionalizing NPOs. In China, NPOs have a big problem in public accountability. With the support of the platform model, this problem could be addressed through a multiple monitoring process as well as enhancing the trust between NPOs and publics. The adaptability of NPOs in the non-profit sector environment has also been improved through the platform model. Therefore, the case of NPI demonstrates that the platform can be adapted to the current situation of China and push the progress of Chinese NPOs' evolution.

## BUSINESS ORIENTATIOIN IN NON-PROFIT SECTOR

A growing subset of Chinese NPOs have started to adopt business models into their operation. This trend has attracted considerable debate. On the one hand, proponents of the business model argue that adopting business strategies in non-profit management is the most effective way to enhance the capacities of organizations (Xu, 2014; Zhang, 2013, Zhu, 2016). The implementation of business model in non-profit context had a big social impact on the society. Moreover, the business model could also help the Chinese non-profit sector to become more professional. On the other hand, some opponents criticize that the business model may not be the ideal model to advance the Chinese non-profit sector. Since business model would intensify unfair competition among Chinese NPOs (Qu, 2016), NPOs cannot rely on business model to solve the relationship with government (NGOCN, 2014). Lastly, adopting business strategies may threaten the inherent and distinctive integrity of the non-profit sector (NGOCN, 2014, Maier et al., 2016), which may influence NPOs operation.

It is clear that adopting a business model can offer potential solutions for managerial issues faced by current NPOs in a more effective way. Evidence from Western countries also highlights the advantages of adopting the market-orientation strategies in the non-profit sector (Choi, 2012; Cooney, 2011). Some NPOs have a business like organizational formation or operation, and some may have the business like goals to direct their operational goals. Thus far, various innovative ideas and a practical model like the platform model can support the Chinese non-profit sector to achieve sustainable development in the long-term. Business orientation may also transform the philanthropic operational dynamic from the traditional practice that follows the fundamental rules to manage organizations and lacks frequent interaction with other organization, to a modernized practice that brings together various ideas from the business sector or other well-developed organizations.

However, we cannot merely focus on the benefits that business-like strategic model potentially brings to the non-profit sector without acknowledging the need to balance the trade-offs in such convergence. It is critical to maintain the value of philanthropy. The implementation of a business strategy is a method or tool for improving performance, and not simply a pathway to marketization. Secondly, utilizing business strategy in the non-profit context does not mean the nature of non-profit is changed. Taking the Horizon Corporate Voluntary Consultancy (HCVC) as an example, it is a grassroots NPO in China, who adopt the business strategy to operate its project since it has been established, and never changed the nature of non-profit. Last but not least, a business strategy is not a panacea. Not every problem can be solved simply by adopting a business-like strategic model. A considerable analysis of the internal management and external environment (political environment, non-profit sector environment) is the first step to decide the organizational strategic model.

## CONCLUSION

In this chapter, we have explored a representative Chinese case: NPI, who has a successful experience on the implication of business strategic model in non-profit setting. From the beginning of its development, the business-oriented strategies have supported its growth and operation. Taking NPI as the evidence, we have argued that the business-like strategic model is feasible in the authoritarian context. There is no any obvious disparity between its implementation compared to democratic regimes. The business strategic model possibly could be regarded as one of the options for organizational sustainable development.

Using the single case study method, we have attempted to dig out the evidence to illustrate the successful implication of business strategic model in China, and guide its further implementation. We applied two analytic frameworks: the balanced scorecard and the policy window. They provide an integrated view to explore NPI and its decision on it strategic planning from internal management system and organizational external environment.

Firstly, the balanced scorecard examines an organizational performance from four different angles. It enables organizational managers to grasp the advantages and disadvantages extant in an organization, and thereby formulate appropriate responses to organizational challenges. Secondly, policy window facilitates the managers to develop better understanding of the organizational external environment. Managers could prioritize organizational plan to respond to issues. Combining both internal and external analysis, managers could appropriately make the decision on organization development. A full consideration of organizational internal and external environment is essential and could ensure organizations make a correct choice of the strategic plan.

The platform model is not only a method to facilitate the development of NPOs. It is a way to enhance the relationship between the non-profit sector and other sectors. In this case, it is observed that the platform model has introduced feasible strategies to Chinese NPOs. The effectiveness and professionalization of NPOs have made considerable progress through the platform model. This model encourages and attracts increased attention from business sector and the government. Their engagement boosts the operation of platform model in our study.

The platform, to some extent, arouses willingness of these two sectors to become involved in nonprofits' developmental process. Most importantly, the Chinese government appears eager to be increasingly involved with the development of NPOs. We believe that the political elements may encourage the application of business in non-profit context, rather than hinder the implementation of it, even under the authoritarian regime. Considering the current Chinese status, the platform model would be a feasible way to practicing the business model in non-profit context. The platform has shed light on both internal and external environments. Adopting the platform model, organizations could identify and respond to the changes effectively. The platform also generates opportunities to Chinese non-profit sector to build a healthier ecosystem. The combination of NSO and platform model enables NPOs mobilize various resources to ensure the success of business model in the Chinese non-profit sector.

This study proves that the business strategic model under the authoritarian regime in China also has a positive effect on organizational performance or management. The business model may diversify the founding sources and enhance the developmental situation of the Chinese NPOs as well as the non-profit sector. The business strategic model is not the only option for NPOs, however, the business oriented strategies and models emphasize and encourage organizations pay an increasingly attention on the relationship with their clients, key stakeholders for their sustainability, like what NPI has done in their operation. A previous study (Hu & Zheng, 2008) also highlights that organizations need to put the customer needs as the top priority. The intimate relationship with their clients could enhance their effectiveness of service delivery. Moreover, the advantage of the business strategic model is taking the external relationship with each stakeholder seriously.

The business strategic model as applied in the non-profit setting can help NPOs to maintain a stable relationship with their stakeholders, particularly with the government, so as to achieve the long term organizational goals. Regarding the Chinese regime, NPOs are expected to have a full consideration of the relationship with the government. Lessons learned from the target organization that the politics elements may generate more opportunities to promote NPOs' growth, in contrast, it may impede the development of NPOs. The implementation of business-like strategic model in Chinese non-profit sector is still in its early stages. Future research may focus on the:

1. Preconditions and process of applying business model, and how this model shapes non-profits behaviours.
2. Potential trade-offs in applying business-like strategies in the non-profit sector warrant further research.
3. More empirical studies have been called for pushing the research and practice to a new stage.

## REFERENCES

Berg, B. (2009). *Qualitative Research Methods for the Social Sciences*. Boston: Allyn & Bacon.

Brown, L. D., & Kalegaokar, A. (1999). Addressing civil society's challenges: Support organizations as emerging institutions. *Institute for Development Research*, *15*(2), 1–20.

Brown, L. D., & Kalegaokar, A. (2002). Support Organizations and the evolution of the NGO sector. *Nonprofit and Voluntary Sector Quarterly*, *31*(2), 231–258. doi:10.1177/0899764002312004

Carroll, T. F. (1992). *Intermediary NGOs: the supporting link in grassroots development*. West Hartford, CT: Kumarian Press.

Chen, J. (2012). *Transnational Civil Society in China: Intrusion and Impact*. Edward Elgar Publishing.

Choi, S. M. (2012). Learning Orientation and Market orientation as catalysts for innovation in non-profit organizations. *Nonprofit and Voluntary Sector Quarterly*, *43*(2), 393–413. doi:10.1177/0899764012465491

Cooney, K. (2011). An Exploratory Study of social purpose business models in the United States. *Nonprofit and Voluntary Sector Quarterly*, *40*(1), 185–196. doi:10.1177/0899764009351591

Cornforth, C., Hayes, J. P., & Vangen, S. (2015). Nonprofit–Public Collaborations Understanding Governance Dynamics. *Nonprofit and Voluntary Sector Quarterly*, *44*(4), 775–795. doi:10.1177/0899764014532836

Dart, R. (2004). Being business-like in a non-profit organization: A ground and inductive typology. *Nonprofit and Voluntary Sector Quarterly*, *33*(2), 290–310. doi:10.1177/0899764004263522

Edward, M., & Hulme, D. (Eds.). (1992). *Making a difference: NGOs and development in a changing world*. London: Earthscan.

Emerson, J., & Twersky, F. (Eds.). (1996). *New social entrepreneurs: The success, challenge, and lessons of non-profit enterprise creation*. San Francisco: The Roberts Foundation.

Fowler, A. (1997). *Striking a balance: A guide to enhancing the effective of NGOs in international development*. London: Earthscan.

Granovetter, M. (1985). Economic action and social structure: A theory of embeddedness. *American Journal of Sociology*, *91*(3), 481–510. doi:10.1086/228311

Guo, C., & Bielefeld, W. (2014). *Social entrepreneurship: An evidence-based approach to creating social value*. John Wiley & Sons.

Hartnerr, B., & Matan, R. (2011). The balanced scorecard: A strategic tool for the non-profit sector. Retrieved from http://www.sobel-cpa.com/resources/white-papers

Hu, Y., & Zheng, W. (2008, October). Market orientation, innovation and performance of non-profit organizations: evidence from China. In *Service Operations and Logistics, and Informatics, 2008. IEEE/SOLI 2008. IEEE International Conference on* (Vol. 1, pp. 429-434). IEEE.

Hvenmark, J. (2013). Business as usual? On managerialization and the adoption of the balanced scorecard in a democratically governed civil society organization. *Administrative Theory and Praxis*, *35*(2), 223–247. doi:10.2753/ATP1084-1806350203

Kaboolian, L.Administration Debate. (1998). The new public management: Challenging the boundaries of the management vs. administration debate. *Public Administration Review*, *58*(3), 189–193. doi:10.2307/976558

Kaplan, R., & Norton, D. (1992). The Balanced Scorecard – Measures That Drive Performance. *Harvard Business Review*, *70*(1), 71–79. PMID:10119714

Katz, M. L., & Shapiro, C. (1985). Network externalities, competitions, and compatibility. *The American Economic Review*, *75*, 424–444.

Kearns, K. (2000). *Private sector strategies for social sector success*. San Francisco: Jossey-Bass.

Keevers, L., Treleaven, L., Sykes, C., & Darcy, M. (2012). Made to measure: Taming practices with results-based accountability. *Organization Studies*, *33*(1), 97–120. doi:10.1177/0170840611430597

Kingdon, J. W. (1984). *Agendas, alternatives and public politics*. Boston: Little Brown.

Kuosmanen, J. (2014). Care provision, empowerment, and market forces: The art of establishing legitimacy for work integration social enterprise. *Voluntas*, *25*(1), 248–269. doi:10.1007/s11266-012-9340-7

Levin, K., Cashore, B., Bernstein, S., & Auld, G. (2012). Overcoming the tragedy of super wicked problems: Constraining our future selves to ameliorate global climate change. *Policy Sciences*, *45*(2), 123–152. doi:10.1007/s11077-012-9151-0

Maier, F., Myer, M., & Steinbereithner, M. (2016). Non-profit organizations beyond business-like: A systematic review. *Nonprofit and Voluntary Sector Quarterly*, *45*(1), 64–86. doi:10.1177/0899764014561796

Martello, M. M., Waston, J. G., & Fischer, M. J. (2008). Implementing a balanced scorecard in a not-for-profit organization. *Journal of Business and Economics Research*, *6*(9), 67–80.

Meyer, J. W., & Scott, W. R. (1992). *Organizational environments, ritual and rationality*. Newbury Park, CA: Sage.

Mosley, J. E. (2012). Collaboration, Public-Private Intermediary Organizations, and the Transformation of Advocacy in the Field of Homeless Services. *American Review of Public Administration*.

NGOCN. (2014). *NGO, market is there, where is fair?* China Development Brief. Retrieved from: http://www.chinadevelopmentbrief.org.cn/news-16622.html

NGOCN. (2015). *Research on government cultivates social organizations and policies innovations*. Guangdong: NGOCN.

Niven, P. R. (2003). *Balanced scorecard step-by-step for government and non-profit agencies*. Hoboken, NJ: Wiley.

NPO Development Centre. (2014). *Report on the status quo of Chinese non-profit support organizations and the list of non-profit support organizations*. Shanghai: Academic Press.

Osborne, S., & Tricker, M. (1994). Local development agencies: Supporting voluntary action. *Nonprofit Management & Leadership*, *5*(1), 37–52. doi:10.1002/nml.4130050105

Pardon, M. (1987). Non-governmental development organizations: From development aid to development cooperation. *World Development*, *15*(Suppl.), 69–77. doi:10.1016/0305-750X(87)90144-6

Pfeffer, J., & Salancik, G. R. (1978). *The external control of organizations: A resource dependence perspective*. New York: Harper and Row.

Qu, C. (2016). *The beautiful word: The dusk of philanthropy. A reflection on the market oriented philanthropy*. China Development Brief. Retrieved from: http://www.chinadevelopmentbrief.org.cn/news-18466.html

Ren, C. R., & Guo, C. (2011). Middle managers strategic role in the corporate entrepreneurial process: Attention-based effects. *Journal of Management*, *37*(6), 1586–1610. doi:10.1177/0149206310397769

Sanyal, P. (2006). Capacity building through partnership: Intermediary nongovernmental organizations as local and global actors. *Nonprofit and Voluntary Sector Quarterly*, *35*(1), 66–82. doi:10.1177/0899764005282480

Scott, W. R., & Davis, G. F. (2006). *Organizations and organizing: Rational, natural and open systems perspectives*. Routledge.

Shea, J. (2011). Taking Non-profit Intermediaries Seriously: A Middle-Range Theory for Implementation Research. *Public Administration Review*, *71*(1), 57–66. doi:10.1111/j.1540-6210.2010.02306.x

Takahashi, L. M., & Smutny, G. (2002). Collaborative windows and organizational governance: Exploring the formation and demise of social service partnership. *Nonprofit and Voluntary Sector Quarterly*, *31*(2), 165–185. doi:10.1177/0899764002312001

Teets, J. C. (2014). *Civil Society under authoritarianism: The China model*. Cambridge University Press. doi:10.1017/CBO9781139839396

Vakil, A. C. (1997). Confronting the classification problem: Towards a taxonomy of NGOs. *World Development*, *25*(12), 2057–2070. doi:10.1016/S0305-750X(97)00098-3

Wang, D. (2015). The summary research of supporting social organization. *Journal of Zhengzhou Institute of Aeronautical Industry Management*, *33*(1), 110–113.

Wang, S. Q. (2012). Non-profit incubator: an important support organization. *The Academic Journal of Chengdu Administrative College*, *5*, 83-88.

Williamson, O. E. (1991). Comparative economic organization: The analysis of discrete structural alternatives. *Administrative Science Quarterly*, *36*(2), 269–296. doi:10.2307/2393356

Xu, J. L., Lu, Y. B., & Cao, F. H. (2014). The construction of non-profit incubators value Chain. China Public Administration, 12, 20-24.

Xu, Y. G. (2014). The discussion of market-oriented philanthropy. Chinese Philanthropic. Retrieved from http://www.chinadevelopmentbrief.org.cn/news-16408.html

Xu, Y. S. (2010). The structural innovation of social organizations. *Research on Organization Management*, *8*, 22-25.

Zeng, K. (2012). The development of the social organization and its incremental layout. *Organization Management and Research*, *7*, 13–17.

Zhang, W. Y. (2013). *Philanthropy need the business logic*. Chinese Philanthropic. Retrieved from: http://sdg.shanda960.com/article/6687

Zhu, Y. (2016). *Three stages of market oriented non-profit donation*. Philanthropic Learning Group. Retrieved from: http://www.chinadevelopmentbrief.org.cn/news-18469.ht

## KEY TERMS AND DEFINITIONS

**GONGOs:** A type of non-profit organization which is established by government. This kind of non-profit organization is more common in China.

**LIREN Platform:** This is one of the main project focusing on community resilience, which is initiated by our target organization (NPI). LIREN is translated from a Chinese word, which means a harmonious community.

**NGOCN:** A website for the communication among all Chinese non-profit organizations. It is one of the famous social platform in China (www.ngocn.net).

**NPI:** A non-profit support organization in China, which is also the only target organization in our study as well as in this chapter (www.npi.org.cn).

**NPO Development Centre:** A non-profit support organization in China that mainly concentrates on organizational capacity building and human resources development (www.npodevelopment.org).

# Compilation of References


Aaker, J., Vohs, K. D., & Mogilner, C. (2010). Nonprofits are seen as warm and for-profits as competent: Firm stereotypes matter. *The Journal of Consumer Research*, *37*(2), 224–237. doi:10.1086/651566

Abate, D., Hoffman, D., Robertson, N., Rogers, A., & Zeppenfeld, G. (2011). *The Use of Social Media in the Workplace.* Mayer-Brown. Retrieved from https://www.mayerbrown.com/public_docs/TheUseofSocialMediainTheWorkplace.pdf

ABC Foundation (1995-2014). *Annual Reports 1995-2014.* New York, NY: Author.

Aboelmaged, M. G. (2010). Predicting e-procurement adoption in a developing country: An empirical integration of technology acceptance model and theory of planned behaviour. *Industrial Management & Data Systems*, *110*(3), 392–414. doi:10.1108/02635571011030042

Acedo, F. J., & Florin, J. (2007). Understanding the risk perception of strategic opportunities: A tripartite model. *Strategic Change*, *16*(3), 97–116. doi:10.1002/jsc.787

Achleitner, A. K., Spiess-Knafl, W., & Volk, S. (2014). The financing structure of social enterprises: Conflicts and implications. *International Journal of Entrepreneurial Venturing*, *6*(1), 85–99. doi:10.1504/IJEV.2014.059404

Achtenhagen, L., Melin, L., & Naldi, L. (2013). Dynamics of business models – strategizing, critical capabilities and activities for sustained value creation. *Long Range Planning*, *46*(6), 427–442. doi:10.1016/j.lrp.2013.04.002

Acılar, A. (2015). The Use of Social Media in the Higher Education Institutions in Turkey: A Case of the Higher Education Institutions in Istanbul. In Strategic Customer Relationship Management in the Age of Social Media (pp. 95-107). Hershey, PA: Business Science Reference. Doi:10.4018/978-1-4666-8586-4.ch006

Acılar, A., & Mersin, S. (2015). Undergraduate Students' Attitudes Toward Facebook Use. *CKS 2015 – Challenges of the Knowledge Society.* Retrieved from http://cks.univnt.ro/download/138_cks_2015.pdf

Adams, J. (1991). Issues in the management of careers. Contemporary Career Development Issues, 1-24.

Adecco Group. (2014). *GlobalRecruiting – A Global Study.* Rapor 2014 Türkiye. Author.

Aghaei, S., Nematbakhsh, M. A., & Farsani, H. K. (2012). Evolution of the World Wide Web: From Web 1 to Web 4. *International Journal of Web & Semantic Technology*, *3*(1), 1–10. doi:10.5121/ijwest.2012.3101

Aguinis, H., & Glavas, A. (2012). What we know and dont know about corporate social responsibility: A review and research agenda. *Journal of Management*, *38*(4), 932–968. doi:10.1177/0149206311436079

Ahokangas, P., & Myllykoski, J. (2014). The practice of creating and transforming a business model. *Journal Business Models*, *2*, 6–18.

Aiken, M. (2007). What is the role of social enterprise in finding, creating and maintaining employment for disadvantaged groups. Social Enterprise Think Piece for the Office of the Third Sector, Cabinet Office, London.

Ajzen, I. (1991). The theory of planned behavior. *Organizational Behavior and Human Decision Processes*, *50*(2), 179–211. doi:10.1016/0749-5978(91)90020-T

Akerkar, R. (2014). *Big Data Computing*. Boca Raton, FL: CRC Press.

Akgün, A. E., & Keskin, H. (2014). Organisational resilience capacity and firm product innovativeness and performance. *International Journal of Production Research*, *52*(23), 6918–6937. doi:10.1080/00207543.2014.910624

Akingbola, K. (2006). Strategy and HRM in nonprofit organizations: Evidence from Canada. *International Journal of Human Resource Management*, *17*(10), 1707–1725. doi:10.1080/09585190600964350

Albareda, L., & Balaguer, M. R. (2007). La responsabilidad social de la empresa y los resultados financieros. Contabilidad y dirección, Barcelona.

Aldashev, G., Jaimovich, E., & Verdier, T. (2016). *Small is Beautiful: Motivational Allocation in the Non-Profit Sector.* ECARES Working Papers.

Alesina, A., & Dollar, D. (2000). Who gives foreign aid to whom and why? *Journal of Economic Growth*, *5*(1), 33–63. doi:10.1023/A:1009874203400

Alexander, J. (2000). Adaptive strategies of non-profit human service organizations in an era of devolution and new public management. *Nonprofit Management & Leadership*, *10*(3), 287–303. doi:10.1002/nml.10305

Al-Ghaith, W. A., Sanzogni, L., & Sandhu, K. (2010). Factors influencing the adoption and usage of online services in Saudi Arabia. *The Electronic Journal of Information Systems in Developing Countries*, *40*(1), 1–32.

Allen, T. J., & Katz, R. (1986). The dual ladder: Motivational solution or managerial delusion? *R & D Management*, *16*(2), 185–197. doi:10.1111/j.1467-9310.1986.tb01171.x

Allyn, D. (2010). Mission mirroring: Understanding conflict in nonprofit organizations. *Nonprofit and Voluntary Sector Quarterly*, *40*(4), 762–769. doi:10.1177/0899764010370869

Al-Somali, S. A., Gholami, R., & Clegg, B. (2009). An investigation into the acceptance of online banking in Saudi Arabia. *Technovation*, *29*(2), 130–141. doi:10.1016/j.technovation.2008.07.004

Alston, L. J., & Gillespie, W. (1989). Resource coordination and transaction costs: A framework for analyzing the firm/market boundary. *Journal of Economic Behavior & Organization*, *11*(2), 191–212. doi:10.1016/0167-2681(89)90013-9

Alsudairi, M. A. T., & Tatapudi, G. (2014). Social innovation: Can it be a strategy for influencing GCC public welfare? *Innovation: Management. Policy & Practice*, *16*(2), 273–282. doi:10.1080/14479338.2014.11081988

Alter, K. (2007). *Social Enterprise Typology*. Retrieved from http://rinovatios.edublogs.org/files/2008/07/setypology.pdf

Alter, K. A. (2006). Social enterprise models and their mission and money relationships. In A. Nicholls (Ed.), *Social entrepreneurship: new models of sustainable social change* (pp. 205–233). Oxford, UK: Oxford University Press.

Alvarado, A., & Schlesinger, M. (2008). Dimesionalidad de la responsabilidad social empresarial percibida y sus efectos sobre la imagen y la reputación: Una aproximación desde el modelo de Carroll. *Estudios Gerenciales*, *24*(108), 37–59. doi:10.1016/S0123-5923(08)70043-3

Amaral, A., Jones, G., & Karseth, B. (2002). Governing Higher Education: National Perspectives on Institutional Governance (Vol. 1). Dordrecht: Springer Science & Business Media.

American Red Cross. (2012a). *American Red Cross FY12 Financial Results*. Retrieved from http://www.redcross.org/images/MEDIA_CustomProductCatalog/m16040150_2012_fiscal_year_auditedFinancialSta tementDocs.pdf

American Red Cross. (2012b). *Superstorm Sandy: One Month Update*. Retrieved from http://www.redcross.ca/cmslib/general/int_news_sandy_update_monthone_2012.pdf

Amin, A., Cameron, A., & Hudson, R. (1999). Welfare as work? The potential of the UK social economy. *Environment & Planning A*, *31*(11), 2033–2051. doi:10.1068/a312033

Amit, R., & Zott, C. (2001). Value creation in E-business. *Strategic Management Journal*, *22*(6/7), 493–520. doi:10.1002/smj.187

Anderson, E. (1985). The salesperson as outside agent or employee: A transaction cost analysis. *Marketing Science*, *4*(3), 234–254. doi:10.1287/mksc.4.3.234

Andreini, D., Pedeliento, G., & Signori, S. (2012). *The customer satisfaction in a nonprofit context: The role of social responsibility and its communication*. Papers of the 37th Annual Macromarketing Conference, Berlin, Germany. Retrieved from http:// macromarketing.org/wp-ontent/uploads/2011/08/Macromarketing2012Proceedings.pdf

Andrew, B. A. (2013, June 18). *How start-ups can tap cash from ordinary people and give the prospect of huge profits in return... What is crowdfunding and how does it work?* Retrieved July 9, 2016, from http://www.thisismoney.co.uk/money/smallbusiness/article-2333399/Crowdfunding-does-work.html

Andzulis, J., Panagopoulos, N. G., & Rapp, A. (2012). A review of social media and implications for the sales process. *Journal of Personal Selling & Sales Management*, *32*(3), 305–316. doi:10.2753/PSS0885-3134320302

Ang, S., van Dyne, L., Koh, C., Ng, K. Y., Templer, K. J., Tay, C., & Chandrasekar, N. A. (2007). Cultural intelligence: Its measurement and effects on cultural judgement and decision making, cultural adaptation and task performance. *Management and Organization Review*, *3*(3), 335–371. doi:10.1111/j.1740-8784.2007.00082.x

Anheier, H. K. (2005). *A Dictionary of Civil Society, Philanthropy and the Third Sector*. Routledge.

Anheier, H. K. (2005). *Nonprofit organizations: Theory, management, policy*. London: Routledge.

Anheier, H. K. (2006). *Nonprofit organizations. Theory, management, policy*. London: Routledge Taylor&Francis Group.

Anheir, H. (n.d.). *Reflections on the Global Economic Downturn, Philanthropy and Nonprofits*. Retrieved from http://www.csi.uni-hd.de/downloads/Anheier%20-%20CSI%20zur%20Krise_EN.pdf

Ansoff, H. I., & Brandenburg, R. G. (1971). A language for organization design: Part I. *Management Science*, *17*(12), B705–B716. doi:10.1287/mnsc.17.12.B705

Antony, J., Kumar, M., & Labib, A. (2008). Gearing six sigma into UK manufacturing SMEs: An empirical assessment of critical success factors, impediments, and viewpoints of six sigma implementation in SMEs. *The Journal of the Operational Research Society*, *59*(4), 482–493. doi:10.1057/palgrave.jors.2602437

Archer, N., & Ghasemzadeh, F. (2007). Project portfolio selection and management. In P. Morris & J. Pinto (Eds.), *The Wiley Guide to Project, Program and Portfolio Management* (pp. 94–113). John Wiley and Sons. doi:10.1002/9780470172391.ch11

Archibugi, D., & Filippetti, A. (2016). *The Retreat of Public Research and its Adverse Consequences on Innovation*. CIMR Research Working Paper Series, Working paper 31. Retrieved from http://www.bbk.ac.uk/innovation/publications/docs/WP31.pdf

Arena, M., Azzone, G., & Bengo, I. (2015). Performance Measurement for Social Enterprises. *VOLUNTAS: International Journal of Voluntary and Nonprofit Organizations*, *26*(2), 649–672. doi:10.1007/s11266-013-9436-8

Arenas, D., Lozano, J. M., & Albareda, L. (2009). The role of NGOs in CSR: Mutual perceptions among stakeholders. *Journal of Business Ethics*, *88*(1), 175–197. doi:10.1007/s10551-009-0109-x

Argandoña, A., (1998). *La teoría de los stakeholders y el bien común*. División de investigación IESE. Universidad De Navarra. Documento de Investigación nº. 355, Enero.

Armenakis, A., & Bedeian, A. (1999). Organizational change: A review of theory research in the 1990s. *Journal of Management*, *25*(3), 293–315. doi:10.1177/014920639902500303

Arnold, J. (2011). *Career concepts in the 21st century*. British Psychological Society.

Arslan, G. (2014). *The Use of Social Media By Labour Unions in Turkey* (Master Thesis). Pamukkale University, Graduate School of Social Sciences, Labour Economics and Industrial Relations Department, Denizli.

Arthur, M. B., & Rousseau, D. M. (1996). A career lexicon for the 21st century. *The Academy of Management Executive*, *10*(4), 28–39.

Arvidson, M., & Lyon, F. (2014). Social impact measurement and non-profit organisations: Compliance, resistance, and promotion. *VOLUNTAS: International Journal of Voluntary and Nonprofit Organizations*, *25*(4), 869–886. doi:10.1007/s11266-013-9373-6

Arvidson, M., Lyon, F., McKay, S., & Moro, D. (2010). *The ambitions and challenges of SROI*. Birmingham: TSRC.

Association of Australian Medical Research Institutes (AAMRI). (2015). *Association of Australian Medical Research Institutes*. AAMRI.

Atler, K. (2016). *Social enterprise typology*. Retrieved May 20, 2016, from http://www.4lenses.org/setypology

Attouni, M. A. K., & Mustaffa, C. S. (2014). How do Non-profit Organizations in Libya Adopt and Use Social Media to Communicate with The Society, The International Conference on Communications and Media 2014 (i-COME14), 1820 October 2014, Langkawi, Malaysia. *Procedia: Social and Behavioral Sciences*, *155*, 92–97. doi:10.1016/j.sbspro.2014.10.262

Atzori, L., Iera, A., & Morabito, G. (2010). The Internet of Things: A survey. *Computer Networks*, *54*(15), 2787–2805. doi:10.1016/j.comnet.2010.05.010

Australian Institute of Health and Welfare. (2007). Health expenditure Australia 2005–06. Health and Welfare Expenditure Series no. 30. Cat. no. HWE 37. Canberra: Author.

Australian Medical Council & Medical Board of Australia. (2013). *The National Internship Framework - Newsletter 1*. Retrieved from http://www.medicalboard.gov.au/News/2013-05-31-joint-newsletter.aspx

Australian Medical Council. (2012a). *List of Australian Recognised Medical Specialties*. Retrieved from http://www.amc.org.au/images/Recognition/AMC-list-of-specialties.pdf

Australian Medical Council. (2012b). *Specialist Medical Colleges*. Retrieved from http://www.amc.org.au/index.php/ass/apo/spp/smc

Australian Medical Students' Association (AMSA). (2015). National Internship Crisis.

Avolio, B. J. (2007). Promoting more integrative strategies for leadership theory-building. *The American Psychologist*, *62*(1), 25–33. doi:10.1037/0003-066X.62.1.25 PMID:17209677

Aziz, H. A., & El Ebrashi, R. (2016). A Business Model Design Process for Social Enterprises: The Critical Role of the Environment. *World Academy of Science, Engineering and Technology, International Journal of Social, Behavioral, Educational, Economic. Business and Industrial Engineering*, *10*(5), 1377–1383.

Baden-Fuller, C., & Haefliger, S. (2013). Business models and technological innovation. *Long Range Planning*, *46*(6), 419–426. doi:10.1016/j.lrp.2013.08.023

Bader, B., Berg, N., & Holtbrügge, D. (2013). Expatriate performance in high-risk countries: Influence of family-related stress. *Academy of Management Proceedings, 50*(1).

Bagnoli, L., & Megali, C. (2011). Measuring Performance in Social Enterprises. *Nonprofit and Voluntary Sector Quarterly*, *40*(1), 149–165. doi:10.1177/0899764009351111

Bailly, F., & Chapelle, K. (2012). The training of jobseekers by non-profit organizations: An analysis based on data from the upper Normandy region of France. *Metroeconomica*, *64*(4), 645–682.

Bandura, A. (1986). Social foundations of thought and action: A social cognitive theory. Englewood Cliffs, NJ: Prentice Hall, Inc.

Bandura, A. (1982). Self-efficacy mechanism in human agency. *The American Psychologist*, *37*(2), 122–147. doi:10.1037/0003-066X.37.2.122

Barkan, T. (2011). *Special Report: How are the members of associations using social media today?* SOCIALSTRAT, Professional Social Media Strategy.

Barker, K. J., DAmato, J., & Sheridon, P. (2008). Credit card fraud: Awareness and prevention. *Journal of Financial Crime*, *15*(4), 398–410. doi:10.1108/13590790810907236

Barnard, C. I. (1938). *The functions of the executive*. Cambridge, MA: Harvard University Press.

Barney, J. (1991). Firm resources and sustained competitive advantage. *Journal of Management*, *17*(1), 99–120. doi:10.1177/014920639101700108

Barr, A., & Fafchamps, M. (2006). A client-community assessment of the NGO sector in Uganda. *The Journal of Development Studies*, *42*(4), 611–639. doi:10.1080/00220380600682009

Barrett, M., Davidson, E., Prabhu, J., & Vargo, S. L. (2015). Service innovation in the digital age: Key contributions and future directions. *Management Information Systems Quarterly*, *39*(1), 135–154.

Baruch, Y. (2006). Career development in organisations and beyond: Balancing traditional and contemporary viewpoints. *Human Resource Management Review*, *16*(2), 125–138. doi:10.1016/j.hrmr.2006.03.002

Baruch, Y., & Reis, C. (2016). How Global Are Boundaryless Careers and How Boundaryless Are Global Careers? Challenges and a Theoretical Perspective. *Thunderbird International Business Review*, *58*(1), 13–27. doi:10.1002/tie.21712

Bassi, A. (2011). *Il valore aggiunto sociale del terzo settore. Verso un sistema di indicatori per la misurazione della performance delle imprese sociali*. Milan: QuiEdit.

Bassi, A., & Vincenti, G. (2015). Toward a new metrics for the evaluation of the social added value of social enterprises. *CIRIEC - España, Revista de Economía Pública. Social Cooperativa*, *83*, 9–42.

Batikas, M., & Bavel, R. (2013). *Assessing the Benefits of Social Networks for Organizations*. Report on the Second Phase of the SEA-SoNS Project, Publications Office. Retrieved from ftp://s-jrcsvqpx102p.jrc.es/pub/EURdoc/EURdoc/JRC85669.pdf

Battilana, J., Lee, M., Walker, J., & Dorsey, C. (2012). In Search of the Hybrid Ideal. Stanford Social Innovation Review, 10, 51–55.

Battilana, J., & Lee, M. (2014). Advancing Research on Hybrid Organizing – Insights from the Study of Social Enterprises. *The Academy of Management Annals*, *8*(1), 397–441. doi:10.1080/19416520.2014.893615

Bauer, T. N., & Taylor, S. (2001). When managing expatriate adjustment, dont forget the spouse. *The Academy of Management Executive*, *15*(4), 135–137. doi:10.5465/AME.2001.5898750

Baur, D., & Schmitz, H. P. (2012). Corporations y NGOs: When Accountability Leads to Co-optation. *Journal of Business Ethics*, *106*(1), 9–21. doi:10.1007/s10551-011-1057-9

Beal, R. M. (2000). Competing effectively: Environmental scanning, competitive strategy, and organizational performance in small manufacturing firms. *Journal of Small Business Management*, *38*(1), 27–47. Retrieved from http://ezproxy.library.capella.edu/login?url=http://search.epnet.com/login.aspx?direct=true&db=buh&an=2716872

Becher, C., Entsch, S., & Frey, M. (2011). (Forthcoming). From wisdom to wisdom of the crowd and crowdfunding. *Journal of Communication and Computer*.

Beck, J., & La Lopa, J. M. (2001). An exploratory application of Scheins career anchors inventory to hotel executive operating committee members. *International Journal of Hospitality Management*, *20*(1), 15–28. doi:10.1016/S0278-4319(00)00035-9

Beecham, R. (2014). Measuring SpICE (Specialist Integrated Community Engagement). *Australasian Journal of University-Community Engagement*, *9*(1), 56–76.

Bekkers, R. (2003). Trust, accreditation, and philanthropy in the Netherlands. *Nonprofit and Voluntary Sector Quarterly*, *32*(4), 596–615. doi:10.1177/0899764003258102

Belleflamme, P., Lambert, T., & Schwienbacher, A. (2010). Crowdfunding: An industrial organization perspective. In *Workshop Digital Business Models: Understanding Strategies* (pp. 25–26).

Belleflamme, P., Lambert, T., & Schwienbacher, A. (2010, June). Crowdfunding: An industrial organization perspective. In *Workshop Digital Business Models: Understanding Strategies* (pp. 25-26).

Belleflamme, P., Lambert, T., & Schwienbacher, A. (2013). Individual crowdfunding practices. *Venture Capital*, *15*(4), 313–333. doi:10.1080/13691066.2013.785151

Bell, M. P., & Harrison, D. A. (1996). Using intra-national diversity for inter-national assignments: A model of bicultural life experiences and expatriate adjustment. *Human Resource Management Review*, *6*(1), 47–74. doi:10.1016/S1053-4822(96)90004-2

Bellostas, A., López-Arceiz, F., & Mateos, L. (2016). Social value and economic value in social enterprises: Value creation model of Spanish sheltered workshops. *Voluntas*, *27*(1), 367–391. doi:10.1007/s11266-015-9554-6

Beltagui, A., Riedel, J. C., & Pawar, K. S. (2008, June). Product—Service transition: Research questions. In *2008 IEEE International Technology Management Conference (ICE)* (pp. 1-8). IEEE.

Bendapudi, N., Singh, S., & Bendapudi, V. (1996). Enhancing helping behavior: An integrative framework for promotion planning. *Journal of Marketing*, *60*(3), 33–49. doi:10.2307/1251840

Bengo, I., Arena, M., Azzone, G., & Calderini, M. (2016). Indicators and metrics for social business: A review of current approaches. *Journal of Social Entrepreneurship*, *7*(1), 1–24. doi:10.1080/19420676.2015.1049286

Bennett, R. (2003). Factors underlying the inclination to donate to particular types of charity. *International Journal of Nonprofit and Voluntary Sector Marketing*, *8*(1), 12–29. doi:10.1002/nvsm.198

Bennett, R., & Savani, S. (2011). Surviving mission drift: How charities can turn dependence on government contract funding to their own advantage. *Nonprofit Management & Leadership*, *22*(2), 217–231. doi:10.1002/nml.20050

Bennett, S., Bishop, A., Dalgarno, B., Waycott, J., & Kennedy, G. (2012). Implementing Web 2.0 technologies in higher education: A collective case study. *Computers & Education*, *59*(2), 524–534. doi:10.1016/j.compedu.2011.12.022

Berg, B. (2009). *Qualitative Research Methods for the Social Sciences*. Boston: Allyn & Bacon.

Bernholz, L., & Richter, L. (2009). *Equity advancing equity: How community philanthropy can build racial and social equity through mission investing*. San Francisco, CA: Blueprint Research & Design and GPS Capital Partners.

Berry, J. W. (1990). Psychology of acculturation: Understanding individuals moving between cultures. In R. W. Brislin (Ed.), *Applied cross-cultural psychology* (pp. 232–253). Newbury Park, CA: Sage. doi:10.4135/9781483325392.n11

Beynaghi, A., Trencher, G., Moztarzadeh, F., Mozafari, M., Maknoon, R., & Leal Filho, W. (2016). Future sustainability scenarios for universities: Moving beyond the United Nations Decade of Education for Sustainable Development. *Journal of Cleaner Production*, *112*(4), 3464–3478. doi:10.1016/j.jclepro.2015.10.117

Bilodeau, M., & Steinberg, R. (2006). Donative nonprofit organizations. Handbook of the Economics of Giving, Altruism and Reciprocity, 2, 1271-1333.

Biolchini, J., Mian, P. G., Natali, A. C. C., & Travassos, G. H. (2005). Systematic review in software engineering. *System Engineering and Computer Science Department COPPE/UFRJ. Technical Report ES*, *679*(05), 45.

Black, J., Boggs, A. M., Fry, H., Jackson, S., King, R., Lodge, M., … Black, J. (2015). *The regulation of higher education*. Academic Press.

Blaikie, N. (2004). Abduction. In M. S. Lewis-Beck, A. Bryman, & T. F. Liao (Eds.), *The Sage Encyclopedia of Social Science Research Methods* (Vol. 1, p. 1). London: Sage.

Bloomberg, L. D., & Volpe, M. (2012). *Completing your qualitative dissertation: A road map from beginning to end.* Thousand Oaks, CA: Sage.

Bogacz-Wojtanowska, E., & Jałocha, B. (2016). The bright side of social economy sector's projectification: a study of successful social enterprises. *Project Management Research & Practice*, *1*(1).

Bonner, T. N. (2002). *Iconoclast: Abraham Flexner and a Life in Learning*. Baltimore, MD: John Hopkins University Press.

Boons, F., & Lüdeke-Freund, F. (2013). Business models for sustainable innovation: State of the art and steps towards a research agenda. *Journal of Cleaner Production*, *45*, 9–19. doi:10.1016/j.jclepro.2012.07.007

Borker, D. R. (2012). Accounting, culture and emerging economies: IFRS in Central and Eastern Europe. *International Business & Economics Research Journal*, *11*(9), 1003–1018.

Borzaga, C., & Defourny, J. (2001). Conclusions: Social enterprises in Europe: A diversity of initiatives and prospects. The Emergence of Social Enterprise, 350-370.

Borzaga, C., & Fazzi, L. (2011). Processes of institutionalization and differentiation in the Italian Third Sector. *Voluntas*, *22*(3), 409–427. doi:10.1007/s11266-010-9159-z

Bos, J. J., & Brown, R. R. (2014). Assessing organisational capacity for transition policy programs. *Technological Forecasting and Social Change*, *86*(1), 188–206. doi:10.1016/j.techfore.2013.09.012

Bouckaert, L., & Vandenhove, J. (1998). Business ethics and the management of non-profit institutions. *Journal of Business Ethics*, *17*(9/10), 1073–1081. doi:10.1023/A:1006071416514

Bowser, B. R. (2015). *A grounded theory approach to creating a new model for understanding cultural adaptation of families in international assignments*. ProQuest Dissertation UMI 3718617. Capella University, Ann Arbor, MI: ProQuest, LLC.

Boyd, D. M., & Ellison, N. B. (2008). Social network sites: Definition, history, and scholarship. *Journal of Computer-Mediated Communication*, *13*(1), 210–230. doi:10.1111/j.1083-6101.2007.00393.x

Boyer, K. K., & Lewis, M. W. L. (2002). Competitive Priorities: Investigating the Need for Trade-Offs in Operations Strategy. *Production and Operations Management Society*, *11*(1), 9–20. Retrieved from http://doi.wiley.com/10.1111/j.1937-5956.2002.tb00181.x

Boyer, K. K., & Pagell, M. (2000). Measurement issues in empirical research: Improving measures of operations strategy and advanced manufacturing technology. *Journal of Operations Management*, *18*(1), 361–374. doi:10.1016/S0272-6963(99)00029-7

Bradley, B. (2004). Foreword. In S. Oster, C. Massarsky, & S. Beinhacker (Eds.), *Generating and Sustaining Nonprofit Earned Income* (pp. xiii–xvi). San Francisco: Jossey-Bass US.

Brammer, S., & Pavelin, S. (2008). Factors influencing the quality of corporate environmental disclosure. *Business Strategy and the Environment*, *17*(2), 120–136. doi:10.1002/bse.506

Brandsen, T., & Karré, P. M. (2011). Hybrid Organizations: No Cause for Concern? *International Journal of Public Administration*, *34*(13), 827–836. doi:10.1080/01900692.2011.605090

Bray, I. (2015). *Using Crowdfunding to Raise Money for Your Nonprofit*. Retrieved July 9, 2016, from http://www.nolo.com/legal-encyclopedia/using-crowdfunding-raise-money-your-nonprofit.html

Brege, S., Stehn, L., & Nord, T. (2014). Business models in industrialized building of multi-storey houses. *Construction Management and Economics*, *32*(1/2), 208–226. doi:10.1080/01446193.2013.840734

Březina, D., Šafařík, D., & Hlaváčková, P. (2013). LM3–Local Multiplier in environmental economics. *Public recreation and landscape protection–with man hand in hand.*

Brignall, S. (2003). *The unbalanced scorecard: A social and environmental critique*. Retrieved from http://www.environmental-expert.com/articles/the-unbalanced-scorecard-a-socialenvironmentalcritique-2943

Brink-Danan, M. (2015). Value and meaning: Paradoxes of religious diversity talk as a globalized expertise. *Language and Communication, 44*, 44-58.

Bronfenbrenner, U. (1979). *The ecology of human development: Experiments by nature and design*. Cambridge, MA: Harvard University Press.

Brooks, A. C., & Wilson, J. Q. (2007). *Who really cares: The surprising truth about compassionate conservatism--america's charity divide--who gives, who doesn't, and why it matters*. New York: Basic Books.

Brooks, P. M., Doherty, R. L., & Donald, K. J. (2001). Expansion and diversification of medical education in Australia, 1951-2000. *The Medical Journal of Australia*, *174*(1), 25–28. PMID:11219787

Brosnan, C. (2010). Making sense of differences between medical schools through Bourdieus concept of field. *Medical Education*, *44*(7), 645–652. doi:10.1111/j.1365-2923.2010.03680.x PMID:20636583

Broughton, A., Foley, B., & Cox, A. (2013). *The Use of Social Media in the Recruitment Process*. Institute for Employment Studies. Retrieved from www.acas.org.uk/researchpapers

Broughton, A., Higgins, T., Hicks, B., & Cox, A. (2009). *Workplaces and Social Networking – The Implications for Employment Relations*. Institute for Employment Studies. Retrieved from www.acas.org.uk/researchpapers

Brown, L. D., & Kalegaokar, A. (1999). Addressing civil society's challenges: Support organizations as emerging institutions. *Institute for Development Research*, *15*(2), 1–20.

Brown, L. D., & Kalegaokar, A. (2002). Support Organizations and the evolution of the NGO sector. *Nonprofit and Voluntary Sector Quarterly*, *31*(2), 231–258. doi:10.1177/0899764002312004

Brown, N., & Deegan, C. (1999). The public disclosure of environmental performance information – a dual test of media agenda setting theory and legitimacy theory. *Accounting and Business Review*, *9*, 21–41.

Brudney, J., & Murray, V. (1998). Do International Efforts to Improve Boards Really Work? The Views of Nonprofits. *Nonprofit Management & Leadership*, *8*(4), 333–348. doi:10.1002/nml.8403

Bryson, J. M. (1988). A Strategic Planning Process for Public and Non-profit Organizations. *Long Range Planning*, *21*(1), 73–81. doi:10.1016/0024-6301(88)90061-1

Bryson, J. M. (1989). *Strategic Planning for Public and Nonprofit Organizations. A Guide to Strengthening and Sustaining Organizational Achievement*. San Francisco: Jossey- Bass Publishers.

Bryson, J. M., Ackermann, F., & Eden, C. (2007). Putting the Resource-Based View of Strategy and Distinctive Competencies to Work in Public Organizations. *Public Administration Review*, *67*(4), 702–717. doi:10.1111/j.1540-6210.2007.00754.x

Bryson, J. M., Gibbons, M. J., & Shaye, G. (2001). Enterprise Schemes for Nonprofit Survival, Growth, and Effectiveness. *Nonprofit Management & Leadership*, *11*(3), 271–288. doi:10.1002/nml.11303

Buhr, N. (1998). Environmental performance, legislation and annual report disclosure: The case of acid rain and Falconbridge. *Accounting, Auditing & Accountability Journal*, *11*(2), 163–190. doi:10.1108/09513579810215455

Bull, M. (2007). Balance: The Development of a Social Enterprise Business Performance Analysis Tool. *Social Enterprise Journal*, *3*(1), 49–66. doi:10.1108/17508610780000721

Bull, M., & Crompton, H. (2006). Business Practices in Social Enterprises. *Social Enterprise Journal*, *2*(1), 42–60. doi:10.1108/17508610680000712

Burger, R. (2005). What we have learnt from post-1994 innovations in pro-poor service delivery in South Africa: A case study-based analysis. *Development Southern Africa*, *22*(4), 483–500. doi:10.1080/03768350500322966

Burger, R., & Owens, T. (2010). Promoting Transparency in the NGO Sector: Examining the Availability and Reliability of Self-Reported Data. *World Development*, *38*(9), 1263–1277. doi:10.1016/j.worlddev.2009.12.018

Cabrera, E. F. (2009). Protean organizations: Reshaping work and careers to retain female talent. *Career Development International*, *14*(2), 186–201. doi:10.1108/13620430910950773

Caesar, P., & Baker, T. (2004). Fundamentals of Implementation. In S. Oster, C. Massarsky, & S. Beinhacker (Eds.), *Generating and Sustaining Nonprofit Earned Income* (pp. 207–223). San Francisco: Jossey-Bass.

Caligiuri, P. M., Hylan, M. M., & Joshi, A. (1998). Testing a theoretical model for examining the relationship between family adjustment and expatriates work adjustment. *The Journal of Applied Psychology*, *83*(4), 598–614. doi:10.1037/0021-9010.83.4.598 PMID:9729928

Caligiuri, P. M., & Tarique, I. (2009). Predicting effectiveness in global leadership activities. *Journal of World Business*, *44*(3), 336–346. doi:10.1016/j.jwb.2008.11.005

Campbell, J., Muijs, D., Robinson, W., & Kyriakides, L. (2003). Measuring teachers' performance: A case for differentiation. *Education, 3*(31), 4-8.

Campbell, D. A., Lambright, K. T., & Wells, C. J. (2014). Looking for Friends, Fans, and Followers? Social Media Use in Public and Nonprofit Human Services. *Public Administration Review, 74*(September-October), 655–663. doi:10.1111/puar.12261

Campos, L., Andion, C., Serva, M., Rossetto, A., & Assumpção, J. (2011). Performance evaluation in non-governmental organizations (NGOs): An analysis of evaluation models and their applications in Brazil. *Voluntas, 22*(2), 238–258. doi:10.1007/s11266-010-9145-5

CanadaHelps. (2014a, August 20). *Lemon Love Ride – A Fundraising Success | CanadaHelps - Donate to any charity in Canada.* Retrieved July 9, 2016, from https://www.canadahelps.org/en/giving-life/fundraising/lemon-love-ride-a-fundraising-success/

CanadaHelps. (2014b, November 5). *Canadian Hero Fund Launches 11 for 11 Campaign | CanadaHelps - Donate to any charity in Canada.* Retrieved July 9, 2016, from https://www.canadahelps.org/en/giving-life/community-happenings/canadian-hero-fund-launches-11-for-11-campaign/

Cantrell-Bruce, T., & Blankenberger, B. (2015). Seeing Clearly: Measuring Skill Sets That Address the "Blurred Boundaries" of Nonproit Management Education. *Journal of Public Affairs Education, 21*(3), 367–380.

Canyelles, J. M. (2009). *Per un territori socialment responsable. Promovent la Responsabilitat Social dels Ajuntaments.* Fundació Pro Penedès. Vilafranca del Penedès.

Canyelles, J. M. (2012). La responsabilidad social de las organizaciones no lucrativas. *Revista de Contabilidad y Dirección, 14*, 129–156.

Cao, X., Vogel, D. R., Guo, X., Liu, H., & Gu, J. (2012). Understanding the Influence of Social Media in the Workplace: An Integration of Synchronicity and Social Capital Theories. *45th Hawaii International Conference on System Sciences*, 3938-3947. doi:10.1109/HICSS.2012.618

Capurro, R. (2005). Privacy. An intercultural perspective. *Ethics and Information Technology, 7*(1), 37–47. doi:10.1007/s10676-005-4407-4

Carbery, R., Garavan, T. N., OBrien, F., & McDonnell, J. (2003). Predicting hotel managers turnover cognitions. *Journal of Managerial Psychology, 18*(7), 649–679. doi:10.1108/02683940310502377

Cãrdoba, D., Jansen, K., & Gonzãlez, C. (2014). The Malleability of Participation: The Politics of Agricultural Research under Neoliberalism in Bolivia. *Development & Change, 45*(6), 1284-1309.

Carmeli, A., & Markman, G. D. (2011). Capture, governance, and resilience: Strategy implications from the history of Rome. *Strategic Management Journal, 32*(3), 322–341. doi:10.1002/smj.880

Carroll, K. M., & Rounsaville, B. J. (2007). A vision of the next generation of behavioural therapies research in the addictions. *Addiction (Abingdon, England), 102*(6), 850–862. doi:10.1111/j.1360-0443.2007.01798.x PMID:17523974

Carroll, T. F. (1992). *Intermediary NGOs: the supporting link in grassroots development.* West Hartford, CT: Kumarian Press.

Carvajal, M., & García, J. (2012). Crowdfunding and non–profit media: The emergence of new models for public interest. *Journalism Practice, 6*(5-6), 638–647. doi:10.1080/17512786.2012.667267

Casadesus-Masanell, R., & Ricart, J. (2010). From strategy to business models and onto tactics. *Long Range Planning, 43*(2/3), 195–215. doi:10.1016/j.lrp.2010.01.004

Castelo, M., & Lima, L. (2008). Factors Influencing Social Responsibility Disclosure by Portuguese Companies. *Journal of Business Ethics, 83*(4), 685–701. doi:10.1007/s10551-007-9658-z

Cavallo, A. (2012). Online and official price indexes: Measuring Argentinas inflation. *Journal of Monetary Economics, 60*(2), 152–165. doi:10.1016/j.jmoneco.2012.10.002

Cellan-Jones, R. (2016, January 20). Zano: The rise and fall of Kickstarter's mini-drone. *BBC News*. Retrieved from http://www.bbc.com/news/technology-35356147

Center for Effective Philanthropy. (2015). *Investing and social impact: Practices of private foundations*. Retrieved March 18, 2016, from http://www.effectivephilanthropy.org/wp-content/uploads/2015/05/Investing-and-Social-Impact-2015.pdf

Chaffee, E. E. (1985). Three models of strategy. *Academy of Management Review, 10*(1), 85–98.

Chaganti, R., & Mahajan, V. (1989). Profitable small business strategies under different types of competition. *Entrepreneurship. Theory into Practice, 13*, 21–35.

Chamberlain, G. (2006). Researching Strategy Formation Process: An Abductive Methodology. *Quality & Quantity, 40*(2), 289–301. doi:10.1007/s11135-005-8094-3

Chang, E. (2005). Employees overall perception of HRM effectiveness. *Human Relations, 58*(4), 523–544. doi:10.1177/0018726705055037

Chapman, J. R. (2015). Fostering career management using career anchor theory in Handbook of career intervention: Vol. 2. *Application*. Washington, DC: American Psychological Association.

Charity Navigator. (2016). *Giving Statistics*. Retrieved July 8, 2016, from http://www.charitynavigator.org/index.cfm?

Charmaz, K. (2006). *Constructing grounded theory: A practical guide through qualitative analysis*. Thousand Oaks, CA: Sage.

Chaudron, G. (2016). Managing the commonplace: Small water emergencies in libraries. *International Journal of Risk and Contingency Management, 5*(1), 42–61. doi:10.4018/IJRCM.2016010104

Chell, E., Spence, L. J., Perrini, F., & Harris, J. D. (2016). Social entrepreneurship and business ethics: Does social equal ethical? *Journal of Business Ethics, 133*(4), 619–625. doi:10.1007/s10551-014-2439-6

Chen, H., Chiang, R. H., & Storey, V. C. (2012). Business intelligence and analytics: From Big Data to big impact. *Management Information Systems Quarterly, 36*, 1165–1188.

Chen, J. (2012). *Transnational Civil Society in China: Intrusion and Impact*. Edward Elgar Publishing.

Chen, T. F. (2009). Building a platform of Business Model 2.0 to creating real business value with Web 2.0 for web information services industry. *International Journal of Electronic Business Management, 7*(3), 168–180.

Chesbrough, H. (2010). Business model innovation: Opportunities and barriers. *Long Range Planning, 43*(2/3), 354–363. doi:10.1016/j.lrp.2009.07.010

Chesbrough, H., & Rosenbloom, R. (2002). The Role of the business model in capturing value from innovation: Evidence from Xerox Corporations technology spin-off companies. *Industrial and Corporate Change, 11*(3), 529–555. doi:10.1093/icc/11.3.529

Child, J. (1972). Organizational structure, environment and performance: The role of strategic choice. *Sociology*, *6*(1), 1–22. doi:10.1177/003803857200600101

Chin, C., Gu, J., & Tubbs, S. (2001). Developing global leadership competencies. *The Journal of Leadership Studies*, *7*(3), 20–31. doi:10.1177/107179190100700402

Cho, C. H. (2009). Legitimation strategies used in response to environmental disaster: A French case study of Total SAs Erika and AZF incidents. *European Accounting Review*, *18*(1), 33–62. doi:10.1080/09638180802579616

Choi, H., & Varian, H. (2012). Predicting the present with Google Trends. *Economic Inquiry*, *88*, 2–9.

Choi, S. M. (2012). Learning Orientation and Market orientation as catalysts for innovation in non-profit organizations. *Nonprofit and Voluntary Sector Quarterly*, *43*(2), 393–413. doi:10.1177/0899764012465491

Chung, E. (2013, June 21). *Charity crowdfunding site launched by Toronto firm - Technology & Science - CBC News*. Retrieved July 8, 2016, from http://www.cbc.ca/news/technology/charity-crowdfunding-site-launched-by-toronto-firm-1.1337335

Clark, B. R. (1971). Belief and loyalty in college organization. *The Journal of Higher Education*, *42*(6), 499–515. doi:10.2307/1979081

Clark, J. (2011). Civil Society in the Age of Crisis. *Journal of Civil Society*, *7*(3), 241–263. doi:10.1080/17448689.2011.604986

Clark, P., & Martinez, L. (2016). Local Alternatives to Private Agricultural Certification in Ecuador: Broadening Access to â€˜New Marketsâ€™? *Journal of Rural Studies*, 1.

Coaldrake, P., & Stedman, L. (2013). *Raising the Stakes: Gambling with the future of universities*. Brisbane: University of Queensland Press.

Coetzee, M. (2008). Psychological career resources of working adults. *Journal of Individual Psychology*, *34*(2), 10–20.

Coetzee, M., & Schreuder, D. (2009). using the Career Orientations Inventory (COI) for internal career orientations in the South African Organisational Context. *South African Journal of Industrial Psychology*, *35*(1), 1–14.

Coetzee, M., Schreuder, D., & Tladinyane, R. (2007). Organisational commitment and its relation to career anchors. *Southern African Business Review*, *11*(1), 65–86.

Cohen, R. (2015, July 2). *The Feds Take Action against Crowdfunding Fraud, and It's About Time!* Retrieved September 12, 2016, from https://nonprofitquarterly.org/2015/07/02/the-feds-take-action-against-crowdfunding-fraud-and-its-about-time/

Coleman, J. S. (1990). *Foundations of social capital theory*. Cambridge, UK: Belknap.

Collis, D. (2000). When industries change revisited: New scenarios for higher education. In Forum futures: Exploring the future of higher education (pp. 103–126).

Collis, D. (1999). When Industries Change: Scenarios for Higher Education. In D. Collis (Ed.), *Exploring the Future of Higher Education* (pp. 47–70). New York: Forum for the Future of Higher Eucation.

Colombo, A. (2008). The Lombardy Model: Subsidiarity-informed Regional Governance. *Social Policy and Administration*, *42*(2), 177–196. doi:10.1111/j.1467-9515.2008.00602.x

Commonwealth of Australia. (2008). *What Makes for Success in Medical Education: Synthesis Report*. Author.

Commonwealth of Australia. (2012). *Department of Health and Ageing Annual Report 2011-2012*. Canberra: Department of Health and Ageing.

Commonwealth of Australia. (2013). *List of Rural Clinical Schools*. Retrieved from http://www.health.gov.au/clinicalschools

Confederation of Postgraduate Medical Education Councils (CPMEC). (2008). *Australian Curriculum Framework for Junior Doctors*. Melbourne: Confederation of Postgraduate Medical Education Councils.

Constantinides, E., & Stagno, M. C. Z. (2011). Potential of the social media as instruments of higher education marketing: A segmentation study. *Journal of Marketing for Higher Education*, *21*(1), 7–24. doi:10.1080/08841241.2011.573593

Cooch, S., & Kramer, M. (2007). *Compunding impact: Mission investing by US foundations*. Boston, MA: FSG Social Impact Advisors.

Cooke, M., Irby, D. M., Sullivan, W., & Ludmerer, K. M. (2006). American Medical Education 100 years after the Flexner Report. *The New England Journal of Medicine*, *355*(13), 1339–1344. doi:10.1056/NEJMra055445 PMID:17005951

Cooney, K. (2011). An Exploratory Study of social purpose business models in the United States. *Nonprofit and Voluntary Sector Quarterly*, *40*(1), 185–196. doi:10.1177/0899764009351591

Corbin, J. J. (1999). A study of factors influencing the growth of nonprofits in social services. *Nonprofit and Voluntary Sector Quarterly*, *28*(3), 296–314. doi:10.1177/0899764099283004

Cordery, C. J., & Baskerville, R. F. (2011). Charity transgressions, trust and accountability. *Voluntas: International Journal of Voluntary and Nonprofit Organizations*, *22*(2), 197–213. doi:10.1007/s11266-010-9132-x

Cornforth, C. (2014). Understanding and combating mission drift in social enterprises. *Social Enterprise Journal*, *10*(1), 3–20. doi:10.1108/SEJ-09-2013-0036

Cornforth, C., Hayes, J. P., & Vangen, S. (2015). Nonprofit–Public Collaborations Understanding Governance Dynamics. *Nonprofit and Voluntary Sector Quarterly*, *44*(4), 775–795. doi:10.1177/0899764014532836

Costa, E., Ramus, T., & Andreaus, M. (2011). Accountability as a managerial tool in non-profit organizations: Evidence from Italian CSVs. *Voluntas: International Journal of Voluntary and Nonprofit Organizations*, *22*(3), 470–493. doi:10.1007/s11266-011-9183-7

Coutts, M. D. R. (2014). *Case study: ABC Foundation*. Retrieved Oct.12, 2016, from http://philanthropy.coutts.com/en/reports/2014/united-states/case-studies/dana-pancrazi.html

Cox, S. A., & Kramer, M. W. (1995). Communication during employee dismissals: Social exchange principles and group influences on employee exit. *Management Communication Quarterly*, *9*(2), 156–190. doi:10.1177/0893318995009002002

Creed, G. S. (2006). *Families in cross-cultural transitions: Psychological adjustment, socio-cultural adaptation and acculturation strategy* (Unpublished doctoral dissertation). University of Northern Colorado, Greeley, CO.

Crespo, F. (2010). Entre el concepto y la práctica: Responsabilidad social. *Estudios Gerenciales*, *26*(117), 119–130. doi:10.1016/S0123-5923(10)70137-6

Crespy, C. T., & Miller, V. V. (2011). Sustainability reporting: A comparative study of NGOs and MNCs. *Corporate Social Responsibility and Environmental Management*, *18*(5), 275–284. doi:10.1002/csr.248

Cronin, P., Ryan, F., & Coughlan, M. (2008). Undertaking a literature review: A step-by-step approach. *British Journal of Nursing (Mark Allen Publishing)*, *17*(1), 38–43. doi:10.12968/bjon.2008.17.1.28059 PMID:18399395

Cumming, D. J., Leboeuf, G., & Schwienbacher, A. (2015). Crowdfunding models: Keep-it-all vs. all-or-nothing. *All-Or-Nothing*.

Cunningham, I. (2008). A race to the bottom? Exploring variations in employment conditions in the voluntary sector. *Public Administration*, *86*(4), 1033–1053. doi:10.1111/j.1467-9299.2008.00752.x

Cunningham, I. (2010). The HR function in purchaser-provider relationships: Insights from the UK voluntary sector. *Human Resource Management Journal*, *20*(2), 189–205. doi:10.1111/j.1748-8583.2009.00112.x

Cunningham, I., & Nickson, D. (2011). A gathering storm: Re-tendering and the voluntary sector workforce. *International Journal of Public Sector Management*, *24*(7), 662–672. doi:10.1108/09513551111172486

Cupitt, S. (2009). *A guide to social return on investment*. Cabinet Office, Office of the Third Sector.

Curtis, L., Edwards, C., Fraser, K. L., Gudelsky, S., Holmquist, J., Thornton, K., & Sweetser, K. D. (2010). Adoption of social media for public relations by nonprofit organizations. *Public Relations Review*, *36*(1), 90–92. doi:10.1016/j.pubrev.2009.10.003

Dacin, M., Goodstein, J., & Scott, W. (2002). Institutional theory and institutional change: Introduction to the special research forum. *Academy of Management Journal*, *45*(1), 45–57. doi:10.5465/AMJ.2002.6283388

Dai, C. X., & Wells, W. G. (2004). An exploration of project management office features and their relationship to project performance. *International Journal of Project Management*, *22*(7), 523–532. doi:10.1016/j.ijproman.2004.04.001

Daley, D. M. (2007). If a tree falls in the forest: The effect of grievances on employee perceptions of performance appraisal, efficacy, and job satisfaction. *Review of Public Personnel Administration*, *27*(3), 281–296. doi:10.1177/0734371X06297621

Dalton, G., Thompson, P., & Price, R. (1977). The four stages of professional careers: A new look at performance by professionals. *Organizational Dynamics*, *5*(1), 19–42. doi:10.1016/0090-2616(77)90033-X

Damm, C. (2012). *The third sector delivering employment services: an evidence review*. Academic Press.

Darby, L., & Jenkins, H. (2006). Applying sustainability indicators to the social enterprise business model: The development and application of an indicator set for Newport Wastesavers, Wales. *International Journal of Social Economics*, *33*(5/6), 411–431. doi:10.1108/03068290610660689

Dart, R. (2004). b. Being 'Business-Like" in a Nonprofit Organization: A grounded and Inductive Typology. *Nonprofit and Voluntary Sector Quarterly*, *33*(2), 290–310. doi:10.1177/0899764004263522

Dart, R. (2004). The legitimacy of social enterprise. *Nonprofit Management & Leadership*, *14*(4), 411–424. doi:10.1002/nml.43

Davenport, T. O. (1999). *Human capital:What it is and why people invest in it*. San Francisco: Jossey-Bass.

Davis, F. D. (1989). Perceived Usefulness, Perceived Ease of Use, and User Acceptance of Information Technology. *Management Information Systems Quarterly*, *13*(3), 319–340. doi:10.2307/249008

Davis, F. D., Bagozzi, R. P., & Warshaw, P. R. (1989). User Acceptance of Computer Technology: A Comparison of Two Theoretical Models. *Management Science*, *35*(8), 982–1003. doi:10.1287/mnsc.35.8.982

de Almeida Biolchini, J. C., Mian, P. G., Natali, A. C. C., Conte, T. U., & Travassos, G. H. (2007). Scientific research ontology to support systematic review in software engineering. *Advanced Engineering Informatics*, *21*(2), 133–151. doi:10.1016/j.aei.2006.11.006

De Castro, M. (2005). La Responsabilidad Social de las Empresas, o un nuevo concepto de empresa. CIRIEC-España. *Revista de Economía Pública. Social y Cooperativa*, *53*, 137–161.

De la Torre, I. (2009). Fundamentos de la responsabilidad social de la empresa. *Revista de Responsabilidad Social de la Empresa*, *1*, 71–86.

De Vos, A., Dewettinck, K., & Buyens, D. (2008). To move or not to move? The relationship between career management and preferred career moves. *Employee Relations*, *30*(2), 156–175. doi:10.1108/01425450810843348

Dedeurwaerdere, T., Admiraal, J., Beringer, A., Bonaiuto, F., Cicero, L., Fernandez-Wulff, P., & …, Luis Vivero, J. (2016). Combining internal and external motivations in multi-actor governance arrangements for biodiversity and ecosystem services. *Environmental Science & Policy*, *58*(1), 1–10. PMID:28149197

Deegan, C. (2007). Organizational legitimacy as a motive for sustainability. In Sustainability Accounting and Accountability. Routledge.

Deegan, C., & Rankin, M. (1996). Do Australian Companies Report Environmental News Objectively? An Analysis of Environmental Disclosures by Firms Prosecuted Successfully by the Environmental Protection Authority. *Accounting, Auditing & Accountability Journal*, *9*(2), 50–67. doi:10.1108/09513579610116358

Dees, G. (2001). *The Meaning of Social Entrepreneurship*. Retrieved from http://www.caseatduke.org/documents/dees_sedef.pdf

Dees, G., & Economy, P. (2001). Social Entrepreneurship. In G. Dees, J. Emerson, & P. Economy (Eds.), *Enterprising Nonprofits: A toolkit for Social Entrepreneurs* (pp. 1–18). New York: John Wiley and Sons Inc.

Dees, J. (2004). Putting Nonprofit Business Ventures in Perspective. In S. Oster, C. Massarsky, & S. Beinhacker (Eds.), *Generating and Sustaining Nonprofit Earned Income* (pp. 3–18). San Francisco: Jossey-Bass.

DeFillippi, R. J., & Arthur, M. B. (1994). The boundaryless career: A competency-based perspective. *Journal of Organizational Behavior*, *15*(4), 307–324. doi:10.1002/job.4030150403

Defourny, J., & Borzaga, C. (2001). *From third sector to social enterprise*. London: Routledge.

Defourny, J., & Nyssens, M. (2008). Social enterprise in Europe: Recent trends and developments. *Social Enterprise Journal*, *4*(3), 202–228. doi:10.1108/17508610810922703

Degli Antoni, G., & Portale, E. (2011). The effect of Corporate Social Responsibility on Social Capital Creation in Social Cooperatives. *Nonprofit and Voluntary Sector Quarterly*, *40*(3), 566–582. doi:10.1177/0899764010362568

DeLone, W. H., & McLean, E. R. (1992). Information Systems Success: The Quest for the Dependent Variable. *Information Systems Research*, *3*(1), 60–95. doi:10.1287/isre.3.1.60

DeLone, W. H., & McLean, E. R. (2003). The DeLone and McLean model of information systems success: A ten-year update. *Journal of Management Information Systems*, *19*(4), 9–30.

Delong, T. J. (1982). Re-examining the career anchor model. *Personnel*, *59*(3), 50–61.

Demil, B., & Lecocq, X. (2010). Business model evolution: In search of dynamic consistency. *Long Range Planning*, *43*(2/3), 227–246. doi:10.1016/j.lrp.2010.02.004

Demsetz, H. (1988). The theory of the firm revisited. *Journal of Law Economics and Organization*, *4*(1), 141–161.

Denhardt, R. B., Denhardt, J. V., & Aristigueta, M. P. (2015). *Managing human behaviour in public and nonprofit organizations*. Sage Publication.

Depree, J. C., & Jude, R. (2007). Ten practical suggestions for terminating an employee. *The CPA Journal*, *77*(8), 62–63.

Desouza, K. C., & Evaristo, J. R. (2006). Project management offices: A case of knowledge-based archetypes. *International Journal of Information Management*, *26*(5), 414–423. doi:10.1016/j.ijinfomgt.2006.07.002

Deutsch, K. W. (1968). Toward a cybernetic model of man and society. In W. Buckley (Ed.), *Modern systems research for the behavioral scientist*. Chicago: Aidine Publishing Company.

Development Trusts Association (DTA). (2008). *Fit for purpose: The Development Trusts Association healthcheck for community enterprise organisations.* Accessed February 6, 2016. http://locality.org.uk/wp-content/uploads/Fit-for-Purpose.pdf

Dey, P., Schneider, H., & Maier, F. (2016). Intermediary Organisations and the Hegemonisation of Social Entrepreneurship: Fantasmatic Articulations, Constitutive Quiescences, and Moments of Indeterminacy. *Organization Studies*, 1–22.

Di Domenico, M., Tracey, P., & Haugh, H. (2009). Social economy involvement in public service delivery: Community engagement and accountability. *Regional Studies*, *43*(7), 981–992. doi:10.1080/00343400701874180

Díaz Garrido, E., Martín-Peña, M. L., & García-Muiña, F. (2007). Structural and infrastructural practices as elements of content operations strategy. The effect on a firms competitiveness. *International Journal of Production Research*, *45*(9), 2119–2140. doi:10.1080/00207540600735480

Dietz-Uhler, B., & Hurn, J. E. (2013). Using learning analytics to predict (and improve) student success: A faculty perspective. *Journal of Interactive Online Learning*, *12*, 16–19.

DiMaggio, P. J., & Powell, W. W. (1983). The iron cage revisited: Institutional isomorphism and collective rationality in organizational fields. *American Sociological Review*, *48*(2), 147–160. doi:10.2307/2095101

DiMaggio, P., & Anheir, H. (1990). The Sociology of Nonprofit Organizations and Sectors. *Annual Review of Sociology*, *16*(1), 137–159. doi:10.1146/annurev.so.16.080190.001033

DiStaso, M. W., McCorkindale, T., & Wright, D. K. (2011). How Public Relations Executives Perceive and Measure the Impact of Social Media in Their Organizations. *Public Relations*, *37*(3), 325–328. doi:10.1016/j.pubrev.2011.06.005

Diver, S. W., & Higgins, M. N. (2014). Giving Back Through Collaborative Research: Towards a Practice of Dynamic Reciprocity. *Journal of Research Practice*, *10*(2), 1–13.

Dixon, S., Meyer, K., & Day, M. (2014). Building dynamic capabilities of adaptation and innovation: A study of micro foundations in a transition economy. *Long Range Planning*, *47*(4), 186–205. doi:10.1016/j.lrp.2013.08.011

DocCheck News. (2012, June 20). *Crowd Funding: The flock instead of public health insurance*. Retrieved September 12, 2016, from http://news.doccheck.com/en/56/crowd-funding-the-flock-instead-of-public-health-insurance/

Doherty, B., Haugh, H., & Lyon, F. (2014). Social enterprises as hybrid organizations: A review and research agenda. *International Journal of Management Reviews*, *16*(4), 417–436. doi:10.1111/ijmr.12028

Dolfsma, W., & Verburg, R. (2008). Structure, agency and the role of values in processes of institutional change. *Journal of Economic Issues*, *XLII*(4), 1031–1053. doi:10.1080/00213624.2008.11507201

Donaldson, T., & Preston, L. E. (1995). The stakeholder's theory of the corporation: Concepts, evidence and implications. *Academy of Management Review*, *20*(1), 65–91.

Dorfman, P., Javidan, M., Hanges, P., Dastmalchian, A., & House, R. (2012). GLOBE: A twenty-year journey into the intriguing world of culture and leadership. *Journal of World Business*, *540*, 1–15.

Dormey, J. (2016). *Going Digital? Harnessing Social Media for Emloyee Voice*. The Involvement and Participation Association.

Dowling, J., & Pfeffer, J. (1975). Organizational legitimacy: Social values and organizational behavior. *Pacific Sociological Review*, *18*(1), 122–136. doi:10.2307/1388226

Dowton, S. B., Stokes, M.-L., Rawstron, E., Pogson, P. R., & Brown, M. A. (2005). Postgraduate medical education: Rethinking and intergrating a complex landscape. *The Medical Journal of Australia*, *182*(4), 177–180. PMID:15720174

Doz, Y. L., & Kosonen, M. (2010). Embedding strategic agility: A leadership agenda for accelerating business model renewal. *Long Range Planning*, *43*(2-3), 370–382. doi:10.1016/j.lrp.2009.07.006

Drakulevski, L., & Nakov, L. (2014). Managing business model as function of organizational dynamism. *International Symposium,* 37-44. doi:10.7595/management.fon.2014.0025

Drevs, F., Tscheulin, D. K., & Lindenmeier, J. (2014). Do patient perceptions vary with ownership status? A study of nonprofit, for-profit, and public hospital patients. *Nonprofit and Voluntary Sector Quarterly*, *43*(1), 164–184. doi:10.1177/0899764012458179

Drexler, M., Noble, A., & Bryce, J. (2013). *From the margins to the mainstream: Assessment of the impact investment sector and opportunities to engage mainstream investors.* Geneva, Switzerland: World Economic Forum.

Dubois, A., & Gadde, L. (2002). 'systematic combining: An abductive approach to case research. *Journal of Business Research*, *55*(7), 553–560. doi:10.1016/S0148-2963(00)00195-8

Duraj, L., Felt, L. J., & Singhal, A. (2014). What counts? For whom? Cultural beacons and unexpected areas of programmatic impact. *Evaluation and Program Planning*, *44*(1), 98–109. PMID:24662404

Du, S., Bhattacharya, C. B., & Sen, S. (2010). Maximizing Business Returns to Corporate Social Responsibility (CSR): The Role of CSR Communication. *International Journal of Management Reviews*, *12*(5), 8–19. doi:10.1111/j.1468-2370.2009.00276.x

Dutta, S., & Bilbao-Osorio, B. (2012). The global information technology report 2012: Living in a hyperconnected world. In I. World Economic Forum (Ed.), *The Global Information Technology Report*. Geneva, Switzerland: SRO-Kundig.

Dutta, S., & Mia, I. (2010). The global information technology report 2009–2010: ICT for Sustainability. In I. World Economic Forum (Ed.), *The Global Information Technology Report*. Geneva, Switzerland: SRO-Kuding.

Dutta, S., Dutton, W., & Law, G. (2011). The New Internet World: A Global Perspective on Freedom of Expression, Privacy, Trust and Security Online. In I. World Economic Forum (Ed.), *The Global Information Technology Report*. World Economic Forum, INSEAD Business School.

Dutta, S., Geiger, T., & Lanvin, B. (2015). The global information technology report 2015: ICTs for Inclusive Growth. In W. E. F. Cornell University, INSEAD (Ed.), The Global Information Technology Report. Geneva, Switzerland: SRO-Kundig.

Earley, C. P., & Ang, S. (2003). *Cultural intelligence: Individual interactions across cultures.* Stanford, CA: Stanford University Press.

Ebrahim, A., & Rangan, K. (2010). *The Limits of Nonprofit Impact: A Contingency Framework for Measuring Social Performance.* Harvard Business School Working Paper.

Ebrahim, A. (2003). Accountability in practice: Mechanisms for NGOs. *World Development*, *31*(5), 813–829. doi:10.1016/S0305-750X(03)00014-7

Ebrahim, A. (2003). Making sense of accountability: Conceptual perspectives for northern and southern nonprofits. *Nonprofit Management & Leadership*, *14*(2), 191–212. doi:10.1002/nml.29

Ebrahim, A. (2005). Accountability Myopia: Losing Sight of Organizational Learning. *Nonprofit and Voluntary Sector Quarterly*, *34*(1), 56–87. doi:10.1177/0899764004269430

Ebrahim, A. (2009). Placing the Normative Logics of Accountability in Thick Perspective. *The American Behavioral Scientist*, *52*(6), 885–904. doi:10.1177/0002764208327664

Ebrahim, A., Battilana, J., & Mair, J. (2014). The governance of social enterprises: Mission drift and accountability challenges in hybrid organizations. *Research in Organizational Behavior*, *34*, 81–100. doi:10.1016/j.riob.2014.09.001

Eby, L. T., Burk, H., & Maher, C. P. (2010). How serious of a problem is staff turnover in substance abuse treatment? A longitudinal study of actual turnover. *Journal of Substance Abuse Treatment*, *39*(3), 264–271. doi:10.1016/j.jsat.2010.06.009 PMID:20675097

Edelman, B. (2015, April). How to launch your digital platform. *Harvard Business Review*.

Edvardsson, B., Tronvoll, B., & Gruber, T. (2011). Expanding understanding of service exchange and value co-creation: A social construction approach. *Journal of the Academy of Marketing Science*, *39*(2), 327–339. doi:10.1007/s11747-010-0200-y

Edvinsson, L., & Malone, M. S. (1997). *Intellectual capital – The proven way to establish your company's real value by measuring its hidden brainpower*. New York: Harper Business.

Edward, M., & Hulme, D. (Eds.). (1992). *Making a difference: NGOs and development in a changing world*. London: Earthscan.

Ehrich, L. C. (2005). *Revisiting phenomenology: Its potential for management research*. Retrieved from http://eprints.qut.edu.au/2893/1/2893.pdf

Eikenberry, A., & Kluver, J. (2004). The marketization of the nonprofit sector: Civil society at risk? *Public Administration Review*, *64*(2), 132–140. doi:10.1111/j.1540-6210.2004.00355.x

Eisenberg, P. (1997). A crisis in the non-profit sector. *National Civic Review*, *86*(4), 331–341. doi:10.1002/ncr.4100860409

Eisenberg, P. (2000). The non-profit sector in a changing world. *Nonprofit and Voluntary Sector Quarterly*, *29*(2), 325–330. doi:10.1177/0899764000292007

Elkington, J. (1997). *Cannibals with Forks. The triple bottom line of 21st century business*. Oxford, UK: Inglaterra.

Ellram, L.M. (1995). Total Cost of Ownership: An Analysis Approach for Purchasing. *International Journal of Physical Distribution and Logistics Management, 25*(8), 4-23.

Emerson, J., & Twersky, F. (Eds.). (1996). *New social entrepreneurs: The success, challenge, and lessons of non-profit enterprise creation*. San Francisco: The Roberts Foundation.

Emma. (2016). *The Videos of the 10 Most Funded Crowdfunding Campaigns Ever*. Retrieved September 11, 2016, from https://ignitiondeck.com/id/the-videos-of-the-10-most-funded-crowdfunding-campaigns-ever/

Enders, B. (2016). *Tax Incentives: An Economic Basis for Charitable Giving | Learning to Give*. Retrieved July 8, 2016, from https://www.learningtogive.org/resources/tax-incentives-economic-basis-charitable-giving

Enterprise, D. T. (2002). *I 'Social. "A strategy for success*. London: DTI.

Equal Employment Opportunity Commission. (2009). *Facts about mediation*. Retrieved from http://www.eeoc.gov/mediate/facts.html

Erdogmus, N. (2004). Career orientations of salaried professionals: The case of Turkey. *Career Development International*, *9*(2), 153–175. doi:10.1108/13620430410526193

Erikson, E. (1968). Youth: Identity and crisis. New York, NY: WW.

Erumban, A. A., & de Jong, S. B. (2006). Cross-country differences in ICT adoption: A consequence of Culture? *Journal of World Business*, *41*(4), 302–314. doi:10.1016/j.jwb.2006.08.005

Espino-Rodriguez, T. F., & Gil-Padilla, M. (2014). The structural and infrastructural decisions of operations management in the hotel sector and their impact on organizational performance. *Tourism and Hospitality Research*, *15*(1), 3–18. doi:10.1177/1467358414553866

Estellés-Arolas, E., & González-Ladrón-de-Guevara, F. (2012). Towards an integrated crowdsourcing definition. *Journal of Information Science*, *38*(2), 189–200. doi:10.1177/0165551512437638

Esterman, T., & Nokkola, T. (2009). *University Autonomy in Europe I Exploratory Study*. Brussels: European University Association.

Esteves, A. M., Franks, D., & Vanclay, F. (2012). Social impact assessment: The state of the art. *Impact Assessment and Project Appraisal*, *30*(1), 34–42. doi:10.1080/14615517.2012.660356

Etzel, M. (2015). Philanthropy's new frontier – impact investing. *Stanford Social Innovation Review*. Retrieved June 1, 2016, from http://ssir.org/articles/entry/philanthropys_new_frontierimpact_investing

European Commission (EC). (2013). *Social economy and social entrepreneurship*. Social Europe guide, Volume 4. Directorate-General for Employment, Social Affairs and Inclusion, March 2013. Accessed November 10, 2015. http://www.sofisam.se/download/18.3453fc5214836a9a472a0430/1411643786917/EU+kommissionen,+Social+Economy+and+Social+Entreprenreurship.pdf

Evers, M. W., Lourenço, C., & Beije, P. (2012). *Main drivers of crowdfunding success: a conceptual framework and empirical analysis*. Erasmus Universiteit.

Farh, C. I. C., Bartol, K. M., Shapiro, D. L., & Shin, J. (2010). Networking abroad: A process model of how expatriates form support ties to facilitate adjustment. *Academy of Management Review*, *35*(3), 434–454. doi:10.5465/AMR.2010.51142246

Farjoun, M. (2008). Strategy making, novelty and analogical reasoning — commentary on Gavetti, Levinthal, and Rivkin (2005). *Strategic Management Journal*, *29*(9), 1001–1016. doi:10.1002/smj.690

Fassin, Y. (2009). Inconsistencies in activists behaviours and the ethics of NGOs. *Journal of Business Ethics*, *90*(4), 503–521. doi:10.1007/s10551-009-0056-6

Fazzi, L. (2012). Social Enterprises, Models of Governance and the Production of Welfare Services. *Public Management Review*, *14*(3), 359–376. doi:10.1080/14719037.2011.637409

Feldman, D. C., & Bolino, M. C. (1996). Career within careers: Reconceptualising the nature of career anchors and their consequences. *Human Resource Management Review*, *6*(2), 89–112. doi:10.1016/S1053-4822(96)90014-5

Firoz, N. M., & Ramin, T. (2004). Understanding cultural variables is critical to success in international business. *International Journal of Management*, *21*(3), 307–323.

Fishbein, M., & Ajzen, I. (1975). *Belief, attitude, intention, and behavior: An introduction to theory and research*. London: Addison-Wesley.

Fisk, N. M., Wesselingh, S. L., Beilby, J. J., Glasgow, N. J., Puddey, I. B., Robinson, B. G., & Smith, P. J. et al. (2011). Academic health science centres in Australia: Let's get competitive. *The Medical Journal of Australia*, *194*(2), 59–60. PMID:21241215

Fisk, R. P., Patrício, L., Ordanini, A., Miceli, L., Pizzetti, M., & Parasuraman, A. (2011). Crowd-funding: Transforming customers into investors through innovative service platforms. *Journal of Service Management*, *22*(4), 443–470. doi:10.1108/09564231111155079

Fitzsimmons, J. A., & Fitzsimmons, M. J. (2006). *Service management: operations, strategy and information technology* (5th ed.). London: McGraw -Hill.

Foster, W. L., Kim, P., & Christiansen, B. (2009). Ten nonprofit funding models. *Stanford Social Innovation Review*, *13*(1), 32–39.

Fowler, A. (1997). *Striking a balance: A guide to enhancing the effective of NGOs in international development*. London: Earthscan.

Franklin, A. L., & Pagan, J. F. (2006). Organization culture as an explanation for employee discipline practices. *Review of Public Personnel Administration*, *26*(1), 52–73. doi:10.1177/0734371X05277335

Fritz, J. (2015, December 4). *How Nonprofits Support Themselves*. Retrieved July 8, 2016, from http://nonprofit.about.com/od/fundraising/a/fundraising101.htm

Froelich, K. A. (1999). Diversification of revenue strategies: Evolving resource dependence in nonprofit organizations. *Nonprofit and Voluntary Sector Quarterly*, *28*(3), 246–268. doi:10.1177/0899764099283002

Fulop, G., Hisrich, R., & Szegedi, K. (2000). Business ethics and social responsibility in transition economies. *Journal of Management Development*, *19*(1), 5–31. doi:10.1108/02621710010308135

Fundly. (2013, February 26). *World's Largest Crowdfunding-for-Good Platform, Fundly, Announces Campaign of the Year Winners*. Retrieved July 8, 2016, from http://www.prnewswire.com/news-releases/worlds-largest-crowdfunding-for-good-platform-fundly-announces-campaign-of-the-year-winners-193240701.html

Fundly. (2016, July 7). *Pricing*. Retrieved July 8, 2016, from http://fundly.com/pricing/

Gair, C. (2009). *SROI act II: A call to action for next generation SROI*. San Francisco: REDF.

Gallego-Álvarez, I., & Quina-Custodio, I. A. (2016). Disclosure of corporate social responsibility information and explanatory factors. *Online Information Review*, *40*(2), 218–238. doi:10.1108/OIR-04-2015-0116

Gálvez, M. M., Caba, M. C., & López, M. (2012). Responsabilidad social y transparencia on-line de las ONG: Análisis del caso español. *CIRIEC-España, Revista de Economía Pública. Social y Cooperativa*, *74*, 207–238.

Gálvez-Rodriguez, M. D. M., Caba-Perez, C., & López-Godoy, M. (2014). Facebook: A new communication strategy for non-profit organisations In Colombia. *Public Relations Review*, *40*(5), 868–870. doi:10.1016/j.pubrev.2014.10.002

Gandía, J. L. (2011). Internet disclosure by nonprofit organizations: Empirical evidence of nongovernmental organizations for development in Spain. *Nonprofit and Voluntary Sector Quarterly*, *40*(1), 57–58. doi:10.1177/0899764009343782

Garavan, T., OBrien, F., & OHanlon, D. (2006). Career Advancement of Hotel Mangers Since Graduation: A Comparative Study. *Personnel Review*, *35*(3), 252–280. doi:10.1108/00483480610656685

García-Mainar, I., & Marcuello, C. (2007). Members, Volunteers, and Donors in Non-profit Organizations in Spain. *Nonprofit and Voluntary Sector Quarterly*, *36*(1), 100–120. doi:10.1177/0899764006293179

Garecht, J. (2016). *How to Use Crowd-Funding Sites to Raise Money for Your Non-Profit*. Retrieved July 9, 2016, from http://www.thefundraisingauthority.com/internet-fundraising/crowd-funding-your-non-profit/

Gareis, R. (2007). Management of the Project-oriented company. In P. Morris & J. Pinto (Eds.), *The Wiley Guide to Project, Program and Portfolio Management* (pp. 250–270). John Wiley and Sons. doi:10.1002/9780470172391.ch6

Garrett, D. F., & Pavan, A. (2012). Managerial turnover in a changing world. *Journal of Political Economy*, *120*(5), 879–925. doi:10.1086/668836

Garud, R., Hardy, C., & Maguire, S. (2007). Institutional entreprenuership as embedded agency: An introduction to the special issue. *Organization Science*, *28*(7), 957–969. doi:10.1177/0170840607078958

Gatzert, N., Schmit, J. T., & Kolb, A. (2016). Assessing the risks of insuring reputation risk. *The Journal of Risk and Insurance*, *83*(3), 641–679. doi:10.1111/jori.12065

Gaynor, G., Morse, J., & Pevzner, M. (2015, October 1). *The Crowdfunding Effect*. Retrieved from http://sfmagazine.com/post-entry/october-2015-the-crowdfunding-effect/

Gebauer, H., & Saul, C. J. (2014). Business model innovation in the water sector in developing countries. *The Science of the Total Environment*, *488-489*(1), 512–520. doi:10.1016/j.scitotenv.2014.02.046 PMID:24612490

Geffen, L. (2014). A brief history of medical education and training in Australia. *The Medical Journal of Australia*, *201*(1Suppl), 19–22. doi:10.5694/mja14.00118 PMID:25047770

Gelbmann, U. (2010). Establishing Strategic CSR: An Austrian CSR Quality Seal to Sub-stantiate the Strategic CSR Performance of SMEs. *Sustainable Development*, *18*(2), 90–98. doi:10.1002/sd.448

George, C., & Reed, M. G. (2016). Building institutional capacity for environmental governance through social entrepreneurship: Lessons from Canadian biosphere reserves. *Ecology and Society*, *21*(1), 18. doi:10.5751/ES-08229-210118

George, G., & Bock, A. J. (2011). The business model in practice and its implications for entrepreneurship research. *Entrepreneurship: Theory & Practice*, *35*(1), 83–111.

Germak, A. J. (2014). Building Nonprofit Capacity: A Guide to Managing Change Through Organizational. *Human Service Organizations: Management. Leadership & Governance*, *38*(1), 116–117.

Ghezzi, A., Cavallaro, A., Rangone, A., & Balocco, R. (2015). On business models, resources and exogenous (dis)continuous innovation: Evidences from the mobile applications industry. *International Journal of Technology Management*, *68*(1/2), 21–48. doi:10.1504/IJTM.2015.068777

Gibelman, M., & Gelman, S. R. (2004). A Loss of Credibility: Patterns of Wrongdoing among Nongovernmental Organizations. *Voluntas*, *15*(4), 355–381. doi:10.1007/s11266-004-1237-7

GIIN. (2016). *What is impact investing?* Retrieved April 05, 2016, from https://thegiin.org/impact-investing/need-to-know/#s1

Gikas, J., & Grant, M. M. (2013). Mobile computing devices in higher education: Student perspectives on learning with cellphones, smartphones & social media. *The Internet and Higher Education*, *19*, 18–26. doi:10.1016/j.iheduc.2013.06.002

Girotra, K., & Netessine, S. (2014). Four paths to business model innovation. *Harvard Business Review*, *92*(7/8), 96–103. PMID:24956873

Gislason, M., & Wilson, J. (2009). *Coaching skills for nonprofit managers: Creating a culture of contribution, self-motivation, accountability, and high performance*. San Francisco: Jossey-Bass.

Glanzel, G., & Scheuerle, T. (2016). Social impact invesitng in Germany: Current impediments from investors and social entrepreneurs perspectives. *Voluntas: International Journal of Voluntary &Nonprofit Organizations*, *27*(4), 1638–1668. doi:10.1007/s11266-015-9621-z

Glaser, M. (2010, November 30). *Fundly + Facebook = Millions in Micro-Donations for Campaigns*. Retrieved July 7, 2016, from http://mediashift.org/2010/11/fundly-facebook-millions-in-micro-donations-for-campaigns334/

Glavas, A., & Mish, J. (2014). Resources and Capabilities of Triple Bottom Line Firms: Going Over Old or Breaking New Ground? *Journal of Business Ethics*, *127*(3), 623–642. doi:10.1007/s10551-014-2067-1

Global Reporting Initiative. (2011). *Guía Para La Elaboración De Memorias De Sostenibilidad*. Amsterdam.

Global Social Venture Competition (GSVC). (2012). *Social Impact Assessment Guidelines*. Accessed February 19, 2014. http://www.iedu.org.cn/gsvc/download/2011_GSVC_SIA_Guidelines.pdf

Godfrey, P. C., & Hatch, N. W. (2007). Researching corporate social responsibility: An agenda for the 21st century. *Journal of Business Ethics*, *70*(1), 87–98. doi:10.1007/s10551-006-9080-y

Goldmark, A. (2012, December 10). *Everyone Chip In, Please: Crowdfunding Sandy*. Retrieved July 8, 2016, from http://www.npr.org/2012/12/10/166742312/everyone-chip-in-please-crowdfunding-sandy

Golensky, M., & Mulder, C. A. (2006). Coping in a constrained economy: Survival strategies of nonprofit human service organizations. *Administration in Social Work*, *30*(3), 5–24. doi:10.1300/J147v30n03_02

Golini, R., Kalchschmidt, M., & Landoni, P. (2015). Adoption of project management practices : The impact on international development projects of non-governmental organizations. *International Journal of Project Management*, *33*(3), 650–663. doi:10.1016/j.ijproman.2014.09.006

Gomez, R. (2013). The Changing Field of ICTD: Growth and maturation of the field, 2000-2010. *The Electronic Journal of Information Systems in Developing Countries, 58*.

Goodhand, J., Hulme, D., & Lewer, N. (2002). Social Capital and the Political Economy of Violence: A case study of Sri Lanka. *Disasters*, *24*(4), 390–406. doi:10.1111/1467-7717.00155 PMID:11138373

Goodwin, Y., & Strang, K. D. (2012). Socio-cultural and multi-disciplinary perceptions of risk. *International Journal of Risk and Contingency Management*, *1*(1), 1–11. doi:10.4018/ijrcm.2012010101

Gore, E. M., & DiGiammarino, B. (2014). *Crowdfunding for Nonprofits*. Standford Social Innovation Review.

Government of Canada, C. R. A. (2012, January 3). *Informant Leads Program*. Retrieved July 8, 2016, from http://www.cra-arc.gc.ca/leads/

Government of Canada. S. C. (2015, December 16). *Infographic: Charitable Giving in Canada*. Retrieved July 8, 2016, from http://www.statcan.gc.ca/pub/11-627-m/11-627-m2015006-eng.htm

Grabenwarter, U., & Liechtenstein, H. (2011). *Search of Gamma---An Unconventional Perspective on Impact Investing*. IESE Business School, University of Navarra.

Granados, M. L., Hlupic, V., Coakes, E., & Mohamed, S. (2011). Social enterprise and social entrepreneurship research and theory: A bibliometric analysis from 1991 to 2010. *Social Enterprise Journal*, *7*(3), 198–218. doi:10.1108/17508611111182368

Granovetter, M. (1985). Economic action and social structure: A theory of embeddedness. *American Journal of Sociology*, *91*(3), 481–510. doi:10.1086/228311

Grant, J. (2004). *Investment Review of Health and Medical Research*. Canberra: Academic Pressa.

Gray, R. H., Owen, D. L., & Adams, C. (1996). *Accounting and accountability, changes and challenges in corporate social and environmental reporting*. Hemel Hempstead, UK: Prentice Hall.

Gray, R., Kouhy, R., & Lavers, S. (1995). Corporate Social and Environmental Reporting: A Review of the Literature and a Longitudinal Study of UK Disclosure. *Accounting, Auditing & Accountability Journal*, *8*(2), 47–77. doi:10.1108/09513579510146996

Greenwood, R., & Hinings, C. R. (1996). Understanding radical organizational change: Bringing together the old and new institutionalism. *Academy of Management Review*, *21*, 1022–1054.

Greenwood, R., Suddaby, R., & Hinings, C. R. (2002). Theorizing change: The role of professional association in the transformation of institutionalized fields. *Academy of Management Journal*, *45*(1), 58–80. doi:10.2307/3069285

Greer, C. R., Lusch, R. F., & Vargo, S. L. (2016). A service perspective. *Organizational Dynamics*, *1*(45), 28–38. doi:10.1016/j.orgdyn.2015.12.004

Grieco, C., Michelini, L., & Iasevoli, G. (2015). Measuring value creation in social enterprises a cluster analysis of social impact assessment models. *Nonprofit and Voluntary Sector Quarterly*, *44*(6), 1173–1193. doi:10.1177/0899764014555986

Grosser, K. (2015). Corporate Social Responsibility and Multi-Stakeholder Governance: Pluralism, Feminist Perspectives and Women's NGOs. *Journal of Business Ethics*, 1–15.

Grossman, R. L., & Siegel, K. (2014). Organizational models for Big Data and analytics. *Journal of Organization Design*, *3*(1), 20–25. doi:10.7146/jod.9799

Gross-Schaefer, A., & Zaller, Z. (1998). The ethics audit for nonprofit organizations. *PM Network*, *12*(4), 43.

Guan, Y., Wen, Y., Xiaohua, S., Haiyang, C., Wei, L., Liu, Y., & Dong, Z. et al. (2013). The role of perceived organizational career management and career anchor. *European Journal of Work and Organizational Psychology*.

Gubler, M., Biemann, T., Tschopp, C., & Grote, G. (2015). How Career Anchors Differentiate Managerial Career Trajectories A Sequence Analysis Perspective. *Journal of Career Development*, *42*(5), 412–430. doi:10.1177/0894845315572891

Guerci, M., Radaelli, G., Siletti, E., Cirella, S., & Rami Shani, A. B. (2015). The impact of human resource management practices and corporate sustainability on organizational ethical climates: An employee perspective. *Journal of Business Ethics*, *126*(2), 325–342. doi:10.1007/s10551-013-1946-1

Gugerty, M. K. (2010). The Emergence of Non-profit Self-Regulation in Africa. *Nonprofit and Voluntary Sector Quarterly*, *39*(6), 1087–1112. doi:10.1177/0899764010372972

Gumport, P. J. (2001). Restructuring: Imperatives and opportunities for academic leaders. *Innovative Higher Education*, *25*(4), 239–251. doi:10.1023/A:1011042522978

Gunz, H., Evans, M., & Jalland, M. (2000). Career boundaries in a 'boundaryless' world. *Career frontiers: New conceptions of working lives*, 24-53.

Guo, C., & Bielefeld, W. (2014). *Social entrepreneurship: An evidence-based approach to creating social value*. John Wiley & Sons.

Gupta, G., & Gupta, A. (2012). International assignments, expatriate adjustment and perceived impact of parent organization support. *Business & Management Review*, *3*(1), 57–65.

Guy, B. S., & Patton, W. E. (2013). The marketing of altruistic causes: Understanding why people help. *Journal of Consumer Marketing*.

Guzzo, T., Ferri, F., Grifoni, P., & Firus, K. (2012). Flood risk awareness: An experiment using school students to inform families and friends. *International Journal of Risk and Contingency Management*, *1*(1), 49–63. doi:10.4018/ijrcm.2012010104

Haddad, M. A. (2011). A state-in-society approach to the nonprofit sector: Welfare services in Japan. *VOLUNTAS: International Journal of Voluntary and Nonprofit Organizations*, *22*(1), 26–47. doi:10.1007/s11266-010-9135-7

Hader, R. (2006). Put employee termination ettiquette to practice. *Nursing Management*, *27*(12), 6. PMID:17159553

Haegeman, K., Spiesberger, M., Veselitskaya, N., Sokolov, A., & Weiss, G. (2015). FTA supporting effective priority setting in multi-lateral research programme cooperation: The case of EUâ€"Russia S&T cooperation. *Technological Forecasting and Social Change*, *101*(1), 200–215. doi:10.1016/j.techfore.2015.04.009

Hafsi, T., & Thomas, H. (2005). Strategic Management and Change in High Dependency Environments: The Case of a Philanthropic Organization. Voluntas. *Voluntas*, *16*(4), 329–351. doi:10.1007/s11266-005-9146-y

Halfpenny, P., & Reid, M. (2002). Research on the voluntary sector: An overview. *Policy and Politics*, *30*(4), 533–550. doi:10.1332/030557302760590369

Hall, D. T. (1996). Protean careers of the 21st century. *The Academy of Management Executive, 10*, 8. doi:10. 5465/AME.1996.3145315

Hall, D. T. (2004). The protean career: A quarter-century journey. *Journal of Vocational Behavior*, *65*(1), 1–13. doi:10.1016/j.jvb.2003.10.006

Hall, H. (2006). Getting over growing pains: Life-cycle analyses help charities deal with the challenges of aging. *The Chronicle of Philanthropy*, *12*(3), 15.

Hamilton, J. (2010). *Medical Education Today: What would Flexner think of it?* Australian and New Zealand Association for Medical Educators (ANZAME).

Hamilton, J., & Vandewerdt, J. M. (1990). The accreditation of undergraduate medical education in Australia. *The Medical Journal of Australia*, *153*, 541–545. PMID:2233477

Hamilton, R., & Brown, D. (2016). Disaster management and continuity planning in libraries: Literature review. *International Journal of Risk and Contingency Management*, *5*(1), 26–41. doi:10.4018/IJRCM.2016010103

Hamline School of Law. (2009). *Faculty, staff, and administration*. Retrieved from http://mitchellhamline.edu/biographies/person/david-larson

Handy, F., Seto, S., Wakaruk, A., Mersey, B., Mejia, A., & Copeland, L. (2010). The discerning consumer: Is nonprofit status a factor? *Nonprofit and Voluntary Sector Quarterly*, *39*(5), 866–883. doi:10.1177/0899764010362113

Hangman, H. (1990). The Economic Role of Commercial Nonprofits: The Evolution of the US Savings Bank. In H. Anheier & W. Seibel (Eds.), *The Third Sector: Comparative Studies of Nonprofit Organizations* (pp. 65–75). Berlin: Walter de Gruyter & Co.

Hansmann, H. (1987). Economic Theories of Nonprofit Organization. *VOLUNTAS: International Journal of Voluntary and Not For Profit Organization*, *89*(2), 93-96.

Hansmann, H. (1980). Role of Nonprofit Enterprise. *The Yale Law Journal*, *89*(5), 835–901. doi:10.2307/796089

Hargrave, T., & Van de Ven, A. (2006). A collective action model of insitutional innovation. *Academy of Management Review*, *31*(4), 864–888. doi:10.5465/AMR.2006.22527458

Harris, B. (2010). Voluntary action and the state in historical perspective. *Voluntary Sector Review*, *1*(1), 25–40. doi:10.1332/204080510X496993

Harrison, D. A., Shaffer, M. A., & Bhaskar-Shrinivas, P. (2004). Going places: Roads more and less traveled in research on expatriate experiences. *Research in Personnel and Human Resources Management*, *22*, 203–252.

Harrison, J. S., Bosse, D. A., & Phillips, R. A. (2010). Managing for stakeholders, stakeholder utility functions, and competitive advantage. *Strategic Management Journal*, *31*(1), 58–74. doi:10.1002/smj.801

Harrow, J., & Mole, V. (2005). I want to move once I have got things straight: Voluntary sector chief executives career accounts. *Nonprofit Management & Leadership*, *16*(1), 79–100. doi:10.1002/nml.91

Hart, C. (1998). *Doing a literature review: Releasing the social science research imagination*. London: Sage Publications.

Hartmann, P. M., Zaki, M., & Feldmann, N. (2014). *Big Data for Big Business? A Taxonomy of Data- driven Business Models used by Start-up Firms*. University of Cambridge Working Paper.

Hartnerr, B., & Matan, R. (2011). The balanced scorecard: A strategic tool for the non-profit sector. Retrieved from http://www.sobel-cpa.com/resources/white-papers

Hatum, A., & Pettigrew, A. M. (2006). Determinants of organizational flexibility: A study in an emerging economy. *British Journal of Management*, *17*(2), 115–137. doi:10.1111/j.1467-8551.2005.00469.x

Haugstad, B. (1999). *Strategy Theory- A short review of the literature*. Retrieved from http://www.kunne.no/upload/Gamle%20publikasjoner/Nedtegnelser/Strategy%20Theory_N0299_Haugstad.pdf

Hazen, T. L. (2012). Social Networks and the Law: Crowdfunding or Fraudfunding? Social Networks and the Securities Laws-Why the Specially Tailored Exemption Must Be Conditioned on Meaningful Disclosure. *North Carolina Law Review*, *90*, 1735–2162.

Healey, P. (1998). Building institutional capacity through collaborative approaches to urban planning. *Environment & Planning A*, *30*(9), 1531–1546. doi:10.1068/a301531

Heffetz, O., & Ligett, K. (2014). Privacy and data-based research. *The Journal of Economic Perspectives*, *28*(2), 75–98. doi:10.1257/jep.28.2.75

Heitzmann, K. (2000). *The role of third sector organizations in specific policy fields: Contrasting non-profit theory and empirical findings—The case of Austria*. Paper prepared for the Fourth International Conference of the ISTR, Dublin, Ireland.

Helmig, B., Ingerfurth, S., & Pinz, A. (2014). Success and failure of non-profit organizations: Theoretical foundations, empirical evidence, and future research. *Voluntas: International Journal Of Voluntary & Nonprofit Organizations*, *25*(6), 1509–1538. doi:10.1007/s11266-013-9402-5

Hemer, J. (2011). *A snapshot on crowdfunding*. Working papers firms and region.

Herbohn, K., Walker, J., & Loo, H. Y. M. (2014). Corporate Social Responsibility: The Link Between Sustainability Disclosure and Sustainability Performance. *Abacus*, *50*(4), 422–459. doi:10.1111/abac.12036

Herr, E. L. (1990). Issues in career research. Methodological approaches to the study of career, 3-21.

Heurlin, C. (2010). Governing civil society: The political logic of NGO–state relations under dictatorship. *VOLUNTAS: International Journal of Voluntary and Nonprofit Organizations*, *21*(2), 220–239. doi:10.1007/s11266-009-9103-2

Hibbert, S., & Horne, S. (1996). Giving to charity: Questioning the donor decision process. *Journal of Consumer Marketing*, *13*(2), 4–13. doi:10.1108/07363769610115366

Hill, C. W., & Jones, T. M. (1992). Stakeholder -agency theory. *Journal of Management Studies*, *29*(2), 131–154. doi:10.1111/j.1467-6486.1992.tb00657.x

Hill, R. (1949). *Families under stress: Adjustment to the crises of war separation and reunion*. New York, NY: Harper.

Hines, F. (2005). Viable social enterprise: An evaluation of business support to social enterprises. *Social Enterprise Journal*, *1*(1), 13–28. doi:10.1108/17508610580000704

Hirsch, F. (2005). *Social limits to growth*. Routledge.

Hobey, E. (2014, July 4). *Fundly: Crowdfunding for the Greater Social Good Interview with Dennis Hu, CEO of Fundly*. Retrieved July 7, 2016, from http://www.crowdfundinsider.com/2014/07/43251-fundly-crowdfunding-greater-social-good-interview-dennis-hu-ceo-fundly/

Hoefer, R., & Sliva, S. M. (2014). Assessing and Augmenting Administration Skills in Nonprofits: An Exploratory Mixed Methods Study. *Human Service Organizations: Management. Leadership & Governance*, *38*(3), 246–257.

Hoffmann, A., & Birnbrich, C. (2012). The impact of fraud prevention on bank-customer relationships. *International Journal of Bank Marketing*, *30*(5), 390–407. doi:10.1108/02652321211247435

Hogan, E. (2008). Does 'corporate' responsibility apply to not-for-profit organizations? In S. O. Idowu & W. L. Filho (Eds.), *Professionals' perspectives on corporate social responsibility* (pp. 271–288). Berlin: Springer.

Hogue, J. (2015, March 23). *Your Crowdfunding Questions, Answered*. Retrieved September 12, 2016, from http://www.crowd101.com/your-crowdfunding-questions-answered/

Hogue, J. (2015, November 23). *How to Set Realistic Crowdfunding Goals*. Retrieved September 11, 2016, from http://www.crowd101.com/setting-realistic-crowdfunding-goals/

Holotescu, C., & Grosseck, G. (2013). An Empirical Analysis Of The Educational Effects Of Social Media In Universities And Colleges. *Internet Learning*, *2*(1), 21–32.

Hopkins, K. M., Cohen-Callow, A., Kim, H. J., & Hwang, J. (2010). Beyond intent to leave: Using multiple outcome measures for assessing turnover in child welfare. *Children and Youth Services Review*, *32*(10), 1380–1387. doi:10.1016/j.childyouth.2010.06.006

Hoque, F. (2016). *Family offices and investing for impact: How to manage wealth, expand legacies and make a difference in the world*. Retrieved June 5, 2016, from http://www.ussif.org/files/Publications/Family_Offices.pdf

Hornsby, A. (2012). *The good analyst, Impact Measurement and Analysis in the Social-Purpose Universe*. Investing for Good.

Hosny, M. I., & Fatima, S. (2012). Facebok in education: Students, teachers, and library perspectives. *Journal of Computing*, *4*(6), 78–86.

House, R. J., & Javidan, M. (2004). Overview of GLOBE. In R. J. House, P. Hanges, M. Javidan, P. Dorfman, & V. Gupta (Eds.), *Culture, leadership, and organizations: The GLOBE study of 62 societies* (pp. 9–28). Thousand Oaks, CA: Sage.

https://www.statista.com/statistics/310218/total-kickstarter-funding/

Hu, Y., & Zheng, W. (2008, October). Market orientation, innovation and performance of non-profit organizations: evidence from China. In *Service Operations and Logistics, and Informatics, 2008. IEEE/SOLI 2008. IEEE International Conference on* (Vol. 1, pp. 429-434). IEEE.

Huang, Z., & Palvia, P. (2001). ERP implementation issues in advanced and developing countries. *Business Process Management Journal*, *7*(3), 276–284. doi:10.1108/14637150110392773

Hugget, J. (2009). *The challenges nonprofits face in the current uncertain economic environment*. Retrieved from http://www.csi.edu.au/assets/assetdoc/985b7df93006c9d4/Lecture%20Series%20No.%206%20-%20Inaugural%20John%20B%20Reid%20Lecture.pdf

Humphreys, J. S., & Gregory, G. (2012). Celebrating another decade of progress in rural health: What is the current state of play? *The Australian Journal of Rural Health*, *20*(3), 156–163. doi:10.1111/j.1440-1584.2012.01276.x PMID:22620481

Hurlburt, M., Aarons, G. A., Fettes, D., Willging, C., Gunderson, L., & Chaffin, M. J. (2014). Interagency Collaborative Team model for capacity building to scale-up evidence-based practice. *Children and Youth Services Review*, *39*(1), 160–168. doi:10.1016/j.childyouth.2013.10.005 PMID:27512239

Hutt, R. (1979). The focus group interview: A technique for counselling small business clients. *Journal of Small Business Management*, *17*(1), 15–19.

Hutzschenreuter, T., & Kleindienst, I. (2006). Strategy-process research: What have we learned and what is still to be explored. *Journal of Management*, *32*(5), 673–720. doi:10.1177/0149206306291485

Huy, Q., & Shipilov, A. (2012). The key to social media success within organizations. *MIT Sloan Management Review*, *54*(1), 72–81.

Hvenmark, J. (2013). Business as usual? On managerialization and the adoption of the balanced scorecard in a democratically governed civil society organization. *Administrative Theory and Praxis*, *35*(2), 223–247. doi:10.2753/ATP1084-1806350203

Ibrahim, S. E. (2010). An alternative methodology for formulating an operations strategy: The case of BTC-Egypt. *Management Decision*, *48*(6), 868–893. doi:10.1108/00251741011053442

Ifinedo, P. (2012). Drivers of E-Government Maturity in Two Developing Regions: Focus on Latin America and Sub-Saharan Africa. *Journal of Information Systems and Technology Management*, *9*(1), 5–22. doi:10.4301/S1807-17752012000100001

Igbaria, M., Meredith, G., & Smith, D. C. (1995). Career orientations of information systems employees in South Africa. *The Journal of Strategic Information Systems*, *4*(4), 319–340. doi:10.1016/0963-8687(95)80002-8

Iida, M., Seidman, G., Shrout, P., Fujita, K., & Bolger, N. (2008). Modeling support provision in intimate relationships. *Journal of Personality and Social Psychology*, *94*(3), 460–478. doi:10.1037/0022-3514.94.3.460 PMID:18284292

Imagine Canada. (2015, March 10). *Tax Incentives for Charitable Donations in Canada with a Focus on the Stretch Tax Credit for Charitable Giving | Imagine Canada*. Retrieved July 8, 2016, from http://www.imaginecanada.ca/sites/default/files/chief_economist_tax_incentives_discussion_paper_03102015.pdf

Imagine Canada. (2016). *Who we are | Imagine Canada*. Retrieved July 8, 2016, from http://www.imaginecanada.ca/who-we-are

Indiegogo. (2012, May 17). *Indiegogo Insight: Nearly 40% of Active Campaigns Receive Money From Multiple Countries - Indiegogo Blog*. Retrieved July 8, 2016, from https://go.indiegogo.com/blog/2012/05/indiegogo-insight-nearly-40-of-active-campaigns-receive-money-from-multiple-countries.html indiegogo.com. (2016, July 7). *How To Raise Tax-Deductible Funds.* Retrieved July 8, 2016, from http://support.indiegogo.com/hc/en-us/articles/202444736-How-To-Raise-Tax-Deductible-Funds

Indiegogo.com. (2016, July 7). *How to Raise Tax-Deductible Funds.* Retrieved July 8, 2016, from http://support.indiegogo.com/hc/en-us/articles/202444736-How-To-Raise-Tax-Deductible-Funds

Ingenhoff, D., & Koelling, A. M. (2007). The potential of Web sites as a relationship building tool for charitable fundraising NPOs. *Public Relations Review*, *1*(35), 66–73.

Inkson, K., Gunz, H., Ganesh, S., & Roper, J. (2012). Boundaryless careers: Bringing back boundaries. *Organization Studies*, *33*(3), 323–340. doi:10.1177/0170840611435600

IRS. (2016). *Instructions for Form 990. Return of Organization. Exempt From Income Tax. Under section 501(c), 527, or 4947(a)(1) of the Internal Revenue.* Internal Revenue Service (IRS). Retrieved June 20, 2016, from the World Wide Web: https://www.irs.gov/pub/irs-pdf/i990.pdf

Issenberg, S. B., Gordon, M. S., Gordon, D., Safford, R. E., & Hart, I. R. (2001). Simulation and new learning technologies. *Medical Teacher*, *23*(1), 16–23. doi:10.1080/01421590020007324 PMID:11260734

Jafarizadeh, B., & Khorshid-Doust, R. R. (2008). A method of project selection based on capital asset pricing theories in a framework of mean–semideviation behaviour. *International Journal of Project Management*, *26*(6), 612–619. doi:10.1016/j.ijproman.2007.09.004

Jäger, U. P., & Schröer, A. (2013). Integrated Organizational Identity: A Definition of Hybrid Organizations and a Research Agenda. *VOLUNTAS: International Journal of Voluntary and Nonprofit Organizations*, *25*(5), 1281–1306. doi:10.1007/s11266-013-9386-1

Jager, U., Hover, H., & Schroer, A., & Strauch, M. (2012). Experience of Solidarity: Why Executive Directors Work for Market Driven Nonprofits. *Nonprofit and Voluntary Sector Quarterly.*

Jałocha, B. (2014). *Zarządzanie portfelem projektów. Koncepcje biznesowe a praktyka organizacji publicznych.* Kraków: WUJ.

Jaskyte, K., & Dresssler, W. W. (2004). Nonprofit organizations studying culture as an integral aggregate variable: Organizational culture and innovation in a group of nonprofit organizations. *Field Methods*, *16*(3), 265–284. doi:10.1177/1525822X03262281

Javalgi, R. G., Hall, K. D., & Cavusgil, S. T. (2014). Corporate entrepreneurship, customer-oriented selling, absorptive capacity, and international sales performance in the international B2B setting: Conceptual framework and research propositions. *International Business Review*, *23*(1), 1193–1202. doi:10.1016/j.ibusrev.2014.04.003

Javidan, M., Dorfman, P. W., de Luque, M. S., & House, R. J. (2006). In the eye of the beholder: Cross-cultural lessons in leadership from Project GLOBE. *The Academy of Management Perspectives*, *20*(1), 67–90. doi:10.5465/AMP.2006.19873410

Jayashankar, P., Ashta, A., & Rasmussen, M. (2015). Analysis: Slow money in an age of fiduciary capitalism. *Ecological Economics*, *116*(1), 322–329. doi:10.1016/j.ecolecon.2015.05.007

Jeffreys, M. R. (2012). *Nursing student retention: Understanding the process and making a difference.* New York, NY: Springer Publishing.

Jegers, M. (2009). Corporate Governance in nonprofit organizations: A nontechnical review of the economic literature. *Nonprofit Management & Leadership*, *20*(2), 143–164. doi:10.1002/nml.246

Jenner, P. (2016). Social enterprise sustainability revisited: An international perspective. *Social Enterprise Journal*, *12*(1), 42–60. doi:10.1108/SEJ-12-2014-0042

Jeyaraj, A., & Sabherwal, R. (2008). Adoption of information systems innovations by individuals: A study of processes involving contextual, adopter, and influencer actions. *Information and Organization*, *18*(3), 205–234. doi:10.1016/j.infoandorg.2008.04.001

Jiménez, G. S., Ongena, S., Peydro, J. L., & Saurina, J. (2014). Hazardous times for monetary policy: What do 23 million loans say about the impact of monetary policy on credit risk-taking. *Econometrica*, *82*, 463–505. doi:10.3982/ECTA10104

Ji-Yong, S. (2014). A study on the determinants of business stability in credit card firms: Evidence from Korea. *Asian Academy of Management Journal*, *19*(2), 105–122.

Johnson, M., Christensen, C., & Kagermann, H. (2008). Reinventing your business model. *Harvard Business Review*, *86*(12), 50–59. PMID:18681297

Jonas, D. (2010). Empowering project portfolio managers: How management involvement impacts project portfolio management performance. *International Journal of Project Management*, *28*(8), 818–831. doi:10.1016/j.ijproman.2010.07.002

Jordan, L. (2003). *Mechanisms for NGO Accountability*. GPPI Research Paper Series No.3. Global Public Policy Institute.

Jordan, L. (2005). *Mechanisms for NGO Accountability*. GPPI Research Paper Series 3. Global Public Policy Institute.

Jugdev, K. (2003). *Developing and sustaining Project management as a strategic basset: A multiple case study using the resource-based view*. University of Calgary.

Junco, R., & Candrainna, C. (2010). *Evaluating sow the courseSmart engagement index predicts student course outcomes*. Purdue University Working Paper.

Jussila, J., Kärkkäinen, H., & Aramo-Immonen, H. (2014). Social media utilization in business-to-business relationships of technology industry firms. *Computers in Human Behavior*, *30*, 606–613. doi:10.1016/j.chb.2013.07.047

Kaboolian, L.Administration Debate. (1998). The new public management: Challenging the boundaries of the management vs. administration debate. *Public Administration Review*, *58*(3), 189–193. doi:10.2307/976558

Kajanus, M., Iire, A., Eskelinen, T., Heinonen, M., & Hansen, E. (2014). Business model design: New tools for business systems innovation. *Scandinavian Journal of Forest Research*, *29*(6), 603-614.

Kanar, C. C. (2014). *The confident Student*. Boston, MA: Wadsworth, Cengage Learning.

Kane, G. C., Alavi, M., Labianca, G., & Borgatti, S. P. (2014). What's different about social media networks? A framework and research agenda. *MIS Querterly*, *38*(1), 274–304.

Kanter, R. M. (1987). *Careers and the wealth of nations: A macro-perspective on the structure and implications of career forms*. Division of Research, Harvard Business School.

Kaplan, A. M., & Haenlein, M. (2010). Users of the world, unite! The challenges and opportunities of social media. *Business Horizons*, *53*(1), 59–68. doi:10.1016/j.bushor.2009.09.003

Kaplan, R. S., & Norton, D. P. (2001). The strategy-focused organization. *Strategy and Leadership*, *29*(3), 41–42. doi:10.1108/sl.2001.26129cab.002

Kaplan, R. S., & Norton, D. P. (2001). Transforming the Balanced Scorecard from Performance Measurement to Strategic Management. Part II. *Accounting Horizons*, *15*(2), 147–160. doi:10.2308/acch.2001.15.2.147

Kaplan, R., & Norton, D. (1992). The Balanced Scorecard – Measures That Drive Performance. *Harvard Business Review*, *70*(1), 71–79. PMID:10119714

Karanikolos, M., Mladovsky, P., Cylus, J., Thomson, S., Basu, S., Stuckler, D., & McKee, M. et al. (2013). Financial crisis, austerity, and health in Europe. *Lancet*, *381*(9874), 1323–1331. doi:10.1016/S0140-6736(13)60102-6 PMID:23541059

Karikari, T. K., Quansah, E., & Mohamed, W. M. Y. (2015). Developing expertise in bioinformatics for biomedical research in Africa. *Applied & Translational Genomics, 6*, 31-34.

Kast, F. E., & Rosenzweig, J. E. (1972). General systems theory: Applications for organization and management. *Academy of Management Journal*, *15*(4), 447–465. doi:10.2307/255141

Katz, M. L., & Shapiro, C. (1985). Network externalities, competitions, and compatibility. *The American Economic Review*, *75*, 424–444.

Kearns, K. (2000). *Private sector strategies for social sector success.* San Francisco: Jossey-Bass.

Kearns, K. P. (1994). The strategic management of accountability in nonprofit organizations: An analytical framework. *Public Administration Review*, *54*(2), 185–192. doi:10.2307/976528

Keevers, L., Treleaven, L., Sykes, C., & Darcy, M. (2012). Made to measure: Taming practices with results-based accountability. *Organization Studies*, *33*(1), 97–120. doi:10.1177/0170840611430597

Kellen, V., Recktenwald, A., & Burr, S. (2013). *Applying Big Data in higher education: A case study*. Arlington, MA: Cutter Consortium.

Kelly, K. S. (2001). Stewardship: The fifth step in the public relations process. In R. L. Heath (Ed.), *Handbook of public relations* (pp. 279–290). Thousand Oaks, CA: SAGE. doi:10.4135/9781452220727.n21

Kendall, J., & Knapp, M. (1995). A loose and baggy monster. An introduction to the voluntary sector, 66-95.

Kendall, J. (2003). *The voluntary sector: Comparative perspectives in the UK*. Psychology Press. doi:10.4324/9780203400128

Keohane, R. O. (2002, May). Political accountability. In *Conference on Delegation to International Organizations* (p. 8).

Kerlin, J. A. (2006). Social enterprise in the United States and Europe: Understanding and learning from the differences. *Voluntas*, *17*(3), 246–262. doi:10.1007/s11266-006-9016-2

Kerlin, J. A. (2013). Defining Social Enterprise Across Different Contexts A Conceptual Framework Based on Institutional Factors. *Nonprofit and Voluntary Sector Quarterly*, *42*(1), 84–108. doi:10.1177/0899764011433040

Kerlin, J. A. (2013). The 501(c)(3) Nonprofit social enterprise. In T. S. Lyons (Ed.), *Social entrepreneurship: how businesses can transform society* (Vol. 1, pp. 27–46). Santa Barbara, CA: Praeger.

Kernot, C., & Mcneill, J. (2011). *Australian Stories of Social Enterprise*. Retrieved from http://www.csi.edu.au/assets/assetdoc/81476e838a4e4d61/Australian%20Stories%20of%20Social%20Enterprise.pdf

Khanagha, S., Volberda, H., & Oshri, I. (2014). Business model renewal and ambidexterity: Structural alteration and strategy formation process during transition to a cloud business model. *R & D Management*, *44*(3), 322–340. doi:10.1111/radm.12070

Khang, D. B., & Moe, T. L. (2008). Success criteria and factors for international development projects: A life cycle based framework. *Project Management Journal*, *39*(1), 72–84. doi:10.1002/pmj.20034

Khan, K., Pattison, T., & Sherwood, M. (2011). Simulation in medical education. *Medical Teacher*, *33*(1), 1–3. doi:10.3109/0142159X.2010.519412 PMID:21182376

Khieng, S. (2014). Funding Mobilization Strategies of Nongovernmental Organizations in Cambodia. *Voluntas: International Journal of Voluntary & Nonprofit Organizations, 25*(6), 1441–1464. doi:10.1007/s11266-013-9400-7

Kickstarter. (2016, July 7). *Kickstarter Stats — Kickstarter*. Retrieved July 8, 2016, from https://www.kickstarter.com/help/stats

Killen, C. P. (2008). *Project portfolio management for product innovation in service and manufacturing industries*. Retrieved September 10, 2011 from http://minerva.mq.edu.au:8080/vital/access/manager/Repository/mq:6279

Kim, D., Chun, H., Kwak, Y., & Nam, Y. (2014). The Employment of Dialogic Principles in Website, Facebook, and Twitter Platforms of Environmental Nonprofit Organizations. *Social Science Computer Review*. Available at: http://ssc.sagepub.com/content/early/2014/01/30/0894439314525752

Kim, L. (2015, January 2). *Most Successful Feel-Good Crowdfunding Campaigns of the Year*. Retrieved September 12, 2016, from http://www.inc.com/larry-kim/most-successful-feel-good-crowdfunding-campaigns-of-the-year.html

Kim, S. E., & Lee, J. W.Seok Eun Kim; Jung Wook Lee. (2007). Is mission attachment an effective management tool for employee retention? An empirical analysis of a nonprofit human services agency. *Review of Public Personnel Administration, 27*(3), 227–248. doi:10.1177/0734371X06295791

Kim, W. C., & Mauborgne, R. (2000). Knowing a winning business idea when you see one. *Harvard Business Review, 78*(5), 129–138. PMID:11143149

Kingdon, J. W. (1984). *Agendas, alternatives and public politics*. Boston: Little Brown.

King, M. A. (2008). A strategic assessment of the higher education industry: applying the Porter's five forces for industry analysis. In *Southeastern Decision Sciences Institute Annual Conference*. Blacksburg, VA: Pamplin College of Business, Virginia Polytechnic Institute and State University.

Kingma, B. (1997). Public Good Theories of the not for profit sector: Weisbrod Revisited. *Voluntas, 8*(2), 135–14. doi:10.1007/BF02354191

Kingma, B. R. (2003). Public Good Theories of Nonprofit Sector: Weisbrod Revisited. In H. Anheier & A. Ben Ner (Eds.), *The Study of the Nonprofit Enterprise: Theories and Approaches*. Kluwer Academic / Plenum Publishers. doi:10.1007/978-1-4615-0131-2_3

Kitchenham, B. (2004). *Procedures for performing systematic reviews* (Vol. 33). Keele, UK: Academic Press.

Kitchenham, B., & Brereton, P. (2013). A systematic review of systematic review process research in software engineering. *Information and Software Technology, 55*(12), 2049–2075. doi:10.1016/j.infsof.2013.07.010

Kloppenborg, T., & Opfer, W. (2002). The current state of project management research: Trends, interpretations and predictions. *Project Management Journal, 33*(2), 5–18.

Knife, K. A. H. N., Haughton, A., & Dixon, E. (2014). Measuring sustainability and effectiveness of social value creation by social sector actors social enterprises within developing countries. *Academy of Entrepreneurship Journal, 20*(1), 1–22.

Knight, B., Robson, S., & House, C. (2007). The value and independence of the voluntary sector. Newcastle, UK: CENTRIS. UK.

Knight, D. K., Broome, K. M., Edwards, J. R., & Flynn, P. M. (2011). Supervisory Turnover in Outpatient Substance Abuse Treatment. *The Journal of Behavioral Health Services & Research, 38*(1), 80–90. doi:10.1007/s11414-009-9198-7 PMID:19949883

Kniveton, B. H. (2004). Managerial career anchors in a changing business environment. *Journal of European Industrial Training*, *28*(6/7), 564–573. doi:10.1108/03090590410549984

Kohler, T. (2015). Crowdsourcing-based business models: How to create and capture value. *California Management Review*, *57*(4), 63–84. doi:10.1525/cmr.2015.57.4.63

Kong, E. (2008). The development of strategic management in the non-profit context: Intellectual capital in social service non-profit organizations. *International Journal of Management Reviews*, *10*(3), 281–299. doi:10.1111/j.1468-2370.2007.00224.x

Konopaske, R., Robie, C., & Ivancevich, J. M. (2005). A preliminary model of spouse influence on managerial global assignment willingness. *International Journal of Human Resource Management*, *16*(3), 405–426. doi:10.1080/0958519042000339570

Koski, C., & Lee, T. (2014). Policy by Doing: Formulation and Adoption of Policy through Government Leadership. *Policy Studies Journal: the Journal of the Policy Studies Organization*, *42*(1), 30–54. doi:10.1111/psj.12041

Kourula, A., & Delalieux, G. (2016). The micro-level foundations and dynamics of political corporate social responsibility: Hegemony and passive revolution through civil society. *Journal of Business Ethics*, 1–17.

Kourula, A., & Laasonen, S. (2010). Nongovernmental Organizations in Business and Society, Management and International Business Research: Review and Implications from 19982007. *Business & Society*, *49*(1), 35–67. doi:10.1177/0007650309345282

Kovacs, N. O., & Wensley, A. (2015). Social media in organizations: Leveraging knowledge sharing. Pannon Management Review, 4(1), 35-65.

Kovacs, G., & Spens, K. (2005). Abductive Reasoning in Logistics Research. *International Journal of Physical Distribution & Logistics Management*, *35*(2), 133–141. doi:10.1108/09600030510590318

Kowal, J., & Roztocki, N. (2013). Information and Communication Technology Management for Global Competitiveness and Economic Growth in Emerging Economies. *The Electronic Journal of Information Systems in Developing Countries*, *57*.

Krashinsky, M. (1997). Stakeholder theories of the not for profit sector: One cut at the economic literature. *Voluntas*, *8*(2), 149–161. doi:10.1007/BF02354192

Krueger, R. A. (1988). *Focus groups: A practical guide for applied research.* Newbury Park, CA: Sage Publications.

Kruschwitz, N. (2011). First look: The second annual new intelligent enterprise survey. *MIT Sloan Management Review*, *52*, 87–89.

Krysiak, Z. (2011). Achieving enterprise stability based on economic capital. *Graziadio Business Review*, *14*(4).

Kuikka, M., & Äkkinen, M. (2011). Determining the Challenges of Organizational Social Media Adoption and Use. *ECIS 2011 Proceedings*. Retrieved 22 February, 2016, from http://aisel.aisnet.org/ecis2011/248

Kuosmanen, J. (2014). Care provision, empowerment, and market forces: The art of establishing legitimacy for work integration social enterprise. *Voluntas*, *25*(1), 248–269. doi:10.1007/s11266-012-9340-7

Kuziemko, I., & Werker, E. (2006). How much is a seat on the Security Council worth? Foreign aid and bribery at the United Nations. *Journal of Political Economy*, *114*(5), 905–930. doi:10.1086/507155

La Piana, D. (2008). *The nonprofit strategy revolution: real-time strategic planning in a rapid-response world.* Fieldstone Alliance.

Laasonen, S., Fougere, M., & Kourula, A. (2012). A Dominant Articulations in Academic Business y Society Discourse on NGO-Business relations: A critical Assessment. *Journal of Business Ethics*, *109*(4), 521–545. doi:10.1007/s10551-011-1143-z

Lagemann, E. C. (1983). *Private Power for the Public Good: A History of the Carnegie Foundation for the Advancement of Teaching*. Middletown, CT: Wesleyan University Press.

Lambert, T., & Schwienbacher, A. (2010). An empirical analysis of crowdfunding. *Social Science Research Network, 1578175.*

Lambert, S., Rothwell, A., & Herbert, I. (2016). Exploring Career Anchors in Shared Service Centres. In *International Workshop on Global Sourcing of Information Technology and Business Processes* (pp. 51-76). Springer International Publishing. doi:10.1007/978-3-319-47009-2_4

Lamson, B. (2013, November 14). *How to Successfully Crowdfund for Your Nonprofit*. Retrieved July 9, 2016, from http://www.huffingtonpost.com/ben-lamson/how-to-successfully-crowd_b_4274202.html

Landsberg, B. (2004). The Nonprofit Paradox: For-Profit Business Models in the Third Sector. *International Journal of Not-for-Profit Law*, *6*(2).

Lane, J. E. (2014). *Building a smarter university: Big Data, innovation, and analytics*. Albany, NY: State University of New York Press.

Lan, H., Zhu, Y., Ness, D., Xing, K., & Schneider, K. (2014). The role and characteristics of social entrepreneurs in contemporary rural cooperative development in China: Case studies of rural social entrepreneurship. *Asia Pacific Business Review*, *20*(3), 379–400. doi:10.1080/13602381.2014.929300

Laudon, K., & Loudon, J. (2012). *Management information systems: Managing the digital firm* (12th ed.). Prentice Hall.

Lawrence, T., Hardy, C., & Phillips, N. (2002). Institutional effects of interorganizational collaboration: The emergence of proto-institutions. *Academy of Management Journal*, *45*(1), 281–290. doi:10.2307/3069297

Lawrence, T., & Phllips, N. (2004). From Moby Dick to Free Willy: Micro-culture discourse and institutional entrepreneurship in emerging institutional fields. *Organization Science*, *11*(5), 689–711. doi:10.1177/1350508404046457

Lawson, K. A., Chew, M., & Van Der Weyden, M. B. (2004). The new Australian medical schools: Daring to be different. *The Medical Journal of Australia*, *181*(11/12), 662–666. PMID:15588204

Lazer, D., Kennedy, R., King, G., & Vespignani, A. (2014). The parable of Google flu: Traps in Big Data analysis. *Science*, *343*(6176), 1203–1205. doi:10.1126/science.1248506 PMID:24626916

Lecy, J. D., & Van Slyke, D. M. (2012). Nonprofit sector growth and density: Testing theories of government support. *Journal of Public Administration: Research and Theory*, *23*(1), 189–214. doi:10.1093/jopart/mus010

Lee, S. (2003). The regulation of fundraising: In search of the public good or an intractable problem of vested interest? *International Journal of Nonprofit and Voluntary Sector Marketing*, *8*(4), 307–314. doi:10.1002/nvsm.221

Lee, T. (2010). The rise of international nongovernmental organizations: A top-down or bottom-up explanation? *VOLUNTAS: International Journal of Voluntary and Nonprofit Organizations*, *21*(3), 393–416. doi:10.1007/s11266-010-9137-5

Lee, T. E., Chen, J. Q., & Zhang, R. (2001). Utilizing the Internet as a competitive tool for non-profit organizations. *Journal of Computer Information Systems*, *41*(3), 26–31.

Lee, T., Johnson, E., & Prakash, A. (2012). Media independence and trust in NGOs: The case of postcommunist countries. *Nonprofit and Voluntary Sector Quarterly*, *41*(1), 8–35. doi:10.1177/0899764010384444

Leinster, S. J. (2011). The history of change in the UK. In P. Cavenagh, S. J. Leinster, & S. Miles (Eds.), *The Changing Face of Medical Education.* Oxford, UK: Radcliffe Publishing Ltd.

Lengnick-Hall, C. A., Beck, T. E., & Lengnick-Hall, M. L. (2011). Developing a capacity for organizational resilience through strategic human resource management. *Human Resource Management Review*, *21*(3), 243–255. doi:10.1016/j.hrmr.2010.07.001

Leong, G. K., Snyder, D. L., & Ward, P. T. (1990). Research in the process and content of manufacturing strategy. *Omega*, *18*(2), 109–122. doi:10.1016/0305-0483(90)90058-H

Leslie, D. W. (1996). Strategic governance: The wrong questions? *The Review of Higher Education*, *20*(1), 101–112. doi:10.1353/rhe.1996.0004

Levin, K., Cashore, B., Bernstein, S., & Auld, G. (2012). Overcoming the tragedy of super wicked problems: Constraining our future selves to ameliorate global climate change. *Policy Sciences*, *45*(2), 123–152. doi:10.1007/s11077-012-9151-0

Levinson, D. J. (1978). *The seasons of a man's life.* Random House Digital, Inc.

Lewis, D., Yerby, L., Tucker, M., Foster, P. P., Hamilton, K. C., Fifolt, M. M., & Higginbotham, J. C. A. et al. (2015). Bringing Community and Academic Scholars Together to Facilitate and Conduct Authentic Community Based Participatory Research: Project UNITED. *International Journal of Environmental Research and Public Health*, *13*(1), 35. doi:10.3390/ijerph13010035 PMID:26703675

Lian, R. G., Jr. (2008). *The potential impact of the Obama administration on the labor and employment legal landscape.* Retrieved from http://washlaborwire.com/2008/11/13/the-potential-impact-of-the-obama-administration-on-the-labor-and-employment-legal-landscape-4

Lichtenstein, B. M. B., & Mendenhall, M. (2002). Non-linearity and response-ability: Emergent order in 21st-century careers. *Human Relations*, *55*(1), 5–32. doi:10.1177/0018726702055001604

Light, P. C. (2004). *Sustaining nonprofit performance: The case for capacity building and the evidence to support it.* Washington, DC: Brookings Institution Press.

Lii, Y. S., & Lee, M. (2012). Doing right leads to doing well: When the type of CSR and reputation interact to affect consumer evaluations of the firm. *Journal of Business Ethics*, *105*(1), 69–81. doi:10.1007/s10551-011-0948-0

Lillis, B., & Sweeney, M. (2013). Managing the fit between the views of competitive strategy and the strategic role of service operations. *European Management Journal*, *31*(6), 564–590. doi:10.1016/j.emj.2012.10.001

Lilly Family School of Philanthropy at Indiana University. (2013). *Leveraging the power of foundations: An analysis of program-related investing.* Retrieved March 20, 2016, from https://philanthropy.iupui.edu/files/research/complete_report_final_51713.pdf

Linder, J. C., & Cantrell, S. (2000). *Changing business models: Surveying the landscape.* Cambridge, MA: Accenture Institute for Strategic Change.

Lindgardt, Z., Reeves, M., Stalk, G., & Deimler, M. (2009). *Business Model innovation.* The Boston Consulting Group.

Lindsay, W. M., & Rue, L. W. (1976). *Environmental Complexity in Long-Range Planning.* Oxford, UK: Planning Executives Institute.

Lin, F., Fofanah, S. S., & Liang, D. (2011). Assessing citizen adoption of e-Government initiatives in Gambia: A validation of the technology acceptance model in information systems success. *Government Information Quarterly*, *28*(2), 271–279. doi:10.1016/j.giq.2010.09.004

Lin-Hi, N., Hörisch, J., & Blumberg, I. (2015). Does CSR Matter for Nonprofit Organizations? Testing the Link Between CSR Performance and Trust worthiness in the Nonprofit Versus For-Profit Domain. *Voluntas*, *26*(5), 1944–1974. doi:10.1007/s11266-014-9506-6

Linnenluecke, M., & Griffiths, A. (2010). Beyond adaptation: Resilience for business in light of climate change and weather extremes. *Business & Society*, *49*(3), 477–511. doi:10.1177/0007650310368814

Lipsky, D. B., Seeber, R. L., & Fincher, R. (2003). *Emerging systems for managing workplace conflict: Lessons from American corporations for managers and dispute resolution professionals*. San Francisco: Jossey-Bass.

Lipsky, M., & Smith, S. R. (1989). Nonprofit Organizations, Government, and The Welfare State. *Political Science Quarterly*, *104*(4), 625–648. doi:10.2307/2151102

Litzky, B. E., Eddleston, K. A., & Kidder, D. L. (2006). The good, the bad, and the misguided: How managers inadvertently encourage deviant behaviors. *The Academy of Management Perspectives*, *20*(1), 91–103. doi:10.5465/AMP.2006.19873411

Lock, M. B., Fansler, C., & Webb, M. (2016). Revolutionary emergency planning: Adding resilience through continuous review. *International Journal of Risk and Contingency Management*, *5*(2), 47–65. doi:10.4018/IJRCM.2016040103

Longoni, A., & Cagliano, R. (2015). Environmental and social sustainability priorities: Their integration in operations strategies. *International Journal of Operations & Production Management*, *35*(2), 216–245. doi:10.1108/IJOPM-04-2013-0182

Lord, R. G., & Maher, K. J. (1991). *Leadership and information processing: Linking perceptions and performance* (Vol. 1). Cambridge, MA: Unwin Hyman.

Lovejoy, K., & Saxton, G. D. (2012). Information, Community, and Action: How Nonprofit Organizations Use Social Media. *Journal of Computer-Mediated Communication*, *17*(3), 337–353. doi:10.1111/j.1083-6101.2012.01576.x

Lovejoy, K., Waters, R. D., & Saxton, G. D. (2012). Engaging stakeholders through Twitter: How nonprofit organizations are getting more out of 140 characters or less. *Public Relations Review*, *38*(2), 313–318. doi:10.1016/j.pubrev.2012.01.005

Lowe, R., & Butcher, T. (1994). The welfare state in Britain since 1945. *Public Administration-London*, *72*(1), 137–137.

Lowson, R. H. (2001). Retail Operational Strategies in Complex Supply Chains. *The International Journal of Logistics Management*, *12*(1), 97–111. doi:10.1108/09574090110806253

Lowson, R. H. (2002). Operations strategy: Genealogy, classification and anatomy. *International Journal of Operations & Production Management*, *22*(10), 1112–1129. doi:10.1108/01443570210446333

Lucas, S. R. (2014). Beyond the existence proof: Ontological conditions, epistemological implications, and in-depth interview research. *Quality & Quantity Journal*, *48*(1), 387–408. doi:10.1007/s11135-012-9775-3

Luke, B., Barraket, J., & Eversole, R. (2013). Measurement as legitimacy versus legitimacy of measures: Performance evaluation of social enterprise. *Qualitative Research in Accounting and Management*, *10*(3/4), 234–258. doi:10.1108/QRAM-08-2012-0034

Mabe, M. R. (2016). Libraries to the rescue. *International Journal of Risk and Contingency Management*, *5*(1), 62–81. doi:10.4018/IJRCM.2016010105

Macnamara, J., & Zerfass, A. (2012). Social media communication in organizations: The challenges of balancing openness, strategy, and management. *International Journal of Strategic Communication*, *6*(4), 287–308. doi:10.1080/1553118X.2012.711402

Magretta, J. (2002). Why Business Models Matter. *Harvard Business Review*, *80*, 86–92. PMID:12024761

Maguire, M. (2009). The non-profit business model: Empirical evidence from the magazine industry. *Journal of Media Economics*, *22*(3), 119–133. doi:10.1080/08997760903129333

Mahat, M. (2016). Strategic positioning in Australian higher education: The case of medical schools. In C. Sarrico, P. Teixeira, A. Magalhães, A. Veiga, M. J. Rosa, & T. Carvalho (Eds.), *Global Challenges, National Initiatives, and Institutional Response. The Transformation of Higher Education* (pp. 119–141). Rotterdam: Sense. doi:10.1007/978-94-6300-675-0_7

Mahat, M., & Coates, H. (2016). Strategic positioning of medical schools: An Australian perspective. *Medical Teacher*, 1–6. PMID:27111532

Mahat, M., & Goedegebuure, L. C. J. (2016). Strategic positioning in higher education: Reshaping perspectives. In J. Huisman & M. Tight (Eds.), *Theory And Method In Higher Education Research*. Bingley: Emerald. doi:10.1108/S2056-375220160000002011

Maher, C. (2009). Managing Career Development in the Not for Profit Sector. Business Leadership Review, 6(4).

Maher, C. (2013). A Qualitative Case Study Approach to Understanding Third Sector Managers' Career Orientations. Work Based Learning e-Journal International, 3(2).

Maher, C. (2015b). Public Policies Impact on Third Sector Social Enterprises in UK Regions. Handbook of Research on Entrepreneurial Success and its Impact on Regional Development, 246-266.

Maher, C. (2016 September). *Managerial Careers in Small Social Enterprise: Contextual Issues*. Paper presented at the 9th Annual Conference of the EuroMed Academy of Business, Warsaw, Poland.

Maher, C. (2015a). Social enterprise managers career path preferences. *International Journal of Globalisation and Small Business*, *7*(1), 59–72. doi:10.1504/IJGSB.2015.069032

Mahmoudi, H., Renn, O., Vanclay, F., Hoffmann, V., & Karami, E. (2013). A framework for combining social impact assessment and risk assessment. *Environmental Impact Assessment Review*, *43*, 1–8. doi:10.1016/j.eiar.2013.05.003

Mahon, J. F., & Murray, E. A. (1980). Deregulation and strategic transformation. *Journal of Contemporary Business*, *9*(2), 123–138.

Mahon, J. F., & Murray, E. A. (1981). Strategic planning for regulated companies. *Strategic Management Journal*, *2*(3), 251–262. doi:10.1002/smj.4250020304

Maier, F., Myer, M., & Steinbereithner, M. (2016). Non-profit organizations beyond business-like: A systematic review. *Nonprofit and Voluntary Sector Quarterly*, *45*(1), 64–86. doi:10.1177/0899764014561796

Mair, J., & Marti, I. (2006). Social entrepreneurship research: A source of explanation, prediction, and delight. *Journal of World Business*, *41*(2), 36–44. doi:10.1016/j.jwb.2005.09.002

Mair, J., & Noboa, E. (2006). How Intentions to Create a Social Venture are formed. In J. Mair, J. Robinson, & K. Hockerts (Eds.), *Social Entrepreneurship* (pp. 121–135). Palgrave McMillan. doi:10.1057/9780230625655_8

Maldonado, M. (2012, August 5). *Crowd-funding campaigns gaining popularity with Canadians*. Retrieved July 7, 2016, from http://www.nationalpost.com/m/wp/news/blog.html?b=news.nationalpost.com/2012/08/05/crowd-funding-campaigns-gaining-popularity-with-canadians

Malloy, D., & Agarwal, J. (2001). Ethical climate in nonprofit organizations. *Nonprofit Management & Leadership*, *12*(1), 39–54. doi:10.1002/nml.12104

Manu, F., & Sriram, V. (1996). Innovation, marketing strategy, environment, and performance. *Journal of Business Research*, *35*(1), 79–91. doi:10.1016/0148-2963(95)00056-9

Mara, C. M. (2000). A Strategic Planning Process for a Small Nonprofit Organization: A Hospice Example. *Nonprofit Management & Leadership*, *11*(2), 211–223. doi:10.1002/nml.11206

Marcuello, C. (2001). *Approaching the Third Sector from a Management Perspective: What Does This Offer? The Third Sector from a European perspective*. University of Trento.

Marcuello, C., Bellostas, A., Marcuello, Ch., & Moneva, J. M. (2007). Transparencia y rendición de cuentas en las empresas de inserción. *CIRIEC-España, Revista de Economía Pública. Social y Cooperativa*, *59*, 91–122.

Mariani, L., & Cavenago, D. (2013). Redesigning Welfare Services for Policies Effectiveness: The non-profit organizations (NPOs) perspective. *Public Management Review*, *15*(7), 1011–1039. doi:10.1080/14719037.2012.758307

Markides, C. C. (2013). Business model innovation: What can the ambidexterity literature teach us? *The Academy of Management Perspectives*, *27*(4), 313–323. doi:10.5465/amp.2012.0172

Marschall, M. (2002). *Legitimacy and effectiveness: civil society organizations' role in good governance*. Paper presented at the poverty reduction strategies forum, Baden, Austria.

Martello, M. M., Waston, J. G., & Fischer, M. J. (2008). Implementing a balanced scorecard in a not-for-profit organization. *Journal of Business and Economics Research*, *6*(9), 67–80.

Martinez, M., & Wolverton, M. (2009a). Analyzing higher education as an industry. In M. Martinez & M. Wolverton (Eds.), *Innovative Strategy Making in HIgher Education* (pp. 45–62). Charlotte, NC: Information Age Publishing.

Martinez, M., & Wolverton, M. (2009b). Enriching planning through industry analysis. *Planning for Higher Education*, *38*(1), 23–30.

Martin, L., & Kettner, P. (1997). Performance measurement: The new accountability. *Administration in Social Work*, *21*(1), 17–29. doi:10.1300/J147v21n01_02 PMID:10166757

Martin, M. (2015). Building Impact Businesses through Hybrid Financing. *Entrepreneurship Research Journal*, *5*(2), 109–126. doi:10.1515/erj-2015-0005

Martín-Peña, M. L., & Díaz-Garrido, E. (2008). Typologies and taxonomies of operations strategy: A literature review. *Management Research News*, *31*(3), 200–218. doi:10.1108/01409170810851294

Marwell, N. P., & Calabrese, T. (2015). A deficit model of collaborative governance: Government–nonprofit fiscal relations in the provision of child welfare services. *Journal of Public Administration: Research and Theory*, *25*(4), 1031–1058. doi:10.1093/jopart/muu047

Marx, J. D., & Carter, V. B. (2014). Factors influencing US charitable giving during the great recession: Implications for nonprofit administration. *American Scientist*, *4*(3), 350–372.

Masanell, R., & Ricart, J. (2007). *Competing through business models*. Working paper no 713, University of Navarra.

Masanet-Llodra, M. (2006). Environmental management accounting: A case study research on innovative strategy. *Journal of Business Ethics*, *68*(4), 393–408. doi:10.1007/s10551-006-9029-1

Maslow, A. H. (1943). A theory of human motivation. *Psychological Review*, *50*(4), 370–396. doi:10.1037/h0054346

Masten, S. E., Meehan, J. W., & Snyder, E. A. (1991). The costs of organization. *Journal of Law Economics and Organization*, *7*(1), 1–25.

Mataira, P. J., Morelli, P. T., Matsuoka, J. K., & Uehara-McDonald, S. (2014). Shifting the paradigm: New directions for non-profits and funders in an era of diminishing resources. *Social Business*, *4*(3), 231–244. doi:10.1362/204440814X14103454934212

Mathooko, F. M., & Ogutu, M. (2015). Porters five competitive forces framework and other factors that influence the choice of response strategies adopted by public universities in Kenya. *International Journal of Educational Management*, *29*(3), 334–354. doi:10.1108/IJEM-12-2013-0187

Matsunaga, Y., & Yamauchi, N. (2004). Is the government failure theory still relevant? A panel analysis using US state level data. *Annals of Public and Cooperative Economics*, *75*(2), 227–263. doi:10.1111/j.1467-8292.2004.00251.x

Mayer-Schonberger, V., & Cukier, K. (2014). *Big data: A revolution that will transform how we live, work, and think.* Boston, MA: Houghton Mifflin Harcourt Print.

Mayer-Schonberger, V., & Cukier, K. (2014). *Big Data: A revolution that will transform how we live, work, and think.* Boston, MA: Houghton Mifflin Harcourt.

McAfee, A., Brynjolfsson, E., Davenport, T. H., Patil, D., & Barton, D. (2012). Big Data. The management revolution. *Harvard Business Review*, *90*, 61–67. PMID:23074865

McClelland, D. C. (1967). The Achieving Society. New York, NY: Free Press.

McConnell, P. J. (2016). Strategic risk management: The failure of HBOS and its regulators. *Journal of Risk Management in Financial Institutions*, *9*(2), 147–162.

McCubbin, H. L., & Patterson, J. M. (1982). Family adaptation to crises. In H. L. McCubbin, E. Cauble, & J. M. Patterson (Eds.), *Family stress, coping, and social support* (pp. 26–47). Springfield, IL: Thomas.

McCubbin, H. L., & Patterson, J. M. (1983). The family stress process: The double ABCX model of adjustment and adaptation. In H. L. McCubbin, M. B. Sussman, & J. M. Patterson (Eds.), *Advances and developments in family stress theory and research* (pp. 7–37). New York, NY: Haworth. doi:10.1300/J002v06n01_02

McDermott, C. M., Markman, G. D., & Balkin, D. B. (2003). Operations strategy and new venture formation. *Management Research*, *1*(2), 195–205.

McGoey, L. (2014). The philanthropic state: Marketâ€"state hybrids in the philanthrocapitalist turn. *Third World Quarterly*, *35*(1), 109–125. doi:10.1080/01436597.2014.868989

McGrath, B. P., Graham, I. S., Crotty, B. J., & Jolly, B. C. (2006). Lack of integration of medical education in Australia: The need for change. *The Medical Journal of Australia*, *184*(7), 346–348. PMID:16584370

McGuire, T., Manyika, J., & Chui, M. (2012). Why Big Data is the new competitive advantage. *Ivey Business Journal*, *76*, 1–4.

McIntyre, T. L. (2004). A model of levels of involvement and strategic roles of human resource development: Professionals as facilitators of due diligence and the integration process. *Human Resource Development Review*, *3*(2), 173–182. doi:10.1177/1534484304265444

McKeon, S. (2013). Strategic Review of Health and Medical Research in Australia – Better Health Through Research. Canberra: Academic Press.

McKinney, R., & Kahn, H. (2004). Lottery funding and changing organizational identity in the UK voluntary sector. *Voluntas*, *15*(1), 1–19. doi:10.1023/B:VOLU.0000023631.74069.d7

McLoughlin, J., Kaminski, J., Sodgar, B., Khan, S., Harris, R., Arnaudo, G., & Mc Brearty, S. (2009). A Strategic Approach to Social Impact Measurement of Social Enterprises. The SIMPLE Methodology. *Social Enterprise Journal*, *5*(2), 154–178. doi:10.1108/17508610910981734

Mcwilliams, A., Siegel, D., & Wright, P. (2006). Corporate social responsibility: Strategic implications. *Journal of Management Studies*, *43*(1), 1–18. doi:10.1111/j.1467-6486.2006.00580.x

Mediation Center. (2009). *Mediation center staff*. Retrieved from http://law.hamline.edu/mediation-center/mediation-center-staff.html

Medical Deans Australia and New Zealand (MDANZ). (2015a). *MDANZ Membership*. MDANZ.

Medical Deans Australia and New Zealand (MDANZ). (2015b). Table 3 (a): Commencing Medical Students 2002-2014 (Australia). MDANZ.

Medina-Borja, A., & Triantis, K. (2014). Modeling social services performance: A four-stage DEA approach to evaluate fundraising efficiency, capacity building, service quality, and effectiveness in the nonprofit sector. *Annals of Operations Research*, *221*(1), 285–307. doi:10.1007/s10479-011-0917-0

Mercado, P., & Garcia, P. (2007). La responsabilidad social en empresas del valle de Toluca (México): Un estudio exploratorio. *Estudios Gerenciales*, *23*(102), 119–135. doi:10.1016/S0123-5923(07)70005-0

Mergel, I., & Bretschneider, S. I. (2013). A three-stage adoption process for social media use in government. *Public Administration Review*, *73*(3), 390–400. doi:10.1111/puar.12021

Meskendahl, S. (2010). The influence of business strategy on project portfolio management and its success – A conceptual framework. *International Journal of Project Management*, *28*(8), 807–817. doi:10.1016/j.ijproman.2010.06.007

Meter, K. (2010). Learning how to multiply. *Journal of Agriculture, Food Systems, and Community Development*, *1*(2).

Meyer-Drawe, K. (1997). Education. In L. Embree, E. A. Behnke, D. Carr, J. C. Evans, J. Huertas-Jourda, J. J. Kockelmans, & R. M. Zaner (Eds.), *Encyclopedia of phenomenology* (pp. 157–162). Dordrecht, Netherlands: Kluwer. doi:10.1007/978-94-017-5344-9_36

Meyer, J. W., & Rowan, B. (1977). Institutionalized Organizations: Formal Structure as Myth and Ceremony. *American Journal of Sociology*, *83*(2), 340–363. doi:10.1086/226550

Meyer, J. W., & Scott, W. R. (1992). *Organizational environments, ritual and rationality*. Newbury Park, CA: Sage.

Mian, A., Rao, K., & Sufi, A. (2013). Household balance sheets, consumption and economic slump. *The Quarterly Journal of Economics*, *128*(4), 1687–1726. doi:10.1093/qje/qjt020

Mignonac, K. (2002). Understanding willingness to accept domestic relocation: The example of French managers. *Career Development International*, *7*(6), 359–370. doi:10.1108/13620430210444385

Milbourne, L., & Cushman, M. (2013) From the third sector to the big society: how changing UK government policies have eroded third sector trust. *VOLUNTAS: International Journal of Voluntary and Nonprofit Organisations*, 1-24.

Millar, R., & Hall, K. (2013). Social return on investment (SROI) and performance measurement: The opportunities and barriers for social enterprises in health and social care. *Public Management Review*, *15*(6), 923–941. doi:10.1080/14719037.2012.698857

Miller, J. G., & Roth, A. V. (1994). A Taxonomy of Manufacturing Strategies. *Management Science*, *40*(3), 285–304. doi:10.1287/mnsc.40.3.285

Miller, K. D. (2002). Competitive strategies of religious organizations. *Strategic Management Journal, 23*(5), 435–456. doi:10.1002/smj.234

Milligan, C. (2001). *Geographies of Care: space and the voluntary sector*. Ashgate.

Millward, L. (2005). *Understanding Occupational & Organisational Psychology*. London: Sage Publications.

Minnesota Council of Nonprofits. (n.d.). *Templates and samples*. Retrieved from http://www.minnesotanonprofits.org/nonprofit-resources/templates-samples

Minnesota Department of Employment and Economic Development. (2006). *An employer's guide to employment law issues in Minnesota*. Retrieved from http://www.mnsbao.com/PDFs/empllaw.pdf

Minnesota Department of Labor & Industry. (2009). *Federal family and medical leave act; state parental leave act*. Retrieved from http://www.doli.state.mn.us/fmla.html

Mintzberg, H. (1973). Strategy-making in three modes. *California Management Review (Pre-1986), 16*(2), 44–53.

Minuchin, S. (1974). *Families and family therapy*. Cambridge, MA: Harvard University Press.

MIT-Brynjolfsson, McAfee, et al. (2015). *Open Letter on the Digital Economy, A group of leading technologists, economists, and investors propose a new approach to help us adapt to new technologies*. Available on: https://www.technologyreview.com/s/538091/open-letter-on-the-digital-economy/

Mitchell, R., Agle, B., & Wood, D. (1997). Toward a theory of stakeholder identification and salience: Defining the principle of who and what really counts. *Academy of Management Review, 22*(4), 853–886.

Moneva, J. M. (2007). El marco de la información sobre la responsabilidad social de las organizaciones. *Ekonomíaz, 65*, 284–317.

Moneva, J. M., & Bellostas, A. (2007). *Accountability en las Entidades sin Fines Lucrativos*. Centros de Investigación de Economía y Sociedad.

Morgan, E., & DiGiammarino, B. (2014, May 22). *Crowdfunding for Nonprofits | Stanford Social Innovation Review*. Retrieved July 9, 2016, from http://ssir.org/articles/entry/crowdfunding_for_nonprofits

Morgan, D. L. (1993). *Successful focus groups: Advancing the state of the art*. Newbury Park, CA: SAGE Publications. doi:10.4135/9781483349008

Morphet, J. (2008). Modern Local Government. *Local Government Studies, 34*(4).

Mosley, J. E. (2012). Collaboration, Public-Private Intermediary Organizations, and the Transformation of Advocacy in the Field of Homeless Services. *American Review of Public Administration*.

Mukhopadhyay, S., & Gupta, R. K. (2014). Survey of qualitative research methodology in strategy research and implication for Indian researchers. *Vision, 18*(2), 109–123.

Mulhare, E. M. (1999). Mindful of the Future: Strategic Planning Ideology and The Culture of Nonprofit Management. *Human Organization, 58*(3), 323–330. doi:10.17730/humo.58.3.975v78735176943v

Mulvey, J. (2013, March 13). *Crowdfunding executive living the dream through his job | MNN - Mother Nature Network*. Retrieved July 7, 2016, from http://www.mnn.com/money/green-workplace/stories/crowdfunding-executive-living-the-dream-through-his-job

Muñoz, P., & Kibler, E. (2015). Institutional Complexity and Social Entrepreneurship: A Fuzzy-Set Approach. *Journal of Business Research*.

Murray, E. A., & Isenman, A. W. (1978, August). *The concept of strategy formulation as a negotiation process.* Academy of Management Meeting.

Musselin, C. (2007). Transformation of academic work: Facts and analysis. In M. Kogan & U. Teichler (Eds.), *Key Challenges to the Academic Profession* (pp. 175–190). Kassel: UNESCO Forum on Higher Education, Research and Knowledge/International Centre for Higher Education Research Kassel.

Nadkarni, S., & Narayanan, V. K. (2007). Strategic schemas, strategic flexibility, and firm performance: The moderating role of industry clockspeed. *Strategic Management Journal, 28*(3), 243–270. doi:10.1002/smj.576

Nair, A., & Boulton, W. R. (2008). Innovation-oriented operations strategy typology and stage-based model. *International Journal of Operations & Production Management, 28*(8), 748–771. doi:10.1108/01443570810888599

Nair, S., Nisar, A., Palacios, M., & Ruiz, F. (2012). Impact of knowledge brokering on performance heterogeneity among business models. *Management Decision, 50*(9), 1649–1660. doi:10.1108/00251741211266732

Nair, S., Paulose, H., Palacios, M., & Tafur, J. (2013). Service orientation: Effectuating business model innovation. *Service Industries Journal, 33*(9/10), 958–975. doi:10.1080/02642069.2013.746670

National Center for Charitable Statistics. (2007). *Number of nonprofit organizations in the United States, 1996–2006.* Retrieved from http://nccsdataweb.urban.org/PubApps/profile1.php?state=US

National Council of Nonprofit Associations. (2004). *Managing nonprofit employees.* Retrieved from https://www.councilofnonprofits.org/tools-resources/managing-nonprofit-employees

*National Health and Medical Research Council (NHMRC).* (2015). NHMRC Advanced Health Research and Translation Centres.

NCN. (2016). *Principles and Practices.* National Council of Nonprofits (NCN). Retrieved June 1, 2016, from the World Wide Web: https://www.councilofnonprofits.org/tools-resources/principles-and-practices

Neave, G. (2012). *The evaluative state, institutional autonomy and re-engineering higher education in Western Europe. The prince and his pleasure.* Basingstoke, UK: Palgrave Macmillan. doi:10.1057/9780230370227

Nebus, J. (2006). Building collegial information networks: A theory of advice network generation. *Academy of Management Review, 31*(3), 615–637. doi:10.5465/AMR.2006.21318921

Neck, H., Brush, C., & Allen, E. (2009). The landscape of social entrepreneurship. *Business Horizons, 52*(1), 13–19. doi:10.1016/j.bushor.2008.09.002

New Economics Foundation (NEF). (2007). *Measuring Real Value: A DIY Guide to Social Return on Investment.* Accessed November 3, 2015. http://www.neweconomics.org/

New Philanthropy Capital. (2010). *Social Return on Investment.* Position Paper, April 2010. Author.

News, M. M. (2016, August 10). *Murray Wimbledon shirt raises £10,000 for Malaria No More UK.* Retrieved September 12, 2016, from http://fundraising.co.uk/2016/08/10/murray-wimbledon-shirt-raises-10000-malaria-no-uk/

Ng, I. C., & Maull, R. (2009, July). Embedding the new discipline of service science: A service science research agenda. In *Service Operations, Logistics and Informatics, 2009. SOLI'09. IEEE/INFORMS International Conference on* (pp. 68-73). IEEE. doi:10.1109/SOLI.2009.5203906

NGOCN. (2014). *NGO, market is there, where is fair?* China Development Brief. Retrieved from: http://www.chinadevelopmentbrief.org.cn/news-16622.html

NGOCN. (2015). *Research on government cultivates social organizations and policies innovations*. Guangdong: NGOCN.

Nicholls, A., & Murdock, A. (2012). The nature of social innovation. In Social innovation (pp. 1-30). Palgrave Macmillan UK. doi:10.1057/9780230367098_1

Nicholls, A. (2006). *Social Entrepreneurship: New Models of Sustainable Social Change*. New York: Oxford University Press.

Nicholls, A. (2009). We do good things, dont we?:'Blended Value Accountingin social entrepreneurship. *Accounting, Organizations and Society*, *34*(6), 755–769. doi:10.1016/j.aos.2009.04.008

Nicholls, A. (2010). Institutionalizing social entrepreneurship in regulatory space: Reporting and disclosure by community interest companies. *Accounting, Organizations and Society*, *35*(4), 394–415. doi:10.1016/j.aos.2009.08.001

Nicholls, A. (Ed.). (2006). *Social entrepreneurship: new models of sustainable social change*. New York, NY: Oxford University Press. doi:10.4135/9781452218557.n489

Nicholls, J. (2004b). *Social return on investment: Valuing what matters*. London: New Economics Foundation.

Nickerson, D., & Rogers, T. (2014). Political campaigns and Big Data. *The Journal of Economic Perspectives*, *28*(2), 51–74. doi:10.1257/jep.28.2.51

Nicolás, C., & Rubio, A. (2016). Social enterprise: Gender gap and economic development. *European Journal of Management and Business Economics*, *25*(2), 56–62. doi:10.1016/j.redeen.2015.11.001

Nisa, S. (2015). Inter-firm differences in the sustainability business model: A study on select firms from agri-food and IT companies. *IUP Journal of Business Strategy*, *12*(4), 35–55.

Niven, P. R. (2003). *Balanced scorecard step-by-step for government and non-profit agencies*. Hoboken, NJ: Wiley.

Nonprofits cut legal risks with better personnel policies. (1996). *Risk Management*, *43*(5), 3–5.

Normann, R. (1977). *Management for growth*. London: John Wiley & Sons.

Northwest Area Foundation. (n.d.). *About us*. Retrieved from http://www.nwaf.org/

NPO Development Centre. (2014). *Report on the status quo of Chinese non-profit support organizations and the list of non-profit support organizations*. Shanghai: Academic Press.

NVCO. (2012). *The UK Civil Society Almanac*. London: NVCO Publication.

O'Connell, F. J., Jr., Hurd, G., & Spurlock, R. (2007). New Form 990 aims for transparency, accountability, and oversight. *Tax Adviser*, *38*(9), 501–502. Retrieved from www.nonprofitlawblog.com/form-990-policies-is-it-better-to-check-yes-or-no

O'Reilly, T. (2005). *What is Web 2.0: Design patterns and business models for the next generation of software*. Retrieved 26 February, 2016, from http://www.oreillynet.com/pub/a/oreilly/tim/news/2005/09/30/what-is-web-20.html

Oberer, B., & Erkollar, A. (2012). Social media integration in higher education. cross-course google plus integration sown in the example of a masters degree course in management. *Procedia: Social and Behavioral Sciences*, *47*, 1888–1893. doi:10.1016/j.sbspro.2012.06.918

Ofstad, A. (2000). *Countries in conflict and aid strategies: The case of Sri Lanka*. Retrieved from http://bora.cmi.no/space/bitstream/10202/248/1/WP2000.18%20Arve-07202007_12.pdf

Oliveira, T., & Martins, M. F. (2011). Literature review of information technology adoption models at firm level. *The Electronic Journal Information Systems Evaluation*, *14*(1), 110–121.

Oliver, C. (1992). Strategic response to institutional process. *Academy of Management Journal*, *16*, 145–179.

Omair, K. (2010). Typology of career development for Arab women managers in the United Arab Emirates. *Career Development International*, *15*(2), 121–143. doi:10.1108/13620431011040932

Omoruyi, F. E. O., & Omiunu, S. E. (2014). Strategies for strengthening vocational skills development programme for women in Benin metropolis. *Journal of Educational Review*, *7*(1), 127–131.

Onat, F. (2010). *Social Media Practices as a Public Relations Application Field: An Analysis About NonGovernmental Organizations. İletişim Kuram ve Araştırma Dergisi*, *31*, 103–122.

Onyx, J., & Maclean, M. (1996). Careers in the Third Sector. *Nonprofit Management & Leadership*, *6*(4), 333–345. doi:10.1002/nml.4130060404

Ordanini, A. (2009, March 23). *Crowd Funding: Customers as İnvestors - WSJ*. Retrieved July 7, 2016, from http://www.wsj.com/articles/SB123740509983775099

O'Reilly, T. (2007). *What Is Web 2.0: Design Patterns and Business Models for the Next Generationof Software*. MPRA Paper No. 4578. Retrieved 23 February, 2016, from http://mpra.ub.uni-muenchen.de/4578/

Organisation for Economic Co-operation and Development (OECD). (2014). *General assessment of the macroeconomic situation*. Economic Outlook, no. 2. Accessed October 6, 2015. http://www.oecd.org/eco/outlook/General-assessment-of-the-macroeconomic-situation.pdf

Orlitzky, M. (2005). Social responsibility and financial performance: Trade-off or virtuous circle. *University of Auckland Business Review*, *7*(1), 37–43.

Ortner, J. (2007). *A Literature Review of Strategy and Complexity Theory*. Retrieved from http://api.ning.com/files/qx6YCvp40dLkRffS1iZUOHb9OVYxoyud8bYyAEBHHLAlob839ZsHYOjDLNNA7zg7Us8QqotWRx4d3AWSv0uC-3TqDNQksP7Nv/aliteraturereviewofstrategyandcomplexitytheory.pdf

Osborne, S., & Tricker, M. (1994). Local development agencies: Supporting voluntary action. *Nonprofit Management & Leadership*, *5*(1), 37–52. doi:10.1002/nml.4130050105

Osterwalder, A., & Pigneur, Y. (2010). *Business model generation: A handbook for visionaries, game changers, and challengers*. Wiley.

Osterwalder, A., & Pigneur, Y. (2013). Designing business models and similar strategic objects: The contribution of IS. *Journal of the Association for Information Systems*, *14*, 237–244.

Osterwalder, A., Pigneur, Y., & Tucci, C. L. (2005). Clarifying business models: Origins, present, and future of the concept. *Communications of the Association for Information Systems*, *16*(1), 1.

Osula, B., & Ng, E. C. W. (2014). Toward a collaborative, transformative model of non-profit leadership: Some conceptual building blocks. *American Scientist*, *4*, 87–104.

Paarlberg, L. E., & Gen, S. (2009). Exploring the Determinants of nonprofit Coproduction of Public Service Delivery The Case of k-12 Public Education. *American Review of Public Administration*, *39*(4), 391–408. doi:10.1177/0275074008320711

Pache, A.-C., & Santos, F. (2012). Inside the Hybrid Organization: Selective Coupling as a Response to Competing Institutional Logics. *Academy of Management Journal*, *56*(4), 972–1001. doi:10.5465/amj.2011.0405

Panel on the Nonprofit Sector. (2007). *Principles for good governance and ethical practice: A guide for charities and foundations*. Retrieved from https://www.independentsector.org/uploads/PrincipleResources/The_33_Principles.pdf

Pardon, M. (1987). Non-governmental development organizations: From development aid to development cooperation. *World Development*, *15*(Suppl.), 69–77. doi:10.1016/0305-750X(87)90144-6

Parker, L. D. (2012). Qualitative management accounting research, Assessing deliverables and relevance. *Critical Perspectives on Accounting*, *23*(1), 54–70. doi:10.1016/j.cpa.2011.06.002

Park, J. H., & Abbott, J. L. (2011). A new approach to expatriate effectiveness: A perspective-taking model for global assignments. *Academy of Management Review*, *91*(1), 1–6.

Pathak, P., & Dattani, P. (2014). Social return on investment: Three technical challenges. *Social Enterprise Journal*, *10*(2), 91–104. doi:10.1108/SEJ-06-2012-0019

Patten, D. M. (1991). Exposure, Legitimacy, and Social Disclosure. *Journal of Accounting and Public Policy*, *10*(4), 297–308. doi:10.1016/0278-4254(91)90003-3

Pearson, R. (1991). *The human resource: managing people and work in the 1990s*. McGraw-Hill Book Co Ltd.

Peattie, K., & Morley, A. (2008). Eight paradoxes of the social enterprise research agenda. *Social Enterprise Journal*, *4*(2), 91–107. doi:10.1108/17508610810901995

Pemberton, C., Herriot, P., & Bates, T. (1994). Career orientations of senior executives and their implications for careers guidance. *British Journal of Guidance & Counselling*, *22*(2), 233–245. doi:10.1080/03069889408260317

Pérez, V., & Mateos, C. (2006). ONG, Internet y Comunicación Alternativa en las ONG dedicadas a la inmigración en España. *Razón y Palabra*, *29*, 49.

Pestoff, V., & Brandsen, T. (2013). *Co-production: The Third Sector and the Delivery of Public Services*. New York: Routledge.

Pfeffer, J., & Salancik, G. R. (1978). *The external control of organizations: A resource dependence perspective*. New York: Harper and Row.

Phusavat, K., & Kanchana, R. (2008). Competitive priorities for service providers: Perspectives from Thailand. *Industrial Management & Data Systems*, *108*(1), 5–21. doi:10.1108/02635570810844052

Pisano, P., Pironti, M., & Rieple, A. (2015). Identify innovative business models: Can innovative business models enable players to react to on-going or unpredictable trends? *Entrepreneurship Research Journal*, *5*(3), 181–199. doi:10.1515/erj-2014-0032

Pitschner, S., & Pitschner-Finn, S. (2014). Non-profit differentials in crowd-based financing: Evidence from 50,000 campaigns. *Economics Letters*, *123*(3), 391–394. doi:10.1016/j.econlet.2014.03.022

Ponte, S. (2008). Greener than thou: The political economy of fish ecolabeling and its local manifestations in South Africa. *World Development*, *36*(1), 159–175. doi:10.1016/j.worlddev.2007.02.014

Popa, A. (2015). Analysis methods procedures for assessing the stability of business entity. *Economy Transdisciplinarity Cognition*, *18*(1), 124–132.

Porter, M. E. (1980). *Competitive Strategy: Techniques for Analysing Industries and Competitors*. New York: Free Press.

Post, J. E., & Mahon, J. F. (1980). Articulated turbulence: The effect of regulatory agencies on corporate responses to social change. *Academy of Management Review*, *5*(3), 399–407.

Powell, T. C. (2001). Competitive advantage: Logical and philosophical considerations. *Strategic Management Journal*, *22*(9), 875–888. doi:10.1002/smj.173

Prahalad, C. K., & Ramaswamy, V. (2004). Co-creation Experiences: The Next Practice in Value Creation. *Journal of Interactive Marketing*, *18*(3), 5–14. doi:10.1002/dir.20015

Priem, R. L., Butler, J. E., & Li, S. (2013). Toward reimagining strategy research: Retrospection and prospection on the 2011 Amr decade award article. *Academy of Management Review*, *38*(4), 471–489. doi:10.5465/amr.2013.0097

Pringle, J., & Huisman, J. (2011). Understanding universities in Ontario, Canada: An industry analysis using Porter's Five Forces Framework. *Canadian Journal of Higher Education*, *41*(3), 58.

Prive, T. (2012, November 27). *What Is Crowdfunding And How Does It Benefit The Economy - Forbes*. Retrieved July 9, 2016, from http://www.forbes.com/sites/tanyaprive/2012/11/27/what-is-crowdfunding-and-how-does-it-benefit-the-economy/#1146a2be4ed4

Project Management Institute. (2008). The Standard for Portfolio Management (2nd ed.). PMI.

Puentes, R., Mozas, A., Bernal, E., & Chaves, R. (2012). E-corporate social responsibility in small non-profit organisations: The case of Spanish Non Government Organisations. *Service Industries Journal*, *32*(15), 2379–2398. doi:10.1080/02642069.2012.677831

Puljak, L., & Vari, S. G. (2014). Significance of research networking for enhancing collaboration and research productivity. *Croatian Medical Journal*, *55*(3), 181–183. doi:10.3325/cmj.2014.55.181 PMID:24891275

Purcell, B. M. (2013). *Big data using cloud computing*. Holy Family University working paper.

Purcell, B. M. (2013). *Big Data using cloud computing*. Holy Family University working paper.

Putnam, R. D. (2000). Bowling alone: America's declining social capital. In *Culture and Politics* (pp. 223–234). New York: Palgrave Macmillan US.

Qu, C. (2016). *The beautiful word: The dusk of philanthropy. A reflection on the market oriented philanthropy*. China Development Brief. Retrieved from: http://www.chinadevelopmentbrief.org.cn/news-18466.html

Qu, S. Q., & Dumay, J. (2011). The qualitative research interview. *Qualitative Research in Accounting and Management*, *8*(3), 238–264. doi:10.1108/11766091111162070

Rad, P., & Levin, G. (2006). *Project portfolio management. Tools and techniques*. New York: IIL Publishing.

Ramakrishna, H. V., & Potosky, D. (2003). Conceptualisation and exploration of Composite career anchors: An analysis of Information Systems Personnel. *Human Resource Development Quarterly*, *14*(2), 199–214. doi:10.1002/hrdq.1060

Ramesh, R. (2010, September 8). *Charitable giving by country: who is the most generous?* Retrieved July 8, 2016, from http://www.theguardian.com/news/datablog/2010/sep/08/charitable-giving-country

Ranci, C. (1994). The Third Sector in welfare policies in Italy: The contradictions of a protected market. *VOLUNTAS: International Journal of Voluntary and Nonprofit Organizations*, *5*(3), 247–271. doi:10.1007/BF02354035

Ranci, C. (2015). The Long-Term Evolution of the Government–Third Sector Partnership in Italy: Old Wine in a New Bottle? *VOLUNTAS: International Journal of Voluntary and Nonprofit Organizations*, *26*(6), 2311–2329. doi:10.1007/s11266-015-9650-7

Rasdi, R.M., Ismaila, M., Uli, J., & Noah, S.M. (2009). Career aspirations and career success among managers in the Malaysian public sector. *Research Journal of International Studies*, (9), 21-35.

Rasoolimanesh, S. M., Jaafar, M., Badarulzaman, N., & Ramayah, T. (2015). Investigating a framework to facilitate the implementation of city development strategy using balanced scorecard. *Habitat International*, *46*(1), 156–165. doi:10.1016/j.habitatint.2014.12.003

Ratty, J. (2015, May 14). *Crowdfunding Charities: 9 of the best UK charity crowdfunds.* Retrieved from http://www.crowdfunder.co.uk/blog/crowdfunding-charities-9-of-the-best-uk-charity-crowdfunds/

Read, A. (2013). *Crowdfunding: an empirical and theoretical model of non-profit support.* Academic Press.

Read, C. (2012). Review of key risk and uncertainty theories influencing contemporary financial economics. *International Journal of Risk and Contingency Management*, *1*(4), 18–27. doi:10.4018/ijrcm.2012100102

Reid, M. F., Brown, L., McNerney, D., & Perri, D. J. (2014). Time to raise the bar on nonprofit strategic planning and implementation. *Strategy and Leadership*, *42*(Iss: 3), 31–39. doi:10.1108/SL-03-2014-0019

Ren, C. R., & Guo, C. (2011). Middle managers strategic role in the corporate entrepreneurial process: Attention-based effects. *Journal of Management*, *37*(6), 1586–1610. doi:10.1177/0149206310397769

Rheingold, H. (1993). *The Virtual Community: Homesteading on the Electronic Frontier.* New York: Addison-Wesley.

Rhoads, J. (2012). *Ready to Interact: Social Media Use by U.S. Hospitals and Health Systems.* CSC. Retrieved from http://assets1.csc.com/health_services/downloads/CSC_Survey_Social_Media_Use_by_U.S._Hospitals_and_Health_Systems.pdf

Richter, L. (2013). Social impact investing at the intersection of health and community development. *National Civic Review*, *102*(4), 67–71. doi:10.1002/ncr.21160

Ridder, H. G., & McCandless, A. (2008). Influences on the Architecture of Human Resource Management in Nonprofit Organizations: An Analytical Framework. *Nonprofit and Voluntary Sector Quarterly*, *39*(1), 124–141. doi:10.1177/0899764008328182

Ridley-Duff, R., & Bull, M. (2015). Understanding social enterprise: Theory and practice. *Sage (Atlanta, Ga.).*

Roaldsen, I. (2014). Dynamic capabilities as drivers of business model innovation - from the perspective of SMEs in mature industries. *International Journal of Entrepreneurship and Innovation Management*, *18*(4), 349–364. doi:10.1504/IJEIM.2014.064212

Roberts Enterprise Development Fund (REDF). (2000). *Social Return on Investment (SROI).* Collection.

Roberts, R. W. (1992). Determinants of Corporate Social Responsibility Disclosure: An Application of Stakeholder Theory. *Accounting, Organizations and Society*, *17*(6), 595–612. doi:10.1016/0361-3682(92)90015-K

Robinson, M., & Riddell, R. C. (1995). *Non-governmental organizations and rural poverty alleviation.* OUP Catalogue.

Rogers, D. A. (2010). *Managing financial risk and its interaction with enterprise risk management.* Wiley.

Rogers, E. M. (1995). *Diffusion of Innovations* (4th ed.). New York, NY: Free Press.

Rokhman, A. (2011). E-Government Adoption in Developing Countries; The Case of Indonesia. *Journal of Emerging Trends in Computing and Information Sciences*, *2*(5), 228–236.

Ronen, J. (2014). On the invariance of accounting principles to business models: A discussion of the Singleton-Green and Page articles. *Journal of Management & Governance*, *18*(3), 707–716. doi:10.1007/s10997-012-9241-6

Rosen, C. C., Harris, K. J., & Kacmar, K. M. (2009). The emotional implications of organizational politics: A process model. *Human Relations*, *62*(1), 27–57. doi:10.1177/0018726708099836

Roth, A. V., & Menor, L. J. (2003). Insights into service operations management: a research agenda. *Production & Operations Management, 12*(2), 145–164. Retrieved from http://search.ebscohost.com/login.aspx?direct=true&db=bth&AN=12334481&site=ehost-live

Rothschild, J., & Milofsky, C. (2006). The centrality of values, passions, and ethics in the nonprofit sector. Special issue introduction. *Nonprofit Management & Leadership*, *17*(2), 137–143. doi:10.1002/nml.139

Royce, M. (2007). Using human resource management tools to support social enterprise: Emerging themes from the sector. *Social Enterprise Journal*, *3*(1), 10–19. doi:10.1108/17508610780000718

Rubaltelli, E., Lotto, L., Ritov, I., & Rumiati, R. (2015). Moral investing: Psychological motivations and implications. *Judgment and Decision Making*, *10*(1), 64.

Ruiz, M., Ríos, A., & Tirado, P. (2009). La responsabilidad social y la crisis económica. ¿Responden las entidades financieras españolas a los grupos de interés? *Revista de Economía Pública. Social y Cooperativa*, *65*, 33–58.

Rungtusanatham, M. J., Choi, T. Y., Hollingworth, D. G., Wu, Z., & Forza, C. (2003). Survey research in operations management: Historical analyses. *Journal of Operations Management*, *21*(4), 475–488. doi:10.1016/S0272-6963(03)00020-2

Russel, J. S. (2015). *Ford Foundations 'Lavish' $196 Million to Push Internet Regulations*. Available on: http://newsbusters.org/blogs/joseph-rossell/2015/02/25/soros-ford-foundations-lavish-196-million-push-internet-regulations

Ryan, P.W., & Lyne, I. (2008). Social Enterprise and the Measurement of Social Value: Methodological Issues with the Calculation and Application of the Social Return on Investment. *Education, Knowledge and Economy*, *2*(3), 223–37.

Rymsza A. (2005). Partnerzy służby publicznej? Wyzwania współpracy sektora pozarządowego z administracją publiczną w świetle doświadczeń amerykańskich. *Kwartalnik Trzeci Sektor, 3*, 53-66.

Sacks, J. (2002). *The Money Trail: Measuring your impact on the local economy using LM3*. London: New Economics Foundation.

Salamon, L. M., Sokolowski, S., & Geller, S. (2012). *Holding the Fort: Nonprofit Employment during a Decade of Turmoil*. Nonprofit Economic Data Bulletin #39. Johns Hopkins University. Available on: http://ccss.jhu.edu/wp-content/uploads/downloads/2012/01/NED_National_2012.pdf

Salamon, L., & Anheier, H. (1997). *The Third World's Third Sector in Comparative Perspective*. Retrieved from http://adm-cf.com/jhu/pdfs/CNP_Working_Papers/CNP_WP24.pdf

Salamon, L., & Sokolowski, S. (2010, July). *The social origins of civil society: Explaining variations in the size and structure of the global civil society sector*. Paper presented at the 9th International Conference of the International Society for Third Sector Research, Istanbul, Turkey.

Salamon, L., & Sokolwski, W. (2003). *Global Civil Society: An Overview*. Retrieved from http://adm-cf.com/jhu/pdfs/Books/BOOK_GCS_2003.pdf

Salamon, L., Sokolowski, S. W., Haddock, M. A., & Tice, H. S. (2012). *The State of Global Civil Societyand Volunteering: Latest findings from the implementation of the UN Non-profit Handbook*. Working Paper No. 49. Baltimore, MD: Johns Hopkins Center for Civil Society Studies.

Salamon, L. M. (1987). Of market failure, voluntary failure, and third-party government: Toward a theory of government-nonprofit relations in the modern welfare state. *Nonprofit and Voluntary Sector Quarterly*, *16*(1-2), 29–49. doi:10.1177/089976408701600104

Salamon, L. M. (2003). *The Resilient Sector: The State of Nonprofit America*. Washington, DC: Brookings Institution Press.

Salamon, L. M. (2010). Putting the civil society sector on the economic map of the world. *Annals of Public and Cooperative Economics*, *81*(2), 167–210. doi:10.1111/j.1467-8292.2010.00409.x

Salamon, L. M., & Anheier, H. K. (1997). *Defining the nonprofit sector: A crossnational analysis*. Manchester, UK: Manchester University Press.

Salamon, L. M., & Anheier, H. K. (1997). *Defining the nonprofit sector: A cross-national analysis*. Manchester, UK: University Press.

Salamon, L. M., & Anheier, H. K. (1998). Social origins of civil society: Explaining the nonprofit sector cross-nationally. *VOLUNTAS: International Journal of Voluntary and Nonprofit Organizations*, *9*(3), 213–248. doi:10.1023/A:1022058200985

Salamon, L. M., & Anheier, H. K. (1999). *The emerging Sector Revisited. A Summary Revised Estimates*. CNP The Johns Hopkins Comparative Nonprofit Sector Project, Phase II.

Salamon, L. M., & Flaherty, S. L. (1996). *Nonprofit law: Ten issues in search of resolution*. Baltimore, MD: Johns Hopkins University Press.

Salamon, L. M., Hems, L. C., & Chinnock, K. (2000). *The Nonprofit Sector: For What and For Whom?* Baltimore, MD: Johns Hopkins University Press.

Salamon, L., & Anheier, H. (1997). The Challenge of Definition: Thirteen realities in Search of a Concept. In L. Salamon & H. Anheier (Eds.), *Defining the nonprofit sector: A cross-national analysis* (pp. 11–99). Manchester, UK: Manchester University Press US.

Salleh, N., Mendes, E., & Grundy, J. (2011). Empirical Studies of Pair Programming for CS/SE Teaching in Higher Education: A Systematic Literature Review. *IEEE Transactions on Software Engineering*, *37*(4), 509–525. doi:10.1109/TSE.2010.59

Samarrokhi, A., Jenab, K., Arumugam, V. C., & Weinsier, P. D. (2015). Analysis of the effects of operations strategies on sustainable competitive advantage in manufacturing systems. *International Journal of Industrial and Systems Engineering*, *19*(1), 34–49. doi:10.1504/IJISE.2015.065944

Samath, F. (2010). *NGO's Brace for Tighter Government Control*. Retrieved from http://ipsnews.net/news.asp?idnews=50507

Sanchez, J. I., Spector, P. E., & Cooper, C. L. (2000). Adapting to a boundaryless world: A developmental expatriate model. *The Academy of Management Executive*, *14*(2), 96–106.

Santos, F. M. (2012). A Positive Theory of Social Entrepreneurship. *Journal of Business Ethics, 111*(3), 335-351.

Santos, F. M., Pache, A.-C., & Birkholz, C. (2015). Making Hybrids Work: Aligning business models and organizational design for social enterprises. *California Management Review, 57*(3), 36–58. 10.1525/cmr.2015.57.3.36

Sanyal, P. (2006). Capacity building through partnership: Intermediary nongovernmental organizations as local and global actors. *Nonprofit and Voluntary Sector Quarterly*, *35*(1), 66–82. doi:10.1177/0899764005282480

Sanzo, M. J., Álvarez, L. I., Rey, M., & García, N. (2015). Business as Nonprofit Partnerships: Do Their Effects Extend Beyond the Charitable Donor-Recipient Model? *Nonprofit and Voluntary Sector Quarterly*, *44*(2), 379–400. doi:10.1177/0899764013517770

Saraniemi, S. (2009). *Destination Branding in a Country Context-A case study of Finland in the British market*. Retrieved from http://www.scribd.com/doc/54035096/3/The-scientific-approach-%E2%80%93-abductive-logic

Sarstedt, M., & Schloderer, M. P. (2010). Developing a measurement approach for reputation of nonprofit organizations. *International Journal of Nonprofit and Voluntary Sector Marketing*, *15*(3), 276–299.

Saxton, G. D., & Guo, C. (2012). Conceptualizing Web-Based Stakeholder Communication: The Organizational Website as a Stakeholder Relations Tool. *Communication & Science Journal*. Available at: http://www.galileoco.com/comSciJliterature/saxtonGuo12.pdf

Saxton, G. D., & Guo, C. (2011). Accountability online: Understanding the web-based accountability practices of nonprofit organizations. *Nonprofit and Voluntary Sector Quarterly*, *40*(2), 270–295. doi:10.1177/0899764009341086

Schalock, R. L., Lee, T., Verdugo, M., Swart, K., Claes, C., van Loon, J., & Lee, C.-S. (2014). An evidence-based approach to organization evaluation and change in human service organizations evaluation and program planning. *Evaluation and Program Planning*, *45*(1), 110–118. doi:10.1016/j.evalprogplan.2014.03.012 PMID:24762778

Schaupp, L. C., & Bélanger, F. (2013). The value of social media for small businesses. *Journal of Information Systems*, *28*(1), 187–207. doi:10.2308/isys-50674

Schein, E. H. (1990). *Career anchors and job/role planning: the links between career pathing and career development*. Academic Press.

Schein, E. H. (1978). *Career Dynamics: Matching Individual and Organisational Needs*. Reading, MA: Addison-Wesley.

Schein, E. H., & Van Maanen, J. (2016). Career anchors and job/role planning: Tools for career and talent management. *Organizational Dynamics*, *45*(3), 165–173. doi:10.1016/j.orgdyn.2016.07.002

Schlesinger, M., Mitchell, S., & Gray, B. H. (2004). Public expectations of nonprofit and for–profit ownership in American medicine: Clarifications and implications. *Health Affairs*, *23*(6), 181–191. doi:10.1377/hlthaff.23.6.181 PMID:15537597

Schneider, C. J., & Trottier, D. (2012). The 2011 Vancouver riot and the role of Facebook in crowd-sourced policing. *BC Studies*, (175): 57.

Schneider, J. A. (2013). Comparing Stewardship Across Faith-Based Organizations. *Nonprofit and Voluntary Sector Quarterly*, *42*(3), 517–539. doi:10.1177/0899764012461399

Schneider, S., & Spieth, P. (2014). Business model innovation and strategic flexibility: Insights from an experimental research deign. *International Journal of Innovation Management*, *18*(6), 1–21. doi:10.1142/S136391961440009X

Schultz, M. D., Koehler, J. W., Philippe, T. W., & Coronel, R. S. (2015). Managing the effects of social media in organizations. *SAM Advanced Management Journal*, *80*(2), 42–47.

Schwedel, M. (2013). *Nonprofit Organizations, Social Media, and Mobile Applications*. (Master's Thesis). Southern Illinois University.

Scott, W. R., & Davis, G. F. (2006). *Organizations and organizing: Rational, natural and open systems perspectives*. Routledge.

Searle, W., & Ward, C. (1990). The prediction of psychological and socio-cultural adjustment during cross-cultural transitions. *International Journal of Intercultural Relations*, *14*(4), 449–464. doi:10.1016/0147-1767(90)90030-Z

Seddon, P. B. (1997). A respecification and extension of the DeLone and McLean model of IS success. *Information Systems Research*, *8*(3), 240–253. doi:10.1287/isre.8.3.240

Sedlarski, T. (2013). New Institutional Economy. Sofia University Press. (in Bulgarian)

Seel, K. (2006). *Boundary Spanning: A Grounded Theory of Sustainability in Canada's Nonprofit Sector*. Retrieved from http://www.mtroyal.ca/wcm/groups/public/documents/pdf/npr06_bound_thesis.pdf

Senanayake, D. (2009). *Sri Lanka's Post-Conflict Transition: Reconstruction, Reconciliation and Aid Effectiveness.* Retrieved from http://www.isas.nus.edu.sg/Attachments/PublisherAttachment/ISAS_Insights_86_29102009120637.pdf

Senses-Ozyurt, S. (2015). Political institutional environment and management culture as determinants of nongovernmental / nonprofit organizations' performance. *International Journal of Organization Theory and Behavior*, *18*(3), 269–303.

Sewell, W. H. Jr. (1992). A theory of structure: Duality, agency, and transformation. *American Journal of Sociology*, *98*(1), 1–29. doi:10.1086/229967

Shah, S., & Corley, K. (2006). Building better theory by bridging the quantitative–qualitative divide. *Journal of Management Studies*, *43*(8), 1821–1835. doi:10.1111/j.1467-6486.2006.00662.x

Shajari, M., & Ismail, Z. (2010). *A comprehensive adoption model of e-government services in developing countries.* Paper presented at the Advanced Management Science (ICAMS), 2010 IEEE International Conference on, Chengdu, China. doi:10.1109/ICAMS.2010.5552982

Shaw, J. B. (1990). A cognitive categorization model for the study of intercultural management. *Academy of Management Review*, *15*(4), 626–645.

Shea, J. (2011). Taking Non-profit Intermediaries Seriously: A Middle-Range Theory for Implementation Research. *Public Administration Review*, *71*(1), 57–66. doi:10.1111/j.1540-6210.2010.02306.x

Sheffi, Y. (2007). *The resilient enterprise: Overcoming vulnerability for competitive advantage.* Boston, MA: The MIT Press.

Sherer, L., & Lee, K. (2002). Institutional change in large law firms: A resource dependency and institutional perspective. *Academy of Management Journal*, *45*(1), 102–119. doi:10.2307/3069287

Sheridan, K. (2011) Measuring the Impact of Social Enterprise. *British Journal of Healthcare Management*, *17*(4), 152–56.

Shivalingaiah, D., & Naik, U. (2008). Comparative Study of Web 1.0, Web 2.0 and Web 3.0. Proceedings of the International Convention on Automation of Libraries in Education and Research Institutions (pp. 499–507). Allahabad, India: CALIBER. Retrieved from http://ir.inflibnet.ac.in/bitstream/1944/1285/1/54.pdf

Shocker, A. D., & Sethi, S. P. (1974). An approach to incorporating social preferences in developing corporate action strategies. In The Unstable Ground: Corporate Social Policy in a Dynamic Society (pp. 76-80). Melville.

Short, J., Moss, T., & Lumpkin, G. (2009). Research in Social entrepreneurship: Past contributions and future opportunities. *Strategic Entrepreneurship Journal*, *3*(2), 161–194. doi:10.1002/sej.69

Sidebotham, E. J. (2005). How to use documentation to decrease the likelihood of litigation. *The Psychologist Manager Journal*, *8*(2), 131–140. doi:10.1207/s15503461tpmj0802_4

Silvanto, S., & Ryan, J. (2014). Relocation branding: A strategic framework for attracting talent from abroad. *Journal of Global Mobility*, *2*(1), 102–120. doi:10.1108/JGM-07-2013-0046

Simmons, J. (2003). Balancing Performance, Accountability and Equity in Stakeholder Relationships: Towards More Socially Responsible HR Practice. *Corporate Social Responsibility and Environmental Management*, *10*(3), 129–140. doi:10.1002/csr.40

Simmons, P. J. (1998). Learning to live with NGOs. *Foreign Policy*, (112): 82–96. doi:10.2307/1149037

Sinclaire, J. K., & Vogus, C. E. (2011). Adoption of social networking sites: An exploratory adaptive structuration perspective for global organizations. *Information Technology Management*, *12*(4), 293–314. doi:10.1007/s10799-011-0086-5

Sinkovics, N., Sinkovics, R. R., & Yamin, M. (2014). The role of social value creation in business model formulation at the bottom of the pyramid–Implications for MNEs? *International Business Review*, *23*(4), 692–707. doi:10.1016/j.ibusrev.2013.12.004

Sisco, H. F., & McCorkindale, T. (2013). Communicating pink: An analysis of the communication strategies, transparency, and credibility of breast cancer social media sites. *International Journal of Nonprofit and Voluntary Sector Marketing*, *18*(4), 287–301. doi:10.1002/nvsm.1474

Skagert, K., Dellve, L., & Ahlborg, G. Jr. (2012). A prospective study of managers turnover and health in a healthcare organization. *Journal of Nursing Management*, *20*(7), 889–899. doi:10.1111/j.1365-2834.2011.01347.x PMID:23050622

Skouloudis, A., Evangelinos, K., & Malesios, C. (2015). Priorities and perceptions for corporate social responsibility: An NGO perspective. *Corporate Social Responsibility and Environmental Management*, *22*(2), 95–112. doi:10.1002/csr.1332

Slack, N., Chambers, S., & Johnston, R. (2001). *Operations management* (3rd ed.). Harlow, UK: Financial Times Prentice Hall.

Smith, S., Windmeijer, F., & Wright, E. (2012). *The effect of social information on charitable donations: Evidence from the (running) field1*. University of Bristol Working Paper.

Smith, B. R., & Stevens, C. E. (2010). Different types of social entrepreneurship: The role of geography and embeddedness on the measurement and scaling of social value. *Entrepreneurship & Regional Development*, *22*(6), 575–598. doi:10.1080/08985626.2010.488405

Smith, K. G., & Grimm, C. M. (1987). Environmental variation, strategic change and firm performance: A study of railroad deregulation. *Strategic Management Journal*, *8*(4), 363–376. doi:10.1002/smj.4250080406

Smith, P. C., & Richmond, K. A. (2007). Call for greater accountability within the U.S. nonprofit sector. *Academy of Accounting & Financial Studies Journal*, *11*(2), 75–87.

Smith, W. K., Gonin, M., & Besharov, M. L. (2013). Managing Social-Business Tensions. *Business Ethics Quarterly*, *23*(3), 407–442. doi:10.5840/beq201323327

Smits, M., & Mogos, S. (2013). The Impact of Social Media on Business Performance. *Proceedings of the 21st European Conference on Information Systems*, 1-12.

SNAP. (2014). *E-Government National Plan 2014-2017, Summary (Resumen del Plan de Gobierno Electrónico 2014-2017)*. Ecuadorian National Government (GNE) - National Secretary of Public Administration (SNAP). Retrieved from http://www.gobiernoelectronico.gob.ec/wp-content/uploads/2015/02/Resumen-Ingl%C3%A9s-PNGE.pdf

Snider, A. (2015). *Impact investing: The performance realities*. Wealth Management Institute.

Snipes, R. L., & Oswald, S. L. (2010). Charitable giving to not-for-profit organizations: Factors affecting donations to non-profit organizations. *Innovative Marketing*, *6*(1), 73–80.

Sobehart, J. R. (2014). Rumour has it: Modelling credibility, reputation and franchise risk. *Journal of Risk Management in Financial Institutions*, *7*(2), 161–173.

Society of Professionals in Dispute Resolution. (2001). *Designing integrated conflict management systems: Guidelines for practitioners and decision makers in organizations (Cornell Studies in Conflict and Dispute Resolution, No. 4). Ithaca, NY: Cornell/PERC Institute on Conflict Resolution and Washington*, DC: Association for Conflict Resolution.

Somers, A. B. (2005). Shaping the Balanced Scorecard for Use in UK Social Enterprises. *Social Enterprise Journal*, *1*(1), 43–57. doi:10.1108/17508610580000706

Sorenson, R. B., & Robinson, S. K. (2009). What employers can do to stay out of legal trouble when forced to implement layoffs. *Compensation and Benefits Review*, *41*(1), 25–32. doi:10.1177/0886368708329213

Sosna, M., Trevinyo-Rodriguez, R., & Velamuri, S. (2010). Business model innovation through trial-and-error learning: The Naturhouse case. *Long Range Planning*, *43*(2-3), 387–407. doi:10.1016/j.lrp.2010.02.003

Southin, T. (2013). *Harnessing the Fundraising Potential of Charitable Crowdfunding in Canada*. Retrieved from http://travissouthin.com/images/pdf/CharitableCrowdfunding-TravisSouthin.pdf

Speckbacher, G. (2003). The economics of performance management in nonprofit organizations. *Nonprofit Management & Leadership*, *13*(3), 267–281. doi:10.1002/nml.15

Spiro, R. J. (2001). Principled pluralism for adaptative flexibility in teaching and learning to read. In R. F. Flippo (Ed.), *Reading researchers in search of common ground* (pp. 92–97). Newark, DE: International Reading Association.

Spremann, K. (1987). Agent and principal. In *Agency theory, information, and incentives* (pp. 3–37). Springer Berlin Heidelberg. doi:10.1007/978-3-642-75060-1_2

Sriboonlue, P., Ussahawanitchakit, P., & Raksong, S. (2016). Strategic innovation capability and firm sustainability: Evidence from auto parts businesses in Thailand. *Journal of Business & Retail Management Research*, *10*(2), 11–29.

Sroypetch, N., & Kleiner, B. H. (2006). How to conduct discipline interviews. *Nonprofit World*, *24*(6), 25–27.

Stake, R. E. (2000). Case studies. In N. K. Denzin & Y. S. Lincoln (Eds.), *Handbook of Qualitative Research* (2nd ed.; pp. 435–454). Thousand Oaks, CA: Sage.

Stanaland, A. J., Lwin, M. O., & Murphy, P. E. (2011). Consumer perceptions of the antecedents and consequences of corporate social responsibility. *Journal of Business Ethics*, *102*(1), 47–55. doi:10.1007/s10551-011-0904-z

StartSomeGood. (2016). *How it works – crowdfunding for non-profits, social entrepreneurs and changemakers*. Retrieved July 9, 2016, from http://ssg.startsomegood.com/HowItWorks

Statistics Canada. (2010). *Charitable giving by Canadians*. Retrieved July 8, 2016, from http://www.statcan.gc.ca/pub/11-008-x/2012001/article/11637-eng.htm

Stecker, M. J. (2014). Revolutionizing the Nonprofit Sector Through Social Entrepreneurship. *Journal of Economic Issues*, *48*(2), 349–358. doi:10.2753/JEI0021-3624480208

Steinberg, R. 2003. Economic theories of nonprofit organizations. In The study of the nonprofit enterprise (pp. 277-309). Springer US. doi:10.1007/978-1-4615-0131-2_16

Steinberg, R. (2006). Economic Theories of Nonprofit Organizations. In W. Powell & R. Steinberg (Eds.), *The Nonprofit Sector: A Research Handbook* (p. 117). London: Yale University Press.

Steinberg, R. (2010). Principal–agent theory and nonprofit accountability. In K. J. Hopt & T. Von Hippel (Eds.), *Comparative corporate governance of non-profit organizations* (pp. 73–125). Cambridge, UK: Cambridge University Press. doi:10.1017/CBO9780511712128.006

Steinmacher, I., Graciotto Silva, M. A., Gerosa, M. A., & Redmiles, D. F. (2015). A systematic literature review on the barriers faced by newcomers to open source software projects. *Information and Software Technology*, *59*, 67–85. doi:10.1016/j.infsof.2014.11.001

Sternberg, R. J. (1982). *Handbook of human intelligence*. Cambridge, UK: Cambridge University Press.

Stevens, S. K. (2001). *Nonprofit lifecycles: Stage based wisdom for nonprofit capacity*. Long Lake, MN: Stagewise Enterprises.

Stewart, R. (2015). A theory of change for capacity building for the use of research evidence by decision makers in southern Africa. *Evidence & Policy Journal*, *11*(4), 547–557. doi:10.1332/174426414X1417545274793

Stewart, T. A. (1997). *Intellectual capital: The new wealth of organizations*. New York: Currency Doubleday.

Stoltz, P. (1997). *Adversity quotient*. New York, NY: John Wiley & Sons.

Strang, K. D. (2010a). *Complexity and project portfolio selection*. Paper presented at the Lille Project Seminars, Helisinki, Finland.

Strang, K. D. (2014c). Nonparametric analysis of global risk management techniques. In Information Resources Management Association (Ed.), Crisis management: Concepts, methodologies, tools and applications (Vol. 1, pp. 687-711). Hershey, PA: Information Science Reference. doi:10.4018/978-1-4666-4707-7.ch033

Strang, K. D. (2016). Exploring Marketing Theories in Business Web Service Procurement Behavior. In IRMA (Ed.), Web-Based Services: Concepts, Methodologies, Tools, and Applications (Vol. 2, pp. 221-250). Hershey, PA: Information Resource Management Association (IRMA). doi:10.4018/978-1-4666-9466-8.ch011

Strang, K. D. (2010b). Education balanced scorecard for online courses: Australia and USA best practices. *Journal of Cases on Information Technology*, *12*(3), 46–51. doi:10.4018/jcit.2010070103

Strang, K. D. (2011a). Applying multidisciplinary logistic techniques to improve operations productivity at a mine. *Logistics Research Journal*, *3*(4), 207–219. doi:10.1007/s12159-011-0058-5

Strang, K. D. (2011b). Portfolio selection methodology for a nuclear project. *Project Management Journal*, *42*(2), 81–93.

Strang, K. D. (2012a). Applied financial nonlinear programming models for decision making. *International Journal of Applied Decision Sciences*, *5*(4), 370–395. doi:10.1504/IJADS.2012.050023

Strang, K. D. (2012b). Group cohesion, personality and leadership effect on networked marketing staff performance. *International Journal of Networking and Virtual Organisations*, *10*(2), 187–209. doi:10.1504/IJNVO.2012.045734

Strang, K. D. (2012c). Man versus math: Behaviorist exploration of post-crisis non-banking asset management. *Journal of Asset Management*, *13*(5), 348–467. doi:10.1057/jam.2012.14

Strang, K. D. (2014a). Dimensional analysis of real estate portfolio selection methods. *Global Business and Economics Review*, *16*(3), 269–265. doi:10.1504/GBER.2014.063069

Strang, K. D. (2014b). Investment selection in complex multinational projects. *International Journal of Information Technology Project Management*, *5*(2), 62–80. doi:10.4018/ijitpm.2014040105

Strang, K. D. (2015a). Exploring the relationship between global terrorist ideology and attack methodology. *Risk Management Journal*, *17*(2), 65–90. doi:10.1057/rm.2015.8

Strang, K. D. (Ed.). (2015b). *Matching Research Method with Ideology and Strategy* (Vol. 1). New York: Palgrave Macmillan. doi:10.1057/9781137484956_4

Strang, K. D. (Ed.). (2015c). *Selecting Research Techniques for a Method and Strategy* (Vol. 1). New York: Palgrave Macmillan. doi:10.1057/9781137484956_5

Strang, K. D., & Alamieyeseigha, S. (2015). What and where are the risks of international terrorist attacks: A descriptive study of the evidence. *International Journal of Risk and Contingency Management*, *4*(1), 1–18.

Strang, K. D., & Vajjhala, N. R. (2015). Impact of Socialized Uncertainty on Group Decisions: An Experiment with Emerging Executives. *International Journal of Risk and Contingency Management*, *4*(2), 45–58. doi:10.4018/IJRCM.2015040104

Streb, Ch. (2010). Exploratory Case Study. In A. J. Mills, G. Durepos, & E. Wiebe (Eds.), *Encyclopaedia of Case Study Research*. SAGE.

Suchman, M. C. (1995). Managing Legitimacy: Strategic and Institutional Approaches. *Academy of Management Review*, *20*(3), 571–610.

Sullivan, S. E., & Baruch, Y. (2009). Advances in career theory and research: A critical review and agenda for future exploration. *Journal of Management*, *35*(6), 1542–1571. doi:10.1177/0149206309350082

Sullivan-Taylor, B., & Branicki, L. (2011). Creating resilient SMEs: Why one size might not fit all. *International Journal of Production Research*, *49*(18), 5565–5579. doi:10.1080/00207543.2011.563837

Super, D. E. (1957). *The psychology of careers; an introduction to vocational development*. Academic Press.

Sutcliffe, K. M., & Vogus, T. J. (2003). Organizing for Resilience. In K. S. Cameron, J. E. Dutton, & R. E. Quinn (Eds.), *Positive Organizational Scholarship. Foundations of a New Discipline* (pp. 94–110). San Francisco, CA: Berrett-Koehler.

Suutari, V., & Taka, M. (2004). Career anchors of managers with global careers. *Journal of Management Development*, *23*(9), 833–847. doi:10.1108/02621710410558440

Szwajca, D. (2016). Strategie zarządzania relacjami z interesariuszami w kontekście ograniczania ryzyka, pogorszenia lub utraty reputacji przedsiębiorstwa. *Research Papers of The Wroclaw University of Economics*, *420*, 324–336.

Takahashi, L. M., & Smutny, G. (2002). Collaborative windows and organizational governance: Exploring the formation and demise of social service partnership. *Nonprofit and Voluntary Sector Quarterly*, *31*(2), 165–185. doi:10.1177/0899764002312001

Tang, L., & Koveos, P. E. (2008). A framework to update Hofstedes cultural value indices: Economic dynamics and institutional stability. *Journal of International Business Studies*, *39*(6), 1045–1063. doi:10.1057/palgrave.jibs.8400399

Tan, J., & Litschert, R. J. (1994). Environment-strategy relationship and its performance implications: An empirical study of Chinese electronics industry. *Strategic Management Journal*, *15*(1), 1–20. doi:10.1002/smj.4250150102

Tapscott, D., Lowy, A., & Ticoll, D. (2000). *Digital capital: Harnessing the power of business webs*. Harvard Business Press.

Tapscott, D., & Ticoll, D. (2003). *The naked corporation*. New York: Free Press.

Taylor, M., & Doerfel, M. L. (2011). Evolving network roles in international aid efforts: Evidence from Croatias post-war transition. *Voluntas: International Journal of Voluntary and Non Profit Organizations*, *22*(2), 311–334. doi:10.1007/s11266-010-9155-3

Teece, D. (2010). Business models, business strategy and innovation. *Long Range Planning*, *43*(2-3), 172–194. doi:10.1016/j.lrp.2009.07.003

Teeni, D., & Young, D. (2003). The Changing Role of Nonprofits in the Network Economy. *Nonprofit and Voluntary Sector Quarterly*, *32*(3), 397–414. doi:10.1177/0899764003254900

Teets, J. C. (2014). *Civil Society under authoritarianism: The China model*. Cambridge University Press. doi:10.1017/CBO9781139839396

Teratanavat, R., & Kleiner, B. (2005). When it's time to say good-by. *Nonprofit World*, *23*(2), 12–14.

Tertiary Education Quality and Standards Agency (TEQSA). (2015). *National Register of higher education providers. National Register breakdown as at August 2015*. TEQSA.

Thatcher, J., & Sharp, L. (2008). Measuring the local economic impact of National Health Service procurement in the UK: An evaluation of the Cornwall Food Programme and LM3. *Local Environment*, *13*(3), 253–270. doi:10.1080/13549830701669005

The Canadian Press. (2012, August 4). *Crowdfunding trend thrust into spotlight by Canadian campaigns - Toronto - CBC News*. Retrieved July 8, 2016, from http://www.cbc.ca/news/canada/toronto/crowdfunding-trend-thrust-into-spotlight-by-canadian-campaigns-1.1136447

The Honorable Peter Dutton Member of Parliament (Minister for Health and Sport). (2014). *Media release: Rebuilding General Practice Training*. Author.

The Interorganizational Committee on Guidelines and Principles for Social Impact Assessment. (1994). Guidelines and principles for social impact assessment. *Environmental Impact Assessment Review*, *15*(1), 11–43.

The King's Fund. (2011). *Social Care Funding and NHS: An Impending Crisis?* London: King's Fund.

The Life You Can Save. (2016). *Ten reasons why people don't donate to charity*. Retrieved July 8, 2016, from http://www.thelifeyoucansave.org/learn-more/common-objections-to-giving

Thomas, A. (2004). The rise of social cooperatives in Italy. *Voluntas*, *15*(30), 243–264. doi:10.1023/B:VOLU.0000046280.06580.d8

Tilling, M. W., & Tilt, C. A. (2010). The Edge of legitimacy Voluntary social and environmental reporting in Rothmans´19561999 annual reports. *Accounting, Auditing & Accountability Journal*, *23*(1), 55–81. doi:10.1108/09513571011010600

TOBB (The Union of Chambers and Commodity Exchanges of Turkey). (n.d.). *History*. Retrieved from http://www.tobb.org.tr/Sayfalar/Eng/Tarihce.php

Tobolowsky, B. F., Mary, S., Hunter, L. A., Schreiner, J., Gardner, N., & Pattengale, J. A. (2009). *Helping sophomores succeed: Understanding and improving the second year experience*. San Francisco, CA: Jossey-Bass Publishing.

Todres, L., & Wheeler, S. (2001). The complementarity of phenomenology, hermeneutics and existentialism as a philosophical perspective for nursing research. *International Journal of Nursing Studies*, *38*(1), 1–8. doi:10.1016/S0020-7489(00)00047-X PMID:11137717

Toland, J., & Yoong, P. (2013). Envisaging the "Big Picture": Information systems researchers. *Australasian Journal of Information Systems*, *18*(1).

Tornatzky, L. G., Fleischer, M., & Chakrabarti, A. K. (1990). *The processes of technological innovation*. Lexington, MA: Lexington Books.

Treem, J. W., & Leonardi, P. M. (2013). Social media use in organizations: Exploring the affordances of visibility, editability, persistence, and association. *Annals of the International Communication Association*, *36*(1), 143–189. doi:10.1080/23808985.2013.11679130

Tremblay-Boire, J., & Prakash, A. (2015). Accountability.org: Online Disclosures by U.S. Nonprofits. *Voluntas. Voluntas*, *26*(2), 693–719. doi:10.1007/s11266-014-9452-3

Trencher, G., Yarime, M., McCormick, K. B., Doll, C. N. H., & Kraines, S. B. (2014). Beyond the third mission: Exploring the emerging university function of co-creation for sustainability. *Science & Public Policy*, *41*(2), 151–179. doi:10.1093/scipol/sct044

Trivedi, C., & Stokols, D. (2011). Social Enterprises and Corporate Enterprises: Fundamental Differences and Defining Features. *Journal of Entrepreneurship*, *20*(1), 1–32. doi:10.1177/097135571002000101

Tschirhart, M., & Bielefeld, W. (2012). *Managing nonprofit organizations*. San Francisco, CA: Jossey- Bass. doi:10.1002/9781119051626

Tuckman, H. (1998). Competition, Commercialization, and the Evolution of Nonprofit Organizational Structures. *Journal of Policy Analysis and Management*, *17*(2), 175–194. doi:10.1002/(SICI)1520-6688(199821)17:2<175::AID-PAM4>3.0.CO;2-E

Tuckman, H., & Chang, C. (2006). Commercial Activity, Technological Change and Nonprofit Mission. In W. Powell & R. Steinberg (Eds.), *The Nonprofit Sector; A research Handbook* (pp. 629–642). London: Yale University Press.

Turco, M. (2014). The multidimensional value measurement: The balanced scorecard and its perspectives of development. *Annual International Conference on Accounting & Finance*, 155-165. doi:10.5176/2251-1997_AF14.65

Ullmann, A. A. (1985). Data in search of a theory: A critical examination of the relationship among social performance, social disclosure, and economic performance of U.S. Firms. *Academy of Management Review*, *10*(3), 540–557.

UN. (2010). *Mid-Year Review-Common Humanitarian Action Plan (CHAP)*. Retrieved from http://reliefweb.int/node/361967

Unerman, J., & O Dwyer, B. (2010). NGO accountability and sustainability issues in the changing global environment. *Public Management Review*, *12*(4), 475–486. doi:10.1080/14719037.2010.496258

United Nations. (2003). *Handbook on Non-Profit Institutions in the System of National Accounts, Studies in Methods, Series F., No. 91*. Retrieved from http://unstats.un.org/unsd/publication/seriesf/seriesf_91e.pdf

Uzunoğlu, E., & Kip, S. M. (2014). Building relationships through websites: A content analysis of Turkish environmental non-profit organizations (NPO) websites. *Public Relations Review*, *40*(1), 113–115. doi:10.1016/j.pubrev.2013.06.001

Vaccaro, A. (2006). Privacy, security and transparency: ICT-related ethical perspectives and contrasts in contemporary firms. In D. Howcroft, E. Trauth, & J. DeGross (Eds.), *Social inclusion: Societal and organizational implications for information systems*. New York: Springer. doi:10.1007/0-387-34588-4_17

Vaccaro, A., & Madsen, P. (2006). Firms' information transparency: Ethical questions in the information age. In J. Berleur (Ed.), *Social informatics: An information society for all?* New York: Springer. doi:10.1007/978-0-387-37876-3_12

Vakil, A. C. (1997). Confronting the classification problem: Towards a taxonomy of NGOs. *World Development*, *25*(12), 2057–2070. doi:10.1016/S0305-750X(97)00098-3

Valcour, P. M., & Tolbert, P. (2003). Gender, family and career in the era of boundarylessness: Determinants and effects of intra-and inter-organizational mobility. *International Journal of Human Resource Management*, *14*(5), 768–787. doi:10.1080/0958519032000080794

Valentinov, V. (2006). Toward an Economic Interpretation of the non-distribution constraint. *International Journal of Not-for-Profit Law*, *9*(1).

Valentinov, V. (2008a). The Economics of the Non-Distribution Constraint: A Critical Reappraisal. *Annals of Public and Cooperative*, *79*(1), 35–52. doi:10.1111/j.1467-8292.2007.00351.x

Vallejo, B., & Wehn, U. (2016). Capacity Development Evaluation: The Challenge of the Results Agenda and Measuring Return on Investment in the Global South. *World Development*, *79*(1), 1–13. doi:10.1016/j.worlddev.2015.10.044

Van Alstyne, M., Parker, G., & Choudary, S. (2016). Pipelines, Platforms and the new rules of strategy. *Harvard Business Review*. Retrieved from https://hbr.org/2016/04/pipelines-platforms-and-the-new-rules-of-strategy

Van Bogaert, D., & Gross-Schaefer, A. (2005). Terminating the employee-employer relationship: Ethical and legal challenges. *Employee Relations Law Journal*, *31*(1), 50–69.

Van der Pijl, K., & Sminia, H. (2004). Strategic management of public interest organizations. Voluntas. *Voluntas*, *15*(2), 137–155. doi:10.1023/B:VOLU.0000033178.54004.e9

Van Everdingen, Y. M., & Waarts, E. (2003). The effect of national culture on the adoption of innovations. *Marketing Letters*, *14*(3), 217–232. doi:10.1023/A:1027452919403

van Fleet, D., & van Fleet, E. W. (2006). Internal terrorists: The terrorists inside organizations. *Journal of Managerial Psychology*, *21*(8), 763–774. doi:10.1108/02683940610713280

van Manen, M. (1990). *Researching lived experience: Human science for an action sensitive pedagogy*. Albany, NY: State University of New York Press.

van Manen, M. (1991). *The tact of teaching: The meaning of pedagogical thoughtfulness*. Albany, NY: State University of New York Press.

Van Puyvelde, S., Caers, R., Du Bois, C., & Jegers, M. (2012). The governance of nonprofit organizations integrating agency theory with stakeholder and stewardship theories. *Nonprofit and Voluntary Sector Quarterly*, *41*(3), 431–451. doi:10.1177/0899764011409757

Van Slyke, D. M. (2007). Agents or stewards: Using theory to understand the government-nonprofit social service contracting relationship. *Journal of Public Administration: Research and Theory*, *17*(2), 157–187. doi:10.1093/jopart/mul012

Vanclay, F. (2003). International principles for social impact assessment. *Impact Assessment and Project Appraisal*, *21*(1), 5-12.

vanderHeiden, P., Pohl, C., Bin Mansor, S., & van Genderen, J. (2015). The role of education and training in absorptive capacity of international technology transfer in the aerospace sector. *Progress in Aerospace Sciences, 76*(1), 42-54.

Vargo, S. L., & Luch, R. F. (2004). Evolving to a new dominant logic for marketing. *Journal of Marketing*, *68*(January), 1–17. doi:10.1509/jmkg.68.1.1.24036

Vargo, S. L., & Lusch, R. F. (2016). Institutions and axioms: An extension and update of service-dominant logic. *Journal of the Academy of Marketing Science*, *44*(1), 5–23. doi:10.1007/s11747-015-0456-3

Varian, H. (2014). Big Data: New tricks for econometrics. *The Journal of Economic Perspectives*, *28*(2), 3–28. doi:10.1257/jep.28.2.3

Vélez, A. M. (2011). Un recorrido hacia la responsabilidad social corporativa. *Revista Ciencias Estratégicas*, *19*(25), 55–74.

Venkatesh, V., & Davis, F. D. (2000). A Theoretical Extension of the Technology Acceptance Model. *Management Science*, *46*(2), 186–204. doi:10.1287/mnsc.46.2.186.11926

Venkatesh, V., Morris, M. G., Davis, G. B., & Davis, F. D. (2003). User Acceptance of Information Technology: Toward a Unified View. *Management Information Systems Quarterly*, *27*(3), 425–478.

Venkatraman, N., & Prescott, J. E. (1990). Environment-strategy coalignment: An empirical test of its performance implications. *Strategic Management Journal*, *11*(1), 1–23. doi:10.1002/smj.4250110102

Venturi, P., & Zandonai, F. (2012). *L'impresa sociale in Italia. Pluralità di modelli e contributo alla ripresa.* Milano: AltraEconomia.

Vickers, I. (2010). *Social enterprise and the environment: a review of the literature.* Third Sector Research Centre Working Paper 22. Universities of Birmingham and Southampton Birmingham.

Vidal, P., Torres, D., Guix, B., & Peña, M. (2005). *La responsabilidad social de las organizaciones no lucrativas.* Centro de recursos del observatorio del tercer Sector. Available at: http://www.galileoco.com/comSciJliterature/saxtonGuo12.pdf

Vidal-García, J., & Vidal, M. (2016). Big Data in financial services. In Effective Big Data Management and Opportunities for Implementation (pp. 217-230). Hershey, PA: IGI Global.

Vidal-García, J., Vidal, M., & Hernandez Barros, R. (2017). Computational business intelligence, Big Data and their role in business decisions in the age of the Internet of Things. In I. Lee (Ed.), *The Internet of Things in the Modern Business Environment.* Hershey, PA: IGI Global.

Vidal, M., Vidal-García, J., & Hernandez Barros, R. (2016). Big Data and business decision making. In M. K. Singh & K. G. Dileep (Eds.), *Effective Big Data Management and Opportunities for Implementation* (pp. 140–157). Hershey, PA: IGI Global. doi:10.4018/978-1-5225-0182-4.ch010

Wadie, N. (2011). Factors Influencing the Adoption of Internet Banking in Tunisia. *International Journal of Business and Management*, *6*(8), 143. doi:10.5539/ijbm.v6n8p143

Walker, J. (2015). Hybrid Organizations: Origins, Strategies, Impacts and Implications. *California Management Review*, *57*(3), 5–13. doi:10.1525/cmr.2015.57.3.5

Walker, R. M. (2014). Internal and External Antecedents of Process Innovation: A review and extension. *Public Management Review*, *16*(1), 21–44. doi:10.1080/14719037.2013.771698

Wang, S. Q. (2012). Non-profit incubator: an important support organization. *The Academic Journal of Chengdu Administrative College*, *5*, 83-88.

Wang, Z. (2006). *Displaced self and sense of belonging: A Chinese researcher studying Chinese expatriates working in the United States.* ProQuest Dissertation UMI 3240429. University of South Florida, Ann Arbor, MI: ProQuest, LLC.

Wang, D. (2015). The summary research of supporting social organization. *Journal of Zhengzhou Institute of Aeronautical Industry Management*, *33*(1), 110–113.

Wang, L., Graddy, E., & Morgan, D. (2011). The development of community-based foundations in East Asia. *Public Management Review*, *13*(8), 1155–1178. doi:10.1080/14719037.2011.619068

Wang, Y.-S., & Liao, Y.-W. (2008). Assessing eGovernment systems success: A validation of the DeLone and McLean model of information systems success. *Government Information Quarterly*, *25*(4), 717–733. doi:10.1016/j.giq.2007.06.002

Ward, C., & Rana-Deuba, A. (1999). Acculturation and adaptation revisited. *Journal of Cross-Cultural Psychology*, *60*(4), 422–442. doi:10.1177/0022022199030004003

Waters, R. D., Burnett, E., Lamm, A., & Lucas, J. (2009). Engaging stakeholders through social networking: How nonprofit organizations are using Facebook. *Public Relations Review*, *35*(2), 102–106. doi:10.1016/j.pubrev.2009.01.006

Waters, R. D., & Feneley, K. L. (2013). Virtual stewardship in the age of new media: Have nonprofit organizations moved beyond Web 1.0 strategies? *International Journal of Nonprofit and Voluntary Sector Marketing*, *18*(3), 216–230. doi:10.1002/nvsm.1469

Waters, R. D., & Jones, P. M. (2011). Using video to build an organizations identity and brand: A content analysis of nonprofit organizations YouTube videos. *Journal of Nonprofit & Public Sector Marketing*, *23*(3), 248–268. doi:10.1080/10495142.2011.594779

Watkins, A., Papaioannou, T., Mugwagwa, J., & Kale, D. (2015). National innovation systems and the intermediary role of industry associations in building institutional capacities for innovation in developing countries: A critical review of the literature. *Research Policy*, *44*(1), 1407–1418. doi:10.1016/j.respol.2015.05.004

WB. (2014). *FY15 World Bank Budget*. Available on: http://www-wds.worldbank.org/external/default/WDSContentServer/WDSP/IB/2014/10/24/000350881_20141024085127/Rendered/PDF/918340BR0R201400disclosed0100230140.pdf

Weerawardena, J., McDonald, R. E., & Sullivan Mort, G. (2010). Sustainability of nonprofit organizations: An empirical investigation. *Journal of World Business*, *45*(4), 346–356. doi:10.1016/j.jwb.2009.08.004

Weidenbaum, M. (2009). Who will Guard the Guardians? The Social Responsibility of NGOs. *Journal of Business Ethics*, *87*(1), 147–155. doi:10.1007/s10551-008-9813-1

Weisbrod, B. (1975). Toward a Theory of the Voluntary Not for profit Sector in a Three-Sector Economy. In E. Phelps (Ed.), *Altruism* (pp. 171–195). New York: Morality and Economic Theory.

Weisbrod, B. (1998). The nonprofit mission and its financing: Growing links between nonprofits and the rest of the economy. In B. Weisbrod (Ed.), *To Profit or Not to Profit: The Commercial Transformation of the Nonprofit Sector* (pp. 1–22). Cambridge, UK: Cambridge University Press. doi:10.1017/CBO9780511625947.003

Weisbrod, B. A. (1977). *The voluntary nonprofit sector*. Lexington, MA: Lexington Books.

Weisbrod, B. A. (1986). Toward a theory of the voluntary nonprofit sector in a three-sector economy. In S. Rose-Ackerman (Ed.), *The economics of nonprofit institutions: Studies in structure and policy* (pp. 1–44). New York: Oxford University Press.

Weisbrod, B. A. (1988). *The nonprofit economy*. Cambridge, MA: Harvard University Press.

Werker, E., & Ahmed, F. Z. (2008). What do nongovernmental organizations do? *The Journal of Economic Perspectives*, *22*(2), 73–92. doi:10.1257/jep.22.2.73

West, D.M. (2012). *Big Data for education: Data mining, data analytics, and web dashboards.* Brookings Institution working papers.

Westmoreland, M. B. (2014). *Five Ways Technology Will Shape the Nonprofit Sector in 2014.* Blackbaud. Retrieved from www.blackbaud.com

White, D. E. (2001). Why do people donate to charity? *The Nonprofit Handbook: Fund Raising, 3.*

White, C., Woodfield, K., & Ritchie, J. (2003). Reporting and presenting qualitative data. In J. Richie & J. Lewis (Eds.), *Qualitative research practice: A guide for social science students and researchers* (pp. 287–320). London: Sage.

White, G. (2005). How to report a company's sustainability activities. *Management Accounting Quarterly*, *7*(1), 36–43.

Wiggins, R. R., & Ruefli, T. W. (2005). Schumpeters ghost: Is hypercompetition making the best of times shorter? *Strategic Management Journal*, *26*(10), 887–911. doi:10.1002/smj.492

Willetts, P. (2009). Non-governmental organizations. Conventions, Treaties and other Responses to Global Issues. London, UK: Encyclopedia of Life Support Systems, 229-248.

Williamson, O. E. (1991). Comparative economic organization: The analysis of discrete structural alternatives. *Administrative Science Quarterly*, *36*(2), 269–296. doi:10.2307/2393356

Willis, J. E. III. (2013). *Ethics, Big Data, and analytics: A model for application.* Instructional Development Center Publications, Purdue University.

Wills, P. (1998). *Health and Medical Research Strategic Review*. Canberra: Academic Press.

Wilson, D. C. (1993). Organizational Structures in the Voluntary Sector: Theoretical Overview. In Issues in Voluntary and Non-profit Management (pp. 149-166). Addison-Wesley Publishing Company.

Wilson, F., & Post, J. E. (2011). Business models for people, planet (& profits): Exploring the phenomena of social business, a market-based approach to social value creation. *Small Business Economics*, *40*(3), 715–737. doi:10.1007/s11187-011-9401-0

Wilson, K. E. (2014). *New Investment Approaches for Addressing Social and Economic Challenges. OECD Science, Technology and Industry Policy, Papers No. 15.* OECD. doi:10.1787/23074957

Wirl, F. (2014). Dynamic corporate social responsibility (CSR) strategies in oligopoly. *OR-Spektrum*, *36*(1), 229–250. doi:10.1007/s00291-013-0319-6

Wirtz, B. W., Pistoia, A., Ullrich, S., & Göttel, V. (2016). Business models: Origin, development and future research perspectives. *Long Range Planning*, *49*(1), 36–54. doi:10.1016/j.lrp.2015.04.001

Witesman, E. M., & Fernandez, S. (2012). Government contracts with private organizations: Are there differences between nonprofits and for-profits? *Nonprofit and Voluntary Sector Quarterly*, *42*(4), 689–715. doi:10.1177/0899764012442592

Wohlgemuth, N. H.-M. (2014). Alternatives to Rural Development: Organic Agriculture and Indigenous Communities in Chiapas, Mexico. *Journal of Latin American Geography*, *13*(1), 67–88. doi:10.1353/lag.2014.0003

Wojciechowski, A. (2009). Models of charity donations and project funding in social networks. In *OTM Confederated International Conferences on the Move to Meaningful Internet Systems* (pp. 454–463). Springer. doi:10.1007/978-3-642-05290-3_58

Wong, A. L. Y. (2007). Making career choice: A study of Chinese managers. *Human Relations*, *60*(8), 1211–1233. doi:10.1177/0018726707081661

World Economic Forum. (2016). *The future of jobs: employment, skills and workforce strategy for the fourth industrial revolution.* World Economic Forum, Geneva, Switzerland.

Wrigley, C., & Straker, K. (2016). Designing innovative business models with a framework that promotes experimentation. *Strategy and Leadership*, *44*(1), 11–19. doi:10.1108/SL-06-2015-0048

Wu, R. (2014, November 24). *5 Best Practices in Nonprofit Crowdfunding*. Retrieved July 9, 2016, from https://www.causevox.com/blog/5-best-practices-nonprofit-crowdfunding/

Wu, S. J., Melnyk, S., & Flynn, B. B. (2010). Operational Capabilities: The Secret Ingredient. *Decision Sciences Journal of Innovative Education*, *41*(4), 721–754. doi:10.1111/j.1540-5915.2010.00294.x

Xu, J. L., Lu, Y. B., & Cao, F. H. (2014). The construction of non-profit incubators value Chain. China Public Administration, 12, 20-24.

Xu, Y. G. (2014). The discussion of market-oriented philanthropy. Chinese Philanthropic. Retrieved from http://www.chinadevelopmentbrief.org.cn/news-16408.html

Xu, Y. S. (2010). The structural innovation of social organizations. *Research on Organization Management*, *8*, 22-25.

Xu, A., Yang, X., Rao, H., Fu, W. T., Huang, S. W., & Bailey, B. P. (2014). Show me the money! *Proceedings of the 32nd annual ACM Conference on Human Factors in Computing Systems*. doi:10.1145/2556288.2557045

Yarnall, J. (1998). Career anchors: Results of an organisational study in the UK. *Career Development International*, *3*(2), 56–61. doi:10.1108/13620439810207536

Yılmazel, M. (2011). *A Content Analysis About Social Media Usage of Charitable Funds Which Activate in Turkey* (Master Thesis). Anadolu University, Graduate School of Social Sciences, Department of Public Relations and Advertising, Eskişehir.

Ying, M. (2012). *Marketing From Social Media Platforms and the Firms That Use These Platforms Effectively* (Master's Thesis). Kadir Has University, Social Sciences Institute.

Yin, R. (1984). *Case study research*. Beverly Hills, CA: Sage Publications.

Yin, R. K. (1994). *Case study research: design and methods* (2nd ed.). Thousand Oaks, CA: Sage.

Yin, R. K. (2013). *Case study research: Design and methods (Applied social research methods)*. Sage Publications, Inc.

Young, D. (2005). *Mission-market tension in managing nonprofit organizations*. Atlanta, GA: Andrew Young School of Policy Studies, Research Paper Series.

Young, D. R. (2006). Social enterprise in community and economic development in the USA: Theory, corporate form and purpose. *International Journal of Entrepreneurship and Innovation Management*, *6*(3), 241–255. doi:10.1504/IJEIM.2006.009877

Young, D. R. (2007). *Financing non-profits: Putting theory into practice*. Lanham, MD: Alta Mira.

Young, D. R., Koenig, B. L., Najam, A., & Fisher, J. (1999). Strategy and structure in managing global associations. *Voluntas: International Journal Of Voluntary & Nonprofit Organizations*, *10*(4), 323–343. doi:10.1023/A:1021434424549

Yunus, M., Moingeon, B., & Lehmann-Ortega, L. (2010). Building social business models: Lessons from the Grameen experience. *Long Range Planning*, *43*(2), 308–325. doi:10.1016/j.lrp.2009.12.005

Yusof, S. W. M. (2010). *Developing Strategy for Customer Value Creation Towards a Professional Services. Academic Press.*

Zaidieh, A. J. Y. (2012). The use of social networking in education: Challenges and opportunities. *World of Computer Science and Information Technology Journal*, *2*(1), 18–21.

Zamagni, S., Venturi, P., & Rago, S. (2015). Valutare l'impatto sociale. La questione della misurazione nelle imprese sociali. *Impresa Soc, 6*.

Zappalà, G., & Lyons, M. (2009). *Recent approaches to measuring social impact in the Third sector: An overview*. Sydney: Centre for Social Impact.

Zatepilina-Monacell, O. (2012). High stakes: U.S. nonprofit organizations and the U.S. standing abroad. *Public Relations Review*, *38*(3), 471–476. doi:10.1016/j.pubrev.2012.02.003

Zeithaml, V. A. (1988). Consumer perceptions of price, quality, and value: A means-end model and synthesis of evidence. *Journal of Marketing*, *52*(3), 2–22. doi:10.2307/1251446

Zeitz, G., Blau, G., & Fertig, J. (2009). Boundaryless careers and institutional resources. *International Journal of Human Resource Management*, *20*(2), 372–398. doi:10.1080/09585190802670763

Zeng, K. (2012). The development of the social organization and its incremental layout. *Organization Management and Research*, *7*, 13–17.

Zhang, W. Y. (2013). *Philanthropy need the business logic*. Chinese Philanthropic. Retrieved from: http://sdg.shanda960.com/article/6687

Zhao, Y., Zu, B., Li, Z., & Li, C. (2014). Corporate social responsibility assessment: A multi-dimensional and dynamic perspective. *Mining Technology*, *123*(4), 230–239. doi:10.1179/1743286314Y.0000000071

Zharp, Z., & Brock, D. (2012). Implementation Through Risk Mitigation: Strategic Processes in the Nonprofit Organization. *Administration & Society*, *44*(5), 571–594. doi:10.1177/0095399711418325

Zhu, Y. (2016). *Three stages of market oriented non-profit donation*. Philanthropic Learning Group. Retrieved from: http://www.chinadevelopmentbrief.org.cn/news-18469.ht

Zincir, O. (2014). *For What Purposes Do Managers Use Social Media? A Conceptual Framework Development Effort* (Master Thesis). Istanbul University, Graduate School of Social Sciences, Business Administration Department, İstanbul, Turkey.

Zlotnikova, I., & van der Weide, T. (2015). Community outreach projects as a sustainable way of introducing information technology in developing countries. *International Journal of Education & Development using Information & Communication Technology, 11*(1), 55-79.

Zorn, M. (2015, November 27). *10 steps to Crowdfunding Success | Vision Launch*. Retrieved September 11, 2016, from http://www.visionlaunch.com/10-steps-to-crowdfunding-success-2/

Zott, C., & Amit, R. (2008). The fit between product market strategy and business model: Implications for firm performance. *Strategic Management Journal*, *29*(1), 1–26. doi:10.1002/smj.642

Zott, C., & Amit, R. (2010). Business model design: An activity system perspective. *Long Range Planning*, *43*(2/3), 216–226. doi:10.1016/j.lrp.2009.07.004

# About the Contributors

**Lindy Lou West** is currently completing a PhD in Accountancy, Finance and Economics at Griffith University, Griffith Business School. She obtained a Masters (Charles Sturt University), Post Graduate (Deakin University) and a B.A. Social Science (Sociology) from La Trobe University.

* * *

**Ali Acılar** is an associate professor in the Department of Management Information Systems, Bilecik Şeyh Edebali University, Bilecik, Turkey. He graduated from the Department of Business Administration at Hacettepe University, Ankara, Turkey, received his MS in Operation Research and Statistics from Rensselaer Polytechnic Institute (RPI), Troy, NY, USA and obtained his Ph.D in Business Administration from Dumlupınar University, Kütahya, Turkey in 2007. His research interest includes information technology usage in SMEs, ethical use of information technology, gender issues in computer ethics, e-commerce and e-government.

**Juana Alonso-Cañadas** is an accounting lecturer at Economics and Business Department in the University of Almeria. Her line of research is focused on the corporate social responsibility and SME business valuation. She has published articles in journals as Business Valuation Review and Valuation Strategies.

**Tomaso Amati** is a research fellow at the Department of Management, Economics and Industrial Engineering of Politecnico di Milano. He completed his MSc in Environmental Engineering in 2011, with a thesis about impact measurements of energy projects in developing countries. At present, his research focuses on social impact measurement models for the social business. He also been working for five years, as project engineer, with "Engineering Without Borders", an associacion specialized in sustainable development and international cooperation with special focus on sustainable resources management, access to energy and water, and environmental sensitization and capacity building in Italy and developing countries.

**Marlene Amorim** is a Professor at the Department of Economics Management Industrial Engineering and Tourism at the University of Aveiro and Pro-rector for Internationalization at the University. She is a member of the Research Unit in Governance Competitiveness and Public Policies. Marlene received her PhD degree in Management from IESE Business School of University of Navarra in Spain, and holds also a Masters in Management of Science Technology and Innovation from the University of Aveiro and a degree in Economics from the University of Porto. Marlene Amorim collaborates as a professor and a project advisor for innovation and entrepreneurship courses offered by the University of Aveiro to university researchers for promoting new business development and start-ups. In recent years she has been involved in several applied projects for the development of social innovation projects including SEFORIS – Social Enterprise as FORce for more Inclusive and Innovative Societies, and several ERASMUS+ projects, such as SES-EU - Social Entrepreneurship Support Europe, and ActYouth - EU Youth: From theory to action. Marlene conducts research in the area of service operations and service quality, notably in topics related to service process design and customer participation in service delivery. She collaborates as a reviewer for the journals and conferences in the field of service management and operations (e.g. Journal of Enterprise Transformation, Caspian Journal of Applied Sciences Research, Annual British Academy of Management Conference, International Conference on Industrial Engineering and Operations Management (ICIEOM) European Marketing Academy Conference, Annual EuroMed Conference).

**Albena Antonova** is lecturer at Sofia University, Faculty of Economics and Business Administration in the field of IST implementation in business and economics. She works on number of research projects, related to technology implementation, serious games, knowledge management and others. Her main research interests include knowledge management, emerging technologies, serious games, business and management education, service science, e-learning and TEL models and methods, e-Business, technology entrepreneurship, open innovations and innovations management and living labs and she has more than 30 publications in the field.

**Marika Arena** is Associate Professor at the Department of Management, Economics and Industrial Engineering at Politecnico di Milano. She teaches Accounting Finance and Control at Politecnico di Milano Her research interests are in three areas: performance measurement; sustainability as a source of competitive advantage, risk management and internal auditing. In these fields, she is author of numerous scientific publications in national and international journals (such as Journal of Cleaner Production, Journal of Small Business Enterprise Development, Leadership and Organization Development Journal, Ironmaking and steelmaking: processes, products and applications). She is member of Tiresia research group.

**Liliana Ávila** is a PhD student and Research Assistant at the Department of Economics, Management, Industrial Engineering and Tourism at the University of Aveiro. She has a Bachelor and a Masters in Management and Industrial Engineering from the University of Aveiro. Since 2012, Liliana has been involved in several projects at the regional level for the promotion of social innovation and entrepreneurship in a straight collaboration with local municipalities, as well as some projects at the international level including SEFORIS – Social Entrepreneurship as Force for More Inclusive and Innovative Societies. SEFORIS is a multi-disciplinary, multi-method international research project on social enterprise funded by the European Commission that aims to understand the role social enterprises play in the development of more inclusive and innovative societies in Europe and beyond. She was the country manager of SEFORIS, the person responsible by the data collection in Portugal. Liliana currently conducts research on social enterprises, namely in topics related to the operations management in such organizations and has presented some communications in academic conferences and project meetings.

**Irene Bengo** is researcher in Management Engineering at Politecnico di Milano, her research focus on performances measurement systems for social business and on reconversion/recycling business model at industrial level. She is project manager of different projects on systems for the generation of employment opportunities for disadvantage. She is adjunct lecturer on “Engineering and Cooperation for Global development” course. She is consultant at MBS company as expert on evaluation systems for gender integration process for Italian Ministry of Labour and consultant at Make a change association as coordinator of “National observatory of Social enterprises”. In 2012 she was national consultant for UNIDO as expert on Social Business and performances measure. Since 2005 she is member of Engineering Without Borders – Milan (ISF-MI) and since 2009 she is President of the association.

**Ewa Bogacz-Wojtanowska**, PhD, is an organizational and management researcher, Associate Professor at the Institute of Public Affairs, Jagiellonian University in Cracow, Poland. Her professional interests are nonprofit and social enterprise management, cooperation among public and non-governmental organization and civil society.

**Bessie Rean Bowser** received her Ph.D. in Organization and Management with a Specialization in Leadership from Capella University. She is a member of Delta Mu Delta International Honor Society in Business, Academy of Management, Text and Academic Author Association, and Institute of Management Consultants. She is CEO of Khayruh Enterprises, established in 1986 to consult entrepreneurs, organizations, and private individuals with a global perspective. She has a Federal Government Administration background as well as a public educational system background. She is a researcher; writes and speaks on issues of cross-cultural adaptation, African-American history, family systems, religion, spirituality, and global unity. She is the author of “A Grounded Theory Approach to Creating a New Model for Understanding Cultural Adaptation of Families in International Assignments” (2015, ProQuest).

**Carmen Caba-Perez** is an Assistant Professor in the Public Management Sector at the University of Almeria. Dr. Caba’s strong research and teaching activity has led to her being accredited as a Full Professor by ANECA (Spain’s National Agency for Quality Assessment and Accreditation). She is author of several articles published in JCR publications including The American Review of Public Administration, International Review of Administrative Science, Social Science Computer Review, Online Information Review, Government Information Quarterly, Public Relations Review, Information Development, etc.

**Sarah Caflisch** received her Master of Arts in Nonprofit Management from Hamline University in 2009, and is a licensed mediator. Caflisch has worked in nonprofit management for close to twenty years, and has served on the board of directors for several family foundations. Currently, she is the Managing Director for a small nonprofit, as well as a consultant with Library Strategies Group.

**Debora Caloni** is a Research Fellow at the Department of Management, Economics and Industrial Engineering at Politecnico di Milano. She has graduated in Management Engineering at Politecnico di Milano, with a thesis about the management of temporary structures’ end of life in mega events. At present, her research and projects focus on social innovation, in particular social impact measurement for social businesses.

**Dario Cavenago** is professor of Management, Department of Sociology and Social Research, Università di Milano-Bicocca. His main research interests lie in the fields of organization and management of non-profit organizations, especially with reference to human capital dynamics, and of services management within welfare systems. He contributed to local development planning and strategic urban planning, with a particular focus on services planning and on the role of non-profit organizations.

**Meena Chavan** is a Senior Lecturer at Macquarie University in the faculty of Business and Economics. She has published in several National and International journals and her research expertise are in the area of International Business and Entrepreneurship.

**Min-Hsiu Chiang** received his PhD from Sol Price School of Public Policy, University of Southern California and is currently Dean of College of Social Sciences and Professor of Public Administration at National Chengchi University (Taiwan, R.O.C). He is founder of the Center for Third Sector and Center for Civil Society and Local Governance at NCCU, Miaoli Community University and Third Sector Foundation. He also severs as the Chief Editor of Third-Sector Review. The areas of his research and teaching include Non-Profit Management, The Third Sector, Research Methodology, Public Policy, Social Enterprise and Social Innovation. Dean Chiang focuses on integration of research group on civil society and Third Sector and communication between academics and practitioners in Greater China.

**Cheryl Chui** is a postdoctoral fellow at the Department of Social Work & Social Administration, The University of Hong Kong. She obtained her undergraduate graduate in International Development Studies at McGill University and went on to complete her doctorate degree at the University of Hong Kong in 2014. Dr. Chui's research interests include state-society relations in China, social enterprises, child welfare and migration.

**María del Mar Gálvez-Rodríguez** is a management lecturer at Economics and Business Department in the University of Almeria. Her line of research is focused on the use of web technologies for an effective management of key stakeholders in organizations. She has published articles in JCR journals such as Voluntas, Public Relations Review and Online Information Review.

**Jessika Graterol-Alfronzo** is a graduate student of Public Administration at Pace University, New York. Jessika earned a Bachelor's degree in Business Administration at the Universidad Católica Andres Bello (Caracas, Venezuela) in 2013. Additionally, she received a certification as a Specialist in Project Management at the Universidad Monteávila in 2015. Currently, Jessika is the Vice-President of the MPA Association at Pace University. Her research interests are: impact investment, public health, social and economic development, and philanthropic strategies.

**Lijun He** is an Assistant Professor of Public Administration, Pace University, New York. Lijun He earned the doctoral degree in Philanthropic Studies with a minor in Nonprofit Management at the Indiana University Lilly Family School of Philanthropy in 2015. Lijun was recognized with the following awards: Wilson Faculty Fellow (2015), Elite 50 graduate (2015), Emerging Scholar by the Association of Research for Nonprofit and Voluntary Sector (2014), a fellow of the Tobias Leadership for Excellence (2013), and as a Ford Foundation and Henry Luce Foundation Research Fellow (2013-2014). Her research interests are entrepreneurship and philanthropy, impact investing, philanthropic ethics,foundation management, and strategic philanthropy.

**Rafael Hernández Barros**, PhD, Universidad Autonoma de Madrid; MBA, IESE Business School. For more than 20 years, Rafael has been working as Senior Manager in front and back office (consulting, operations and finance) management roles in the financial services industry, and is currently Financial Support Director at Aon Spain, business support area on financial strategic planning and corporate compliance. As a Professor, He undertakes regular lecturer assignments about Financial Management and Corporate Finance at master's and bachelor's levels at Universidad Complutense de Madrid and Universidad Carlos III de Madrid, and his academic activity includes research in finance and risk management, done in institutions such as IESE Universidad de Navarra, Cass Business School (City University London), Universidad Autónoma de Madrid and Universidad Complutense de Madrid. His recent research work has been published in The Journal of Business Economics and Management, The Geneva Papers on Risk and Insurance or The Operational Risk Journal, among others; and He also serves as board member and editor-in-chief in some other international journals. Rafael is author of the book "Gestión del Riesgo y Fundamentos Prácticos de Solvencia", published by Editorial Complutense. He is also founding partner, adviser and consultant to several organizations and start-ups.

**Beata Jałocha**, PhD, is an Assistant Professor at the Institute of Public Affairs, Jagiellonian University in Cracow, Poland. Her main research interests are: projectification, project management in public and non-governmental sectors, critical participatory action research.

**Lucy Jordan** works at the intersection of social policy and population studies. Her professional and research experience emphasizes market-state-civil society strategies to address social protection needs of poor and working-poor families including access to education, employment security, family support and provision of services to vulnerable populations in emerging economies. Dr Jordan also holds an appointment as senior research associate at the Centre for Social Development in Africa (CSDA), University of Johannesburg.

**Tony Kandaiya** is currently Director of an International not for profit organisation. He has worked collaboratively with Meena Chavan on this international case study.

**Marian Mahat** has more than twenty years of professional and academic experience, spanning several Australian universities, the Australian Federal and local governments, the LH Martin Institute for Tertiary Leadership and Management, the Melbourne Centre for the Study of Higher Education (MCSHE), as well as the private sector. Marian has made a significant contribution to higher education both at institutional and national levels through developing evidence-based strategic policy, providing advice to institutional leaders and policy makers as well as conducting analyses of issues affecting the higher education sector. Marian's research interests include strategic leadership and management in higher education, quality assurance and performance indicators in higher education, university rankings and league tables, and student experience and learning outcomes. Marian was past Treasurer and Membership Secretary of the Australasian Association for Institutional Research.

**Chi Maher** lectures at St Mary's University, Twickenham, London. She has published a book, book chapters and several research papers in national and international scientific journals. Besides those academic activities, she has many years' experience of developing and managing projects in the public sector and the third sector. Dr Maher is an award winner of the Westfocus Enterprising Business Award and a recognised Fellow of the Higher Education Academy.

**Amir Manzoor** is a senior faculty member in MIS/Finance Area at Bahria University, Karachi, Pakistan. He did MBA in General Management from Lahore University of Management Sciences (LUMS), Pakistan and an MBA in Finance from Bangor University, UK. He has about 10 years of corporate experience and more than six years of teaching experience. His research papers and book chapters have been published in reputed journals (such as SAGE Open) and by publishers (such as IGI Global). Amir has authored six books three of them adopted as reference texts in various reputable universities around the world. His research interests are in the areas of technology use for competitive advantage, quantitative analysis, management of academic institutions, and financial modeling.

**Laura Mariani** is assistant professor of Management and Accounting at the Department of Management, University of Bologna. She holds a PhD in Management of Small and Medium Enterprises from the University Carlo Cattaneo – LIUC, and a BSc in Management from Catholic University of Milano. Her research interests focus on Third Sector, welfare services design and evaluation, performance management, management of healthcare organization.

**Alan Pettigrew** has Bachelor of Science and Doctor of Philosophy degrees from the University of Sydney and is a Fellow of the Australian Institute of Company Directors. He has held senior academic and executive appointments at the Universities of Sydney, Queensland, and New South Wales. He was Vice-Chancellor and CEO of the University of New England from 2006 to 2009. From 2001 to 2005 Professor Pettigrew was the inaugural CEO of the National Health and Medical Research Council (NHMRC) of Australia. Professor Pettigrew is a Professorial Fellow of the L.H. Martin Institute at the University of Melbourne. He is a member of the Council of the QIMRBerghofer Medical research Institute and is Chair of the Board of the Illawarra Health and Medical Research Institute. He is also Chair of the Board of the Western Australian Data Linkage Infrastructure Project. Professor Pettigrew served on the Cooperative Research Centres Committee for five years up to 2015. He was also an adviser to the Chief Scientist of Australia (2010-2014) and has actively contributed to national policy discussions on research and higher education. Professor Pettigrew has served as a consultant on international higher education and research training projects supported by the World Bank, the OECD and the Swedish International Development Agency. He has been engaged as a consultant by the NHMRC and the Australian Research Council as well as by eleven Australian universities advising on leadership, management and research strategy. Professor Pettigrew participates in and leads various research leadership training programs offered by the L.H. Martin Institute in national and international settings.

**Louis Sanzogni** is a Senior Lecturer in the Department of International Business and Asian Studies at the Griffith Business School. His research expertise includes business and organisational intelligence technologies and diffusion of innovation modelling, information access, knowledge acquisition and the technology that supports information access and knowledge acquisition. With more than 30 years' industry and academic experience, Louis is widely published in the area of business and organisational intelligence technologies and currently teaches business processes, enterprise mobility, and operations management.

**Laura Saraite** is Degree in Finance and Accounting and Master in Accounting and Corporative Finance. Currently, PhD student in the University of Almeria. In addition she has received a scholarship of Departmental Collaboration in Economics and Business Faculty of Almeria.

**Nayeth Solorzano Alcivar** is a PhD Candidate in the Information System field (under final examination process) at the Department of International Business and Asian Studies at Griffith University. She has been appointed as Adjunct Professor at Griffith University, and she is Professor of Escuela Superior Politécnica del Litoral (ESPOL), in Ecuador. Her main area of interests is in IS Research Methodology; IS/ICT Adoption studies; IS management. She is particularly researching the challenges and issues of applying and adopt IS in Public Organizations.

**Beata Maria Staszewska** is a Ph.D. Candidate at Kozminski University - Warsaw. She holds Masters degree in Psychology from the Maria-Curie Skłodowska University. She also completed Postgraduate Management Studies from the Lublin University of Technology and the University of Illinois at Urbana-Champaign. She was a business trainer, strategy consultant and an author of methodologies, which created possibilities for social research using ICT systems (including Equal Programme). Currently, works as CEO of Recreation Park Zoom Nature. She specializes in management strategy, human resource management and industrial psychology, and studies leadership, dynamic capabilities and knowledge management. Her current areas of strategic management interest are a business model and business model development. She is particularly interested in the application of the management strategy theory into business practice.

**Kenneth Strang** has a Doctorate in Project Management (business research, high distinction), an MBA (honors), a BS (honors), as well as a Business Technology diploma (honors). He is a certified Project Management Professional® from Project Management Institute, and is a Fellow of the Life Management Institute (distinction, specialized in actuary statistics and pension systems), from Life Office Management Association. Ken has over 220 publications (100 of those are sole-authored and appear in peer-reviewed journals). he has won many honors including the Highly Commended Emerald Literati Award. His research interests include: Leadership, multicultural elearning, marketing new product development, knowledge management, ebusiness project management and risk management. He designs and teaches multidisciplinary subjects in business and information technology, in class and online (distance education), at an accredited university. He also supervises PhD and doctorate students. He is associate/area editor on several journals and he serves as editor-in-chief of the International Journal of Risk and Contingency Management. He has been CEO/President aof private and non-profit organizations. Currently he is the CEO of APPC Research and he is a professor in the school of business and economics at the State University of New York.

**Kilian Tep** is currently a junior student at the Pforzheimer Honors' College, Pace University studying Economics and Computer Science. Kilian is a member of two Parisian youth-based think-tanks: Open Diplomacy, an organization focusing on international relations; and Econ+, a community-based think-tank focusing on economic issues. His research interests are poverty alleviation, entrepreneurship, sustainable development, and societal change through technology.

**Javier Vidal** is an Assistant Professor of Finance, University of Valladolid. Spain. He graduated with a BSc in Management from Queen´s University Belfast, MSc in Finance from Aston Business School, MA in Economics from Autonomous University of Madrid, PhD in Financial Economics from Complutense University of Madrid and has been postdoctoral fellow at the Harvard Business School.

**Marta Vidal** has a BSc and MBA from ESADE Business School, is a PhD student in Management at Complutense University, and is an Assistant Professor of Management at European University of Madrid.

**Xunyu Xiang** is a year three PhD Candidate in the Department of Social Work and Social Administration at The University of Hong Kong. His research interest focuses on nonprofit governance, and the collaboration among nonprofit organizations. He conducts research on Support Organization and nonprofit collaborations. He has published in Social Work that is a journal in Mainland of China.

# Index

# E



# F



# G



# H



# I



# L

## M



## N



## O



## P



## R

## S



## T



## U



## V

# Purchase Print + Free E-Book or E-Book Only*

Purchase a print book through the IGI Global Online Bookstore and receive the e-book for free or purchase the e-book only! Shipping fees apply.

**www.igi-global.com**

## Recommended Reference Books

ISBN: 978-1-4666-4707-7
© 2014; 1,862 pp.
List Price: $1,476

ISBN: 978-1-4666-6236-0
© 2014; 508 pp.
List Price: $236

ISBN: 978-1-61520-789-3
© 2011; 556 pp.
List Price: $212

ISBN: 978-1-4666-6579-8
© 2015; 316 pp.
List Price: $156

ISBN: 978-1-4666-8159-0
© 2015; 345 pp.
List Price: $160

ISBN: 978-1-4666-5146-3
© 2014; 311 pp.
List Price: $164

*IGI Global now offers the exclusive opportunity to receive a free e-book with the purchase of the publication in print, or purchase any e-book publication only. You choose the format that best suits your needs. This offer is only valid on purchases made directly through IGI Global's Online Bookstore and not intended for use by book distributors or wholesalers. Shipping fees will be applied for hardcover purchases during checkout if this option is selected.

Should a new edition of any given publication become available, access will not be extended on the new edition and will only be available for the purchased publication. If a new edition becomes available, you will not lose access, but you would no longer receive new content for that publication (i.e. updates). The free e-book is only available to single institutions that purchase printed publications through IGI Global. Sharing the free e-book is prohibited and will result in the termination of e-access.

Publishing Information Science and Technology Research Since 1988

IGI GLOBAL DISSEMINATOR OF KNOWLEDGE

www.igi-global.com | Sign up at www.igi-global.com/newsletters | facebook.com/igiglobal | twitter.com/igiglobal

Stay Current on the Latest Emerging Research Developments

# Become an IGI Global Reviewer for Authored Book Projects

## The overall success of an authored book project is dependent on quality and timely reviews.

In this competitive age of scholarly publishing, constructive and timely feedback significantly decreases the turnaround time of manuscripts from submission to acceptance, allowing the publication and discovery of progressive research at a much more expeditious rate. Several IGI Global authored book projects are currently seeking highly qualified experts in the field to fill vacancies on their respective editorial review boards:

**Applications may be sent to:**
development@igi-global.com

Applicants must have a doctorate (or an equivalent degree) as well as publishing and reviewing experience. Reviewers are asked to write reviews in a timely, collegial, and constructive manner. All reviewers will begin their role on an ad-hoc basis for a period of one year, and upon successful completion of this term can be considered for full editorial review board status, with the potential for a subsequent promotion to Associate Editor.

If you have a colleague that may be interested in this opportunity, we encourage you to share this information with them.

www.igi-global.com

# InfoSci®-Books

A Database for Progressive Information Science and Technology Research

## Maximize Your Library's Book Collection!

Invest in IGI Global's InfoSci®-Books database and gain access to hundreds of reference books at a fraction of their individual list price.

The InfoSci®-Books database offers unlimited simultaneous users the ability to precisely return search results through more than 68,000 full-text chapters from nearly 3,000 reference books in the following academic research areas:

Business & Management Information Science & Technology • Computer Science & Information Technology
Educational Science & Technology • Engineering Science & Technology • Environmental Science & Technology
Government Science & Technology • Library Information Science & Technology • Media & Communication Science & Technology
Medical, Healthcare & Life Science & Technology • Security & Forensic Science & Technology • Social Sciences & Online Behavior

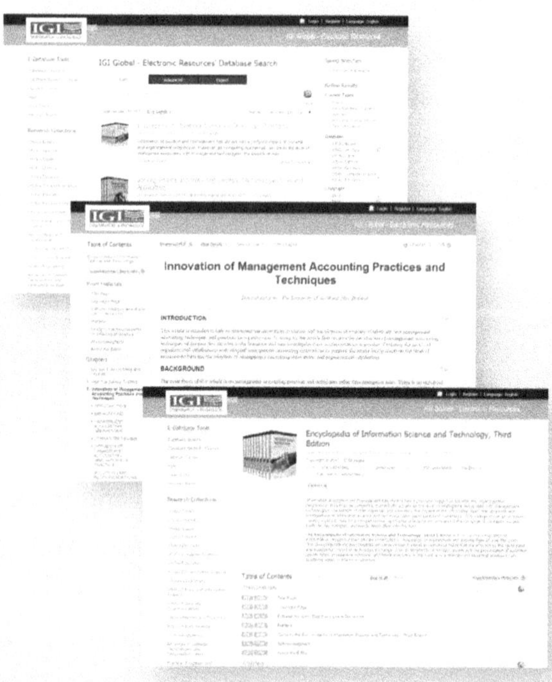


**Peer-Reviewed Content:**

- Cutting-edge research
- No embargoes
- Scholarly and professional
- Interdisciplinary

**Award-Winning Platform:**

- Unlimited simultaneous users
- Full-text in XML and PDF
- Advanced search engine
- No DRM

**Librarian-Friendly:**

- Free MARC records
- Discovery services
- COUNTER4/SUSHI compliant
- Training available

**To find out more or request a free trial, visit: www.igi-global.com/eresources**

IGI GLOBAL
DISSEMINATOR OF KNOWLEDGE
www.igi-global.com

IGI Global
Proudly Partners with
eContent Pro

## eContent Pro specializes in the following areas:

**Academic Copy Editing**
Our expert copy editors will conduct a full copy editing procedure on your manuscript and will also address your preferred reference style to make sure your paper meets the standards of the style of your choice.

**Expert Translation**
Our expert translators will work to ensure a clear cut and accurate translation of your document, ensuring that your research is flawlessly communicated to your audience.

**Professional Proofreading**
Our editors will conduct a comprehensive assessment of your content and address all shortcomings of the paper in terms of grammar, language structures, spelling, and formatting.

## IGI Global Authors, Save 10% on eContent Pro's Services!

**Scan the QR Code to Receive Your 10% Discount**

The 10% discount is applied directly to your eContent Pro shopping cart when placing an order through IGI Global's referral link. Use the QR code to access this referral link. eContent Pro has the right to end or modify any promotion at any time.

Email: customerservice@econtentpro.com

econtentpro.com

www.ingramcontent.com/pod-product-compliance
Lightning Source LLC
LaVergne TN
LVHW062103300926
849161LV00010B/2365
* 9 7 8 1 5 2 2 5 2 5 3 7 0 *